W. P. Tamsh.

f-7

THE MEMOIRS OF

Anthony Eden

EARL OF AVON

The Reckon- ing

COMPANION WITH THIS VOLUME

FULL CIRCLE

FACING THE DICTATORS

THE MEMOIRS OF

Anthony Eden

EARL OF AVON

The Reckon-ing

WITH MAPS

HOUGHTON MIFFLIN COMPANY BOSTON

The Riverside Press Cambridge

1 9 6 5

ACKNOWLEDGMENTS

I HAVE, once again, to thank Mr. David Dilks for his help in the preparation of Book One of this volume. Miss Anne Orde has given me the benefit of her experience on Books Two and Three, while Mr. Antony Grant has assisted throughout the volume. I am grateful to Lieutenant-Colonel E. N. W. Bramall for both general and detailed advice on several chapters. I would also like to thank Miss Pocock, my secretary, who typed the volume.

I am grateful to Countess Wavell for permission to print the preface which Field-Marshal Earl Wavell had written for our projected book on the Greek campaign. I am also grateful to other friends who have allowed me to use quotations from letters.

The official documents printed in this volume are Crown Copyright, which is legally vested in the Controller of Her Majesty's Stationery Office, and I am obliged for permission to reproduce them.

FOREWORD

THIS VOLUME of my memoirs deals with the span of time extending from my resignation as Foreign Secretary in Mr. Chamberlain's Government, to the end of the second world war. At the outbreak of that war I joined the Government as Dominions Secretary. When Mr. Churchill was appointed Prime Minister in May 1940, I became Secretary of State for War, which office I held until the end of the year. I then returned to the Foreign Office for the longest of my three periods as Secretary of State, until the summer of 1945. For half this time I was also Leader of the House of Commons. Four and a half years were spent as a member of the War Cabinet, and for the whole of the tenure of Mr. Churchill's Government I was a member of the Defence Committee. This last shouldered for some years the daily burden of the conduct and strategy of the war.

In wartime, diplomacy is strategy's twin. The demands of allies are urgent, the susceptibilities of neutrals, friendly or otherwise, scarcely less important. Between 1939 and 1945 these made incessant calls upon my time and entailed much travel. In all I journeyed three times to Athens and Moscow, twice to Washington and Quebec, four times to Cairo, once to Ankara, as well as to the Conferences at Tehran, Yalta, San Francisco and Potsdam. I also made shorter visits to France and Italy. My mission to the Middle East at the beginning of 1941 with General Sir John Dill, to advise on the British Government's decision to go to the aid of Greece, had far-reaching consequences and is treated fully in this volume.

During the course of the war I had frequently to deal with President Roosevelt, General de Gaulle and Marshal Stalin as well as with Mr. Cordell Hull and Mr. Molotov. Some of these exchanges were lively enough, but the man who bulks largest is Sir Winston Churchill, with whom I worked constantly and round the clock and whom I grew to love throughout our general agreement and occasional difference.

As in the other two volumes, I have made use of my telegrams and despatches, as well as minutes to the Prime Minister and other colleagues, my purpose being to give the reader the unfolding pattern as I saw it and wrote and spoke about it at the time. This account is based largely on unpublished material. To avoid being repetitious I have, wherever possible, refrained from reprinting those of my despatches already used in other records of these years. I have also drawn upon diaries and notes which, though separately kept, were, on the occasion of some of my more important journeys, a useful personal record. There has been no pruning or amendment of my comments of the time to make them wiser with twenty years more of knowledge and experience. I have even occasionally allowed judgment of men and events to stand which I would now modify, by hindsight, because I thought it better that the reader should have my reflections as I formed them and set them down. Where my subsequent opinions are stated they are clearly shown to be such.

The only excisions I have made in these notes and diaries, and they are few, have been to avoid unnecessary pain to persons still living. Posterity can rustle them out if it wishes; they will serve only to sharpen or deepen the account told here.

This volume is the story of my part in the reckoning which fell upon us and which was encouraged by the appeasement policies of the democratic powers. Hitler's actions determined the war and Mussolini sought to profit by it. The effort which Great Britain had then to make accelerated a process which must anyway have grown with the years, the transference of power, for a phase at least, from Western Europe to the United States and Soviet Russia.

AVON

August, 1964
Fyfield Manor,
Pewsey, Wiltshire

CONTENTS

MAPS

BOOK ONE

The Fatal Slope

1

THE DICTATORS MAKE READY
February–May 1938

My resignation — Herr Hitler's ambitions — Austrian struggles
— Herr von Ribbentrop says goodbye — The *Anschluss* — Brit-
ain holds aloof — My letters on the Anglo–Italian Agreement —
M. Daladier in England — I return to the House of Commons
— An unexpected interview

ON THE NIGHT of February 20th, 1938, I found myself at the age
of forty an ex-Foreign Secretary. Waking up the next morning I
realized that this was the first day for over six years when I had no
Minister's work to do. A sense of deprivation came over me and I
felt wretched at having to leave the Foreign Office. I had enjoyed
every moment of the work there, it was the breath of life to me.
Not only would I now rarely see friends with whom I had worked
daily for so long, but I had also a conceit, which I hope was pardon-
able, that I could do the job if only I could have my way.

In spite of this, my chief sentiment was one of relief at having cut
the painter with the Government. I had resigned because I could
not agree with the foreign policy which Mr. Neville Chamberlain
and his colleagues wished to pursue. The opinions, especially of
the senior among them, had become increasingly at odds with my
own, and these were the colleagues with whom I had to deal. Every
detail became a negotiation in the Cabinet before it could be a
factor in our foreign policy. This was an impossible situation.

I had now to consider what my political course should be. To
continue my arguments from a back bench in the House of Commons during the next few weeks could not have any decisive consequence. The Cabinet, with some doubters, had taken its decision
and now events must speak. When the attempt to negotiate with
Signor Mussolini and Herr Hitler failed to produce results of value

would be the moment to point the moral and try to influence British foreign policy.

My action had gained support in the Liberal and Labour Parties as well as in my own, and I had some encouragement to form a new party in opposition to Mr. Chamberlain's foreign policy. I considered this once or twice during the next few months, only to reject it as not being practical politics. Within the Conservative Party, I, and those who shared my views, were a minority of about thirty Members of Parliament out of nearly four hundred. Our number might be expected to grow if events proved us right, but the more complete the break, the more reluctant would the newly converted be to join us.

The Labour Party, though anti-Chamberlain and ready to speak against the dictators, was not yet prepared to face the consequences, especially in rearmament, which it continued to oppose until the outbreak of war. Many Liberals were also tangled in the same contradiction. Such disparate elements as these could not form a party. On the other hand, the call for national unity and for a corresponding effort in armaments to meet the growing dangers was more likely to be heeded if voiced by men who believed in it with conviction, whatever their party. Their numbers, as well as their authority, might then influence events.

These opinions were shared by Lord Cranborne, who, as Under-Secretary at the Foreign Office, had resigned with me, and by the few Conservatives with whom he and I were in contact. Meanwhile, I decided to go abroad and set out for my sister's villa at Cap Ferrat in the South of France.

★   ★   ★   ★   ★

On the day of my resignation, Hitler addressed the Reichstag. His speech was an open avowal that Germany would shortly demand more territories. He spoke of two countries on Germany's borders, proclaiming that they held more than ten million Germans. None could miss the reference to Austria and Czechoslovakia. While lavishing praise upon the Austrian Chancellor, Dr. Kurt von Schuschnigg, for working to improve relations, Hitler said no word about Austria's independence.

During my tenure of the Foreign Office, I had always insisted that any "settlement" with Germany must be wide-ranging and must include disarmament. This was in accordance with the principle I had laid down on Lord Halifax's return from Berchtesgaden: "If we do not get, we shall not give." It was also the reason why I told my colleagues on the day of my resignation that we should adopt a stiffer attitude towards colonial concessions after the Führer's bullying of Schuschnigg on February 12th. Admittedly this attitude had its critics. For instance it caused Mr. Robert Barrington-Ward, Deputy Editor of *The Times,* to write of me in a private note on the evening of my resignation: "He really has no heart for any kind of direct talks with the dictatorial powers."

British and German documents on foreign policy published since the war show that His Majesty's Government, during the vital year between my resignation and the Nazi entry into Prague, ceased to apply my maxim and showed a readiness to negotiate with Hitler piecemeal. Only rarely have the bitter fruits of a misconceived policy been gathered so speedily.

When the full import of the Hitler–Schuschnigg interview was known, the earlier instructions to Sir Nevile Henderson, our Ambassador in Berlin, to approach the Nazi Government tentatively about a general settlement should have been cancelled. However, the German account* of the Chancellor's meeting with the Ambassador reveals that Hitler showed little interest in colonies. I had expected this, believing that his immediate ambitions were European. Doubtless, he would take colonies if he could get them without trouble, but as I had told M. Van Zeeland in 1936, Hitler wanted them largely for reasons of prestige. In any event, he had other prey to stalk for the present.

★　★　★　★　★

A few days after I resigned, *The Times* published a leader welcoming Lord Halifax to the Foreign Office and containing a reference to the fact that he was a relation of Sir Edward Grey and would bring to the Office the qualities that statesmen had commanded, which were more needed than those of "the ingenious

---

* *Documents on German Foreign Policy, 1918–1945;* Series D, Vol. I, No. 138.
Full details of all references and sources noted in the text can be found on pages 663 ff.

diplomatist." This seemed to me rather hard, as Lord Halifax's father, my mother and Sir Edward Grey were all the grandchildren of three Grey brothers, the eldest of whom was the Prime Minister of the Reform Bill.

At that time, the *Yorkshire Post* stood out from most Conservative newspapers in supporting the stand which Lord Cranborne, Mr. J. P. L. Thomas, my Parliamentary Private Secretary, and I had taken. Mr. Arthur Mann, its editor, wrote to me on February 28th:

> I shall continue to think you were right until we have proof to the contrary. The Chamberlain line of approach to the dictators seems to me highly dangerous and unless it succeeds, its effect on this country will be damnable.

To the question whether Neville Chamberlain or I was right in the policies we advocated, I replied, with too much pessimism, on March 1st:

> It is very difficult to establish these things convincingly by experience. To explain what I mean in this instance, Mussolini is so hard pressed that I feel it difficult to believe that the Government will not be able to get an arrangement of some sort which, to outward appearances at least, will seem fairly satisfactory. Our position, of course, was that as good, or better, results could have been obtained by our methods with much less risk than the Government have chosen throughout. This, however, can never be proved, since the course we advocated has not been followed.

In the event, the agreement which the Government reached with Mussolini was to prove even less satisfactory than I had expected.

Meanwhile, Sir Nevile Henderson did not appear to anticipate any immediate difficulties. He wrote to me from Berlin, expressing formal regret at my resignation, but adding that it might make things easier for him, as the Germans always regarded me as a *Deutschenfresser.** By Germans, Henderson no doubt meant the Führer and the Nazis.

* A devourer of Germans.

At this stage Hitler still hoped that Austria would fall into his hands, rotted from within. He intended that the Austrian administration, already infiltrated by Nazis, should be steadily eaten away until a "peaceful solution" was effected; naked force was to be used only if other methods failed. Hitler had not scrupled to tell Schuschnigg this at Berchtesgaden on February 12th. The Austrian Chancellor, who thought that he had safeguarded his country's independence by his agreement to "establish neighbourly good relations," did not give in without a struggle.

Strangely enough, when I saw the Austrian Minister in London during my last days as Foreign Secretary, on February 17th, the memorandum he gave me was in no sense alarmist, nor did it convey any impression of the crude violence of Hitler's behaviour to Schuschnigg. The reason for this playing down of the odious truth is obscure. No overt military preparations had yet been made by Germany and possibly Schuschnigg and his Minister thought that to give Britain the brutal facts so soon would only result in a protest, which would intensify Hitler's rancour against the Austrian Government.

On February 24th Schuschnigg insisted in a public speech that Austrian independence must be preserved. Thereupon Nazi agitation and lawlessness were loosed in a campaign timed to reach its climax a month later. Schuschnigg's reaction was robust. He would not surrender an atrophied Austria and announced on March 9th that a plebiscite would be held on the following Sunday, so that the Austrian people might decide their fate. If, as Hitler asserted repeatedly, the vast majority of Austrians longed for the *Anschluss,* this fact would be demonstrated. The principle of self-determination was being neatly used to turn the tables on Hitler.

It was at this moment that Ribbentrop was making his farewell rounds as Ambassador to Britain. On the decisive day, March 11th, he attended a luncheon offered to him at No. 10 Downing Street, an unusual compliment, where Mr. Chamberlain gave him a message for Hitler which Ribbentrop transmitted as follows:

> It had always been his [Chamberlain's] desire to clear up German–British relations. He had now made up his mind to realize this aim. He requested me to tell the Führer that this was his sincere wish and firm determination.

Ribbentrop replied to the Prime Minister with his usual gramo-phone record of Hitler's good intentions, but this happy atmosphere did not last. Before the luncheon was over news arrived of the German threat to invade Austria if the plebiscite were not called off.

Lord Halifax recorded that when Mr. Chamberlain spoke to the Nazi Ambassador of the extreme gravity of the situation, Ribben-trop replied that he had no information, but that he would return to the Embassy and get into touch with Berlin. Later, when Lord Halifax called upon the Ambassador, a secretary came in with a message to say that Schuschnigg had resigned and Herr Artur von Seyss-Inquart was now Chancellor. The news, according to Halifax, supplied the text for a further harangue by Herr von Ribbentrop to the effect that this was really much the best thing that could have happened; Halifax would surely agree that it was the object of them all to see peaceful solutions of obstinate problems.* Schu-schnigg's offer to resign and to postpone the plebiscite had no effect. Hitler was determined to stage his triumphal entry in force.

While the clouds were gathering over Austria, I remained in the South of France, reading the French newspapers and listening to the Vienna wireless. One day when I tuned in, I heard Hitler's entry into Linz, the hypnotized chants of the crowd, *"Ein Volk, ein Reich, ein Führer,"* and Hitler's frenzied speech proclaiming the *Anschluss.* Schuschnigg had shown courage, but there was nothing he could do and no one to help him. France was in the throes of yet another ministerial crisis, Signor Mussolini had chosen his course and had not, in any event, the power to stop Hitler, while in Britain this deed only imposed a temporary check on the optimism of the appeasers.

Henderson telegraphed on March 12th that:

> . . . everything that could be done, short of direct threat of force, was done here to save Austria from consequences of Doctor Schuschnigg's ill-conceived and ill-prepared folly.

These were harsh terms for the majority of hapless Austrians and their brave leader, whose crime had been to suggest that his people

* *Documents on British Foreign Policy, 1919–1939;* Third Series, Vol. I, No. 44.

should determine their own future. For having understood the true Nazi menace, as His Majesty's Ambassador in Berlin singularly failed to do, Dr. Schuschnigg was to undergo seven years of imprisonment; Henderson abused him instead of clamouring for his release.

Fourteen years later, when I was Foreign Secretary again and the guest of the Austrian Government in Vienna, I had to remind myself that my opposite number, Dr. Figl, always so friendly and debonair, despite the anxiety I knew he felt about his country and its fate under allied occupation, was another victim who had been flung into a concentration camp in 1938. There he had stayed, often under brutal treatment, until the end of the second world war. Some of Hitler's harshest cruelties were reserved for those in the country of his birth who withstood him with a lonely courage. They deserve to be remembered.

★　★　★　★　★

In March 1938, the successful invasion of Austria should have pointed the danger for Czechoslovakia, even to the obtuse. Of course the Nazi Government was prolific in reassurance, Göring giving his word of honour to Dr. Vojtech Mastný, the Czech Minister in Berlin, that "developments in Austria would have no detrimental influence on the relations between the German Reich and Czechoslovakia." Germany, he protested, wanted to improve their mutual relations. No confidence should have been placed in these words, especially as they were accompanied by at least one sharp warning in the Nazi press in reference to my own resignation:

> Three weeks ago, on the occasion of the change at the Foreign Office, the English Prime Minister announced a realist policy and repeatedly defended a common-sense attitude. Germany wonders whether after Monday's interlude he will return thereto.*

In other words, Mr. Chamberlain must please disinterest himself in all that was happening in Central Europe.

* *Essener National Zeitung,* March 14th, 1938.

The French Government were not slow to note and move. On March 15th their Ambassador in London, M. Charles Corbin, called on Lord Halifax. He spoke of the peril to Czechoslovakia from German attack. He feared that if the British Government did not specify what they would do in the event of such an attack, their silence would be taken throughout Europe to mean that they were not interested and would acquiesce in whatever happened. The results might be disastrous and his Government hoped that the British would take account of these dangers.

The response was tepid. On March 24th, the British Government took note before Parliament of the promises Germany had given to Czechoslovakia and Chamberlain repeated the definition of our obligations, which I had given to my constituents at Leamington in November, 1936. He added a general warning that where peace and war were concerned, legal obligations were not alone involved. If war broke out, it would be unlikely to be confined to those who had assumed such obligations.

These words would have had more influence if the preparations for our help in Europe had been steadily advanced, but here we had gone backwards. By the time I left office, the Prime Minister had agreed to start conversations with France. Unfortunately these never fulfilled the purpose I had advocated of concerting our joint preparations and showing a red light to Berlin. This failure was in part due to the coolness our Chiefs of Staff displayed, once the Foreign Secretary's pressure was withdrawn.*

His Majesty's Government could have ended this confusion. In the aftermath of anxiety about Nazi intentions created by events in Austria, the British public might have been alerted and prepared to support the French Government's position. Hitler could have been warned that, though Czechoslovakia was militarily weaker as a result of the occupation of Austria, Britain was prepared to join with France if that country were called upon to fulfil her treaty obligations. In other words, the British Government could have led up to a position from which, if Hitler had continued with his intransigent tactics, they might have given a guarantee to Czechoslovakia comparable to that which they were to give a year later to a more remote Poland, after Czechoslovakia had fallen.

* *Facing the Dictators*, page 501.

The guarantee once given, they could reasonably have discussed the problem of the Sudeten Germans with their French and Czech allies.

There was, however, no hope of this, Chamberlain being wrapped in his design to get on terms with the dictators and to be the arbitrator in all obtruding differences. Nothing was further from his mind than to impress the British people with the truth that events in Central Europe were their business. Yet if Hitler were now to digest Czechoslovakia, and later Poland and even Russia, I knew that he would then have a stranglehold upon the very existence of Britain and France. It would be at Hitler's whim to turn, irresistible, against the West. Meanwhile, Mussolini would try to keep pace with his overbearing partner by intrigue and adventure in the Mediterranean, the Middle East and the Balkans. The pillage in the Far East would be left to Japan.

★   ★   ★   ★   ★

At this time, as his speeches and letters show, Chamberlain did not believe that a policy of rallying the remaining free nations to resist Hitler and Mussolini was either desirable or practical politics. As a result, the Prime Minister and his colleagues expended much time and good intention in an effort to resolve what they chose to look upon as a local racial problem in Czechoslovakia. We know now that Herr Konrad Henlein and the Sudeten Nazis were subsidized by Berlin from the start. Their whole activity was aimed at building a Trojan horse by means of which the Nazis would penetrate and destroy the citadel. Reading the documents of this period is a melancholy business, with British policy vacillating between pressure upon the Czechs to make more concessions towards autonomy for the Sudeten Germans, and paler warnings to Berlin not to press matters too far. Naturally the Germans observed the pressure upon the Czechs and ignored the warnings.

I had been conscious, while in the Government, of being regarded as too provocative in my statements on the conduct of the dictators. Chamberlain in particular felt this. When I had stated in November, 1937, that while we offered co-operation to all, we would accept dictation from none, he noted in his diary:

Mussolini had been more than usually insolent with his offensive remarks about bleating democracies, and his outrageous allusion to the Colonies. But Anthony should never have been provoked into a retort which throws Germany and Italy together in self defence, when our policy is so obviously to try and divide them.*

I have never discovered the names of the powers whose attitude was so menacing that Germany and Italy would be "thrown together in self defence."

While I was Foreign Secretary, I had sensed that some of my colleagues also thought my speeches too alarmist, with their emphasis on the calamities which would attend a final breakdown of international order. They considered such language exaggerated and likely to be resented by the electors. In fact, I had found my audiences deeply concerned and prepared to heed harsh truths. With the greater freedom I now enjoyed, I was determined to multiply my warnings.

The true state of mind of my critics was probably best expressed by Sir Kingsley Wood, who in a burst of candour confessed to me, shortly after the war broke out, that he was never able to convince himself that Hitler would really fight when the moment came. It is hardly surprising that this attitude failed to convince Hitler that we would fulfil our own obligations.

★　★　★　★　★

After the rape of Austria, the Prime Minister continued his pursuit of Mussolini. In his diary, he wrote on March 19th:

It is tragic to think that very possibly this [the *Anschluss*] might have been prevented if I had had Halifax at the Foreign Office instead of Anthony at the time I wrote my letter to Mussolini. . . .†

This showed that the Prime Minister did not understand that

* Keith Feiling: *Life of Neville Chamberlain.*
† op. cit.

what decided Mussolini's policy was power. Once engaged in Abyssinia and Spain, Mussolini could not defend Austria and exchanged his interest there for Nazi help in Spain, making a bargain of necessity. It should also have been evident to Mr. Chamberlain then, as it was soon confirmed, that Signor Mussolini and Count Ciano took a lofty and disdainful view of their British negotiations. Our eagerness was regarded by the Duce as exemplifying decadence. Ciano's diary, at an early phase of the negotiations, expresses it well:

> Chamberlain is more interested than we are in achieving agreement — this is the card on which he has staked his political future, if not that of the whole Conservative Party.*

This same zeal for an agreement weakened British representations against Italian intervention in Spain. If we wanted an agreement so much, why should the Fascist leaders pay any attention to our remonstrances? Proof of this was given in March, when Lord Halifax rightly decided to protest against the air-raids on Barcelona. According to Count Ciano's account, Lord Perth, our Ambassador in Rome, handed to him a note calling attention to the recent bombing attacks, and adding that they might prejudice the continuation of Anglo–Italian talks. Ciano replied suavely that the operations were initiated by General Franco, not by the Italian Government; but he noted privately in his diary:

> The truth about the air-raids on Barcelona is that the orders for them were given to Valle by Mussolini . . . Franco knew nothing about them, and asked yesterday that they should be suspended for fear of complications abroad. . . . Mussolini . . . wasn't very worried when I informed him of Perth's *démarche*. In fact, he said he was delighted that the Italians should be horrifying the world by their aggressiveness for a change. . . .†

It is strange that this regime should have been thought fit support

* *Ciano's Diary, 1937–1938.*
† op. cit.

for any policy and humiliating that British Ministers should have scraped to get it.

★ ★ ★ ★ ★

I arrived back in England on April 4th, a few days before the Anglo–Italian talks were completed. By their terms, Mussolini pledged himself to evacuate his volunteers from Spain, giving an assurance that he sought no privileged position there. He also undertook to withdraw from Libya troops which, as I wrote to Mr. Winston Churchill, were probably sent there in the first place for their nuisance value. Great Britain virtually accepted Fascist fortifications in the Mediterranean, while agreeing not to fortify Cyprus without prior consultation; a surprising condition, since no check was to be placed on Mussolini's preparations. We promised to raise at Geneva the *de jure* recognition of the Italian conquest of Abyssinia, but no clause in the Agreement was to take effect until the Spanish question had been settled. This condition was not observed. No firm commitment was given about hostile propaganda, which was merely described as being "inconsistent with good relations," so it continued, if more covertly.

I set out my views of these developments in a private letter to Mr. Rupert Beckett, chairman of the *Yorkshire Post:*

> The Government were, I think, mistaken in opening conversations in Rome under the conditions they did, and in pursuing conversations in Berlin after the Berchtesgaden interview with Schuschnigg. The mentality of the two dictators being what it is, those actions were construed by them as weakness. The union of Germany and Austria might have been inevitable in some form at some time, but the impression of weakness created by British foreign policy accelerated both these events. And so now, while firmness in foreign policy cannot, perhaps, prevent events, it can delay them, and delay is most important. The sum of my criticism of Chamberlain's foreign policy is that his too patent eagerness to come to terms with the dictators encourages their aggressive tendencies. Queen Elizabeth once wrote to the Danish Ambassador: "I

would have the King of Denmark know that England hath no need to crave peace."

When we come to home affairs the position is no less anxious. Our rearmament programme is clearly inadequate to the dangers that confront us. If we are to live, other than on sufferance, in the next few years a united national effort is called for on a scale comparable to that being put forth by the dictator countries. For this a national leader is called for. Neville Chamberlain has none of the necessary attributes. He is essentially a party man, revels in the party battle, and lacks the imagination and personality for the wider appeal. Under his leadership the National Government will not win the next General Election, and were we confronted with a dangerous domestic crisis, strikes and such like, his methods and outlook would probably result in fierce internal controversy.

For these reasons I believe that it would be wrong to lend active support to the Government in its present form — at least I cannot give it — for I am convinced that in policy and personnel they are unequal to the situation, perhaps the gravest we have known for centuries. . . .

It may be true that the *Yorkshire Post* has sniped at the Government. I am sure that it is no less true that by their frank exposure of the plans of the dictators and the risks that accrue in consequence to the British Empire, they have done an immense service. Incidentally they are not quite alone — the *Glasgow Herald* and *Birmingham Post* have been scarcely less outspoken. The London press has been sycophantic, but I am sure that the *Yorkshire Post* more truly represents national uneasiness. It would be a tragedy, I feel sure, if they were to cease to cry "wolf," as Roberts did before the war.

How the internal situation is to be remedied is at present hard to tell, but that it must be remedied if we are to emerge through this ordeal, which will prove to be not of one year but of several, I am convinced. The greatest risk of the moment is complacency. The British people are only too ready to believe that the international situation is easier, when it is not. We are still islanders in mind, though we have long since ceased to be so in a military sense.

If I seemed to you reluctant, as indeed I am, to consider re-joining the present Government, it is because I felt when I was in it increasingly out of tune with the blind optimism of the majority of my colleagues. It would be impossible for me to return to play the part of the ostrich, or to cheer on a party warfare which I regard as stupid, if not criminal, at this time.

Hence I must wait; but while I wait I must speak out, for unless some of us, to whom the nation will lend at least passing attention, are prepared to do so, we can neither pave the way to that greater national unity that must come, nor do our duty by our countrymen.

I wrote to Mr. Churchill on April 16th:

[The Anglo–Italian Pact] is in many respects a strange document, for it does not apparently enter into force at once. It may not do so for many months and in the interval much may happen. There is not . . . to be a marriage as yet, but only the announcement of the banns, coupled with the admission that there is a just impediment. The Italian part of the bargain seems to consist principally of the re-affirmation of pledges, which up to now they have consistently broken, and which they are breaking today. . . .

Fundamentally, however, I suppose that one's attitude towards negotiations with either Germany or Italy depends upon what one's conceptions are of the ambitions of these two Powers. As to Germany, you know my views. As to Italy, I do not believe that Mussolini has abandoned his dream of creating a *Mare Nostrum*. If so, every step we take in negotiations with Italy must be judged from the standpoint of whether or not it has facilitated Mussolini's main plan. I only hope we shall not fulfil the statement which I saw attributed to Mussolini in the *New Statesman* the other day. "Chamberlain will let me conquer Spain and then pay me to get out," or words to that effect.

Quite naturally the Government will make all they can of the Agreement, even though it is as yet only of a hypothetical character, but I find it hard to believe that it will arouse great enthusiasm in the country, while amongst those who care ardently about the Spanish issue, it is likely to be interpreted as giving Mussolini and Hitler a free hand to finish their campaign.

Mr. Churchill's reply deplored the Agreement. I wrote to him again on April 22nd:

It has now become clear that, as I expected, Mussolini continued his intervention in Spain after the conversations in Rome had opened. He must be an optimist indeed who believes that Mussolini will cease increasing that intervention now, should it be required to secure Franco's victory.

As a diplomatic instrument, the Pact embodies a machinery which is likely to be found very troublesome to work. It is not to come into force until after the Italians leave Spain. It may be, however, that many months will elapse before that occurs, and since what is important is not the presence of Italian infantry, but the authority of their experts and the Germans, it will be difficult to establish with certainty that the withdrawal has taken place. But maybe some do not mind much about that.

Then there is the Italian position in Abyssinia which, from what I hear, so far from improving grows steadily worse. I am afraid that the moment we are choosing for its recognition will not benefit our authority among the many millions of the King's coloured subjects. . . .

The most anxious feature of the international situation, as I see it, is that temporary relaxation of tension may be taken as a pretext for the relaxation of national effort, which is already inadequate to the gravity of the times.

It was not until nine weeks after my resignation that I made another public speech. This was on April 26th, when the Royal Society of St. George invited me to propose the toast of "England" at their annual banquet. My speech, which was broadcast to the United States as well as at home, restated my beliefs and warnings.

★　★　★　★　★

A few days later, on April 29th and 30th, Anglo–French official talks took place in London. The British record, now published, shows how encouragement was given to the further misfortunes soon to descend upon us. The French Ministers were left with no illusions about the lack of British armed power to back their word and ours. The Prime Minister refused to commit Britain to the despatch of an army to the Continent and admitted that the tiny force which might be sent would not be fully mechanized. Lord Halifax told the visitors that, in our existing military situation, it would be impossible to preserve the Czech state, if Germany decided "to take hostile steps."

Mr. Chamberlain, according to the official record,

> had asked himself whether the picture was really so black as M. [Edouard] Daladier [Prime Minister of France] had painted it. For his part he doubted very much whether Herr Hitler really desired to destroy the Czech State or rather a Czech state. He doubted whether at the present moment he wished to bring about the "Anschluss" of the Sudeten districts with Germany, and he thought that the reason why Herr Henlein had not in his speech demanded the "Anschluss," which was desired by his own followers, was that he had received advice from Berlin not to do so.

In reply to this spate of facile prophecy, M. Daladier remarked, with truth, that if the common policy of France and Great Britain was inspired by sentiments of weakness, the only result would be to precipitate renewed violence and ensure further success for the use of forceful methods. He feared that time was against us, if we allowed Germany to achieve a new success every few months, increasing her material strength and her political strength with each advance. If this continued, countries which were now hesitating would feel compelled to submit to the hegemony of Germany and then, as we had been warned in *Mein Kampf,* Germany would turn west.*

This was a miserable time for those who believed that they understood the international situation more thoroughly than did the

* *Documents on British Foreign Policy, 1919–1939;* op. cit., No. 164.

Government. A hazy optimism prevailed in official quarters. Ministerial speeches abounded in confidence that Europe would be pacified and in warnings of the danger of dividing the Continent into two opposing *blocs*. This was a pleasant ideal, but remote from the facts. So far as I know, none of the thirty or so dissident Conservatives, and certainly not I, wished to align all democracies against all dictatorships, with some of which we enjoyed friendly relations. But the cleavage already existed, not of our creating; it was between those who kept their word and upheld international law and those who used their words to cloak their next aggression, those who had growing appetites and those who had not. No mellifluous phrases could obscure the consequences of these realities.

Nonetheless, our rearmament still went forward on the basis that there could be no interference with normal trade, and unemployment was still rife. Even the docile House of Commons of that time felt much agitated by our slow progress in equipping the country with an adequate air force. An angry debate on May 12th convinced the Prime Minister that the Secretary of State for Air, then Lord Swinton, must be a member of the House of Commons.

★   ★   ★   ★   ★

Soon after this I went to the House for the first time since the debate on my resignation. I took the corner seat on the third bench below the gangway, usually reserved for Ministers who have resigned. A while later, the Government Chief Whip, Captain Margesson, came and said that the Prime Minister would like to have a word with me. I waited in my seat for a few moments, so that my departure from the Chamber should not be too closely linked with the Chief Whip's approach to me, and repaired to the Prime Minister's room. Mr. Chamberlain received me in a very amiable fashion and, in the course of our talk, expressed himself, considerably to my surprise, in confident terms about the international scene, particularly about relations with Mussolini. The Italian Agreement, he believed, would soon come into force. He hoped that then I would be able to rejoin the Government, not of course at the Foreign Office, but in some other department agreeable to me. He hinted at the Admiralty.

I was embarrassed by these advances, for I had noticed nothing in the international news to make me believe in the improvement which the Prime Minister saw. At the same time I did not want to be rude in the face of an invitation which was obviously friendly in intention. I replied that although I had not, of course, his sources of information, I was sorry that I could not yet discover the improvement in Anglo–Italian relations which he had mentioned. Chamberlain assured me that this was taking place and so I added: "Well, perhaps we had better see first how all this works out. If the future is as good as you believe, we can, if you wish, have a talk again." The Prime Minister assented cheerfully. I left his room perplexed, but I kept my own counsel and war broke out before we spoke again alone.

2

DRAMA OF THE MUNICH DAYS
June–October 1938

Optimism over Czechoslovakia — My talks with Lord Halifax —
I urge action — My letter to *The Times* — Mr. Neville Cham-
berlain's first visit to Germany — The Godesberg ultimatum —
M. Jan Masaryk's distress — Mr. Chamberlain's second visit to
Germany — The Munich Agreement — Dangerous assumptions

By MIDSUMMER, Nazi agitation against Czechoslovakia had reached
a new pitch of violence. This state, created by the Versailles settlement of 1919, included substantial minorities, Germans, Poles and
Ruthenes. The authors of the Treaty, when defining its boundaries, had not insisted on the principle of nationalism at the cost of
strategic necessity, believing that if the new state were to be viable,
it must enfold the whole of Bohemia. It is mistaken to claim, as
some of Chamberlain's apologists have done, that Czechoslovakia
could not in any event have continued to exist. It had already
done so for nearly twenty years. Czech policy towards minorities,
under Tomas Masaryk and Eduard Beneš, was more liberal than
most. Nor could Nazi Germany pose with truth or even plausibil-
ity as the protector of minorities. Ruthless pogroms on a terrible
scale were soon to lay bare their horror before the world.

The Sudeten Germans, numbering about three and a quarter
millions, inhabited the mountainous border region which formed
Czechoslovakia's natural defence against Germany. Like the Austrians, they were far from unanimous in desiring closer links with
the Nazi state. However, as Hitler's power waxed, the voice of
Sudeten Nazis led by Konrad Henlein grew more strident. The
published documents now attest that Henlein's supposedly moderate programme was a well-conceived fake. He followed the Führer's
instructions always to ask for more than could be given, masking

21

any move against Beneš with a show of reasonableness. Much of this could have been surmised in the summer of 1938.

There was no need to guess at Italian policy. Despite repeated and solemn engagements, Mussolini increased his intervention in Spain, evidently indifferent to the fate of the much vaunted Anglo–Italian Agreement, which had still not entered into force. He decided that two thousand volunteers, double the usual number, should leave for the Civil War in June and a further two thousand in July. We read in the Italian Foreign Minister's diary for June 21st, 1938:

> I informed him [Mussolini] that the Volunteer Corps will go into action in Spain very soon. He is pleased. He . . . absolutely refuses to compromise — we shall not modify our policy towards Franco in the smallest degree and the agreement with London will come into force when God pleases. If indeed it ever will.*

Believing that the danger of domination by the dictators, or European war, was now very near, and that the Government were failing to warn the country and the British Commonwealth, I said to my constituents on June 11th that the optimism which was being shown was unfounded:

> There is today less liberty in Europe than there has been at any time for centuries. Whatever else the Great War did, it did not make the world safe for democracy. . . .
> We are still far from understanding the extent of the dangers that confront us. Therein lies the chief cause for national anxiety today, and not in any failing in the British character or people.
> You may gain temporary appeasement by a policy of concession to violence, but you do not gain lasting peace that way. It is a grave delusion to suppose that you can. Even more untrue is it to suggest that those who would have wished to see our country take a firmer stand in the last six months on behalf of the principle of good faith in international relations

---

* *Ciano's Diary, 1937–1938.*

SWITZERLAND

FRANCE

BELGIUM

HOLLAND

North Sea

LUX- LAND

R. Rhine

RHINE-

Cologne
Godesberg

Frankfurt-on-Main

Stuttgart

Nuremberg

G E R M A N Y

R. Weser

Hanover

Bremen

Lübeck
Hamburg

R. Elbe

Leipzig

Potsdam
Berlin

Frankfurt

Stettin

Baltic Sea

R. Oder

W. Neisse

Breslau

UPPER SILESIA

Neisse

Danzig

Königsberg

EAST PRUSSIA

LITHUANIA

AUSTRIA

Munich

Berchtesgaden

Linz

R. Danube

Vienna

Bratislava

Budapest

C Z E C H O S L O V A K I A

Prague

Teschen

Cracow

R. Vistula

Warsaw

P O L A N D

Lublin

MOLOTOV-RIBBENTROP LINE

LINE A

Lwow

LINE B

CURZON LINE

Bialystok

HUNGARY

ROUMANIA

CENTRAL EUROPE
Areas of Czechoslovakia ceded in 1938

would thereby have plunged this country into war. The very reverse is the truth.

The Nyon Agreement to suppress piracy last September was an instance of firm and timely action by this country which contributed to avert the danger of war. Nor was Nyon the only instance in our history. Retreat is not always the path to peace. Our greatest interest is the preservation of peace, but the more general the disrespect of international engagements, the greater the danger to peace.*

The last two paragraphs of this speech express a conviction I have never ceased to hold, but its application is seldom popular when it is most necessary, as in 1938 and in more recent times.

Many persisted in seeing the Sudeten problem as an isolated one. Amongst this myopic band Mr. Geoffrey Dawson, editor of *The Times,* was prominent. On September 7th that newspaper carried a leading article which suggested:

> It might be worthwhile for the Czechoslovak Government to consider whether they should exclude altogether the project, which has found favour in some quarters, of making Czecho-slovakia a more homogeneous state by the secession of that fringe of alien populations who are contiguous to the nation with which they are united by race.

This thinly veiled surrender was promptly disavowed by the Foreign Office, though Munich was later to match or exceed it.

It was a national misfortune that at this period *The Times* had no Foreign Editor.† Nor, contrary to custom, was there a member of the Foreign Service among Neville Chamberlain's private secretaries. To have any specialist knowledge of foreign affairs was to be quite out of fashion; it was the day of the uninhibited amateur.

---

* *Foreign Affairs,* page 279.
† See *The History of The Times,* Vol. IV, Part ii, a candid and indispensable commentary on the period.

★   ★   ★   ★   ★

When the House rose, my wife and I and my elder son went for a motoring tour in Ireland, and it was while there that I received several messages from Sir Robert Vansittart, Chief Diplomatic Adviser to the Government, warning me of the growing danger of the Czech situation and advising my return for a talk with the Foreign Secretary. I complied and arrived back in London on September 8th, when I wrote at once to Jim Thomas:

> Here things look black, even very black, I am afraid. *The Times* bloomer may be a loosening of the stone that sets off the avalanche. No one can tell.

I saw Lord Halifax at the Foreign Office on the afternoon of September 9th. I had taken with me some notes, which, at his request, I read over to him. In these I wrote that it was important to make a further communication to the German Government and that this time it should be delivered to Hitler in person. This communication should say three things. First, we considered that the latest Czech proposals marked a big advance and that they should constitute a fair basis for settlement; the German Government should be asked to inform the Sudeten Germans that this was their opinion also. Secondly, it was inconceivable that if a conflict were to break out in Central Europe, it could be localized. Thirdly, if there were a European conflict and France was involved, we should be involved also "up to the neck." Halifax replied: "Great minds are thinking alike, for my mind is moving on just such a project and indeed I was going to speak to Neville about a draft today." He asked for my notes and I wrote out a copy of them for him.

I then made two further suggestions: that the Opposition leaders should be consulted, and that some action should be taken, either by the concentration of ships or by other means, to demonstrate to the German Government that we were in earnest. I added that I suggested this because I thought there was a danger that Hitler still did not understand our real position. Whereas the words which His Majesty's Government used might be twisted or ignored, any action we took must at once be reported to him. Halifax replied that the Cabinet had already considered this, but that the weight of opinion had been against it. I said I was sorry to hear it. I wrote in my diary:

> *September 10th:* It appeared from the *communiqué* issued today that though the Government had actually drawn up a communication to the German Chancellor on the lines of the notes that I had given, they then had decided not to send it. I assume on Henderson's advice. If this advice was given I believe it to be wrong.

On September 11th I again saw Lord Halifax, who confirmed my reading of what had happened. He remarked that I would have seen from the newspapers that he had been considering the question of the movements of ships. The press had already announced that four minelayers, then in reserve, were to be commissioned, while the First Minesweeping Flotilla was to be brought up to full complement and placed under the orders of the Commander-in-Chief, Home Fleet. Halifax added that the question was whether the Government should do a little more.

I understood him to refer to destroyers and strongly urged that they should, pointing out that this would be effective not only in Berlin, but also in other capitals which might wish to draw Berlin's attention to the dangers of the situation. I said we ought to make evident military movements, because of the distinction between our commitment to defend France and Belgium against unprovoked aggression and France's treaty obligation to Czechoslovakia. Here was an opening which Nazi manœuvre would do its best to exploit, since it was always Hitler's purpose to isolate France from us.

A sense of this danger necessarily influenced the conduct of French policy, then in the hands of M. Edouard Daladier and M. Georges Bonnet. Daladier was well-intentioned, but not as firm as his appearance suggested. Bonnet was accommodating to the point of weakness and sometimes of equivocation.

★   ★   ★   ★   ★

I decided to write to *The Times* pointing out the dangers of any hesitation in making Britain's position clear. My letter appeared on September 12th, the day after my last meeting with Halifax:

Your Diplomatic Correspondent writes in your issue of to-day of the difficulty that confronts the Government here in explaining to the German Government the effect that an attempt at a violent solution of the Sudeten German problem might have in this country. He has given expression to an apprehension widely held. It would be the gravest of all tragedies if, from a misunderstanding of the mind of the British people, the world were once again to be plunged into conflict.

We have often been told that the war of 1914 would never have come about had the attitude of this country been clearly understood in time. Whatever we think of this statement it is the duty of each one of us, press and public as well as Government, to take every step in our power to prevent such a repetition of tragedy. For this reason I set before you the salient points of the Central European situation as they appear to me today.

(1) A settlement of the Sudeten German problem by conciliation is of the utmost urgency in view of the growing realization of the far-reaching consequences of any resort to a decision by armed force in Central Europe.

(2) The Czechoslovak Government in their most recent proposals have shown their sincere desire to go very far to meet the grievances of the Sudeten party. It should not be impossible to evolve from these proposals a settlement acceptable to all.

(3) It is a dangerous illusion to assume that once a conflict had broken out in Central Europe it could be localized. The experience of recent history goes to prove the contrary.

(4) The friendship and understanding between this country and France can neither be weakened nor broken. In any international emergency that threatened the security of France this country would be found at the side of the French Republic, whatever the consequences. Such a decision would not be taken upon grounds of sentiment or of past history, but because upon the security of France the security of this country ultimately depends.

I also wrote to Halifax about the failure to make the further naval preparations we had discussed the day before:

I was sad that the press today made no mention of the positive step you said last night we might take. The second instalment: maybe the Government are merely taking it, and letting those principally concerned know. But I cannot help feeling it could only be useful.

Another suggestion, might it not perhaps be well to take some preliminary anti-aircraft defence measures? So far as I can recollect at least forty-eight hours is required to man these, and a few precautionary moves might prove salutary abroad, as well as reassuring at home.

★   ★   ★   ★   ★

A violent speech from Hitler at Nuremberg on this same day confirmed my worst forebodings. In this crisis, it was my aim to influence our country's policy to match closely that of France; we were too much involved in Europe to be mediators and we could not rally opinion that way. It is often argued that more forceful action was not possible at the time of Munich because opinion, especially in the Dominions, was not ready for it. If this is true, it was largely due to the British Government's fascination for the role of honest broker instead of "honest facer of truths." *

Taking a hand in direct negotiation between aggressor and victim requires the utmost firmness and vigilance, if it is not to lead to a series of engulfments. Great Britain had now, over Czechoslovakia, placed herself in the position I had always tried to avoid.† The Government had sent Lord Runciman as an investigator to Prague. By doing so they had committed themselves to mediation without undertaking to uphold the result. Consequently, the effect of Runciman's intervention could only be to weaken France's ally and breed hesitation among other watchful nations. All those threatened by the bullying of a militant dictator must, I considered, be encouraged to stand together. No mediation could promote this.

On the morning of September 14th, I telephoned to Lord Halifax, suggesting that the British and French Governments

* See *Facing the Dictators*, page 178.
† See *Facing the Dictators*, page 503.

should issue a public statement, either jointly or on the same lines. It would emphasize the gravity of the situation and repeat in durable form the warning of dangerous consequences if Germany resorted to violence. I also asked whether it might not be possible to secure corresponding action by Soviet Russia. When Halifax wanted to know whether I contemplated taking this country farther than the Government had already taken it, I replied that I hoped we should get nearer to the point of saying that if the French were in, we should be in. Casting a fly over the Foreign Secretary, I remarked that I understood we had said rather more in private than in public. Halifax denied this.

★　★　★　★　★

Within hours there followed the first of Mr. Chamberlain's visits to Germany, a prelude to the bloodless victory won by Hitler at Munich. After this initial encounter at Berchtesgaden, the Prime Minister accepted the principle that those frontier areas where the Germans numbered more than fifty per cent of the population should be transferred to the Reich. This solution was pressed by Chamberlain upon Daladier and Bonnet, who came to London for talks on September 18th. It involved the disruption of Czechoslovakia as a military and economic entity. On the next day my friend M. Jan Masaryk, the Czech Minister in London, telephoned to me.

> *September 19th:* . . . He stated that there seemed to be a profound misapprehension here if it was thought that Czechoslovakia could accept anything like the proposals foreshadowed in the Press this morning. . . .
>
> Monsieur Beneš had telephoned to him and pointed out that there was no possibility of the Czech Government accepting the concessions which were apparently to be demanded of her. "Of course," added Monsieur Masaryk, "we know nothing, except that we have been sold."
>
> Monsieur M. added that he had spoken in this sense to Lord Runciman, Lord de la Warr and myself.
>
> I suggested to him that if he had a message from Monsieur

Beneš it would be wise to refer it to the F.O. at once so that Lord Halifax might be aware of it.

I felt scarcely less uneasy than Masaryk and wrote privately to Halifax to tell him at once how deeply distressed I was to read the accounts which had appeared in the press, during the last two days, of the outcome of the Anglo–French conversations in London. Nothing official, I added, had appeared and I could only hope that what the press had published was not accurate for, if it were, I could only look to the future with increased apprehension.

On the evening of September 23rd I told my constituents at Stratford-upon-Avon:

> Nobody will quarrel with the Government's wish to bring about appeasement in Europe. . . . But if appeasement is to mean what it says, it must not be at the expense either of our vital interests, or of our national reputation, or of our sense of fair dealing.
>
> For our own people the issue becomes clarified. . . . They see freedom of thought, of race, of worship grow every week more restricted in Europe. The conviction is growing that continued retreat can only lead to ever-widening confusion. They know that a stand must be made. They pray that it be not made too late.

This speech was broadcast to the United States and warmly endorsed by Bonar Law's son, Mr. Richard Law, who called to see me the next day, as Mr. Chamberlain was returning from his second visit to Hitler at Godesberg. Law said that at the time of my resignation, he had thought I was wrong. Now, however, he realized that I was right and would support me in any action I might decide to take. He begged that I should not be influenced by fear of the motives which people might impute to me. I asked him about the state of the party. His own impression was that a minority shared his view. A still smaller minority maintained that the Prime Minister was right, while the majority were miserably unhappy and would now follow an alternative lead, if given one.

When news reached me of the Godesberg ultimatum I was

grieved that a British Prime Minister should undertake to forward such terms to Prague, as to an evil-doer. Hitler now required not merely the cession of German-speaking districts, but also the immediate military occupation of a larger area. Our Fleet had still not been mobilized and the Führer's intuitive flair for exploiting his opponent's weakness had emboldened him to press his advantage. At luncheon-time on September 24th, Masaryk telephoned again to my London home and begged me to see him at once.

September 24th: He came round immediately and brought with him the text of the Godesberg proposals which [Sir Alexander] Cadogan [Permanent Under-Secretary at the Foreign Office] had just given him.

He was in a state of great distress and reiterated several times that his Government could not accept them. He thought it incredible that the Prime Minister of Great Britain could forward such a document to a friendly power.

I tried to invent some comfort by pointing out that the significance of the proposals depended largely upon the map and that therefore he must not make any too hasty judgment.

I did not tell Masaryk what I thought myself and that it was incredible that such terms could be recommended to H.M.G. and most unfortunate that they should be forwarded by Chamberlain to Prague. Even without the map their tone was only too apparent.

In the circumstances I advised Masaryk to ask to see the Foreign Secretary at once and to get from him the necessary map and an expression of the Government's attitude to the proposals. Masaryk then made the appointment from my house.

At six o'clock that evening, General Sir Louis Spears, who had for many years been a friend of the Czech Minister, telephoned to let me know Masaryk's report. Halifax, in speaking to him of the proposals, had emphasized the Prime Minister's conviction, on his return from the interviews with Hitler, that if only Hitler could get what he wanted in the Sudeten areas, he would then be satisfied.

On Masaryk expressing his incredulity that anyone could believe such a thing, Halifax had merely repeated the statement.

Captain Harry Crookshank, then Secretary for Mines, came to see me after dinner and told me that he would have to resign from the Government. Neville Chamberlain's foreign policy had been, in his view, disastrous, and he could not possibly endorse it to his constituents. Though Crookshank was not a member of the Cabinet, his attitude no doubt had an influence on some of his colleagues when their position stiffened against the terms next day.

On the morning of September 25th, when I had read the forecast of the terms in the press, I decided to telephone the Foreign Office and try to speak to Halifax. As he had not yet arrived and a Cabinet was imminent, I left a brief message asking that the Government should not endorse the terms, if they corresponded in any way to what was published in the press.

A succession of visitors came to see me during that day. One of these was Sir Alexander Hardinge, King George vi's Private Secretary, who called during the afternoon. I told him that in my view the Godesberg proposals would be looked upon as the last straw. The Prime Minister's remark, "It is up to the Czechs now," had been most unfortunate and ill-timed. Alec Hardinge suggested that if we got through this crisis without a war, we should then reorganize ourselves and put part of our industry on a war basis. I agreed, but expressed doubt as to whether this was possible without a truly National Government. Labour should be invited to cooperate. Hardinge seemed to agree. He said he thought Neville Chamberlain would have to continue as Prime Minister. I replied that this might be, but the Labour Party would probably find such a thing difficult after the experiences of recent months.

★   ★   ★   ★   ★

Meanwhile the British Cabinet had decided that the Godesberg *diktat* was too much. The Fleet was finally mobilized on September 27th and by the next day war seemed imminent. I was in my seat in the crowded House of Commons when Chamberlain described the course of events. A scrap of paper was passed along to him. He glanced at it and then announced that Hitler had invited Mussolini, Daladier and himself to Munich. Members of all parties rose to their feet, cheered and waved their order papers. I did not feel I could take part in this scene, neither did Churchill, neither did Mr. Leopold Amery. As one who witnessed it all from a seat under the gallery, wrote, "there doubtless were others." * This was so.

On paper, the Munich Agreement which resulted from this meeting of the four heads of Governments was more plausible than the Godesberg terms. In practice, the Czechs suffered as badly under the one as they would have done under the other. Worst of all was Mr. Chamberlain's conviction, perfectly sincere in my opinion, that he was in the way to bringing about world appeasement. The negotiations were concluded in the early hours of September 30th. Later that morning, taking Hitler to one side, Chamberlain had asked whether he would be willing to sign a declaration. The Chancellor, of course, assented, and the two men thereupon put their names to the following document:

> We, the German Führer and Chancellor, and the British Prime Minister, have had a further meeting today, and are agreed in recognizing that the question of Anglo–German relations is of the first importance for the two countries and for Europe.
>
> We regard the agreement signed last night, and the Anglo-German Naval Agreement, as symbolic of the desire of our two peoples never to go to war with one another again.
>
> We are resolved that the method of consultation shall be the method adopted to deal with any other questions that may concern our two countries, and we are determined to continue our efforts to remove possible sources of difference, and thus to contribute to assure the peace of Europe.

Of this Mussolini remarked: "You do not refuse a glass of lemonade to a thirsty man." † The French Ministers were not invited and did not take part in the exercise.

The Prime Minister, on returning home, waved this piece of

* R. W. Seton-Watson: *A History of the Czechs and Slovaks.*
† *Ciano's Diary, 1937–1938.*

paper to the crowd at Heston airport and in Downing Street called
the Munich Agreement "peace with honour. I believe it is peace
for our time." Seven months later, the Anglo–German Naval Agreement was denounced by Hitler. Eleven months later we were at
war.

★   ★   ★   ★   ★

Here was the tragic failure of these days. A defence could be
made for the Munich surrender as the price to be paid for our
military weakness. There is no defence for such a misreading of
Hitler's mind as to believe its authors had "at last opened the way
to that general appeasement which alone can save the world from
chaos," as Chamberlain wrote in a personal letter on October 2nd.*
I do not suppose for a moment that the Prime Minister was deliberately deceiving the British public or his private correspondents.
He believed that Hitler had no more territorial ambitions, yet the
Führer and the Duce had offered no concession. The Prime Minister's proposal that Hitler should join him in appealing to the
Sudetens and Czechs for moderation was refused, showing that the
situation was only as much out of control as the Führer wished it to
be. His comment to Ciano no doubt revealed his thought:

> The time will come when we shall have to fight side by side
> against France and England. All the better that it should hap-
> pen while the Duce and I are at the head of our countries and
> still young and full of vigour.†

Mussolini has been credited with the authorship of the Munich
terms. These, it is argued, he would never have proposed but for
the goodwill engendered within him by the Anglo–Italian Agreement. I thought at the time that it was more probable that he had
made this move because he thought it in his interest. We now
know that he was only acting as a stooge and was putting forward
the draft proposals supplied to the Italians from Berlin. They had
been telephoned to Mussolini the previous night. The rest was
elaborate comedy.

* Feiling: op. cit.
† *Ciano's Diary, 1937–1938,* September 29th, 1938.

After Munich, Chamberlain could have come home and said in effect: "The position in Europe is still very grave and depends much upon us. I am determined that Great Britain shall not find herself in such a humiliating position again and am therefore resolved to spend much more freely on rearmament and to broaden the basis of my Cabinet." We should then have been behind him to a man and so, I am sure, would British and Commonwealth opinion, once educated in the facts.

I have never blamed the British and French Governments for not supporting Czechoslovakia to the point of war, though I think it would have been to their nations' advantage to have done so. On the other hand, the argument for Chamberlain's Munich policy rests on the dangerous assumptions that demands for self-determination, whatever their true source, should override accepted international boundaries and that the threat of force should excuse a failure to fulfil international engagements. Doubtless Chamberlain little realized how his attitude at Munich would influence the future. Certainly it had its effect upon the fate of Poland.

When the first relief at being spared a total war had passed away, the British people would have been more than ever ready to make sacrifices, if the issues had been explained to them. No firm lead and no sufficient acceleration in our defence preparations were forthcoming from the Government, for the reason that the Prime Minister did not believe them to be necessary. Great Britain was bewildered, uncertain what to believe. Truncated Czechoslovakia, demoralized France, disillusioned America, vulnerable Poland, small nations and lovers of freedom everywhere were the associates and co-partners of our loss.

3

THE EDEN GROUP
October 1938–March 1939

The Group is formed — Sir Sidney Herbert's speech — Disarray among the smaller powers — Mr. Chamberlain's satisfaction — I speak in Cardiff — Italian violations — *Arbeit macht frei* — A luncheon with Mr. Joseph Kennedy — My visit to New York — Meeting with President Roosevelt in Washington — Mr. Chamberlain and Lord Halifax go to Rome — "The tired sons of a long line" — The Nazis enter Prague — I warn the House of Commons — The Group asks for conscription — Colonel Beck calls upon me

THE ANGLO–ITALIAN negotiations and Chamberlain's encounters with Hitler should have exposed to all the contrasting approach to foreign policy of the democracies and the dictators. For us, diplomacy's object was the patient removal of dangers, an end to be achieved by compromise and goodwill. For them, the object was to expand their territories by means of bluster and blackmail and at the minimum cost. Every advance made good was the jumping-off ground for the next demand.

During the summer of 1938, a number of Conservative Members of Parliament who shared the same opinions about the threatening international dangers, met together to discuss them and to consider what action should be taken. I used to preside over these gatherings. No minutes were kept and there was no compulsion to follow any decisions reached, though we kept to fixed topics which we met to discuss. Gradually our numbers and influence grew. Outside, this floating membership was variously dubbed "The Eden Group," or by the Government Whips' Office, "The Glamour Boys."

At first we met at Mr. J. P. L. Thomas's house in Westminster, or occasionally at that of Mr. Mark Patrick, who shared with Thomas the unofficial secretarial duties. Patrick had been Sir Samuel Hoare's Parliamentary Private Secretary, but he had come to disagree emphatically with the policies of his former chief. By the end of the year there were between twenty and thirty of us. They included, in addition to Thomas and Patrick, Duff Cooper, Cranborne, L. S. Amery, Paul Emrys Evans, Wolmer, Richard Law, Edward Spears, Harold Macmillan, Harold Nicolson, Ronald Tree, Sidney Herbert, Hubert Duggan, Robert Bower, Derrick Gunston, Dudley Joel, Anthony Crossley and Ronald Cartland. The last two were soon to be killed, to the impoverishment of their country's leadership.

This group was a fair cross-section of the party; some had held high office, others were to do so, either in the war or later. Our discussions were entirely free-for-all and not burdened by either the prolix or the tedious, nor did our widely spaced ages seem to inhibit anybody. I may have been prejudiced, but I thought this a good company in which to be.

During the autumn and winter of this year, many of the group had to face considerable difficulties in their constituencies, where some of their leading officers were ardent supporters of Mr. Chamberlain and of Munich. This led to argument and correspondence, to meetings of the local executive committees and, occasionally, of party supporters, when the discussion was often hot and the voting close. One of our liabilities was that no Conservative newspaper in London or southern England was sympathetic to our opinions, while several were actively hostile. As a result, it was not easy for a Member of Parliament without a national following to sway the critical and convince the doubting, against the power of the Party machine and the general sentiment for peace.

At times these battles were fought out with bitterness; both Lord Cranborne and Mr. Thomas, for instance, had to face continuing opposition in their constituencies. Differences of this depth of feeling are rare in the history of the Conservative Party. In the period from Munich to the outbreak of the war they inflicted wounds which took years to heal.

I was too young to remember, except in general terms, the bitter periods of the Ulster crisis before the first world war, when members of the Conservative and Liberal Parties would not meet even at the dinner table. This later period of Munich was in some ways more disagreeable because the tensions were within our Party. Altercations were frequent and could even lead to blows, as when the late Lord Salisbury had his face slapped by an overwrought Conservative Member of the House of Commons.

North of the Trent those who shared our opinions fared better, for there we had the staunch support of the *Yorkshire Post,* whose editorials showed unremitting hostility to the practice of appeasement. At the time this was often attributed to the influence of Mr. Rupert Beckett. This was only so to the extent that he supported its editor, Mr. Arthur Mann, whose firm opinions and prophetic judgments were held with a faith which was not to be daunted.

★   ★   ★   ★   ★

An immediate consequence of the Munich Agreement was to create noticeable over-confidence among its less-informed enthusiasts. "Well, one result of this business," declared Sir Kingsley Wood, "is that we shall hear no more of Anthony Eden." There was also support for a General Election, which at least went far enough to cause some of us to consider what our course should be in such an event. I determined that I would then stand as an independent Conservative. Mr. Winston Churchill told me that he would do the same, for there was a prospect of an official party candidate being adopted against him.

Wiser counsels prevailed, however, about the propriety of an election, influenced I have no doubt by a remarkable speech by Sir Sidney Herbert, the much respected Member for the Abbey division of Westminster. He was in sadly failing health; I can see him now, standing at the corner of the front bench below the gangway, leaning heavily on his stick and in evident physical difficulty. The House had filled up as his name appeared on the tape early in the evening of October 4th, the second day of the Munich debate. He began by giving the Government clear warning that, while all felt gratitude and relief at what the Prime Minister had done, there were many who could not give a vote of confidence in what seemed a grave and even desperate humiliation. He went on to declare:

There could be no greater iniquity in the world than to force a General Election on the people of the country at this moment. . . .

We have talked long enough about "the years which the locusts have eaten." I was led to suppose that the locusts had stopped nibbling about two years ago, but I can hear their little jowls creaking yet under the Front Bench.

The debate was of a high standard, opening with Mr. Duff Cooper's courageous and raking speech of resignation. I thought that Richard Law was the most effective speaker in the three days. Mr. Lloyd George thought so too, when I talked with him near the end of the debate. Law was brief, closely reasoned, and spoke with the burning sincerity of the converted. The change of opinion had a dramatic effect which could even be compared with Mr. Churchill's indictment and its searing comment: "We have sustained a total and unmitigated defeat."

Those who most admired Mr. Chamberlain's brave first flight at the age of seventy and felt a human relief because the crisis was at least temporarily evaded, should at least have had some anxiety about what was to come next. Such was certainly my thought at the time, as I expressed it in a speech during the debate:

It does not seem to me that it is so important to consider whether we should praise or blame those proposals, as it is to examine what the conditions were that caused the British Government to press such proposals on a friendly nation, and to consider once more what steps we are to take now to see that we do not have to play so unpleasing a role again.

I was critical of the option terms of the Agreement. I was trying, I said,

to put myself in the position of a German Jew or a German Social Democrat in those areas, knowing that, by the 10th [October], German troops would enter. Even though there might remain with me a power to opt later, I feel that I would rather make assurance doubly sure. . . . What is happening today is something like a panic flight of these unhappy people from a rule which they dread.

From the White Paper, it appeared that there was some favourable modification in the Munich proposals, compared with those of the Godesberg ultimatum. I reserved judgment on this until I could see how it worked out from the reports of the Commissions which were to be set up. In the event, it worked out very badly.

I pointed out that "the Czechoslovak State has accepted these proposals, drastic as they are, and has thereby given evidence of its desire for peace," and asked:

> Surely the House will be agreed that foreign affairs cannot indefinitely be continued on the basis of "stand and deliver!" Successive surrenders bring only successive humiliation, and they, in their turn, more humiliating demands.*

Most of the members of our group had decided that we could neither support the Government motion on Munich, nor the Opposition amendment, and that we should therefore abstain. Mr. Churchill had told me that he and Mr. Brendan Bracken would do the same. The Prime Minister's final speech on the third evening, however, was firmer and displayed fewer illusions. In particular, he declared that rearmament must go forward. I do not know the reason for this change of mood or emphasis. Maybe it was the outcome of a conversation which Amery told me that he had had with him before his speech, or quite simply it was to rally the doubters whom Chamberlain must have known to exist in his own ranks. Whatever the cause, it brought some comfort to us, but not to the point where we could support the Government, having no confidence that the Agreement would be observed or that a resolute attitude would be maintained by Ministers. Any hopes we might have had faded after a few days, when it became apparent that rearmament was not to be speeded by a fuller use of national resources or even by a Ministry of Supply.

* *Foreign Affairs,* pages 286–99.

★   ★   ★   ★   ★

The Munich Agreement had its baleful consequences throughout Central Europe. Smaller powers, sensing that the initiative lay with Hitler, inclined perforce towards him. Poland yielded to the temptation to take a hand in the pillage and seized the Teschen area, thereby alienating opinion in the west. On October 10th I received a visit from Count Raczynski, the Polish Ambassador in London, who was a friend of mine and a devoted servant of his country. On this occasion, however, I could not agree with him.

October 10th: I left Raczynski in no doubt as to what I thought of recent Polish behaviour, and in mitigation he maintained that once we had legalized Germany's seizure of Sudetenland, Poland could hardly be blamed. He added "If, however, you and France had stood firm by Czechoslovakia, we would not have touched Teschen, but would have declared our neutrality, and ultimately, I have no doubt have come in on your side." In the main his appeal was that Poland should not be abandoned on account of her recent behaviour. The encirclement of Germany was no longer possible, but Poland could still be useful as a check on Germany.

I understood this and reported the conversation to Halifax, who later saw Raczynski.

The same day, the Netherlands Minister, Baron van Swinderen, doyen of the Diplomatic Corps and a man of unrivalled experience in his profession, asked to see me, ostensibly in order to thank me for undertaking the chairmanship of the Dutch–Polish Arbitration Board.

October 10th: He was in the depths of gloom. Germany had carried all before her at Munich. The final boundaries of the Czech State were worse than those at Godesberg. He did not see how Czechoslovakia could survive. Germany was now all-powerful from the North Sea to the Black Sea. She had secured the hegemony of Europe. The balance of power, which had been the traditional British policy for three centuries, had now ceased to exist.

While not expecting anything in the nature of an attack, the Minister said that inevitably his country would be under strong pressure from Nazi propaganda. The position of Denmark was worse.

Van Swinderen feared that France's internal condition was very unsatisfactory; the future of Europe now depended upon our ability to make a supreme national effort.

I had not talked with the Prime Minister during these months, but, feeling that the Foreign Secretary's view was more nearly in accord with mine than Chamberlain's, I asked him for an interview shortly after Munich and we had an hour's conversation at the Foreign Office:

> *October 11th:* [Halifax] said that he was very unhappy and counting the hours to the time when he should leave the office. The choice had been a very cruel one, but he still thought the Government had chosen the lesser of the two evils. He then spoke of the future at home. I told him that in my own view, the proper solution was a National Government, in the broadest sense, to include Labour and Liberals. We would not go much faster in armaments without some form of mobilization of industry. Clearly our present pace was far too slow. Mobilization of industry would require the co-operation of Labour, even if Labour was to refuse, Neville's position would be much stronger.
>
> Edward agreed, and had urged this course on Neville on their return from Heston [airport]. At the time, however, Neville was not prepared to be rushed. Edward had wished the action to be taken before the debate in the House of Commons. Though anxious for such a solution himself, I did not think he considered that Neville Chamberlain was likely to favour it. Horace Wilson, I gathered, was against it.

It is my belief that the Foreign Secretary did again try to persuade Chamberlain of the wisdom of this course, perhaps using my insistence upon wartime powers for rearmament as a lever, to which I would certainly not have objected. But although Halifax probably pressed as hard as it was in his nature to do, he did not insist, as he could have done, for Chamberlain could never have faced the loss of a second Foreign Secretary. We know Chamberlain's reaction to Halifax's efforts because, after receiving from him an account of our talk, the Prime Minister wrote of me:

> What makes him [Eden] think it possible to get unity is my insistence on the necessity for rearmament, and the news that I didn't like Hitler personally. He leaves out, or chooses not to see for the moment, that the conciliatory part of the policy is just as important as the rearming.*

On rearmament, essential steps were not being taken and the Prime Minister was writing at the end of October that a lot of people were "losing their heads and talking and thinking as though Munich had made war more, instead of less, imminent." †

No doubt I was numbered amongst this panicking group, roundly condemned by Hitler in a speech on October 9th:

> It only needs that in England, instead of Mr. Chamberlain, Mr. Duff Cooper or Mr. Eden or Mr. Churchill should come to power, and then we know quite well that it would be the aim of these men immediately to begin a new world war.

Many years later, when speaking at Blackburn in October, 1950, before the General Election, I had cause to cast my mind back to these weeks. After the meeting my Chairman, Colonel Robert Mottershead, said that the last time he had seen the hall filled to capacity was when Neville Chamberlain spoke there shortly after Munich. As they were walking towards the platform the Prime Minister had made a remark which he had remembered ever since: "You know, whatever they may say, Hitler is not such a bad fellow after all." He had not known whether Chamberlain was speaking seriously. I told Colonel Mottershead that I had no doubt Chamberlain was speaking seriously; it was no joke.

★   ★   ★   ★   ★

Our group accepted that the pace of rearmament could not be

---

* Feiling: *Life of Neville Chamberlain.*
† op. cit.

sharply quickened unless the national economy were geared to the needs of the hour. I told an audience at Cardiff on October 14th:

> The gaps in our defences and the public demand for a speeding up of our rearmament, arise from the fact that the armament industry in this country and in France is being operated on a peacetime basis. Any talk about overtaking arrears and filling gaps has little meaning unless we face the simple truth that, in the totalitarian states, armaments are being piled up on a basis which we have hitherto only consented to adopt in time of war.

I thought that this was what Lord Baldwin had had in mind when he said in the House of Lords a week before: "I would mobilize our industry tomorrow."

In terms of day-to-day politics, the Government could afford to ignore these and like arguments, and did so, for their position was strong. The Cabinet's policy was supported in Parliament by a large majority. Our group at no time numbered forty, even with Churchill and Bracken, and after Hitler's occupation of Prague. The nation was admittedly confused, but by no means convinced that Chamberlain and those who supported him were in error. Most members of the group had to be active in their constituencies even to hold their own where their influence was strongest. There was little possibility as yet of proselytizing. Chamberlain and his colleagues certainly did not, at this period, base their defence of Munich on the grounds that time must be bought for rearmament. That justification was to come later. For the moment, the nation's best energies were held in check, while reassuring statements about our armed strength were freely issued.

★　　★　　★　　★　　★

At the beginning of November, the Prime Minister announced that the Anglo–Italian Agreement would now come into force. It could not be pretended that its preconditions had been fulfilled, for Mussolini had not abated seriously his intervention in Spain. On the contrary, he had intensified it, especially in the air. I told the House of Commons on November 2nd that I could not vote for the Agreement, and drew attention to the many reports of the terrible punishment inflicted upon the Spanish Government forces by newly arrived German and Italian air units. The Fascist press had made no attempt to conceal this, they gloried in it and listed their bombing raids in which more than five hundred aircraft had joined.

"The presence of each and all of those aeroplanes," I commented, "is a direct violation of the Non-Intervention Pact." The raids were continuing, I said, at the very time our debate was being held. When the Anglo–Italian Agreement had been signed in April, His Majesty's Government declared that they regarded "a settlement of the Spanish question as a prerequisite of the entry into force of the Agreement." It was not possible, I argued, to pretend that this condition had been fulfilled. We had waived it and nothing was going to disguise that fact from the world. I said of the Axis powers:

> We are constantly giving, and they are constantly taking. I am reminded of the charity collectors in *The Hunting of the Snark*—they collect, but they do not subscribe.*

Soon after the debate, it was made known that the Prime Minister and Foreign Secretary would visit Rome early in the New Year.

In the interval, vom Rath, a young member of the German Embassy staff in Paris, was shot by a Polish Jew. Immediate and wholesale reprisals were ordered by Hitler and unconditionally approved by Mussolini. Innocent victims in their thousands were despatched to concentration camps, there to perish or to labour long years under the sardonic banner *"Arbeit Macht Frei,"* work makes you free. The blame for the murder of vom Rath was spread wider, the *Angriff* exclaiming:

> The Jewish murder-urchin Grynsban also assumed the post of a world improver and avenger. Thereby he took the same line as is pursued by Messrs. Churchill, Eden, Duff Cooper

* *Foreign Affairs,* pages 300–9.

and their associates, indefatigably and in the most varied fashion, in association with the international of Jews and Freemasons.

My condemnation of the wholesale reprisals brought further blasts of anger in the Nazi press, which saddened me still more for the victims of an unspeakable tyranny.

★   ★   ★   ★   ★

One day towards the end of November the American Ambassador, Mr. Joseph Kennedy, whom I did not then know personally, telephoned to invite me to luncheon for a private talk. I accepted and over our meal my host asked me about an invitation which I had received from the National Association of Manufacturers in the United States to attend their annual conference and to be the chief speaker at the dinner held at its conclusion in New York. I explained that with reluctance I had, for a number of reasons, refused the engagement. The Ambassador asked me earnestly to reconsider this decision. He said that opinion in his country had been critical of the Munich Agreement and that many Americans were, in consequence, anti-British. In view of my known views, he thought that I could render an important service by speaking in the United States just then.

I explained why I thought this difficult for me. I could not defend policies with which I did not agree; on the other hand I was not prepared to criticize the Government of my country in a foreign land. The Ambassador replied I could go and say just that. He was sure that the American people would understand my position and would welcome a speech from a British visitor with the opinions I held. I could do much good to the relations between our two countries. I also understood from the Ambassador's comments that Lord Halifax, at least, would welcome my acceptance. After some further discussion, I thanked Mr. Kennedy for the trouble he had taken in the matter and said that I would reflect upon the advice he had given me.

The next day I cabled my acceptance to Mr. Charles Hook, the President of the Association. There was not much time to make the arrangements and a strike on the *Normandie,* in which ship I had booked my passage, made matters worse. I transferred to the *Aquitania,* armed with a case of champagne from the Ambassador, but this ship was only due in New York the day before the dinner. As ill fortune would have it, we ran into extremely rough weather and at one point the Captain told me sadly that he would not be able to make New York until early in the morning of the day after my speech was due. However, feats of seamanship and a supreme effort of the engines of that grand old ship achieved the seemingly impossible, to the considerable discomfort of the passengers, and we reached Battery Point about an hour before the dinner was due to begin. There I was taken off in a tug, rushed across the harbour and through the streets of New York to the Waldorf Astoria with the sirens sounding, certainly not a modest entry into the great city. A swift change of clothes and I was conducted through several overflowing rooms in which the assembled company was already dining. It was something of an ordeal to have to be introduced and to say some words of greeting at each of them in turn. By the time we reached the main dining-room I was feeling more than a little bewildered, but my humour was restored by being greeted to the unexpected strains of *Land of Hope and Glory,* so reminiscent of a party conference at home.

During a hurried dinner, for we were due on the air for a nation-wide hook-up, the photographers were incessantly active, as it seemed to me, at every mouthful I swallowed. Public figures in England were not yet used to such insistent attention and I was getting rather restive under the barrage when a note was handed to me. It ran: "Whatever you do, don't mind the photographers." It was signed by Mr. Noël Coward, who was at one of the tables nearby in the audience and gave me this kindly hint.

In my speech I did not ask the Americans to pull our chestnuts out of the fire, but I spoke of "the gathering storm," and of the failure to destroy militarism after the last war. We knew that we were destined to live "in a period of emergency of which none could see the end," but we intended to hold fast to our faith and to defend it. All this seemed to evoke the response in the audience and the press which Mr. Kennedy had counted upon.

Congress added its stamp of approval by printing my speech in its Congressional Record on a proposal by the Chairman of the Foreign Relations Committee, Senator Pittman. In doing so, the Senator added, among generous comments, that he had never known a foreigner coming to his country unofficially who had been more cordially received.

In Washington on the morning of December 13th, I had my first meeting with Mr. Sumner Welles, United States Under-Secretary of State, who received me in Mr. Cordell Hull's absence. Of all contemporary Americans, Mr. Welles seemed to me to have the widest knowledge of European problems, together with a lucid mind which I grew to respect.

After a short talk he led me across to the White House to present me to Mr. Roosevelt. We spoke for three-quarters of an hour, freely if somewhat discursively. I sensed that the President might have been slightly embarrassed about how to take this visitor who was not in agreement with his own country's foreign policy. In any event he was correct in avoiding that topic, while expatiating on the inferiority of the air-power of Britain and France compared with Germany's. He kept insisting that we should strengthen ourselves in the air, and described his own intention to increase the armaments of the United States.

We also spoke of Jewish migration to Palestine, then becoming more pressing with the plight of the unhappy refugees. In a reference to Japan the President was firm that he would not recognize that country's conquest of Manchukuo, despite the Japanese attempt to make an economic *bloc* with China and the victim of aggression, but he gave no glimpse of any positive American policy either in the Far East or in Europe. Probably, I reflected, he preferred to play it by ear. This has its limitations in diplomacy. The plan for a conference of powers which he had put forward in January, and which had led to such sharp differences between Mr. Chamberlain and myself, was not mentioned.*

Roosevelt displayed all the charm I had been led to expect, both in this conversation and at a shorter meeting over tea with Mrs. Roosevelt, but at the end I did not feel that I knew the man any better than when I first crossed his threshold.

* *Facing the Dictators,* Book II, Chapter XII.

My memory of this week in the United States, which my critics dubbed the visit of a film star, was one of much friendliness, mixed with anxiety, from the American people about what was to come and a wish to know more, tinged with a reservation about whether any European could really give a dispassionate account of that storm-darkened continent. My comfort was a farewell message in the leading article of a New York newspaper entitled "As a Friend Departs."

★ ★ ★ ★ ★

Chamberlain and Halifax arrived in Rome on January 11th. This visit must, in any circumstances, have been a delicate operation. The Fascist purpose was evident, to divide Britain from France and to aid this process by denigrating the French Government and people in any way possible. The stage has been well set in the Chamber of Deputies in Rome. At the conclusion of a speech by the Italian Foreign Minister, Ciano, on November 30th, the deputies cried out in well-ordered spontaneity, "Tunis, Corsica, Nice, Savoy, Jibuti," an unpleasant curtain-raiser, one would have supposed, for France's principal ally.

M. François-Poncet, the brilliant French diplomatist now transferred as Ambassador to Rome, recorded:

> One might have considered in these conditions, that his [Mussolini's] eager approach towards Great Britain was suspect, that he was aiming less at restoring friendship between Britain and Italy than at harming Anglo–French understanding; that he was intending to divide the democratic powers and to weaken them before the enemy, namely, the totalitarian powers. . . . In truth, he was working no longer for peace but for Germany. His attitude, at all events, was such that London should have taken exception and have warned him that Britain would not separate herself from France and that the cause of the two countries was the cause of peace. . . .
> As for the British visitors, they did not think fit to offer me openly and in public those remarks of sympathy which would have been most timely, because they would have shown that

the Franco–British alliance was an established fact and could not be shaken.*

In the circumstances, it is hardly surprising that, after Chamberlain's departure, Ciano gave instructions to mount a steadily increased propaganda against France. Of the Duce's attitude, the perspicacious Ambassador writes:

> Far from prompting the Duce to greater moderation, the British Ministers' visit to Rome seemed to have made him more impudent. The instructions he had given about me were not softened. I remained in quarantine.†

As the Ambassador had noted, no impression of firmness was left on Fascist minds by the British statesmen. On the contrary, the Duce crisply concluded that Chamberlain and Halifax were not made of the same stuff as Sir Francis Drake and the other magnificent adventurers who created the British Empire:

> These, after all, are the tired sons of a long line of rich men, and they will lose their empire.‡

The Fascist leaders certainly acted up to the opinions they had formed, and confirmed their decision to enter into full alliance with Germany and perhaps with Japan.

A strange feature of this visit was the complacency with which the British Prime Minister apparently regarded its outcome. "I am satisfied," he wrote on January 15th, "that the journey has definitely strengthened the chances of peace. To give first my impressions of Mussolini, I found him straightforward and considerate in his behaviour to us. . . ." §

The only conclusion that can be drawn from this self-satisfaction is that the four senior members of the Cabinet, Chamberlain, Halifax, Simon and Hoare, "The Big Four" as Hoare extravagantly

---

* A. François-Poncet: *Au Palais Farnèse*. Author's translation.
† op. cit.
‡ *Ciano's Diary, 1939–1943.*
§ Feiling: op. cit.

dubs them,* sincerely believed that Munich had secured peace. Certainly, easygoing peacetime methods still prevailed in our preparations for the conflict, which, it should have been clear enough, was fast approaching. A few weeks after his return from Rome, the Prime Minister was to write privately to Lord Tweedsmuir that he felt conscious of some "easing in the tension . . . a greater sense of brightness in the atmosphere." †

For my part, I felt only a sense of oppression and imminent peril, so that I warned my hearers at a National Service rally in Birmingham later in the same month that it was attractive but dangerous to live in a world of make-believe. To some governments, I said, force was now the sole determining factor in politics. It might seem to many that we had been too long listening-in to the moods of others. It was more than time to make plain our intentions and, while we had no desire to order the lives of others, we had every intention of ordering our own.

These warnings, as I knew well, grated on the ears of the Government, though not upon my audiences, which grew constantly larger and more responsive. The Government were soon to point the contrast once again. On March 10th, Sir Samuel Hoare, after, he tells us,‡ consulting the Prime Minister, spoke to his constituents of the creation of a "Golden Age" of peace and material well-being, to be brought about by Hitler, Mussolini, Stalin and the Prime Ministers of France and Great Britain, working together. On the previous day, Chamberlain had told the Lobby Correspondents of the House of Commons that Europe was settling down to a period of tranquillity, and spoke of the possibility of a general limitation of armaments. The Foreign Office could not conceivably have shared this euphoria and Lord Halifax was driven to protest to the Prime Minister.§

★   ★   ★   ★   ★

It happened that on the very day that Chamberlain was speaking to the Lobby Correspondents in the House of Commons, the

* Lord Templewood: *Nine Troubled Years*, page 301.
† Feiling: op. cit.
‡ Templewood: op. cit.
§ Feiling: op. cit.

Czech Government dismissed the Slovak Prime Minister, Monsignor Joseph Tiso, and despatched troops to occupy Bratislava. Upon this, Tiso appealed to Hitler. Now, I thought, the Führer might find his opportunity.

Churchill and I were together in the House of Commons when news came of the Nazi entry into Prague. Only a few minutes before, we had been discussing a cartoon in *Punch* which showed John Bull awakening, while a nightmare figure labelled "War Scare" escaped through the window. Behind John Bull's head was an almanac with the date March 15th. The caption described him as saying, "Thank goodness that's over," while an explanatory note in brackets added: "Pessimists predicted another major crisis in the middle of this month."

Retribution for this myopia had been swift, but the question now was what the Government would do. Would they continue to try to find excuses for Hitler's conduct, or would they at last accept that no trust could be placed in his assurances and try to rally the remaining anti-Axis powers, a task now becoming every week more difficult. Reluctantly, we still thought the first course quite conceivable and for the moment it seemed that we were right.

The next afternoon, March 16th, I said in a debate in the House of Commons that we were meeting in a situation of gravity amounting almost to tragedy. There could be no doubt about the character of Germany's action. We had been given no shred of evidence of ill-treatment of the remaining German minorities in Czech territory, although the French and British Governments should have been told, under the Munich Agreement, if the matter were serious and urgent. My conclusion was that "these grievances which are now being paraded are largely imaginary and are evidence adduced to justify illegitimate action after the event."

All hopes that the new Czech state would be stronger than the old, and Hitler's undertaking that he had no ambitions towards any territories where there were no German-speaking peoples, had now been proved false. I went on to give a quotation from *Mein Kampf*, interpreting much in recent events which might otherwise have been veiled to us:

A wise victor will, if possible, always impose his claim on the defeated people stage by stage. Dealing with a people that has

siderable group of nations, small as well as great. They sit
round a table. You endeavour to draw this line. It is pretty
certain, apart from any other consequences, that every nation,
certainly every small nation, would wish to draw the line so
as to include within the protected area its own country. It is
certain that every one of the members of this conference would
insist, quite naturally, that his own area, and the whole of it,
must be within the line of protection. Does that mean then
that this country, this Parliament, should be committed to an
assurance of support by force of arms of that very long and
varied frontier?

This was exactly what the British Government were soon to hasten
to do, from Poland to Roumania and Greece.

Simon further objected that Britain should not enter into extensive indefinite commitments, and argued that the control of our
foreign policy would then depend not on this Parliament and
country, but "upon a whole lot of foreign countries." He contended, with what I thought a strange perverseness, that recent
acquisitions of territory had not altogether strengthened the German Reich, giving Austria as an instance and adding: "I do not
feel at all sure that the Sudeten Germans will be an unmixed
blessing." Simon did not show a glimmer of understanding, even
then, after the occupation of Prague, that the Sudeten Germans
had been simply a pretext for Hitler's seizure of the whole country.
He appeared to feel no responsibility for the Czech post-Munich
frontiers which the British Government had guaranteed, and ended
by saying that Chamberlain still intended to pursue his policy, as
did his colleagues.

★ ★ ★ ★ ★

This speech was in tune with the opinions of many supporters
of the Government, who were still taking what was apparently the
official line, by saying that no change of policy was called for. The
Chancellor's reply seemed to me deplorable and all in my group
thought the same. We felt that if this were really the Government's
attitude, we could not now give them even tacit support. No doubt

grown defeatist — and this is every people which has volu
tarily submitted to force — he can then rely on this fact th
in not one of those further acts of oppression will it see
sufficient reason to take up arms again.

In the previous autumn, I continued, the country had been stil
far from understanding the challenge that confronted it. There
were then two views,

> but surely, today, after recent events no two views are possible.
> Is there any Member in any part of the House now who be-
> lieves that after those events we shall have more than another
> brief respite, perhaps briefer than the last, before further
> demands are made, before another victim is arraigned and
> before that victim is again faced with the alternative of resist-
> ance or surrender. . . . I am convinced that if the present
> methods in Europe are to be allowed to continue unchecked
> we are heading straight for anarchy, for a universal tragedy
> which is going to involve us all.

I recalled my warning of the autumn, that in a situation so serious the time for party controversy had gone. In the days immediately after the Munich crisis a Government of all parties might
have been formed to prevent its recurrence. No greater contribution could be made now, I said, than that this, the greatest democracy in Europe, should unite and make a national effort without
parallel in its history. Our duty was to consult with all those
nations who were like-minded with us about where we should make
our stand and, "having determined that, to make with them at
once the military plans to give effect to our decisions."

Sir John Simon replied for the Government in a speech which
proved that nothing had been learnt so far. There was no new
spirit in it; Hitler might not have entered Prague. He dismissed
my suggestion that the peace-loving nations should now consult
together and lay their defensive plans:

> Let us imagine the nature of the commitment involved by
> this. We should get to the conference, I should hope, a con-

some of this sentiment percolated through to members of the Government, from outside Parliament as well as from within. The country could hardly have accepted the rape of Czechoslovakia and the denial of Hitler's recent pledges as just another minor incident to be explained away by some clever legal special pleading. The next evening the Prime Minister made a speech in Birmingham which bore little relation to Simon's.

The Eden group now joined with Churchill in tabling a resolution in the House of Commons on March 29th. We asked for the immediate introduction of conscription, for the formation of a National Government, and that "such a government should be entrusted with full powers over the nation's industry, wealth and manpower, to enable this country to put forward its maximum military effort in the shortest possible time." We mustered thirty-six signatories.

Within a few days came the reply: a resolution in the names of one hundred and eighty Conservative Members of Parliament, giving full support to the Prime Minister and insinuating that the signatories of our resolution were trying to divide the nation. Neither motion was debated, for the ugly facts had compelled the Government to alter course abruptly. Guarantees were hurriedly offered of the exact description which had been ridiculed by the Government spokesmen in Parliament only a fortnight before.

On March 31st, Chamberlain announced in the House of Commons:

> In the event of any action which clearly threatened Polish independence and which the Polish Government accordingly considered it vital to resist with their National Forces, His Majesty's Government would feel themselves bound at once to lend the Polish Government all support in their power. They have given the Polish Government an assurance to this effect.

This, I thought, was the only course now left open to us, but it was a far from happy one. At last the Government had apparently abandoned their continuing attempt to appease the insatiable, but the decision had been taken in haste and without any plan as to how help could be brought to Poland by Britain and France. It seemed unlikely that the Chiefs of Staff had had time for serious examination of the strategic possibilities, which were slender enough. Meanwhile, throughout the year Germany was strengthening her Siegfried Line and using the Skoda works of captured Czechoslovakia, the most powerful armaments factory in Europe after Krupps, to swell her strength in armour and other weapons. The Nazi occupation of Czechoslovakia marked an important shift in power to the Axis, materially as well as geographically.

That night I was in Newcastle, speaking at a National Service rally. While endorsing the Prime Minister's new pledge to Poland I added:

> We cannot afford any more relaxation. I hope to heaven we have no more optimistic speeches about golden ages. We can all of us recognize the golden age when we see it.

Nine months later I presided in the House of Commons over a dinner to French deputies.

January 29th, 1940: [M. Yvon] Delbos, [M. Paul] Bastid and one or two others spoke of the past. They all took the view that, while war could not probably have been avoided in any circumstances, we should have been much better placed from every angle, including American co-operation, had the cause of war been the German invasion of Czechoslovakia rather than the German invasion of Poland.

Delbos in particular maintained that he should have resigned at the same time as myself. We had carefully worked out our rearguard action and had we been allowed to follow out our plans he thought that Austrian events would have been postponed until the autumn and Czechoslovakia until the following year. Immense pressure was put upon him in the Cabinet not to resign at the time, but he had no doubt now that he had made a mistake in giving way to it. Had he resigned, the new phase of appeasement, which Chamberlain ushered in, would have been pulled up short at the start.

★   ★   ★   ★   ★

At the beginning of April 1939 the Polish Foreign Minister, Colonel Beck, paid a visit to Great Britain. He asked to see me on the fourth of that month, and came to my London home immediately upon leaving the Prime Minister. The following are the salient points in a record of the conversation which I made at the time and sent to the Foreign Secretary:

> First Beck emphasized that Poland would in no circumstances submit to German rule, nor be included within the German sphere of influence. At the moment the Polish Government was controlled by an inner Cabinet of four, and at a recent meeting they had all been agreed as to this and had determined that they would rather see half the country devastated than submit to German rule. . . .
>
> Colonel Beck continued that it was difficult to express these sentiments in an official conversation without appearing to boast, but he begged me to believe that they represented the truth. As to armaments, Poland was making good progress and had even sold us some anti-aircraft guns. The morale of the country was excellent. If I could go to Warsaw, as he wished that I could, he would be proud to convince me of that. The city, which in normal times was inclined to a certain light-hearted irresponsibility, was now grimly determined.
>
> M. Beck explained to me that his Government welcomed the declaration of His Majesty's Government, and were prepared to reciprocate the assurances given to them. I would recollect how patient he had been over and over again in seeking to come to terms with Germany, but there were limits and those limits had now been reached. A halt had to be called, and so far as the Poles were concerned it would be called.
>
> Some little time ago the German Ambassador had complained to him that Poland had a large force in arms in the neighbourhood of Danzig. "You negotiate then," the Ambassador had complained, "under the menace of bayonets." M. Beck had replied that if this was so Poland was only copying the methods used by Germany herself.
>
> In reply to a question, M. Beck expressed the belief that the result of his visit and of the agreement reached in London would be to deter Germany from taking any further step

against Poland. Germany would be angry and would bluster, but there was nothing she could do. He himself thought that the efficiency of the German army had been greatly exaggerated. Reports at the disposal of the Polish authorities went to confirm this.

In reply to a question of mine on the subject of Russia, M. Beck replied that if we chose to make an arrangement with Russia ourselves that would be no affair of Poland's. He believed, however, that if Poland and Russia were to be included together in an arrangement with the Western Powers now, the effect might be to provoke Germany to instant aggressive action.

In reply to questions about Roumania, M. Beck maintained that if Poland, Britain and France were to enter into an arrangement with Roumania now it would have the effect of finally driving Hungary into the arms of Germany. M. Beck professed to have some hopes that Hungary was not yet entirely subservient to the Axis. He laid emphasis on Hungarian national pride and pleaded that the moment was not yet ripe for such an arrangement with Roumania, though he admitted that the occasion might subsequently arise.

In my covering letter to Halifax I observed:

> The least satisfactory part of our talk, as also the briefest, concerned Roumania. I could not help feeling that Beck was far from anxious that Roumania should be placed on a similar footing to Poland. In part this may be due to Poland's predilection for the role of a great power, in part also to the fact that Poland is more anxious to ensure her own absolute safety than that of her neighbours. By this I do not mean that Beck or the Polish Government are shortsighted enough to ignore the fact that if Roumania is attacked by Germany, Poland would also be involved. Maybe the Polish calculation is the more limited one that, if there is to be a conflict in Eastern Europe, Poland would prefer that Roumania rather than herself should be the first victim.
>
> As you know, I worked with Beck for many years and my impression of this conversation was that he spoke with a much

greater frankness than has been habitual with him, of the relation of Poland with His Majesty's Government. It was only
in respect of third parties and particularly of Roumania that
he seemed to cloak himself in those ambiguous phrases which
he had always at his command.

★   ★   ★   ★   ★

As M. André Dunoyer de Segonzac wrote in this spring of 1939
across my copy of his drawings of the battle front in the first world
war: *Ces dessins de guerre que nous avions la naïveté de croire "la
dernière."*

4

WAR

April–September 1939

The Fascists invade Albania — A talk with M. Gafencu — National Service again impeded — Mr. Molotov replaces Mr. Litvinov — I offer to go to Moscow — *Les Conférences des Ambassadeurs* — The Territorial Army — I rejoin my Regiment — Mr. Hore-Belisha is vexed about armour — Declaration of war — The first air-raid sirens — I accept the Dominions Office

THE NAZI ENTRY into Prague on March 15th and the consequent Western disarray gave Mussolini the opportunity to practise some aggression on his own account. Ciano wrote in his diary a week later:

> Chamberlain has sent a letter to the Duce. He expresses his concern over the international situation and asks the Duce's help in re-establishing mutual trust and ensuring the continuance of peace. Mussolini will answer after striking at Albania. This letter strengthens his decision to act because in it he finds another proof of the inertia of the democracies.*

Mussolini chose Good Friday for his invasion of Albania, of which intention the British Government appear, surprisingly, to have had no advance warning from any source, for the Prime Minister was fishing in Scotland and the Fleet dispersed. The official reaction was a mild protest, while the Prime Minister lamented in a letter:

> I am afraid that such faith as I ever had in the assurances of dictators is rapidly being whittled away.†

* *Ciano's Diary, 1939–1943*, March 23rd, 1939.
† Feiling: *Life of Neville Chamberlain.*

Nevertheless, Lord Perth was instructed to hand in a memorandum of which Ciano wrote that it "might have been composed in our own offices." * This was the nadir of the policy of appeasement.

Mussolini had not invaded Albania on its own account; his purpose was the same as Communist China's when recently invading Tibet, to obtain a strategically dominating position in the area. In an attempt to counter the growing dangers, guarantees were now handed out by the French and British Governments to Greece and Roumania. Although the commitments were multiplying, the resources to fulfil them were still failing, so was a national effort to provide them. In Britain there was no National Service and no Ministry of Supply. This was hardly the way to show Hitler and Mussolini that we meant business, at a time when their continuing illusions about our willpower could only end in war.

On April 24th, I found that the Roumanian Foreign Minister, M. Gafencu, shared my frame of mind. I had had luncheon with Lord Halifax at the Foreign Office and in a talk with Gafencu afterwards, I found him more resolute than most of his countrymen. He feared that Hitler would attempt yet another grab, because of his failure to understand Britain's seriousness of purpose.

Towards the end of April the Government at length made a modest beginning with National Service. Men of twenty years of age were to be called up, about three hundred and ten thousand in all. The political significance to Europe of this gesture was unhappily dimmed by the action of the Labour and Liberal oppositions in voting against the bill to give effect to it. This was the worst mark against them in their conduct before the war. Sir Archibald Sinclair argued that such action was superfluous and contrary to British tradition. Mr. Attlee declared that we could not provide a great continental army in addition to the greatest fleet in the world and a rapidly growing air force. In the event we had to and, as late as June 1944, Britain and the Commonwealth had a larger man-power in the field than the United States.

These criticisms of National Service must have been agreeable reading to Hitler, who had on April 3rd already given instructions to prepare for an attack against Poland at any time from September 1st. The insolence of the Nazi Government was growing with

* Ciano: op. cit.

its success and, on April 28th, Hitler announced, without apology, that the German–Polish Treaty of Arbitration was now dead and that Danzig wished to return to the Reich and must do so. In the same speech he denounced the Anglo–German Naval Agreement, which Mr. Chamberlain had named as the touchstone of goodwill on his return from Munich only seven months before.

Even these events did not persuade Labour and Liberal members to support National Service, or to abstain. I made an appeal that the bill should be passed without a division, to show the nations more immediately threatened that we were determined to resist aggression, but opposition ears were deaf.

★ ★ ★ ★ ★

The British Government having now adopted a policy more akin to my own, the possibility that I might rejoin the Cabinet was sometimes canvassed as the year 1939 drew on. This I did not want to do and could not even consider, unless Cranborne also returned with me. I learnt that the Foreign Secretary was favourably disposed and it appears that he had approached Chamberlain earlier in the year on the subject, when Chamberlain wrote privately, and truly, that I could not for the moment re-enter the Cabinet, since the real difference was still there. He added that my return might even tempt the dictators "to break out now, before the democracies had further strengthened their position." *

The same apprehensive reasoning was applied to prevent Churchill's inclusion in the Government. It was, probably, never practical politics for either of us to join a Government whose leaders still upheld opinions so divergent from our own. Even then, there were signs that the new-found resolution was not entirely supported in No. 10 Downing Street. Early in May, 1939, I received a letter from a friend in the Foreign Office:

I'm afraid "appeasement" may be rearing its ugly head again from across the street — there is a strong wind blowing from there, as you may have noticed. However, I hope and trust it will be firmly resisted from our side. But it is a nasty feel-

* Feiling: op. cit.

ing and the explanation, I think, of why there is no broadening of the Government in view.

In any attempt to rally the peace-loving nations of Europe, Russia's position was capital. The Munich Agreement had been made without consulting Moscow and must, I feared, have gravely undermined Mr. Maxim Litvinov's position as Soviet Foreign Minister. Stalin was the arbiter of Russian policy and he might, as I had told my colleagues in the autumn of 1937, come to terms with Hitler at any moment. The repeated public expression of hatred for each other's systems and intentions could be swiftly expunged in dictatorships.

There was, however, little hope of any determined British effort to enlist the Soviets. The French would have been willing enough, for it had been their traditional policy to call in Russia to redress the military might of Germany. But, since Munich, the leadership of Anglo–French policy had rested with Britain, amongst whose Ministers antipathy towards Russia rivalled misjudgment of Nazi Germany. This was not based on any long-term dread of Soviet power, for Russian military prowess was derided, but on a failure to apprehend the danger of Nazi–Soviet connivance and the mortal peril in which this must place the surviving democracies of Western Europe.

★   ★   ★   ★   ★

Early in April, 1939, immediately after the guarantee had been given to Poland, I suggested to Chamberlain and Halifax that, in order to make a beginning with the Soviets, we should make use of the fact that France, Russia, Turkey and ourselves were all parties to the Straits Convention. The four countries might, I thought, issue some form of joint declaration, perhaps about preserving the *status quo* in the Eastern Mediterranean. Lord Halifax replied that the difficulties were too great and I did not press the idea, though I still think it provided a possible opening.

The negotiations which had begun with Moscow early in April were not, in my opinion, being driven forward with sufficient zest, and I heard with dismay on May 3rd that Litvinov had been replaced by Molotov. A few hours before I knew of this, I had spoken to my constituents about the need for an early and complete understanding with France and Russia. "Let us remember," I added, "the words of Mr. Churchill, whose exceptional talent the nation will wish to see employed in its service at this time, that 'we have a common cause.'"

The talks dragged on through this unhappy month of May. Ministers kept expressing confidence in their outcome, while the Russians occasionally put it about that they did not trust our good faith. When the House of Commons debated foreign affairs on May 19th, I said that it would be a gain to peace if an understanding could be arrived at between our country, France and Russia, and the sooner, the more complete, the more far-reaching that agreement, the better.

Recalling our commitments, I argued that it would be folly not to build the most powerful deterrent in our power. Compulsory National Service on the one hand and an arrangement with Russia on the other would be such a deterrent.

I realized that the difficulty lay in the fears of the smaller powers, for whose position, however, the Russian proposals made as much allowance as ours. Indeed, the British and French drafts had so far dealt only with the countries bordering on Russia. I suggested that a widening of the pact's scope, to cover the whole of Europe, would place Russia's neighbours on the same footing as others and render the idea of an agreement less invidious to them. The pact would not come into operation in respect of Russia's neighbours or in respect of anybody else except with their consent or at their invitation.*

This was going rather faster than the Government had it in mind to do at that time, but I was sure that if we were to do business at all, we must do it quickly.

Wishing to further my ideas without publicity, I went to see Halifax and suggested that he should go to Moscow himself with

---

* Extracts from this speech, giving my judgment on relations with Soviet Russia at that time, are printed as Appendix A.

the least possible delay. I could see that he did not like the idea, so I pointed out that the Prime Minister and he had both gone to see Mussolini and that Stalin would expect treatment at least comparable with that which Mussolini had received. These considerations counted with any country; they were especially important in Russia, which, as a revolutionary power, was sensitive in such matters. However, the Foreign Secretary's reluctance persisted, so that after some further talk I told him that I would be prepared to go myself. I had been the only British Minister to visit Stalin and it would not therefore seem so extraordinary if I went again. Of course, if the Government were to consider this, we would have to determine the terms of reference together so that there could be no misunderstanding about what I was to do. Halifax pondered the proposition and seemed to like it. He said that he would certainly put it to the Prime Minister and I thought it his intention to recommend it. I soon heard, without surprise, that Chamberlain would not agree.

Later, when I told Mr. Churchill what I had done, he thought that I had been rash and that my position as an emissary for this Government would have been a very difficult one. No doubt that was true, but I felt the issue to be so critical and weighty in the scales of peace and war that the risk had to be taken, if the Government would accept it.

I was under no illusions about Stalin's motives. By now, the British and French bargaining position had been weakened. In every sense we scarcely carried the guns. Hitler could offer Russia at least a temporary peace, while if Stalin came to terms with us, he must expect that the Führer might at any moment direct his vengeful fury eastwards. If I had gone to Moscow, I should have tried to persuade the Russians that any agreement with Germany would be dearly bought, while we might still, by girding ourselves for fresh exertions, successfully halt Germany if she broke loose again. The most stubborn difficulty must have been to arrive at any arrangement acceptable to Poland, Roumania and the Baltic States, all of which countries believed that if Soviet troops once entered their lands, they would never leave again. However, if the joint undertaking of the three powers had been available to any future victim of aggression in Europe, the deterrent would have been created and the Ribbentrop–Molotov pact, perhaps, frustrated. Soviet Russia might not then have passed, even temporarily, into the Nazi camp.

★   ★   ★   ★   ★

In the early summer of 1939 I was asked to go to Paris and make a speech in a series called *Les Conférences des Ambassadeurs.* I accepted and this turned out to be a more intimidating business than I had expected. The Théâtre de Marigny, on the Champs-Elysées, was engaged for the occasion, and M. Paul Reynaud, then Minister of Finance, presided. A repeat performance being called for, M. Edouard Herriot, then President of the Chamber of Deputies, took his place. My message was the constancy of Britain at the side of her ally and the dangerous vanities of appeasement. I said:

> The peoples of France and Britain . . . are peaceful people. They hate war. But to hate war and to fear war is not the same thing. No policy that is based upon fear, no policy that appeals to fear, is a policy that a great people can follow and survive. Such a policy will certainly not be countenanced by the British people at this time. It is important that there should be no mistake about that anywhere. . . . Clearly if we do not adopt conscription, other nations will doubt our purpose. We must stop these doubts. That is why we have agreed to this reversal of our traditions as we would to any other that might be necessary. We believe that this is the most effective way to prevent war.
>
> Where will all this lead to? We know that in a long war the resources at our disposal in wealth, raw materials and man-power, would give us final superiority. But this is not enough; we would rather not put it to the test. Everywhere, warlike preparations are being speeded up. We must not, however, think of the horror as inevitable. We still have time to stop on the fatal slope, and to reflect. . . . The greatest tragedy of all would be if, from a stubborn refusal to realize

that we are sincere, some further act of aggression were undertaken which would unleash a world war.*

In a speech at the end of June, 1939, Lord Halifax declared with
renewed emphasis that the first object of British foreign policy
must be to resist aggression. I congratulated him, while writing to
Arthur Mann:

> Though the situation is clearly desperately serious, in some
> ways I feel less anxious, because surely we are at last on the
> right lines? If we can really make Germany believe that we
> will fight, then we may at long last be able to do something
> to prevent an outbreak of war.

Addressing a crowd of nearly forty thousand at a National Service
rally in Ealing on July 1st, I repeated this argument. I noticed
that the tougher my words, the louder the cheering. Parliament,
however, adjourned on August 3rd after an acid debate occasioned
by the Prime Minister's refusal to agree that provision should be
made for its early recall.

The mood of the Government still failed to match the hour. Its
senior members woefully lacked that sense of purpose and leadership which was to mark Mr. Churchill's administration. Mr.
Chamberlain seemed unable to adapt himself with sympathy to the
only course which the nation could follow in unity. He thus undermined his own position and that of the Government, especially in
the House of Commons. He seemed brusque and narrow, while
the renewed rumours of an early General Election caused bitterness within and between the parties, at a time when a leader with
a more sensitive political touch would have been striving to
assuage dissension.

If Hitler were to allow us to fight an election, my friends and
I could not, of course, stand as candidates supporting Chamberlain's record in foreign policy. On August 12th I wrote to Jim
Thomas, asking him to begin to collect material from Ministers'
"sunshine" speeches which I regarded as dangerous deception. On
the same day I sent letters to Richard Law and Lord Cranborne:

* *Freedom and Order,* pages 21–6. French text.

The indications seem to me to point to the Government appealing to the country in November, unless there should be some major upheaval meanwhile. I think that we should now consider our attitude should such an appeal be made, for we do not want to be taken by surprise at the last minute.

It is of course possible that an attempt will be made to reconstruct the Government on wider lines before appealing to the country, but let us suppose the worst from our point of view and that the Government go to the country as they are now, with all the old team, and seek to get a renewal of their mandate.

I do not feel that I myself could, in these circumstances, support such an appeal. There are, no doubt, many in the House and tens of thousands in the country, similarly placed. What then should our attitude be? Ought we to form a group of our own? Would we stand as Independent Conservatives? Would we seek to create a new party? What should our relations be with Winston?

These seem to me to be some of the questions which will require urgent thought within the next few weeks. In any event we shall have to have a clear statement of our own views in respect of the past and our intentions for the future.

So far we have done virtually no propaganda and have allowed charges to be made against us which we have made no attempt to refute. I am not saying that this was wrong in the past but the time has now definitely come, I think, when we should consider a reply.

During these days I felt that I should take some step to make contact again with friends in my Regiment. I was not so old as to rule out active service, should war break out, as seemed increasingly possible. After reporting at the Rifle depot at Winchester, I got into touch with the War Office to ask what I could best do. At that moment a decision was taken by the Government to double the Territorial Army.

This was not wise because, while it resulted in a rapid growth in the numbers of the army, there was not the staff to train the recruits or the equipment to put into their hands, so it was an apparent rather than an effective increase. However, the expansion involved the Territorial battalions of my Regiment and, in consequence, I was asked if I would serve as second-in-command of a battalion of the Rangers affiliated to the King's Royal Rifle Corps. Though I only had a brief previous connection with the Territorial Army, I gladly accepted and there followed some strenuous days at our drill hall off the Tottenham Court Road in London.

We had little in the way of accommodation, few experienced officers or non-commissioned officers and scarcely any equipment. Large numbers came forward, but my vivid memory of those days is of the quality of the men presenting themselves. We were soon picking and choosing. All the would-be riflemen were volunteers and there were among them clerks from banks and insurance offices and recruits from every walk of life, with not a glimmer of hesitation about what they wanted to do. They wished to serve and to give every moment of their spare time to training themselves.

Physically they were superior to their fellow volunteers as I remembered them twenty-five years before; they had made use of their better opportunities. One afternoon a few weeks later, when in camp, I took a detachment on a bathing parade to the Solent. They swam off eagerly, apparently to the Isle of Wight. I thought some of them would get into difficulties and summoned a boat to watch out, but none had need of it, a contrast I reflected to what we could have done in the first war. The standard of intelligence was also high, so that I was hardly surprised when I learnt a year or two afterwards that nearly three hundred of the recruits to this one unit later qualified for commissions.

The selection of junior officers presented us with some problems, despite the many volunteers. We were soon told that we must consider none without military experience. One evening when we were in camp I heard that a friend of mine, the artist, Rex Whistler, had called to see me. As a personality he had always seemed to me much of a piece with his painting, delicate, sensitive and witty. I was therefore the more impressed at his evident eagerness to join us immediately. I warmly shared his wish, but on consulting higher authority, was firmly told that he had not the necessary qualification and that no exception could be made. When I reluctantly gave Whistler this news, he was utterly crestfallen and I miserable at my failure. I was to see him several times in the next few years when he came to stay with us at our house in Sussex, on his leaves from another regiment, until he went into action overseas and was killed.

For my own instruction I was given an opportunity to learn the work of an armoured unit, which was eventually to be my battalion's role and, for this purpose, I was attached to the 2nd Battalion of the 60th Rifles, which formed part of the 1st, and then only, Armoured Division. I was made welcome and was soon the instructed spectator of many exercises on Salisbury Plain. What I saw then of the equipment of even this division, which must be indispensable if we were ever to send an expeditionary force to France, greatly disturbed me. It also led to an altercation with the then Secretary of State for War, Mr. Leslie Hore-Belisha.

One evening when I had to return to the House of Commons for an important vote, Hore-Belisha spoke to me pleasantly and asked me how I was getting on. I told him of my attachment to the 1st Armoured Division. "Ah," said Hore-Belisha, "they at least have everything they need." I assured him that unhappily they had not. His whole attitude immediately changed and an incredulous and vexed expression came over his face. I continued my explanations, but he clearly had no patience with them and our interview ended badly.

During these days in camp, visitors as well as messages came to me from time to time, Mr. Churchill being a frequent correspondent. An unexpected caller one afternoon was Sir Ronald Campbell, our Ambassador to France, who took a few hours off for a talk with me. Though resolute in his loyalty to the *Entente,* Campbell was not without his anxieties about the French political scene. Paris could hardly be expected to be firmer than London when almost all the impact of war must fall upon France. We lamented our minuscule contribution on land.

One evening when we were marching back to camp after some exercises, I saw Colonel Bobbie Erskine, then G.S.O.I of our division, watching us from the roadside with a stranger beside him. Later I asked Erskine who his companion had been. "Didn't you recognize him? He recognized you all right. He was the German Military Attaché."

In the early morning of August 24th I remember well a rustling and a strange sense of eventfulness which brought me to my tent door, as it did others. The daily papers had just arrived with news of the Nazi–Soviet Pact. I was asked by another officer what this would mean in terms for us. I had to say that it meant war.

★　　★　　★　　★　　★

Earlier in the same month, Ciano and Ribbentrop had met. I suppose that the foreign policy of two great allies has never in modern times been in the hands of men at once so sycophantic and without scruple. "Well, Ribbentrop," asked Ciano, "what do you want? The Corridor or Danzig?" "Not that any more," Ribbentrop replied, "we want war." *

This remark seems to me to express correctly the responsibility for the second world war. It did not take much foresight to know of Hitler's ambitions, which were revealed in *Mein Kampf* and made possible by Germany's geographical position. Probably the Führer accepted that he would have to fight France; it may be that he and Mussolini never understood that Britain's reluctance did not mean defeatism. War could now have been avoided only if we had continued to appease to the point of surrendering our national existence. A disastrous result of Chamberlain's policy was that Hitler and Mussolini could believe we were weak enough to acquiesce in their designs. The Führer was wont to talk disparagingly of his enemies as the little worms he saw at Munich; they would be too cowardly to attack.

British policy had been persistent to the point of obstinacy. The price had now to be paid.

On the night of August 29th, I said in a broadcast to the United States:

> Our obligations to Poland will of course be honoured; not only because our pledged word has been given, but also because it is now universally understood that something of

* *Ciano's Diary, 1939–1943.*

much greater significance is at stake than the determination of one frontier or even the freedom of one people, however brave.

The world has to choose between order and anarchy. For too long it has staggered from crisis to crisis under the constant threat of armed force. We cannot live for ever at the pistol point. The love of the British people for peace is as great as ever, but they are no less determined that this time peace shall be based on the denial of force and a respect for the pledged word.*

★   ★   ★   ★   ★

On September 1st the Territorial Army was placed on active service and, on our return from camp, my battalion found itself charged with the protection of a number of key bridges over the Thames. The newspaper hoardings were placarded with notices of the attack on Poland and, as I visited our posts, I reflected unhappily upon that country's plight. While I supposed that a declaration of war against Germany by France and ourselves must soon follow, I was far from clear what effective action the Western Allies could take, even if they had the will, of which I was doubtful. Yet if they made no move, Poland must in time be overrun, with fearful calamity to herself and damage to the reputation of her allies. I wondered what would happen then.

Against this background, I was not convinced what my own course should be. Even if asked to go back into the Government as it was at that time, I did not want to accept. I knew that my return would not be welcome to the Prime Minister and most of his senior colleagues; they would only tolerate it in response to public demand. Nor did I believe that such a Government, modified only by the addition of Mr. Churchill and myself, could lead us in a war. I had been advocating a National Government for months past; none could pretend that the existing administration, so amended, would be anything of the kind.

I saw Mr. Churchill frequently in those days and told him my thoughts, but he would not accept my reluctance to rejoin. I had no right to go on soldiering, he argued, my place was in the Govern-

* *Freedom and Order*, pages 36–9.

ment. We could effect much more there together. On the evening
of September 2nd we had another talk, when Mr. Churchill told
me of an interview he had had with the Prime Minister. Chamberlain offered him a seat in the War Cabinet and he had asked
whether I was also to be invited to join the Government. Mr.
Chamberlain had replied: "Yes, certainly, one of the major offices
of state." Churchill had not been told which, but he had no doubt
that Chamberlain would send for me.

On the morning of September 3rd my political group assembled
in Ronald Tree's house to await the Prime Minister's statement.
When it came, it seemed rather the lament of a man deploring his
own failure than the call of a nation to arms. Afterwards I started
to walk to the House of Commons with Duff Cooper and Derrick
Gunston. As we approached Parliament Square the air-raid sirens
wailed. We stopped and I observed, perhaps foolishly, "Where do
we go from here?" Whereupon Duff Cooper drew himself up and
answered typically: "To the House of Commons, of course." We
continued on our way, until Louis Spears picked us up in his car
and drove us into Palace Yard. Here we found a number of
Members assembled underneath the archway outside one of the
Ministers' entrances. Presumably they were supposed to be taking
cover, though actually they were as vulnerable there as anywhere.
We then went through on to the terrace until the false alert was
over, when we trooped into the Chamber to hear Chamberlain
repeat his declaration that the country was at war.

In the afternoon my summons came. There was a great crowd
of people in Downing Street when I drove into it. They seemed
glad to see me there again. Chamberlain invited me to come back
into the Government and asked me if I was prepared to do so. I
replied that we were now at war and I was therefore ready to
give any help that I could. He said that he wanted me to take the
Dominions Office which, he claimed, would now have a special
importance in view of the contribution which the Dominions, in
their loyalty, were likely to offer. I replied that I would be glad
to do this. Chamberlain continued, speaking with some embarrassment, that there was one difficulty about the War Cabinet itself.
He wished to keep it small and the service Ministers would have to
be included. In the circumstances, he could not offer me a seat in

the War Cabinet, but I would be a constant attender at their meetings. I asked whether this meant that I could make any contribution to the discussions and he said that, strictly speaking, these should be limited to what I had to say about the Dominions, but he did not expect that this restriction would be at all rigidly enforced.

While I liked the idea of working with the Dominions, I could feel no enthusiasm for the general arrangement of the Government, nor for my own somewhat anomalous position in the Cabinet. If it had not been for the emergency of war, nothing would have induced me to return. The next few months, until Mr. Churchill formed his Government, were for me uneasy because, though I was a spectator of most War Cabinet proceedings, I had no real part in them. It is always disagreeable to be neither fish nor fowl, but in war those considerations do not count.

I told Churchill of my talk with the Prime Minister. He shared my sentiments, and said that we must keep in touch, which we did from that evening, for twenty-five years.

BOOK TWO

Endurance

1

POLAND FIGHTS ALONE
September–November 1939

The Dominions enter the war — Our complicated relations with
Eire — The Empire Air Training Scheme — Poland vanquished
— Allied war aims — Mr. Maisky defends Soviet policy — A visit
to the French and British fronts — I am disturbed by what I see
— The Maginot Line — "They shall not pass"

MY FIRST DAY at the Dominions Office was September 4th, 1939.
The High Commissioners came to see me and we arranged to meet
every afternoon, so that I could give them information of the War
Cabinet's proceedings and we could consult together. Within a
matter of days Canada, Australia and New Zealand had declared
themselves at war with Germany and offered to raise and equip a
division apiece for service at home and abroad. To Australia and
New Zealand I had telegraphed that we must get ready for a long
war, which would call for all our resources, whether Japan's neutrality were friendly or reserved.

The Union of South Africa presented a more chequered aspect.
Before the outbreak of war, the South African Prime Minister,
General James Hertzog, had shown marked sympathy for the German cause. When I had read of these opinions, I was reminded of
an incident which I had witnessed on my first visit to Chequers in
November 1926. Mr. Stanley Baldwin was then Prime Minister.
During the Imperial Conference, General Hertzog and Mr. W. L.
Mackenzie King, the Prime Minister of Canada, had been his
principal guests for a weekend. The South African had appeared
understanding in speech as well as gracious in manner, "a gentle
creature" Baldwin called him. We knew, nonetheless, how perverse
his mind could be, at least to British judgment. At that moment
the controversy was at its height over what flag the Union was to

fly. Encouraged, no doubt, by the easy exchanges of that weekend, the British Prime Minister was on the steps of Chequers saying good-bye to Hertzog, when he quizzically added: "and please take care of the flag." With characteristic suppleness Hertzog kept the old flag, added a new one, and flew both together.

General Jan Christian Smuts did not share Hertzog's opinions, but he skilfully preserved a façade of unity within the Government, until Hitler's invasion of Poland set off a startling chapter of events in South Africa. The Prime Minister would have been obliged to summon Parliament to confirm his country's entry into war; but not to confirm its neutrality. He had, however, overlooked the ten-year rule by which the term of the elected members of the Senate expired on September 6th. As a result, Parliament had to be called together to pass the legislation needed to prolong the life of the Senate and met on September 2nd, the eve of the British declaration of war. General Hertzog's Cabinet at once split on the issue of belligerency. The Governor-General, Sir Patrick Duncan, said he could not grant the Prime Minister a dissolution if General Smuts were able to form a majority government and the difference had, therefore, to be fought out in Parliament. There, on the day when I took over the Dominions Office, Smuts won by a majority of eighty votes against sixty-seven.

On receiving this news, the South African High Commissioner, Mr. te Water, came to see me. He immediately confirmed his personal sympathies by saying that General Hertzog understood his people better than General Smuts did. He hoped that the new Prime Minister would succeed in finding a formula upon which all sections of South African opinion could unite, for, given time and the influence of Germany's actions, South Africa's co-operation would grow rapidly. But he greatly feared the consequences of a split between Hertzog and Smuts. While I listened to the High Commissioner's comments, I did not think it necessary to conceal my satisfaction at the turn of events which brought General Smuts back to the office of Prime Minister. There was no man living whose wisdom I respected more.

A Government was formed in Cape Town committed to a declaration of war, which was proclaimed on September 6th. With a slender majority Smuts had to manœuvre warily, but he contrived to give us valuable help in the Empire Air Training Scheme and in other ways, even before Mussolini's acts of war. It was this signal, with its African consequences, which enabled him to despatch an expeditionary force at the moment when our need was greatest.

★ ★ ★ ★ ★

Infinitely more complicated and querulous were relations with Eire, as the Irish Republic was then called. Nominally a Dominion, with the King still signing Letters of Credence for the appointment of its representatives to other countries, Eire had declared itself a neutral, wished to be accepted by us as such, and yet asked for a consignment of arms of various kinds at a cut rate. Our dealings bristled with the possibilities of trouble, some serious, others in lighter relief.

It so happened that Mr. Éamon de Valéra and I had worked together in years gone by at many meetings of the League of Nations. I liked him personally and we were often of the same mind on international problems, always excluding, of course, the six counties of Ulster. When I had been on holiday in Ireland a few weeks before Munich, Mr. de Valéra asked me to luncheon in Dublin, where we talked over old times as well as present dangers. Now that I was at the Dominions Office, he greeted me with kindly messages sent through Mr. Dulanty, Eire's astute and experienced High Commissioner, and through Mr. Walshe, the head of the Eire Department of External Affairs, who soon visited me.

However, to guard against possible differences, I was convinced that we must have a diplomatic representative in Dublin. A characteristic negotiation followed, Eire asking for an Ambassador and we declining anything so portentous for a country still in name a part of the British Commonwealth. Eventually a "Representative" was offered and accepted, Sir John Maffey doing the work with patience and skill.

As the weeks passed, it became increasingly evident that the Government of Eire wanted to do anything it could to be helpful, provided such action did not conflict with their doctrine of neutrality which, I had to admit, the great majority of the Irish people wished to see preserved. One of our earliest problems was connected with the soldiers, sailors and airmen from Eire who had volunteered to serve in His Majesty's Forces. When these went on leave, their presence in uniform was held to be hardly consistent with neutrality, yet Mr. de Valéra did not want to stop them coming home or even to stop others from enlisting, as they continued to do. Some method had to be found of allowing these men to travel to and fro, while taking account of the susceptibilities of a neutral. Eventually we evolved a scheme. Dumps of civilian clothes were provided at Holyhead, where servicemen travelling on leave to Ireland could change into them, resuming uniform on their return. This little device was endorsed by the Cabinet and worked smoothly through the war years.

There was, however, no humour in the danger to merchant ships of all countries caused by the activities of German submarines off the coast of Eire. To meet this we gradually established some useful, if unofficial, co-operation, which was of service to the Admiralty. But no minor contrivance could compensate for the loss of the Irish ports and of Berehaven in particular. The Agreement of April 25th, 1938, had surrendered their use, and the resultant toll in ships and lives was to be cruel and hard to bear. The same British convoys brought supplies to Eire, and this not unnaturally rankled, in particular with the Royal Navy. Small wonder that the seizure of the ports by force should have been considered by the Cabinet in October 1939, and only abandoned with reluctance by Mr. Churchill, as First Lord of the Admiralty. It is more difficult to understand why so complete a surrender had been accepted in the first place. A puzzling feature of the whole business, the First Lord's civil staff told me, was that at the time the Admiralty did not seem to have made any strong protest.

★　★　★　★　★

It was at one of my daily meetings with the High Commissioners that both Mr. Vincent Massey for Canada and Mr. Stanley Bruce for Australia brought up the question of what the Empire could contribute in the air. They thought that it was this arm, with its scope for individual venture and gallantry, which would make the most appeal to their countrymen. It was decided that I should write to the Secretary of State for Air, Sir Kingsley Wood, tell him this, and suggest an informal discussion about what might be done.

When Massey informed me that his Government would like to be hosts if a good plan emerged, I arranged a joint meeting with the British departments concerned in my room at the Dominions Office. This was the origin of the Empire Air Training Scheme, under which our own would-be pilots and navigators, together with those of Australia and New Zealand, went to Canada in their thousands for training, while the South Africans and the Rhodesians had like schemes of their own. The figures were to swell, until the schools in Canada were supplying about eleven thousand pilots and seventeen thousand aircrew every year. There had never been an effort like it in the world before and its contribution to victory was capital.

I was far from happy at the inactivity we and the French had displayed while Hitler's armies swept to victory in Poland under the wings of air power but, on September 12th, the Supreme War Council had been emphatic in their negative. On October 1st, Ciano met Hitler in Berlin and the conquest of Poland was complete. Without help and attacked from east and west, courage alone could not withstand overwhelming aircraft and armour. The Führer had already begun on his next move. During the previous fortnight he had been transferring the bulk of German forces to the western front; the offensive against France was being prepared.

Hitler's timing was now at its best and he skilfully combined peace overtures with his aggressive plans. On October 6th he spoke to the Reichstag assembled in the Kroll Opera House, exultantly describing the victory over Poland, where the new "settlement" to be made would be a "final" revision of the Treaty of Versailles. Incredibly, Hitler appears to have believed sincerely that these proposals for the abandonment of our ally, Poland, would be heeded. Colonies were also demanded and their restoration was put into the first place; it seemed evident that the claim was now for more than those territories previously under German rule.

M. Daladier's reply on October 10th was to the point. "France," he declared, "has taken up arms against aggression, and will not lay them down until she has positive guarantees of security, of a security which will not be called into question every six months."

On September 28th the Dominions had asked, on Mr. Bruce's initiative, for immediate discussion between the High Commissioners and members of the War Cabinet about the peace offensive which Hitler was expected to launch and a meeting was arranged for six o'clock that evening. When the Prime Minister, Lord Halifax and I met the High Commissioners, a statement of policy on our war aims was worked out to be used as a basis for the reply to the Führer. The first essential, it was decided at the meeting, was to convince the world that we were fighting solely to free Europe from Hitler and the Nazi regime and that we were not prolonging the war in our own material interests.

Meanwhile I had already expressed myself in general terms on this topic in a broadcast to the nation on September 11th:

> There can be no lasting peace until Nazism and all it stands for in oppression, cruelty and broken faith, is banished from the earth.
> For some of us, the challenge has come a second time in our generation. There must be no second mistake. Out of the welter of suffering to be endured, we must fashion a new world that is something better than a 'stale reflection of the old, bled white.*

As before, these ambitions were to prove easier to express than to fulfil.

After several days of exchanges with the Dominions, and in accord with their opinion, the Prime Minister replied to Hitler soon after Daladier:

> It is no part of our policy to exclude from her rightful place in Europe a Germany which will live in amity and confidence with other nations. . . .
> The peace which we are determined to secure, however,

* *Freedom and Order,* pages 41–5.

must be a real and settled peace, not an uneasy truce interrupted by constant alarms and repeated threats. What stands
in the way of such a peace? It is the German Government, and
the German Government alone.

Even so, General Smuts telegraphed on the evening of the 11th,
after I had recorded in my diary that "at 8 o'clock in the evening
it seemed as though everything was satisfactory," to express his regret at the absence of any clearly stated war aims. His was not a
lone voice in asking for a more specific declaration.

This topic of war aims led to some argument between the allies,
but at this stage to no acrimony. The French, who had already
suffered so much, wanted to ensure that Hitler once disposed of,
they could not be attacked by Germany again. The Dominions,
from their remoter geographical position, felt that the more explicit the definition of war aims the more effective it would be in
uniting their own peoples in support of the war. This resulted in
intermittent discussion while I was at the Dominions Office.

Personally I understood French motives for being chary of a
return by stages to President Wilson's Fourteen Points which, despite good intentions, brought a legacy of misunderstanding after
the first world war. In October, some senior members of the Government, believing that Hitler's mind might still be open to negotiation, considered a settlement with Germany more likely if the
terms were not precisely defined. This was a lingering relic of past
appeasement policies. I did not share their opinions, but I did fear
that with so many viewpoints, there was at least danger that to
define too closely might be to divide too sharply.

The position of the Government at this time was by no means a
happy one. Some of the senior Ministers, notably Sir John Simon
and Sir Samuel Hoare, were much under criticism for their earlier
policies. The Dominion High Commissioners would voice their
feelings about them to me, vigorously if unofficially. The Government were, of course, exclusively drawn from the Conservative
Party and its allies, nor was the best use being made of the talent

available from those ranks. The Prime Minister was still resentful towards his critics and at a meeting of the War Cabinet, my diary records:

> *October 4th:* Neville Chamberlain showed a flash of his old vindictiveness when Leo Amery's name was suggested for a job. I had passed it up on a slip of paper, though the suggestion was originally [Lord] Hankey's [Minister without Portfolio] and Neville pushed it away with an irritated snort.

Hoare showed the same reaction from the other side of the table,

> in contrast to Winston and Edward Halifax, the last of whom had the bright idea of adding Duff's [Cooper] name to the list. Neville Chamberlain at once said vehemently that he thought neither of them would be at all suitable. It was a revealing little explosion.

This rancour was not dimmed even after Chamberlain's resignation as Prime Minister. When, as Lord President, he had to swear in Lord Cranborne as a Minister, he would not speak a friendly word.

Wishing to make clear my view of our war aims, I told Parliament in concluding the debate on the Address on December 6th, 1939:

> Hitler himself is not a phenomenon; he is a symptom; he is the Prussian spirit of military domination come up again. National Socialism was originally conceived in militarism, and it believes only in force. From the beginning, it has organized its people for war. It is the most barren creed that was ever put before mankind. Therefore, if it is allowed to triumph there will be no future for civilization, no future for our debates, no future for our suggestions and no future for the suggestions that have been made by hon. Members opposite.

During this autumn I had given some thought to the kind of world we could hope to build after the war. For those of my generation who had seen the failure which followed the earlier catastrophe, it was natural that we should wish to provide, in so far as we could, against the repetition of this disillusionment. I spoke, in the same speech, of the future:

> The war will bring about changes which may be funda-
> mental and revolutionary in the economic and social life of
> this country. On that we are all agreed. In fact, every war has
> done so, and, since the rise of industry in the modern sense of
> the term, the upheaval has been all the greater. We saw this
> after the Crimea, a minor war for this nation as compared with
> the one that we are fighting now. It brought about a complete
> reform of the War Office, but, fortunately, we can do that now
> without a war. It brought about other changes. It brought
> about the beginning of our medical system, and the beginning
> of the nursing system in this country.
>
> Again, the Boer War disclosed the poor standard of health
> of the recruits; it brought home to all concerned the standard
> of health at that time . . . which resulted in the beginning of
> the school medical service. So it was in the last war.*

In a letter to Lord Halifax I enlarged upon the international aspect of these same problems. I agreed that we had two sets of war aims, the negative and the positive. The former

> to ensure that Europe is not subjected to Nazi rule. The only
> way to do this is to destroy Hitlerism and all that it stands for.

But we had, I suggested, to aim at something wider:

> If the supreme effort which we shall have to make to win this
> war is to be worth while, we cannot be content with merely
> attempting to restore the world situation to what it was before
> war broke out. We must do better next time; as well is not
> good enough.

To achieve this, I looked forward to a solution

> on the lines of some form of European federation. This would
> comprise a European defence scheme, a European customs

* *Freedom and Order,* pages 47–53.

union and common currency. All these projects may seem somewhat wild now, but they are in truth little more than the extension of Briand's conception of a European union.

I did not suggest that the detailed proposals described should be included in our war aims, but I thought that we should bring home to our own people, as well as to other nations, that we were fighting for something more worthwhile than our own interests, "or even the re-creation of the world as we knew it two months ago."

These ideas were slow to develop after the war. I had no direct part in them until my return to the Foreign Office in the early nineteen-fifties. Then we brought Italy and western Germany into closer union by enlarging the Brussels Treaty and making its terms general against any aggressor within its membership, instead of directing them against our former foes. We also negotiated successfully to bring western Germany into N.A.T.O. Federation was less attractive, with its merger in a European Parliament at a time of French political uncertainties and a large communist minority in Italy. Where our heritage of a free Parliament is at issue, caution cannot be censured and may prove surer as well as safer.

★ ★ ★ ★ ★

Early in October, 1939, the Soviet Ambassador, Mr. Ivan Maisky, asked me to luncheon. I knew him well and respected him as a man who wished, I believed sincerely, to improve relations between our two countries. I suspected that the Stalin deal with Hitler, dreadful as its consequences had been, was a measure of Soviet fear of Nazi power and a temporizing action. I thought it prudent to accept the invitation, having first got the agreement of the Foreign Secretary, who asked me to take the opportunity to sound Maisky about our representation in Moscow. On this I reported to Halifax that Maisky showed no enthusiasm for a politician of the Left as ambassador, saying, wisely as I thought, "that the representative should have the confidence of his Government. . . ." He added that the important factor was the personality of the man. His occupation in ordinary life, he thought, was of secondary significance.

I began our conversation by telling my host that I remembered a luncheon during 1935,* in the country near Moscow at Mr. Litvinov's house, at which Mr. Maisky was also present, when the butter was stamped "Peace is Indivisible." I also remembered the warning that was uttered, so far as I could recollect, to Mr. William Strang of the Foreign Office, when he brought his knife too near that magic formula. It did not seem to me possible to reconcile those words on the butter pats with the policy which the Soviet Government appeared to be pursuing at the present time.

Mr. Maisky replied that he remembered the occasion perfectly, but that he did not think the evolution of Soviet policy was very difficult to understand. He complained that the Foreign Secretary had not visited Moscow in 1939, though the Soviet Ambassador had himself indicated that such a visit would have been welcomed. I replied that this might have been just as well, in view of what had happened afterwards and in view of Russia's present attitude. Maisky retorted that if the visit had taken place, the position would have been different. He also remarked adversely upon the small staff and the dilatory travel of the British military mission of that time.

As I expected, Maisky defended Russia's actions in Poland and the Baltic States† on the grounds that it was essential "that certain vital strategic points should be under her own control." He claimed that his country's demands had not been grasping. The Soviet frontier with Poland even now included less territory than Tsarist Russia had held. As for the Baltic States, the problem was once again strategic. In a world such as this, "where wild beasts are loose, every country has to take certain precautions for its own safety." I replied that this did not justify the Soviet action in Finland, which country enjoyed great sympathy all over the world.

After further argument on this topic and that of the Baltic States, we discussed the interpretation of neutrality, a very important matter for us. Maisky protested that Soviet Russia was as ready to trade with Britain as with any other belligerent. He thought our discussions on timber and rubber were a useful beginning. I reminded him that when I had visited Moscow four years before, we had agreed that the interests of our two countries were nowhere in

* *Facing the Dictators,* page 158.
† See page 107.

conflict; the Ambassador said that was still the position. In this I feared that Maisky's wish was father to his thought.

Finally the Soviet Ambassador put out some feelers about the possibility of peace with Germany but, seeing no encouragement, did not persist. Probably he was by then a little out of touch with the true interpretation of the Muscovite gospel. No doubt Mrs. Maisky was right to say that her husband had always been anxious for improved Anglo–Russian relations and that recent events had been a disappointment to him. I reported this conversation to Halifax and, with his agreement, I did not lose touch with Maisky.

★ ★ ★ ★ ★

The Prime Minister had appointed Lord Hankey, Admiral Lord Chatfield, Minister for Co-ordination of Defence, and myself as a small Cabinet Committee to handle Dominions questions. On September 14th we decided to invite each of the five participants in the war to send a Cabinet Minister to Europe. We had to tread warily, so as not to seem to be preparing for a meeting of Cabinet Ministers of the British Commonwealth; Mr. Mackenzie King would not have welcomed any likeness to the Imperial War Cabinet of 1917–18.

All the Dominions accepted and their representatives assembled in London by the end of October. They were well chosen. The Canadian Government sent a senior Minister, Mr. Thomas Crerar, so did New Zealand, in the person of Mr. Peter Fraser, her deputy Prime Minister. Mr. Richard Casey from Australia and Mr. Deneys Reitz from South Africa had impressive war records, Reitz having been in addition a brilliant leader of Commandos against us under General Smuts in the South African war. I had long admired his book, *Commando,* a lively masterpiece of military adventure. India was represented by Sir Muhammad Zafrullah Khan, who was already known to me and was to be a friend for twenty years and more.

The preliminaries in London consisted of meetings with the Chiefs of Staff and with British Ministers. About one of these, presided over by the Prime Minister, Reitz was to write caustically: "It might have been a meeting of some suburban county council discussing the rates." * But the chief interest for our guests and for me was a visit to France and to the French and British fronts.

A journey by destroyer and motor car brought us to Paris at eleven in the morning of November 10th. We drove at once to the fortress of Vincennes, where General Maurice Gamelin, the Allied Commander-in-Chief, gave us a smooth and practised account of his dispositions in front of a large-scale map. I was not proud of the minute British contribution represented by two small Union Jacks on pins amidst a forest of Tricolours. Gamelin had every confidence in the Maginot Line, but little in the Belgian refusal of staff talks to determine how to defend the area between the northern end of the Maginot Line and the sea.

The Prime Minister, M. Daladier, received us in the afternoon and told us that he was expecting an early German attack. He attributed the delay to the enemy's hope of dividing Britain and France. To me it seemed that the weather was a more probable cause. Our two countries, Daladier said, had tried to appease, but Hitler could not be appeased and the French people saw that they might have once again to rebuild their homes, rebuilt only twenty years ago.

The next morning was Armistice Day. We spent it driving across the Somme battlefield, where memories from the last war were still vivid for me. Reitz and I were familiar with the same grim sector, from Delville Wood forward to Factory Corner and the Gird Ridge. Would events repeat themselves, I wondered. It seemed improbable. No war begins where the last left off, but I could not conjecture what form it was going to take, only be sure that air-power must influence, and might transform, the new campaign, and be troubled at our lack of armour, all the more so after Poland's experiences.

We reached the headquarters of our Commander-in-Chief, General Lord Gort, at Habarcq near Arras, in time for luncheon. On this day I began to understand the problems which confronted our defence. Air Vice-Marshal C. H. B. Blount, who was in command of the Air Component, told us that he had no aerodromes "properly so-called" at his disposal; several were already waterlogged and

* Deneys Reitz: *No Outspan*.

abandoned. That evening Gort dined with us and we had some talk of his dispositions and prospects. I had much respect for Gort, not only on account of his gallantry, but for his firmness of character and decision, even though it seemed that a smaller command, of a division or an army corps, would have better suited his qualities. As always, he was cheerful and confident, while not minimizing his difficulties which included some serious shortages in equipment.

On November 12th we met the two corps commanders, Lieutenant-General Sir John Dill and Lieutenant-General Alan Brooke, and some of the divisional commanders, while making an extensive tour of the British sector. What I saw on this journey was not what I had expected. Our line was thinly held and, though much work was going on, the defences were still patchy. This was in part due, as I told the Cabinet on my return, to our extended front, which left less man-power at our disposal than the French could command in some of their sectors. The two British divisions in the line were together holding a front of fourteen thousand yards, about the same length as the Fifth Army had held in March 1918. This seemed to me ominous, for I had been there and experienced the German breakthrough and its consequences.

I was not surprised to find Dill uneasy at the general layout, nor was there any certainty that the British Expeditionary Force would ever fight in these defences, indifferent as they then were. If Belgium were invaded, we were to go forward to the support of a thinly spread Belgian army, which seemed a doubtful proposition unless we had command of the air.

When the day was over, I compared notes, particularly with Reitz and Casey, and found that they shared my misgivings. Reitz was later to write of his own impressions of his drive with Casey:

> We shook our heads at what we saw. The new line, under hurried construction, seemed an amateurish affair. The trenches were shallow, the concrete domes the French had built at intervals of eight hundred yards contained only a single anti-tank rifle apiece and the loophole faced sideways with no frontal view. We thought the psychological effect on troops unable to see ahead of them would shake their morale, and taking it all round we did not like the look of things. . . .

We were taken over Mont de Bouvines, an obsolete fortress dating from 1870, now held by British troops, and we watched a maze of muddy trenches and tank traps being haphazardly scooped out by steam shovels.*

The next morning we travelled south through villages and towns which had become household names in the first world war and were soon to be destroyed again. Finally, after Verdun and Metz, we came to the headquarters of the French Third Army, where General Condé received us. He gave an account of his front and the prospects, which seemed to me coldly realistic. It was at this time a strange twilight war, with artillery fire restricted to counter-battery work on either side. The Germans fired shell for shell with the French guns and No Man's Land was patrolled by the opposing armies, without, it seemed, much contact.

Condé did not think an attack by the German army through Holland and Belgium likely before the spring. The Germans would husband their resources in oil and other supplies for that big operation. They might also hope, in Condé's opinion, that the six months' interval would cause boredom and dissension in our ranks. The Allies, he warned, must not underestimate what the German effort might be at that time, for they could not expect to have achieved air parity.

There was a sense of drama in the Maginot Line: fortresses which seemed immensely strong, two British soldiers unexpectedly in charge of an observation post, a fervent confidence that could be felt. After General Sivot, who commanded the Metz sector of the line, had made a short speech, to which I replied, he came across, took off the bronze badge which he, like all his men, was wearing and pinned it to my coat. It showed a gun in a fortress and bore the legend "They shall not pass."

As far as visitors could see, there was nothing wrong with either the defence or the morale of the defenders, but this was hardly likely to be the pivotal point of any German attack. On the way northward again, I asked to make a short stop at Verdun and visited the War Memorial with the Sous-Préfet of the province. A crowd of civilians and soldiers in the streets gave me a welcome I was to remember in the darker days ahead.

* op. cit.

I had always felt that Munich was harmful to French morale, because of the ambivalence it created; France was called to arms and then her forces were stood down. When, at the outbreak of war, mobilization was ordered a second time and the major offensive on the western front was long delayed, the French again expected to be demobilized. In a democracy, soldiers cannot be called up twice in as many years and left inactive without consequences. I was glad that Britain had been fortunate enough to escape the ordeal, though this was scarcely to her credit.

2

CHURCHILL TAKES OVER
December 1939–May 1940

Mr. Casey and Mr. Reitz report to the Prime Minister — Mr.
Hore-Belisha blames the Commander-in-Chief — Arrival of the
Canadian troops at Greenock — A conversation with Admiral
Darlan — I fly to Cairo — Arrival of the Anzacs at Suez — The
Egyptian Prime Minister and King Farouk — The inspiration
of the Commonwealth and Empire — Mr. Sumner Welles wants
an arms agreement — Russia attacks Finland — German invasion
of Norway and our failure — Herr Hitler strikes at the Low
Countries — Mr. Churchill becomes Prime Minister — I go to the
War Office

ON OUR RETURN to London, Reitz and Casey asked to see the Prime
Minister to make their report to him. This was arranged and
Reitz opened the conversation, he tells us, by describing the Gort
Line and its French equivalent, as well as our experiences in that
area during the 1914–18 war. He said to Chamberlain: "Sir, if you
will pardon my saying so, the Germans will go through there like
a knife through cheese." *

Reitz left the interview under the impression that, though he
and Casey had argued the matter, they had made no progress. This
was not entirely true. The Prime Minister later asked me what I
thought, when I told him that I had little to add to what I had
already said to the War Cabinet. I thought the morale of our
troops high, but I endorsed the verdict of Casey and Reitz about
the weakness of the line. This, I told Chamberlain, was not due
to any fault on the part of the defenders, but simply to the fact
that they were too extended on the ground to build trenches and
pillboxes with their existing resources, where and when they

* Deneys Reitz: *No Outspan.*

needed them. As a result of these exchanges, the Prime Minister and the War Cabinet began to think that some further report on the state of the defences on the British front was needed.

At this time the Secretary of State for War, Mr. Hore-Belisha, was himself in France and, on his return, he reported to the War Cabinet that generally speaking our defences were very strong, although he saw, to his surprise, only two new pillboxes under construction. Another visit followed, this time by the C.I.G.S., General Sir Edmund Ironside, and I have no doubt that its purpose was to chcek up on the diverse opinions which were being expressed. The arrangements for this journey appear to have been made without much consideration for the Commander-in-Chief. Certainly there were some hard feelings between Lord Gort in France and the War Office at home. This would not have mattered had Gort's relations with Hore-Belisha been good. Unfortunately they were not.

Before events developed thus far, Hore-Belisha had asked me to come to see him, when I could only repeat what I had stated before. Considerably to my surprise, the Secretary of State then put the blame on Gort who, he said, "has everything he asked for." Hore-Belisha appeared resentful, as though he himself were being criticized in some way, all the more, perhaps, because he had chosen Gort as C.I.G.S. He told me that he had made the appointment to popularize the army and help recruiting: "A Viscount and a V.C." I showed my incredulity. Belisha continued that I did not understand what his difficulties had been. He had inherited an army in the doldrums and he had to stimulate recruiting. His colleagues gave him little enough help; he had never had the money he needed. His was always the service that was sacrificed. This was true enough, but he was also too inclined to give optimistic accounts to the Cabinet, which would later blame him when they did not appear justified.

Hore-Belisha would not, for instance, accept my account of the condition of the equipment of the 1st Armoured Division, which I knew because I had been training with it. According to his statements in Cabinet, this division was always on the point of leaving for France, but in the event it never did so until after the main engagement, and the British Expeditionary Force had to go into action without the support of its own armour. Later when the consequence of this failure was evident and Mr. Churchill was Prime Minister, he several times spoke to me, blaming himself for not taking up and pressing my earlier questions upon our colleagues. He had no need, as I told him, for any such reflection, for his hands had been full enough at the Admiralty.

Unhappily, though Mr. Hore-Belisha had some good qualities as a War Minister and showed courage in enforcing National Service, attention to detail, however important, was not one of them. It was a weakness of his that being very publicity conscious, he was too eager about appearances and too indifferent about what lay behind them.

On December 1st, 1939, the Secretary of State for War spoke to us of the serious deficiency in infantry tanks. The position was indeed deplorable. On that day there were still only seventy infantry tanks in France out of a total requirement of more than two hundred. Four hundred and sixty-one would be needed by the end of February, 1940, and only one hundred and thirty would then be ready to go overseas. Mr. Hore-Belisha spoke of the use of a French design which was being rapidly produced, to which the Minister of Supply, Mr. Leslie Burgin, replied that he had only just been informed of this War Office opinion.

I proposed that our Armoured Division should be equipped with French tanks, in order to relieve the dangerous situation created by the lack of both anti-tank guns and armoured fighting vehicles with the British army in France. It was admitted that, even in May, 1940, we should still be one hundred and sixty-six cruiser tanks short of our needs. As a result, if an emergency arose, the brigades of the Armoured Division might be sent overseas separately. It was a sorry tale, for which the blame did not rest on the War Minister alone. More than two years earlier, before my resignation from the Government, I had advocated that we should arrange with the French for the use of the Char "B" tank because of my conviction that our own plans for production were too backward.

★ ★ ★ ★ ★

Before the year ended I had my first experience of the British Commonwealth gathering itself for war. On the morning of

December 17th, 1939, Massey and I arrived in Greenock, where the Commander-in-Chief's barge was waiting to take us on board his flagship, H.M.S. *Warspite*. Soon the convoy from Canada began to arrive and we went on to the fo'c'sle to watch the ships pass, a most spectacular sight. A number of our men-of-war were in line ahead, their convoy duty over, including H.M.S. *Hood*, the most graceful ship afloat. The troops themselves had crossed the Atlantic on board several famous liners, the *Empress of Britain*, the *Aquitania* and others, some of which were later to be sunk by enemy action. As each liner passed, the crews of the ships of the Home Fleet cheered and the troops replied lustily, while the flagship's band played *O Canada*.

In the evening of December 20th, 1939, Mr. Churchill gave a dinner at the Admiralty for Admiral Darlan, then Chief of the French Naval Staff. I sat at the guest of honour's left hand and Darlan recalled the days we had spent together at the Nyon Conference in 1937, of which he seemed proud. Ever since that Conference, he said, he had watched my policy at the Foreign Office and had been in complete accord with it. In the last two years, however, Frenchmen had found it difficult to understand our foreign policy. Though he said this, Darlan's chief criticism seemed to me to be directed not so much at the British leaders as at the French, for lacking the determination to steer a firm course and hold us to it.

The Admiral mentioned that on a previous visit, in the same room in which we were dining, he had been told that the British could not sleep easily in their beds as long as there was a French submarine in the Channel. To this foolish and unfriendly comment, Darlan had charitably replied that he had always taken the view that our fleet could not be too strong. At that moment, my sympathies were with Darlan.

After our guests had departed, my host and Kingsley Wood spoke to me about a pending reconstruction of the Government. Churchill repeated his desire that I should go to the War Office. They were both strongly opposed to the possibility, then apparently being canvassed, that Hoare should be put in charge of economic affairs. Kingsley Wood, who had become very friendly to me, insisted several times that Hoare's stock had never been so low.

The project that I should go to the War Office was strongly pressed, particularly by Churchill, within the next week or two. Halifax as well as Kingsley Wood favoured the idea, which I, too, would have liked. Despite all my interest in Dominion affairs, it was the army which I wanted to serve in war-time. For a while it looked as though the appointment might be offered to me, but the Prime Minister was against it, which was probably fortunate for me. Mr. Oliver Stanley was appointed and was soon involved in the unhappy outcome of the Norwegian campaign. This was not his fault, but he was the incumbent and therefore the victim. I do not flatter myself that I could have done any better; these are the chances of politics.

★　★　★　★　★

Since I was to stay at the Dominions Office, I thought I should fly out to Egypt to meet the Australian and New Zealand troops on arrival, as I had done the Canadians in Britain. I mentioned the idea to Edward Halifax who telegraphed to the Ambassador, Sir Miles Lampson, recommending it. Lampson replied that he was sure the visit would be excellent from every point of view and helpful to him personally. I then spoke to the Prime Minister on the subject. He was not enthusiastic, but the plan was approved at a second attempt, thanks to Halifax's support.

As it was not flying weather on February 9th, when I reached the aerodrome from which I was due to take off, I drove to Portsmouth and telephoned to Mr. Churchill at the Admiralty, who put a destroyer at my disposal. Mr. Harold Balfour, Parliamentary Under-Secretary for Air, was on his way to visit the Royal Air Force in the Middle East and travelled with me. The only ship available came in from patrol duty as we waited on the quay. I felt sorry for the crew having to turn back into that tempestuous sea, but they were so eager that they made up for a very rough journey. There being no train from Le Havre, we drove on through the night to Paris, arriving at three in the morning. Two hours later, after a dawn breakfast at the Embassy, we continued the journey by air, reaching Cairo in the afternoon of February 11th.

During a preliminary talk at the Embassy, Lampson suggested that I should go round to the Palace immediately and sign my name in the King's book. So far, no public announcement had been made about my visit, but the Ambassador felt sure that the King would soon learn of my arrival and it would only be polite to perform this act of courtesy at once. As it was a Sunday afternoon, it was unlikely that any European would be there. I agreed and we drove to the Palace. Just as I had done the deed, someone entered the room. Lampson introduced us. It was the Italian Minister. I have never seen expressions of incredulity, horror and polite inquiry chase themselves so rapidly across the features of a diplomat. The poor man could hardly believe his eyes and clearly wondered what mischief I was up to. However, Lampson was fully equal to the occasion and invited him to the Embassy during my visit when we had a harmless and amiable conversation.

The next morning I flew off from Cairo for Suez with the Ambassador and General Sir Archibald Wavell in an antique and slow-moving aircraft, which was all that the Commander-in-Chief had at his disposal to travel from place to place over his enormous command. This was my first chance of a talk to Wavell, whom I had never met before. He told me of his recent meetings with General Maxime Weygand, the Commander of the French forces in the Near East, with whom he was evidently on good terms. I was impressed by Wavell's quiet but firm analysis of his many responsibilities; he made no attempt either to gloss over the shortcomings of his command or to complain about them. He just told a straightforward story. I liked him from the first meeting and our friendship was to grow very close and last until his death.

The New Zealanders were the first to arrive at Suez, in the *Empress of Canada,* when the Ambassador read out a message from the King, which I had brought with me. They were a sturdy lot. In the afternoon it was the turn of the Australians to steam up the Canal and we went on board the *Otranto* to greet their first contingent. These two visits were for me an unforgettable experience. The cheerfulness and outspoken enthusiasm of the men, their splendid physique and the spirit in which they had made this journey, expressed Empire loyalties more eloquently than fine speeches. I had been to Australia and New Zealand fourteen years before, but this meeting took my thoughts back farther, to the month of April 1918, a dark period in the first world war, when we had been in the line alongside the Australians at Villers-Bretonneux, and to September 1916 and the capture of Flers in the Battle of the Somme, when the New Zealanders had been on our left. No tougher fighting neighbours could be dreamed of.

In the next two days I inspected an Indian Brigade camped in the desert near Mena. This was my first close view of Indian troops and I liked their quiet but combative purpose. It was no surprise when, later that year, General Wilson told me that the 4th Indian Division was the equal of the best infantry in his command. I also flew to Palestine to see two or three Australian camps, as stimulating an experience for me as greeting the first contingent on board ship. The arrival of the Anzacs, unexpected by the Egyptians, and the surprise of my visit, gave a dramatic touch to these events.

The 1st Battalion of my own regiment was in the citadel at Cairo and their commanding officer, Lieutenant-Colonel "Strafer" Gott came to see me one evening at the Embassy. The last occasion we had met was at a regimental dinner in the summer of 1939, when I was out of office. As a guest I had given a short but, I hoped, realistic account of events abroad. Gott now reminded me that after the meal he had come up to me and asked: "Do you think there will be a war?" I had replied: "Yes, within a year." Now he told me how he had been grateful for that prediction. He had rejoined his battalion on its arrival in Egypt and had done everything he could to get it ready for war. This battalion was soon to form part of the Desert Rats.

Sir Miles Lampson handled my political duties with a deft touch. First the Prime Minister, Ali Maher, came to luncheon with us alone at the Embassy and we had a long talk late into the afternoon. Ali Maher told me that just as all the parties in Egypt endorsed the Anglo–Egyptian Treaty, so did they now wish to give any help they could to the Allied cause. I thanked the Prime Minister and said I had heard since my arrival in Egypt that it was thought we underrated the strength of the enemy. This was not true. We knew that Germany was the greatest military power in the world and were exerting ourselves accordingly. The Prime Minister was worried because Mussolini was strengthening his defences extensively in Libya. This and other information which his Government had received was causing them uneasiness. My reply that our reports

showed that, for the present, Italy desired to maintain her neutrality, brought him no comfort. He clearly thought that Mussolini was
waiting and watching with hostile intent and I could not deny him
with any conviction.

I had known King Farouk since he was a young cadet at Wool-
wich, when I had been a guest at parties given for him and his
mother, Queen Nazli, at English country houses. These occasions
had passed off smoothly, the success of one evening being a game of
hunt-the-slipper which the Queen appeared to find both exhilarating
and original. Now I was to have an audience of him and present a
message from King George vi. As I reported to the Foreign Office,
the King lacked neither confidence nor brains, but he was opinion-
ated, a tendency abetted and encouraged by sycophantic minions.
A certain jealousy of his position also made him reluctant to take
advice. "Unhappily," I commented, "there is no Egyptian Mel-
bourne to guide and warn."

On this occasion, however, he was all out to please and his observations were shrewd. He was deeply suspicious of Mussolini's intentions and unshaken by any official assurances Lampson or I could
muster to allay them. He was also nervous of our weakness in the
Sudan, a state of affairs, as I was soon to learn, made worse by the
British Government's reluctance to offend Mussolini. This had
curbed Wavell's plans to expand the Sudan Defence Force, which
would have been invaluable in the emergency soon to arise.

The audience over, Lampson held a large reception for the leaders
of all political parties. This gave me the chance to meet again each
signatory of the Treaty we had put our names to in London in August 1936, and many more besides, and to end my visit by partaking
in a massive photographic group of beaming goodwill.

After Palestine, I returned to Malta on my homeward flight,
where a large crowd demonstrated vociferously their loyalty and support of the Allied cause, thus concluding a happy journey.

★   ★   ★   ★   ★

On the evening of my arrival back in England, February 19th, I
had an audience of the King, before attending a small dinner party
at Buckingham Palace, at which the guests were all Ministers. The
King seemed pleased with my journeys, so did my colleagues. That
afternoon I had made a brief statement to the House of Commons,

when one enthusiastic but confused Member of Parliament said to me that the visit was "an inspiration and the most important flight since Munich."

Ten days later, I travelled north to speak at a public meeting in the Philharmonic Hall, Liverpool. There I tried to tell in one incident of the spirit of the British Commonwealth which the Nazis had so misjudged:

During the flights which I made recently in the course of my visit to the Middle East, we landed to refuel on one occasion upon an aerodrome in a very remote spot. There was scarcely more than a handful of people present, none of them Europeans. The only other machines on the ground at the time were two single-seater fighters of a British make. We went up to them and spoke to the two young pilots, one of them turned out to be a Scot from Lanarkshire and the other a South African from Johannesburg. From the opposite ends of the world these two men had come as volunteers to serve the same cause, and here on this remote aerodrome we met for a few minutes' conversation before each flying our separate ways, we northward, they back to the east from which they had come.

There seemed to me to be a message in this chance meeting. What is it that has brought these men, Canadians, Australians, New Zealanders, South Africans, across the world? What is it that has moved them to leave their homes, their work, their factory or farm in their tens of thousands and offer man's proudest gift, his service as a volunteer? It is something more than sentiment, deep as no doubt that sentiment is. It is something stronger even than the ties of kinship, strong as those ties are. It is because, as one of them put it himself, in the simplest but most expressive terms: "It seems there is a job of work to be done." Just so. Though separated by thousands of miles of ocean, these men, who might very well have been excused had they failed to appreciate the extent of the peril that pressed in the first instance upon us, saw clearly from the first. They understood the issue, and it is this clear perception, the vision of the men beyond the seas who see truly, that should give us courage now.*

* *Freedom and Order*, pages 56–63.

These thoughts and feelings are passing from our ken, sometimes through circumstances and sometimes through our own fault. We are the poorer for it.

★   ★   ★   ★   ★

The New Year, 1940, opened darkly for the Allies. It is true that, during the few months' respite which lasted until the Nazi invasion of Denmark and Norway and the Low Countries, we gained an increase in supplies, particularly of aircraft. But the war effort was still muted. Neither the Liberal nor Labour Parties would join the Government, while the War Cabinet was dominated by old men, who, with the vigorous exception of Mr. Churchill, were doubtfully suited to their appointments. Though changes were frequent, there was still no concert between Government and people, and no national confidence, while the country became restless and critical.

The Members of Parliament were themselves conscious of this. Mr. Paul Emrys Evans wrote to me on March 17th:

When you joined the Government we all hoped that a Coalition was not far off, that we should have a real War Cabinet and that the only opposition we should have would be the Pacifists, whether they lived in Mayfair or on the Clydeside. As it is, Parliament is going on almost exactly as if we were at peace. The Whips are just as busy, the attention of the Government is taken up on matters quite unconnected with the war. . . . All this seems to show a lack of understanding of the realities and perils of the situation, and the Government must take the main share of the responsibility. They seem to enjoy keeping up antagonism against the Opposition and indeed against those of us, on our own side, who have not seen eye to eye with them in the past.

The same day after luncheon with Edward Halifax, I had some talk with him about the domestic situation and the Government. We were neither of us content with its composition and authority. I told Halifax that there were few men in the Cabinet itself who had support in the country. The majority were civil servants or more or less discredited politicians. The main issue which I thought the Prime Minister had got to face, if he wished to reconstruct his Government, was whether he was prepared to create a Minister of Defence to represent the services in the Cabinet and to offer the job to Winston Churchill. Halifax said that, for his part, he would be prepared to face this.

I next heard of changes in a talk with Mr. Churchill after a Cabinet on April Fool day, 1940. I had previously seen Sir Alexander Hardinge at Buckingham Palace about some routine business and I found him unhappy at the news. Hoare was to go to the Air Ministry, Kingsley Wood changing places with him. Lord Chatfield was to drop out:

April 1st: Cabinet is thus eight. There are a series of other swops, a game of musical chairs.

Winston saddened and disgusted. He has not been consulted, only informed. He much wanted me to go to the Air Ministry, asked me if I would if there were still a chance. I said that I would go where it was thought I could give most useful service. As he knew I would have liked War Office and would have felt more confidence there, but it was for my colleagues to say. Winston maintained that the news would be very ill received. Public confidence would not be increased, airmen would not like it. He had told [Admiral Sir Dudley] Pound [First Sea Lord] who had been unable to conceal his consternation at Sam's appointment.

I agreed that the public would not welcome appointments and added that I thought the Government would not be well placed to meet the rough weather that must lie ahead. But Neville had his particular friends and would stick to them as long as he could and longer than the country wished. He had only accepted Winston and me because he could not avoid it.

Winston maintained that there would be more chances, many more, on this rough voyage and sought to hearten himself in this strain, and no doubt me too. But he was worried and depressed, which is not wonderful.

★　★　★　★　★

The military direction of the war was not happily organized and attempts to improve it resulted in a series of permutations and combinations, none of them satisfactory. From the outbreak of war Lord Chatfield had presided as a co-ordinating Minister over a committee of the service Ministers. At the beginning of April 1940, Mr. Churchill was appointed to a position with much the same authority. A week later, at Churchill's suggestion, the Prime Minister took the responsibility for presiding over defence discussions. Then, at the beginning of May 1940, more authority was given to the First Lord of the Admiralty. None of this produced good results, nor could it, because in war the Defence Minister must have continuing power and direction under the War Cabinet, and it is desirable that this should be exercised by the Prime Minister himself.

In all these matters I was only on the fringes. I enjoyed my work with the Dominion High Commissioners and with their Governments, but my position in the Cabinet was highly anomalous, not to say humiliating. Two years before, I had been a principal figure in the Cabinet, now I was back again, not because my former colleagues wanted me to join them, but because the country had judged me to be right and them wrong in the controversy over my resignation. I was only there on condition that I took no effective part in anything outside the work of my department. So far as the Cabinet was concerned, I was a constant attender and not a participant. As such I merely had a close view of the events which followed.

★   ★   ★   ★   ★

In March, 1940, Mr. Sumner Welles paid visits to Rome, Berlin, Paris and London to try to establish what were the chances of bringing the war to an end. He has written dispassionately about this episode and has acidly condemned Senator Borah, the most purblind of isolationists, for dubbing the lull in hostilities the "phoney" war and for condemning the "failure of Great Britain and France to undertake the offensive" as "somehow reprehensible." "This feeling," commented Mr. Welles, "was almost sadistic. It had in it something of the 'boos' howled out by the spectators at a prize ring when the two contestants are not putting on as bloody an exhibition as they have paid to witness." *

* Sumner Welles: *The Time for Decision.*

I had known Sumner Welles from my Washington visit and I respected his capacity for international affairs. He and the United States Ambassador, Mr. Joseph Kennedy, came to see me at the Dominions Office on the afternoon of March 12th. Welles began by asking me whether I saw any way out of the existing deadlock. I replied that I did not, save in the defeat of Germany and the establishment of a regime in that country in whose good faith other nations could have confidence. Welles said that he had expected me to give that answer and he then began to examine whether some scheme of disarmament could be worked out while the armies still held their positions.

Hitler, he explained, had spoken to him at length about disarmament and alleged that he had several times made proposals which had been turned down, in particular one "for a mutual pooling of armaments by Britain, France and the United States." Had I any recollection of this scheme? I replied that I had none and that to the best of my belief no such suggestion had ever been made. It was certainly in conflict with the general trend of Hitler's sentiments, which were antagonistic to international collaboration. Many of us had worked at disarmament projects in the past and I had no doubt that a plan could be evolved. The real difficulty was to find the will to work it and confidence between those taking part in it. It seemed to me inconceivable that a nation could have confidence in the good faith of Nazi Germany, in an arms convention any more than in any other form of treaty. I had found that even the best of schemes could soon be shipwrecked on international mistrust. The mistrust of Hitler today was infinitely greater than the mistrust of Germany in 1935.

The Ambassador, Mr. Kennedy, then spoke in very gloomy terms of the economic state of the world and of the consequences to the prosperity of all nations of a failure to solve our problems. We had all of us been living on our fat for long enough. The British Empire had assets in many parts of the world, but we could not realize them. The standard of life everywhere would go steadily down unless peace could be made.

I replied that I was not qualified to argue with the Ambassador on economic questions, but it seemed to me that if Hitler were allowed once more to demonstrate that aggression did pay, then there would be no future for any free people in Europe. The truth was that Hitler's conception of how the world should live was quite different from ours. He thought a Germanic hegemony good for Europe. We knew that under such a rule, life would not be worth living. Mr. Welles said that he fully appreciated what I had said, both on this occasion and at our previous meeting, but he was thinking of the hatreds which must be created, if once hostilities broke out with real vigour, and he repeated his conviction that man should be able to devise some means of avoiding this worst catastrophe.

The conversation turned to peace conditions and I told Mr. Welles I did not believe that the terms, when imposed, should provide for an indemnity or reparations. Those provisions in the Treaty of Versailles had, I thought, been a serious mistake. I hoped he would let me emphasize to him one contrast between our position and that of the dictator states. For a dictatorship it was comparatively easy to turn from peace to war and back again. For a democracy the position was otherwise. Our peoples loved peace and were reluctant to take up arms. This applied more particularly to an organization spread all over the world like the British Commonwealth. We were now engaged on what we knew to be a life or death struggle. It would put us to an unfair disadvantage to ask us to stay our hand, though such an appeal would not present the same difficulties for Nazi Germany. The United States as a free people would, I felt sure, themselves understand this distinction.

Mr. Welles did not contest what I had said. At the same time he seemed unwilling to accept my refusal to believe in the possibility of an arms agreement. The truth was that military domination was only part of Hitler's creed. With it went nihilism, a deliberate willingness to gamble everything in the knowledge that he might bring the whole of western Europe, including Germany, to ruin.

In the early months of 1940, much of the time of the War Cabinet was taken up with the problems of Scandinavia. There was first the question of the iron ore from Sweden, which travelled in winter south from Narvik to German ports through Norwegian territorial waters. Mr. Churchill had advocated that we should mine those waters to force the ships out on to the high seas, where their cargoes could have been dealt with as contraband. The difficulties in this course were ethical as well as practical, and accepted as such by Churchill, in a war which we were fighting for the rights of small nations. There was also the question whether a military enterprise should be made ready, and perhaps launched, in support of this mining action. In the event, the argument went back and forth for months and no decision was taken, until a few days before the delivery of the German attack which had been mounted much earlier.

- Into this confused scene obtruded a darker tragedy. Having first demanded bases in the Baltic States of Latvia, Estonia and Lithuania, Soviet power then installed suitably submissive governments to obey its will. Under the then secret terms of the Ribbentrop–Molotov Pact, Finland had also been allotted to the Russian sphere of interest, though Hitler may not have expected the consequences to be so grievous and immediate.

Early in October 1939, Moscow began to make demands on Finland for the leasing of the port of Hangö, one of the country's capital defences, as a Russian naval and air base, and for concessions of territory in the Rybachiy peninsula, including the Arctic port of Petsamo, and for islands in the Gulf of Finland. The Finnish Government refused, and on November 30th the Soviet attacks began. They made little progress except at Petsamo, in the far north, and failed completely before the stubborn defence of the Mannerheim Line. The spectacle of the Finnish people battling successfully against such odds was acclaimed by the free world, but it also made new demands upon the limited resources of the Western Allies, faced with the menacing uncertainty of Hitler's plans for the spring of 1940. Public opinion began to call for aid to the Finns.

Sympathy was not the only motive in Allied assistance to Finland. The route for any reinforcement lay through Narvik and implied the control of Germany's supplies of iron ore. The League of Nations had approved the despatch of help to Finland, so that to cross northern Scandinavia became perfectly correct international behaviour. France offered troops and we made ready to contribute bombers from our straitened resources. In spite of which, aid would only have been possible if Sweden and Norway had granted passage.

After the fate of Poland, however, small countries were not eager for Anglo–French assurances of help, unless it were close at hand

and not always then. The proffered activity came to naught, because Sweden and Norway were not prepared to expose themselves to Russian wrath by allowing anything more than the most gingerly departure from strict neutrality, so that the only reinforcement was a few volunteers. This did not avail against a Soviet assault with armour, aircraft and heavy artillery which, in March 1940, at length smashed the Mannerheim Line. The Finns could then do no more than make terms with Moscow.

I thought that the cynical Nazi connivance in these deeds must be publicly condemned and said at Liverpool on February 29th, 1940:

> Not Russia only but Germany also, bears a terrible responsibility for what is happening in Finland at this hour. Hitler and Ribbentrop, these men and their policies alone made Stalin's aggression possible. Stalin is the aggressor in Finland, Hitler the abettor.
>
> It seems strange to think now how many hours I used to spend listening to the present German Foreign Secretary when he was Ambassador in London, when he used to expound to me, as indeed he did also in public many times, the dangers and horrors of Bolshevism. He was never tired of expatiating on this theme. Soviet Russia, this untouchable with whom Nazi Germany could not sit down at a conference table, this leprous thing, this cancer. Many a time the British people were taken to task because we, it was alleged, did not understand the extent of our peril. We did not appreciate, we were told, the realities of the European situation. Only Hitler could do that. He, alone, we were assured, stood as a bulwark between Britain and Red Russia. But for the Hitlerian St. George the Red Dragon would have swallowed us long since. So ran the German fable with its many variations.
>
> And what has happened now? The Red Dragon has taken the Hitlerian St. George for a ride. It may be that one day in the not so distant future the German Foreign Minister may have need to recall his own warnings.*

French opinion was more disturbed even than British at the defeat of Finland. Our failure to take an initiative seemed menacing

* *Freedom and Order*, pages 56–63.

to those who were keeping an army of many millions in the field, with nothing to show for it but the dislocation of a nation's life. There was also a natural desire on the part of the French Government to keep the war out of France, and an impatience that their ally's sea-power had effected nothing.

When, on April 9th, the Nazi invasion of Norway was loosed without warning on that peaceful land, even graver questions had to be faced and answered. Should help be sent and where and how? For a while a landing to seize Trondhjem was a popular course, but Admiral Sir Charles Forbes, Commander-in-Chief, Home Fleet, was, I think, right in his reluctance to endorse it. It would have been wiser to concentrate on taking and holding Narvik. As it was, our limited forces were too widely spread in several enterprises, all of which failed, in part because there was confusion of thought as to what should best be done. There were changes of plan almost every day.

Exaggerated hopes were held of what sea-power could do along the Norwegian sea coast where the ground favoured defence, but it was soon proven that without effective air cover it could do little except to add to the Royal Navy's annals of superb courage. These misfortunes, seen in the light of the main German invasion of the Low Countries and France, were not an unmixed evil, for the commitment of maintaining military and air defences in Norway would have drained our resources. At the time, however, they were the cause of much distress and brought about the downfall of the Government.

★　★　★　★　★

Men who had read the signs so differently, could hardly work together easily:

April 10th: On the way back from an official dinner in the City, called in at Admiralty War Room. Winston found me there and carried me off to his room. He is indignant with Sam [Hoare] whom he suspects of being eager to score off him, Winston, and whom he regards as unsuited to inspire the Air Force at a time like this. "A snake" and some stronger epithets.

The gallantry of individual feats of arms brought a flash of pride
and happiness to the nation, but could not redeem the growing
criticism of the Government's conduct of the war:

> *April 14th:* Greatly relieved to hear of *Warspite*'s successful
> dash into Narvik. It was a bold deed, brilliantly executed. We
> seem to have done much damage, and gained much glory at a
> critical time, but I hope that great ship will not be called to run
> any comparable risk again.

The Government were themselves conscious of the mounting tide
of opinion against them, and at the Cabinet on May 1st much of the
time was spent by colleagues rehearsing their defence of our withdrawal from southern Norway. I could not help murmuring to
John Anderson my curiosity as to whether Hitler's supreme councils
were also conducted in this fashion. I had to speak in the City that
day and uttered my now usual warning against underrating the
enemy, made the more necessary by the Prime Minister's recent reference to Hitler as having "missed the bus."

The final debate in the Government's life took place in an atmosphere of sour disillusionment with undertones of bitterness. Mr.
Churchill did all he could to redress the balance, but the issue was
decided in the minds of the House before the final speech and the
life of the Chamberlain Government was over. Though the end had
been painful, I felt some relief that it had happened before the great
events which were clearly pending when Hitler's offensive was
launched. Next day:

> *May 9th:* Winston rang me up about 9.30 and said that he
> wanted to see me as soon as possible and while shaving he re-
> hearsed to me the events of the previous evening. He thought
> that Neville would not be able to bring in Labour and that a
> national Government must be formed. Later I lunched alone
> with him and Kingsley [Wood], when they told me that Neville
> had decided to go. The future was discussed. Kingsley thought
> that W. should succeed, and urged that if asked he should make
> plain his willingness.

I was surprised to find Kingsley Wood there giving a warning that Chamberlain would want Halifax to succeed him and would want Churchill to agree. Wood advised: "Don't agree, and don't say anything." I was shocked that Wood should talk in this way, for he had been so much Chamberlain's man, but it was good counsel and I seconded it.

Meeting had been arranged for 4.30. Some talk with Oliver [Stanley] and K.W. at intervals during day. Dined with Winston when he told me he thought it plain N.C. would advise King to send for him. Edward [Halifax] did not wish to succeed. Parliamentary position too difficult. W. had made it plain he hoped N.C. would stay, would lead House of Commons and continue as leader of party. W. would be Minister of Defence as well as P.M. W. quiet and calm. He wishes me to take War.

I told Mr. Churchill that I would do as he asked, but I knew that the position would be difficult. The state of the army was inglorious, through no fault of its own and, despite all my admiration for Churchill, I expected that relations with him might be choppy. In this I was unduly apprehensive, for he was indulgent to me and no two men could have worked more closely together.

May 10th: Roused at 7.40 for Cabinet at 8.0 a.m. Germans have violated neutrality of Holland, Belgium and Luxembourg. No detailed news at present. Report soon after that all changes postponed; it seemed for some time. After 11.30 Cabinet N.C. made statement to us of what had been his intention, as W. had told me. Added that new attack must cause hold-up, only temporary. He had communicated with Attlee in this sense, who had accepted. He had asked Attlee to put out notice which would include support of Government *pro tem,* but when announced on tape it did not say more than support of war effort. Horace Wilson was specially indignant about this. This impressed many present with difficulty of prolonged delay, especially as conditions for change might become more rather than less difficult. For P.M. there was also risk to personal position if appearance of clinging on were given. K.W. took that view, but no one expressed it.

Just before the 11.30 Cabinet, I was talking to Maurice Hankey when Simon came up and said he understood that despite the attacks in Flanders, Churchill was pressing for early changes in the Government. He was indignant. Hankey commented quietly but firmly: "Personally, I think that if there are to be changes, the sooner they are made the better." My diary continues:

> After the afternoon Cabinet, P.M. told us he had thought matters over and, since Labour had by then said yes to service under another P.M., he proposed to see King that evening. Expect W. will be sent for.

The next morning, May 11th, Mr. Churchill asked me to call in before going to the Dominions Office. He seemed well satisfied with the way events were shaping in the war and in the formation of the Government, and told me that he hoped to be able to publish the first list of Ministers that evening. We had some discussion about these. On May 12th, I had my farewell meeting with the High Commissioners. They seemed as genuinely sorry as I was at parting. I had been planning to visit each of the Dominions in turn, starting with Canada. The date for this journey was fixed and now the defeat of the Chamberlain Government and its consequences ruled it out for me.

The first list of Churchill's Ministers had appeared that morning. These were: Chamberlain, Lord President; Attlee, Lord Privy Seal; Arthur Greenwood, Minister without Portfolio; A. V. Alexander, First Lord of the Admiralty; Archibald Sinclair, Secretary of State for Air; myself, Secretary of State for War. We were summoned to the Palace at noon to be sworn into our new offices:

> *May 12th:* It was a strange party. Owing to some new and rather silly convention, explained to us by the Clerk to the Privy Council at interminable length, Sinclair and I and Alexander had to take the oath before N.C. instead of before the King.

This was an added embarrassment. I had a short conversation with Chamberlain, who looked ill and was clearly hating it all. He said that he was staying in the new Government with a heavy heart; he was depressed that at such a critical time we should be considering questions of personalities. Though Chamberlain could hardly be blamed for not understanding, much more was at stake than this; it was win or lose.

3

THE BATTLE OF FRANCE
May–June 1940

The fighting in Belgium — Paratroops and the Home Guard —
Anxious news from France — General Ironside's remark — Number seventeen at roulette — The allied armies are severed — The
attack on Calais — M. Reynaud's visit to London — Dunkirk —
The nation's spirit — The Prime Minister and I in France —
Meeting with the French Government and high command — M.
Reynaud on Marshal Pétain — Problems of equipment at home
and the Middle East — Mr. Churchill's view — Mr. Lloyd George
at the War Office — A talk with Mr. Maisky

IN THE AFTERNOON of Whit Sunday, May 12th, I took over from
Mr. Oliver Stanley at the War Office and met the Chief of the Imperial General Staff, General Ironside. Together we looked at the
map and exchanged some uneasy comments on the deep advance
which our forces were then making in Belgium towards the line
of the River Dyle.

This situation was a legacy of the failure to complete joint plans.
All British and French efforts to prepare their advance to the rescue
of Belgium had only resulted in variants of the Belgian Government's official reply of September 29th, 1939. Even at that date
they had not expected an invasion of their country. The Belgian
Government believed, so M. Paul-Henri Spaak argued, that there
were greater risks in holding staff talks than in waiting upon events.

This refusal to make ready against an almost certain event was
a sad mistake, for Hitler was not the man to need an excuse for
an act of aggression, nor would he be provoked because his victim
prepared to defend himself with the help of his neighbours. So
beguiled were the Belgian King and Government, that they would

not even say what they intended to do if the Netherlands were attacked.

The French Command, conscious of its numerical inferiority and the slender British contribution, was ready to pay a price for the help of the twenty Belgian divisions, but no close staff work was possible. The result was missed opportunities all round. The negative Belgian attitude never allowed their own forces to be used to best advantage, while General Gamelin planned on assumptions which were not fulfilled.

The Belgian army could not make an effective defence along the Albert Canal, as Gamelin had hoped, nor had the anti-tank fortifications between Louvain and Namur been built, though he appears to have counted upon them. The declaration by the Belgian Government that Brussels was an "open town" was serious for the B.E.F. Lord Gort had planned to use roads passing through the outskirts, though not the centre, of the city. Despite M. Spaak's protests, Gort was obliged to persist in his intention, for lack of alternatives. Altogether there were many loose ends and their cost was high. As Colonel Charles de Gaulle wrote, without being heeded, some years before: "The pattern of a war is set in times of peace." *

The next morning, May 13th, the news began to look bad. The Germans were outflanking the Dutch defences. In Belgium, Liège fell, which seemed sudden to me, who remembered so vividly the gallant and prolonged defence of its forts in the first world war. We had yet to learn how much the pace had changed. More serious still were reports that the Germans were approaching the Meuse through the Ardennes.

Marshal Pétain had argued that this countryside was not practicable for armour in modern war, and it was said that his confidence had influenced the failure to extend the Maginot Line farther north to guard against this threat. I was not surprised by his opinion, for our advance had lain through the Ardennes at the end of the first world war, soon after the fighting had finished. It was winter time and the conditions had been hard for man and beast. Now, modern armour and transport were to make nonsense of all physical difficulties and of Pétain's judgment. The misplaced

* Charles de Gaulle: *The Edge of the Sword.*

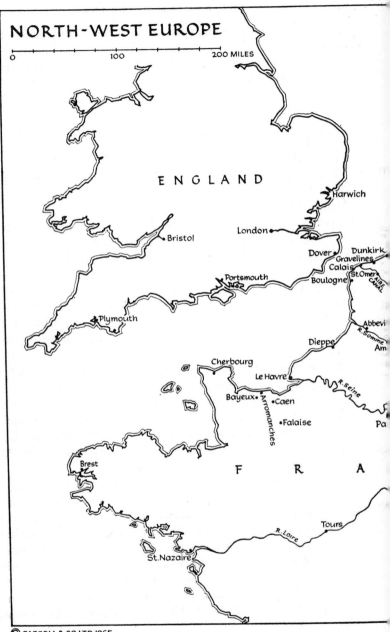

NORTH-WEST EUROPE

0   100   200 MILES

E N G L A N D

Harwich

London

Bristol

Dover
Dunkirk
Gravelines
Calais
St.Omer
Boulogne
AIRE CANAL

Portsmouth

Abbevi
R.Somme
Am

Plymouth

Dieppe

Cherbourg

Le Havre

Bayeux
Caen
Arromanches
R.Seine
Falaise
Pa

Brest

F   R   A

Tours
R.Loire

St.Nazaire

© CASSELL & CO LTD 1965

confidence had not only misled the French. As late as March 27th, the British Chiefs of Staff considered that the Allied forces then in the field should be capable of halting a German offensive against France.

★　　★　　★　　★　　★

From Holland and Belgium came reports of the extensive German use of paratroops. The preliminary work on a scheme to combat this menace had already been done when I reached the War Office and I decided to talk to the nation on this subject on May 14th, two days after I took over. This was the origin of the Home Guard:

> The purpose of the parachute attack is to disorganize and confuse, as a preparation for the landing of troops by aircraft. The success of such an attack depends on speed. Consequently the measures to defeat such an attack must be prompt and rapid. . . .
>
> Since the war began, the Government have received countless inquiries from all over the Kingdom from men of all ages who are for one reason or another not at present engaged in military service, and who wish to do something for the defence of their country. Well, now is your opportunity.
>
> We want large numbers of such men in Great Britain, who are British subjects, between the ages of seventeen and sixty-five, to come forward now and offer their services in order to make assurance doubly sure. The name of the new Force which is now to be raised will be "The Local Defence Volunteers." This name describes its duties in three words. It must be understood that this is, so to speak, a spare-time job, so there will be no need for any volunteer to abandon his present occupation.

I then spoke to those who proposed to volunteer and told them:

> When on duty you will form part of the armed forces, and your period of service will be for the duration of the war. You

will not be paid, but you will receive uniform and will be armed. You will be entrusted with certain vital duties for which reasonable fitness and a knowledge of firearms is necessary. These duties will not require you to live away from your homes.

In order to volunteer, what you have to do is to give in your name at your local police station; and then, as and when we want you, we will let you know. This appeal is directed chiefly to those who live in country parishes, in small towns, in villages and in less densely inhabited suburban areas. I must warn you that for certain military reasons there will be some localities where the numbers required will be small, and others where your services will not be required at all.

Here, then, is the opportunity for which so many of you have been waiting. Your loyal help, added to the arrangements which already exist, will make and keep our country safe.*

I had expected the response to this appeal to be prompt. In fact it was overwhelming, the first recruit arriving within four minutes of the end of the broadcast. It was quite impossible to deal with the number of volunteers who flocked to join, still less to provide them with weapons. But this was only a beginning and the answer which mattered had already been given. The Local Defence Volunteers acted as a catalyst, giving point to the nation's will to resist. As the years passed, the volunteers recorded long periods of service which were often dreary, but always devoted, with only one reward, the knowledge that "The Home Guard," as it was re-christened, closed a gap in our defences which must have been dangerous and could have been fatal.

★   ★   ★   ★   ★

Enemy air power soon dominated the battle in France. One of the first personal telegrams I received from the Commander-in-Chief on May 13th said that it was essential to reinforce with additional fighter squadrons those in action

* *Freedom and Order,* pages 71–3.

[who] have been fighting for three days with great success but cannot continue at this pressure. We have to support in the air not only the B.E.F. but also our Allies who have suffered heavy air attacks. In this battle our main defence in the air is fighters. Reinforcing squadrons will retain their entity and can be called home at short notice if required. Temporarily, for limited period, additional squadrons can be maintained with ground staffs now in France. I earnestly hope War Cabinet will decide to give additional air assistance which, in my judgment, is essential for Allied success in the coming battle.

Scarcely less important was the use to be made of our bomber force. In those early days of the fighting the War Cabinet decisions were not always those for which the War Office asked. On the afternoon of May 13th, in agreement with the C.I.G.S., I contended that the decisive land battle had already begun and asked that we should concentrate on winning the battle and use the bomber force on the marshalling yards and communications of the German army. We could not, I said, direct too great an attack upon them.

The decision I had asked for was, however, postponed, the Air Staff and the Prime Minister preferring more distant targets such as oil refineries and the Ruhr. Some argued that the battle had not yet fully developed, others were reluctant to open up air attack against industrial targets in the Ruhr for fear of inviting retaliation. To the C.I.G.S. and me this did not seem to be the issue. We wanted every bomb dropped where it would tell most for the battle in France.

Two days later the heavy bombers came into use, but still the majority of them were employed against oil targets, which could not conceivably affect the actual fighting. From the point of view of the army, it was also soon evident that our troops were at a disadvantage for lack of the dive-bombers which the Germans used so efficiently in close support. This was even more serious than the preference of the War Cabinet and the Air Staff for targets for the heavy bombers which were deep in Germany, but it must take much longer to remedy. Once again, no lesson seems to have been learned from the experience of Poland, nor were the intervening nine months used to the best advantage. It was in truth only after Mr. Churchill became Prime Minister that the nation and the services began to be effectively organized for war, and by then the guns were going off.

For the time being our appeals for additional fighter squadrons were also rejected, the Chief of the Air Staff maintaining that sixty fighter squadrons were needed for the adequate defence of this country, whereas we had only thirty-nine. Within a few days, the lowering picture of the battle enforced second thoughts and, by May 17th, the War Cabinet had decided to send ten more squadrons across the Channel. When these arrived twenty British fighter squadrons were operating in France, or over it from airfields in Kent, which was twice the modest number available at the opening of the German offensive.

By May 31st very little was left of the first ten squadrons and our total air strength was, we reckoned, outnumbered by the Germans two and half to one. Eventually all but ten of the fifty-three fighter squadrons existing in May 1940 had been in action in France at one time or another. So selflessly had they done their duty that, when the Prime Minister and I were at Briare on June 11th, nearly a thousand aircraft had been lost, half of them fighters.

Even if, in the weeks of fighting in France and Belgium, the allied armies could not always understand the full extent of the effort being made, there can be no question that the fighter squadrons of the Royal Air Force did more even than was asked of them. The Battles, with which the medium bomber squadrons were mostly equipped, were not good aircraft and they suffered cruelly heavy losses in sorties of desperate courage. Only the tactical employment, at this time, of the heavy bombers remains open to criticism.

★　★　★　★　★

During the next week, my waking hours were entirely occupied with the details of the struggle raging in France, frequent Cabinet meetings and repeated emergencies. I wrote:

May 18: News no worse this morning, but seems to me too early to call it better. P.M. and C.I.G.S. gave, however, optimistic survey to Cabinet. Less German air activity yesterday. I still regret that we do not concentrate our bombing on military targets, advancing troops, columns of transport, etc.

Later the same day:

An hour's sleep in the sun in the Park then back to the office. The German thrust towards the sea continues and the French 1st and 9th Armies seem badly broken up. No counter-attack has materialized or made progress except one from Laon which appears to have met no opposition. Meeting with Winston and Chiefs of Staff at Admiralty 10.30. Decided to send Dill [now Vice-C.I.G.S.] tomorrow at dawn to see Reynaud [Prime Minister of France] and Georges [principal allied commander under Gamelin] to try to learn latter's plan and give him our view.

May 19: An interminable day of glorious weather and grim news. Reached the office after a walk as usual. Some discussion of troops from India and evacuation of civilians from Gib. Then to Cabinet at 10. Situation reports revealed continued drive on Abbeville and the sea. Meeting at office decided withdraw eight regular battalions from India and replace by eight or twelve territorials. Just going to join Edward [Halifax] for lunch when C.I.G.S. sent for me urgently to report message from Gort, actually talk with [Lieut.-Gen. Henry] Pownall [Gort's Chief of Staff], that French 1st Army on his right had faded away and that he proposed to base himself on Dunkirk, hold a semi-circular line through St. Omer, Aire Canal and fight it out with his back to the sea. C.I.G.S. did not like this at all and thought Gort should try to fight his way through to Amiens. Later message from Pownall showed Gort only contemplated this as last resort if French failed to fill or hold gap about Cambrai, Le Cateau and Valenciennes, which now threatens his communications.

Went to No. 10 and Admiralty House to find P.M. and N.C. [Chamberlain] had left London for a few hours. Found [Sir Edward] Bridges [Secretary to the Cabinet] and summoned them back. Lunch at War Office and talk with C.I.G.S. Agrees we must try to re-establish contact with French. If only they would stage good counter-attack from Chauny, Gort's very dangerous position would be eased. Winston and Cabinet took C.I.G.S. view and latter leaves tonight for Gort's Headquarters. C.I.G.S. and I much talk at luncheon. Agreed that if French army really had lost fighting value, no preparation of ours could have decided issue. He lamented Belisha's many errors and lateness of our preparations. N.C. had not decided on a continental army until April last year after Germans had taken Prague.

On our return from the Cabinet, as we walked up the ugly staircase of the War Office to my room, Ironside said to me: "This is the end of the British Empire." He spoke the words flatly and as a mere statement of military fact. He did not believe that we could hold out alone for more than a few months. I argued against this, but more from instinct than from reason; militarily I did not see how he could be gainsaid.

One day at the War Cabinet when the news had been more than usually discouraging, the Prime Minister looked at me across the table and remarked: "About time No. 17 turned up, isn't it?"

After I had resigned from Mr. Chamberlain's Government and was staying with my sister on Cap Ferrat, I used occasionally to see Mr. Churchill on the Riviera. One evening, when we met in the Casino at Cannes I was playing roulette. He joined me and asked what number I was on. I said "No. 17." We backed it and after one or two failures the number turned up. We left our stakes and it turned up again and we withdrew, well content.

The first clear picture of unfolding events came in a letter which Sir John Dill sent to me on May 19th. He had found General Gamelin at General Georges' headquarters. Dill already judged that the German drive was definitely towards the Channel ports, the probable axis being Calais. When he had suggested striking northwards towards the Aisne, Gamelin and Georges replied that they had no forces with which to do this and that the Germans were pressing them near Montmédy. Two counter-attacks were in operation or contemplated, the first from Laon by the *Groupement de Gaulle*, the first time I had ever heard that name. The second counter-attack was from Le Cateau, which had been my brigade's last engagement in the first world war.

Dill reported Gamelin and Georges as tired and the calm of their headquarters as almost oppressive, after eight days of intense activity. Probably there was nothing much left for the French High Command to do but wait to see how the battle turned. The main enemy, Dill concluded, was the tank; all our resources, including air, should be devoted to its destruction.

An hour or two before the despatch of this message, Dill had telegraphed a sad commentary on the unpreparedness of our own armour. He had just seen M. Reynaud, who was very gloomy, expecting a thrust of enemy armoured vehicles towards Amiens. In discussing the arrival of our 1st Armoured Division, Dill telegraphed that Reynaud used the expression "to be late is to die." Unhappily we were late and this splendid division was never in action as such during this campaign.

At five o'clock on the evening of May 22nd, Lord Gort's A.D.C., Lord Munster, telephoned to me from a point on the Belgian coast with a message from the Commander-in-Chief. The situation, he reported, was very grave. All the lines of communication of the B.E.F. were cut. There was a serious shortage of food and munitions. Above all, there was no co-ordination between ourselves and the French on our right flank. "The Co-ordinator has had an accident and co-ordinates no longer." This was a veiled reference to General Billotte, who had died as a result of a motor-car accident when leaving a meeting with the King of the Belgians and General Weygand. I asked what had happened at that meeting the day before and learnt that Gort had taken no part in it, owing apparently to a failure to tell him where to rendezvous. General Blanchard was appointed to succeeed General Billotte in command of the northeastern group of armies, which included the Belgians and the British.

Lord Munster's message seemed to me a deadly commentary on the increasing confusion which we had neither the authority nor the reserves to mend. The only hope was a joint offensive from the north and south, if there were the will and the means to mount it. General Weygand had replaced General Gamelin in supreme command and he assured the meeting of British and French Prime

Ministers at Vincennes on May 22nd that it could be done. A later telephone conversation with General Weygand's headquarters even told of progress in the south, including the capture of Péronne, Albert and Amiens.

Unhappily these reports proved to be unfounded. Before we knew this, I had become uneasy about the fate of the Weygand plan, and telegraphed to Gort, giving him latitude to withdraw to the Channel ports if the attacks on his communications compelled him to do so. In this event he should let us know at once, so that we could tell the French and also make naval and air arrangements to assist him.

★   ★   ★   ★   ★

The developing threats to Gort's communications made it more than ever important to hold the Channel ports. Two Guards battalions were sent to garrison Boulogne on May 22nd, while the only remaining trained British infantry in the country, a battalion each of the King's Royal Rifle Corps (60th Rifles) and the Rifle Brigade which formed the support group of the 1st Armoured Division, a battalion of the Royal Tank Regiment and a territorial motor-cycle battalion of the Queen Victoria Rifles, were sent under the command of Brigadier Claude Nicholson to Calais. The Guards battalions were withdrawn from Boulogne on instructions from the Government on the night of May 23rd–24th. The attack on Calais was already in progress that evening, as the British forces landed on the quay, and some of their equipment was never unloaded. The main German assault developed in the morning of May 24th and, after a day of continuous fighting, the garrison retired to the inner town.

Next morning, Admiral Sir James Somerville came into my room at the War Office to tell me that the night before he had been in Calais harbour with his destroyers, that the town was on fire and that, if any of the garrison were to be withdrawn, we should have to act that evening. The C.I.G.S. and I went across to see the Prime Minister and reluctantly agreed that the garrison must hold out until the last, so vital had it by then become to delay the German armoured advance along the coast to Dunkirk. We should have seen this more clearly and sooner, when Boulogne was evacuated.

I sent a message to Nicholson, telling him that the ultimate defence of Calais was of the highest importance and that we were confident that he and his gallant regiments would perform an exploit worthy of the British name. The garrison continued their resistance until the night of the 26th, withstanding attacks by two German armoured divisions.

The Calais decision was one of the most painful of the war, for I had served with one of the regiments and knew personally many of those whose fate I had now to decide. The next day, while Ironside and I were still grieved at what we had had to do, General Percival, who was then Assistant C.I.G.S., came into my room. He brought an intercepted German message and remarked: "Here is the justification for your decision." The message was an instruction from the German High Command to an armoured division, then moving eastwards against Gort's communications, to change direction and reinforce the troops attacking Calais. The order added that Calais must be reduced at all costs.

In the press of war, I thought no more of this incident for some time, until later in the summer when General Dill, by then C.I.G.S., was staying with me in a house I had taken in Kent. General Sir Andrew Thorne, commanding the South Eastern sector of the Home Command, was discussing with us the defence of his area against the invasion which we thought might soon take place. In the course of our talk the conversation turned on the events at Calais and I told Dill and Thorne the story of the intercepted message. I wrote this note of what Thorne then said:

> What an extraordinary thing. That now explains something I have never understood. The Division I was then commanding, the 48th, was defending the flank of the British Army as it was retreating into the Dunkirk perimeter and to do that we were holding, amongst other places, the position on Cassel Hill, which has a wonderful view over the whole surrounding plain of that part of Flanders.
>
> From the heights of the hill a number of German armoured vehicles could occasionally be seen probing along our extended

front, but they turned away whenever actively engaged by us; particularly so after the very severe handling they got in their first attempt on Cassel. The one thing I feared, of course, was a massed attack by German armour. What astonished me was that this was never made, when success was almost assured, and Dunkirk would have been at their mercy.

We now know of Rundstedt's decision, supported by Hitler, not to engage the German armour too deeply at Dunkirk, but the delaying action at Calais played its part, certainly disruptive, perhaps decisive.

★　　★　　★　　★　　★

With the northern French, Belgian and British armies cut off from those south of the Somme, it became increasingly evident that there was no choice left. On May 25th I drafted a telegram, which the Prime Minister approved, to Lord Gort. I told him our information showed that the French offensive could not be made in sufficient strength to hold out any prospect of a junction with his army in the north. If this happened, I wrote:

> you will be faced with a situation in which safety of B.E.F. will be predominant consideration. In such conditions only course open to you may be to fight your way back to west where all beaches and ports east of Gravelines will be used for embarkation. Navy would provide fleet of ships and small boats and R.A.F. would give full support. As withdrawal may have to begin very early, preliminary plans should be urgently prepared. You should also consider urgently security of Ostend and Dunkirk. . . . Prime Minister is seeing M. Reynaud tomorrow afternoon when whole situation will be clarified, including attitude of French to the possible move. . . .

M. Reynaud came to London on May 26th, when the Prime Minister unfolded to him at two sessions the military situation as we saw it. Reynaud was a courageous man and never during the coming weeks, when I saw him on several occasions, did he fail to confront the worst. He was not a man to pretend and he brought us disturbing accounts of Marshal Pétain's already burgeoning defeatism. If, said the French Prime Minister, a large part of his country were occupied by the enemy, Pétain would be likely to come out in favour of an armistice.

We made no comment, but at Mr. Churchill's request I then took part with Reynaud in drafting a telephone message to Weygand. In this the French Prime Minister told the General that the reports received from the front showed that the offensives from the north and south could not succeed in joining up. Reynaud's message continued that he had told us that Weygand had given Blanchard full freedom of decision. He asked the Commander-in-Chief to give Blanchard formal authority at once to order a withdrawal towards the ports.

I reported these decisions to Gort the same afternoon. My message to him concluded: "You are now authorized to operate towards coast forthwith, in conjunction with French and Belgian armies."

★　　★　　★　　★　　★

That night I wrote to the Prime Minister to remind him that we had ourselves told the Belgians nothing about the change of plan, though we had authorized Gort to take steps to do so. I suggested that he advise the King personally to send this news, or that he do so himself. I feared lest our withdrawal should crack the Belgian resolve, already weakened by defeat.

The French Command had no direct contact with the northern armies, while we were comparatively well-informed about their plight, which perhaps explains why the Belgian surrender the following night appears to have taken French Ministers entirely by surprise. Maybe it was particularly alarming to those who wished to keep France in the battle, as though coming events were casting their shadows before.

It should be remembered that at this time the intention was not to extract any forces permanently from the battle, but to use sea-power to rescue them from threatened encirclement and bring them back into the battle farther west. But the French Command must be made to understand what we were doing or there would be bitterness and talk of betrayal.

Therefore, on May 27th, I sent a telegram to General Sir Richard Howard-Vyse, head of our military mission at General Weygand's headquarters, telling him that it was necessary to consider the destination of the B.E.F. and of any French forces evacuated from the northern ports. It would, I explained, help us to receive an early indication of the view of the French authorities, especially about the positions in France to which they wished these units to be transferred. I suggested that he should speak to General Weygand, to make plain to him that we had every intention to continue the struggle side by side with our Allies.

★　★　★　★　★

Inevitably the difficulties of the retreat to Dunkirk, which was an admission of overwhelming defeat for the allies, were increased by the surrender of the Belgian army in the night of May 27th–28th. I remember a conversation with the Prime Minister during one of the more anxious of these evenings. Certainly neither of us believed then that so large a proportion of the British and French armies could be saved from Dunkirk. It has always seemed to me something of a mystery that the Germans did not press their advantage more vigorously against the perimeter of Dunkirk, or make any persistent attempt to bomb Dover.

My own belief was and remains that the Germans were chiefly concerned to ensure the defeat of the French armies. Their main effort was directed to the destruction of their principal opponent on land. In this they were probably right, from the point of view of textbook strategy. They were wrong psychologically. Hitler had not allowed for so swift a victory and he was not ready to change fronts to deal with his lesser opponent. For the moment, the German forces were like a man who in a rough-and-tumble has knocked out his larger opponent more quickly than he expected. He stumbles over the body before he can regain his balance and turn to look for his smaller foe.

After Gort had been ordered home by the Government, General Harold Alexander was left in charge of the rearguard at Dunkirk and handled its dangers with the unhurried ability we later associated with his campaigns in Burma and Africa. The last message I received from the B.E.F. was from him. He told me of the extreme danger which threatened his force. I agreed to immediate evacuation, but asked him to give French troops equal facilities with our own to get away. His work done, Alexander came to report to me in my room at the War Office as soon as he reached England. After he had given me an account of what had passed I congratulated him and he replied, with engaging modesty: "We were not pressed, you know."

★　　★　　★　　★　　★

Immediately after Dunkirk, I visited a number of camps in different parts of the country in which the returned troops of the B.E.F. had been hurriedly quartered. I had half expected some questioning or complaint, for there was enough to criticize. Our infantry had had no armour to support them; even its equipment had revealed some woeful shortages. But the mood of the officers and men showed none of this. On the contrary, their temper was that of victors, with no sign that they had had to retreat during days of continuous fighting before an overwhelmingly stronger enemy. I felt that having measured their opponent in these conditions, they were convinced that, given the weapons, they could match and outfight him. Even those brigades which had suffered the heaviest casualties, notably the 5th Brigade of the 2nd Division, were as confident and resolute as their more fortunate comrades. For me the hours I could spend among these men were a tonic, for there was in them the temper of those who knew they could not be beaten, whereas in Whitehall I had only too much reason to reckon how heavy must soon be the odds.

It was about this time that Mr. Churchill told me he had seen the King who said that I had seemed in wonderful spirits. When his Majesty asked me why, I had said: "Now we are all alone, Sir. We haven't an ally left." It was in this mood of exaltation that on June 2nd I broadcast to the nation an account of the battle of the ports, proclaimed the nation's refusal to accept defeat as the guarantee of final victory and concluded:

Our duty in this country is plain. We must make good our losses and we must win this war. To do that we must profit by the lessons of this battle. Brave hearts alone cannot stand up against steel. We need more planes, more tanks, more guns. The people of this country must work as never before. We must show the same qualities, the same discipline, and the same self-sacrifice at home as the British Expeditionary Force have shown in the field.

The nation honours with proud reverence those who fell that their comrades might win through. The innumerable actions, the countless deeds of valour of the last week, cannot all be recorded now. Each will have its place in history. Soldiers, sailors, airmen, who gave their lives to help — theirs is an immortal memory. Their spirit must be our banner, their sacrifice our spur.*

These days at the War Office seemed all too short for the work which had to be done. The principal commands had to be changed to give opportunity to the younger men who had fought in France and to prepare against possible attempts at invasion. I saw the commanders, both the departing and their successors, to explain what we were doing and why. The Prime Minister advised me to write letters to those who would have to go, but I said that I would rather see them and I am glad that I did for all except one took it well.

Then there were the priorities for equipment among the divisions returned from Dunkirk. During these weeks I had a chart before me on my table, showing by weapons the progress in rearmament of each division. By this means I could keep a close watch on any delays in delivery, which constant consultations with the Ministry of Supply, under Mr. Herbert Morrison's intelligent administration, enabled us to remedy from an unprecedented national output. Added to this were frequent discussions with Sir John Dill, who had become C.I.G.S. on May 27th, about the situation in France and the position of our remaining forces there, and the daily sessions of either the Defence Committee or the War Cabinet, or both. Sometimes the War Cabinet met two or three times a day.

* *Freedom and Order,* pages 74–7.

Soon after Mr. Churchill took over as Prime Minister, the Defence Committee had been transformed. It was presided over by him and attended by the service Ministers and their Chiefs of Staff, the Foreign Office being represented by the Permanent Under-Secretary.

Gradually the system further evolved until, with my return to the Foreign Office, the attendance usually consisted of the Prime Minister, Mr. Attlee and myself, with the three service Ministers and their Chiefs of Staff. Later it consisted of the same three members of the War Cabinet, the Chiefs of Staff, sometimes with, sometimes without, the service Ministers. The War Cabinet not wishing to be informed of the details of our plans, this Defence Committee became a most important instrument in the conduct of the war and continued to be so, although the number of meetings fell in 1942. Later, the meetings between the Prime Minister, as Minister of Defence, with the Chiefs of Staff alone became more frequent, but whenever these discussions had a political complexion, as they usually did, it was the Defence Committee which handled them on behalf of the War Cabinet.

★　★　★　★　★

As long as the French armies remained in the fight, we had an obligation to reinforce them as rapidly as we could. This raised the question of the command of the new Expeditionary Force, an invidious assignment in the circumstances. On June 3rd, I wrote to the Prime Minister:

> You will see among the Chiefs of Staffs' recommendations, the constitution of a B.E.F. This is clearly right, but I hope that no decision will be taken at the Cabinet about its command until you and I have had a word together.
>
> The new B.E.F. will, to start with anyway, be of Corps size and there is perhaps something to be said for a commander of that rank. Brooke has done brilliantly and it might be that he should go out first. I have no decided view as yet, but I wanted to enter this *caveat* now, and not take a decision until you and I and Dill have spoken together.

General Alan Brooke was in fact chosen and did all that man could do in the short interval, although our meeting with the French Command at Briare soon showed how near was the end of resistance.

On June 9th the Prime Minister mentioned to me that he would have to visit France again and wanted me to accompany him, with General Dill. Two days later we took off in the unbroken sunshine of that summer for Briare on the Loire, motoring from there to the Château de Muguet. I felt almost ashamed of our ordered escort of Hurricanes as we landed on the airfield, with its scattered confusion of odds and ends of aircraft. The château was small, civilized and typical, an easy and agreeable home with one telephone in the back passage. It seemed ominous to me that this, with a train in a nearby siding, was the headquarters of the French army at war.

M. Reynaud received us, firm and courteous despite the strain. We soon got down to discussion across the dining-room table; Pétain, Reynaud, Weygand facing Churchill, Dill and me, with interpreters. General Georges joined us later. We talked for almost three hours, the discussion hardly advancing matters. The speakers were polite and correct, but although at that time the Maginot Line had not been attacked, it was soon evident that our French hosts had no hope.

Early in our talks, Weygand described the military situation, explaining how he had attempted to block a number of gaps in the line. He believed he had succeeded and, for the moment, the line held, but he had no more reserves. Somebody asked what would happen if another breach were made. "No further military action will then be possible," Weygand replied. Reynaud at once intervened sharply: "That would be a political decision, *Monsieur le Géneral.*" Weygand bowed and said: "Certainly." Georges told us that the French had altogether only some one hundred and ninety-five fighter aircraft left on the northern front.

When the moment came for Mr. Churchill to tell the French that we would go on with the struggle, if necessary alone, I watched the expressions opposite. Reynaud was inscrutable and Weygand polite, concealing with difficulty his scepticism. Marshal Pétain was mockingly incredulous. Though he said nothing, his attitude was obviously *C'est de la blague.* Once in our discussion, Churchill, in his eagerness to convey his meaning, broke into French, at the same time looking earnestly at Reynaud. Since Reynaud spoke good English, the manœuvre was of doubtful effect, but it led to a moment of some confusion when, at the end of one such passage, Reynaud murmured absently: *"Traduction."*

Despite all the difficulties, our dinner, though simple, was admirably cooked and served. Reynaud presided, with Churchill on his right, Weygand sat opposite and I on his right. As we were taking our places, a tall and somewhat angular figure in uniform walked by on my side of the table. This was General Charles de Gaulle, Under-Secretary for Defence, whom I had met only once before. Weygand invited him pleasantly to take a place on his left. De Gaulle replied, curtly as I thought, that he had instructions to sit next to the British Prime Minister. Weygand flushed up, but made no comment, and so the meal began.

I had Marshal Pétain on my other side. Conversation was not easy. His refrain was the destruction of France and the daily devastation of her cities, of which he mentioned several by name. I was sympathetic, but added that there were even worse fates than the destruction of cities. Pétain rejoined that it was all very well for Britain to say that, we did not have the war in our country. When I said that we might have, I received an incredulous grunt in reply. With General Weygand my talk was perfectly friendly and consisted mainly of a discussion about our available forces in Britain and what we were doing to speed their training. I had little cheer to give him.

Weygand was something of an enigma. He had a famous reputation, crowned by his victory with Pilsudski over the Bolshevik forces in 1920. I had met him on several occasions, most recently early that year in the Middle East, and always found him friendly, quick and receptive, a modest man carrying his fame without affectation or conceit. He worked well with General Wavell, for the two men understood each other. I was glad when I heard that he had been called back to France to take over the supreme command. He achieved little, but probably no man could. At this stage, though always correct and courteous, he gave the impression of resigned fatalism. He was certainly not a man to fight the last desperate corner.

There was little room in the château, so Dill and I slept that night in the train. The next morning the Prime Minister and I were standing with Reynaud on the porch of the château in the sunshine, talking before breakfast. Reynaud was canvassing with regret the decision he had felt compelled to take to put Pétain into the Government. At that moment the Marshal appeared, walking towards us across the grass. "He looks buoyant this morning," commented Reynaud. "There must be some bad news [des nouvelles néfastes]." There was.

We left the French headquarters with the certainty that effective resistance could not last much longer. As I flew low over Brittany, hedge-hopping above the lovely French countryside in June, I felt a great sadness and wondered whether I should ever see this land again. It scarcely seemed probable. We had returned in separate aircraft, Mr. Churchill and General Ismay in one, Dill and I in the other. The cloud was thick when we took off, so the Royal Air Force could not escort us. There were anxious moments because the Germans were reported trying to intercept us. We knew nothing of that at the time, only sorrow and a sense of vacancy.

★   ★   ★   ★   ★

That afternoon, which was my birthday, the Prime Minister reported to the Cabinet, but before I went round to the meeting I had time to send him a letter:

June 12th, 1940.

I have been thinking over our experiences of the last twenty-four hours and I am more than ever convinced that the chances of Reynaud's survival and of France staying in the war are to a large extent dependent upon the attitude of the United States. If Roosevelt could go a stage further and break off relations with Germany, even without declaring war, if such an action be possible, he would perhaps give our hard-pressed French friends just that spice of encouragement they need.

I do not know whether it is possible for you to telegraph personally to Roosevelt in this sense. But your relations with him are so good, and he is so heart and soul with us, that may be the risk could be taken. It is, perhaps, only fair to Roosevelt to give him the true picture as we see it, and I believe that picture to be that only a further step by United States can keep France in the war, though even that may not suffice.

My own sentiment was that the French armies could not hold out for more than a few days. I knew that the Prime Minister shared this opinion from the talk we had had after the Briare meeting. We must expect that Reynaud would have to make way for Pétain, or another, who would call for an armistice. In that event, the essential was to ensure that the armistice was not the prelude to something worse, a treaty of peace. For we had to hope not only that the French fleet would be saved, but that France would continue to fight in North Africa and elsewhere. I sent a note to the Prime Minister:

> You will keep in mind the vital distinction between armistice and peace. The former is military, the latter political. We could consent to France asking for former under military duress. We could never agree to her making *peace*. Holland has not made peace nor Norway.

★   ★   ★   ★   ★

While the situation in France inevitably preoccupied the War Cabinet, I had also much in mind the dangers in the Middle East, where our forces were thin enough on the ground in any event. If French resistance were to collapse, our position would at once become precarious if Mussolini entered the war against us, as seemed daily more probable. The jackal would want to be in at what he smelt was the kill.

These considerations brought me into some controversy with the Prime Minister, who was impatient at the delay in bringing home eight battalions from Palestine. He had sent me a sharp minute on this subject on June 6th, complaining that while it was natural that Wavell should have his own point of view, "Here we have to think of building up a good army in order to make up, as far as possible, for the lamentable failure to support the French by an

adequate B.E.F. during the first year of the war." He drew attention to the forty-seven divisions brought into action at the end of
the first world war, with twelve battalions each, compared with the
nine of the modern division. "We are, indeed, the victims of a
feeble and weary Departmentalism." *

This seemed to me an over-simplification of our problems, for
Wavell's preoccupation with the loss of his eight battalions would
have still more force if the French collapsed. The consequence of
this would at once be felt if fighting were to break out against
Wavell's command, perhaps on several fronts at once. In my reply
the same day I explained that I was arranging a shuttle of battalions
to and from India with a view to getting our regular battalions
home, and gave the reasons for my Middle East anxieties. The
Chiefs of Staff had already advised against the withdrawal of battalions from that theatre. I wrote:

> The considerations which were put forward by the Chiefs of
> Staff from the angle of our commitments in the Middle East
> still hold good. Indeed they have been reinforced by telegrams
> which I have received from General Wavell. He makes it clear
> that there is no margin in the Middle East to cover the wide
> responsibilities which he has to face. . . .

The emphasis of Mr. Churchill's exordium was on a build-up in
terms of battalions at home, excusably enough for the moment, but
I had to redress the balance. It was all too easy at the War Office
to understand how bare was the cupboard of equipment and that
this, and not more men to equip, was our instant problem everywhere.

Symbolic of our condition at home at this time was a report
which I sent to the Prime Minister after a visit on June 23rd to
XII Corps under General Thorne, defending the counties of Kent,
Sussex and Surrey, a key area in any German invasion. I wrote:
"There is no anti-tank regiment nor anti-tank gun in the whole of
this Corps area." There were also, of course, no tanks, for we had
no cruiser or infantry tanks serviceable and with fighting units at
that time. This same report referred also to another unresolved

* Winston S. Churchill: *The Second World War*, Vol. II.

problem which was to occupy much of my time in the next few months, air co-operation:

> At present the Commander-in-Chief has a few medium bomber squadrons, I think only four, under his command, and neither Commands* nor corps have any; nor do these formations control any dive-bombers. It would enormously add to the efficiency of our defence if co-operation between the army and the air force could be made possible with lower formations in the army than G.H.Q. If the Germans attack this country, we may be certain that their infantry and tanks will once again work in the closest collaboration with the German dive-bombers. We have at present no means and no method of meeting this threat.

The demands upon us for equipment kept mounting alarmingly. Virtually everything had been lost in France except rifles, yet the calls to equip new units multiplied daily. For instance, another minute had reached me on June 6th from the Prime Minister, saying that the Netherlands Ministers wanted to form a Dutch brigade, which was to be furnished with as much equipment as possible. The Prime Minister wanted a weekly report on how this was progressing. This was laudable, but our own trained and battle-proven regular divisions had to come first.

★   ★   ★   ★   ★

If the Prime Minister was exigent, he was also thoughtful and having heard, I suppose, that excessive demands were being made upon me in Parliament as well as in the War Office, on July 10th he sent me this letter:

> The same kind of intense Parliamentary pressure arose after the last war when I was in your shoes. The problem of demobilization raised not hundreds but thousands of questions which M.Ps. had a right to ask. I protected myself by appointing my

---

* This referred to the geographical Commands into which England was divided.

very able Parliamentary Private Secretary, Mr. McCallum Scott, to be a kind of "Members' friend." I let him use my room at the House of Commons, and he sat there all the time for hours on end seeing Members and keeping them away from me.

This arrangement was commended to the House by me, and it was found to work very well. The precedent could be looked up, and might be of help to you. You have, however, also two Under-Secretaries in the House of Commons, and perhaps one of these could be nominated as the shock-absorber.

I entirely agree that you yourself should keep clear of minor business, so as to have plenty of time for the large issues of strategy, and the general problems of organizing the Army. I am afraid I have had to add to your labours by sending you numerous letters and Minutes.

As soon as the intense pressure allowed, I tried to escape for a few hours every week, often on Saturday, to visit the army in some part of the country. For this purpose I had at my disposal a Flamingo aircraft. This was a lovely machine, the forerunner of the Devon and the Dove. I made scores of flights in it during the summer, until the excessive interference of German aircraft in southern England caused the Secretary of State for Air to forbid me its use.

★   ★   ★   ★   ★

In the summer of 1940, I had two unexpected visitors at the War Office. The first was Mr. Lloyd George, who in a conversation in the lobby of the House of Commons one day said he would like to come over to the War Office for a talk. We had become friends in the last three years and he had sent me messages of encouragement. I had always thought him a great war Minister, so I welcomed the opportunity and, when Lloyd George arrived, we indulged in a broad and lively survey of events and prospects. Later I took him along to the C.I.G.S.'s room to introduce him to Dill. When Lloyd George had entertained us with his reminiscences of some earlier occupants of that office, we returned to my room and he remarked that I was fortunate in my soldiers. Men like Dill and Wavell were clearly outstanding and of a very different calibre from those with whom he had had to work. I said that I had not known the generals of the 1914–18 war, except from the point of view of a subaltern in the trenches, but I did know these men and I had the highest opinion of their quality.

A little later I had a message from the Soviet Ambassador, Mr. Maisky, hinting that he would like to come to see me. I thought it prudent to have a word with the Prime Minister about this, because I felt that if I were to see Maisky, it would be necessary to put him pretty fully into the picture. It was likely that the Soviet Government were well informed about our dispositions and resources anyway, and to have a discussion with their Ambassador without telling him anything could do more harm than good. The Prime Minister shared my opinion and, with the Foreign Secretary's consent, I asked Maisky to come round.

After I had given him an account of the position, the Ambassador, who seemed pleased at being treated with so much confidence, said that in return he would now tell me of a despatch he had recently sent to his Government. He had told them that Britain would not collapse as France had done, because the spirit of the people was quite different. He did not think that Britain would be defeated in the war. On the other hand, though he believed we could withstand all Hitler's attacks, he did not see how we could win the war. I saw nothing to quarrel about in this as a neutral's judgment of events.

Some years later when I was in Moscow, I attended a Red Army concert at which I sat next to Molotov. I mentioned this incident, and asked him if he recalled getting such a despatch. He said that he certainly did and that they had been impressed in Moscow by Maisky's reporting of the situation. It was the first confident forecast which the Soviet Government had received that Britain would be able to hold out, which was why he remembered it.

4

MEN AND WEAPONS

June–October 1940

General Wavell wants a War Council — He asks for more equipment — General Wavell's uneasy relations with the Prime Minister — He is called to London — Mr. Churchill is partly reassured — Lend-lease and the Arsenal of Democracy — The Battle
of Britain — The Prime Minister considers troop dispositions —
Reinforcements to the Middle East are accepted — Mr. Churchill
contemplates Cabinet changes — "You can keep your Dill"

ONE EVENING during these June days, the C.I.G.S. and I were conferring alone together in my room at the War Office about the
position of our forces in the Middle East and the army's part in
the war, which the British Commonwealth and Empire would now
have to wage alone. We agreed that it was in North Africa that
our fighting must be done. Nowhere else could Britain get to grips
with the enemy on land. We could not foresee when a landing in
Europe would be practicable again, but our sea-power, using ex-
terior lines, made it possible to build up our strength in Egypt
and in the Western Desert. This was the theatre where the army
must prove itself.

I told Dill that I did not think that the army's reputation or
that of its leaders stood very high with the nation. Dill agreed and
spoke of Hore-Belisha with a bitterness which surprised me. He
had done damage to the army that could not be repaired in years,
Dill said, commanders had come to look over their shoulders. I
continued that we must make no mistake about the man to be in
charge in the Middle East. He must be the very best; we had the
whole field to choose from. Dill replied that he regarded Wavell as
the finest general in the British army and he would be his choice.
I said that I would back him on this.

141

SPAIN

Barcelona

AZORES: 700 MILES

Cadiz
Tangier
Gibraltar
Ceuta
Algiers
Bizerta

MADEIRA

Rabat
Casablanca
Oran
Tunis
PANTELLERIA
MAL

Marrakesh

MOROCCO

TUNISIA

Tripol

CANARY ISLANDS

ALGERIA

TRIPOLITANIA

RIO DE ORO

L

Dakar

FRENCH WEST AFRICA

GAMBIA

PORT. GUINEA

R. Niger

Kano
TAKORADI A
Ft. Lam

Freetown
SIERRA
LEONE

L I B E R I A

GOLD
COAST

N IGERIA

Lagos
Takoradi

FRE

NORTH & CENTRAL AFRICA

0   500   1000 MILES

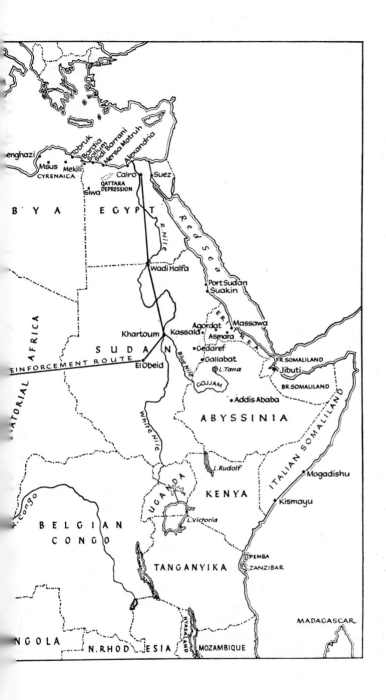

Benghazi
Msus • Mekili • Tobruk
Bardia
Sollum
Sidi Barrani
Mersa Matruh
Alexandria
CYRENAICA
Cairo • Suez
QATTARA DEPRESSION
Siwa

B Y A   E G Y P T

R. Nile

R e d   S e a

Wadi Halfa

Port Sudan
Suakin

AFRICA

Khartoum   Kassala
Agordat • Massawa
Asmara
S U D A N
Gedaref
El Obeid   Gallabat
L.Tana
GOJJAM

E R I T R E A

FR.SOMALILAND
Jibuti
BR.SOMALILAND

REINFORCEMENT ROUTE

ATORIAL

White Nile

Blue Nile

• Addis Ababa

A B Y S S I N I A

I T A L I A N   S O M A L I L A N D

L.Rudolf

U G A N D A
K E N Y A
• Mogadishu
• Kismayu

Congo

B E L G I A N
C O N G O
L.Victoria

T A N G A N Y I K A
PEMBA
ZANZIBAR

MADAGASCAR

NGOLA
N.RHOD ESIA
NYASALAND
MOZAMBIQUE

On June 18th General Wavell telegraphed to the C.I.G.S. suggesting that a war council should be set up in the Middle East, working under the general direction of the War Cabinet at home. It might comprise representatives of South Africa, India, Australia, France, if French Africa were still fighting, and possibly Egypt. Dill replied, asking for more details, which Wavell gave on June 29th, but two days later he reversed his advice, fearing that his plan would take so long to become effective that it would delay his reinforcements. He substituted a suggestion that a sub-committee of the War Cabinet should be given the task of keeping close watch on the area.

The Chiefs of Staff were not enthusiastic. They accepted that it was urgent to reinforce Wavell, but reminded him that they had to keep back enough equipment to meet a probable air offensive and even invasion of Britain. Two months might pass before they could start to release it for the Middle East. Even so, there was wisdom in Wavell's plans which were later to be adapted and used.

★ ★ ★ ★ ★

On July 4th, the Italians captured Kassala and Gallabat in the Sudan, on the Eritrean and Abyssinian frontiers. British forces were locally so weak that I felt anxiety lest the Italians, with a quarter of a million men in Abyssinia, should mount a drive upon Khartoum if weather conditions allowed. There was only about a brigade to withstand them.

On the same day, Wavell telegraphed that he had in his whole command only one incomplete armoured division, two very incomplete divisions and another fit only for policing duties. He concluded: "My essential needs are more armoured troops, more anti-tank guns and other artillery." To meet a possible German and Italian attack, he wanted two armoured divisions and a corps of three divisions. I discussed this situation with the Prime Minister, and Dill did so with the other Chiefs of Staff. We had little enough to propose and, on July 8th, after totalling up the meagre help I could offer, I told Wavell: "An insurrection in Abyssinia would greatly assist your task. No doubt every effort is being made to further this, despite difficult weather conditions." I asked for his views and concluded: "You will share our keen desire to strike at Italians, especially if they should attempt advance from Kassala on Khartoum." Wavell's reply was robust and comprehensive, showing that he was already considering the reinforcement of the Sudan

> to enable counter-offensive to be taken but distances and rainy season are difficulties. . . . We can hold on all right while you defeat German invasion, unless there is very heavy air concentration on Egypt, and we are doing what we can to harass Italians, who are not very formidable.

★ ★ ★ ★ ★

The loss of the French military contribution, upon which we had counted in many parts of the Middle East from Syria to Somaliland, our own slender resources and how to stretch or fortify them, formed the topic of several discussions between the Prime Minister and myself at meal and other times during these weeks, when the threat of the invasion of our own island loomed large. On one occasion, when I was deploring the earlier failure to double the strength of the Sudan Defence Force, whose fighting quality we rated so highly, Churchill remarked: "If you lose Khartoum your name will live in history." It is fair to add that when, some years later, I reminded Mr. Churchill of this comment, he shook his head and said: "My dear, I would never have said that to you."

On July 11th the Prime Minister agreed to give me the help of a Cabinet Committee to handle the innumerable Middle East problems. Mr. Leo Amery and Lord Lloyd, representing India and the Colonies respectively, were the other members, with myself presiding. In addition, the Dominions Secretary, Lord Caldecote, the Chiefs of Staff, and Mr. R. A. Butler, Under-Secretary at the Foreign Office, were often present as well as military officers and officials.

This Committee was never popular in Whitehall and its advice was often unpalatable, but I have no doubt that the Prime Minister was right to set it up. In a short life it focused attention and compelled action to help a more distant theatre, at a time when the claims of an impending invasion of Britain must otherwise have devoured all we had. Perhaps some unhappy errors could have been spared us if a committee of comparable authority had been appointed for the Far East later in the year.

Shortages of equipment mattered most and could be mended least. Each had its tail of consequences. Malta could not be used until the scale of defence, particularly in anti-aircraft guns, had been improved, and Wavell's shortage of anti-tank guns was chronic. Even the 7th Armoured Division, later famous as the Desert Rats, lacked much equipment. The Royal Air Force also had to be strengthened, while Wavell's policy of minor offensives could not be kept up because of a shortage of ammunition.

On July 23rd the Commander-in-Chief had to report that, unless his needs in this and other respects were met within the next three months, his army's position would be at risk. In another telegram, on July 30th, he said that there were practically no replacements or spare parts even for the vehicles of the Armoured Division:

> We cannot continue indefinitely to fight this war without proper equipment and I hope the Middle East requirements will be delayed no longer.

The next day Wavell reported that he must evacuate Sollum:

> *July 31st:* Sad but not unexpected. He is short of equipment and has all our troubles and his own to boot. Discussed with [Maj.-Gen.] Carr [Assistant C.I.G.S.] and [Maj.-Gen.] Pope [Director of Armoured Fighting Vehicles] the despatch of what we could to help him, especially armoured cars, one of our worst weaknesses.

July 22nd was a typical day in that summer:

> Heavy office work in morning. Two-hour Cabinet. Archie [Sinclair, Secretary of State for Air] lunched with me and we had some talk of our respective problems. . . .
>
> Saw M.Ps. with their various problems in the afternoon. Then to Winston in the garden at No. 10. He was pleased that our changes* had gone so well. I told him that War Office got noth-

---

* General Sir Alan Brooke succeeded General Sir Edmund Ironside as C.-in-C. Home Forces. Lieutenant-General Claude Auchinleck succeeded Brooke as G.O.C. Southern Command.

ing but kicks anyway. . . . We then talked of Ireland and he approved my visit to the North. Neville [Chamberlain] asked to see me, and also expressed satisfaction at way changes had gone. He was anxious to let de Gaulle loose somewhere. I could ask nothing better.

Army Council got through much business.

July 25th: Long Middle East Committee. Fair progress.

Dined with Winston. Violent tirade after about Middle East and Wavell and at times heated altercation, George [Lloyd] and Max [Beaverbrook], Dill and [Maj.-Gen.] Ismay [Prime Minister's chief staff officer]. Bed 1.30 a.m.

My discussions with the Prime Minister were embarrassed at this time by what I feared was his increasingly critical attitude towards the C.I.G.S., of whom I thought highly. Sir John Dill had an exceptionally fine mind, but he could also be tense. While he was always correct in his attitude to the Prime Minister, he was not so ready to adapt his moods to those of Churchill, which could succeed each other with a bewildering if engaging rapidity. Dill never lacked personal charm, but it was not in his character to be aware of it, still less to employ it to ease any discussion about which he cared. I had had an example of the growing rift between these two men in a complaint which the Prime Minister had already made to me. We were not, he considered, receiving from Dill the help which we had expected. For the moment I was able to reassure him, but the Prime Minister's doubts were not altogether resolved.

★ ★ ★ ★ ★

On July 28th our Middle East Committee made a number of recommendations to the Cabinet, the most important of which were: (1) The whole of the Indian division, previously to be sent to Basra, should be placed at General Wavell's disposal. (2) Preparations should be put in hand at once for the despatch of a second armoured division to the Middle East and it should leave as soon as the dangers of invasion had lessened. (3) The Australian and New Zealand Governments should be invited to despatch to the Middle East any forces they could spare after meeting their commitments in the Far East. (4) No financial considerations should be allowed to stand in the way of fomenting rebellion in Abyssinia. Two days later the Chiefs of Staff went through our points and agreed with them all.

I had spent that morning seeing troops in Northern Ireland, but the real purpose of my visit was to meet Major-General Sir Hubert Huddleston, then in command of the area. I thought that if he were fit enough to stand the climate again, about which Dill had some doubts, he would be the man to take over as Governor-General of the Sudan. I was much impressed by him and, as he seemed keen on the job and confident that he could do it, I took him out with me to Cairo when I flew there two months later. He brought new life to the country.

On July 29th, the Cabinet met in the War Room underneath the building at Storey's Gate known as the annexe. I was already complaining of the stuffy atmosphere, for I always detested working there; not least because I sat in line with the Prime Minister and not opposite him as in the Cabinet room, where I could see his expression. I did not like to argue out of the side of my mouth.

There seemed to me to be something unearthly about emerging from our subterranean chamber on a night when enemy aircraft were alive and the sky was lit with countless flashes. I remember how, two months afterwards, I drove back late with Dill through Parliament Square, when St. Margaret's Church was ablaze like a fiery furnace. I did not expect that even the stone walls would be standing the next day.

After the Cabinet of July 29th the Prime Minister asked me to talk to him alone. He spoke of a Government reconstruction, following on Chamberlain's illness. One alternative, he said, was to bring me into the War Cabinet but, from my own point of view, he thought I might prefer to stay where I was, since there was no more important work to be done anywhere. I said that I would much prefer to stay at the War Office, and would be very sorry to be told to move, though I would do as he wished. Churchill agreed that I should remain.

These days also saw the beginning of a long period of argument with the Prime Minister about General Wavell's merits. Churchill did not know the Commander-in-Chief personally, and was naturally impatient of the sprawling character of our Middle Eastern dispositions and the many men required in the workshops at the base and on lines of communication to keep modest forces in the field. At this time, too, the army had won no battle, which did not incline my other colleagues to be enthusiastic, and so it seemed to me that I was constantly defending the reputations of men unjustly assailed. On one occasion Chamberlain remarked to me with wry sympathy after one of our Cabinets: "I'm sorry, Anthony, that all your generals seem to be such bad generals."

Dill and I felt that there must be a limit to this chastisement of the army, the more so as it took place before the representatives of the other services. Accordingly, after a Cabinet meeting in the House of Commons, we stayed behind to see the Prime Minister and told him that if Wavell and his commanders continued to be singled out for criticism in this way, which we thought most unjust to them and damaging to the army, we could not accept it and would both have to go. Churchill gave us a soothing reply, but thereafter the balance was better kept.

Early in August I came to the conclusion that we might gain some important advantages if Wavell could come home for a few days, meet the Prime Minister and talk over his difficulties with us. Dill liked the idea and I mentioned it to Mr. Churchill, who at once agreed.

August 8th: Long talk alone with Wavell at 10 a.m. when we reviewed his resources and tasks. He was in good heart, but the deficiencies are shocking. We shall have to make him up a parcel of what we can scrape together and send it out soon. There is then the question of the route.

Our talk over, we had a meeting of the Middle East Committee and the Chiefs of Staff. I thought then that Wavell's account was masterly and it is even more so in retrospect. He admitted that if the Italians were to bring up a large force, some withdrawal would be necessary for a while. The real danger would not arise until German armour and motorized units appeared. The outcome of this meeting was a strong recommendation by our Committee and the Chiefs of Staff that the despatch of convoys taking reinforcements to the Middle East should be hastened.

The next day, after inspecting our troops and defences in East Anglia, I drove to Chequers and joined in a conference with the Prime Minister, Dill and Wavell. This went reasonably well, even though Churchill still kept, I thought, his reservations about Wavell. The Commander-in-Chief was not a man who could be drawn out, or one to make a special effort to please, but there was agreement as to what should be done. It was decided that the War Office should prepare a note of the armoured and other forces which we felt ought to be sent at once to the Middle East, accepting the risks at home. The next day Dill did this and sent it across to the Prime Minister with what Mr. Churchill later called my "ardent approval":*

1 Cruiser Tank Battalion (52 tanks)
1 Light Tank Regiment (52 tanks)
1 Infantry Tank Battalion (50 tanks)
48 Anti-Tank guns
20 Bofors Light A.A. guns
48 25-pdr. Field guns
500 Bren guns
250 Anti-Tank rifles
Ammunition for the above and some
Anti-Tank mines.

The Middle East Committee and the War Cabinet agreed to this list. The only remaining discussion was whether the convoy should go round the Cape or through the Mediterranean. On this we finally settled that the Cape was preferable, unless Wavell on his return considered an Italian attack imminent, which in the event he did not. The War Office, and in particular the C.I.G.S., deserve the credit for asking for so bold a transfer of essential equipment from our still limited resources, but this does not detract from the Prime Minister's share, for his was the final responsibility.

Wavell announced the good news in a cable to Lieutenant-General Sir Henry Maitland Wilson, who was in command in his absence, adding that "further reinforcements will be sent as soon as possible." The Middle East Commanders were, however, doomed

* *The Second World War,* Vol. II.

to disappointment, as was often to be their lot in these early years of war. August 13th was Hitler's *Adlertag,* "Day of the Eagle," the official beginning of the air offensive against this country. The call for arms to defend our island became urgent and absolute. Fortunate are those British commanders to whom chief responsibility falls in the later years of a war, when there is enough equipment to go round.

Personal relations continued to be a complication. On August 12th my diary records of a Defence Committee with Wavell in attendance: "A very long and exhausting sitting with Winston beginning at 10 p.m. and finishing at 2 a.m. or later." There was first an argument with the Admiralty whether after all the armoured troops should not go through the Mediterranean, "then long discussion about Wavell's dispositions. P.M. most anxious to move this battalion here and that battalion there. At the end he took me into the garden and we continued argument." All this was not novel to Dill or to me, but to Wavell it was.

> *August 13th:* Found Wavell waiting for me at 9 a.m. He was clearly upset at last night's proceedings and said that he thought he should have made it plain that if the Prime Minister could not approve his dispositions and had not confidence in him he should appoint someone else. He was anxious to get back to his command if this were desired. He and I and C.I.G.S. then made a review of situation and I sent the Prime Minister note asking for a talk today and rang up Ismay in same sense. Prime Minister sent message agreeing to the three of us at 5.30. At 4 p.m. another message came that he only wanted C.I.G.S. and me at 6.

Later came a letter which, though friendly in tone, dealt with a number of detailed questions and disturbed me by the lack of confidence it showed in Wavell. The Prime Minister wrote that while favourably impressed with Wavell in many ways, he did not feel in him that sense of mental vigour and resolve to overcome obstacles, which was indispensable to successful war. Instead, he found tame acceptance of a variety of local circumstances in different theatres, which was leading to a lamentable lack of concentration upon the decisive point. Mr. Churchill also proposed the transfer of two West

African brigades to the Sudan, of the South African brigade to Egypt, and of six regular battalions, Australian troops and half the regular cavalry regiments from Palestine, to Egypt.

Unfortunately there was little to be gained by movements of troops at this time unless they were trained and equipped. Weapons not men were the open sesame to victories. I replied:

> Thank you for your letter in which you tell me that you will have to consult further with the Admiralty before reaching a conclusion upon the armoured reinforcements. I am myself convinced that this reinforcement should be sent to Egypt even if it has to go round by the Cape, for it is the measure of help which will best enable Wavell to defeat the enemy in the Desert where he would, and should, fight him.
>
> The next most important contribution that we can make from here to any forthcoming operations in the Middle East is in the supply of equipment. Wavell is at present short of all the weapons which go to make up a modern fighting force. As you know, his armoured division is a division only in name, and consists of four regiments and two motor battalions. He is short of anti-tank weapons, anti-aircraft weapons, guns, carriers and Brens for all his forces.
>
> Until he receives sufficient supplies of these he cannot fully equip his Australian and New Zealand forces, who have now been under training for more than a year, nor use them effectively. Furthermore, until this equipment reaches him, Wavell will scarcely be able to relieve the British battalions at present on internal security duties, for he has neither the equipment for those battalions nor the guns and other supporting units which he needs to make them into an effective fighting force under modern conditions.

I then dealt in detail with the four points raised by the Prime Minister, explaining that in every instance the usefulness of these suggestions was governed by the shortage of equipment. I added in manuscript:

> Dill and I were much perturbed at your judgment of Wavell. Neither of us know of any General Officer in the army better

qualified to fill this very difficult post at this critical time. As
you know, we have made changes in almost every command,
and I am sure that you will believe me when I write that I
should not hesitate for a moment to ask you to agree if I
thought that a change was called for in the Middle East. I still
hope that our conversation tomorrow will enable you finally to
remove any lack of confidence you may have felt in Wavell.

In the event we met that evening when Dill and I told the Prime
Minister that we did not share his judgment of Wavell:

August 13th: . . . discussion was long and difficult. C.I.G.S.
made it quite plain that he agreed with Wavell [about his dis-
positions], and we both tried to impress upon Winston that equipment rather than man-power was the key to the situation.
Eventually Winston said that he would address us some questions
and that we would discuss the answers to them tomorrow.

We continued our exchanges. At one time the Prime Minister
was taking the view that Wavell was "a good average colonel," a
phrase he often used to me about him, "and would make a good
chairman of a Tory association." But Wavell had always been
anti-appeasement and was a Winchester scholar of repute, as I
argued in reply. This brought little comfort to Mr. Churchill who,
I learnt, did not much care for Winchester or its products, except
Sir Edward Grey. I felt sure that Wavell had exceptional ability
and Dill shared this opinion, though he admitted that he was perhaps on occasion, inclined to be lethargic. If Dill's judgment were
sound, I reflected, Wavell would certainly have been stirred up.

The truth was that Churchill never understood Wavell and
Wavell never seemed to encourage Churchill to do so. When the
Commander-in-Chief elaborated his plan for the defence of Alexandria I was not impressed by it and Mr. Churchill clearly abom-
inated it. "As the plan was described," the Prime Minister told
someone afterwards, "I noticed Anthony become more and more
uneasy. His face grew longer and longer, and his eyelids rose and
fell more and more rapidly." All the same, I could not blink at the
fact that we had no other commander as good.

August 15th: More Wavell talks, when Winston told me he must stay another day. I was against this, for Wavell is doing no good here and should either return or be replaced. Winston asked me who was a possible alternative. I said Auchinleck, he agreed. But we both felt that we had not sufficient evidence to compel a change which at the moment might have very bad effect on morale throughout Middle East. At a further meeting of us four in the afternoon, Winston suddenly agreed that Wavell should leave tonight.

This presumably showed that the Prime Minister had been convinced. I was much relieved and, though Mr. Churchill's doubts were from time to time revived, there was no further serious question of Wavell's replacement during the remainder of my tenure of the War Office.

★   ★   ★   ★   ★

Several times during these August days, the Prime Minister spoke to me about the composition of the War Cabinet. He was troubled about it. On one occasion he remarked that he had asked me, then Sinclair, then Beaverbrook, but none of us wanted to come in because it meant leaving our jobs. At another time, having spoken to me very generously about my work, he asked me where the other men were he could bring in. He did not know them, did I?

Again, after a dinner on August 22nd to some American generals, from which I did not get away till two in the morning, the Prime Minister said that he was worried about supply problems and wanted to put Lord Beaverbrook in charge of the lot. The burden of supervision was too much for him. He would like to put Ernest Bevin into the War Cabinet. I spoke in favour of this. Then, was I satisfied with my present post? There were many who would like to see Halifax leave the Foreign Office, would I like to go there? To Churchill . . .

August 22nd: [The] Foreign Office was a contracting job and the War Office expanding. I replied I would prefer to stay where I was. Winston seemed relieved. "I know where I can find another Foreign Secretary, he is here in the room with me; but

where I am to find another Secretary of State for War — can any-
one tell me that? After all he must know something of the work.
Yet, if Edward were to go, you would have to go to Foreign
Office."

★ ★ ★ ★ ★

The ability of the Royal Navy to escort the convoys upon which
Britain's life depended was tried to the limit during this summer.
Matters were made worse because the Government had not laid
down any destroyers during 1938, apparently owing to Treasury
pressure for economy which, almost unbelievably, was accepted.
The United States Government were now straining neutrality in
our favour and Mr. Churchill was continually pressing them to
further efforts. He asked, among other things, for the loan of fifty
or sixty destroyers, and this scheme was discussed between London
and Washington.

The negotiations did not go smoothly, nor did I altogether approve of the details of the final settlement. At one time the suggestion was put forward in Washington that the entire British West
Indies should be handed over for the cancellation of our war debts.
I thought this less than friendly bargaining. At another, the destroyers were to be exchanged for a public assurance that the British
fleet would sail to North American waters if Hitler gained control
of the United Kingdom. The Prime Minister rightly protested that
such an announcement would have a "disastrous effect" * on British
morale. The West Indian bases alone were certainly worth more
than fifty or sixty old destroyers.

The sweeping nature of the first American demands caused some
delay in the negotiations. Local patriotism in the West Indies was
justifiably affronted. By August 14th, however, the agreement was
settled, to be ratified at the beginning of the following month. Our
desperate straits alone could justify its terms. The age and condition of the fifty destroyers made unexpectedly large demands upon
our dockyards. Only nine ships were available before the end of
1940, by which time our own naval construction was catching up
on our losses.

* op. cit.

Help on a larger scale was soon to be forthcoming. Re-elected President on November 5th, Mr. Roosevelt suggested almost at once plans to open "the Arsenal of Democracy" for Great Britain. In March 1941 the cash-and-carry basis of British purchasing in the United States was abolished, and the principle of lend-lease sanctioned by Congress. Later the same month documents handing over bases in Newfoundland, Bermuda and the West Indies were signed.

★ ★ ★ ★ ★

Meanwhile I was following up the decisions taken earlier in August. In a minute to the Prime Minister on August 21st I wrote:

> We are now preparing plans for the shipment of men and material to the Middle East. Even if the three armoured units are passed through the Mediterranean, there is still a considerable consignment of equipment, especially guns, due to General Wavell. This must follow as rapidly as practicable, and will assist in the equipment of the remainder of the Australian Division.
>
> Next, we should prepare now for a convoy to leave in September, which convoy would take either Australian or New Zealand forces, now here, fully equipped to Egypt, or further armoured units or both, according as the situation in the Battle of Britain develops in the next few days. Preparations for this convoy have already begun. We have also in mind the preparation of a regular series of subsequent convoys to carry further contingents of arms and equipped troops, including perhaps a British division. Recent developments in Greece point to the likelihood of further calls upon our Army in the Middle East, and we cannot plan too early.

On August 26th I sent the Prime Minister two minutes, as well as replying to one of his about Commandos:

> Wavell's reports indicate no likelihood of an immediate offensive against Egypt. The accounts from the Sudan-Eritrean border are, however, by no means so reassuring, and I am glad

to see that Wavell is taking early steps to reinforce his troops in the Sudan. The essential for us in all these land operations in the Middle East is to gain the six to eight weeks we need to concentrate sufficient force. To achieve this we need to harass the Italians in Eritrea as we have already done with good effect in Libya.

I have, therefore, asked Dill to ask the Chiefs of Staff to examine —

(1) Whether there is effective air action we can take against the Italian rail-head in Eritrea.

(2) Whether the bombardment of Massawa [chief port in Eritrea] is a possibility from the sea (this is another aspect of a problem previously examined, viz., whether it were possible to land at Massawa).

(3) Whether it might be desirable to follow up any action that is possible in these spheres by an attack on Kassala, which, were it successful, would throw the Italian offensive out of its stride.

I feel sure that you will not mind my having asked Dill to put these ideas before the Chiefs of Staff.

To this the Prime Minister replied: "I am very glad you have done so."

★　★　★　★　★

Before France collapsed, I had rented a small but attractive old black and white house in the downs behind Elham in Kent, only a few miles from Dover. If I had planned to choose an observation post for a German invasion, it was ideal. Sir John Dill was often able to come down for a night during the weekend, when we would have informal talks with the local commanders, or visit some point on the coast, or one or other of the units engaged in its defence. Here we had front seats for a view of the Battle of Britain and from mid-August onwards there were frequent air battles overhead, sometimes while we were playing tennis. There was great excitement one day while I was in my bath. One of our fighters and a Messerschmitt had a battle over the garden. It looked as though the German as he crashed must hit our house. Actually his plane fell in the wood a few hundred yards behind, and he baled out in front, between us and the village. By the end of August, however, I thought it wise to move my wife and two sons to the greater security of Oxfordshire, while I continued to use the house as a private look-out.

★   ★   ★   ★   ★

The fact that Sir Archibald Sinclair and I were neither of us members of the War Cabinet sometimes had vexing consequences. For instance, it was a chance remark by Sinclair at a Cabinet meeting on September 13th which told me that the Cabinet had decided nine days before to delay the despatch of Hurricanes to the Middle East. However justified the decision, I was concerned not to have known about it. The fault was mine, because the minutes were circulated; but the pressure of events was such that there was excuse for my ignorance. The delivery of fighters to the Middle East involved even more argument than the forwarding of equipment for the army, and all through the latter half of September our Committee was tabling its requirements and urging its needs upon the Prime Minister. When there were differences, they were not so sharp as they appear in recital, because they were of degree, not of principle. Nor did Churchill resent pressure as he did sycophancy. He could take care of himself and arrive at the right answer.

September 15th saw a decisive turn in the Battle of Britain, though we did not yet know how completely. I think it was a month earlier that I went across to see the Prime Minister and, our business over, I sat on in the Cabinet room with him while reports came in of the air battle which was developing. Squadron after squadron of the Royal Air Force went up to engage the enemy and still the Luftwaffe kept coming. The news was scrappy at first and still more squadrons were called for, until it seemed that they had all been committed. As we listened and conjectured, things looked very stern, with the odds heavy against us. At last Churchill announced that he would drive to Fighter Command Headquarters and I went back to the War Office, neither of us yet knowing that this was to be one of the critical days of the war and end in victory.

Dill and I lunched with the Prime Minister on September 16th. It was intended that we should discuss the Middle East; in effect the talk was of air-raid warnings and how to regulate them.

In a brief talk with Winston afterwards he was vehement against sending anything more to Middle East. "I do not know what you are thinking of," etc., etc.

That same evening a telegram reached me from Wavell which relieved what had been one of my principal anxieties:

> Have just returned from Sudan where arrival of reinforcements has removed danger of any major Italian offensive and should enable our attacks to be developed when weather permits.

Two days later the argument was still being pursued. The Prime Minister telephoned to me in the evening to postpone agreement to the despatch of the 6th Australian Division to the Middle East. In my diary I called this "really maddening," because all the arrangements had been made and their Government had been told. I believed that the Australians would be better placed with their countrymen. "They cannot," I wrote, "decide the Battle of Britain; they might decide the Battle of Egypt." The Prime Minister, on the other hand, so I wrote in my diary, complained that I was always trying "to get him to send more men than he wanted to the Middle East."

On reflection I do not consider that these differences were in any way surprising. From the army point of view, the Middle East was the theatre where we had to develop our greatest power. The Prime Minister had wider responsibilities. The delays at which I tilted seldom lasted long and, on September 20th, the Prime Minister accepted that the convoy should sail on October 2nd so that, I wrote, "we must make up a really good packet for Wavell, even though it cannot contain all we would wish."

One night the Prime Minister, after a meeting with the Chiefs of Staff and service Ministers, called me into his room:

September 24th: He told me that I ought not to be so violent with him, for he was only trying to help me. I told him that he

was for ever nagging at the Army and was unjust to it. He retorted that he was far harder on the Navy, which I did not accept. Then he spoke of the Government's future. Neville was
very ill, cancer, and would have to give up soon. When he did,
he [Churchill] must bring another Tory into War Cabinet, and
I was only one country would accept. If Edward [Halifax] were
willing to become Lord President, he would like me to go to
Foreign Office. If not, I should be Lord President and help him
with matters of defence. I told him that he knew that I did not
wish to leave War Office. He agreed but said he could not have
only one service Minister in War Cabinet and asked if I had any
suggestion for War Office. . . . We left it that we would think
matters over.

★   ★   ★   ★   ★

Sometimes the location of my weekend home had its comic side.
On Sunday, September 22nd, I was working quietly through some
papers, when the Prime Minister sent me a message that President
Roosevelt had telegraphed saying three o'clock that afternoon was
zero hour for the German invasion. If I thought I should come
back, he would give me dinner. I replied that it was wet and blowing and I felt quite safe. I went to the top of the hill which overlooked the Channel and afterwards sent a further message, reporting it was so rough that any German who attempted to cross the
Channel would be very sea-sick. The next day the puzzle of Roosevelt's warning was resolved. The President of the United States
used from time to time to send pieces of information which he
thought might be useful to us in our embattled island. But this
time the code had got mixed and the invasion of Britain should
have read the invasion of Indo-China, which proved true enough,
and fateful.

During the same weekend I set out my thoughts on the enemy's
political and military plans, after reading accounts of a meeting
between Ribbentrop, Ciano and Mussolini in Rome. These I em-
bodied in a memorandum* which I sent to the Prime Minister and
Lord Halifax, to urge that we should take the admittedly serious

* This memorandum is printed as Appendix B.

risks involved and despatch further fully equipped forces to the
Middle East. In a covering note to Mr. Churchill I explained that
it was an attempt to take stock at a critical hour, adding: "If Hitler
chooses tonight to attempt to invade us it will be out of date before
you read it." To Lord Halifax I wrote:

> It seems to me essential that we should continue to pile up
> our effort in the Middle East. A few Wellingtons may achieve
> much there, they can decide nothing here.

This paper brought a reply on September 24th which referred
first to the Far East. The Prime Minister protested at the two Indian brigades being kept there against what he considered the unlikely threat of a Japanese siege of Singapore. He was critical of
the alleged waste of troops in Kenya and Palestine, and in the
Middle East Command in general. Finally he was disquieted by
the position in Malta, which might be attacked by a large force
from Italy.

To this I replied * on the same day:

> It seems to me difficult to maintain now that the Japanese
> threat to Malaya is not serious. . . . There is every indication
> that Germany has made some deal with Japan within these last
> few days, and it seems, therefore, wise to make some provision
> for the land defence of Singapore, even though in present con-
> ditions that must be more modest than we would like.

In fact Japan signed the Tripartite Pact with Germany and Italy
three days later. I added that if Singapore were to be defended as
a naval base, we must command a sufficient proportion of the
mainland also. I then examined the question of the forces in Kenya
and the Sudan in detail. The stronger forces in the Sudan, I said,
showed that Wavell shared our opinion that its defence was more
important than that of Kenya. The number of troops in Palestine
had been greatly reduced, while the total number of battalions
held in reserve and for internal security in Alexandria, Cairo and
on the Canal, was no more than seven. I agreed that the apprecia-

* This memorandum is printed in full as Appendix C.

tion of the Governor of Malta had certainly been pessimistic, but an attempted invasion supported by the Italian fleet would surely give the Royal Navy the opportunity of which it had dreamed.

★   ★   ★   ★   ★

The complexity of these matters, their importance to the survival of our military action in the Middle East and the dangerous strains they imposed on our defences at home, were set out in the further memorandum which I sent to the Prime Minister on October 2nd. In this I told him of the plans I wished to lay for further convoys to the Middle East. I proposed making certain changes in the dates and sailings,

> to give us a considerable capacity which we would suggest using to despatch the following formations:
> (a) Remainder of 2nd Armoured Division, i.e.
>   2 Cruiser Tank Regiments
>   2 Light Tank Regiments
>   Support Group
>   Divisional Headquarters
>   A total of 11,000 personnel.
> (b) 1 Australian Brigade.
> We would propose that the fast convey should still sail on November 17th as previously arranged. This would be composed of liners and would include a number of personnel — Gunners, Field and A.A., Sappers, Signals, Artisan Workshops, etc. — for which Wavell has asked. If the Admiralty were able to find escorts on this basis, Armoured Division should reach Suez on the 14th December, and liners a few days later.
> We have now to weigh the balance of risk in sending these Armoured Units. We had on 29th September 179 Cruiser Tanks in this country. To send these units would leave us with 79, plus October production. We have at present here 318 Light Tanks; this arrangement would leave us with 198. We have at present here 259 "I" Tanks, and this number is being added to at an average rate of 12 to 15 a week. Cruisers are coming out at the rate of about 9 a week. There is also the

Support Group, for which work special training is required, and if the 2nd Armoured Division's group is sent, only the reformed Calais Rifle Battalions would remain.

There is this further difficulty, that if the remainder of the 2nd Armoured Division is to leave this country in a month's time, their vehicles will need thorough overhauling and preparation for the Desert before they go. To enable this to be done they will have to be withdrawn from their battle stations within the next few days.

We have given this subject the most careful thought here and on balance we believe that it is right that the 2nd Armoured Division should be sent as here proposed. We should be compelled as a consequence, in the event of invasion, to rely to an increasing extent upon "I" tanks, though the small output of Cruisers would gradually improve the situation in that respect also, but there is accumulating evidence of German assistance to Italians in Libya, and should this eventuate within the next two months, the presence of these additional armoured forces may just turn the scales in Egypt.

I have spoken to Commander-in-Chief [Gen. Sir Alan Brooke] on this subject and, in the circumstances, he does not feel that he can resist this decision.

I have not dealt here with the possibility of passing any or all of these Armoured Units through the Mediterranean. If this were possible, there would be a saving in time of, I think, something between three and four weeks.

The Prime Minister and the Defence Committee approved the next day. Beyond question the decision was right.

It was some time before the ban on Hurricanes for the Middle East was lifted. The War Cabinet discussed the matter again on September 23rd, but we extracted no more than that the Secretary of State for Air should produce a table showing the proposed reinforcements from August to November. These did not include Hurricanes, though our air forces in Egypt were so much weaker in numbers than the Italian.

The argument had to be pressed. With the Middle East Committee's agreement, I prepared a memorandum for the War Cabinet on September 27th. This paper asked that our planned air reinforcements to the Middle East should be resumed, though even this would still leave us in a position of dangerous weakness. The Chiefs of Staff supported me, despite the demands of the Battle of Britain. So did Halifax, Attlee and Greenwood, while Sinclair gave figures showing that the position in Britain was better since the beginning of the month and the deficiencies in the Middle East grave. Lord Beaverbrook, as Minister of Aircraft Production, admitted a considerable improvement as regards fighters in this country since September 1st. Nevertheless, he was strongly opposed to further withdrawals of either fighters or pilots. The Battle of Britain was the only battle which counted, in his opinion, and he was well entitled to that opinion, for his energy and single-mindedness played a galvanizing part in its outcome.

So the argument continued, until the Prime Minister agreed to the withdrawal from this country, and preparation for overseas, of the aircraft suggested in the Secretary of State for Air's list. Though this was only part of what I wanted, I proposed to the Cabinet to make a programme setting out the forces and equipment we would send to the Middle East, month by month. We could then, I explained, ask General Wavell for a related plan of campaign. Until Wavell knew definitely and for months ahead what he was to receive, he had no chance to plan in advance. I also suggested that it might be convenient for one of us to go out from this country to the Middle East to discuss these matters on the spot. These opinions found favour with my colleagues and it was agreed that they should be further examined by the Prime Minister and the Ministers concerned.

★   ★   ★   ★   ★

Meanwhile I pressed Wavell's still unsatisfied and ever more urgent needs upon the Secretary of State for Air. On October 4th I wrote to him:

> The co-operation between Wavell and the Air Officer Commanding in Chief, Middle East could not be better. . . . The

uncomfortable truth, however, remains that our Air Force in Egypt and in the Sudan is even at present heavily outnumbered. . . . You will recall how great, perhaps decisive, was the part played by the German Air Force against the French Army in May. Proportionately, aircraft will, I believe, prove even more important in fighting in the Desert in Africa. Dive-bombing may be an unpleasant experience for troops fighting in comparatively enclosed country; it must be still more difficult to endure where cover or concealment is so much harder to contrive. . . .

This letter is, therefore, a plea to you to consider whether, despite the very heavy calls upon you for the Battle of Britain, it might not be possible for you to spare some further reinforcements for the Middle East. . . .

The Prime Minister, to whom I had sent a copy, asked warily whether my proposal was additional to the programme agreed the week before. I replied that it was and explained:

As with all African problems, this is another question of the balance of risks. As we get stronger here, which, with bad weather, our own production and American help, we can surely hope to do, we may feel bold enough to send more help to the Middle East, where . . . flying conditions will be as good as they will be bad over England in the next few months. . . .

The following day I expressed my concern to the Middle East Committee who summed up their opinion in a memorandum I sent to the Cabinet:

(a) That our air forces in the Middle East are already inferior to the Italian forces opposed to them. That, in the event of strong German air reinforcements reaching that area, the whole of our position in the Middle East would be imperilled.

(b) That in the event of enemy attacks upon Greece or Turkey, it is of vital importance that we should be able to afford some assistance to these countries in the air as well as at sea. Meanwhile, our strength in the Middle East may very well determine the attitude of both countries.

(c) For these reasons, the Committee do not consider that the present policy of replacement is sufficient. They are informed that on technical grounds new squadrons cannot operate in the Middle East, unless the necessary ground staff are sent out beforehand. The Committee urge that this should be done at once.

The next day the Prime Minister announced my visit to the Middle East at a Cabinet meeting. I would, he said, be meeting General Smuts and would see the Turkish military mission which had already arrived. At the same time he directed the Chiefs of Staff to consider my memorandum.

Their reply, on October 12th, was that to send additional squadrons to Egypt would seriously delay bringing those at home up to strength. The Royal Air Force in the Middle East could, however, be reinforced immediately by expanding its first-line strength and sending new fighters and bombers to replace obsolete types. These total reinforcements would equal six new squadrons. Three days later the Defence Committee endorsed the Chiefs of Staff's recommendations, but they were not enough and it would have done no harm to have delayed a little in bringing the home squadrons up to strength.

As for what had been promised, a decision in London was very different from an aircraft in the Middle East, whether it went by sea round the Cape, or through Takoradi. For instance, to ship the fifty special vehicles, the five hundred tons of stores and one thousand five hundred men needed by four squadrons would take three and a half months. Aircraft flying into Egypt across Africa on the Takoradi route at times sucked into their engines so much sand that they had to be stripped right down. The new programme had not had any appreciable effect before the Italian invasion of Greece threw fresh strains on our exiguous Middle East resources. We were forever trying to stretch too small a blanket.

★ ★ ★ ★ ★

There were occasional light interludes however stern the pressure. On August 7th I had luncheon with Halifax.

Edward told me a good story. He had sent Winston a confidential paper *re* Ministry of Economic Warfare in which he forecast opposition from them to a course he wished to pursue. Winston sent the paper on to M.E.W., result, explosion from [Hugh] Dalton [the Minister]. When Edward remonstrated at such indiscretion, Winston said, "I only marked the paper 'M.E.W.,' it seems he has mewed."

One morning at the Cabinet our far-seeing Minister of Food, Lord Woolton, warned us that owing to shipping difficulties there could be no more imports of sardines. The Cabinet accepted this blow with an exchange of rueful glances. From where I sat opposite the Prime Minister, however, I could hear him quietly rumbling to himself: "I shall never eat another sardine."

Lord Morrison of Lambeth, in his autobiography,* says the Prime Minister's relationship to me was that of father and son. This account of a discussion, which took place before the Cabinet changes following Mr. Chamberlain's resignation, illustrates how close we were:

September 30th: Winston sent for me about 5 p.m. to ask me whether I would join his Cabinet as Lord President, or stay where I was. I asked which he would like me to do. He said that he preferred that I should decide for myself. I asked what the duties of Lord President would be. He said there might be some revision in an upward direction, but mainly those Neville had carried out and entirely domestic. He added that, as I knew, he had hoped to be able to offer me Foreign Office, but Edward [Halifax] clearly did not want to move to Lord President and he feared that if he suggested it, Edward would ask to go altogether, which Winston did not want at the moment Neville was leaving. I asked for an hour or two to consider, but said that my present inclination was to stay where I was. Winston seemed to agree and said future was mine anyway. We then went to Cabinet where a noisy and discursive discussion on man-power and supply took place.

After dinner wrote Winston a note saying I would do as he

* Lord Morrison of Lambeth: *An Autobiography.*

wished, but if he left choice to me I was content to stay where I was. Winston sent for me before note was delivered and I took it over with me. Found him depressed because Max [Beaverbrook] is suffering from asthma and will not take on Supply which is in a mess. This was holding up all his arrangements. I told him that if he wished for help in defence I was ready to do anything I could, even to give up War Office to be Lord President. I would then sit with Chiefs of Staff and him on Defence Committee, and could perhaps relieve him of much. Winston appeared to like this. He reiterated that he was now an old man, that he would not make Lloyd George's mistake of carrying on after the war, that the succession must be mine. John Anderson could clearly not "be in the way" in this respect. He admitted that Kingsley's [Wood] appointment would not be popular, but said the Chancellor must be in Cabinet if financial control was to be kept. . . .

October 1st: I spoke of Bobbety [Cranborne] and urged his qualification for Dominions Office rather than candidate Winston had selected. Winston doubted whether B's health would stand it. I told him that I had recently caused inquiries to be made of Lady S. [Lady Salisbury, Lord Cranborne's mother] and received good report. Eventually, though Winston had made up his list, he agreed and asked me to ring up David [Margesson, the Chief Whip] and tell him, which I did. This last was Tuesday night when, not having heard from Winston all day and having gone to bed, I was fetched round after midnight in pyjamas. I protested that I was in bed, but W. said he must talk over his list with me. I found David and K.W. [Kingsley Wood] leaving.

Winston said that he had thought over defence suggestion and had reluctantly decided to turn it down. It would make too many cogs in the machine and I should be in an uncomfortable position, which is perfectly true. He referred to my two letters, the latter written late Monday night after our talk. "Your two very sweet letters, so generous and worthy of the occasion." He lamented that he could not give me Foreign Office and thus bring me into War Cabinet and seemed distressed at this. "It is not what I want," he repeated many times. He thought at Foreign Office I could help much with U.S.A. I begged him not to worry about all this. Said with truth that I was happier where I was.

He said: "We shall work this war together" and began to talk of future projects and Smuts' view on Dakar, which I pointed out had been modified by a later telegram he had not seen. He said: "You can keep your Dill!" So that is the end, I hope, of that long battle. We parted in the early hours.

5

WAVELL'S COMMAND
October–November 1940

I fly to Cairo again — Discussion on strategy — Transjordan —
Meeting with Amir Abdullah — I visit Jerusalem and Suez —
The Western Desert and our soldiers — Hopes of an offensive
— German ultimatum to Greece — I meet General Smuts in
Khartoum — Haile Selassie's war — My telegram to Mr. Churchill
on Crete — An argument on priorities

I LEFT LONDON for Cairo on the morning of October 11th, with General Huddleston and Major Cecil Sugden, who was to act as my military assistant. We drove first to Wilton House, near Salisbury, its lovely rooms truncated by plywood partitions and now the headquarters of Southern Command. There I discussed with General Auchinleck the question of his appointment as Commander-in-Chief in India:

> *October 11:* He clearly does not want to go, which is natural,
> though he did not deny immense importance of the post these
> days. Much more in the centre of things than last war. A. is
> impressive, steady, level-headed and tough. One feels one could
> be sure of a straight opinion from him at all times.
>
> Some talk with Huddleston on the long drive to Plymouth.
> He thinks that we are too weak in Sudan and are short of specialist weapons. . . . I share his view about our strength in
> Sudan, and so to some extent does Dill. Dined in R.A.F. mess
> [at Plymouth] and on board our flying boat [a Sunderland of the
> Royal Australian Air Force] at 10 p.m. Surprisingly comfortable
> and all would have been well, but for H's snoring which is the
> most alarming sound I ever heard. I can at least now reassure
> Dill that H. does not suffer from insomnia.

October 12th: In the morning woke up off the coast of Spain to a dead calm sea. Some trouble with head winds so that we did not approach Straits until 3 p.m. I climbed into top turret of plane and standing there could see whole panorama displayed in brilliant sunlight. It was so clear that Ceuta seemed little more than five or six miles from Gib. The rock itself, viewed from above in perspective in this way, lay out into the Straits, much more significant than when approached by sea.

A perfect landing and then to Government House. Some talk with [Lieut.-Gen. Sir Clive] Liddell [the Governor and Commander-in-Chief] of refugees and his other problems. Also with Mason Mac [Maj.-Gen. Mason MacFarlane, his second-in-command] who seems resolute and confident. A short sleep followed by Sam's [Sir Samuel Hoare, Ambassador at Madrid] arrival. He seemed delighted to see someone from home. He had nothing new to tell except that Spaniards do not expect any Italian offensive in Africa for another month. He bemoaned the difficulty of his task, the tortuous delaying tactics of the Spaniards. I asked him if Beigbeder [Spanish Foreign Minister] would stay. He replied that the man himself was convinced of it; but I had the impression that others were not quite so sure. Sam and everyone else here was emphatic upon the effect our resistance alone in Britain has had on world opinion.

October 13th: After dinner continued our flight to Malta which we reached about 7.30 a.m. I again had a splendid view of our approach from my conning tower. We learnt later that we had flown too far to the south, and had been with difficulty reached by radio and redirected.

Spent the whole day in Conference with [Lieut.-Gen. William] Dobbie [the Governor] and tour of island and visits to troops. It was unhappily difficult to see much of the last who were in small detached posts. Not greatly enamoured of dispositions for defence which seemed to me to concentrate too much on beaches. No depth and too small a mobile reserve. All the men I saw certainly seemed fit and cheerful, but in some battalions officers appeared to be only a moderate lot. . . . The company commanders too old and too sedentary. We must give the good youngster his chance and make it for him.

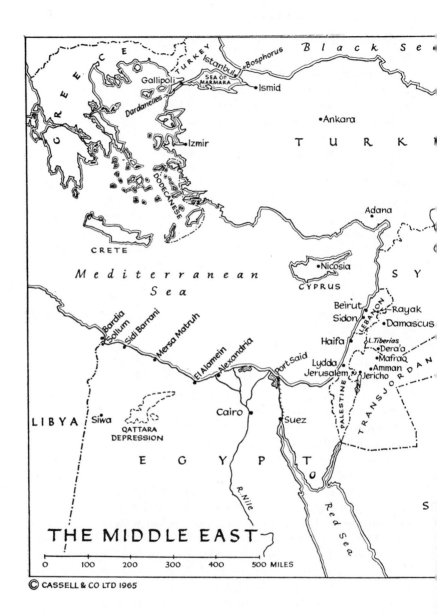

THE MIDDLE EAST

0   100   200   300   400   500 MILES

© CASSELL & CO LTD 1965

October 14th: Left Malta early in morning of 14th and crossed the coast of Egypt between Alexandria and Matruh in brilliant sunshine. Our Australian boys had never been to Egypt before and their instructions for landing in the Nile were more than vague. They were told to approach city from south, on no account to fly over it, to circle round second tower on Heliopolis road, of which I was only vaguely aware and they, of course, not at all. However, we decided bravely to ignore all this, and we flew gaily over Cairo without being shot at and plomped down firmly but gracefully on the Nile.

I was met in a launch by the Ambassador, Sir Miles Lampson, General Wavell and the Air Officer Commanding-in-Chief, Air Chief Marshal Sir Arthur Longmore. We went direct to the Embassy garden landing stage.

★   ★   ★   ★   ★

On my first afternoon I saw the Turkish military mission and sent the following telegram to the Prime Minister about my meeting with them:

> The Turkish representatives, whose attitude was throughout most friendly, expressed themselves as favourably impressed by the number of troops and organization of defence in Egypt. They said that they had visited Mersa Matruh and other areas in the Western Desert and were confident of our ability to hold an Italian attack.
>
> In the course of the conversation which ensued I gave the mission some account of the reinforcements which we had already sent to the Middle East and indicated that more would follow. After consultation with Commander-in-Chief, I offered to arrange for technical British Military Missions to go to Turkey from Egypt to assist Turks in the maintenance of army equipment and in training with it. The mission seemed to welcome this offer and undertook to communicate it to the Marshal [Çakmak], who they felt sure would be glad to consider it most favourably. I anticipate that Turks will also ask

for permission to send technical liaison officers to Egypt, if so,
I propose to agree to this request. . . .

On this first evening I had a preliminary talk with Wavell and
Longmore at which Lampson was present. They gave me a general account of the situation from which I singled out air reinforcements as most badly needed.

On the next morning I first saw Wavell alone, when he described
the military dispositions he had made to meet a further Italian attack. When this phase of our discussion was over I said to him:
"But what if the Italians do not attack? Have we any plans as to
what to do then?" Wavell gave me one of his quiet, appraising
looks and replied: "Wilson will be here in a few minutes and I
think you should hear the answer to that question from him." In
due course General Wilson arrived. I had known him since the
first world war, when he had been a staff officer in 41st Division,
which included the battalion in which I served as a subaltern and
later as adjutant. We had all liked him in those days, because of
his approachability and understanding of what was expected of an
infantry battalion in the battle of the Somme. Perhaps I was too
young then to understand also that his quick capacity for decision
was the expression of a first-class military brain. Dill had told me
before I left that, in his opinion, Wilson's was probably the best
tactical mind among our principal commanders at that time.

Wilson explained the situation in detail and for three hours we
discussed his dispositions in the Western Desert, the enemy's probable intentions, our present counteraction and future plans. He
estimated that the maximum strength the Italians could deploy
against Matruh was three divisions, the limiting factors being
water and communications. He thought it unlikely that, of these
divisions, any one would be a complete armoured division, because
Italian tactics differed from ours and the Germans. They used
their armoured troops in conjunction with columns of infantry and
mobile artillery.

At that time the enemy was being continually harassed by
patrols of our armoured cars, mobile artillery and infantry carried
in trucks. The tanks of 7th Armoured Division were being rested
with a view to their re-employment against any further enemy ad-

vance. Wilson anticipated that if the enemy resumed his advance from Sidi Barrani, the nature of the country would probably force him to move in two widely separated columns. This advance would be continually harassed and the enemy would be held in front of Matruh while 7th Armoured Division attacked his southern column in the flank. Dumps of petrol and water had been so sited in the desert that this Division would always be able to keep south of the enemy and attack his flank. Wilson gave me details of the forces available, which he considered sufficient to meet the threat opposed to him and to enable him to defeat it, provided he was assured of adequate air support.

We then discussed future offensive operations and Wilson confirmed Wavell's judgment of the role which infantry tanks could play in the fighting, "much more important," as I telegraphed to the Prime Minister on October 15th, "than we had thought." For that reason, in my telegram to Mr. Churchill I asked that a second battalion should be sent out and that at least one company should be made available in time for the November convoy. This company would be off-loaded at Port Sudan and used in a projected offensive against Kassala. My telegram concluded: "Much hope that you may be able to give us this extra help." The Prime Minister at once responded.

In a later telegram, sent next day, I told the Prime Minister that it was hoped offensive operations could be launched on a serious scale in January, "but the possibility of such operations being undertaken with a fair prospect of success depends upon the provision of certain items of equipment and particularly M.T. [motor transport]. I shall bring back full details of these." It also depended upon air reinforcements, about which I telegraphed home at length.

The following personal telegram to the Prime Minister sent on the evening of October 16th sums up my conclusions at that point:

Our journey out was uneventful and Mussolini clearly does not command the air over the Mediterranean. I am already very glad to have made the journey for I have found a number of problems affecting all three Services in respect of which I think that I have been able to help. Lampson seems delighted at the visit and states that it will have a stiffening effect on Egyptians. A considerable number of points have arisen which, though not of the first importance, will require regulation. These I will refer to you on my return home.

As regards the military situation in its widest aspect, there can be no doubt that air reinforcement is the essential. A.O.C. here has frequently represented to Air Ministry that determined Italian air offensive, more particularly if carried out with German support, would entirely overwhelm his three forward fighter squadrons. Number of Italian fighters seen in one patrol now often exceeds our total strength available in these forward squadrons. I know that you have this problem much in mind and appreciate difficulty of in any way weakening our fighter strength at home, but I am sure that A.O.C., who has greatly impressed me with his grasp and vigour, in no way exaggerates his present weakness.

Politically whole situation here would be immeasurably improved if we were able to gain some military success. Most hopeful field for this in the near future would appear to be Sudan and I trust that the "I" tanks for which I have asked can come in the November convoy. This is most important, since psychological moment for striking on that front may easily come shortly. Plans for an offensive for the capture of Kassala are being worked out by the Sudan Command, and Wavell and I will go into this fully when we are at Khartoum. Abyssinian revolt is going better than had been expected, but may well soon require stimulus of a military success on our part. Of course Italy may by some offensive of her own upset any plans we make, but this must not prevent us laying our own plans. I propose to spend several days in the Western Desert with Wilson. So far I am impressed with his command of the situation and plans to meet it, but you may be sure that I shall take nothing for granted.

To this message I received a heartening reply:

Have read all your telegrams with deepest interest and realization of value of your visit. We are considering how to meet your needs. Meanwhile continue to master the local situation. Do not hurry your return.*

This same day I was able to fulfil another part of my duties by visiting the vast ordnance shops at Abbasiya.

October 16th: It would be difficult to find a more striking example of the advantage of a "neutral" Egypt. There are acres of inflammable and invaluable material. Fortunately plans are now far advanced to spread these risks and a great part of the works is being moved elsewhere. Organization seemed efficient. Saw something of desert-worn and sand-gritted tanks back from their toil.

I was somewhat taken aback when the officer-in-charge reminded me that we had not yet let Egypt have any tanks for reserve. "In theory," I commented afterwards, "he is quite right, of course, but few of the folk out here have any conception how low are our stocks of equipment at home." The ignorance was widespread and it would have been dangerous to try to correct it, even among the higher ranks of commanders in the Middle East, for there was always the hope that Hitler might share it. This officer had not understood that there were no tanks in reserve at home, and that each one we sent out around the Cape was adding to the calculated risk in the British Isles.

★ ★ ★ ★ ★

After a day spent seeing troops in Palestine I left, early on the morning of October 18th, with Wavell by car for Transjordan. We talked of the country and politics and persons and also of Meredith and George Moore, so that the time passed very happily until we were beyond Jericho.

October 18th: The valley of the Jordan is here most impressive, even if the river itself is only the expected muddy trickle.

* *The Second World War*, Vol. II.

The Mount of Temptation fairly deserves its association. On such a morning the country can cast its spell.

At Allenby bridge [Sir Alec] Kirkbride [the British Resident] met us and I drove with him to Amman. He has been in this country ever since the [first world] war, speaks excellent Arabic and has an understandable affection for this country and its peasant people. The drive with him had no dull moment. Amman itself is a bustling and, after Arab fashion, thriving capital.

My driver, a young sergeant in the Palestine Police, hooted and nosed and cajoled his way skilfully through the thronged streets until we reached the Amir's Palace.

A guard of honour was drawn up before the door. This was a detachment of the Arab Legion, very smart and of good physique, their crusader helmets adding a touch of distinction to an olive tinged khaki. They carried their colour, and a band of brass and drum and pipes played the national anthem as we drove off. Set in these remote mountains at such a time, it was a moving moment.

Abdullah met us on the doorstep, and Wavell and I and [Lieut.-Gen. Philip] Neame [commanding in Palestine and Trans-jordan] retired to his room for some talk, coffee and a smoke. Abdullah was courteous and friendly in the extreme. The Turk-ish Consul, whom he had seen the day before, had affirmed the determination of his people to resist and had spoken scornfully of the Russians who, he had declared, could not effectively help either side. Their troops on the Turkish border were miserably ill-equipped.

Abdullah asked of the attitude of Egypt and I have the im-pression that Arabs generally would be much more whole-hearted in the war, if Egypt would declare war.

On leaving Abdullah we went to Kirkbride's house, where we discussed increasing the strength of Trans-Jordan Frontier Force, Legion and Desert Patrol. We told him to go ahead and under-took to ask London for authority at once. Then to aerodrome where we saw Desert Patrol, the toughest looking lot of Bedouin

Arabs ever I saw. Glubb has a remarkable control over them. Their clothes are well chosen. Bedouin skirt, coloured sash and head-dress, the whole slung about with innumerable bandoliers. They have two armoured cars, the rest Chevrolets, large open cars.

Took to the air again and landed at Mafraq, where saw Trans-Jordan Frontier Force commanded by [Lieut.-Col.] Peter Wilson, who was at Eton with me. He looked splendid in his pale blue shirt, scarlet sash, khaki shorts and Arab head-dress. More Arab than any Arab, and ready for a John drawing. He spoke with an infectious enthusiasm of his men which is easy to understand. They are recruited from all nations and all parts of Palestine and are not Bedouin, as Desert Patrol. They would operate on the army flank as an organized formation. Discussed increase in force and problems that this will raise. Left by air for reconnaisance of Syrian frontier and problems that presents at Dara Gap, Lake Tiberias and along the coast. Neame explained his plans.

Reached Haifa at lunch-time after a bumpy flight and the most exhilarating day yet.

Later in the afternoon I spoke to one of the local commissioners who complained

[that] Arabs had no cause to fight for and regarded this war as no affair of theirs. Egypt gave no lead. I asked whether a declaration that we intended to free Libya from Italian rule, without further defining the future, would help at all. He said "Yes, definitely."

This I was to do fifteen months later, on January 8th, 1942, having in the interval met the Sayid Mohammed Idris el Senussi, most impressive in his dignity and wisdom. He is now the venerated head of the Libyan kingdom.

The same evening, October 18th, I flew to Lydda and motored to Jerusalem. At dinner that night with General Neame I sat next to General Sir Thomas Blamey, commanding I Australian Corps and enjoyed my talk with him:

He was measured and shrewd in his comments and understanding of Wavell's problems. In particular he made no complaint that Australians were split [between Egypt and Palestine].

Early next morning I flew to Suez and, after visiting the Royal
Army Medical Corps and a good Indian convalescent camp, I made
arrangements with Wavell to "see the chief doctor before leaving,
in order to discuss medical plans generally."

Luncheon followed with Baron Louis de Benoist, Agent-General
of the Suez Canal Company. He had rallied to de Gaulle at the
hour of the French armistice, at considerable risk to his family,
who were then still in France. With Benoist I had some talk of
the attitude of his countrymen:

> *October 19th:* He agreed that neither Pétain nor Weygand
> had ever conceived that we could carry on without them. He
> could not understand Pétain ever having brought Laval into the
> Government, whom he regarded as wholly evil. Opinion in oc-
> cupied France was moving in our favour.

After luncheon, at my suggestion,

> [we] borrowed a launch from Benoist and slipped across to see
> a company of the Highland Light Infantry opposite. A cheerful
> and fit looking lot of men.
> Then to Free French, by whom I was immensely impressed. It
> was not only men on parade but alertness and smartness of those
> in camp that caught the eye. They are not the Legionary type
> of professional fighter so much as the best of young Frenchmen.
> It was moving to see them; they ask nothing but to fight. . . .
> Motored to R.A.F. repair shops where Longmore showed us
> round. They are preparing for larger force they soon hope to
> have. A good lot of men as R.A.F. always are.

★ ★ ★ ★ ★

I returned by air to Cairo, flying low over Tel el Kebir to view
the large ordnance workshops. But my day was by no means over;

I was soon engulfed in a large party for Egyptian politicians of every opinion, expertly staged by the Ambassador.

Spoke to P.M., Nahas, Ahmed Maher, whom I thanked for his attitude, and a score of others. As a general rule they did not speak well of internal situation in Egypt, and many of our friends were either openly or covertly critical of the Palace. King is certainly non-co-operative and maybe anti-British, but it is difficult to know how much his attitude is governed by fear and how much by malice. . . . There is probably at least a spice of hate too.

After this party, I drove by car with the Ambassador, his wife and Arthur Longmore to Port Tewfik, where we had an excellent dinner in the desert washed down by iced Australian beer. The next day, Sunday, I was able to have a few hours rest, then motored back with Longmore, for whose clear mind I felt increasing respect. I found him cool and co-operative throughout.

October 21st: Western Desert. Flew with "Jumbo" Wilson and his A.D.C. and landed near [Lieut.-Gen. Richard] O'Connor's [commanding Western Desert Force] headquarters. He met us with [Air Commodore Raymond] Collishaw, the vigorous and forceful Canadian who runs R.A.F. so efficiently. Collishaw showed us over his headquarters and discussed plans and resources, after which we motored to O'Connor's where we are to spend three nights. . . . O'Connor is a most attractive personality. So young for his years as to give the impression of having never grown up. Yet a very gallant and dashing leader, I feel sure.

October 22nd: Lovely early morning swim with O'Connor. White sand and clear blue sea; the most wonderful bathing I have ever known. Would have loved to dawdle.

Jumbo and I and his A.D.C. set off in three Lysanders for Siwa. We were each in the observer's place, and had our Lewis guns ready for action. As we started a Military Policeman offered me his pistol, which I rejected and regretted the moment I was in the air and realized that if I were forced down I was unarmed.

We had an escort of three Gladiators and made the journey to Siwa without mishap. Qattara depression is strange country to fly over. Looks from the air like a caramel pudding with cream edging.

On arrival we were met by the commander or adviser of the Egyptian garrison, a lively and entertaining individual and by Freddy [Capt. J. F. C.] Mellor who commands company of 60th now at Siwa. Officers and men seemed to like the place. They were all deep brown, almost black in colour, but very fit and cheerful. They gave us a champagne luncheon, we having prepared to arrive with sandwiches. . . . I much enjoyed my outing. Talked to a Rhodesian platoon, a fine body of men.

Siwa itself when approached across the desert is for all the world like a cinema city in the sand. *L'Atlantide* to the life. Great rocks, almost hills, rise sheer out of the plain for no apparent reason, they would be militarily most difficult to penetrate, each rock being a natural fortress with cover for Brens, anti-tank rifles etc. Within this natural fortress is the oasis, with ample water, rich date palms, a few sheep, and a few thousand, three, I think, inhabitants. One great rock is full of tombs of Roman days, and it is queer to contemplate in contrast the tanks half hidden under the palm trees.

We saw some of the Egyptian troops and their commanders. All our people were agreed that they would not fight if seriously attacked. Mellor told me that one of the Egyptian officers had rejected his suggestion for an improved site for his anti-tank gun on the ground that he would have no chance to get it away from there when he wanted to. The men are Sudanese and good material, some of the younger officers struck me as keen.

Unfortunately our impression of some of the elder officers was not so reassuring.

Of our return to the coast I wrote:

The last stage of our flight petrified me, for both our three Lysanders and the escort flew together in compact formation, with our plane as the centre-piece. I was scared to death, but the airmen were delighted with themselves!

Spent two hours with [Maj.-Gen. Bernard] Freyberg going round New Zealand detachments. I had seen these men before when they first arrived last February, but they are improved out of all knowledge, in physique and all respects. They were very cheerful but longing to be in a battle.

October 23rd: After an early morning bathe, Jumbo and I flew forward of Matruh and met [Maj.-Gen. Michael O'Moore] "Dickie" Creagh [commanding 7th Armoured Division] and Gott and other commanders. Latter now commands Support Group [7th Armoured Division]. We held an informal conference where they frankly stated their wants. Impressed by all of them. Creagh is a delightful little man, sympathetic and keen. He is far from well and is suffering from some bug in the liver. Gott has come on tremendously since he has been given his larger command and gave us a valuable appreciation of Italian fighting value, which he was well qualified to do, since he commanded our rearguard in our withdrawal from Italian frontier. He said that Italians showed some courage during their advance, but that they were ill-trained and their tactics wretched. We had taken a heavy toll of them. He was sure that if we could be put in a position to attack them, they would fall an easy prey. This appeared to be the general opinion.

After the conference I motored round as many positions as possible and saw units of 7th Armoured Division, including some tank units and 3rd Hussars, recently arrived from home. As a whole there were few complaints and the men looked fit enough save for many desert sores. One sergeant, who had been in the desert for long, complained of the food and in particular the absence of desert vegetables. We are going to try to remedy this; it is a problem of transport. I spent more time than was scheduled on this, but Creagh encouraged me in my breaking of the rules. . . .

After dinner a talk in O'Connor's dugout with Jumbo and him. O'Connor brought out his ideas for an offensive, if ever opportunity allows. Jumbo made his comments. It is obvious that their plans are further advanced than I had understood from Wavell. I told them what we were sending out and approximate dates of arrival which seemed to hearten them greatly. I did all I could to encourage them.

If Italians come on, as they hope they will, battle of Mersa Matruh and Negamish Nullah can be fought according to plan, but it is what to do if he does not come on, and our offensive plans then, that we are now discussing.

I spent the morning of October 24th on a tour of the Matruh defences, followed by a hurried luncheon at O'Connor's headquarters and a flight back to Cairo.

★   ★   ★   ★   ★

That night the Ambassador and I dined with the Prime Minister. Hassan Sabri told us of a "first-class row" which he had just had with King Farouk, arising out of some quite infantile suspicions in His Majesty's mind about, so the Prime Minister said, certain protocol suggestions. According to Hassan Sabri's account, in a stormy forty-five minutes he had rounded upon the King and told him that such baseless accusations were intolerable and that he would be delighted to return to private life, adding that, if he did, His Majesty might find that his tenure, too, was affected. The Prime Minister told us that the King had caved in and that he had been much strengthened by the event.

We then discussed the situation at Siwa, about which the Prime Minister showed every readiness to reach an arrangement with our military authorities. As Lampson telegraphed that night, I shared his opinion that Hassan Sabri was himself loyal to the Allied cause. For instance, when talking of King Farouk, he said that if it came to a showdown, he would be prepared to invite His Majesty to take a sea trip: "the rest would be up to us."

The next few days were spent seeing 6th Australian Division, the Black Watch, which was Wavell's own regiment, and other contingents. Most dramatic of all was a parade of the Polish Brigade. These men, so far from their own land, so isolated by language, climate and ways of life, were yet compactly sufficient to themselves and unmistakably military material of the finest quality.

Now, when I look back over those days with their kaleidoscope of brief meetings with so many men of all three services and several nations, my chief recollection is of their health and confidence. While none could tell when the battle would come or where, all seemed quietly to feel, though few would say, that the issue was not in doubt. Critics may condemn this sentiment as smugness or conceit. I thought it stimulating, increasingly so as I found it shared by those who had already been in battle, as the next few weeks were to show.

★   ★   ★   ★   ★

I continued to be concerned at the delay in the arrival of air reinforcements. Dill had sent me a telegram on October 21st, telling me of plans for the despatch of more troops, should the month pass without invasion. For the air, he could only say that the Chief of the Air Staff, Sir Cyril Newall, had re-examined the programme for the Middle East, "but is at present unable to do more than replace obsolete aircraft by modern and increase number of aircraft per squadron." I felt that this was not enough and telegraphed on October 26th to Dill:

> I am frankly disappointed in what you tell me about air reinforcements. Position here in that respect remains most serious. A.O.C.-in-C. has again emphasized to me that he is not at present in a position to give the army effective support if serious military operations develop. It would help him and us if authority could be given to the A.O.C.-in-C. to raise three complete new squadrons, as suggested in my telegram of October 16th. . . .
>
> The Air Force here has, by brilliant tactical skill, maintained a bluff which may at any moment be called, but for successful defence, let alone any question of offensive military operations in the near future, it is essential that air reinforcements should at least keep pace with those on land. At present they are not doing so.

This question of air reinforcements was the weak point in our defences. We were never able to make up for the postponements of the early autumn and new demands were soon upon us.

October 28th: Woken at an early hour by telegram from [Sir Michael] Palairet [our Minister in Athens] announcing ultimatum to Greece. Had begun to hope that season was so far advanced that this adventure might be postponed until the spring. As it is we are not in a position to give effective help by land or air, and another guaranteed nation looks like falling to the Axis.

Talked to Wavell on telephone when we decided to continue on our way to Khartoum, though he would have to start back earlier. Later he telephoned that [Admiral Sir Andrew] Cunningham [Naval Commander-in-Chief] had asked to see him, and we agreed that he should fly to Alexandria and back, before we started south, and report to me at aerodrome. No room for Miles [Lampson] in plane, nor can we afford even ten minutes delay if we are to make Khartoum before dark.

Wavell reached aerodrome just before noon. He and I and Wilson had a talk. He showed me suggested telegram to London and action proposed re Crete. At my suggestion he added appeal that since battalion was being sent to Crete from Egypt, Malta's requirement of an extra battalion might be met from the other end. Acting A.O.C.-in-C. also undertook to examine possibility of bombing Italy, e.g. Taranto, by landing [to refuel] in Greece.

Then left for Khartoum which we only just made before dark. For the most part an uninteresting desert flight. Smuts and [Lieut.-Gen. A. G.] Cunningham and [Lieut.-Gen. D. P.] Dickinson [handing over East Africa Force to Cunningham, November 1st] already arrived. Smuts and I and Wavell had a talk together when we discussed general strategy. Smuts repeated several times that our first task was to create an army in Middle East to replace Weygand's. Everything depended upon that. As to East Africa, if we could knock out Italians there we should free important forces, including South African, for operations elsewhere.

After dinner we held a full conference, over which I asked Smuts to preside, and discussed and decided general lines of conduct of campaign in this part of the world.

Lieutenant-General William Platt, General Officer Commanding the Sudan, reported that the Italians had a quarter of a million troops under arms in Italian East Africa, against which we had in the Sudan two regiments of artillery, ten infantry battalions, one company of tanks and the Sudan Defence Force, a total of 28,000 men. In spite of this disparity, Platt was confident of his ability to prevent any serious enemy threat from Kassala, which was the most likely point of attack. We discussed possible offensives and General Smuts made the point that attacks elsewhere, especially from Kenya, must synchronize with any action we took against Kassala. The Italians had an enormous territory to guard and limited resources. It would be sound strategy to keep them guessing where the blow was to fall, to make them stretch their forces to the limit. Smuts spoke of the importance of securing Kismayu, a port in Italian Somaliland, before we advanced into Abyssinia.

I then raised the question of timing and suggested early November for the attack on Gallabat, and early January for those on Kassala and Kismayu. We considered the Prime Minister's proposal to withdraw a West African brigade from Kenya, to avoid sending a brigade of white troops to Freetown. Smuts said there was no immediate threat to Freetown and we agreed that if this withdrawal took place, we could not stage the offensive on Kismayu. I undertook to explain the position to the Prime Minister and, in the event, the brigade remained.

It was agreed that Smuts and Cunningham should fly off the next day to reconnoitre and decide whether the Kismayu project could be launched before the rains. On their return they informed me that it could, and we decided that it should be carried out early in 1941.

October 29th: Smuts and I had some private talk last evening and this morning. He was in splendid health, most cheerful and friendly. We spoke of men and events at home. Smuts was warm in his appreciation of Winston, a great fellow. How ill was Chamberlain, was his resignation really health or diplomatic. When I told him how ill Neville was, Smuts murmured: "Poor fellow," and then in speaking of Neville's foreign policy continued: "He must have been very badly advised. It is extraordinary that anyone could have been so deeply deceived." He was particularly critical of Neville's confidence in Hitler's signature and their joint manifesto after Munich.

As to his own position, Smuts was confident. His trouble was the existence in South Africa of what he called a "middle-west opinion"; real isolationists who did not think that the war was any concern of theirs. These were far more of a problem than pro-German element represented by [Mr. Oswald] Pirow [former Defence Minister]. [Gen. Sir Pierre] Van Ryneveld, Smuts' Chief of Staff, with whom I also had some talk and whom I liked very much, was vehement in his denunciation of Pirow, under whom he had to work for many years. He maintained that if Smuts had not won in Parliament when war broke out, there would have been fighting in the country.

Smuts could not have been more helpful or reasonable in his demands for equipment. The conversations as a whole were as satisfactory as could be.

Khartoum was still hot, even in the lofty rooms of the Palace which Kitchener had rebuilt. We were glad to sleep on the roof and to be wakened by the sun as it rose over the desert.

★   ★   ★   ★   ★

Our conference was resumed at nine o'clock in the morning. Command questions were discussed and we agreed on a proposal to ease Wavell's already too onerous burden. Smuts then gave us encouraging news of the expansion of his South African forces, but once again equipment was in short supply.

October 29th: After Smuts had flown away about 11.30, we adjourned to Platt's office where we went through his plans in detail until luncheon.

Our host Huddleston is far from well and retired to bed with lumbago. His arrival here had a tonic effect, and I only hope that his health will stand the strain of the climate. In the afternoon I inspected West Yorkshire Regiment, which was short of officers and under strength in men. Drafts have not been sent for these [British] battalions [forming part of 5th Indian Division], which is foolish.

Went on to see one of the companies of the Sudan Defence Force which has recently done good work at the front. They have some home-made armoured cars armed with "boys" and Bren, and have quite rightly a nice conceit of themselves. My only regret is that we have not more such. They are ideal for this country, but a surprising reluctance to offend Mussolini, and later a difficulty in finding the right type of Arabic-speaking officer, caused delays. A 7th Company is now being formed and I urged Platt to make all speed he could to ten companies.

Between tea and dinner Wavell and I called on the Negus. It is clear that the rebellion goes better than we had dared to hope, and no less clear that there is a sad lack of co-ordination and, I gather, to some extent perhaps, of interest on the part of the military here. Wavell not satisfied either. As a result, we had a meeting of all concerned after dinner which was at times a stormy affair. Wavell began the indictment and I followed it up. I fear that they must all have regarded me as intolerable, but there are times when it does little good to sit down to a pleasant evening party and I deliberately wanted to stir our folks up.

Haile Selassie was engaged in a war of liberation and I was determined that we must help him without stint. Naturally the Emperor was confident that, once he could cross the frontier, his subjects would rise in his favour. I did not doubt that, but I was anxious to make sure that we did not move prematurely. A revolt which was crushed with heavy losses to the Emperor's supporters would hardly help our cause or his. What I needed was an English officer who would work in close contact with the Emperor and act as his staff officer. Then, an active column working in concert with Haile Selassie might achieve something useful.

When I was back in Cairo I had some discussion with Wavell and we agreed upon what we wanted. One day Wavell mentioned that he had been looking out for an officer for the job. He thought he had the man, quite a young officer, his name was Major Orde Wingate. Did I know him? I said I did and that we had met on several occasions in London. Wavell then sent for him and we had a probing discussion on the scope and purpose of the enterprise he was to lead. Thus began a new phase in a remarkable military career.

★   ★   ★   ★   ★

October 30th: 7.0 a.m. Left early for Butana Bridge with Platt and Sugden in a civil machine of Platt's that has done its million miles. The plane was small and the flight bumpy, especially the last bit which was flown at 500 ft. Glad to arrive.

Heartened by all I saw at Butana Bridge. Defences good and troops determined and in high spirits. Talked to as many of the Indians as I could and to our own gunners. The latter were delighted with themselves for they had twice taken their guns forward to shell Kassala from short range, had plastered the place most effectively and though the Italian had fired back with all he had and more, they had suffered not a scratch. Not unattractive country at Butana Bridge, like big game country, though there is actually little game. A good Brigadier in charge, and a bright young intelligence officer who was resident in Kassala at the time of the Italian occupation. He was confident that morale of enemy was low, and we were told of desertions, bad food, etc.; all of which I received with caution, though I hope that there is some truth in it.

On to Gedaref, where we were met by [Maj.-Gen. Lewis] Heath [commanding 5th Indian Division] who, poor man, had lately smashed himself up by driving his car into a camel at night. This is the aerodrome where Italians lately shot up a number of our machines; their charred remains were a doleful framework. The price of over-confidence. I liked Heath, who is big, *pondéré* and, I should think, sound. After luncheon we made a hurried tour of Indian battalions, which were splendid, and had all too brief a glimpse of the Essex. From what I saw, I should judge a good battalion. Some of our gunners, though, looked very sorry for themselves. They had been pricked by a poisonous thorn that abounds in these parts and almost all had arms or knees in bandages, some both. Platt will have to develop a hill station, if our people are to fight here and keep fit.

Discussed plans with Heath in the car. Talked to Commander, Royal Artillery and others, then quite good flight back, during which I slept. An encouraging day. Wavell left in the morning to return to Cairo.

October 31st: Rather puzzled to hear nothing from London in reply to my telegrams about my movements, so continued my programme and flew to Port Sudan. Last part of flight over hill country and Suakin which looks an attractive old walled village. P.S. itself a Turkish bath. The air felt hot even in the aeroplane as we approached. Actually the temperature was much lower than Khartoum. 94° instead of 108° but it seemed infinitely hotter, so damp is the atmosphere. When I got back I found that my keys had rusted in my pocket.

An uneventful tour of troops. Worcesters seemed fairly cheerful, a splendid battery of Ulster A.A. gunners were certainly so. I was delighted with them. [John] Marriott, who is Brigadier and was G.S.O.3 when I was Brigade Major, tells me that these men have had a day or two each in the hills. Determined that we must concentrate upon developing one of these stations. Also we should be able to get the men fresh fruit and vegetables; oranges at any rate.

Flew back to Khartoum in early afternoon. Still no word from London, so preparations go ahead for our flight west early tomorrow. [Plans had been made to fly by Lagos and West Africa.]

Platt dined and we had some further talk of position and plans. I have sent full telegram home which he has endorsed.

These few days in the Sudan showed me how far our forces, thin as they were on the ground, had already gained local superiority over the enemy, who seemed sprawled and perhaps conscious of impending defeat in a hostile land, which Fascist numbers could not subdue.

November 1st: Telegram arrived an hour before we were due to start urging my return to Cairo. It seems one had arrived two days ago in my own cypher. Cairo had not advised Khartoum this method could be used and cypherers here had been struggling in vain. A silly muddle.

Set out north at once. A long and dull flight with a break at a most unprepossessing aerodrome at Wadi Halfa. Wavell met me and I went with him to luncheon. We are both apprehensive lest the cries from Greece should result in our being asked to divert any part of our very small resources from here. Sent in the evening a full telegram stating my view, both about Crete and Greece.

This I despatched to the Prime Minister:

> Have arrived in Cairo and held preliminary conversation
> with C.-in-C., A.O.C.-in-C., and H.M. Ambassador. There is
> full agreement here as to the importance of preventing capture
> of Crete by Italians.

I then gave an account of the preliminary steps which had been
taken, including the despatch of a battalion by cruiser for Crete,
as a follow-up of the two advance parties which had already arrived. A further force consisting of brigade headquarters and another battalion, together with heavy and light anti-aircraft batteries,
some sappers and other units was ready in Egypt for embarkation.
A squadron, part fighters, part bombers, was to be sent as soon as
aerodrome facilities were available. All of these could only be
spared with difficulty. My telegram continued:

> It is difficult to estimate the probability of Italian attack
> upon Crete. As seen from here it does not seem likely that
> this will be attempted until Greece is overrun, nor possible for
> Italians to execute with success while the British Fleet is at sea.
> I should even have thought it unlikely that an attempt at a
> landing would be made while the British Fleet was still able to
> operate in the Eastern Mediterranean.
>
> As regards air reinforcements to Crete itself, A.O.C.-in-C.
> has at present nothing more available to send, except at the ex-
> pense of his force in the Western desert. As I have already
> frequently emphasized, this force is at present too weak to allow
> A.O.C.-in-C. to give effective support to the army should a major
> battle develop. . . . Enemy aircraft yesterday raided Mersa
> Matruh more heavily than they have done for weeks. They
> were probably testing out our defences and hoping to find that
> we had already weakened them by diverting forces to Greece.
> A further difficulty in basing aircraft in Crete is that Crete at
> present possesses only one aerodrome which can be made serv-
> iceable. Crete is very vulnerable to air attack, not only from
> Italian bombers from Libya but also from fighters operating
> from the Dodecanese. To attack Italian aerodromes in Libya,
> as we are doing from well-organized bases in Egypt, is therefore

an important if indirect help for defence of Crete. If British squadrons were based on Crete, vulnerability of aerodrome must result in high percentage of losses on the ground.

I summed up my conclusions on Crete: (a) Its first line of defence was the Mediterranean Fleet and (b) we should be prepared to reinforce with infantry to the extent which I had suggested; we should not deplete our air force further, for we were too weak to afford a high percentage of losses on the ground. I continued:

> As hostilities develop between Italy and Greece, we must expect further persistent calls for aid by air force and army to Greece. It seems essential that we should be clear in our minds on this main issue now. The following are my conclusions.
>
> We cannot, from Middle East resources, send sufficient air or land reinforcements to have any decisive influence upon course of fighting in Greece. To send such forces here, or to divert reinforcements now on their way or approved, would imperil our whole position in the Middle East and jeopardize plans for offensive operations now being laid in more than one theatre.
>
> After much painful effort and at the cost of grave risks, we have, so far as our land forces are concerned, now built up a reasonably adequate defensive force here. We should presently be in a position to undertake certain offensive operations which, if successful, may have far-reaching effect on course of the war as a whole. It would surely be bad strategy to allow ourselves to be diverted from this task and unwise to employ our forces in fragments in a theatre of war where they cannot be decisive.
>
> I am anxious to put before you in detail at the earliest date the dispositions and plans which have been worked out here, and propose therefore not to proceed to West Africa but to return home by the shortest route leaving here on the third.

I wrote in Cairo that night about a day which had dawned for me in Khartoum:

November 1st: I feel absolutely confident that this telegram gives the line we should follow. I am less certain unhappily that we shall stick to it. Telegram was dictated and sent after a preliminary talk with Wavell and Longmore.

★ ★ ★ ★ ★

On the morning of November 2nd, I had a conference with Wavell and sent a telegram to the Prime Minister confirming that I proposed to leave for England. I also saw an American attaché who had arrived in Cairo via Berlin. He gave me an account of five hours spent in a shelter at night and said the bombing had been a most unpleasant experience. The morale of the civilian population was good, of the army, fair.

During dinner a telegram came from the Prime Minister in reply to mine of the previous day. He told me that the Greek situation must now be held to dominate others and that aid to that country must be attentively studied, lest the whole Turkish position be lost, through the proof that England never kept her guarantees. The Prime Minister suggested that I should stay in Cairo for at least another week, while these questions were being studied and we made sure we had done our best from both ends. Across this I wrote: "Egypt more important than Greece. Enemy air in Libya unaltered."

November 2nd: My main purpose in wishing to go [home] was to give them picture here which they have not got, details of certain projects we have in mind and, above all, try to stop folly of diverting men, aeroplanes and material from here to Greece. Disturbing telegram, in all senses, arrived. It seems that Greece is now to dominate the scene. Strategic folly.

There followed a somewhat tense argument with London about my return. The next morning I held a conference in which Andrew Cunningham, Wavell, Longmore and Lampson took part. All were of the same opinion, Egypt was strategically vital, while Greece was not. We were barely strong enough in Egypt as it was and our weakness in the air would speedily become dangerous. The Italian attack on Greece, which seemed anyway not to be fully driven at that time, might well be intended as a diversion. Everyone present

agreed with the telegram I had already sent to the Prime Minister
and the conference adjourned while I drafted a later edition:

> All strongly of the opinion I should return home as rapidly
> as possible in order to put whole position as seen from here
> before you. Earnestly hope you will agree to this. Propose to
> leave tomorrow morning. Perfectly prepared to fly back here
> if required after I have seen you, but am convinced that this
> meeting between us is most urgent. It is impossible to explain
> position and plans fully by telegram.

This brought me a reply which excusably showed some bewilder-
ment as to why I could not telegraph the essential points I had in
mind. The reason was the overriding demands of secrecy upon
which Wavell was, rightly, most insistent. Even cyphers are not
always absolutely safe.

November 3rd: [Admiral] Cunningham stayed to luncheon.
I like him more and more. He is shrewd as well as fiery, and
cheerful good company.

In the afternoon discussed with Wavell need for giving home
a clearer picture of our military position and plans and the consequences of any withdrawal for Greece. Decided to send two
further telegrams.

I gave the Prime Minister details of the reasons why we did not
think an Italian attempt on Crete was likely in the near future,
"nor unless and until Greece is overrun." I also told him that the
Commanders-in-Chief were strongly of the opinion that the defence
of Egypt was the crux of our whole position in the Middle East.
From the strategic point of view, they thought that the security
of Egypt was the most important commitment and must take
precedence of any attempt to save Greece. It was also essential if
we were to retain the support of Turkey.

We had been troubled by optimistic reports from London of
what we could do to reinforce Greece and so I added a final paragraph to my telegram:

In view of the very limited extent to which, with the best will in the world, we can now help Greece, all here are greatly perturbed at impression being given by statements from London that air support is being given and British troops have landed. The former is limited to one squadron on its way and the latter to one battalion at Crete. We much hope that instructions can be given B.B.C. and others, especially Reuters, not to raise hopes which cannot be realized.

I wrote in my diary:

November 3rd: These we drafted and despatched a few minutes only before tirade from Winston. This included such assertions that Athens was more important than both Khartoum and Kenya, etc. Accused us of pursuing safety-first tactics, etc. The weakness of Winston's telegram is that I have for long been urging the despatch of air reinforcement here. It was the burden of letters to him and to Archie [Sinclair] before I left England. I failed to secure it, and now we are to send to help Greece from our insufficient air forces here.

The weakness of our policy is that we never adhere to the plans we make. If we had ever thought to help Greece, we should long since have laid our plans accordingly. Instead of which we took a deliberate decision not to do so, and then go back on it and seek to improvise out of air, at the expense of air-power! High-sounding phrases only make matters worse.

Merely telegraphed in reply to Winston's vehement telegram that we had said our say before receiving his and would await his comments.

In a further attempt that night to persuade the Prime Minister to let me come home, I telegraphed hinting, but not proclaiming, our plans, which I doubled with an appeal to the C.I.G.S. In spite of this, November 4th was mainly a day of waiting, which I used in the morning to hold a conference with Wavell and Longmore. In the evening a telegram arrived from the Prime Minister stating his demands on us. We were to send at once to Greece one Gladiator squadron and two more Blenheim squadrons. If necessary, a second battalion was to be sent to Crete. He concluded by saying that we should not abandon our special plan, though some post-ponement might be necessary. This was the last thing we were prepared to do, because to delay must be to miss our opportunity. I commented:

> *November 4th:* [These demands] are heavy, but they have no doubt been modified by our own strong warnings. What is melancholy is that we once again enter here the period of grave risk to a vital artery and these new commitments have an uncanny habit of growing despite all promises that they will not.

Early next day a telegram arrived from the Chiefs of Staff, supported by an appeal from Dill. They backed up the Prime Minister's instruction to draw upon our resources in Egypt. Aerodromes were to be prepared for the operation in Greece of the three Blenheim and two fighter squadrons. They added that it was appreciated that this plan would leave Egypt very thin for a period, but they would try to make it as short as possible. We telegraphed accepting reluctantly the additional risks they asked us to face:

> Withdrawal, though it will hamper arrangements made in Western Desert, will not entirely dislocate them. But any increase in commitment or attempt to hasten rate of despatch to Greece beyond that now laid down in C.O.S. telegram No. –, will mean serious risk to our position in Egypt.
>
> Uncertain factor still remains date by which air reinforcements, particularly fighters, arrive in Egypt to replace those sent to Greece. Experience hitherto shows that previous forecasts have not been fulfilled, and time-table is sadly behind. Now feel that there is nothing further I can do here and propose leave here tomorrow morning by air.

November 5th: Final conference with Wavell and Wilson, who both seemed deeply grateful for the very little I have been able to do.

Saw Yugoslav Minister who brought me a message of thanks from Prince Paul for the information I had sent him, much of which was new to him. He did not conceal his surprise that the Greeks had fought so well, and thought that the Italians had been equally taken aback. That remains to be seen.

Wavell came to see me, as I was dressing for dinner, with further last-minute problems, including a question concerning the size of his command, now raised by a mysterious African conference which appears to be sitting in India! We agreed to hold to arrangement made with Smuts, as a start anyway.

Both Wavell and Longmore do not believe in anything more than a local offensive against Egypt in the near future. I pray that they may be right.

November 6th: A night's reflection left me more troubled than ever about air situation here. It is a further worry that we are short of A.A. guns. Showed Wavell and Longmore two telegrams which I wanted to send. They clearly were not keen, so redrafted them in the Sunderland and sent them as one telegram from myself from Malta.

Said goodbye to all our friends in Egypt with real reluctance. Sped down the Nile in the launch in brilliant sunshine. A good but slow flight to Malta. Eight and a half hours. Saw Crete and its adjacent isles en route, but did not land.

6

DESERT VICTORY

November–December 1940

A discussion on air reinforcements — Trouble over weapons from
the United States — Operation "Compass" — Our plans in East
Africa — Victory at Sidi Barrani — Lord Halifax Ambassador to
Washington — I return to the Foreign Office

THE AIR JOURNEY home from Malta was by Sunderland, slow and
uneventful. I reached England on November 8th and went at once
to see Sir John Dill at the War Office. When I had shown him,
with the help of a map, the proposed plans for the offensive in the
Western Desert, we repaired together to the Prime Minister who was
then working in a disused Underground station in Down Street, off
Piccadilly.

Churchill gave me an affectionate greeting and was soon eagerly
asking for my news. As I cautiously explained Wavell's projects,
the Prime Minister's enthusiasm grew and he began asking for the
operations to take place soon. I explained the limitations, which
were principally the need for aircraft reinforcements, the time required for the detailed preparations, and the moon. Dill, observing the Prime Minister's gusto, repeated some words of warning I
had used about the enemy's numerical superiority in the air as well
as on land. Though he accepted these, the Prime Minister did not
that night allow them to lower his spirits, while we talked of all
I had seen and learnt.

The next day, November 9th, after a further discussion with Dill
and the discharge of some arrears of work at the War Office which
had been awaiting my return, I left for Ditchley, Mr. Ronald Tree's
beautiful house in Oxfordshire where the Prime Minister stayed
every full moon, when Chequers might have been a target. There
we continued our talk and Churchill agreed to the despatch of a

telegram to Wavell, saying that I had given a full account of his plans, and assuring him of our full support in any offensive action he might be able to take against the enemy, whatever its outcome might be.

While I was at Ditchley I had some discussion with the Prime Minister about our air position. Basing myself on a reckoning of our strength in the Middle East which he showed me, I wrote this minute:

> Thank you for allowing me to see attached. Position in Egypt is — or shortly will be — worse than here appears.
>
> (1) Of 2 Gladiator Squadrons one is due to leave for Greece. Total fighter strength in Egypt will then be —
> 1 Squadron Hurricane ⎫
> 1   "   Gladiator ⎬ Western Desert
> 1   "   Hurricane   Alexandria and Cairo
>
> (2) A total of 3 Blenheim Squadrons is due to go to Greece. One has gone, but two more should be so marked [this out of a total of four squadrons].
>
> A disturbing feature is that fighter position will not improve for some time, since the moment enough machines arrive to form a new squadron, a second Gladiator Squadron has to go to Greece.
>
> I cannot help wishing that this move of a second Gladiator Squadron should not be automatic, and that Longmore should be asked to report when sufficient reinforcements have arrived to replace it. We could decide in the light of events then whether it should go to Greece or stay in Egypt.

When I got back to London I found an appeal from Longmore to the Air Ministry in almost exactly the same terms and using the same figures as I had given the Prime Minister. Although the Air Ministry had rejected this request to keep the second Gladiator squadron, I approached the Prime Minister again the next day, November 11th, adding at the end of my minute: "The arrival of Italian pilots here makes me anticipate more than ever that German pilots will appear in Libya."

At a Defence Committee meeting that night, the Prime Minister finally accepted my suggestion that before despatching the second squadron to Crete, Longmore should be entitled to present his case for retaining it. So careful an argument about so small a formation as one squadron of fighters points to our meagre resources of those days.

On November 12th I gave the War Cabinet a full account of my experiences in the Middle East, and a review of our dispositions and intentions in every theatre of Wavell's wide command, from the Western Desert, deep into the Sudan and beyond into Kenya. I summed up by recalling Wavell's strategy as he had expressed it:

First, to ensure the security of Egypt by the defeat of the Italian forces now threatening it.

Secondly, to foster rebellion in Abyssinia and, by raids and local offensives from Sudan and Kenya, to seek to liquidate the Italian forces in East Africa. We should thus remove threat to Red Sea and liberate our forces now engaged there for use in other theatres.

Thirdly, to build up forces to assist Greece, Turkey and other Middle Eastern countries.

★   ★   ★   ★   ★

The period of waiting, before Wavell's offensive could get under way, was an uneasy one. The Prime Minister was still impatient with the army, not entirely understanding the modern maintenance problems of motor transport, tanks and aircraft, operating in a country of desert spaces and devoid of industrial capacity. I was apt to resent these assaults and did not, perhaps, make enough allowance for the confidence I could feel, because I had seen the men who were to handle the job, and knew their mood.

November 20th: Found telegram that Winston wanted to send to Wavell which is partly repetition of what I have already sent, with his approval. Telephoned and tried to persuade him to let me handle the business. Some acrimony, not much success.

November 25th: Dined with Winston when we had some talk of future plans. We were alone. Champagne and oysters in his bedroom. I told him that if "Compass" [operation in Western Desert, December 1940] went reasonably well, we should need to determine future dispositions, after discussion with C.-in-Cs. on the spot and Greeks and possibly Turks. We could not leave an army inactive in Africa. Should we reinforce Greeks, if so where, Salonika? And what could these men achieve? I suggested I should pay another visit. We must continue to hammer Italians either in Africa, or Europe or both. Winston agreed generally. He felt that "Compass" might influence attitude of all these countries; this is true, though one must not place too high hopes on "Compass," which is at present a limited operation.

On November 30th I sent the Prime Minister a brief letter on his birthday:

Many and happier returns of the day. Very few men in all history have had to bear such a burden as you have carried in the last six months. It is really wonderful that at the end of it you are fitter and more vigorous, and better able than ever to guide and inspire us all.

You do not know how you heartened me on Monday night by your comment that never in your life had you felt more equal to tackle your work. All the same, take care of yourself.

I have just read in a telegram a rumour that Italians in Libya are short of water and generally in trouble, and I feel better. So do we clutch at straws. Bless you; thank you for all your kindness to me, and may we yet celebrate the last stage of a long hard road travelled *la main dans la main*.

The next day I received a manuscript reply of thanks which ended: "I am very grateful to you for all your help and comfort."

★   ★   ★   ★   ★

One of the subjects to which I had to give much attention in those weeks was the supply of weapons due to be delivered to us from the United States. A telegram from Sir Walter Layton, on a mission to Washington from the Ministry of Supply, disturbed me.

It appeared to show that the orders we had put in five months before, under our "A" programme to equip fifty-five divisions, were only to be given priority after the full United States rearmament programme and also after programme "B" to equip ten new British divisions with American weapons.

This reversal of priorities, which had been put forward by the Americans on October 23rd, would have hamstrung us. We could not do without supplies of British types of weapons under programme "A," for they were to replace the losses we knew we must suffer from German bombing, whereas programme "B" enabled the United States Government to place orders for armaments which were only legitimate at that time under cover of British commands. I could not accept that our immediate needs should be sacrificed on account of this and wrote to the Prime Minister on November 30th that "the United States Administration is pursuing an almost entirely American policy, rather than one of all possible aid to Britain."

I admitted that these troubles were not the responsibility of Mr. Arthur Purvis, the Canadian Director of the British Purchasing Commission; but I suggested that we should be represented in the United States by a Minister with the full authority of the War Cabinet.

In a message to the Prime Minister the day before, I had made an alternative proposal to strengthen our military representation in the United States:

> We need a senior General with experience of the problem to head our Mission. He must have the necessary Staff Officers with him and seek to educate American military opinion, as well as to secure that our own needs are met.

As my confidence in Purvis grew, it did not abate my wish for the highest military representation in Washington, which eventually was brilliantly fulfilled by the appointment of General Sir John Dill. His work with the United States Chiefs of Staff and his close friendship with General Marshall were decisive factors in the final victory.

On December 4th I saw the new Minister of Supply, Sir Andrew

Duncan, who had been appointed ten days before my departure for
Egypt:

> I found him sympathetic, understanding, energetic. He will,
> I am sure, do us well. He was bitter in condemning failure to
> order in U.S.A. at outbreak of war. If this had been done, they
> would be making our types now. As it was, having started on
> their types, it would be the devil and all to get them to make
> ours, even if theirs were inferior. He wanted me to pay a visit
> to U.S.

This failure was brought home to me when Brigadier-General
Raymond Lee, the United States Military Attaché, came to see me
the next day. He had been at all times helpful. I tried to impress
upon him the difficulty in which we were placed, because his country would not make our types of weapons. He could not offer me
much comfort. I knew that the fault was chiefly ours, for as far
back as 1937 I had been trying to persuade the War Office to place
these very orders and they had not been willing.*

From the moment that Hitler launched his offensive in France
and Flanders in May 1940, the effectiveness of dive-bombers and
our lack of them was seared into our minds at the War Office.
I discussed our needs with Lord Beaverbrook, Minister of Aircraft
Production, who wrote to me on June 8th:

> The only way is to buy more from the United States. Fifty
> machines are coming now, and I will telegraph to the Agents
> of the Ministry in North America to do all they can to find
> more for immediate delivery.

I told him that "we all feel here that we could not be in better
hands." Lord Beaverbrook ordered two hundred American Vultee
dive-bombers for delivery in January. I asked the General Staff and

* *Facing the Dictators,* pages 481–2.

the Air Staff to study the details of their employment, replying to Beaverbrook:

> I am most grateful to you for your help in this matter and personal interest in it. I am confident that the provision of this tactical air support is of the first importance.

I asked Sir Archibald Sinclair to form the dive-bombers into squadrons as soon as they arrived. These squadrons were to receive training in army co-operation and I offered Army pilots for the purpose, which was accepted. Administrative difficulties caused delay, but I was able to tell the House of Commons on November 12th of the arrangements which led, a few weeks later, to Army Co-operation Command.

> *November 29th:* Lunched with Brooke [Commander-in-Chief Home Forces]. All his staff there. Afterwards we discussed his plans and dispositions in his room. He believes in likelihood of German attempt at invasion in spring, and so do I. We had some talk previously with his air liaison officer. It is evident that matters are not satisfactory in that sphere. Even the dive-bombers are not to continue to work with us. They are to be lent sporadically. We agreed that meeting with Air Staff would be necessary to clear matters up.

In the desert, however, Longmore solved the problem brilliantly. Having been allotted Lysanders for army co-operation, he realized that they would have been shot down in no time by the Italian C.R. 42, so instead he made a few Hurricanes available to work with General O'Connor's forces. This arrangement was highly successful during Wavell's offensive, "Compass," and was the beginning of what was later the Tactical Air Force.

★　★　★　★　★

After a Defence Committee I wrote:

> *December 4th:* W. asked for news of "Compass" and was indignant that I had not asked date. He was also critical of army

and generals. "High time army did something," etc. I made it plain that I did not believe in fussing Wavell with questions. I knew his plan, he knew our view, he had best be left to get on with it. This did not suit W. Dill was very angry at his attitude.

The next day I spent a large part of the morning setting down an account of our future plans in East Africa for the Prime Minister. The most effective means of developing an offensive against the Italians, I wrote, was to further the rebellion in Abyssinia. Three columns were operating in the country. Colonel D. A. Sandford was already deep into the Gojjam country, halfway between Lake Tana and Addis Ababa. Pressure at Gallabat had attracted enemy forces and minor activity would be kept up to hold them there. Preparations were being made for an attack upon Kassala in February, if additional troops could be provided, which would depend upon the outcome of "Compass." I explained: "the importance of the capture of Kassala is that it opens up possibilities of advance into what is militarily the most tender spot in Italian East Africa," Eritrea.

For Kenya I described plans for a strongly offensive policy northeast of Lake Rudolf on the Abyssinian border. From the point of view of the Abyssinian rebellion, this would yield a better dividend than the capture of Kismayu, which was the next phase of the programme. It was to be achieved in two stages, the first before the rains, in February, and the second after, in May. I concluded:

> For all these operations against Italian East Africa in the next two months, on a wide front stretching from Kassala to the mouth of the River Tana, our Command there will have need of, and should make good use of, all the troops at present at their disposal. I therefore propose that the West African Brigade shall remain available at least until the rains begin in February. The British battalions in West Africa would be relieved then, either by a West African Brigade now in Kenya, or by new West African battalions which are now being trained locally.
>
> In all this I have made no mention at all of air forces. As you know, Longmore has rightly closed these towards the north,

with the result that the present air forces available for all operations against Italian East Africa are very light indeed.

Events exceeded my expectations. General Platt's forces, with the 4th Indian Division, withdrawn from the Western Desert after the first of Wavell's victories at Sidi Barrani early in December, occupied Kassala on January 19th. General Cunningham had proposed to postpone the whole of his operation against Kismayu until after the rains and Churchill and Smuts were bitterly disappointed. In January, however, Cunningham was cheered by news of the Libyan victories and strengthened by additional transport from South Africa. He felt able to adhere to the plans originally agreed between us at Khartoum, and during the second half of February took Kismayu and Mogadishu, both in Italian Somaliland. In April Asmara and Addis Ababa fell, the Emperor entering his capital in May. Thus the first victim of aggression by one of the Axis powers was also the first to come into his own again.

On the night of December 5th we held a Defence Committee to discuss "Workshop," an operation for an attack on the small Italian island of Pantelleria, half-way between Sicily and Tunisia.

December 5th: So far there is no plan worthy of the name. My present feeling is same as [Air Chief Marshal] Portal's [now Chief of the Air Staff], a four to one chance to win an even money risk.

I advocated asking Wavell and Cunningham where they would like to use this force, perhaps in North Africa. After the discussion the Prime Minister took me into his room.

Winston unhappy at plan being turned down. Sang Roger's [Keyes] praises, and proposed I should go out to command in Middle East. Wellesley had gone straight from Parliament. I declined very firmly.

This suggestion, made more than once, displayed Mr. Churchill's imaginative flouting of convention and fondness for historical precedents.

★   ★   ★   ★   ★

General Wilson launched his attack in the early morning of December 9th. The first reports were inevitably scrappy, but at least there was no bad news. After twenty-four hours the omens for a victory at Sidi Barrani looked favourable, but we still kept our fingers crossed.

December 11th: After luncheon two telegrams just before Dill went off. These showed continuing uncertainty in Sidi Barrani area, but we are closing in. Six thousand prisoners by last night.

As I was reading a later telegram which showed us still closer to Sidi Barrani but situation still obscure, [Lieut.-Gen. Sir Robert] Haining [V.C.I.G.S.] came in with a brief but triumphant message that Sidi Barrani had been captured with large numbers of prisoners. 7th Australian Brigade and support group manœuvring to cut off enemy in Sofafi area. Three generals captured. Rang Winston, who congratulated me warmly on a great victory. Spoke to Jack Dill later, who was delighted. Sent a joint telegram to Wavell. It all seems too good to be true.

For the next five days O'Connor pursued the enemy as far as Bardia, which fell on January 5th. Tobruk was captured on January 22nd and Benghazi on February 6th, completing a dazzling chain of victories.

December 12th: Winston rang up early in morning and complained that we were not pursuing enemy and had much to say about missed opportunities. After an angry riposte from me, it emerged that he had not seen telegram that appeared during night giving details of further plans. But this is all symptomatic of his distrust of local leaders which to my disappointment is not abated at all. He even went so far as to say when I saw him later that this showed we should have held Somaliland. I replied: "That is most ungenerous at this moment, you know that we had not a gun there." "Whose fault was that?" Winston retorted. Our talk was less cordial than usual.

After all it was the elimination of the larger French forces in their Somaliland which exposed ours and the appeasement of Mussolini which had left us so weak; certainly not the Prime Minister's responsibility, nor the policy I had wanted before I resigned in 1938.

On December 16th Mr. Churchill held a conference at No. 10 Downing Street on our arms orders from the United States, with Lord Beaverbrook, Sir Archibald Sinclair, Mr. A. V. Alexander, Sir Kingsley Wood and myself. Matters were not going well for the army and we all felt the time had come to air our discontent. We would rather not have programme "B" at all than agree to it being placed before programme "A." Our point was taken and, in the event, the Americans did not enforce these priorities to our disadvantage.

After dinner the Prime Minister told me that Mr. Lloyd George would not have the Washington Embassy, which he had offered him on the sudden death of Lord Lothian. Lord Horder, his doctor, had ruled him out, but he had been flattered by the invitation.

Early the next morning there arrived from Wavell an excellent appreciation of his plans. I sent a telegram of approval at once, before argument could confuse it. After a Defence Committee the Prime Minister summoned Kingsley Wood, Sinclair and myself to his room at midnight and discussed the Washington appointment. He was in great form because of the outcome of the battle in the Western Desert. His preference was for Lord Halifax, and for me to take his place at the Foreign Office. Sinclair and Wood thought my return to the Foreign Office would have a great effect in Britain and in the United States. I went home sad at the thought of leaving the soldiers. I thought, too, that I would like to stay on the Defence Committee, which was in fact what happened.

Lord Halifax came to see me the next evening. He told me that the Prime Minister had asked him whether he would like to go to Washington and he wanted to know my mind. Personally he did not want to go, both he and Lady Halifax would prefer their Yorkshire home. He understood that the Prime Minister wanted to send a public figure and he thought that right, but he believed that what little use he might be at home lay in restraining Mr. Churchill. Eventually we agreed that only a Prime Minister could decide these things.

December 19th: Winston read his statement to the House in morning, which went well, including a picturesque description of a cavalry charge "sword in hand" by Australians in desert.

Dined with Winston when we had talk of Edward [Halifax] and Washington etc. W. said that E. had now made it clear to him that on personal grounds he did not want to go and that on public he was doubtful if it was right, but P.M. must decide. W. was sure that it was right he should go, moreover he much wanted me back at F.O. I asked if E. had suggested anybody else. No, except hints that as result of my talking with E., I might like to go. I said NO! I had said no more to E. than that in wartime all must go where sent.

We then spoke of the War Office, for which I had previously suggested Oliver Lyttelton, whom I again commended. When the Prime Minister asked for more names I proposed Lord Trenchard. For that day my diary concluded:

Winston was tired but cheerful. We spoke of the dark days of the summer. I told him that Portal and I had confessed to each other that in our hearts we had both despaired at one time. Winston said: "Yes. Normally I wake up buoyant to face the new day. Then I awoke with dread in my heart."

Next day my wife and I lunched with Lord and Lady Halifax:

December 20th: When Edward saw us out he said: "I am afraid you have let me down," with a smile and I replied: "What do you mean? I only told Winston that I was not keen to go, while you told him I was." Edward retorted: "I only said that I thought you might hate it a little less than myself!"

After more work in the afternoon, I left by car for Chequers, where I found Lord Gort. The Prime Minister arrived soon afterwards and told me that he had written definitely to Halifax. He realized I did not want to move, but there was, he said, really no comparison between the importance of the two offices. He was sure that the moves were right. Churchill was very tired and had a headache. He said that he found these personal matters between friends exhausting. All the same he would not go to bed until 2 a.m. and we discussed possible Mediterranean and African developments with Gort.

December 21st: Rumours, in *Daily Mail* more than rumours, of impending changes. Roosevelt as yet knows nothing and his *agrément* was hurriedly telegraphed for.

Saw Winston before I left. He was in bed and said he felt perfectly fit again. We discussed my successor. "O.L. [Oliver Lyttelton] or D.M. [David Margesson]" as Winston put it. I favoured the former. Winston suggested that I should have Under-Secretary in House of Lords and suggested a name. I said I thought this unnecessary and would prefer that Bobbety [Cranborne, then Dominions Secretary] should represent me in Lords. Winston liked this plan. When I left O.L. seemed virtually settled.

I heard no more on this subject, but Margesson was appointed. My seven months at the War Office had been as dramatic as could be imagined. From my arrival, while the opening shots were being fired in the Battle of France, through the threat of invasion of the British Isles and the early dangers from our weakness in the Middle East, to Wavell's victories, every day and often every hour had been crammed with historic incident. My heart had been in the work. Now I was to open the second and longest of my three spells as Foreign Secretary.

Though my feelings were mixed, I knew that there could not really be any argument and that my responsibility must be greater as Churchill's colleague at the Foreign Office, than as his subordinate with the army. In wartime diplomacy is strategy's twin. There is a strict interplay of interests. I could only hope that I would do the job so that others would feel, as Churchill wrote, that I was "like a man going home." *

* *The Second World War,* Vol. II.

7

THE DECISION ON GREECE
January–February 1941

The Italians driven back from Greece — Herr Hitler's Balkan
plans — We advance in the Western Desert — Herr Hitler's
orders for Sicily and Bulgaria — General Metaxas dies — A bad
flight to Cairo with Sir John Dill — My "sealed orders" — General Wavell favours a Greek campaign — He appoints General
Wilson to the command — Athens — A moving interview with
the Greek Prime Minister — Anglo–Greek decision to hold the
Aliakhmon line — Prince Paul of Yugoslavia hesitates

MUSSOLINI'S LATEST aggression against Greece was paying no divi-
dends. The Italian onslaught collapsed almost at once and a
vigorous Greek counter-offensive soon drove the enemy back over
the frontier into Albania, four squadrons of the Royal Air Force
playing their daring part in these engagements. On November 11th
a brilliant thrust by our naval air arm had put half the Italian
battle fleet out of action at Taranto. These events and their consequences were soon to engage me at the Foreign Office as they had
done at the War Office before.

Meanwhile, Hitler was maturing his own plans for the Balkans
and Russia. As early as November 4th he reflected that he might
have to come to the rescue of the Fascist excursion against Greece,
which he described as a "regrettable blunder." On November 12th
he ordered the German Army Staff to prepare for an advance
through Bulgaria in order to occupy the northern Greek mainland.
Molotov was in Berlin from November 12th to 14th, and Hitler
tried to use this opportunity to deflect Russian interest from his
Balkan scheming. He proposed the signature of a new German–
Soviet agreement, with protocols defining the Russian sphere of
interest as "south of the national territory of the Soviet Union in

the direction of the Indian Ocean," while offering Russia freedom
of passage for her warships through the Turkish Straits.*
   This was tempting bait, but Molotov would only swallow it if he
could get his other demands as well. Russia, he firmly indicated,
was closely interested in the Balkans. The official Soviet reply was
more explicit, Bulgaria must accept a Russian guarantee and a
Russian base within reach of the Straits. In addition, the Soviets
wanted German troops withdrawn from Finland, the Japanese to
renounce their right to concessions in North Sakhalin, and the area
"south of Batum and Baku in the general direction of the Persian
Gulf" recognized as the centre of Soviet aspirations.† For this disagreeable revival of the Russian appetite, as well as the danger
which he foresaw of a British intervention in the Balkans, Hitler
thought it convenient to blame Mussolini. He wrote to him:

> The situation which has now arisen has very grave psycho-
> logical and military repercussions which it is important to
> understand clearly. . . .
>   With Russia, too, it is more difficult to bring about an agree-
> ment on interests and to divert Russian ambitions towards the
> east.
>   M. Molotov showed, on the contrary, an increased interest
> in the Balkans. . . .
>   England is now obtaining a number of air bases which bring
> her into close proximity to the oilfields of Ploesti, and likewise
> also within striking distance of all southern Italy.‡

   The Führer's plans were soon recast. He called off preparations
for an advance through Spain upon Gibraltar, being thwarted by
General Franco's refusal to fix a date for Spain's entry into the war,
and having also new engagements elsewhere. On December 13th
Hitler issued his orders for the attack on Greece through Bulgaria
and, five days later, for the campaign which broke his power, the
attack on Russia. There remained the problem of the Yugoslavs.
If possible they must be coaxed; the carrot of Salonika was there-

---

* *Documents on German Foreign Policy;* Series D, Vol. XI, Nos. 325–6, 328–9.
† op. cit., No. 404.
‡ op. cit., No. 369, Hitler's letter to Mussolini, Nov. 20th, 1940.

fore dangled before them, but pressure was also applied to make them join the Tripartite Pact.

On New Year's night I was in the Foreign Office after dinner, when the Prime Minister summoned me to discuss a telegram to President Roosevelt. Kingsley Wood and Beaverbrook were also there. When we had done our work and the others had gone, Churchill took me on to the roof. It was raining and the firing that evening was slight. I could not help wondering what fate would have in store for us before the next New Year's day came around.

★   ★   ★   ★   ★

Throughout the war I had audiences of King George VI and these were always easier than they had been during my earlier spell as Foreign Secretary, when I had not known His Majesty so well. When I saw him in January, the King spoke of Halifax's departure and I told him that, for Halifax's own sake, it was wise; he had many critics and they were hunting him. The King nodded and agreed with a later remark of mine, that we ought to have had three-party government much sooner. It was not made easy for him, King George said, to meet the Labour leaders. Eventually he had told Chamberlain that he must see Attlee and Greenwood from time to time or he would never get to know them.

January 4th: Good news of five thousand prisoners at Bardia. It looks like being a race whether we can cause complete defeat of Italians in Libya before Germans loose their attack on Greeks as I feel sure they mean to do.

The Greeks were now held up in Albania by bad weather and lack of transport and supplies. Inevitably their requests for help in war material multiplied and, in trying to meet them, we had to consider the prospect, which at that moment seemed imminent, of a German advance through Bulgaria.

To counter this, the Defence Committee decided on January 8th to approach the Greeks about the despatch of British forces to Salonika. General Ioannis Metaxas, the Greek Prime Minister, refused, arguing that such a reinforcement would merely provoke a German attack without being strong enough to repel it. The Greek Government were ready to make plans, he said, but did not want British troops to arrive until they were in sufficient strength for attack as well as defence. This was much more than our resources could provide. The Yugoslav Government improved upon the Greek reluctance, telling Athens that if the British sent troops to Salonika, and so provoked a German attack, they might have to let the Germans advance through Yugoslavia.

The Defence Committee, therefore, decided on January 20th not to press the Greeks, but to allow Wavell to continue his advance as far as Benghazi and, at the same time, tell him to start building up a mobile reserve which could be used as occasion required, to go either to Greece or to Turkey, or for other operations in the Mediterranean.

January 20th: Dined with Winston and Clemmie [Mrs. Churchill] alone. W. in very good form and clearly encouraged by his most successful Clyde trip. He had been through all three I.L.P. [Independent Labour Party] seats and warmly welcomed everywhere.

He was pleased I was at Foreign Office and asked me to confess I was also. I did so. "For," said W., "it is like moving up from fourth form to the sixth."

We had long meeting of Defence Committee. . . . W. was reluctant to give up a certain favourite project of his [the capture of Pantelleria]. I talked to him of this again after the meeting. He admits it cannot now be carried out, but is very irritated against Chiefs of Staff for not having done it sooner.

News of Italian withdrawal from Kassala came in during evening. Winston maintained at dinner that this was "Anthony's strategy." Which, of course, is nonsense, but I did have to struggle with him to prevent him forbidding Wavell to move 4th Indian Division south, as we had planned. Anyway if we can advance to Agordat [in Eritrea] this should be important contribution to finishing up Italian East African resistance.

★   ★   ★   ★   ★

A few days earlier, on January 11th, Hitler had taken further decisions. Mussolini, he considered, could not be allowed to collapse under the weight of the defeats which British and Greeks were dealing him. The Führer issued orders for German forces to go to the help of the Italian army, both in the desert and in Albania. An armoured formation, soon to become famous as the Afrika Korps, was got ready for Tripolitania, but Hitler did not tell Mussolini of this until April 5th. The other force was prepared for Albania, to join up with the main German advance through Bulgaria, but it was later countermanded.

On January 11th, German air force units began to operate against the British from Sicily. Their power soon demonstrated that Benghazi could not be relied upon as a supply port for any advance upon Tripoli.

Meanwhile Hitler had to soothe the Russians, who did not like the stories reaching them of a German build-up in Bulgaria. The Soviet Ambassador in Berlin was told that the concentrations were only directed against the British and the Greeks and had nothing to do with the Straits. But in all these plans and projects, Yugoslavia held the master geographical position and Hitler had not yet succeeded in winning over the Yugoslav Government. For their immediate reckoning, therefore, the German High Command had to accept that they would not be able to use the Yugoslav railways for the attack on Greece.

January 29th: A heavy day, during a great part of which I was afflicted by a most unpleasant headache. News of Metaxas' death, a heavy blow. A small country like Greece cannot be expected to produce two such men in a generation, and the political field is sparse.

A long conversation with Maisky in the afternoon and later with [Sir Malcolm] Robertson about reform of office. De Gaulle followed him about N. African problems, Bobbety [Cranborne] about Abyssinian ones, and then a Cabinet. After which more work until a hurried dinner with Charles [Ponsonby, my Parliamentary Private Secretary] at Brooks's. Then Chiefs of Staff Committee at 9.30 which continued until midnight and talk with Winston until one and work in my room until two.

We all feel that we are having our good days in Africa but that there is much rough weather ahead in Central Mediterranean and Balkans. Turkey is the key and we must intensify our efforts there. We discussed my going to Turkey. Portal very keen if it can be managed. Winston also anxious that I should see Wavell who he feels is insufficiently aware of Balkan dangers.

Events were soon to prove that this was not so.

General Metaxas had prepared his country for the war he believed inevitable, and led it with a remarkable discrimination and courage. With his death the Greek Government grew apprehensive about the country's ability to withstand the Fascist weight in numbers, and still more so about Nazi intentions. On February 8th the new Greek Prime Minister, M. Koryzis, gave Sir Michael Palairet, the British Minister in Athens, a note suggesting that we should fix the size and composition of the forces which we were prepared to send to Greece. We could then see, he explained, whether they would be enough, with the Greek forces, to check a German attack and encourage the Turks and the Yugoslavs to come into the war.

Within the last few days Mr. Churchill had offered to send air forces to Turkey, but the Turkish President had refused, on the familiar ground that to admit British units before a German attack, would precipitate it. Even so, Turkey still loomed larger in my mind than Greece.

In contrast to the previous autumn, the desert battle had now been fought and won. If a secure flank could be established at Benghazi, forces would be released for use elsewhere. Moreover, German infiltration into Bulgaria posed a threat which had not existed in the autumn of 1940. We could attempt to meet this by help to Greece or Turkey. We could not do both.

On the morning of February 10th I sent the Prime Minister a detailed minute with more question marks in it than was my habit. No doubt, I wrote, he would be reviewing the military position after the fall of Benghazi and deciding upon military strategy. My questions were those upon which we must clear our minds from the political angle. The capture of Tripoli would have political as well as military advantages, for example proximity with the French and Weygand. If, on the other hand, circumstances compelled us to halt the advance at Benghazi, what effect would this decision have upon our ability to send help to Greeks and Turks? How much could we send and when could it arrive? I judged the Greeks would say:

> "We are willing to accept any British force you care to send, but you yourselves will wish to make sure that that force is adequate for its task." Can we, in any circumstances, send such a force to Greece? If so, when will it and the necessary shipping be ready? If not, what material can we send for use by the Greek forces?

Having once again given first priority to our obligations to Turkey "as the buttress of our defence in the East," I wrote of the good political effect upon Turkey which would result from completing "the old programme of equipment which is heavily in arrears" and from preparing the ten air force squadrons recently offered for despatch to Turkey. I concluded:

> What worries me most about the Balkan situation is the position of Greece. Clearly if and when Germany has established herself in Bulgaria she will threaten Greece. Greek forces are inadequate to make any effective defence of the Macedonian front. Is it conceivable that we could send and maintain sufficient forces to fill this gap? I should fear not. Or can we hope that by reinforcing Turkey and preparing our aerodromes there we could develop a sufficient threat against the German flank to make the latter hesitate to engage himself heavily in Greece? Clearly the threat to the German flank is more effective if Turkey can maintain herself in Europe, or better still, advance into Bulgaria. Is it our present advice to Turkey that she should pursue either of these courses, or is it our view that the only sound strategy available to her is to withdraw to Asia and to use the Bosphorus, Sea of Marmora, and the Dardanelles as an anti-tank ditch?

The Defence Committee met that night and first considered the pros and cons of an advance upon Tripoli, deciding against this.

Then it discussed the situation in the Balkans and Turkey, and whether our forces should be offered to Greece or to Turkey. The Turkish Government had recently refused our offer of air support; Koryzis had said again that Greece would resist a German attack at all costs and had suggested that the size and composition of what British forces could be sent to Greece should now be determined. We also had to take into account the guarantee which had been given to Greece by Mr. Chamberlain's Government on April 13th, 1939. If another country to which we had given such a pledge were to fall to the Axis powers without a real British effort to prevent it, the effect, especially in the United States, must be deplorable.

The Committee decided to concentrate on building up a force to help Greece. Such a decision would probably limit to Eritrea for the time being our coming East African offensive, but this was accepted. There was no division of opinion about the conclusion.

Meanwhile much detailed work was necessary. Military and political action would have to be closely co-ordinated on the spot. The Defence Committee decided that the C.I.G.S. and I should go at once to Cairo to put this decision into effect.

★   ★   ★   ★   ★

Mr. Pierson Dixon, of the Southern Department of the Foreign Office, and my Principal Private Secretary, Mr. Ralph Stevenson, travelled with me, while Brigadier Mallaby accompanied Dill.

February 12th: A strenuous final morning. Answered questions in the House, and attended luncheon given for me by Maisky. Had difficulty in getting away from this and shedding Dalton in time to catch special at 3.40. Hardly a secret departure, the train being drawn up at No. 1 platform, a space railed off and a crowd assembled.

Uneventful journey [to Plymouth] during which I got through some papers and slept. A lovely evening, but learnt to our disappointment that the weather was bad at Gib. and we could not start.

February 13th: A day of waiting with what patience we could muster. A sunny morning and afternoon when we crossed to Mt. Edgcumbe and walked in the park, discussing policy. In the evening the wind got up and there was no hope of leaving though we hung on from hour to hour. A disturbed night. Amongst other incidents Winston rang up at 1.30 a.m. to say that we were not to start until following evening. I had to collect station commander and with his help induce Winston to let us act as we thought fit.

February 14th: Luncheon with Admiral, when at length news reached us that the weather was improving and we should get off tonight. A destroyer is on its way from Derry, but we all pray not to have to use it in these mountainous seas. Dill and I filled in the time by going to "The Two Dictators," which disappointed us. After dinner, and clearing up final papers which had come from London, we boarded our Sunderland. An Australian boy [Flight Lieut. Havyatt] in command, who had been second in command on my last return trip, and a grand crew. Took off in pretty difficult conditions at 11.30 p.m. A terrific flight. Met. people proved all wrong, and whereas first part of flight was difficult, second, expected better, was infinitely worse. At one time storm was so violent that we could make scarcely any headway, instruments ceased to function properly and we were hopelessly astray. I managed to sleep pretty well despite all this and had no idea how bad things were, until I was roused about 7 a.m. with cheerful tidings that pilot feared he had not enough petrol to reach Gib. He could, however, put in to Cadiz, where we should be interned, should he do so.

Went up and had a talk to pilot and navigator, as far as one could have a talk in these conditions. Gathered that there was a chance that we might reach Gib. and decided we should take it. Dill had been very ill during this period but he agreed with decision, and later went up himself, talked to pilot again and confirmed it. A little later, I went up again and found that we had done a little better in last half-hour, having made forty miles at the cost of fifty gallons. Seventy-five miles remained to do, on one hundred gallons, so we should just do it. Suggested to pilot that he should send message to Gib. telling of our troubles and asking them to send destroyer out to pick us up if we were compelled to force land in Straits. We had earlier agreed that if Straits were too rough and petrol at that stage was clearly not enough, we should put in at Tangier and try with Gascoigne's [British Consul-General at Tangier] help to bluff our way out. There were many other adventures. We drained two tanks dry and had to switch to reserve tanks, engines conking out in interval and we losing height rapidly. But engines picked up again all right.

We eventually landed with forty gallons to spare, about ten minutes' flying at the pace of our consumption during part of our flight. We should not have made it, if our pilot had not been really splendid, and the navigator and every member of the crew. They were most of them very sick, but kept going somehow. On one occasion pilot had to cut a corner and fly over Portuguese territory to save vital mileage and petrol. Sunderland that preceded us was piloted by very experienced Wing Commander [Francis Fressanges] who said that in twenty years' flying he had never met flying conditions to compare with these and that no machine but a Sunderland could have stood up to them. The Sunderland that followed us is lost.

Physically the discomfort was much less than in my Prague–Cologne flight, but it was a queer sensation sitting trussed in one's lifebelt and contemplating the alternatives of internment or drowning. One felt strangely detached and could review it all dispassionately and conclude that one had had a very good full life. But the crew were all such boys.

Flight Lieutenant Havyatt, Royal Australian Air Force, was later killed in action.

February 15th: A bath and shave and drink and we were ready for a late luncheon at 2.30. Sam and Maud H. [Hoare] here, otherwise Govt. House party only. Slept in afternoon until near dinner. Weather too bad to go on tonight.

February 16th: A meeting in morning when we discussed plans for help to Spain should need arise. Gave lines for draft to P.M. which we later discussed, amended and approved. Lunched with Admiral. Weather still bad and no chance to leave tonight.

I had "sealed orders" which the Prime Minister had entrusted to me with solemnity and relish when I left, with the injunction that I must not open them while I was still in the country. I broke the seals at Gibraltar, which was not so dramatic as it sounds because I had discussed the contents at length with Mr. Churchill during the previous days. My instructions provided that my principal object must be to send speedy help to Greece. To this end I was to initiate any action which I might think necessary with the Commander-in-Chief, Middle East, and with the Greek, Turkish and Yugoslav Governments. I was to consider what was the minimum garrison required to hold the western frontier of Libya and Benghazi, and what measures should be taken to make Benghazi a main naval and air base.

When in Athens I was to make the best possible arrangements I could with the Greeks. I was to try to keep the War Cabinet informed, or ask their help as far as possible, but in an emergency I must act as I thought best. I was to deal direct with the Yugoslav and Turkish Governments, with the object of making both countries fight at the same time or do the best they could. While our first duty was to fight, and if necessary to suffer, with Greece, the interests of Turkey at the second stage were no less important to us than those of Greece. I was to gather together all the threads and propose continuously the best solutions for our difficulties and not be deterred from acting on my own authority if the urgency was too great to allow reference home.

February 17th: Sam and Maud [Hoare] left. We still unable to get off. Read *War and Peace,* walked about the rock, and gazed at the storm through the window. Telegraphed to Malta to ask them to send Glenn Martins to fetch us. Said they had only one and that was needed for an operation by C.-in-C. Mediterranean. Then telegraphed please send a Wellington bomber. Answer, Wellington could not take off with necessary load of petrol.

During this enforced delay, Dill and I had some talk about our orders and how to fulfil them. While Dill did not believe in a campaign for Tripoli, he was concerned for Turkey, which he rated strategically above Greece. We were both of us troubled at the

slow progress of our journey. Time was so important and we did
not know what Wavell's own sentiments might be about the political and military decisions we must now take. If he had different
views from ours and those of the Defence Committee, our delay in
reaching Cairo and exchanging opinions with him could be dangerous.

As Yugoslav policies must so closely influence any decisions we
might take I had sent on February 15th a message to Prince Paul,
Regent of Yugoslavia, suggesting I should meet him in southern
Serbia. The Regent refused, fearing that a meeting would be too
dangerous; later attempts to get him to change his mind also failed.
I regretted this, for, as old friends, we could have talked frankly
together and I could have told him of our plans in more detail
than was possible in the letters I wrote to him. But whether I
could have given him more resolution is another matter, for on the
day before my message was sent, the Yugoslav Prime Minister and
Foreign Minister had meetings with Hitler and Ribbentrop at the
Führer's house in the Obersalzberg.

Though already enmeshed, the Yugoslavs were still wriggling to
avoid committing their country to the Axis, and proposed mediation to stop the Italo–Greek war. If this could be contrived, they
said, the British would leave Greece and the Balkan States could
join together in a neutral *bloc*. The Nazis were contemptuous of
this attempt to reverse events, as well they might be, with their
grip tight on Roumania, their entry into Bulgaria due to begin in
another fortnight and their plans for attacking Russia already laid.

February 18th, Gibraltar: After another depressing morning, a
sudden improvement in the weather about lunch time. Hopes
rose as the afternoon wore on and I came back from a walk to
learn that we were to take off at 6 p.m. We did so, in a pretty
choppy sea. Earlier part of flight fair, but it soon became rough
and we were flung about without respite until we reached Malta
about 3 a.m. A difficult landing and then found ourselves left tied
up to a buoy in a rough sea. I have never felt a more uncomfortable sensation. Neither Dill nor I having had one wink of
sleep we became mildly irritated that nobody came to take us off.
Learnt later that one of the causes was that old Dobbie had

put off himself on the launch, had felt ill on the way and launch had then been ordered to take him back again. After vehement wireless messages, we were at last rescued and reached Palazzo Dobbie three and a half hours after landing at Malta. We learnt on reaching shore that there was another Sunderland available to take us on and decided to leave the same morning.

February 19th: Two hours sleep, wash, bath and breakfast and off to join our Sunderland. On the way Dill and I spoke to a gathering of officers of the garrison. A difficult take-off, for it was still blowing hard, but a smooth flight to Suda Bay in Crete. I should have explained that during breakfast Air O.C. arrived and said that reports from Egypt as to weather were so bad, sand storms etc., that we could not land there, but urged us to go on to Crete and spend night on board a warship there. I found it difficult to believe Egyptian weather could be so bad as to stop us landing, but accepted his advice, refusing a suggestion that we should stay in Malta. I stipulated though that a message should be sent to Suda telling us latest weather forecast.

At Suda found *York* and Jack's [Egerton] ship *Bonaventure.* Went on board with C.I.G.S. and Jack showed us over his ship. Portal's brother commands *York.* Seemed to me a very good man. We were to have dined and slept with him and all arrangements had been made, but we felt that we must press on. Reached Cairo about 11 p.m. which is pretty good time, twenty-nine hours from Gibraltar.

The Ambassador and Wavell met us, and Dill and I had a few words with the Commander-in-Chief at the landing stage before going on to the Embassy. Wavell looked at us with the contemplative expression that he sometimes wore and remarked: "You have been a long time coming." We felt this reproach rather unjust and murmured our explanation. He nodded and then came the comment: "As you were so long I felt I had to get started, and I have begun the concentration for a move of troops to Greece." Dill and I exchanged a glance, relieved that Wavell's mind was apparently in tune with our instructions. Two months later, when I was back in London, I received unexpected confirmation of this. Dill showed me a memorandum which Wavell had written that day, before our arrival in Cairo, strongly in favour of going to the help of Greece.

After supper I had some talk with the Ambassador, read the telegrams from home, and finally had a discussion with Colonel William Donovan. He had been touring the Balkans for the United States Government and was able to give me a first-hand account of recent developments. His blunt speech in those countries had been useful and I was grateful to him for waiting several days to see me. I asked him to send the President a message emphasizing that any action we might take in the Mediterranean would overstrain our shipping resources and inviting him to help if he could.*

February 20th: Met three Commanders-in-Chief and Dill at Wavell's office where we went into a three-hour session. There was agreement upon utmost help to Greece at earliest possible moment. There is grave risk in this course and much must depend on speed and secrecy with which it can be carried out. But to stand idly by and see Germany win a victory over Greece, probably a bloodless one at that, seems the worst of all courses. If we are to act we must do so quickly and we decided at a conference at Embassy later in the day that we would propose ourselves for a secret conference in Greece on Saturday.

Much discussion about Turkish position. [Gen. James] Marshall-Cornwall and [Air Vice-Marshal T. W.] Elmhirst [both of whom had recently been to Turkey as members of a mission for staff talks] gave doleful account of state of Turkish readiness. They do not know how to use technical arms and their operational efficiency in the air is very low. All this led Wavell to take the view, which Dill did not share, that Turks would be more a liability than an asset at present time.

February 21st: [Admiral] Cunningham put other point of view well when we discussed whole matter again this morning. "Would the Germans like best that Turks should stay out?"

Another full discussion this morning with C.-in-C's found us all agreed on line with Greeks and our plans laid. Greeks have accepted visit.

After the meeting I sent the Prime Minister a telegram describing our interim conclusions:

* *Foreign Relations of the United States, 1941;* Vol. II.

Dill and I have exhaustively reviewed situation temporarily*
with Commanders-in-Chief. Wavell is ready to make available
three divisions, a Polish brigade and best part of an armoured
division, together with a number of specialized troops such as
anti-tank and anti-aircraft units. Though some of these . . .
have yet to be concentrated, work is already in hand and they
can reach Greece as rapidly as provision of ships will allow.
This programme fulfils the hopes expressed at Defence Committee that we could make available a force of three divisions
and an armoured division. In order to do this we shall have to
place a severe strain on administrative services and have to
improvise widely. You can be sure that we are not being bound
by establishments laid down. In fact, we could not possibly
make available such a force in so short a time if we were.

Gravest anxiety is not in respect of army but of air. There
is no doubt that need to fight a German air force, instead of
Italian, is creating a new problem for Longmore. My own
impression is that all his squadrons here are not quite up to
standard of their counterpart at home. Having been very
hardly worked in chasing Italians these last months, some of
them are tired and . . . the supply of modern aircraft still
leaves much to be desired. Many good troopers are still
mounted on wretched ponies. We should all have liked to approach Greeks tomorrow with a suggestion that we should join
with them in holding a line to defend Salonika, but both
Longmore and Cunningham are convinced that our present
air resources will not allow us to do this. Dill and I are not
prepared to take a final decision until we have discussed the
matter with the Greeks.

As regards general prospects of a Greek campaign, it is, of
course, a gamble to send forces to the mainland of Europe to
fight Germans at this time. No one can give a guarantee of
success, but when we discussed this matter in London we were
prepared to run the risk of failure, thinking it better to suffer
with the Greeks than to make no attempt to help them. That
is the conviction we all hold here. Moreover, though campaign is a daring venture, we are not without hope that it

* This word may have been wrongly decyphered.

might succeed to the extent of halting the Germans before
they overrun all Greece.

It has to be remembered that the stakes are big. If we fail
to help the Greeks there is no hope of action by Yugoslavia,
and the future of Turkey may easily be compromised. Though,
therefore, none of us can guarantee that we may not have to
play trump cards . . .* we believe that this attempt to help
Greece should be made. It is, of course, quite possible that
when we see the Greeks tomorrow they may not wish us to
come. If so, a new situation will have been created in respect
of which we will have to think afresh. But all my efforts will
be concentrated on trying to induce Greeks to accept our help
now.

We have discussed the question of command. Dill, Wavell
and I are all agreed that we must select a figure who will command respect with the Greeks and exercise authority over the
Greek officers with whom he will have to work. It is also necessary to choose a first-class tactical soldier. We have, therefore,
decided that the command should be given to Wilson, who will
be replaced in the military governorship of Cyrenaica by
Neame, at present commanding in Palestine. . . . Wilson has
a very high reputation here among the general public, as well
as amongst the soldiers, and his appointment to lead the forces
in Greece will be a guarantee to the Greeks that we are giving
of our best.

That same night Dill sent the following message to General Haining, the V.C.I.G.S.:

I came out here with firm idea that forces sent to Greece
would inevitably be lost and that we should concentrate on
help to Turkey. I have now heard views of three Commanders-
in-Chief, Marshall-Cornwall and Heywood [the army member
of our Military Mission in Greece]. It has been made clear to
me by them: —

(a) That Turkey will not fight at our bidding.
(b) That she may fight if we show that by helping Greece
we can stem a German advance.

* The text is obscure at this point, one group being undecypherable.

(c) That there is a fair military chance of successfully holding a line in northern Greece if we act at once.

(d) That Yugoslavia will not fight unless Turkey fights and that the converse is very likely true.

I have concluded that our only chance of preventing the Balkans being devoured piecemeal is to go to Greece with all that we can find as soon as it can be done. The risks are admittedly considerable but inaction would in my view be fatal.

It is not yet possible to see what line we should aim at holding in Greece but I doubt very much whether Salonika could be covered. If this proves to be so after our discussion with Greeks tomorrow we may still be able to hold a line covering northern Greece and giving Yugoslavia a bolt-hole through the Monastir Gap.

The greatest risks are shortage of air forces and A.A. units, strain on administrative services, and fact that "Mandibles" * cannot be completed until concentration in Greece is well under way or even finished.

Shipping needs can only be met by holding ships from convoys arriving here and further difficulty is mining in Suez Canal which is not yet fully under control. This makes it increasingly urgent to complete "Mandibles" and all energies are being directed to this end.

Line to take with Turkey is dependent on what Greeks reply to our proposals. Turkey as an ally would inevitably demand war material which we cannot supply and her forces are not really fit to meet Germans. Nevertheless I think we must try to persuade (but not bully) her to come in now as this will be her last chance. There are those who consider that Turkey in the war would be liability and would prefer to see her remain neutral.

Have had long talk with Donovan. He clearly thinks that help for Greece is urgent.

Though the force to be sent to Greece was a high proportion of the army's total strength in the theatre, the percentage of armour

* A plan for capturing the Dodecanese, which was postponed because the transport of the force to Greece occupied all available shipping and naval resources.

to be called upon was relatively small, one brigade, and it was armour which was expected to play the decisive part in any revival of desert warfare.

★ ★ ★ ★ ★

February 22nd: Left aerodrome at 8 a.m. for Athens. Smooth and pleasant flight *via* Tobruk where we met Jumbo Wilson and made tour of Italian sheds and workshops while aeroplane re-fuelled. Islands and Greece itself looked lovely in the sunlight as we flew in. Motored with all discretion, Generals being disguised in civilian hats and overcoats, to Tatoi, the King's country Palace. The King met us, and asked me for a talk alone when he told me of his troubles. He had worked hard to re-create his country since his return and now all was to be destroyed by German attack. He was determined to resist.

King George of the Hellenes was resentful of some rumours which he had heard to the contrary. There was not a word of truth in any such suggestion. His Majesty then said that he wanted me to have a word with his Prime Minister, alone, before we got down to discussing plans. I told the King that as we had come on a military mission, to decide whether or not there was a military operation which we could carry through together, I was reluctant to begin with a political discussion with the Prime Minister. The King replied that he was not asking me to say anything, but that the Prime Minister had something he wanted to say to me. It would not take more than a few minutes. I could not refuse and we were thereupon put into a small ante-room together.

I can see the scene in my mind now. M. Koryzis produced a piece of paper which he read out in French and then handed to me. The declaration said that Greece, having given our spontaneous guarantee and having received our valuable help on the unprovoked aggression of Italy, was our faithful ally. She was determined to continue the struggle at our side until final victory. The resolve of the King and the Government, shared by the whole Greek people, applied no less to an attack by Germany than to the struggle against Italy. The statement ended:

But let me repeat once again that whatever the future holds in store, and whether there is any hope of repelling the enemy in Macedonia or not, Greece will defend her national soil, even if she has to do so alone.

Looking back now upon the events of those days, I have no doubt that this modest little display of dauntless courage had been staged by the King. Irked by the rumours to which he had referred, he had been firm to explain his country's true intent, before the British representatives could say a word. It was all of a piece with the sense of duty which invariably guided King George, with the result that he made no single mistake in these months of ordeal, where many a cleverer man would have tripped.

We then went in to the meeting, at which the chief Greek repre-sentatives were the King, M. Koryzis and General Papagos. Our side consisted of myself and Dill, Wavell, Longmore and a member of Cunningham's staff, Heywood, Palairet and Pierson Dixon. I began by giving an account of the situation in the Balkans as it had appeared to the British Government in London the week be-fore. The Germans had assembled a striking force in Roumania. We believed this to consist of twenty-three divisions of which three were armoured, supported by between four hundred and five hun-dred aircraft. The German infiltration into Bulgaria had gone far, technicians in plain clothes were busy establishing their air organi-zation on Bulgarian aerodromes. If the reports just received were correct, the Germans were likely to cross the Danube at any mo-ment. Their motives were to subdue Greece and immobilize Tur-key. By extending their power over the Balkans, the Germans sought to strike a decisive blow at the British position in the Near East.

I explained that when the Greek Government had, on February 8th, appealed to the British Government for help and counsel, we had considered what we should do. Our Ministers, with the Chiefs of Staff in London and the three Commanders-in-Chief in Cairo, had agreed that we ought to offer all the help we could to Greece at the earliest possible moment. If action were to be taken, we must move with speed and in the utmost secrecy. I then gave de-tails of the forces we could send, by land, sea and air.

M. Koryzis said that Greece was determined to defend herself against attack from all quarters; any aid which Great Britain could give her was warmly welcomed. He did, however, wish to draw our attention to the danger of precipitating a German attack. We should first consider whether the Greek forces and those that Great Britain could provide would be sufficient to give effective support to Greece, in view of the dubious attitude of Yugoslavia and Turkey. The Prime Minister emphasized that he raised this as a purely military and not as a political question. He also asked what we thought the attitude of Yugoslavia and Turkey was likely to be.

I told M. Koryzis that we did not know what those two countries would do. Sir John Dill and I were to visit Ankara and hoped to get an indication then. We should have to explain to the Turks that our help to Greece meant that we could not give Turkey the military aid she was expecting. We could hope Turkey would understand that Britain helped her best by helping Greece. I emphasized that it was important that we and the Greeks should take our decisions independently of the attitude of Turkey and Yugoslavia, since if we waited to find out what they would do, it might be too late to organize an effective resistance to a German attack on Greece. We then adjourned for the military to do their work.

At the military meeting General Papagos said that:

[he] realized the extreme importance of time, which made it impossible to wait for Yugoslavia and Turkey to declare themselves. He had therefore asked his Government for permission to begin the withdrawal [to the Aliakhmon line*] as soon as possible and, in any case, before a German move made the withdrawal look like a retreat. It could be made to appear that the Greek troops were being sent to reinforce the Albanian front. Troops would be withdrawn first from rear areas in Macedonia, then, if agreed with Turkey, from Thrace, and lastly from the frontier of Macedonia. The time required to withdraw the troops from Thrace and Macedonia was twenty days.

When the withdrawal was complete, the Greeks would have

* This line ran from the mouth of the Aliakhmon river through Veria and Edessa to the Yugoslav frontier.

thirty-five battalions on the Aliakhmon line, plus one division, motorized, at Larissa, and possibly one more from reserve. It would then be possible to withdraw the right of the line in Albania.

There would then remain only frontier guards and light covering troops on the Bulgarian frontier. Those would fight to the last in all positions prepared for all-round defence; from other positions they would withdraw after delaying action. A plan had been prepared for demolitions in Eastern Macedonia, to be carried out by detachments of troops left for this purpose. A similar plan was under consideration for the Vardar valley. . . .

If Yugoslavia said tonight that she was going to fight, the Greeks would hold the Nestos line and ask the British to land at Salonika and Kavalla. Asked if the Greeks could cover disembarkation at Salonika, General Papagos said they would do their best: there were ten heavy and thirty-two light A.A. guns at Salonika. If the Aliakhmon line was held, these guns would remain at Salonika till the last phase of the withdrawal to the line. . . .

The Germans would need twenty days, if the demolitions had been made, from the time of crossing the frontier before they could be ready to attack the Aliakhmon line in sufficient strength. The line was naturally strong and the thirty-five Greek battalions with the British forces offered should be able to hold it. There were no fortifications, but the field works constructed by the troops themselves should suffice.

When the British military representatives came to tell me the result of their discussion with the Greeks, we all agreed that unless we could be sure of the Yugoslavs joining in, it was not possible to contemplate holding a line covering Salonika. In view of the doubtful attitude of Yugoslavia, we considered that the only sound plan from the military point of view was to stand on the Aliakhmon line.

★   ★   ★   ★   ★

I dined with the King in a small party, including his brother and sister-in-law Prince and Princess Paul of Greece. The presentations were somewhat mumbled by the King, English fashion, and I was preoccupied by the discussions of this extraordinary day. After dinner there was some talk about German behaviour in the war and I made comments which, though no doubt critical, did not seem unduly so to me in the atmosphere of that time. As we left for the final meeting of the conference, the King said somewhat quizzically to me: "Rather severe on my sister-in-law, weren't you?" I had to confess that, though struck by her beauty, I had not known who she was, which was not a good mark for my diplomacy.

At our final meeting to review our discussions, General Papagos himself began his report with the statement that

> in view of the dubious attitude of the Yugoslavs and Turks, it was not possible to contemplate holding a line covering Salonika, and that the only sound line in view of the circumstances was the line of the Aliakhmon.

The General followed this up by declaring the importance of the Yugoslav attitude, upon which depended the choice of the line to defend Greece. General Wavell, who spoke next, left no doubt that, in view of the time factor as well as the attitude of Yugoslavia and Turkey, the Aliakhmon line must be preferred. Later, after discussion about what could be done to enlist Yugoslav help, I asked that the decision be taken on whether preparations should at once be made, and put into execution, to withdraw the Greek advanced troops in Thrace and Macedonia to the line which we should be obliged to hold, if the Yugoslavs did not come in. Our minutes record that it was agreed that this should be done.

It never occurred to the British representatives either then or later that the Aliakhmon line was not the one which we must hold. A variant would only have been possible if the Yugoslavs had promptly declared their intention to enter the conflict, which we none of us expected, and if we and the Greeks had then had time to make detailed plans with them for the co-operation of our forces. When, years later, General Papagos wrote* that the decision on the line to be held in Greece was only intended to be taken after we discovered the Yugoslav intentions, Wavell and I discussed this

* *The Battle of Greece, 1940–1941.*

apparent misunderstanding. We were both at a loss to comprehend how there could have been doubt in the mind of the Greek Commander-in-Chief.

His account spurred us to set down our own and we planned to write a book to which Wavell would contribute the military chapters and I the political. Unfortunately his death in 1950 put an end to this idea. Nothing survives except the Preface, which was his writing.*

At the end of the discussions at Tatoi, I said that we must be sure about one thing: did the Greek Government really welcome the arrival of British troops in the numbers and on the conditions proposed? We should have to set preparations in train immediately and we did not want anyone to think that we were forcing our help on the Greeks. M. Koryzis was visibly moved and said at once that the Greek Government accepted with deep gratitude the help we had offered and entirely agreed with the plan put forward by the military representatives. The War Cabinet in London later endorsed these proposals.

We also spoke with the Greeks about how I should deal with the Turkish Government when I visited Ankara in a few days' time, and discussed how to get into touch with Prince Paul of Yugoslavia. It would have been too risky to send a staff officer to inform him of our decisions. Instead I instructed our Minister in Belgrade, Mr. Ronald Campbell, to tell Prince Paul that a German advance on Salonika seemed certain and that it was urgently necessary for us to know what Yugoslavia's attitude would be. I also suggested that the Prince Regent should send M. Dragiša Cvetković or M. Alexander Cincar-Marković, the two Ministers who had just been to Germany, to meet me in Athens or Istanbul. During the next two months Campbell and his small staff in Belgrade had to live and work at high pressure in an atmosphere of mounting tension. They never faltered in advice or action and the Minister's influence played a decisive part in shaping events.

When Prince Paul saw Campbell, he toyed once more with the idea of meeting me himself, but finally turned it down on the ground that it would cause "great trouble." He told our Minister that he found it very difficult to answer my question about what

* Printed as Appendix D.

Yugoslavia would do, without knowing what we intended to do.
It would have been scarcely possible to tell him, even if I had been
able to see him; nor would anything I could have said been likely
to influence his decision. We now read that on February 24th his
confidential emissary, Stakić, told Mussolini that the Prince had
become convinced Britain could not win the war and that he must,
therefore, make an agreement with Italy, which of course meant
Germany, too.*

February 22nd: I authorized Wavell to set his plans in motion
and Dill and I worked until 3 a.m. preparing messages for London. From first to last Greek attitude has been entirely resolute.
They are determined to resist whoever attacks. Only doubt was
whether to accept arrival of British troops now, or to await German attack and then call for them.

Our chief anxiety is in respect of the air. Longmore is much
weaker than I had thought and much weaker than he should be.
Flow of aircraft out to him has been recently most disappointing.
It must be speeded up at all costs, and I only pray that the Hun
gives us the time.

In any event our decision was the only one possible. On this
I have no doubt.

* *Documents on German Foreign Policy;* Series D, Vol. XII, No. 85.

8

A BYZANTINE SITUATION
February–March 1941

In Ankara — Defensive rather than offensive — I reprimand the
Yugoslav Ambassador — The Germans enter Bulgaria — General
Papagos' misplaced hopes — The Greek withdrawal is delayed —
My letter to Prince Paul of Yugoslavia — We are committed in
Greece — General Smuts backs the decision

FROM ATHENS we flew back to Cairo. After forty-eight hours there,
Dill and I set off by air for Adana, travelling on by train to Ankara.
We had decided, in a conference in Cairo with the Commanders-in-
Chief, that we would give the Turks the details of our visit to
Athens, of the Greek will to resist an attack by Germans or Italians
and of our determination to help them.

This I did at a meeting with the Prime Minister, M. Saydam, the
Minister for Foreign Affairs, M. Saraçoğlu, and Marshal Çakmak,
a much respected figure who was the Turkish Chief of the General
Staff. M. Numan Menemençoğlu, whose temperament was a natural
negative, made the fourth in this formidable team which faced Dill
and myself and our Ambassador, Sir Hughe Knatchbull-Hugessen.

The Turkish Government accepted and indeed approved our
decision to give help to Greece, but commented through Marshal
Çakmak that the German preparations could be equally well interpreted as being directed against the Straits. The Marshal feared
that the German intention might be to make a feint at Greece,
while aiming the decisive blow against Turkey. The Ministers
pleaded that their country was so weak in armoured vehicles and in
the air that it could not intervene if the Germans moved against
Greece, even though the Turks knew it would be their turn next.
Dill and I had to admit that the Turkish army was by all reports
a defensive and not an offensive force. The best I could get was

GREECE AND THE BALKANS

0   50   100   150   200   250 MILES

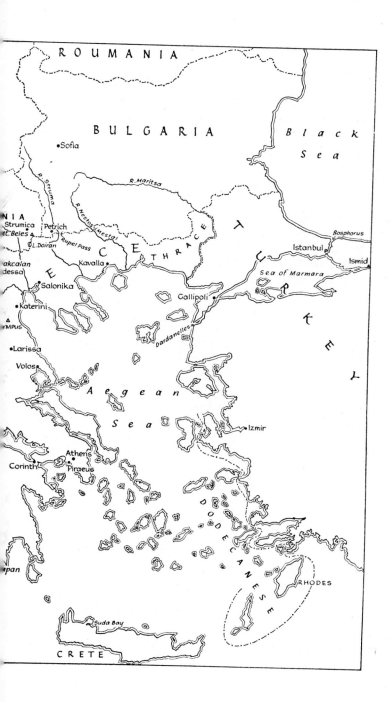

ROUMANIA

BULGARIA

•Sofia

Black
Sea

R.Maritsa

R.Struma

R.Nestos(Mesta)

NIA
Strumica •Petrich
t.Beles
•L.Doiran   Rupel Pass

akcalan
dessa

•Kavalla

THRACE

Bosphorus

Istanbul•

Ismid

•Salonika

Sea of Marmara

•Katerini

•Gallipoli

MPus

Dardanelles

•Larissa

Volos•

A e g e a n

*Izmir

S e a

Athens•
•Piraeus

Corinth•

DODECANESE

pan

RHODES

•Suda Bay

CRETE

an assurance that the army would fight bravely if attacked and that the Government were ready to concert common action with Yugoslavia. M. Saraçoğlu also agreed that we could tell the Greeks that the Turkish Government approved the plan which we had drawn up at Tatoi for assistance to Greece.

My talk with the President of the Republic, M. Ismet Inönü, whom I respected as a man and as Atatürk's chief subordinate commander, yielded nothing new except that the Turks said they were convinced that the Germans would ultimately seek a decision at their expense. This may have been true, for we now know that the German navy favoured an attempt to get control of Turkey in order to put the whole Mediterranean under Nazi sway, as Marshal Çakmak had predicted. Fortunately for the Turks, this intention was never approved by the Führer, who decided in November 1940 to take no action against them.

I admitted to the President that we should be receiving heavy blows in the next few months, and I asked him whether he thought we were right to send troops to Greece. Inönü replied that it was necessary for us to do so and that opinion in Turkey was unanimous in our favour. M. Saraçoğlu proclaimed a distrust of Yugoslavia which our efforts in the following weeks failed to allay, perhaps because he found the pretext useful to his own diplomacy.

Sir Stafford Cripps, then our Ambassador in Moscow, flew down to Ankara to meet me, encouraged by the action of the Soviet Government, usually so neutral in such matters, in placing an aircraft at his disposal. We had some talk of Anglo–Soviet relations and, more usefully, of what we could do to reduce the suspicion between Russia and Turkey. This had a sequel.

★　★　★　★　★

On February 27th I heard from Campbell that a message from the Yugoslav Government was on its way to Ankara. I was therefore surprised when the Yugoslav Ambassador arrived late at the reception Knatchbull–Hugessen was giving at our Embassy, and proved not only to have been having dinner beforehand at the Italian Embassy, in company with the German Ambassador, Herr Franz von Papen, but also to have left his message behind. I had to ask him to go home to fetch it. It was a lamentable document, amounting to a confession that Yugoslavia could not take a definite position and begging that we would not insist on her doing so. I said to the Ambassador that the attitude revealed by the message was purely negative. It was, in a way, worse than that adopted by Roumania. I had expected to hear that Yugoslavia found herself in a difficult position, that she was anxious to defend her independence and territorial integrity and to pursue a helpful policy, but that she wanted to know, before assuming a definite attitude, whether Great Britain was able to assist her in any way. Instead of which, Yugoslavia was without a positive policy.

I was bitterly disappointed, I told the Ambassador. If I could have seen Prince Paul, I would have informed him of what had passed between us and the Turkish Government. I felt, however, that I was being held at arm's length, the Yugoslav attitude being so prudent as to deny discussion. I added that Hitler's activities in the Balkans were encouraged by the lack of co-operation between Turkey, Yugoslavia and Greece. If they had shown a united front, the Germans would have hesitated long before moving against them. To this the Yugoslav Ambassador made the stock reply that such collaboration between the remaining members of the Balkan Entente might well have provoked action by Germany. I replied that I sympathized with him for having to deliver so deplorable a message to me.

★　★　★　★　★

Flying in those days was a chancy business. I had already promised to return to Athens once more, this time publicly, but the day scheduled for our arrival was spent instead in a special train at Ismid. While we were thus incarcerated, Bulgaria joined the Tripartite Pact and Nazi forces began to move into the country openly. The Germans had done what they could to soothe Russian fears. They had given advance warning and had been profuse in assurances that the move was only directed against us and the Greeks.

The Soviet Government were not, however, to be comforted and Molotov held a characteristic interview with the German Ambassador in Moscow, repeating over and over again that Germany's action was out of keeping with the Russian proposals of the previous November and that Bulgaria belonged to Russia's "security zone."* Moscow also put out a public statement saying that these events would lead to the "expansion of the sphere of the war" and Bulgaria's inclusion in it, which was true enough and as Hitler intended.

The Turkish authorities had given me permission to fly over the Dardanelles, which lay on our route to Athens. Once again we were in a Sunderland of the Royal Australian Air Force, I beside the pilot, with Dill and Air Marshal Elmhirst in the cabin below. We began to lose height abruptly over Gallipoli, so that I could view the site of bitter fighting in the first world war. The Air Marshal wanted to know, were we taking evasive action? Dill answered that he fancied it was only the Secretary of State taking over the controls.

Although we had been expecting this German move into Bulgaria, it gave point to our renewed conversations in Athens, which were soon to bring us bad news. When we arrived at our Legation, we were met by General Heywood with the information that the Greek withdrawal to the Aliakhmon line had not begun and that General Papagos now said it was too late to carry it through, because of the risk to his troops of being caught on the move. Heywood also told us that no troops had been withdrawn from Albania. His impression was that General Papagos had been hoping against hope that the Yugoslavs might be willing to come in, thereby enabling a line to be held which would cover Salonika. Papagos, Heywood thought, was afraid that the army's withdrawal would scare the Greek population in Macedonia. By the same token, the reason why no troops had been transferred from Albania was that their morale would have suffered. I had no doubt that Heywood was right in this last judgment and that the motives for the change in the attitude of the Greek Commander-in-Chief were political; they were still very grave.

Two British officers had just made a reconnaissance of the Aliakhmon line. They reported it to be naturally strong, but needing much work on communications, particularly in order to be able to deploy the artillery. This was just the task which we

* *Documents on German Foreign Policy;* Series D, Vol. XII, Nos. 108, 121.

had agreed with the Greeks should be set in hand at our previous meeting. Meanwhile there was barely a division of Greek troops on the line.

We discussed this damaging situation at once at a meeting with the C.I.G.S. and Longmore, which was also attended by Wavell's Chief of Staff, General Arthur Smith, Admiral Cunningham's representative, and Sir Michael Palairet. I recalled what had been decided by all concerned at our meeting at Tatoi, and said that evidently there had been an unfortunate misunderstanding, due to General Papagos' hopes that Yugoslavia would in fact enter the war. I asked Dill what course we should now take with the Greeks, from the military point of view. The C.I.G.S. said that it would be unsound to hold any line other than the Aliakhmon, or to hold that with less than eight divisions plus one in reserve. The British force alone would not be enough to do this and the Greeks must therefore provide the balance. Longmore pointed out that the Germans would not arrive in strength through the passes for some little while, probably at least a month. There should thus still be time to withdraw the Greek forces.

This proved to be a sound judgment, but ten days had been lost and we now entered upon a series of long and painful meetings with the Greeks, from the night of March 2nd to the night of March 4th, which I summarized in a telegram to the Prime Minister:

On arrival here we found a changed and disturbing situation and the atmosphere quite different from that of our last visit.

General Papagos had on the last occasion insisted strongly that the withdrawal of all troops in Macedonia to the Aliakhmon line was the only sound military solution. We had expected that this withdrawal to the Aliakhmon line had already begun. Instead we found that no movement had in fact commenced, Papagos alleging that it had been agreed that the decision taken at our last meeting was dependent on the receipt of an answer from Yugoslavia as to their attitude. He now stated that in view of the German entry into Bulgaria, the withdrawal was no longer possible since his troops would risk being caught on the move. Moreover, both he and the King stressed the fact that a withdrawal from Macedonia now must have serious internal political consequences by causing panic among the civil population. Papagos also stated that it was quite impossible to make any withdrawals from the Albanian front since his troops there were all exhausted and greatly outnumbered.

I went on to explain that Papagos therefore wanted to hold the line of fortifications near the Macedonian frontier with four divisions, though he accepted that they could not hold out for long. He also wanted to remain where he was on the Albanian front. This seemed a decision of despair as he almost admitted. The telegram continued:

> He proposed that British troops should, as they arrived, be moved up piecemeal to the Macedonian frontier line, although it was unlikely that they could arrive in time. We naturally refused to accept this proposal, which was so entirely different from the conditions under which we had agreed to send our forces. We telegraphed to the Commander-in-Chief Middle East to come to Athens for discussion. He arrived yesterday, March 3rd, and discussions have been practically continuous during afternoon and evening of March 3rd and today, March 4th. As attitude of Papagos was unaccommodating and defeatist, we had to enlist the aid of the King who was, throughout the very trying discussions which followed, calm, determined and helpful.
>
> By a process, which at times painfully resembled the haggling of an oriental bazaar, we were finally offered three Greek divisions, 12th from Macedonia, 20th from Florina and newly formed motorized division, together with battalions from Western Thrace, provided Turks would agree to release them and they arrived in time, to hold position on Aliakhmon line until reinforced by British troops.
>
> We were thus faced with following alternatives:
>
> (a) To accept the plan of Papagos to which he constantly returned, of attempting to dribble our forces piecemeal up to Macedonian frontier.

(b) To accept three Greek divisions offered for Aliakhmon line, the equivalent of about sixteen to twenty-three battalions instead of thirty-five we had been led to expect on our previous visit, and to build up our concentration behind this. Against this we had to set the delay likely to be imposed by defence of Rupel and other passes by the three divisions remaining in Macedonia.

(c) To withdraw our offer of military support altogether.

We were agreed that course (a) could only lead to military wavering while course (c) seemed equally disastrous, because it would inevitably lead to the rapid elimination of Greece from the war and because of the effect which the abandonment of Greece would have throughout the Near and Middle East as well as in the Empire and America. Moreover we should have been faced with considerable difficulties in withdrawing our air force and other troops already in Greece.

We therefore agreed after some misgivings to solution (b), but with the proviso that the command and organization of the whole Aliakhmon line was entrusted to General Wilson as soon as he was in a position to take it over. This was agreed to.

Military advisers, while recognizing the dangers and difficulties of this solution, did not consider it by any means a hopeless proposition to check and hold the German advance on this line, which is already strong with few approaches. At the worst, it should always be possible to make fighting withdrawal from this line through country eminently suitable for rearguard action.

Most depressing feature of the situation is the attitude of Papagos who, deprived of guidance of Metaxas, seems to have lost confidence. At final interview, however, after we had taken the decision, he seemed to recover.

We are all sure that we have in a very difficult situation arrived at correct decision. These two days have been indescribably anxious, but now that decision has been taken, there is a marked improvement in the general atmosphere of the Greek side. The hard fact remains that our forces, including Dominion contingents, will be engaged in an operation more hazardous than it seemed a week ago. You will no doubt decide on any communications to be made to the Dominion Governments. . . .

Later. We have just heard that the Turkish Government agrees to release of the Greek troops.

The conclusions which, as a precaution, we caused to be agreed in writing and signed by Dill and Papagos, were as follows:

The following decisions were taken as a result of the discussions between the Greek and British High Commands held at Athens on the 2nd, 3rd and 4th March, 1941:

1. The Greek Army will leave in Macedonia three divisions to defend the prepared positions on the Nestos–Rupel line.
2. The Greek Army will concentrate, with all possible speed, on the position Mt. Olympus–Veria–Edessa–Kajmakcalan (called the Aliakhmon position) the following forces:
   (a) 12th Division from Western Thrace, already moving towards the west by train.
   (b) 20th Division from Florina.
   (c) 19th Motorized Division from Larissa.
   (d) Seven battalions from Western Thrace, provided that the Turkish Government agree to release them as requested by the Greek and British Governments.
3. A separate Greek Commander will be appointed forthwith for these forces.
4. The British forces will be despatched as rapidly as shipping will permit to Piraeus and Volos.
5. The British forces will concentrate on the Aliakhmon position, on which it is intended that the Graeco–British forces should give battle
6. The command of all forces on the Aliakhmon position will be entrusted to Lieutenant-General Sir H. M. Wilson under the high command of General Papagos. The date on which General Wilson assumes his command will be settled by General Papagos in consultation with him, and will depend on the arrival of General Wilson's Headquarters and the establishment of his communications.

That night Dill and I sent a further telegram to the Prime Minister:

Military problem is essentially one of time and space.

Reports from Bulgaria suggest that the Germans may arrive on the Greek frontier in sufficient strength to deliver an attack during the next six or seven days. Rate of German advance will of course depend on the weather and the date of attack may also be affected by need of building up dumps of supplies and ammunition near the Greek frontier.

Resistance which Greek divisions can be expected to put up in prepared positions on Nestos–Rupel line should delay the Germans for some days. There will then be further advance of one hundred miles from Rupel Pass before contact is made on Aliakhmon position. Time required for this advance should be considerably increased by demolitions which Wilson will prepare as rapidly as possible.

Concentration of three Greek divisions on Aliakhmon position should be complete within five days. The seven battalions from Thrace require a further five or six days to complete concentration, Aliakhmon position itself needs considerable work on communications and defences.

Concentration of British forces on Aliakhmon position will be as follows:

Bulk of one armoured brigade and one New Zealand infantry brigade between 16th and 19th March. Bulk of a second New Zealand infantry brigade about 26th March. New Zealand infantry division should be complete in essential men and weapons by the end of March. Subsequent programme is not yet arranged.

All possible measures are being examined to speed up the programme including the use of Greek ships for transport of British forces from Egypt.

The question of bombing German communications in Bulgaria was discussed yesterday with the Greeks. Their attitude is that to avoid retaliation no attack should be made during concentration of Anglo–Greek forces. If, however, Germany attacks

Greece by land or air during this concentration, bombing will begin at once.

Thus the margin is narrow and the risk considerable. Nevertheless . . . this risk appears to us the least dangerous of the three possibilities with which we were faced.

★   ★   ★   ★   ★

By this time Dill and I felt that the die was cast. Not only had we an air force of nine squadrons in Greece with anti-aircraft guns and crews, but the administrative advance party of the land force had already arrived. The first convoy of troops was due to sail from Alexandria the next day, March 5th. Inevitably these decisions caused us much anxiety in Athens, where Dill and I and Longmore worried at them long and deeply. I decided that it would be invaluable to have a fresh mind upon the scene, in the clarity of whose judgment I had the greatest confidence. So I telegraphed to General Smuts, asking him whether he could come to meet me in Cairo, telling him of the choice of evils with which we were faced and the doubtful outcome of whatever decision we took. Smuts replied at once with characteristic courage that he was coming.

On reflection, I have no doubt that it was the political implications of withdrawing Greek troops from Macedonia which proved too much even for the stalwart intentions of the Greek Government. Possibly, if we had foreseen them, we could have dotted the i's and crossed the t's more fixedly at Tatoi; but I doubt if this precaution would have had the necessary consequences. To uncover Salonika, Greece's second greatest city, and expose the Macedonian plain to an unhindered German advance, was probably more than even this people, whose courage had been so superb, could have endured.

The truth was that the feebleness of Prince Paul's Yugoslav Government had been a bitter disappointment to the Greeks. The Prime Minister made this all too plain to me as soon as I saw him on March 2nd, while the King had no confidence that the men in power in Yugoslavia would take any firm decision. Campbell had come down from Belgrade at my request and saw Koryzis, but he could give him little comfort. He still thought it possible that

Prince Paul might privately have decided to help and advised me to tell him secretly of our plans for Greece. I therefore wrote a letter for Campbell to take back to Belgrade:

Athens, 3rd March, 1941

Sir,

Mr. Ronald Campbell has joined us here and has given me a full report of the situation in Yugoslavia and of Your Royal Highness's difficulties and anxieties. Believe me, I do most deeply sympathize with you and understand how you must feel as a trustee called upon to confront and take decisions which must affect the whole future life of your people.

As we see it, Germany's objective in the Balkans is to subdue Greece and to immobilize Turkey. If Germany could achieve these dual objects and in the course of so doing occupy Salonika and dominate the Straits, Yugoslavia would be at Germany's mercy. Yugoslavia's fate must then surely be like that of Roumania, bit by bit her independent national life would be choked out of her and then Italy would take her pound of flesh from the helpless victim. This seems clearly to be the inevitable sequence of events unless we can take steps together to prevent it, as I am confident that we can.

Germany has now made the first move to achieve these results. It has been made abundantly clear to me in my visits to Turkey and Greece that neither is prepared to be the dupe of German assurances, and I have no doubt that Turkey and Greece if attacked will resist by force.

As Mr. Campbell will have told you, my colleagues in London thought it advisable that I should come out here with Sir John Dill and discuss on the spot with General Wavell and our Greek and Turkish allies the decisions to be taken. As you know, Sir, I had much hoped to have a like conversation in secret with you, for I should then have been able to describe to you in person and in detail the decisions to which we have come and the steps which we propose to take to give them effect. In the circumstances Mr. Campbell will shortly be able to inform you of the decisions to which we have come.

To sum up, I am so certain that a passive Yugoslavia, once

completely surrounded, will be subjected to all the well-known German methods of bleeding and disruption, that I have no hesitation in urging you most earnestly to decide to resist this evil and to join with us and Greece in an attempt to withstand it. What, Sir, would the result of the other course be? To endure German rule now in its most contemptuous form, and at the end of the war to lie for many years under the evil after-effects of a German occupation, rendered all the more pernicious and disruptive because it has not been resisted. In such conditions the soul of a people must suffer.

In choosing the alternative to resist with us, hard though it may be for the moment, you and your people will at least know that you have done all in your power to avoid the far worse fate that has befallen Roumania and Bulgaria. You will then be able to face the future with the greater courage and hope, rooted as they will be in your own splendid traditions and brave deeds. Could this not be made plain to any who, in some parts of your country, fail to see matters in their true light?

Anthony Eden

I instructed Campbell to give the Prince Regent an outline of our plans to help the Greeks, including the fact that we were going to deploy our forces west of Salonika, which would be only temporarily covered by the Greek army; the successful defence of Salonika must therefore depend largely on Yugoslavia. I did not ask Prince Paul to commit himself blindly, but time was short. We would have been glad to discuss plans with the Yugoslavs if they had sent a staff officer to Athens at once. I also authorized Campbell to tell the Prince Regent that we thought that a case could be made at the peace conference for revising the Italo–Yugoslav frontier in Istria, if Yugoslavia were our ally. This, for what it was worth, was intended as something of a bait for the Croats and Slovenes.

★   ★   ★   ★   ★

These days in Athens were strained and unnatural. My visit was then publicly known and the crowds took every opportunity to cheer happily. I had to respond, while in my heart I felt wretchedly anxious at what the next weeks must bring. In one interval I visited a military hospital, preparing myself for sad sights of suffering, but these round-headed, dark-haired little soldiers were so lively, brave and confident after their Albanian victories, that they gave me heart.

Dill and I returned to Cairo on March 6th. Here we received telegrams from Mr. Churchill and the Chiefs of Staff expressing grave doubts about the wisdom of our decision to go on with the despatch of our troops to the Aliakhmon line. We discussed these with the three British Commanders-in-Chief. Although both Longmore and Cunningham were unhappy about the risk they foresaw of losing most of the convoy ships and most of our air forces in Greece, all three agreed that, despite the dangers involved, the decision taken in Athens was the only possible one and that we should go ahead. Dill said that the situation was grimmer than we had thought. All the same, he saw no alternative but to persist with our plans. If we could get into our positions before the Germans arrived, there was a good chance of holding them. If the Germans arrived first, it should be possible to withdraw the majority of our forces without great loss.

Wavell agreed with this. The results of success, he said, would be incalculable and might alter the whole aspect of the war. I said that if we withdrew from the operation now, we would have lost the last chance of bringing Yugoslavia into the war and the effect on Turkey could not be measured. We decided that I should send an interim reply to the Prime Minister saying that the question had been re-examined with the three Commanders-in-Chief and that we were unanimously agreed that, in spite of the heavy commitments and dangers involved, especially in view of our limited naval and air resources, the right decision had been taken in Athens.

Later in the evening, we had another discussion with Smuts and General Van Ryneveld, the South African Chief of General Staff, Lampson and the three Commanders-in-Chief. Smuts said that whatever we did, we were confronted with the gravest risks. After the recent change in our luck, he would be most reluctant to see a setback. He did not set much faith in possible action by either Turkey or Yugoslavia, which left the Greeks and ourselves. The Greeks had done better than could have been expected and the public opinion of the world was on their side. If we did not stand by them we should be held up to ignominy. But they had not carried out the arrangements made at Tatoi and time had been lost. The question was whether our troops could arrive on the Aliakhmon line soon enough and it seemed doubtful whether the four Greek divisions on the frontier could hold the German advance for long. We were faced with a dilemma, but it was too late for retreat. We had made a provisional arrangement and had started to carry it out, we could not now back out. If the weather held up the Germans, there was a good chance that we would be in sufficient strength on the Aliakhmon line in time to hold it. It might be said that a German victory in the Balkans would be a great setback to our cause, but the setback would probably be worse if we stood aside and did not help.

As the discussion proceeded, Wavell, Dill and Longmore explained the reasons for our decision. Smuts endorsed Dill's refusal to go up to the Bulgarian frontier. We were right to stick to a plan which was tactically sound and he repeated that he saw the greatest objections to our retracting now. I said that the work of the Royal Air Force had greatly helped the Greeks to resist the Italians and that I considered we had in fact been committed to help Greece once we had sent our squadrons over there.

One of the considerations which troubled me most was that such a large proportion of the British forces to be engaged would be Australian and New Zealand troops. But there was no way of avoiding this. Wavell told us at this meeting that he had informed General Freyberg and General Blamey of the change in the situation and of the greater dangers involved. Both of them, he reported, seemed to be ready to face these and neither had shown any sign of wanting to back out.

Smuts offered to provide another squadron of the South African Air Force from Kenya to relieve a further squadron from Egypt to go to Greece, and to press Mr. Churchill for more aircraft from England. After all, he said, if the Germans were sending air reinforcements to the Balkans they would have less to use against the United Kingdom, and he very much doubted whether they now meant to invade England.

Fortified by General Smuts' opinion, I sent the Prime Minister a telegram the next morning which fully rehearsed our discussions and conclusions since our return to Cairo and Smuts' arrival. Even before this, the War Cabinet had in fact taken their bleak decision in London, to accept our advice and assume responsibility for its outcome.

9

COUP D'ETAT
March–April 1941

Yugoslavia draws nearer to the Nazis — I again appeal to the Prince Regent — Meeting with M. Saraçoğlu in Cyprus — I give our Ambassador in Belgrade the signal — *Coup d'état* in Yugoslavia — Hitler has to postpone Operation "Barbarossa" — I return to Athens — General Papagos wants to change strategy again — The new Yugoslav Government wavers — Abortive meeting at Florina — A Russo–Yugoslav pact of friendship — The Germans invade Greece and Yugoslavia — Bad news from the Western Desert — The defence of Tobruk — Rommel's offensive

DILL AND I had originally planned to return home from Cairo soon after our second visit to Athens. Bad weather held us up and then we decided that it would be better to remain on the spot for as long as there was any chance that either of us could influence, or visit, Belgrade. I could not stop thinking of Yugoslavia. This was the country with the best and largest army in the Balkans and with an air force which, though made up from many makes of aircraft, far exceeded in total the strength of any other Balkan country, and indeed our own in that theatre of war.

On March 4th, while I was still in Athens, the Prince Regent had gone to Berchtesgaden to see Hitler and to be told that, if Yugoslavia did not secure her claim to an outlet to the Aegean in time, the opportunity would not come again.* Reports of this possibility had reached me through our Legation in Athens, though it was Göring whom the Prince Regent was then said to be visiting. I mentioned this one day when at luncheon with the King of Greece. One of Prince Paul's relations, who was present, indignantly denied the rumour and declared that the Prince had made up his mind to

---

* *Documents on German Foreign Policy, 1918–1945;* Series D, Vol. XII, No. 130.

stand with Britain and Greece, it was only the moves that were in doubt. Afterwards when we were alone, I expressed my regrets to the King if I had inadvertently cast suspicion where it was not deserved. He shook his head sadly, adding "I expect that your reports are only too true."

More arresting was the information which reached me from the Americans at the end of March: Hitler had also told the Prince Regent that he was going to attack Russia in June or July. This was a half-truth, for he had already laid his plans to launch "Barbarossa," as the operation for the invasion of Russia was called, in May.

On March 7th, the Yugoslav Government asked Hitler and Mussolini for assurances that their country's sovereignty and territorial integrity would be respected if it joined the Tripartite Pact. They tried to impose conditions: they should not be asked to give military help, no troops would pass through their country during the war and their "interests in a free outlet to the Aegean Sea through Salonika" would be taken into account in the reorganization of Europe.* The next ten days were spent in bargaining about these assurances, but Hitler would give no undertaking not to call for Yugoslav troops, except for the campaign against Greece.

Yugoslav contacts with us remained faint. Even when on March 8th Major Pericić, an officer of the Yugoslav General Staff, came to Athens, it was only to seek answers to seven questions. These he put at two meetings with General Papagos and our military representatives. They concerned the help we could give to Yugoslav forces retreating south to the Aegean and west to the Adriatic. He had nothing to say about Yugoslav plans. In reply Pericić was told that we would do all we could to remedy his country's deficiencies in equipment. He was also reminded that if the Yugoslavs would attack the Fascist forces in Albania, they could gain large stocks of equipment, make communications up and down the Adriatic much easier and release Greek troops and Greek and British air forces to fight the Germans.

Campbell, usefully backed by the United States Minister in Belgrade, continued his evocation of the Prince Regent and the leading Yugoslavs. On my instructions, he asked the Government to agree

* op. cit., No. 131.

to a visit from either Dill or myself. But once again, on March 15th, the answer came that a visit was not feasible. Nor did we hear a word of Yugoslav comment on Major Pericić's visit to Athens.

The Greek Government, while steadfast in their purpose to resist the Nazi attack, heavy as the odds must be, made a last effort to spare their country this more terrible ordeal. As we now know, they attempted an unofficial approach to the German Government, later followed by an official one, suggesting that Germany might take the initiative in mediating between Greece and Italy and so restore peace to the Balkans. But nothing of this kind was in Hitler's plans.* At the same time, Mussolini tried to thrust himself into events by launching a new offensive in Albania on March 9th. This failed, but the tired Greek army became still more extended and still less able to transfer troops to meet the impending German attack.

★　　★　　★　　★　　★

Dill and I had remained in Cairo and kept in close touch with Turkey. The Prime Minister agreed with our action. I telegraphed to him on March 15th:

> You will have seen . . . that I am doing all in my power to encourage Yugoslavia and to stiffen Turkey, so that she in her turn may stimulate Yugoslavia. The hand is an extraordinarily difficult one to play. Commanders-in-Chief, while anxious that Yugoslavia should fight with us, are of the opinion that Turkey's entry into the war at this stage would constitute a military liability which they do not wish to incur. You may be certain that we will not leave here until we are satisfied that we have done all that we can in the diplomatic and military spheres, but once that stage is reached, as it is likely to be about the middle of next week, we both wish to return home. There will then be nothing more that we can do and should need arise one or other of us can always come out again later.

* op. cit., Nos. 170, 179, 180, 189.

However, Dill and I did discuss with Longmore, Wavell and Lampson, the question of another visit to Ankara. The Commanders-in-Chief maintained their reluctance to see Turkey in the war. Only if a Turkish declaration of war proved essential to bring in the Yugoslavs, did Wavell think we should press for one. In this I am sure that he was right. We therefore agreed that I should arrange a political discussion with M. Saraçoğlu and try to get the Turkish Government to make a firm statement publicly against any further acts of aggression in the Balkans. We could then use this with the Yugoslavs.

While these arrangements were going forward, an Anglo–Turkish meeting became even more pointful when Campbell reported that the Yugoslavs were weakening. There was a danger, he thought, that their Government might be on the point of signing a non-aggression pact with Hitler. With Greek consent, I gave him authority to say that such a pact must include a German promise not to attack Salonika. This was not because we expected the Nazis to give, still less to keep, their word, but because such a request, which it was reasonable for the Greeks to insist upon, would be an obstacle to agreement between the Yugoslavs and the Germans.

On March 15th the Yugoslav Prime Minister told Campbell the Germans had suggested that the Yugoslavs should themselves take Salonika. According to his account, M. Cvetković had replied that for Yugoslavia, the best guarantee for Salonika's future was that it should remain in Greek hands. In fact, we now know that, on March 12th, the Yugoslavs had asked the Germans to guarantee them "territorial connexion" with the Aegean through Salonika.*

In yet another effort to influence the Prince Regent, I decided on March 17th to send a letter to him in Belgrade, by the hand of Mr. Terence Shone, who was then the much-trusted Minister in our Embassy in Cairo, but had previously served in Yugoslavia.

I gave Prince Paul an account of the decisions taken by His Majesty's Governments in the United Kingdom and the Dominions to strengthen the forces at the disposal of their Commanders in the Middle East, and told him that air reinforcements, in particular, were arriving in growing volume. The passage of the Lend-Lease bill would hasten the supply of material aid, including aircraft,

* op. cit., No. 156.

direct from the United States to the Middle East. After recounting
the progress of our East African campaign, I explained how the end
of Italian resistance in East Africa would release our naval, land
and air forces for operations elsewhere and continued:

> The attitude that you and your Government have taken up
> means that the German military authorities must take into ac-
> count that a further aggression in the Balkans may bring them
> into conflict with Yugoslavia, Greece and Turkey, backed by
> all the resources that we can bring to bear. It seems to me of
> the first importance to hold this position, for as long as you,
> Sir, and your Government can do this there is always a chance
> of checking the German threat to the independence of Yugo-
> slavia, Greece and Turkey before ever that threat develops into
> military action.
>
> I feel sure that there can be no vestige of doubt in your mind
> that to come to an arrangement with Germany now would be
> to sacrifice the strong position you have built up and would
> lead step by step to Yugoslavia suffering the fate that has al-
> ready overcome Roumania and Bulgaria.

After recalling the "valuable munitions of war and supplies of
all kinds" awaiting the Yugoslavs in Mussolini's Albanian protectorate, where Italian morale was low and, "only two nights ago, the
Fleet Air Arm sank a ship in Valona Harbour," I summed up this
part of my message: "It is indeed certain that with the passage of
time Italy will become an increasingly heavy burden upon Germany," and concluded:

> I was very sorry not to be able to see Your Royal Highness
> and to discuss all these matters with you. Apart from all politi-
> cal considerations, it would have been like old times to have
> had a full talk together. I know how difficult it is to arrange
> this, but I am optimistic enough to hope that events may yet
> make it possible.
>
> I am particularly sorry that Sir John Dill has not had an
> opportunity to meet your General Staff. . . . If there were still

any possibility of your Government being able to agree to receive a visit by Sir John Dill and another Staff Officer from here, Dill, Wavell and I are convinced that such a talk would be of the greatest value to both our countries.

Mr. Shone, who bears this letter, is already well known to Your Royal Highness and he is fully acquainted with our minds too. I therefore hope that you will find it possible to see him. He bears with him to you, Sir, the thoughts and heartfelt good wishes of us all.

The Prince Regent's reply, after his talk with Shone, though very friendly, showed a continuing repugnance towards any meeting. I was more sorry than surprised, but at least I had done all I could to persuade the Prince to resolve his dilemma, cruel and admittedly none of his own making, in the way which would best have served his people and his dynasty.

★ ★ ★ ★ ★

Wavell and Dill reconnoitred the Western Desert on March 17th. I had wanted to go with them, but Dill was firm that the advice which they would have to give was military and that it would be better for me and them if I had no part in it. If I went, it would be argued that I had influenced them. In the event, they felt no uneasiness as a result of what they saw.

On the morning of March 18th I flew to Cyprus. The arrangements had been made in the utmost secrecy, with the result that when I had been in the air a few minutes, the pilot sent me back a message. "Where to, Sir?" I arrived in the island just before noon, landing a few minutes ahead of M. Saraçoğlu. We motored together to Government House, where we went into conference, Knatchbull-Hugessen and Pierson Dixon helping me. We discussed the Yugoslav attitude and Saraçoğlu told me the opinion of the Turkish General Staff, that the Germans would not risk attacking Greece if Yugoslavia stood firm and fortified the Monastir Gap. He argued that this might divert the German attack on to Turkey, but added that the Turks were prepared to risk this.

Having said so much, Saraçoglu could hardly refuse my suggestion that his Government should send an encouraging message to
Belgrade. The form of the message, however, melted in discussion
from a declaration that Turkey would regard an attack on Salonika
as a *casus belli* if Yugoslavia would do the same, to a message suggesting an exchange of views about the threat to Salonika. I made
sure that the news of this message was conveyed at once to the
Yugoslavs, but in the end the Turks never delivered it, pretexting
the political uncertainties in Belgrade.

In one particular Saraçoğlu gave me better news. When I had
seen Sir Stafford Cripps in Ankara, we had agreed on a plan to try
to improve relations between Turkey and Moscow. Cripps had
followed this through, telling M. Vyshinsky of Turkish fears of
Soviet intentions. As a result, Saraçoğlu gave me the text of an
assurance his Government had received from the Russians, which
said that if Turkey were attacked, she could count on Russia's
"complete understanding and neutrality." The Turks had replied
to the same effect and the assurances were published a few days
later.

After luncheon, Saraçoğlu and I went for a drive about the island.

March 18th: A long talk with S. both there and back. He is
absolutely confident of a British victory and regards the fact that
Hitler is now concentrating on secondary objective in the Balkans
as proof of it. Even if he overruns Greece and Turkey, Hitler can
obtain no decision that way. Hitler should make a most generous
offer of peace, even telling us to state our own terms, and seek
thereby to weaken will of our public and American, but he was
not the man to do this. He was concerned about aircraft position
and I told him that I was moving heaven and earth to get more
sent out here. It would help us enormously if we could gain a
few more weeks. S. thought that we should, even another month.

The next morning the Turkish Foreign Minister and I left Government House to drive by way of Nicosia to the aerodrome. All
went well for a mile or so, but in the square in the centre of the
town the cheering crowd was so thick that it brought our car completely to a stop. I became rather anxious, because I felt responsi-

ble for Saraçoğlu's safety and he was a sitting target for a fanatic or enemy agent. At that moment there was a cry above the cheering and a spout of warm blood splashed over the front of the car and the windscreen. I could not guess what had happened, but told the driver that as the main road was blocked by the press of people we should take another to the aerodrome. This we did and we would not have got through the throng otherwise, for the Governor and the Ambassador, who were in a pilot car, had to take refuge in a police station. The blood turned out to be that of a sheep sacrificed in honour of my guest:*

Saraçoğlu was, I think, quite pleased and it was certainly an amazing spontaneous demonstration which took the Governor by surprise, he having expected only a few groups of people clapping!

★   ★   ★   ★   ★

While we were in Cyprus events moved rapidly to a crisis in Yugoslavia. On the eve of my arrival in the island, M. Cincar-Marković told the German Minister that the Crown Council had decided in principle to join the Tripartite Pact; but the details of the German and Italian assurances to be given to Yugoslavia were not yet settled.† Nor were they settled in the country itself, for when the decision came before the full Cabinet on March 21st, three Serb Ministers resigned. The next four days were filled with Yugoslav attempts to postpone their fate and a German ultimatum on March 22nd giving them until the 25th to sign.‡

So uncertain was the outcome that, on the day of the ultimatum, a German High Command directive for the operations against Greece still left open the possibility of a Yugoslav advance on Salonika. Hitler's original orders had laid down the occupation of the Greek mainland north of the Aegean as the first objective and the rest of the country as might be necessary. Greek resistance and the arrival of British forces were already influencing Nazi

* Full Circle, page 394.
† Documents on German Foreign Policy, 1918–1945; Series D, Vol. XII, Nos. 173, 175.
‡ op. cit., No. 192.

plans. The new orders said that more troops were to be made available for the occupation of the mainland, including the Peloponnese, and some of the islands. This could only be done by using forces hitherto earmarked for the attack on the Soviets. One of the five prongs of the advance, that in the south from Roumania, was therefore cut out of "Barbarossa." *

On our side I was desperately searching for ways and means to encourage the national spirit which I was sure was strong in Yugoslavia. I knew from Cripps that Moscow and Belgrade had recently discussed a military alliance and, on March 22nd, I instructed him to find out whether the Russians would be willing to encourage the Yugoslavs to resist. Although Vyshinsky did not like talking about this with Cripps, he took the suggestion seriously. While explaining to the Yugoslav Minister in Moscow that the Soviet Government could do nothing in the matter, as the issue seemed to be settled already, he added that if this turned out not to be true, the Soviets would be ready for further discussion.

By now Belgrade was rife with rumours, for the people of Yugoslavia, especially the Serbs, were becoming increasingly incensed at the prospect of being handed over by surrender to Hitler and Mussolini. We had for some time been supporting one of the Serb parties, which had a Minister in the Government. He had taken the lead in resigning over the Pact. On March 21st, Campbell telegraphed to ask me whether he should threaten to break off relations with Yugoslavia if the Government signed the Tripartite Pact, and so encourage the opposition to overthrow the Government and annul their signature. If I agreed, the Ambassador wanted to know when would it suit me, from the military point of view, for this to be done.

I replied at once to Campbell's inquiry that I did not favour a threat to break off relations, for I had never known such methods to produce results. He was, I considered, doing invaluable work on the spot and we should only lose by withdrawing him. As for a *coup d'état,* I needed to know more about its practical possibilities, because such events could hardly be improvised. My telegram continued:

* op. cit., No. 195.

How do you assess possibilities of success as result of your soundings? I agree that upon present information suggested *coup* would have to be staged at the moment of reaction caused by signature and this may be very soon. . . .

From the military point of view it is more important that Yugoslavia should deny passage, if necessary by force, to German troops than that she should declare war if Greece is invaded through Bulgaria. Germans will certainly wish to attack Greece, either through Petrich and valley of Vardar, which would turn Greek positions on Rupel Pass, or through Monastir Gap, which would threaten allied position and imperil Greek army in Albania. Advance through Monastir Gap is the danger which we most fear. So long as Yugoslavia is resolute to refuse passage, it should now be difficult for the Germans to direct the attack on Greece with good prospects of success. Doubt as to Yugoslav attitude on this score is most probably a cause of present German quiescence.

Much will depend upon the Commander of Southern Yugoslav army. Have you any contacts with him or information as to his attitude? So long as he refuses passage to Germans he is our friend. What would be effect on him of a *coup d'état*? While I would stop at nothing to ensure that Yugoslavs fight to deny passage to Monastir Gap, I do not yet know enough to estimate the effect of a *coup* or chance of ensuring this.

But the next day, when I learnt of the malleable situation in Belgrade caused by the resignation of the three Ministers, I telegraphed again to Campbell, giving him authority to act on his own if he had no time to consult me. I said:

. . . In considering [the chances of a successful *coup d'état*] you should bear in mind that rather than allow Yugoslavia to slip by stages into German orbit, we are prepared to risk precipitating German attack. . . .

On the morning of March 24th, I heard from Campbell that Hitler had delivered an ultimatum to Yugoslavia to sign the

Tripartite Pact. Since there was clearly nothing to be done with the Prince Regent, I sent a telegram to Campbell recognizing this and adding:

> You are authorized now to proceed at your discretion by any means at your disposal to move leaders and public opinion to understanding of realities and to action to meet the situation.
> You have my full authority for any measures that you may think it right to take to further change of Government or regime, even by *coup d'état*.
> Any new Government formed as a result of these events and prepared to resist German demands would have our full support. You may secretly so inform any prospective leaders in whom you have confidence.

Before leaving Cairo I had to reply with more restraint to suggestions from Campbell about promising military supplies.

> As those with whom you are in touch will be aware, British forces are now established in Greece. These forces include anti-tank, anti-aircraft and armoured units. Yugoslav army, if they fight with us, will thus be fighting side by side with British forces armed with equipment mentioned in your telegram.
> It would be impossible to transfer this equipment from our troops to Yugoslav troops, nor would the latter without a period of training, as suggested, make effective use of these highly specialized weapons. Furthermore there is no other source from which we can at present supply equipment of this nature. . . .

★ ★ ★ ★ ★

Having done all that it lay in our power to do from Cairo, the C.I.G.S. and I began our homeward flight on March 25th. As we took off from the Nile, the Yugoslav Ministers were in Vienna signing the Tripartite Pact, and receiving from Hitler and Ciano assurances that "in the new settlement of the frontiers in the Balkans the interests of Yugoslavia in a territorial connection with the Aegean Sea, through the extension of her sovereignty to the

city and harbour of Salonika, are to be taken into account." *
This was black treachery at the expense of the menaced Greek
neighbour. The Yugoslav Government's surrender to Hitler's demands might be excused because its ruler and members were weak
and spiritless, the additional demand for an ally's great port and
rich territory cannot be.

Talking with Ciano after the ceremony, Hitler said that it was
satisfactory that Yugoslavia's position was now defined. If her
attitude had still been uncertain, an operation against Greece
"would have been an exceedingly irresponsible undertaking militarily." † This was just what we wanted to make it. Hitler also
admitted to Ciano that internal conditions in Yugoslavia could
become complicated again. So indeed they proved to be.

Sir John Dill and I were in Malta on our homeward way, but
still battling with bad weather, as these schemes were mounted.

March 27th: Spent a stimulating morning with R.A.F. First to
see Hurricane pilots who were the centre of much activity, landing and taking off all round us. A splendid lot of men, most of
them volunteers. Particularly impressed by squadron leader
named Lambert. Then to Luqa where we viewed the damage
and the Wellington graveyard which is certainly a most depress
ing sight. Maynard is an enthusiast for pens for his cattle, but
I should judge that mortality among Wellingtons at Luqa must
always be heavy.

On the way back called on tank detachment. . . . The men
seemed cheerful, though wishing that they were in Greece.

Just before luncheon local press telephoned to say that there
had been *coup d'état* in Belgrade, Government out, Paul fled
and a pro-ally administration established. Magnificent news
which so delighted me that I almost hugged Lady Dobbie! Col-
lected Dill and Service Chiefs and we agreed that right course
was to leave for Athens by Sunderland tonight.

Complication that Italian fleet is out and something of a naval
engagement is expected off Crete at dawn. We should, however,
pass Crete long before this.

* op. cit., No. 205.
† *Ciano's Diary, 1939–1943.*

This turned out to be the Battle of Cape Matapan.

The national pride of the Yugoslavs had revolted against the shame of their country's submission to the Axis. Their anger turned against the dictatorial, mainly Serbian, regime which had brought them to this pass. Campbell meanwhile did everything in his power to encourage the more robust among the politicians and the military through his many useful contacts. His authority would have been negligible if there had not already been evidence that Britain was redeeming her pledge to Greece.

In the early hours of March 27th the *coup d'état* took place, the young King Peter was proclaimed and a new Government containing Ministers of all the Yugoslav nationalities set up. The presence of British and Dominion forces in Greece had directly influenced events in Yugoslavia.

Hitler's reaction was fury. By mid-afternoon he had announced to Göring, Ribbentrop, the High Command and Army staffs his decision to "smash Yugoslavia militarily and as a state." No inquiries about foreign policy were to be made of the new Government and no ultimatum presented; any Yugoslav assurances would be taken note of, but could not be trusted. The attack was to begin as soon as the troops could be ready. It must be carried out with such strong forces that Yugoslavia would collapse in the shortest time; Turkey would thus be deterred from intervening. Politically, too, the blow was to be "inexorable." Hitler had already that morning promised Hungary and Bulgaria their share of the body, the Croats would be given political autonomy and Italy would get the Adriatic coast.

All this entailed another and still graver decision. The date for launching "Barbarossa," Hitler decreed, would have to be postponed for up to four weeks.* It was in fact postponed for more than five weeks, from May 15th to June 22nd. Although we could not know it then, this in itself justified the sufferings of Greeks and Yugoslavs, British and Dominion troops in the final reckoning. Karl Ritter, German Foreign Office liaison officer with the High Command, later summed up the consequences of the postponement in these words:

* *Documents on German Foreign Policy, 1918–1945*; Series D, Vol. XII, Nos. 217, 215, 216.

This delay cost the Germans the winter battle before Moscow and it was there the war was lost.*

He had reason to know. The postponement of "Barbarossa" on account of Hitler's decision to attack Yugoslavia was admitted by the Russian historian V. T. Fomin in 1957.†

Before we flew off from Malta I telegraphed to Campbell:

Warmest congratulations on your share of this most happy turn of events.

Please telegraph, to reach me on arrival at Athens, your appreciation of the situation and your views on how we can best help. What we most desire is to establish contact with members of new Government and with army and air force leaders. From every point of view, by far the most valuable means of doing this would be by meeting in Belgrade and I earnestly hope that it may now be possible to arrange this. Failing this, meeting might be held at some place in southern Serbia. If visit by us to Yugoslavia is not practicable, I shall be glad to see Yugoslavia representatives with sufficient powers in Athens and I have no doubt that Greek Government would likewise welcome them.

While change of Government in Yugoslavia must have disjointed the Germans' plans, it is of first importance that we should make the utmost use of the time thereby gained to concert our own plans against all eventualities.

March 28th: As we were leaving about 1 a.m. wire arrived from Winston suggesting that we should leave for Cairo, so we have had much same reaction. Good flight. At dawn suddenly dived to sea level on sighting aircraft. Went up to see what had happened and found we were off Crete! Pilot had apparently not been told anything of Italian fleet or of report that Italian aircraft were to make a dawn assault on island. We flew on quite

---

* D. C. Poole: "Light on Nazi Foreign Policy"; *Foreign Affairs,* XXV, October 1946.

† *Voprosui istorii,* No. 6, June 1957.

happily, aircraft turned out to be Swordfish [of the Fleet Air
Arm] and we saw no other. Sat in second pilot's seat all the way
from this point to Athens, flying myself a small part of the way.
Dawn breaking over the islands, very beautiful in a soft grey
light with many clouds. There is a transparency about the light
here which cannot be described or painted.

Palairet met us on arrival. After a bath held a conference at
which Dill, Wilson, Palairet, airman and Admiral were present.

★   ★   ★   ★   ★

One development upon my return disturbed me. General Wilson
told Dill and myself that General Papagos now had the idea of
moving the Greek divisions which were on the Aliakhmon line up
to the frontier again, leaving our forces alone on the line. He had,
however, been unable to get into touch with the nearest Yugoslav
army commanders and neither he nor we knew what the Yugoslav
intentions were. I telegraphed to Campbell that Dill and I wanted
a meeting with a representative of the new Yugoslav Government
at the earliest possible moment.

Later in the morning we saw the Greek Prime Minister and
Papagos. The latter now had an ambitious plan for forming a
continuous front from the Adriatic to the Black Sea. To make this
possible he proposed joint Greek and Yugoslav action to clean up
Albania, and to ask the Turks to take over the defence of western
Thrace. He also wanted to move all available British and Greek
forces forward into eastern Macedonia, on the supposition that we
should be obliged to defend Salonika if the Yugoslavs came in.
I pointed out that we still did not know what the Yugoslavs were
going to do and that we must first try to make arrangements with
them. We could then see about the Turks, but I did not think that
they would be inclined to fight for Salonika. The Turkish Government had so far failed to take any initiative with the Yugoslavs. Dill
and Wilson supported me, underlining that we must not advance
from the Aliakhmon position until we knew Yugoslav intentions.
There for the moment the matter rested, no move being immediately ordered.

In the evening I had a conversation with the King of the Hellenes, who was very cheerful about Greek morale. He said that his people now felt they could take on anybody, but he was not very confident about what might happen in Yugoslavia. It would be very difficult, he thought, to bring the new Government to early and definite decisions. We were soon to learn the wisdom of this judgment.

In the first flush of enthusiasm after the *coup*, the new Yugoslav Prime Minister, General Simović, had sent a message to the British Air Attaché in Belgrade to say that the army was now being fully mobilized and would be concentrated in the south, and that an attack on the Italians in Albania was imminent. A statement was being issued that Yugoslavia remained faithful to her policy of neutrality, but this was only to gain time. The implication in this telegram, that the Yugoslav army was not already fully mobilized, disturbed me because it was contrary to the impression conveyed to us more than once by the previous Government, that the Yugoslavs had already taken this action, as the Turks had done many months before.

Two days later Yugoslav policy was already being toned down. The General now told Campbell that the Government were not going to denounce the Tripartite Pact, although they would not ratify it, if it needed ratification. Salonika, the General stated, was a vital Yugoslav interest and if it were attacked the Yugoslavs would attack the Germans in Bulgaria and the Italians in Albania; but they would not make a public declaration of their intentions. Campbell thought that the new Government would resent any assumption on our part that they had definitely ranged themselves on the side of the democracies. This backing and filling would not have mattered so much if we had had time to straighten out our joint plans for defence, but I was sure that we could not have more than a few days to spare before Hitler's blow fell. Despite our efforts, we failed to bring home to the new Yugoslav Government the degree of their peril.

March 29th: A disappointing day. Shone should have left about noon and reached us about 4 p.m. but at luncheon we learnt he had crashed near Salonika, sabotage being suspected. Nobody hurt, but relief plane had to be sent. Meanwhile message came that he bore satisfactory news, only to be followed later by message that hot water bottles were needed and position not so good.

Shone arrived about 7 p.m. and gave us his account. P.M. had right ideas, but has many troublesome politicians in his large Cabinet. He should be able to bring them along, but hitch over my visit is typical of what we must expect. Shone brought answer "Yes," Jevtić [the Foreign Minister] put a spoke in and P.M. went back on his acceptance. Maddening.

March 30th: On reflection during night decided essential was to establish contact, so telegraphed Ronnie [Campbell] to return to charge, and if they would not have me, to accept Dill if he could get this.

March 31st: Yugoslavs accepted Dill and he left for Belgrade. Work and conversations in Athens.

Dill and I agreed what he should tell the Yugoslavs, General Papagos concurring. Our forces, he would say, were consolidating on the Aliakhmon line, but we understood that the Yugoslavs would wish Salonika to be defended. The city was now covered by Greek forces and we would strengthen these, if we were assured that Yugoslavia would undertake to fight in the event of a German attack on Greece and, in particular, to act against enemy communications in the upper Struma valley. The Yugoslavs should also co-operate with the Greeks in clearing Mount Beles west of the Rupel Pass and attack the Italians in Albania from the north and east. Dill would suggest staff talks between the Yugoslavs, the Greeks and ourselves, and would point out that since political decisions would also have to be taken, it was very desirable that I, too, should be asked to Belgrade.

I spent the afternoon with [Air Vice-Marshal John] D'Albiac [Air Officer Commanding in Greece] seeing his squadrons. A splendid lot of men as R.A.F. always are. I wish to God that we had a fair proportion of them out here. Air Ministry have been remiss in not keeping a steady flow going by sea.

This was perhaps an impatient judgment, delivered from the receiving end.

April 1st: Message from Dill showing good news at start, later qualified, but there are to be some staff talks at Florina [on the Greek–Yugoslav frontier] on 3rd, which shows some progress.

★ ★ ★ ★ ★

When Sir John Dill met General Simović, General Ilić the Minister of War and the acting Chief of the General Staff in Belgrade on the evening of March 31st, he found them worried about the internal situation of the country and determined to avoid provoking a Nazi assault. On both these grounds they refused to take any action in Albania before a German attack on themselves, which they thought more probable than one on Greece. They were quite ready to hold staff talks, however, and agreed to sign a brief statement saying that if Yugoslavia were attacked by Germany, the British Government would give her all the aid in their power and that, if the Germans attacked Greece and not Yugoslavia, the Yugoslav Government would join with us in giving Greece all the aid in their power. The Yugoslavs asked for air support from our bases in Greece and for war material. Dill inquired what was happening about the Tripartite Pact and was told that the Yugoslavs regarded it as having lapsed, but were leaving it in suspense.

Next morning, however, the General Staff refused to agree to the statement Dill had prepared, without putting in an amendment limiting Yugoslav help to Greece to the case of a German attack west of the Struma. Dill in turn refused to accept this and asked to see Simović again. He now found the Prime Minister quite unwilling to sign anything that would commit the Yugoslav Government. He said that if he asked his Government to accept such obligations, or if I came to Belgrade, there would be a split and the home front would disintegrate.

No other Ministers knew of Dill's visit. The C.I.G.S. had already discovered that the General Staff did not know his identity and thought that he was one of Wilson's divisional commanders. The staff talks, now fixed for April 3rd, the Prime Minister said, could only be to exchange views and must not lead to a military convention. Simović added that he could do no more unless the Government changed their mind or the Germans attacked Yugoslavia or

Salonika. Even an attack on Salonika would only bring in the Yugoslavs if it passed the Struma.

April 2nd: Dill arrived back about 10.30, fairly satisfied with his talks, though as so often happens in the Balkan lands, second thoughts meant a retreat from first positions bravely taken up.

★ ★ ★ ★ ★

Meanwhile the consequent movements of German troops were soon revealed to us. On March 30th Mr. Churchill sent me his judgment on the situation:

> My reading is that the bad man concentrated very large armoured forces etc. to overawe Yugo and Greece and hoped to get former, or both, without fighting. The moment he was sure Yugo was in the Axis he moved three of the five panthers [Panzer divisions] towards the Bear, believing that what was left would be enough to finish Greek affair. However, Belgrade revolution upset this picture and caused orders for north-west move to be arrested in transit. This can only mean in my opinion intention to attack Yugo at earliest or alternatively act against the Turk. It looks as if heavy forces will be used in Balkan peninsula and that Bear will be kept waiting a bit. Furthermore these orders and counter-orders in their relation to the Belgrade *coup* seem to reveal magnitude of design both towards south-east and east. This is the clearest indication we have had so far.

When I received this telegram, I discussed it with Dill and asked what he would do as a soldier if he were in Hitler's position. He said that if the Nazis had made up their mind that a conflict between them and Russia was inevitable, then, from the purely military standpoint, they would be wise to move now rather than next year, despite any withdrawal of forces they might have to make for the Balkans.

April 2nd: Greek P.M. and Papagos came round, when we agreed that Dill and I and P. should go to Florina for talks, but D. and I would not appear.

Mystified during day by telegram from Wavell which, when referring to reluctance to send staff officer to our talks, speaks of enemy attack in Western Desert. We know nothing of this from any other source.

General Wilson, with whom Dill and I spoke of this report, was not perturbed, for he considered that our dispositions ought to enable us to deal with it. "We should have them where we want them," was his comment, but he could not know what changes had been made since he left, particularly in the location of the armoured division.

Caught train in Athens at 5 p.m. Was rather late and horrified to find red carpet and large crowd for a departure which I had thought secret. Travelled through superbly beautiful scenery which held me entranced until nightfall. This country is much lovelier than anything I had ever imagined.

April 3rd: Woken up at 6 a.m. after a very poor night by Freyberg climbing on the train at Katerini. Sat with him and Dill and Wilson while train wound itself along the front. Much work has clearly been done, and the position is naturally very strong.

Reached our destination, a few miles beyond Edessa, about noon. Dill and I got off there and train carried others to Florina. Saw a cruiser tank battalion who are having trouble with their tracks. . . .

Saw some medium gunners. Very fit and soldierly and cheerful. Talked to the men and it turned out that they had been at Beaulieu camp with us in 1939.

Even more beautiful than yesterday in scenery and weather. Lunched by roadside overlooking a lake which was a softer coloured and less sophisticated Annecy.

Drove on in afternoon to Edessa, [Brig. H. V. S.] Charrington's [Armoured] Brigade Headquarters and a picturesque old Turkish town with numerous cascades tumbling down the mountain side. Scenery still as glorious as ever. On to a village ten miles further east when we saw Rangers [King's Royal Rifle Corps] and Northumberland Hussars. . . . All in best of spirits.

Back to Edessa to learn that Jugs had not turned up and train had gone on to frontier in hope of contacting them. After a tortuous journey over the worst of tracks, reached frontier station only to find train was a mile further on. Eventually our pilot train came back to fetch us and we clambered aboard to find everybody in a bad temper after a day of futile waiting.

Jugs eventually arrived 10.30 and left at 2 a.m. Conference patchy and no definite plans laid.

General Janković, the chief Yugoslav representative, was only authorized to discuss certain points about common action in the event of an attack on Salonika, and the plan he put forward was based on such faulty information about the size and dispositions of the British and Greek forces that it could not be used. When General Wilson insisted on being allowed to reconnoitre the Doiran–Strumica area where the plan suggested our forces should concentrate, Janković could only promise to refer back to Belgrade. He gave the same reply when General Papagos suggested that army and air force representatives should be sent to Athens to continue the conversations. He refused to give any information about the disposition of the Yugoslav forces, except in the south-east, where there were four divisions, and on the Albanian frontier, where there were also four. Although we knew that these were forty thousand strong and therefore twice the size of an ordinary division, General Janković emphasized that the Yugoslav divisions were not designed to repel an armoured attack.

Meanwhile a telegram from Campbell told me that the Yugoslav Government were trying to renew contact with the German and Italian Governments, in order, they told Campbell, to gain time to finish their preparations. I did not suppose that this manœuvre would achieve anything.

★ ★ ★ ★ ★

During the week since the *coup* I, and the Foreign Office at home, had made several attempts to induce the Turkish Government to give the Yugoslav Government political support. I telegraphed to our Ambassador at Ankara:

. . . while the attitude of the Greeks is steadfast and that of Yugoslavia improves, Turkish policy becomes increasingly equivocal.

These equivocations, I wrote:

> may be due as you maintain, to military unpreparedness. I have myself full confidence in the loyalty of Minister for Foreign Affairs and in the intentions of the President of Republic, but are you certain that there are no other malign influences at work? . . .
>
> It is common ground that strategically Turkey's role is to remain on the defensive. But we have never agreed that politically she should play a negative part. . . .

The new Yugoslav Government now asked the Turks to receive a staff officer and inquired whether they would regard an attack on Salonika as a *casus belli*. M. Saraçoğlu asked Knatchbull-Hugessen for advice on how to deal with this awkward question. He was in favour of consultation with the Yugoslavs and well aware that a definite statement that Turkey would not automatically go to war over Salonika would have a very depressing effect on them. On the other hand he could not lead them to suppose that Turkey would fight in the event of such an attack. Hugessen consulted me and I replied:

> . . . Best contribution Turks could make at the moment would be (a) to create a diversion by troop movements on Turco–Bulgarian frontier and (b) to assure Yugoslav Government that in the event of a German attack on Yugoslavia directed towards Salonika, Turkey would at least declare war.
>
> I do not ask Turkish Government to undertake offensive action in these circumstances, since limitation of Turkey's present capacity for offensive action is well understood between us. . . .

The Turkish Government refused to accept these suggestions and were unconvinced by any arguments in favour of political action. The knowledge that we were anxious to avoid any further commitments was a handy pretext for their attitude.

One consequence of the Belgrade *coup d'état* was that discussions were once more opened between Soviet Russia and Yugoslavia. A pact of friendship was actually signed on April 5th, a few hours before the German attack and was no doubt intended as a gesture of encouragement to the Yugoslavs. Yet it was puzzling that Stalin, who had hitherto shown himself so prudent to avoid any move likely to antagonize Hitler, should suddenly have taken so defiant, if ineffective, a step. It must have formed another item in the score that Hitler was chalking up against the Kremlin. This was, indeed, the one specific example of the "hostile policy of the Soviet Government toward Germany" cited by Ribbentrop in his final interview with the Soviet Ambassador, Mr. Vladimir Dekanozov, in the early hours of June 22nd.*

Later in the war, I asked Stalin why he had made this move. His answer was that there was not really any new risk in it, because the Russians were fairly sure by then that they were going to be attacked. Secondly, he wished to make a gesture of solidarity at that time to a fellow Slav nation. The first part of his explanation did not satisfy me, because I remembered the Soviet reluctance, shown many times by Maisky, to give any credence to reports that they were going to be attacked. Though this could have been only a front, I am not convinced that it was. It looks as if this were a rare occasion when Stalin allowed his head to be influenced by his heart.

★   ★   ★   ★   ★

April 4th: Report of attack morning 5th [the attack on Greece and Yugoslavia took place on April 6th]. Since nothing could be done further, trains started back at 2 a.m. and, urged on by me, contrived to reach Larissa at noon. Flew on to Athens, where I found telegram from Winston with a "prayer" to go to Cairo at once. We were most reluctant, and telegraphed accordingly, but decided anyway to await his reply.

As the evening wore on, more and more alarming telegrams arrived from Archie [Wavell, about Cyrenaica]. Most disturbed by them. Either his Intelligence has greatly underestimated German strength or something has gone badly wrong with his own operations. Failure of armoured brigade is particularly difficult to understand, though there are reports of mechanical defects.

April 5th: Awake most of the night turning these anxious

* *Documents on German Foreign Policy, 1918–1945;* Series D, Vol. XII, No. 664.

thoughts over in my mind. In weighing the balance of risks in sending help to Greece, not one of the military ever expressed doubt as to ability to hold in the west. The anxiety was all for those going to Greece. But Egypt is the base upon which everything depends, and to lose it would be worst calamity. In circumstances, decided I would return via Egypt today and spend night in Cairo.

Woke Dill up about 7 a.m. and put these proposals to him. He agreed. We summoned D'Albiac, made other preparations and left, miserably, by air for Cairo about 1 p.m. To kill my thoughts I flew the Lockheed myself from Crete to Alexandria. Difficult because weather was hazy and all had to be done by instruments, as at night. Hurricane intercepted us at Alexandria, and did a victory roll when they recognized our machine.

Miles [Lampson] and [Air Marshal Arthur] Tedder [Deputy Air Officer Commanding-in-Chief Middle East] met us with information that position was less serious than it had appeared. Archie joined us later at Embassy and brought us more disturbing news. There is still no accurate information of whereabouts of our armoured troops. All the same, Archie does not want either to stop the Poles or to recall cruisers [tanks] from Greece. Latter would in any event have been most difficult and if the reports of a German offensive tomorrow are correct, almost impossible.

April 6th: After a slightly better night, up early and went to Gezira for a swim. News reached us while there of German invasion of Greece and attack on Jugs, as foretold.

Some consultations with Archie and Dill, when I listened to a rehearsal of pros and cons of making a stand at Tobruk. Full conference in afternoon when three C.-in-C's, Dill and Arthur Smith rediscussed the stand at Tobruk. Arguments well put by Wavell and alternatives exhaustively examined. There is no obvious choice but as discussion proceeded, a stand at Tobruk gradually emerged as favourite. Both Longmore and Cunningham supported this conclusion for their own services. Doubt is whether effective arrangements for a stand there can be made in time.

Late in evening Wavell came in with grave telegram from

Neame advising preparations for stand further back if Tobruk cannot be held. He was without information of recent events at Mekili which has been attacked. First attack repulsed. There is clearly much confusion in our commands, due in the main to a breakdown of communications, as occurred in France last year. . . .

April 7th: Sat up till early hours discussing situation. A wretched night and an early talk with Dill who told me that liaison officer had just returned with a terrible tale of muddle about Msus [half-way between Agedabia and Mekili].

It seemed that the local commander, on information which turned out to be false, blew up the dump at Msus prematurely. When our armoured brigade fell back on it to refuel, there was nothing for them and many were immobilized.

The defeat in the Western Desert in the spring of 1941 was not, of course, caused by the sudden removal of troops to Greece against the advice of the military commanders, but was due to a faulty appreciation by the command of the speed and strength with which Rommel could mount an offensive west of Benghazi. There was also a serious lack of experienced desert commanders in the forward area when the fighting began. Wilson had been withdrawn for Greece, O'Connor was commanding in Egypt and 7th Armoured Division, under Creagh, was resting. By the time the men who knew the desert and had proved themselves in handling armour had reached the scene of action, the losses and consequent disorganization had caused terrible chaos.

Later in morning went round to see Archie who had received report from [Brigadier A. F.] Harding, B.G.S., that O'Connor and Neame* were missing. Rest of report confused but not wholly bad. . . . Mekili apparently still in our hands. [Maj.-Gen. J. D.] Lavarack [commanding 7th Australian Division] was there. I was

* Lieutenant-General Neame took over as G.O.C.-in-C. Cyrenaica when General Wilson was appointed to command the British force in Greece. Lieutenant-General Sir R. O'Connor was commanding British troops in Egypt. On April 2nd General Wavell sent for General O'Connor with the intention of putting him in command in Cyrenaica, but then decided to leave General Neame in command with General O'Connor to help and advise him.

much impressed by his calm and grip of situation and readiness to take command at Tobruk. He and Wavell are to fly up tomorrow.

Before Wavell left for the desert he saw Dill and me off on our homeward flight. He came out in the launch to our flying-boat, and as we were about to get on board remarked to the C.I.G.S.: "I hope, Jack, that you will preside over my court-martial." After being once again held up at Gibraltar, we reached London and more bad news, on April 10th.

10

GAINS AND LOSSES
April–May 1941

War in the Balkans — Rashid Ali seizes power in Iraq — The
Nazis intervene too late — H.M.S. *Hood* is sunk — The evacuation of Crete — The enemy active in Syria — Turkish troops on
the frontiers — My minute to Mr. Churchill on the Middle East —
The British and Free French enter Syria — The character of
General de Gaulle — Failure of Operation "Battleaxe" — General Auchinleck succeeds General Wavell — Mr. Lyttelton appointed Minister of State in the Middle East — Mr. Wendell
Willkie visits Britain — Herr Rudolf Hess' fantastic flight —
Reform of the Foreign and Consular Services — I speak on post-
war economic plans

THESE WERE DAYS when Hitler's friends in every part of the world
had cause to be in a buoyant mood, for Rommel's offensive had
outmanœuvred us in the Western Desert and his armour appeared
to swoop at will. In the Balkans the Germans had invaded Greece
and Yugoslavia before General Wilson's troops were all in position.
One division of the three which Wavell had advised should be sent
to Greece, and the Polish brigade, had to remain to face the threat
in Cyrenaica. The rapid collapse of Yugoslav resistance left the
flank of the Aliakhmon line open and the Greek army was battle
weary after its long winter campaign.

To these external factors must be added the crippling shortages
which had hampered our operations since the beginning of the war.
The Royal Air Force performed prodigies of valour in Greece but
was heavily outnumbered by the Germans and Italians, so that a
long and complicated line of supply lay open to enemy attack. Our
troops also suffered from faulty equipment, some of the tank tracks

failed, while the Germans had specially trained mountain troops
and more up-to-date weapons.

April 20th: Winston rang me up from Ditchley in evening and
asked me to go to London and "take command" of situation in
respect of Greece and help to Wavell. I motored up after a
scratch dinner and we had meeting of Chiefs of Staff who had
already had some general instructions from Winston.

Next day, after the Cabinet, a Defence Committee meeting at
noon discussed the position in Greece. Later I saw the Greek Minister, who told me that his people felt wounded by British argument
whether or no they had been worth helping. Certainly there was
no recrimination from the Greeks, who behaved grandly and sped
the parting troops with flowers, as they had greeted their landing.

April 27th: Winston broadcast after dinner. Another good
effort in admirable perspective. I am sorry, though, that he based
help to Greece solely on *noblesse oblige.* A war in Balkans was
not what Hitler wanted.

★　　★　　★　　★　　★

Abreast of Rommel's successes, on April 2nd the pro-Axis Rashid
Ali had seized power in Iraq by a *coup d'état,* while the Regent fled
for refuge to a British gunboat at Basra. Hitler now decided to
send Rashid Ali what he called "arms of the best quality," but fortunately it was not easy for him, even at the height of his power, to
get them there.

If Hitler was to be checked, Iraq had to be under a government
friendly to Britain. Oil pipelines traversed the country, while the
airfields at Habbaniya near Baghdad and Shaiba near Basra were
indispensable for our communications with India. The right to
these bases rested on the Treaty of 1930, which also entitled us to
pass troops through the country.

In the summer of 1940, when at the War Office, I had wanted to
send a brigade to Basra, but the immediate needs of the Sudan
ruled that out. Now the Government of India responded to an ap-

peal for help. The first Indian troops began to land at Basra on April 18th, but it was the news of the arrival of the next echelon which forced Rashid Ali's hand. The Iraqi army and air force besieged the principal Royal Air Force station, Habbaniya, from April 30th for a week; they were just too late. The first of the Indian troops had already joined the garrison. Together, they beat off all attacks.

On May 2nd the Defence Committee decided to return Iraq temporarily to Middle East Command. Not surprisingly, Wavell did not at all like this addition to his already far spread commitments. He telegraphed home to complain of the new baby which had been landed in his lap, but having made his protest he put together a force, which entered the country from Transjordan ten days later.

Nazi aircraft flown into Baghdad from Mosul arrived after the Royal Air Force had destroyed the Iraqi planes. On May 18th the main British column reached Habbaniya. Only on May 23rd did Hitler issue the order:

> I have therefore decided to advance developments in the Middle East by giving support to Iraq.
>
> Whether and how the English position between the Mediterranean and the Persian Gulf shall in due course be finally destroyed, in connection with an offensive against the Suez Canal, will only be decided after "Barbarossa." *

This Directive, by its date and by the clause "after 'Barbarossa'" explains the Nazi failure in Iraq. Obsessed by the coming struggle with Russia, the German Command intervened too little and too late.

The tense character of these lonely and still critical days inevitably found expression in the War Cabinet.

May 24th: Naval battle has developed in Denmark Straits and there is an agonizing report that *Hood* has been sunk. The Navy must avenge her on *Bismarck* which is reported to have been hit. Poor *Hood*, the loveliest ship to look at in all the Royal Navy and for many years to millions its emblem.

* *Documents on German Foreign Policy, 1918-1945;* Series D, Vol. XII, No. 543. Retranslated from German text.

The pursuit was prolonged and two days later I was writing:

May 26th: A most gloomy day. *Bismarck* appears to have been lost. We face defeat in Crete and make little progress towards Baghdad. The worst Cabinet we have had yet in evening. Winston was nervy and unreasonable and everyone else on edge. An absurd row as to whether we should publish convoy losses or not, which ended in what Max afterwards described as a two minutes silence.

The next day came the reassuring news that *Bismarck* had been sunk. Reports from Iraq were better, too, and on May 31st the Chiefs of Staff met in my room at the Foreign Office to agree on the armistice terms for that country, also to discuss Russia and a number of other questions. I called it a useful meeting.

June 1st: [The Prime Minister] rang me up in morning to discuss Iraq situation and told me Cretan evacuation was at an end. . . . Winston said he wanted to overrule C.-in-C. Mediterranean and carry on another night, but he had found that Wavell had already issued orders to capitulate. The naval losses are heavy. *Calcutta* to add to a long list.

In the first days of June the Regent of Iraq returned to his capital amid popular acclaim. For the rest of the war the loyalty of this linked strategic area was no more in doubt. The recovery of our position in Iraq might seem a small set-off for the loss of Crete, but its effect upon the Middle East was crucial.

★   ★   ★   ★   ★

The dangers in Syria during this early summer of 1941 ran parallel to those in Iraq and were related to them. Towards the end of April I wrote in a minute at the Foreign Office: "I have never been happy about our negative Syrian policy, but it has proved difficult to evolve any effective positive action." The reason had been that Syria and the Lebanon were at this time ruled by the French Government at Vichy, so that any action we took to forestall German and Italian intentions had to take account of the position of the Free French, as well as of Arab opinion inside and outside the country. Nazi agents were enterprizing and enemy aircraft might try to use Syrian aerodromes to refuel while carrying troops to Iraq.

Longmore was conscious of this risk which he voiced at a discussion held in Cairo on April 15th with de Gaulle and Catroux, General Spears, head of our mission with the Free French, and our Ambassador, Sir Miles Lampson. De Gaulle told this meeting that he planned to take possession of Beirut, Damascus and the aerodrome at Rayak with Free French forces and rightly said that once this had been done, there would be little or no resistance. He asked for British assistance with lorries and mechanized forces, since he had few or no tanks, and for some aircraft.

When this conference was reported to me, I minuted that an unsuccessful attempt at a *coup d'état* in Syria would be disastrous, but if we could put together a sufficient force to ensure success, I was prepared to risk the strain on our relationship with Vichy. It was a question of men and materials, and I asked the Chiefs of Staff to give their opinion as quickly as possible.

They replied that any Free French *coup* against the Syrian administration must be ruled out absolutely, because at present General Wavell had neither the tanks nor the aircraft required and if he had, he would use them for even more imperative tasks elsewhere. For the moment we had to do the best we could by diplomatic means. I therefore instructed our Consul-General at Beirut, Mr. Godfrey Havard, to warn General Henri Dentz, Vichy High Commissioner and Commander-in-Chief, against a possible German airborne attack on Syria. To this Dentz replied with duplicity on April 29th that his orders were to resist all aggression.

Our warnings were timely, because Berlin and Vichy were arranging at this date to build up a supply of arms in Syria for passage to Rashid Ali and for German aircraft to stage there on their flight to Iraq. I decided to call in American help to redress the balance of Vichy's double dealing. On May 12th I told Washington of General Dentz' declaration to our Consul at Damascus that his instructions did not provide for a German occupation, but that if such orders came, he would obey them. I asked the United States Government to do anything it could to stiffen Vichy resistance to

German activity in Syria. I also applied the threat of counter-action to the Vichy French and said in the House of Commons on May 15th:

> Detailed information at the disposal of His Majesty's Government shows that the French authorities in Syria are allowing German aircraft to use Syrian aerodromes as staging posts for flights to Iraq. His Majesty's Government have in consequence given full authority for action to be taken against these German aircraft on Syrian aerodromes. . . .

Deeds followed the threat and, on May 19th, Lampson telegraphed that our bombing attacks on airfields at Damascus had been welcomed and that the Arabs were impressed by the show of force. Lampson went on to relay the information that Vichy forces were withdrawing from Syria into the Lebanon. If this was so, he wanted to know whether the Free French battalions could immediately enter Syria, with or without any available British detachments. This prompted the following minute from me to the Prime Minister on the same day:

> From our present information my own view would be that we should tell Lampson that if he and the C.-in-C. estimate that the going is good, then the Free French should be given the chance to do what they can.

The Defence Committee favoured the course I proposed, but then came a hitch. Wavell, with his many preoccupations, telegraphed that to try to occupy Syria with an insufficient force would be a dangerous operation to which he was opposed. As against this, we had to weigh the air force opinion that German occupation of Syrian aerodromes would double the strain on the Royal Air Force in Egypt. Our Embassy in Cairo added that the political effect on Egypt would be most unfortunate and upon Turkey no less so.

The conclusion about Turkey was certainly just, because, as I told the War Cabinet on the afternoon of May 19th, the Germans were at that moment making a strong diplomatic offensive in Ankara. Von Papen, the German Ambassador, was cajoling the

Turks with tales of the unreliability of Russia as a friend and using the fate of Poland as a warning. The War Cabinet shared my apprehensions and that night I sent the Prime Minister a fuller minute:

> I think I should put before you certain political considerations in connection with the recent developments in Syria and Iraq.
>
> Apart from the intrinsic importance of Iraq to us as a line of communication and of Syria as Palestine's northern neighbour, these developments cause me most concern on account of their influence on Turkey's policy. So far, Turkey has held fast to the Anglo-Turkish Alliance and, for the present at least, appears to wish to continue to do so. Our Military Attaché at Ankara reports that the Turks are concentrating troops on the Iraqi and Syrian frontiers and are asking us in return for our plans for dealing with the situation in these recalcitrant countries. It seems that the Turks expect to have completed their concentrations by the end of the month.
>
> It seems to me essential that we should make a plan of our own and that we should take the Turks to a large extent into our confidence. The mobile brigade has evidently had difficulties in its approach to Habbaniya and I confess that I had not appreciated when the Defence Committee recommended this move that its development would take so long. The delay has enabled German arrivals to hearten the Iraqis. I presume, however, that we can still expect that our forces will shortly be able to enter Baghdad and enable us to set up a friendly Government there. The problem of northern Iraq and of Syria will then remain.
>
> On his western flank General Wavell is engaged in a battle in the Western Desert. I do not know what forces remain available to him to concentrate in Palestine and when he can hope to have a sufficient force there to advance into Syria. We have as yet no reports of the results of General Catroux's appeal to the French in Syria but, unless that response is good, I should not have supposed that the Free French battalions alone would suffice.

On the other hand, the forces which it is possible to employ on either side in the Western Desert are presumably limited and, though I should be the first to admit the importance of the battle there, its course will not, I hope, prevent us from making a plan to deal with the situation in Syria and Iraq, which plan would take account of the Turkish attitude. . . . If once the Germans are able to establish themselves in any strength in Syria and in Iraq, and succeed in organizing a part of the Arabs against us, Turkey will be effectively surrounded and it would indeed be difficult then to count upon her enduring loyalty. This morning's telegrams show that pressure by Germany on Turkey is being intensified by every means. In the order of our urgent commitments I would, therefore, place very high the need for determining a plan to meet the Syrian danger.

Taking a long view, there is this further consideration: if, as a result of her isolation, Turkey were to cave in and allow the passage of German troops into Syria, Germany would presumably be able to accumulate in due course important armoured forces in Syria and Iraq. These forces would not be limited by the difficulties of communication and supply which hamper any forces advancing on Egypt from the west, and a more formidable German army could then be maintained and employed from Syria than from Tripoli. The only way to stop this is for Turkey to hold fast, and the only way to ensure that Turkey holds fast is to deal at the earliest possible moment with the situation in Syria and in Iraq.

I discussed with the Defence Committee on May 27th the question of whether we should ask the Turks to take a hand. It would have been best, I argued, to do the job ourselves but, as General Wavell did not think that we could go farther than Damascus, Rayak and Beirut, it looked as though we should try to get the Turks to occupy the northern part of the country. Their advance into Syria would complicate our plans with the Arabs, who would suspect that the Turks had come to stay. On the other hand, Nazi pressure was strong and some discussions were on foot between the Germans and the Turks.

On balance I favoured trying to get the Turks in, at the expense of temporarily estranging the Arabs. I was not at all sure in my own mind that the Turks would accept the bait, for fear of the consequences upon their relations with Germany. If so, our offer would have pleased them without doing any harm, though we should not get their active help. This rather devious conclusion was agreed by the Committee and I was authorized to tell General de Gaulle, but no one else within the Free French movement.

The stakes were high. If Germany were to control Syria, Turkey's back door would be unguarded. If, on the other hand, the Allies were in control, even the loss of Cyprus would not be so serious. As the First Sea Lord pointed out, we could then hammer the Germans, if they were in occupation of Cyprus, as they had hammered us in Crete. Although we did not know it at the time, the Nazi losses in airborne troops during the capture of Crete had been so heavy that Hitler was hesitant about mounting such an operation again. This stood us in good stead when Malta was threatened a year later.

The Turks, who had met us to the extent of halting their talks with the Germans for the time being, were not ready to do more than move troops and heavy artillery to the Syrian frontier. This was helpful, but the collapse of Rashid Ali's rebellion was even more so. Nazi activities in Syria waned until, by the beginning of June, German air forces were withdrawn, presumably to prepare for the Russian campaign. It may also have seemed to Hitler a skilful move to leave the British and Free French face to face with the Vichy forces. So might the resolution and the bitterness of Vichy be fortified.

For us the decision to take the hazard presented Wolfe's dilemma: "There is such a choice of difficulties that I am myself at a loss how to determine."

On the morning of May 20th I discussed Syria, and a draft by General Catroux for the independence of the Levant States, with the Chiefs of Staff. We concluded that the Free French troops should be moved up to the Syrian border as soon as possible and should be given transport and such other support as could be contrived. General Wavell was to be told to let the Free French enter Syria if he thought there was any chance of their success. The declaration of independence might need some amendment but, this done, it should be given out at once and supported by His Majesty's Government.

The Defence Committee met after midday and endorsed our conclusions which I telegraphed to Lampson:

> It is clearly desirable that we should be associated with General Catroux's action, and we wish to give him all political help in our power. You have authority to support his declaration and associate His Majesty's Government with it.

When informed of this change of policy to active intervention in Syria, General Smuts sent a particularly encouraging reply on May 21st, supporting the decision and telling us that he had been about to telegraph, himself, urging just this course of action.

Since the Vichy French in Syria seemed wholly committed to Germany, General Wavell moved reinforcements into Palestine and proposed that General Wilson should advance into Syria with a force of Imperial and Free French troops. This was approved by the Defence Committee on May 27th.

On June 4th I held a meeting in my room at the Foreign Office with Margesson, Dill and Portal, together with Foreign Office representatives:

> *June 4th:* We discussed Syria, pros and cons. There was much anxiety. Maybe we are too late for surprise and too early in the sense that our force is not large. Against this must be set the fact that it must be some time, a month at least, before our forces can be larger; meanwhile French will have time to consolidate, get their breath and German help. Vichy has sold out, and there is nothing to be hoped from Weygand [Vichy High Commissioner in North Africa]. A useful discussion, the general consensus being in the end in favour of going ahead with what must be a gamble.

This was reported to the Defence Committee, who endorsed our judgment.

In the early morning of June 8th, British and Free French forces under the command of General Wilson crossed the Syrian frontier. There was nothing half-hearted about the resolve of the Vichy

French troops and the fighting was hard, with many casualties on both sides. In the second week our advance had almost come to a standstill and by June 22nd only Sidon and Damascus had been captured. But the Anglo–French campaign was skilfully led and fought and in its last phase held the initiative, so that on July 11th General Dentz had to ask for an armistice.

Its signature did not mark the end of controversy, for though there was no dispute on our part that the Free French should take over the political control of the country, the Prime Minister and I were insistent that the Arab population should not be made to feel that they had merely exchanged one set of French masters for another. Our position was all the more involved because as long as British forces were in occupation of the country, ultimate authority had to remain with the British Commander-in-Chief. De Gaulle was watchful lest we should try to supplant the French in their favoured position in the Levant, nor were French suspicions of our intentions in Syria ever wholly allayed.

This controversy was the theme of many discussions between de Gaulle and myself during the war. I had the most sincere admiration for this great Frenchman's qualities. To know him was to understand how exaggerated was the picture, often created of him in the public mind, of arrogance and even majesty. This facilely mistook the man. In intimate conversation de Gaulle could be direct but dispassionate, perhaps because he was in the true sense a dedicated man, his country absorbing his whole being. His selflessness made it possible for him to keep the flame of France alive when in political or more diplomatic hands it must have flickered out.

Yet de Gaulle was the victim of his qualities, for the fervour of his faith made him at times too suspicious of the intentions of others. The schemes and the greed not infrequently attributed to Britain and its leading personalities in those years were many of them insubstantial myths. We did not want Madagascar, nor Syria, nor Jibuti, nor to succeed to the French position, there or elsewhere. On the most egoistic grounds of national advantage, it was to our interest that France should be strong and that the French empire should survive, if possible intact, but I doubt if General de Gaulle ever believed this. Maybe we saw further than he thought; perhaps if we had had to fight as desperate a corner, we too should have believed that all men's hands were against us.

De Gaulle could be generous in his sentiments. For example, after signing the agreement about Madagascar with me on December 14th, 1942, he paid tribute to *"la loyauté entière dont venait de faire preuve notre bonne et vieille alliée l'Angleterre."* *

As the war unfolded we were to have experience enough of de Gaulle's tenacity. If it made him seem contumacious, especially to our American allies, perhaps we should have learnt from it. Some of the faults of later years might have been avoided if we had shown more of the same spirit.

★ ★ ★ ★ ★

In the months of May and June the question of the military command in the Middle East began to loom once again. After a Defence Committee which had gone on until midnight, Beaverbrook and I repaired to Churchill's room, where we found Attlee and Margesson. The Prime Minister posed the question:

May 10th: He was in favour of changing Auchinleck and Wavell about. Max agreed as Amery had already done. The other three of us were more doubtful. As I knew the men best, I found the advice not easy to give. I have no doubt that Archie has the better mind, but one does not know how he is bearing the strain and one cannot tell, though some of his recent reactions seem to indicate that he is flagging. In the end I weakly counselled delay and asked to wait for Crete result. Winston agreed there was not unanimity.

During dinner on May 13th, the Prime Minister talked to me about the Middle East and said he would give much to have me out there. I answered that I had already lost enough tail feathers on my last effort. He was indignant in denial: "You were defended."

This was certainly true, especially of Churchill himself, but there was also something in the advice which Lord Tyrrell gave me when

* Charles de Gaulle: *Mémoires de Guerre;* Vol. II.

he came to see me on June 6th. He begged me not to go abroad again without sufficient force at my back. I told him that I had been perfectly conscious of the danger, but that in war-time one could hardly consider personal reputations. He agreed, but told me not to do it again, all the same.

That night I dined alone with the Prime Minister. Beaverbrook, whom I found there, told me that I had made a mistake in leaving the War Office for the Foreign Office. Anybody could hold the Foreign Office. He also thought the time had come for the reconstruction of the Government. Later the Prime Minister, whose affection for Beaverbrook was a blend of sincere admiration and of a generation of political experiences shared together, remarked that his friend had not now enough to do.

Churchill was resentful of press and political criticism of the evacuation of Crete. He cited the *Daily Mail, Daily Herald,* Hore-Belisha and others, I thought with reason. An earlier comment of Attlee's about Parliament had force: "They showed no sign to wish to debate our entry into Baghdad." These were not easy days for those at the top.

June 6th: Winston talked a good deal about the past. He reiterated that I should have chosen a bigger issue for resignation, but admitted for first time that a Foreign Secretary is not a free agent in these matters. "He has to conceal what he would most wish to make public, and make public what he would most wish to conceal."

★ ★ ★ ★ ★

Meanwhile the desert news was not good. General Wavell had for some time been preparing an offensive, "Battleaxe," urged on by the Prime Minister, who, as was his buoyant nature, had set the highest hopes upon the operation.

June 18th: "Battleaxe" has failed. For the first two days all went well, though we lost many tanks. On the third came a strong counter-attack, carried out in part by German tanks brought from Tobruk. Infantry were extricated, but we have lost more than a hundred tanks. We had air superiority throughout the battle. My own conviction is that we had not enough armoured fighting vehicles for the job. Gott was nearer success last month. Winston rang me up, very sad, and later in the morning asked me to go over and discuss situation.

He also showed me a personal telegram Roosevelt had sent him

> which indicated that his last two actions [freezing German and Italian assets, and closing German consulates] had received wide support. Some comfort in a dark hour. With Libyan failure and Turkish signature with Germany the hour is anxious. Syria looks better.

The Turkish Government had eventually given way, to the extent of signing on this day a treaty with Germany which appeared damaging to us at the time, but its terms were in fact anodyne.

At the end of June a pause in the fighting in the Western Desert provided an opportunity for a decision on the change of command in the Middle East, if one was to be taken. I knew, of course, what was in the Prime Minister's mind and I feared that Wavell must have felt the burdens which he had had to carry in the last few months, with the numerous campaigns strung from the Western Desert through Crete, Syria and Iraq to East Africa. I had experienced the close friendship between Dill and Wavell and, when I realized that a decision was near, I talked to Dill about it and asked his opinion. Reluctantly he had to admit that a change could not be resisted. He thought the Commander-in-Chief tired and that he knew it himself. I accepted this judgment as final so far as I was concerned. General Wavell was replaced by General Auchinleck on July 5th and, a little later, took up his Command in India.

This change did not, however, resolve the parallel problem which the Prime Minister and I had discussed so many times. Our political representation in that theatre of the war had been the subject of a further talk with Mr. Churchill on May 29th. He said that if I could be there, this would suit him, but it was not possible. We agreed that anyone who did not enjoy his confidence would be useless. Finally, on June 28th Mr. Oliver Lyttelton went out as representative of the War Cabinet, with the title of Minister of State in the Middle East, which appointment was without blemish.

★   ★   ★   ★   ★

The first months of 1941 saw new contacts with several Americans, some of whom were to play a large part in forthcoming events.

January 10th: [Mr. Harry L.] Hopkins came to see me in the morning. We had met before at Washington and I liked him. He gave me messages from R. [Roosevelt] and H. [Hull] and told me that R. was determined to get his bill [Lend-Lease] through Congress and would succeed. The bulk of the country was behind him. He [Hopkins] had come to fill the gap until the new Ambassador was appointed. I told him that everything United States could deliver before May was worth double anything after. This seemed rather to depress him.

I told Hopkins in answer to his questions that I thought Hitler more likely to attack the Greeks than to attack Turkey through Bulgaria.

Meanwhile the President had encouraged his unsuccessful competitor to visit Europe, which event proved important to us.

January 28th: Max [Beaverbrook] gave a banquet for [Wendell] Willkie. Successful party, with some brief speechmaking. I believe Willkie to be sincere in his desire to help us, though as a personality he has none of the charm of Hopkins. The latter is quiet, subtle, with a sense of humour. W. is big, self-confident, gives the impression of a successful lawyer. H. speaks with all the added appeal of a man who appears not to want to, W. with the healthy pleasure of a man who likes to hear his own voice.

Soon afterwards Willkie came to see me at the Foreign Office, when I modified my first opinion. His friend, Mr. John Cowles, was with him. Willkie plied me with questions, amongst other things about communism in Britain. I was able to assure him that our communists were an insignificant minority and suggested that in order to find out what the British people really thought, he should speak to them whenever he got the chance. After our talk, I took him down in the lift to the side door near my room at the Foreign Office, and as we stepped out a workman was patching some broken windows after an air-raid. "There," I said, "you can make a start now." Willkie walked up to him and asked a few questions. The man had no idea who Willkie was. "How do you feel about this war?" "How d'yer mean?" Willkie persisted: "Want to go through with it?" The man looked at him quickly: "Hitler ain't dead yet, is he?" and turned back to his work. I could not have staged it as well.

I saw Willkie again towards the end of his tour and he said he had followed my advice. Among the scores he had questioned, he had only met one who wished to chuck the war. She was an Irish housemaid in an hotel.

Of a short visit to Chequers when Willkie was the Prime Minister's guest, together with Beaverbrook and Attlee, I wrote:

February 1st: Much talk until 1.15 a.m. when I retired exhausted. I believe that they went on until after 2. Liked Willkie better. I am sure he is sincere in his desire to help and belief in our cause, while the courage of our people has moved him deeply. It has been a great gain to us that he should have come.

February 2nd: We all sallied forth for a short walk in afternoon, Winston protesting mildly, but eager to show us Happy Valley, into which he wishes to pour a waterfall, electrically driven!

The appointment of Mr. John G. Winant on February 6th as United States Ambassador to the Court of St. James's was an important event. In welcoming him publicly a while later, I said of him:

He cares much for his work, little for party politics, not at all for himself.

We soon established an easy relationship. With the passage of time, it became so close that we could agree together which parts of our conversations should be on record for the information of our two Governments and which for ourselves alone. This understanding persisted throughout the war and the records show that it was never broken. John Winant was very often my guest at Binderton, the house in west Sussex of which I was to buy the lease in the late summer of this year, so that my sons could spend their school holidays there and my wife and I could have some occasional relaxation.

My visits to Chequers during the war were rare, because the constant late hours of the Defence Committee, together with the demands of the Foreign Office and, subsequently of the leadership of the House of Commons as well, would not allow an after luncheon break for a siesta. I just had to have some regular hours. The Prime Minister was indulgent about this and only at one or two very critical stages of the war was the summons to Chequers regarded as overriding.

April 12th: Motored to Chequers, arriving just before dinner. Winant and Harriman there, two of the most delightful Americans I have met. That at least was my first reaction. They must have thought us a funny party. Winston in his rompers in which he had apparently travelled from South Wales. Dill and I and Winston had some talk after dinner about general situation and Libya in particular. Dill wants to hold back one of the four battalions of "I" tanks, much to my surprise, on the grounds that we were short of trained crews here. My only regret is that we have not included a battalion of cruisers.

★　　★　　★　　★　　★

In the early hours of Monday, May 12th, the Prime Minister telephoned to me, but I had been tired that weekend and my wife refused to wake me. The Prime Minister accepted this, but left a message that he wished to see me as soon as I got to London. There followed what my diary describes as an incredible day. Churchill told me that the Duke of Hamilton had tried to contact Sir Alexander Cadogan at the Foreign Office but that he, Churchill, had intercepted him and taken him to Ditchley.

May 12th: Hamilton's story was that a German airman had landed in a M 110 in his former constituency, giving name of

Horn and asking to see him. When Hamilton contacted him he
revealed himself as [Rudolf] Hess [Deputy to the Führer]. Hamilton produced a number of photographs [which Hess had
brought with him] and showed them to me. I said that they
appeared to be of Hess. The Prime Minister was much impressed,
not having believed story.

I told Mr. Churchill that I would like to take the Duke of Hamilton across to the Foreign Office and have the photographs checked.
There Cadogan and I heard the full account and I suggested that
we should send at once for Mr. Ivone Kirkpatrick, who knew Hess.
Kirkpatrick identified the photographs as well-known ones of Hess
and we decided to fly him with Hamilton up to Scotland to see the
visitor. The Prime Minister agreed.

During dinner came German wireless communiqué about Hess.
Winston rang up, immensely excited and wanted us to issue something at once.

I went round to see him and eventually a statement was agreed
about midnight. How much we should tell of Hess' confused ob-
sessions posed quite a problem:

> *May 14th:* Winston rang me up late at night with text of state-
> ment he wants to make in House tomorrow about Hess, quoting
> trend of his statements. I protested, urging Germans must be
> kept in dark as to what Hess had said. Winston then demanded
> alternative draft and I struggled out of bed and produced it and
> telephoned it. A few minutes later Winston telephoned he did
> not like it and Duff [Cooper, Minister of Information] was much
> upset. On the other hand Max [Beaverbrook] agreed with me.
> Which was it to be, his original statement or no statement. I re-
> plied: "No statement." "All right, no statement" (crossly!), and
> telephone was crashed down. Time 1.30 a.m.

A few days later the Prime Minister reverted to his projected
statement about Hess, this time at the Cabinet, but nobody liked it,
so that nothing came of it. Lord Beaverbrook told me afterwards

that we might have to "strangle the infant" a third time, but fortunately it was not reborn.

The incident of Hess' arrival was one of the strangest personal dramas of the war. The flight itself was a brave undertaking most skilfully executed. What lay behind the man's clouded mind is still conjecture. It has been suggested that he felt dismay at the prospect of a German attack on Russia and its consequences, and was trying to make an effort to stop the war before this happened, but there is no evidence that Hess knew Hitler's plans.

More probably his sudden venture was due to the influence of Karl Haushofer, a professor of geopolitics and the latter's son, Albrecht, who had been anglophiles. By his pseudo-science, Haushofer had once adduced historical and geographical arguments for German expansion which suited Nazism very well. Hess inspired Hitler with them and they had their place in *Mein Kampf*. It now appears from a memorandum* of Haushofer's that, from September 1940, he had been discussing with his son and with Hess peace moves towards England without having much faith in their success. A letter to the Duke of Hamilton from the son having received no reply, Hess apparently decided to fly to Scotland himself. The timing seems to have been fortuitous. Hess had a sanguine belief in the power of Dukes in Britain which also illustrates the fanciful ignorance of foreign countries in Hitler's most intimate circle of leadership.

The drama of Hess' escapade never ceased to fascinate the Russians, who found it difficult to believe that there was not something sinister behind it, in which the British Government were in some way implicated. Over and over again within the next few years I was cross-questioned about it by Molotov, by Mr. Shvernik, a member of the Politbureau and later President of the U.S.S.R., while Stalin would on occasion throw out a grumbling aside. Though I told them all the details and offered to show them the dossier of Hess' statements I doubt if they were ever really satisfied that the incident was as unexpected and inexplicable to us as to them.

* *Documents on German Foreign Policy;* Series D, Vol. XII, No. 500. See also same series Vol. XI.

★   ★   ★   ★   ★

Shortly after my return to the Foreign Office, two reports occupied my attention and interest. I decided that I must now take in hand the reform of the Foreign Office and Diplomatic and Consular Services, formidable though this was likely to prove. These services were thought to have suffered in the last few years from the rather narrow field of recruitment and from lack of expert economic and commercial knowledge. Even if these criticisms were exaggerated, some changes in the structure of the Foreign Service would be needed in the post-war world. Since these could not be made hastily, it was time to start deciding what they should be.

As a first step I asked Sir Malcolm Robertson to look at a number of suggestions which had been made, and to put forward any other reforms which he might think necessary. Sir Malcolm was well fitted for the part. He had retired some years earlier in favour of a business career, while still Ambassador at Buenos Aires, so that he was not personally involved in the recent history of the Diplomatic Service.

After he and I had discussed the possibilities, Robertson wrote a report recommending the amalgamation of the Consular Service with the Foreign Office and Diplomatic Service. He advised introducing a broader system of entry and increased grants and allowances, so that the best men could be sent to any post without financial hardship.

I agreed with these recommendations and brought them before the War Cabinet on June 2nd. Though the amalgamation could not be introduced until after the war, I asked my colleagues to approve in principle those reforms which involved legislation and the immediate expenditure of public money. They included a pension scheme, by which I set much store, which would enable a senior officer who proved unsuited for the highest posts to be retired on pension by the Foreign Secretary. Under the existing regulations, I had the power to put any member of the Foreign Office and Diplomatic Service en disponibilité, but since he then received no pay, this weapon was so harsh that it was rarely used. A pension scheme such as I now proposed would make it possible for me and for my successors to act with more freedom and without injustice, and would speed up the promotion of able younger men.

The Chancellor of the Exchequer, Sir Kingsley Wood, did not

like this plan, but after considerable debate my scheme of reform was approved, and I was able to tell the House of Commons of my intentions in general terms. Much detailed work still remained to do, but in January 1943 I laid before Parliament a White Paper containing proposals for legislation. These became law that year, and entered into operation at the end of the war. I have no doubt that they were necessary and resulted in a better balanced Foreign Service at the period when we needed it most.

The second report had been prepared a few weeks before I took over as Foreign Secretary again. Mr. John Maynard Keynes had written for the Foreign Office a memorandum exposing the fallacious Nazi promises of an economic and financial paradise, which was being paraded by Hitler in support of his New Order. In this paper Keynes included proposals for the post-war economy. I thought the whole exercise useful, minuting in the Foreign Office that we should put it to good purpose soon.

> I am prepared to write to the Chancellor in this sense. . . . Some day I shall have to make my first speech as Foreign Secretary (2nd phase!) and if I can do so without unduly plagiarizing the professor, I should like to say something on these lines. It represents my sentiments, though my knowledge is less than anyone's.

Keynes now visited Washington and had a useful talk to the President on post-war economic plans, which included what I had in mind to say about them. On May 24th I spoke to Mr. John Winant, the United States Ambassador, who told me that the President was to broadcast four days later. Roosevelt might well develop the same theme, which he considered was all to the good. I told Mr. Winant that, according to our reports, American opinion was waiting, even flagging, for a lead. He agreed and thought, from some cryptic comments which Mr. Harry Hopkins had let fall on the telephone from Washington, that a lead was to be expected.

On the morning of May 28th a telegram arrived from Halifax, reporting that the President did not much like what I had to say, because it was too British or too European. Halifax did not think that the President's criticisms had much substance, but added that any reference in my remarks to Roosevelt's own address would help. The President's personal reactions made the Foreign Office ask me to cut out all the ideas inspired by Keynes, but I refused, though I did offer Roosevelt some incense. This speech dealt with post-war economic affairs in Europe, and had significance as the first declaration by a British government to espouse Arab unity.* Halifax telegraphed that my words having had a very good press in the United States would be "useful in counteracting rumours circulating that our silence about Hess connotes peace talks through him." So little was our temper understood even by our best friends.

* *Freedom and Order,* pages 102–111.

BOOK THREE

Alliance

1

RUSSIA IS ATTACKED
April–December 1941

Anglo–Russian relations — I warn Mr. Maisky of Germany's intentions — Sir Stafford Cripps at Chequers — Our pessimistic
estimates of Russian strength — The Nazis attack Russia — I try
to draw Soviet and Polish Governments together — Russia and
Britain secure the trans-Iranian railway — Argument with Russia
pro and con a second front — A dinner at the Ritz — Sir Stafford
Cripps demands to come home — Sir Alan Brooke succeeds Sir
John Dill as C.I.G.S. — Harsh messages from Mr. Stalin — My
projected visit to Moscow

WHEN I RETURNED to the Foreign Office from the Middle East on
April 10th, Britain's relations with the Soviet Union were high on
my list of priorities. The Russian signature of a pact with the new
Yugoslav Government showed that the Soviets would, when it
suited them, consider helping countries which were threatened by
Nazi attack. We were also receiving increasing evidence of German
preparations for an attack on Russia. In the circumstances, I
thought the time had come for a smoothing-out of relations between
our two countries.

A difficulty was that the Russians wanted us to acknowledge their
grab, in 1940, of the Baltic States of Estonia, Latvia and Lithuania.
We were pledged not to give *de jure* recognition to the changed
position of any state, even if we had wished to do this, which we
did not. Nor could we give up their gold, then in Britain, still less
their ships which formed a part of our shipping pool. The Russians,
for their part, gave no sign of making any contribution to agreement. They just argued that it was necessary to clear up the Baltic
question before our relations could improve. It has always been
the Soviet method to ask for substantial concessions on differences,

while holding out nothing more than a hope that, if these are made, the atmosphere for more general negotiations will improve. These were the tactics which they now employed.

On April 16th Mr. Maisky came to see me. He was accompanied by a young individual I had never seen before, who was introduced as a Counsellor and who was present throughout the conversation, though he took no part in it. He seemed to be a Kremlin shadow set to watch upon Maisky. We had a general discussion and I told the Ambassador of recent developments in Libya and the Balkans, while he told me of the Russo–Japanese Neutrality Pact, which his Government hoped had lessened the chances of war in the Far East.

I then informed Maisky of the reports we had received of Hitler's interview with the Prince Regent of Yugoslavia at the beginning of March, at which Hitler had spoken strongly, first against Turkey and then against Russia. This conversation, I felt sure, was symptomatic of a determination made plain in many ways. In the light of it, I had thought that Maisky and I should have a talk. The Ambassador showed some readiness for this and asked me to reflect upon and table what we could do, accepting my reply that I was not prepared to contemplate a gesture only on Britain's part. Afterwards I concluded my record with the comment:

> It is always difficult to know how much Maisky is informed of Soviet policy. Outwardly, his attitude is one of readiness to negotiate; nothing was to be gleaned from the expression of his watch-dog.

Sir Stafford Cripps, on his own initiative, had held a general conversation with Vyshinsky about the same time. There, for the moment, I thought we should let matters rest, for, if the Russians made no approach after my conversation with Maisky, this would show that they were not yet prepared to revise their policy towards Germany. Nor were they. On the contrary, the Soviet Government began to make a series of appeasing concessions to Hitler. They suddenly accepted the German interpretation of the boundary line in Lithuania, a change of attitude which the German Chargé d'Affaires in Moscow described as "very remarkable." * They

* *Documents on German Foreign Policy, 1918–1945*; Series D, Vol. XII, No. 351.

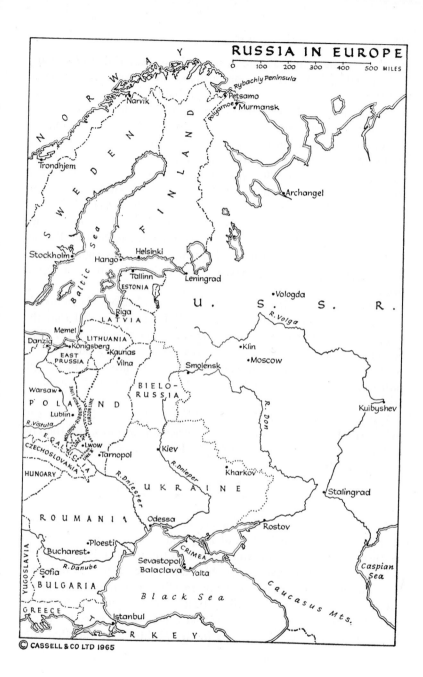

RUSSIA IN EUROPE

0   100   200   300   400   500 MILES

N O R W A Y

S W E D E N

F I N L A N D

Rybachiy Peninsula

Narvik

Petsamo

Polyarnoe

Murmansk

Trondhjem

Archangel

Baltic Sea

Stockholm

Helsinki

Hango

Tallinn

ESTONIA

Leningrad

Riga

LATVIA

Vologda

U. S. S. R.

R. Volga

Memel

Danzig

LITHUANIA

Königsberg

Kaunas

EAST PRUSSIA

Vilna

Klin

Moscow

Smolensk

BIELO-RUSSIA

Warsaw

P O L A N D

Lublin

R. Vistula

MOLOTOV-RIBBENTROP LINE

CURZON LINE

R. Don

Kuibyshev

G A L I C I A

CZECHOSLOVAKIA

LINE A

Lwow

LINE B

Tarnopol

Kiev

R. Dnieper

Kharkov

HUNGARY

R. Dniester

U K R A I N E

Stalingrad

R O U M A N I A

Odessa

Rostov

Ploesti

Bucharest

CRIMEA

R. Danube

Sevastopol

Balaclava

Yalta

Caspian Sea

YUGOSLAVIA

Sofia

B U L G A R I A

Black Sea

Caucasus Mts.

G R E E C E

Istanbul

T U R K E Y

© CASSELL & CO LTD 1965

speeded up their deliveries of grain and raw materials to Germany and ceased to put pressure on Finland to transfer the Petsamo nickel concession. All of which was probably more important than Stalin's fulsome embrace of the German Ambassador on the railway station in Moscow, with the Japanese Foreign Minister looking on.

None of the Russian caresses had any effect on Hitler, who had made up his mind. He would not even listen to his wise Ambassador, Count von der Schulenburg, when he saw him at the end of April. On the contrary he wanted to know what kind of devil had possessed the Russians to conclude the Friendship Pact with Yugoslavia, adding that it was not yet clear who had pulled the strings in the overthrow of the Yugoslav Government, England or Russia. In his opinion it had been the English. Hitler was right, though his judgment ignored the impact of his dragooning upon a proud people.

Schulenburg explained the Soviet pact with Yugoslavia as merely a declaration of Soviet interest in the Balkans and added that the Russians had not had a hand in the *coup d'état* in Belgrade. The Soviets were most eager to make concessions. Stalin's purpose, the Ambassador thought, was to correct "the recent mistakes in foreign policy which led to a cooling off of the cordiality of German–Soviet relations." *

With the atmosphere then prevailing in Moscow, it is not surprising that I got no answer to my suggestion of talks. By the end of May I was so uneasy that I thought I must make another attempt to re-establish contact.

★　★　★　★　★

On June 2nd I again sent for Maisky. He came with his shadow still beside him. I spoke first of Iraq and complained of the Soviet gesture of appointing an Ambassador to the usurper Rashid Ali. I told Maisky that the action we had taken over Iraq was only one example of our determination not to allow our position throughout the Middle East, including Iran and Afghanistan, to be attacked or undermined. We knew that the Germans were intriguing in every possible way against us in the Middle East and that they

* Op. cit., Nos. 423 and 468.

hoped by these activities to bring British and Soviet interests into conflict. There was no reason why they should succeed. The Ambassador agreed. I then explained that, from the information available to us, it was clear that Germany was making considerable concentrations of land and air forces against Russia. No doubt the Ambassador was better informed than I could be on this subject, but I thought I should tell him of my information and tell him also that we were continuing to reinforce our army and air force in the Middle East by all possible means.

Maisky thanked me for the information I had given him and said he would like to ask a few questions. Did we now consider that we had the Iraqi situation well in hand? I replied, yes. Were we equally sure that we could deal with the situation in Syria? I said we knew of the danger, which we were now better placed to meet, as a result of events in Iraq. He then asked for information about the strength of the German air force which had been used against us in Crete. He appeared to consider that about one thousand aircraft had been used. I did not disagree with his estimate, but confirmed that German losses had been heavy.

Maisky then inquired whether I was convinced that the information which I had given him about German concentrations against Russia was accurate. I replied that I had given it to him in good faith and believed it to be correct. Maisky accepted that it might be so, but said he found it very hard to believe that Germany contemplated taking military action against the Soviet Union. After all, that would be a very big undertaking. The Soviet army was well equipped and would not have to fight with sticks, as it did last time. Hitherto Germany had never been called upon to fight large armoured formations. If she fought Russia, she might find that her ten armoured divisions had to face as many as fifteen armoured divisions.

At the time I was sceptical about this figure, wrongly, as it turned out. While Maisky delivered his statement with emphasis, I had a feeling that he might be trying to convince himself as he went along. When he suggested that these German concentrations could be part of a war of nerves, I agreed that it was quite possible the Germans hoped by these means to force concessions from the Soviet Government, which it was not in their national interest to give. Although I did not say so to Maisky, this was just the development which I wished to help him to guard against if I could.

Three days later we met again:

> *June 5th:* Had long talk with Maisky. There is tremendous German pressure on Soviets. I continue to believe that latter will give way unless their skin is asked of them.

On June 9th, as the reports of the German preparations against Russia became still more specific, I wrote to the Prime Minister:

> All the information points to German concentrations against Russia being pressed with the utmost speed and vigour. I have been thinking whether there is any action we can take to encourage Russian resistance. . . . But diplomatically there is no further action we can take until Maisky gives me some reply to my message of last week.
>
> I see in the Intelligence Reports that the Germans are said to have withdrawn a part of their fighter defence from northern France. If these reports are confirmed, would it not be desirable that we show the maximum possible air activity over France and the Low Countries in the next few days? With our forces in the Middle East fully engaged it is about all we can do.

I also raised the question in the War Cabinet on the same evening. I suggested that, should Maisky revert to the subject of the German concentrations, I would say that if Russia became involved in war with Germany, we would do all that we could, for example, by air action in the west, to draw off German air forces.

My colleagues agreed with this suggestion and I spoke in these terms to Maisky when he asked to see me on the following day. He told me that no negotiations, either economic or political, were at present in progress between the German Government and his own. Russia still regarded her relations with Germany as governed by the Non-aggression Pact of 1939 and felt no anxiety about the German concentration of troops. Maisky brought me no answer about Russian policy in the Middle East, but he did say with astonishing frankness that, provided all went well for us in Syria, the moment would be propitious for attempting to make progress in Anglo–Soviet relations.

On June 13th I had a further talk with the Soviet Ambassador, when I told him that in the past forty-eight hours the information reaching us had become more significant. The troop concentrations might be for the purpose of a war of nerves, or they might be for the purpose of an attack on Russia. I did not know, but we were bound to consider, in the light of this very formidable build-up, that conflict between Germany and Russia was possible. We thought it right to tell the Soviet Government what, in such an eventuality, we would be prepared to do. We would be ready to send to Russia a military mission representing all three services, not because we pretended to any superiority in the art of war over Soviet commanders, but because it would be composed of officers who had had the most recent experience in actual combat with the German forces. We thought that might be useful. We should also be prepared to discuss Russia's economic needs at once, and certain technical details such as routing and transport.

The Ambassador said he would communicate what I had told him to his Government, but he betrayed no personal reaction to the message and still professed not to believe in the possibility of a German attack. The atmosphere of the conversation was stiff, in keeping with a Tass communiqué published the same day, which dismissed all the rumours of impending war as "obvious absurdity" and propaganda, concocted by forces which had an interest in the extension of hostilities. "In the opinion of Soviet circles," it said, "the rumours of the intention of Germany to break the [Soviet–German Non-aggression] Pact are completely without foundation."

Sir Stafford Cripps had returned from Moscow for consultations:

June 16th: Luncheon to Cripps at Savoy, Jack Dill, Portal and Alexander. Both J.D. and P. were convinced that Hitler intends to smash Russian military power now, and that he is right to do so. Stafford Cripps thinks we should do better if Soviet is not involved this year and remains a potential threat. This I do not think Hitler will permit. Russia will either have to accept crushing terms of "collaboration," or be attacked.

Maisky and I had done what we could in our respective posts, but, when the German attack fell on Russia a week later, our relations with the Soviet Government could certainly not be described as friendly. They were eased but not transformed now that our two countries were fighting the same enemy.

★   ★   ★   ★   ★

As our Intelligence had shown the German attack on Russia to be imminent, the Prime Minister asked me to come to Chequers on Saturday, June 21st, for the weekend. We had some talk after dinner about the consequences for us should the attack really take place. Our advisers were pessimistic about what the Russians could do. Cripps excused the Soviet appeasement of the Nazis on the grounds of their extreme weakness. Every day must count for them. He had told the War Cabinet on June 16th that the prevailing view in diplomatic circles in Moscow was that Russia could not hold out against Germany for more than three or four weeks. Dill, in conversation with me, hoped for a few weeks longer, but thought we should be unwise to count on more than six or seven.

When I went to bed that night I had no clear view on these matters, only the conviction that for the Germans to have to suffer losses in Russia, even for a spell, on a scale far exceeding those they were now enduring, must ease some of the strain upon us. Not until the Russians were invaded did I realize the immense power of the Nazi fighting machine on land. Though the Battle of Britain had been for us the first brave, decisive victory of the war, we had to thank sea-power for our solitary survival for so long.

The next morning at about half-past seven the Prime Minister's valet, Sawyers, came into my bedroom and said: "The Prime Minister's compliments and the German armies have invaded Russia." Thereupon he presented me with a large cigar on a silver salver. I put on my dressing-gown and went along to the Prime Minister's bedroom. We savoured the relief, but not for me at that hour the cigar, and discussed what was immediately to do. Churchill said he would speak to the nation that night and tell them that we intended to treat the Russians as partners in the struggle against Hitler. I said that I thought that I should see Maisky and speak to him on behalf of the Government. The Prime Minister agreed and suggested that I should summon the Ambassador to the Foreign Office during the morning. After this, I could return to Chequers and tell him what had passed. We could then discuss his broadcast.

When Maisky entered my room at the Foreign Office, he was this time alone and seemingly serene. He described the Nazi attack as sheer banditry. Then, in reply to a question from me, the Ambassador said he expected to receive a response to our suggestion of military and economic missions within a few hours. He then plied me with his own questions. He wanted to know if he could assure his Government that our position and our policy were unchanged. He felt certain Germany would seek to combine offensive action against Russia with a peace move towards the Western Powers. Could the Soviet Government be assured that our war effort would not slacken? I replied that he could certainly give his Government this assurance, and indeed could go further and say that, so far from slackening our war effort, we should intensify it. He would have seen in the newspapers that morning that our air force had fought a successful action over France. That initiative had been deliberately taken in an attempt to ease the situation for Russia.

When the Ambassador went on to speak of his anxieties about the United States, I suggested he should have a conversation with Mr. Winant, who had just returned from America.

Behind this Russian interrogation was the fear that we would stand inactively watching their life-and-death struggle, as they had watched ours. It was almost as much for this reason as because they needed help, that the next six months were filled with Soviet requests, even demands, for a second front, for enormous quantities of material aid, for British troops to fight in Russia and for a political treaty. We on our side knew the limits within which we could give help to the Russians. These were unfortunately narrow, and both costly and cruel in their loss of life.

On June 30th, Maisky asked me to define the scope of Anglo–Russian collaboration; whether it was to be military only, or military and economic, or military and economic and political. I said that both the Prime Minister, in his broadcast on June 22nd, and I, in my speech in the House of Commons on June 24th, had made it clear that we would give all the military and economic help that we could, but political collaboration was a more difficult question. Did the Soviet Government want an alliance, or something less far-reaching. Maisky said he thought that they would like to discuss our countries' respective policies in areas like the Middle East, where both had interests. I replied that I saw no difficulty in this and reminded him that I had suggested such an exchange of opinions even before the German invasion.

★   ★   ★   ★   ★

My immediate purpose, even during the first weeks after the Nazi attack on Russia, was to restore relations between the Polish Government, now in exile in Britain, and the Soviet Government. The Russians in their invasion and occupation of eastern Poland had carried off as prisoners large numbers of Polish soldiers and civilians. Now that this collusion had not spared the Soviets from attack by Hitler, they had, I thought, an obligation to create a new relationship with the ally on whose behalf we had declared war on Germany.

General Sikorski, the intrepid Polish Prime Minister, played his part with a statement, on June 23rd, that an understanding could be reached between the two countries if the Soviets would recognize the relations established between them by the Treaty of Riga in 1921, and release Polish deportees and prisoners of war to fight the common enemy.

The reply which Maisky brought to me on July 4th was patchy. National Committees of Poles, Czechs and Yugoslavs were to be set up in Russia. These would have facilities to form national military forces. It followed, Maisky said, that the Polish prisoners of war in Russian hands would be released. The rest was vaguer, with references to an independent Polish national state and a possible treaty to form a common front against Germany.

When I saw General Sikorski on the same day, he thought the development in Soviet policy significant, but proposed that the Polish Government should send a representative to Moscow, adding that there was no need for a Polish National Committee. Equally it was unnecessary to discuss the Polish frontiers at present. Poland only required that the Soviet Union should nullify the treaties made with Germany in 1939. I passed on these reasonable comments to Maisky.

Two days later, on July 6th, the Soviet Ambassador met General Sikorski in Sir Alexander Cadogan's room at the Foreign Office. Maisky undertook to submit to his Government five points which summed up the Polish position:

(1) Discussion of frontiers to be left aside for the moment, provided the Russians denounced the treaties with Germany of August and September 1939;
(2) Normal relations to be resumed between the two Governments and a Polish Ambassador appointed to Moscow;
(3) Poland would then be prepared to collaborate in the common fight against Germany;
(4) A Polish army to be formed on Soviet territory, to be transported elsewhere if desired;
(5) Polish military and political prisoners to be released.

Our political collaboration with the Soviets made some progress during these July days. Cripps saw Stalin on July 8th and found that all the Russians wanted in the way of an agreement at the moment was a pledge of mutual help without precise statements about quantity or quality, and an undertaking on both sides not to conclude a separate peace. We accepted and the declaration was signed in Moscow a few days later.

July 9th: Russian military mission called on me at 10.30 chaperoned by Maisky. The General [Golikov] impressed me as quick, direct and keen. The whole party, though somewhat motley, had a vigorous, business-like air. The General brought me a tough message from Stalin, and gave a more cheerful picture of Russian prospects than Stalin had given to Cripps.

Not surprisingly, the Polish negotiations presented far more difficulties and meetings with either Maisky or Sikorski, or both, were frequent. There was also the complication of the American position.

July 21st: A morning of struggle with Poles and Russians. Perhaps made a little progress. A luncheon of sandwiches (caviar!) at the office. Then work on Belgian broadcast.

Hopkins and Winant came to see me. They told me that Roosevelt was most eager that we should not commit ourselves to any definite frontiers for any country before the peace treaty. H. said that U.S. would come into the war and did not want to find after the event that we had all kinds of engagements of which they had never been told. Winston was clearly not interested in the peace and H. had therefore been told to speak urgently to me. I explained our position, and that I was as eager to keep my hands free as anybody, but the spectacle of an American President talking at large on European frontiers chilled me with Wilsonian memories.

The Agreement between the Russians and the Poles was finally signed on July 30th. General Sikorski's statesmanship deserved any credit that might be due for this. Our part was only patient diplomacy tinged with anxiety for what the future must hold for the Poles as the weaker partner.

★　★　★　★　★

Having done what I could to ease relations between Poland and Russia as two sovereign states, the British and Soviet Governments had now to face the situation which had developed in Iran. German agents had been active there for some time, but now that the Soviets were under Nazi attack, the railway across the country became of capital importance as the only practicable land route from the Persian Gulf for the despatch of supplies to Russia. The northern Arctic route, though shorter, was more vulnerable to enemy attack as well as being climatically brutal. The Iranian route could not be secure while Nazi agents were free to subvert and sabotage. These men were formidable. We had recently had an experience of what they could do in Bulgaria and we dared not risk a repetition of growing German authority in the vital geographical area from which we drew our oil supplies.

As a result, I accepted that the British and Soviet Governments had no choice except to exert joint pressure to expel these German agents. When this pressure failed, I reluctantly agreed to the forces of the two countries entering Iran from south and north and in September they advanced on Tehran. The trans-Iranian railway thus became available and secure for the rest of the war. Its carrying capacity, at first limited, was improved by energetic American enterprise, until it played its part in the transport of essential war supplies from Britain and the United States to Soviet Russia.

Next in importance was the Turkish position, now that Britain and Soviet Russia were fighting alongside. As a result of exchanges with Moscow, each of our countries gave the Turkish Government, in August, assurances that we would not make an agreement detrimental to Turkey's essential interests with any Government at war with Germany. The Turkish Government were thus caressed, but not entirely reassured.

All was not the making of diplomatic plans; there were interludes.

August 2nd: I spent a heavenly two hours working in garden. Tore myself away most reluctantly to motor to Chequers, for meeting with Chiefs of Staff at 6 p.m. Found P.M. and Auchinleck sitting in sun in garden and was told they had tried to stop me because meeting was off until after dinner. Winston shortly retired for his sleep and A. and I had a gossip. He asked me about people in Middle East, but I was reluctant to say much about soldiers there for I just don't know. He thought Jumbo [General Wilson] very good but a little slow for a big offensive and was inclined to favour Cunningham [appointed to command the Eighth Army on September 24th], whose campaign in East Africa was certainly brilliant. He thought highly of Gott [commanding 7th Armoured Division from September 2nd] among juniors and of a Black Watch man [Lieut.-Gen. Neil Ritchie, who became Auchinleck's Deputy Chief of General Staff] of whom I have heard Dill speak well.

A. is determined not to risk another fiasco like that of May in Western Desert. He says that if an opportunity offers before end of October he will seize it; if not, he must collect necessary tank forces to strike really effective blow when he is ready. This seems to me sound sense but Winston finds it unpalatable and urged earlier action.

Later in the month Soviet protests about our help began. We had, Maisky said, turned down the suggestion of a second front.

He had no wish to argue about that, but at least we might give more aid in supplies, especially aircraft. The Soviet Government were grateful for our promise of two hundred fighters, but this was a small contribution in the scale of Russia's enormous losses. Seven hundred thousand men had been killed and wounded, between four thousand and five thousand aircraft and about five thousand tanks had been lost. The Russians also wanted to know our plans and ideas on the general strategy of the war. I agreed that this, like supplies, was certainly a subject for discussion between the two Governments. If the Soviet Government were suspicious of the sincerity of our desire to help them, Maisky should disabuse them of this at once. Geography imposed difficulties which could not simply be dismissed, but we had already sent help and were going to send more. We then doubled the number of Hurricanes.

★   ★   ★   ★   ★

I now tried to get a few days' holiday in the country, but it was soon interrupted. On the afternoon of September 4th, Sir Alexander Cadogan rang me up to say that Maisky was delivering a message to the Prime Minister from Stalin that evening and Mr. Churchill had particularly asked that I should be there, so I drove back again to London. Stalin's message was a cry for help. Things had gone badly for the Soviet forces in the Ukraine and at Leningrad. The relative stabilization of the front which the Russians had achieved three weeks before had broken down, owing to massive German reinforcements. The Germans were transferring all their forces with impunity. "As a result," wrote Stalin, "we have lost more than one half of the Ukraine and in addition the enemy is at the gates of Leningrad." He called for a second front that year in the Balkans or France, to draw off thirty to forty German divisions, as well as for enormous supplies of aluminium, tanks and aircraft. Without these two forms of help, Stalin declared, the U.S.S.R. would suffer defeat or would lose any capacity to give help in the struggle by its own operations.

Maisky, in delivering this message, spoke sombrely about the seriousness of the situation. The Prime Minister explained to him the various reasons which made it impossible for us to operate on the Continent in such a way as to draw off German forces from the Russian front. He then arranged for the Ambassador to have a meeting with the Chiefs of Staff and myself the next day, in order to receive fuller information.

Mr. Churchill and I had some talk after Maisky had left, when Sir John Dill joined us. Dill took a grim view of the Russian military position, especially at Leningrad. Anxious as the Prime Minister and I were to help the Russians, we had to admit that the case against a landing in France was overwhelming, above all because of the power of the German air force, if Portal had estimated it aright.

The next day a dogged and worried Maisky came to a meeting with the Chiefs of Staff and myself. The situation on the Russian front was critical, he repeated, and the time had come for Britain to take risks to help the Soviet Union to continue the struggle. He asked the Chiefs of Staff to give him their views on the formation of a front, either in France or in the Balkans. He said that the size of the British force he had in mind was fifteen to twenty divisions.

The Chiefs of Staff replied that there was no operation we could mount which would result in drawing any important German forces from the east. There were still more German divisions in France than we could land there and they would have local air superiority. We could not land sufficient forces to remain in France and would be driven out without the Germans having to withdraw anything from the eastern front. To collect the shipping necessary to land fifteen to twenty divisions would be an almost insuperable task and would imperil our position in the Middle East. These arguments against a landing in France applied even more strongly to the Balkans. The Chiefs of Staff told Maisky that, if they saw any possibility of achieving his object, the many and serious difficulties in landing a force on the Continent would have to be overcome, but they could see no such possibility. I wrote that night that the Soviet Ambassador had stated his case well. Neither side had been shaken in its convictions, but I thought that Maisky had at the finish a clearer perception of our weakness and limitations.

The War Cabinet met immediately afterwards. We considered whether we could promise to supply from our own production half the tanks and aircraft for which Stalin had asked and invite the

Americans to provide the other half. After a further meeting with
the Minister of Aircraft Production and the Chiefs of Staff, the
draft of the Prime Minister's reply to Stalin was agreed.

September 5th: Maisky was then summoned. First of all Winston spoke to him roundly but kindly, as only he can combine, about Soviet propaganda here in favour of second front, and said only result would be rough reaction and recrimination all would wish to avoid. Maisky said he understood, but pleaded that when asked he could not say that he was satisfied with our help when in fact he was not. All this while final draft was being typed. Maisky was, I think, pleased with it, and we finished up by calling in Max's help to find some aluminium, of which Russians want 30,000 tons, pretty well at once it seems!

To celebrate this, Winston insisted on a restaurant dinner and carried Max and self off to Ritz. Very good dinner, oysters, partridge etc. and good talk. Winston at top of his form. Talk much of past events, some long past. Winston said that he would like best to have F.E. [Smith, Lord Birkenhead] back to help him. Not F.E. of last years, but F.E. about '14 or '15. Next he would like A.J.B. [Balfour].

Max told Winston that if he had played his cards well when he was at Admiralty early in last war, especially with Tory party, he could have been P.M. instead of Lloyd George. Winston agreed. He described as toughest moment of his life when he learnt that Lloyd George did not propose even to include him in his Cabinet. He had dined, with Max, with Lloyd George the night Lloyd George had been given the commission and had assumed from this Lloyd George would ask him. He had even urged Max to ask for Postmaster General, when Max had actually Board of Trade in his pocket, and Max had been detailed to break the bad news to Winston.

Max girded at me for not understanding my strength when I resigned and for coming back as Dominion Secretary. He said that had I played my hand strongly, I must have succeeded Neville. Winston said I was right to take Dominions Office. My own feeling about it all was that I do not truly believe my own contribution at any time to be so overwhelmingly good as to be prepared to drive it *à outrance.*

Mr. Churchill more than once remarked to me that, though he himself had not thought so at the time, he realized that he had been fortunate to be out of the Government for so long in the thirties. He explained that when one is a member of an administration one has inevitably to yield in opinion to some extent for the sake of the team. He had been spared all that.

★ ★ ★ ★ ★

One difficulty throughout this period was that the Russians believed, or affected to believe, that it was possible for us to make an important diversion by landing at some point in sufficient strength to draw off the Germans, or alternatively to send twenty-five divisions to fight in Russia. All our explanations about action on our own account on the continent of Europe, though often repeated to Mr. Maisky in London, failed to shake the Kremlin. Lord Beaverbrook's mission with General Ismay to Moscow, in which he was joined by Mr. Averell Harriman, concerned itself chiefly with supplies. Judging the atmosphere unfavourable for military discussions, Beaverbrook decided to stick to his own last.

> *October 10th:* Max returned in morning and Winston and I heard his account. Very lively and entertaining and, he clearly maintains, satisfactory. He believes that Stalin will fight on, come what may, and that he hates Hitler, which he certainly did *not* in 1935, with cold fury. . . .
> Motored to Chequers in the afternoon, Russian news looking bad. . . .
> Party was only Max, Harriman and self. We had much gossip about Moscow. Harriman told me privately that Stalin had spoken of an alliance after the war and proposed it to Max. He thought S. would be offended if we did not return some reply.
> After an interlude for films, more talk about Russia and plans to aid, our production and American etc.

Gradually Stalin began to apprehend part at least of the situation. On September 15th Mr. Maisky delivered a message from him to Mr. Churchill suggesting that, if the establishment of a second front was impossible, perhaps another method could be found to give the

Soviet Union military help, either through Archangel or through Iran. Maisky told me on September 29th that he hoped in due course British troops would appear in the Caucasus and perhaps also in southern Russia. He was sure that the presence of even a few British troops would make a great difference to Russian morale.

We were always looking round for ways to help the Russians. The Prime Minister was keen on a plan for a landing in northern Norway. I was not, and preferred another for attacking Sicily in conjunction with General Auchinleck's forthcoming offensive in the desert. It was eventually agreed to study this.

On October 17th, I took up Stalin's mention of a treaty of alliance and told the Ambassador that I would be glad to hear any Soviet proposals. However, in spite of our earlier explanations to Maisky, Stalin persisted in his demand for large-scale British military support in south Russia. Indeed, it became apparent that, because there had been no military discussions at the Moscow conference on supplies at the end of September, the Soviet Government were contending that we had never answered the proposal made to Mr. Churchill on September 15th. Mr. Molotov had complained of this to Sir Stafford Cripps on October 23rd.

We discussed the whole question in the War Cabinet on October 27th. Lord Beaverbrook was sure that, in the talks in Moscow, Marshal Stalin had not pressed strongly either for the despatch of British troops to fight in Russia or for the creation of a second front. I told Mr. Maisky next day that we regretted that Molotov had turned down our offer of a token force for the Caucasus, made by me to Maisky on October 16th. I also pointed out that, from a military point of view, it would be foolish to send a small force far into Russia, where it could do nothing to influence the course of the battle and would merely create additional problems of supply and maintenance. It would only help to choke the routes that were open to us for sending war material to Russia.

October 29th: Attended a meeting of Supply Committee for Russia, Max in the chair. Matters seem to be going fairly well, though I fear congestion later at Archangel.

It seemed by now that explanations given to Maisky were not always passed on to the Kremlin, or at least were not accepted there.

The British Government decided therefore to make another offer of military talks. The Prime Minister suggested to Stalin on November 4th that Wavell and General Paget, Commander-in-Chief designate Far East, should visit Russia, and Maisky spoke to me twice on the same day about this visit. Would the two generals be in a position to discuss future plans, he first asked. I replied that they would. Later the Ambassador spoke again about the need for a final answer to Stalin's request for British forces for Russia. Would Wavell be able to discuss this? I replied that there should be no misunderstanding on this issue; Stalin had asked for twenty-five to thirty divisions and the Prime Minister had made it plain that this was quite outside our powers. On the other hand, the Soviet Government had turned down our offer to relieve Russian troops in Iran and to send a small force to the Caucasus.

Maisky persisted, asking whether, if Stalin said he did not want a British force in the Caucasus but would welcome one, say, at Rostov, this was a matter the generals could discuss. I replied that Wavell would be able to discuss such a request and would, no doubt, explain how this question was related to the delivery of those supplies for which the Russians were asking so urgently.

★ ★ ★ ★ ★

Many times in the war I had occasion to notice the continuing resentment of Soviet leaders about British intervention during the civil war of 1918–19. They would often tease Mr. Churchill about it, not always in friendly fashion. No doubt they remembered that the Caucasus was one of the regions where we had played a part then. They feared that nationalist feeling among the mountain peoples might flare up again and take an anti-Soviet shape. Something of this kind did in fact happen when the Germans reached the Caucasus a year later. After the war, whole peoples paid a terrible price for having allowed their dream of independence to lead them into collaboration with the enemy.

November 4th: Meeting at 10 p.m. with Winston and Chiefs of Staff. Dickie [Mountbatten] appeared in his new role [Commodore Combined Operations]. Then talk about Far East, Russia and other plans. Altogether a useful evening. Winston said he was off tomorrow evening until Monday [November 10th] and would I mind the shop and call together Chiefs of Staff if need be. Later we talked over whiskies in his room, particularly of Wavell and Paget's projected visit to Moscow. I suggested it might be useful if I went sometime. Winston agreed. Both thought it better after results of "Crusader" [the forthcoming offensive in Libya] were visible. Timetable thus a little difficult. Depends upon how long Stalin takes to reply.

The Foreign Office sent Mr. Averell Harriman's notes of his and Lord Beaverbrook's conversations with Stalin to Sir Stafford Cripps. The Ambassador was incensed not to have heard the details before. He appeared to believe that we in London had paid little attention to Stalin's remarks and telegraphed that he could see no use in staying any longer in Russia. I replied that all Stalin's points were being dealt with. I had asked Maisky to find out what Stalin had in mind about an alliance and had told him we were ready to carry our war-time collaboration with the Soviet Union into the peace settlement and beyond. But we did not think it was practicable at this stage to formulate our peace aims for discussion with our allies more definitely than had been done in the Atlantic Charter. I told Cripps that I hoped to be able to visit Russia myself at a not too distant date.

November 11th: Winston told me that he had had a difficult morning in House, fifteen questions and many supplementaries. He felt resentful. Maisky came to see us both at noon, to give Stalin's answer. This was sharp and critical, though I believe the presentation to be worse than the substance. Anyway Winston was, excusably, very angry and pretty rough with Maisky.

In evening before dinner Winston and I and Max [Beaverbrook] discussed whole business, Max and I being the men of peace. Meanwhile there will surely be more trouble with Cripps, whose one idea is to come home and play a part here.

Dined with Winston, Brendan [Bracken, Minister of Information] only other present. W. talked of future and suddenly said that if anything happened to him I should have to take over.

Brendan approved. Announcement was repeated later when Chief Whip [Mr. James Stuart] and P.J. [Grigg, Permanent Under-Secretary of State for War] came in. I am unhappy that Jack Dill is to be moved [from being C.I.G.S.]. I am convinced that Winston underrates him. He did not consult me on this, merely remarking that he had taken his decision and adding: "I know that you will not agree."

Margesson rang me up that evening to tell me that a decision had been taken that Dill should go, and to speak to me about his successor. He said that he thought that it should be Sir Alan Brooke, but that there was some pressure for Major-General Archibald Nye, now Vice-Chief of the Imperial General Staff, as the younger man. I said that I was sure Brooke was the answer. I held a high opinion of Nye, but he did not have Brooke's experience of command. Margesson seemed relieved to be confirmed in his own judgment.

A few days later Sir John Dill wrote to me:

. . . It is sad to leave the Army that one loves in the middle of a war, particularly at a time when one knows one has its complete confidence and even its affection. I leave in great sadness but with no bitterness.

May I say how greatly I value your friendship and with what pleasure I look back upon the days when we worked so closely and I think successfully together in bringing the Army through its most difficult period. . . .

★ ★ ★ ★ ★

Later we were to become only too familiar with the harsh tone of Marshal Stalin's messages to the Prime Minister, but the first example made a very disagreeable impression on the War Cabinet. We disliked the way Stalin linked acceptance of a visit by General Wavell and General Paget with his insistence on discussing war aims and post-war policies, which the two generals would quite obviously not be qualified to do. Stalin also showed himself irritated by our delay in declaring war on Finland, Hungary and Roumania, which had joined with Germany in attacking Russia. The War Cabinet decided that the message should not be answered until Maisky had had time to report home on its reception.

November 14th: A morning of many interviews with Ambassadors. In a talk with Maisky I was indiscreet and told him he had better get a message from Molotov which would enable me to build a bridge again. He said that he would try. . . .

A talk at F.O. about Russia, Cripps' troubles etc. We thought that it would on whole be better that Cripps should stay until I arrive out there.

During this discussion, a summons came to go to see the Prime Minister, who was indignant with Cripps and wanted him home at once to tell him so. Beaverbrook was also summoned. Like me he did not want Cripps home, but rather that he should be empowered to negotiate about the post-war settlement, though he did not think that anything would come of this.

Winston said he would not have me go to Moscow to keep Cripps quiet. I said that there had never been any question of that anyway. After more talk we decided to put issue to War Cabinet alone at special meeting on Monday. Winston is impressed with the strength of our hand in dealing with Stalin. His need of us greater than our need of him, I must not go to Moscow except the red carpet is out, etc. There is much force in all this.

There was, however, also the Prime Minister's reluctance to consider post-war problems at all. This was natural enough in one who had to bear the principal burden of the conduct of the war, but it was a position which would become increasingly hard to hold with allies, American as well as Russian, who wanted to do just this.

After further discussions in the War Cabinet on November 17th, I telegraphed to Cripps, who had referred to the need to give Stalin a clear answer on war aims, the post-war settlement, and military collaboration:

I give the clear answer that we are prepared to join in both discussions. We have no idea of "turning these points down"; but if "a clear answer" means that we are to give Stalin at once a clear statement of our conception of war aims and post-war organization of peace . . . I must say that simply cannot be done.

I went on that we had not ourselves determined what our conditions and problems would be, nor could we go ahead without the United States. But I hoped that the discussion would help toward agreement.

On November 20th Maisky brought me an apology from Stalin about the manner of his last message. The next afternoon I attended a meeting with the Prime Minister at which Beaverbrook and Attlee were also present, when we discussed the Russian position anew. The Prime Minister favoured a personal telegram to Stalin in which he would suggest a visit from me. I told him that I was not keen to go, unless the political ground had been prepared. The others, however, favoured the visit now, and after some modification the text was sent off. The message said:

We shall be willing in the near future to send the Foreign Secretary, Mr. Eden, whom you know . . . to meet you at Moscow or elsewhere. He would be accompanied by high military and other experts, and will be able to discuss every question relating to the war, including the sending of troops not only into the Caucasus but into the fighting line of your armies in the south. Neither our shipping resources nor the communications will allow large numbers to be employed, and even so you will have to choose between troops and supplies across Persia.

I notice that you wish also to discuss the post-war organization of peace. . . . The Foreign Secretary will be able to discuss the whole of this field with you.

A few days later, I talked over the military part of my mission to Moscow with the Prime Minister and the Chiefs of Staff. It was bleak. Since our offer to send a brigade group to the Caucasus had been turned down by the Russians, the battle in Cyrenaica had begun. The British offensive had been launched on November 18th and at first all went well, but Rommel once again countered strongly and by the date of our meeting our forces had failed in their first attempt to relieve Tobruk. Auchinleck had replaced General Cunningham by General Ritchie, in command of the Eighth Army. In these conditions the Chiefs of Staff were unwilling to make any firm offer of troops for Russia; every available man might be needed for the Libyan battle.

I understood this, but the decision was embarrassing, as I told the Chiefs of Staff, because the Prime Minister had informed Stalin that we could offer a small force to co-operate with the Russians on the southern front. Now that it was very difficult to do this, it might, I suggested, be wiser to defer my visit until the horizon was clearer. However, that evening:

> *December 3rd:* Max [Beaverbrook] came to Defence Committee talk about Russia. Quite a useful discussion. We all agreed that it would be wrong to send a small land force to South Russia as things are at present. Max suggested offering tanks and aeroplanes instead and maintained that Stalin would much prefer these. It was agreed that this should be examined. Max suggested five hundred tanks and five hundred aircraft.

The next day the War Cabinet approved a memorandum I had prepared for Stalin and gave me authority to hand it to him. I explained that my purpose in this document was to exorcize certain suspicions from Stalin's mind. These were that we wished to exclude Russia from an Anglo–American scheme for a post-war settlement, that in making peace we should ignore Russian interests, and that we were not ready to take sufficiently strong measures against Germany, when the fighting was over, to render her harmless for many years to come. I proposed to meet this state of mind by a joint declaration proclaiming our mutual agreement to collaborate, not only in making the peace settlement, but in maintaining it.

In addition to this declaration, I told my colleagues that I should have to be ready to discuss with the Russians the future of Germany, post-war reconstruction, reparations and the possibility of confederations between certain smaller European states. I thought that Stalin might raise the question of Russia's western frontiers, but I would have to decline to go beyond the first two clauses of the Atlantic Charter. All this was agreed to.

The Chiefs of Staff's paper admitted the difficulty of dissipating Soviet suspicions, but asked that we should try to persuade the Russians that our strategy was based on military and naval necessities and not on merely selfish interests. This was clearly not going to be an easy job, but I was encouraged in it by the support of General Nye, who was to accompany me with staff officers from the War Office and the Air Ministry. Even more important was the offer I was authorized to make of ten squadrons of the Royal Air Force to operate on the southern flank of the Russian armies. These squadrons were to be withdrawn from the Libyan battle at the earliest moment when success had been gained.

2

THE BEAR
December 1941

I set out for Russia — A telephone call at Invergordon — Pearl
Harbour — Arrival at Murmansk — First interview with Mr.
Stalin in Moscow — Reparations and post-war frontiers — Mr.
Stalin sums up the Russian position — Second interview — Mr.
Stalin shows his claws — I visit the battlefront — Third inter-
view — Mr. Stalin relents — Russia and Japan — A banquet

I SET OUT from Binderton on my Arctic journey to Russia on the
morning of December 7th. I had chosen a strong delegation from
the Foreign Office to accompany me, including Sir Alexander Cadogan, the Permanent Under-Secretary, Mr. Oliver Harvey, who
had again become my invaluable private secretary, and the resource-
ful and tireless Mr. Frank Roberts of the Central Department.
Mr. Maisky travelled with us to take part in the talks. As Permanent Under-Secretary and therefore my principal official adviser,
Cadogan was at all times wise and thorough. These qualities, and
his exceptional experience, enabled him to take much of the burden
off me.

I left Euston on a lovely afternoon, but during the long journey
northward I began to feel chilled and sick. When I reached Invergordon at 8 o'clock the next morning I saw a doctor, who diagnosed
gastric influenza, the only time I was ill during the war in Europe.
Soon after, a naval officer said that the Prime Minister wanted to
speak to me on the telephone; this, he explained, meant going to
his headquarters. I was reluctant, for I felt miserable and wanted
to get straight on to the destroyer and make for Scapa and my
cruiser. I thought it would need all my strength anyway. However,
ill as I was, I felt that I must take the call, the more so when I was
told that the United States Ambassador was with the Prime Min-

ister. Mr. Churchill told me what he knew of the Japanese attack on Pearl Harbour. He was quite naturally in a high state of excitement. I could not conceal my relief and did not have to try to. I felt that whatever happened now, it was merely a question of time. Before, we had believed in the end but never seen the means, now both were clear.

Mr. Churchill began laying plans. He said he must go to the United States at once. I saw the force of this, but I did not imagine we could both be away and was not sure that the Americans would want him so soon. I felt that my visit to the Russians was important and that they would be resentful if it were postponed. Reluctantly I asked what Mr. Churchill wanted me to do. He replied at once that I must carry on with my journey, while he crossed the Atlantic. I demurred, saying that I did not see how we could both be away at once. He said we could. The emphasis of the war had shifted, what now mattered was the intentions of our two great allies. We must each go to one of them. I should repeat every telegram from Moscow to him and he would do the same at his end. After some more exchanges, Mr. Churchill added: "Wait a minute, someone else wants to speak to you." Gil Winant came on the line. It was good to hear the relief in his voice as he acclaimed our decisions and wished me God speed. I knew that in his heart he was acclaiming something else too. The United States and Britain were now allies in the war against Japan.

December 8th: Left by destroyer for Scapa. A fine ship, *Somali,* and mercifully a smooth passage. Reached *Kent* after four hours' cruise. Found Commander-in-Chief [Home Fleet, Admiral Sir John Tovey] on board. Since I had a temperature I was bundled into bed.

December 9th–12th: These four days at sea—moderate weather. I spent nearly all the time in bed, battling with this wretched 'flu. Very tedious. Up on Thursday 11th and held conference and dined, all of which was probably a mistake for I had a wretched night.

We saw nothing of our Russian guests throughout the voyage. They remained immured in their cabin, from which was wafted from time to time a breeze of what appeared to be ether. If they were anæsthetizing each other, they were wise.

While at sea I received a telegram from the Prime Minister, telling me that we should have urgently to reinforce Malaya with aircraft from the Middle East. In view of the changed circumstances, I could not offer Stalin the ten squadrons of the Royal Air Force, as we had planned before I left London. I accepted this as an inevitable decision, but the prospects for my mission looked bleaker still.

★   ★   ★   ★   ★

December 12th: Arrived off Murmansk in a thick fog. Clearly no possibility of flying on today. Maisky went ashore to investigate and reported choice of train or aircraft, former taking sixty hours. In view of uncertain weather consensus of opinion favoured train.

On the Ambassador's return he asked if he could speak to me privately for a few minutes. We went into my cabin, where Maisky put a small black bag on the table and made a little speech. Stalin, he said, was anxious that I and those accompanying me should not be embarrassed while we were in Russia by the controversy then prevailing between our two countries about the rouble exchange rate. He wished, therefore, to put a sum at my disposal in roubles which I could use without reservation.

Maisky then opened the bag and took out package after package of notes which he set down in rows before me. I was agape at so much wealth and asked Maisky to thank Mr. Stalin for the hospitable thought which had prompted this action. I assured him, however, that we could meet our expenses without having to put him to this trouble and that we should not have need for the currency. The Ambassador seemed quite downcast at my reply but, when I persisted in it, replaced the roubles and relocked his bag.

December 13th: Russian delegation, Admiral, General, etc., came aboard about noon, I still feeling far from well. After luncheon we left the *Kent* in half-light and whirling snowstorm, a most eerie proceeding. "Pipe," says captain to chilled mariners, who do their manful best and we clamber down the side into the bowels of a warm and greasy tug. So, farewell England. A few minutes and we are alongside and step ashore to a most picturesque scene. Still this uncanny half-light. A line of soldiers in their sheepskin uniforms making a smear of ochre, decked out by the flags of the two nations, over-bright, rather cheap and new, as the only splash of colour, behind them log huts, unfinished shacks, a few idle spectators who as black smudges brave the scuds of snow. The bands strike up. We salute, and the usual ceremonies take place. The men look very young. The effect of the whole scene is surprisingly beautiful. Soon we are packed into cars and off for sixteen-mile drive to Murmansk. Soviet soldiers mount guard at intervals along the half-dark route. No better testimony to Soviet man-power.

As we topped the hill above Murmansk, the clouds lifted and the harbour looked most beautiful in its semi-circle of hills and half-lights. The colour of a pale pearl grey and of a fairy texture. Quite indescribable and unpaintable, the air crisp and fresh. This Arctic scenery has a beauty which is the exact antithesis of the Christmas card of tradition. Soft, melting half-tones. Nothing brittle or garish.

Boarded our train at once on arrival at Murmansk and left at 4 p.m., heavily guarded.

This protection was, we were told, due to the fact that we had to travel near the Finnish frontier, but it was the anti-aircraft defence which most surprised me. Between every two of our carriages was an open truck in which was mounted an anti-aircraft gun with its crew. The cold which these men had to endure when moving at a fair pace through these Arctic temperatures must have been cruel, even though the crews were changed frequently, I think every two hours. I felt astonishment and admiration at the powers of endurance which could survive such an ordeal. From Murmansk I telegraphed to Mr. Churchill:

Deeply grieved at the loss of H.M.S. *Prince of Wales* and H.M.S. *Repulse*.

Agree that in present conditions we can promise the Russians nothing beyond quotas already pledged.

I will do all I can to impress on Stalin importance of our Libyan operations and our determination to press on with them. Need for clearing a passage through Mediterranean is increased by Japanese naval predominance in the Pacific and potential threat to Indian Ocean.

Arguments for limiting our fighter offensive over France must now be strong. If you decide to forgo this in order that Libya and Far East may be fed, I feel confident that Stalin would understand. . . .

God speed to your journey from us all.

December 14th: Woke up late after indifferent night to find my carriage flooded with sunshine. We have made good progress during the night. Had two good walks during the day. Second time the equivalent of 45 degrees of frost or fifteen below our zero. But it did not feel very cold, for there was no wind.

December 15th: More good progress during night and welcome news at breakfast that we should make Moscow tonight. Vologda reached about noon and we stamped about for a good half-hour on the platform there. 45 degrees below zero. Really felt the cold this time. Stafford Cripps boarded train in evening. We eventually reached Moscow about 11.30 p.m. Molotov and others met us and we went through usual military ceremonies, complicated somewhat by glare of scores of cinema lights which completely blinded us, so that I almost stumbled over the guard of honour.

December 16th: Read telegrams and worked in morning. Far Eastern situation looks ugly. Russian and Libyan news good. Our first interview with Stalin at 7 p.m. It continued until nearly 11 p.m. In the concluding stages tea and cakes were brought in but nobody took much interest in them, except Cripps. After about half an hour's interval brandy followed with zakoushka and champagne in which many toasts were drunk. All was friendly. Stalin is a quiet dictator in his manner. No shouting, no gesticulation, so that it is impossible to guess his meaning, or even the subject of which he is speaking until the translation is given. Maisky was a good interpreter. Cripps made a full record of all that passed so I don't go into all that here. Late to bed.

★　　★　　★　　★　　★

At this first meeting Stalin gave me the drafts of two short treaties. One was for a military alliance during the war, the other provided for common action to solve post-war questions in Europe and
to prevent renewed aggression by Germany. Both these treaties
were to be published, but the second one was to have a secret protocol dealing in some detail with European frontiers.

Stalin's suggestions for this protocol showed me that the hope
we had held in London, of being able to confine the discussion of
frontiers to the general terms of the Atlantic Charter, had been
vain. Russian ideas were already starkly definite. They changed
little during the next three years, for their purpose was to secure
the most tangible physical guarantees for Russia's future security.

Stalin proposed that Poland should expand westwards at Germany's expense. Other occupied countries were to return to their
old frontiers, Austria being restored, while the Rhineland and possibly Bavaria would be detached from Germany. The Soviet Union
would regain her frontiers of 1941 with Finland and Roumania
and would recover the Baltic States. Her frontier with Poland
would be based on the Curzon line.* Stalin also wanted the right
to establish bases in Finland and Roumania with a guarantee for
the exits from the Baltic. The Soviet Government would not object, he said, to Britain establishing bases in Denmark and Norway.

Stalin then put two questions. What were our views about repa-
ration by Germany for the damage she had done, and how were we
to keep peace and order in Europe after the war. He suggested a
council of the victorious powers, with a military force at its disposal.
The Soviet Union would have no objection if some European countries wished to federate.

I told Stalin that I agreed with much that he had said about
post-war Europe. The British people were determined that every
possible military measure should be taken to prevent Germany
breaking the peace again. Exactly how this was to be done would
have to be gone into carefully. There was no doubt that some kind
of military control over Germany would be necessary and that Great
Britain, the Soviet Union and the United States, if they would
help, would have to undertake it.

* The eastern frontier for Poland proposed at the time of the Paris Peace Con-
ference in 1919–20, with alternatives at the southern end. From 1921 to 1939 the
Russo–Polish frontier ran considerably farther to the east. The Ribbentrop–
Molotov line of 1939 lay somewhat farther to the west. See map on page 307.

On the partition of Germany, I said, the British Government had not taken a decision either way. There was no objection to it in principle. Nor had we closed our minds to a separate Bavaria or Rhineland; we were certainly in favour of an independent Austria. I could not commit my colleagues on these matters without first consulting them, but when I had done this, the discussion could be carried a stage further through our Ambassadors. So far as reparations were concerned, I was sure, from our experience after the last war, that we should be against any money reparations; the restitution by Germany of goods taken away from occupied territories was another matter.

I then explained to Stalin that I could not agree to the secret protocol without reference to the Cabinet and added:

Even before Russia was attacked, Mr. Roosevelt sent a message to us, asking us not to enter into any secret arrangement as to the post-war reorganization of Europe without first consulting him. This does not exclude our two countries from discussing a basis for the peace. Mr. Roosevelt was worried because he had heard that I had offered the Yugoslav Government some territorial extension, and he was nervous about this, as he did not want the United States to go to the peace treaty and find that a lot of matters had been settled without their knowledge.

STALIN: But there are many questions relating to the safety of our two countries which can be discussed between us.

EDEN: We can discuss matters between us, but ultimately, for the purpose of the peace treaty, the Soviet Union, Great Britain and the United States of America must all come in and agree with one another on the principal world affairs.

STALIN: I agree.

I then suggested that before we spoke of military plans, we ought to clear up a political point. Should we try to combine our two documents, or what course did Stalin propose.

STALIN: I think that what you have submitted is a kind of declaration, whereas ours are two agreements. A declaration I regard as algebra, but an agreement as practical arithmetic. I do not wish to decry algebra, but I prefer practical arithmetic, and I think in the present circumstances, when Hitler is boasting to everyone of all the treaties he has managed to obtain, it would be wiser to have treaties between the two countries, and our documents are in that form.

EDEN: Perhaps I could take the two treaties as a basis and see if there is anything in our document which it is worth while incorporating in the two treaties.

STALIN: What about the attachment of the secret protocol?

EDEN: My difficulty is that I cannot sign such a document without consulting my colleagues, and we have not as yet applied our minds to these problems.

MAISKY: Not even the Soviet frontiers?

EDEN: I couldn't do this without consulting the Prime Minister and also talking to the Americans. We could give an answer when I get back to London, which I could communicate to Mr. Maisky, and then we could continue with the discussion.

I went on to explain that apart from the question of the United States we had, of course, to consult the Dominions, who were with us in the war and were helping us and who would, rightly, expect to have their say about any arrangements for national frontiers after the war.

STALIN: Perhaps it would be possible to do it in London by an exchange of notes.

EDEN: We should have to tell the United States of America if we were deciding upon anything so important in its effect upon Eastern Europe and, in any case, I think it would be much wiser for us to tell them about it.

STALIN: I am quite agreeable to your informing America, and I would be very glad if the United States would participate.

EDEN: I doubt whether they would do that. It is best to let me consult the Prime Minister when I get back and then let you know what are his views. I can assure you that we are entirely realistic in our determination to stop the Germans from repeating their aggression, and I very much hope that you fully understood that.

STALIN: I agree with the proposal. What I want to underline is that I want to come to an agreement with you on this so as to have a united front on these problems.

EDEN: We have not yet worked this out ourselves. We have not yet even discussed it in the Cabinet. I have yet to discuss the question of Poland and East Prussia with the Prime Minister.

STALIN: I quite understand. My desire is to establish that the war aims of our two countries are identical, as then our alliance will be all the stronger. If our war aims were different, then there would be no alliance.

EDEN: I agree. I see no reason why our war aims should be different, but these frontier questions I must discuss with my colleagues. My object will be to seek to reconcile the war aims of the two countries. There may be some points on which there are differences.

Stalin then spoke of the possibility of dividing Germany, and giving Poland the lands up to the Oder.

EDEN: There is a difficulty in cutting up Germany unless the movement for it comes from within the country, as you may cause an irredentist movement to unite the country again, rather like the *Anschluss*.

STALIN: These kind of conceptions brought us to the present war. Would you like to try another attack by Germany?

EDEN: I think that is rather an over-simplification of the causes of the war.

Stalin then changed the subject, revealing an opinion on German aid to Japan which was to prove unfounded.

STALIN: My military advisers believe that Germany has given the Japanese about 1,500 aircraft. They are not absolutely certain about this, but they have several good reasons to believe it; and that German pilots are working for Japan as well.

EDEN: Certainly the Japanese have shown more skill in the air than we expected.

STALIN: We had experience with air fighting with Japan, and also we have carefully observed it in China for a very long time, and I have come to the conclusion that this is not really a Japanese war. I think some of the Japanese pilots were trained in Germany, and others are Germans.

EDEN: How do you think the aeroplanes got there?

STALIN: Probably through South America. Certain South American States, if they do not encourage, at least do not discourage these activities, and Spain and Portugal might also help.

EDEN: I am grateful to you for this information. I would like to look into it.

STALIN: I cannot give you absolute proof, but have good reason to believe it.

EDEN: I am certain that the attacks on the *Prince of Wales* were pressed with great skill and determination and were as good as any of the German attacks upon our warships.

STALIN: And then there is the reason that for the last six weeks we have noticed a considerable decrease of German aviation on our front, also we know that the arrival of new German aircraft on our front is very small, whereas the German production is from 2,000 to 2,500 a month. Where are they going?

EDEN: We thought that refitting and the weather might account for some of it, also some have been sent to Libya, but not such a quantity as you mention.

STALIN: In Libya the Germans have less aviation than the British and the number is not very great. Nor is it on our front. Where then is the German aviation?

EDEN: Perhaps I can tell you now that when I left England I hoped to offer you ten squadrons from our Air Force to co-operate with yours at your front as soon as progress with Libyan operations allowed, but since I left London I heard that these extra squadrons would have to go to Singapore as the air attack there is very heavy.

STALIN: I fully understand and I have no objection.

EDEN: It is a great disappointment to us.

STALIN: I fully realize the position and that the situation has changed. We also have had our difficult periods.

EDEN: I very much appreciate the spirit of your answer, and if the wheel goes round again we shall be very glad to help.

STALIN: What about tanks?

EDEN: They will go on coming just the same. The anxiety I have is about American production. I am afraid they will reduce delivery to us in tanks and in aircraft. For instance, in the Middle East we are reinforcing our air units from America and sending you the Hurricanes which would otherwise go to the Middle East. If the Americans stop their supplies the position will become a very anxious one.

It was possible that now they were in the war, the United States would not have armaments to spare. I then gave Stalin a description of the British military situation, based on a note which the Chiefs of Staff had prepared for me.

STALIN: Now what would you like to ask me about our military situation?

EDEN: I would like to have a general view of how it is developing and what you think is likely to be your plan through the winter and in the spring.

STALIN: The war policy of the Soviet Union has so far been that of a fighting retreat. We have defended every district and every point so as to wear down gradually the German forces.

The moment has now arrived when the wearing-down process has reached the point where the Germans feel the pinch. The German soldiers are tired. Their Commanders hoped to finish the war before the winter and they made no preparations for a winter campaign.

This December the German army has shown itself tired and ill-clad and just at this time new Soviet armies and formations reached the front. These reinforcements created the possibility for the change over at the front which you have noticed during the last two weeks. The Germans attempted to dig themselves in, but were not inclined to make very strong fortifications. Our troops were able to break through and now we have the possibility of attacking; counter-attacks have gradually developed into counter-offensives. We shall try and carry this on all through the winter.

When the new German formations will be ready to come to the front, I don't know. Just now the Germans are reorganizing their old forces and making new formations. It is difficult to say when this will be; in any case probably not for two months, so we have two months in hand. In any case our army will try to carry on an offensive all through the winter. It is difficult to say how far we shall move forward, but that will be our policy until the spring.

We have now the air superiority, but not a very great one. The Germans still have a great superiority in tanks, and tanks are vitally necessary for us, especially Valentines, which we have found to be much better for use in the winter. The Matilda will be all right in the summer weather, but the engine is too weak for winter conditions. We shall go ahead on all fronts. In the south the position is quite satisfactory. The bringing in of fresh reinforcements was the cause of the recent successes. The German army is not so strong after all. It is only because it has an enormous reputation.

Mr. Stalin and I discussed many other topics. One was the Japanese war, when I remarked that there would be great difficulties for us in the Pacific, especially in view of the loss of our battleships. Stalin seemed to take this as a hint. He immediately said that, unfortunately, the Russians could do nothing to help us there. I made it clear that I had not in any way intended to suggest such a thing. Stalin continued: "I appreciate your attitude. We can do nothing now, but in the spring we shall be ready, and will then help." He volunteered that the antagonism between Russia and Japan could only be settled by force, in his opinion the Japanese would weaken themselves by the dispersal of their efforts.

We also spoke of our military mission and I suggested that all was not well in their relationship with the Russians. Stalin said that he realized that the mission were dissatisfied and he thought they had reason to be. The difficulty was that there were not too many generals and they were all very overworked and had not even time to sleep. Cripps explained that the trouble lay with the Liaison Department and that, when contacts were established with the actual operational staffs, all went swimmingly. Stalin then suggested that the mission should come to Moscow from Kuibyshev and I at once accepted this.

December 17th: Talks between Alec and Maisky during morning when texts were elaborated and agreed. Motored to Sparrow's Hill with Cripps and went for a short walk there. Much building has been done on outskirts of Moscow since I was last here.

On my return Maisky said S. had had urgent business thrust upon him, I gathered a conference of generals, and that our business must be put off until midnight, or tomorrow, whichever I preferred. I said: "Midnight." I asked M. whether texts had been approved; he replied: "Except for one or two alterations of a minor character." He thought all would be well.

When we resumed the talks, Maisky was immediately proved wrong. The conversation, which up to that moment had been smooth in character, suddenly changed and Stalin began to show his claws. He opened by asking for our immediate recognition of Russia's 1941 frontiers as the Soviet frontiers in the peace treaty. When I explained at length that I was not able to promise such a thing, Stalin retorted that, in that event, he would rather have no agreement. I replied that the Prime Minister had made a statement publicly to the whole world that we would not recognize changes made during the war. This was said when Germany was advancing and was really to the advantage of the U.S.S.R. Obviously I could not now decide this issue of frontiers although, as I had said, I was prepared to take it up when I returned to London.

> STALIN: If you say that you might well say tomorrow that you do not recognize the Ukraine as forming part of the U.S.S.R.

> EDEN: That is a complete misunderstanding of the position. It is only changes from the pre-war frontiers that we do not recognize. The only change in the Ukraine is its occupation by Germany, so of course we accept the Ukraine as being part of the U.S.S.R.

I then tried to explain about our relationship with the Dominions:

> EDEN: Let me take the case of Canada and the question of the frontier between Poland and Russia. Canada has sent us hundreds of thousands of soldiers to help in the war and if they were to hear tomorrow that I had agreed upon the Polish–Russian frontier, without any consultation with them, they would have every right to the strongest complaint. No Minister who did a thing like that could survive for twenty-four hours.

> STALIN: I certainly do not want to demand the impossible from you and I fully realize the limitation of your powers, but I am addressing myself to the British Government and I am genuinely surprised. I thought that the Atlantic Charter was directed against those people who were trying to establish world dominion. It now looks as if the Charter was directed against the U.S.S.R.

To this I later replied:

> EDEN: If you were asking for the frontiers which existed in 1939, before the war broke out between us and Germany, there would be no difficulty at all, but now you are asking for frontiers which differ from those of 1939 in various places. I have

taken a note of that and will report it to my Government, but I cannot see how these agreements that it is proposed to sign will make it any more difficult for us to give you the answer that you want.

STALIN: It makes it look as if I should have to come cap in hand.

EDEN: Not at all, I don't understand that. These are documents of perfect equality and don't represent the conferring of anything by either party upon the other.

MOLOTOV: We are talking of common war aims, of what we are both fighting for. On one of these important aims, our western frontiers, we have no support from Great Britain.

December 17th: The argument continued at length without either side giving way, but I had some hope at the end that I had persuaded him of impossibility of his demand. Cripps, who was most complimentary about my handling of the talk, and I think for the first time thought that there might after all be something in this rather flotsam Tory, and Alec both thought so.

December 18th: But the morrow proved us wrong. We met again at 7 p.m. I had not gone to ballet, meanwhile, to avoid publicity, but for another walk and drive with Stafford C.; quite pleasant. But this snow and grey skies are depressing.

Our evening meeting with Stalin proved completely abortive and I was considerably irritated at what I thought Stalin's unreasonable attitude.

At one moment he spoke of our agreement with Turkey:

STALIN: I am surprised at your having a treaty with Turkey and now creating a difficulty as to having a treaty with us. If you have any difficulty in entering into a treaty with us, then it is much better to say so.

EDEN: That is not the question at all. It is simply a matter of time. The Turkish treaty took many months to negotiate.

I went on to explain that I could now sign an agreement, but not a treaty until the Dominions had been consulted and had acceded

to it, when the treaty could be signed in London in proper form
and ratified. Stalin accepted this, but soon made other difficulties
and I had to repeat many times that we could not now recognize
the Russian frontiers of 1941, because they affected other countries,
one of which, Poland, was our ally. I told Stalin that I could not
agree to definite frontiers without breaking pledges I had already
made to other people, and I was not going to do that. Stalin merely
said: "It is a pity." Molotov was most unhelpful, and the close of
our discussion frigid.

★　　★　　★　　★　　★

As I drove back to our hotel with Cripps and Cadogan, I said
that our car was the one place where we could be pretty confident
of not being overheard. I thought that we should show our dis-
satisfaction at our treatment in no uncertain terms when we got to
our rooms. Probably microphones had been installed and, if so, we
might give these the benefit of our feelings. The others agreed and
on arrival I walked up and down our sitting-room complaining of
Soviet behaviour and sharply regretting that I had made the journey to Moscow. My conclusion was that, with the best will in the
world, it was impossible to work with these people even as partners
against a common foe. The others joined in the chorus.

Whether this exercise had any influence I cannot tell, but a few
hours later Maisky telephoned about my earlier request to go to the
front. This I had made, because I was eager to see something of
the conditions and, if I could, of the recent fighting. So far my
request had not been met. Maisky reported that Mr. Stalin had
now given the necessary order to take me to Klin. The Ambassador,
who had been clearly unhappy throughout the interview of that
day, added that he hoped I would go because he believed that a
break in the talks would do good on both sides. I said that I was
quite ready and would wish to take General Nye with me. This also
was accepted. Cripps nobly volunteered to stay behind to give
Molotov a lecture.

December 19th: We left hotel at 8 a.m., Maisky and I and Nye
in one car. Our military mission came with us. A drive of about
four hours, broken by one good walk, brought us to Klin. Some

signs of fighting on the road as we neared the town. Several
broken down tanks, a few shell-torn trees and many demolitions.
The scorched earth policy appeared to have been unevenly carried out. Sometimes almost a whole village would be standing,
more often two-thirds of it had gone, and now and again everything. Most of the houses are built of wood, the chimneys only
being brick so that when they are burnt, gaunt brick fingers
point to the sky. The effect is more ghoulish than total destruction would be.

From the looks of it, most of the armoured fighting has taken
place on or beside the main Moscow–Leningrad road. We motored through Klin and on some dozen kilometres along that
road, after which we had to turn back though still some thirty
kilometres from the front. The German army has retreated fast,
for it was only on Monday [December 15th] that they were still
fighting in Klin. On the way back we stopped at what had evidently been the scene of a pretty sharp little engagement north
of Klin. There were a few Russian tanks knocked out and a big
German tank which appeared to have received a direct hit at the
base of the turret. In the ditch at the side of the road were perhaps a score of corpses, stiff and swollen, which the Russians appeared to contemplate with considerable satisfaction.

Back to Klin which is pretty well battered and burnt, yet a
considerable number of civilians about. We were taken to see
Tschaikovsky's house which the Germans had treated roughly,
using books and music for fuel. The old custodian was still there
and very voluble in his indignation. Then to a late but large
luncheon with much vodka and caviar. I sat next to the Russian
general who had described to us the battle for Klin. He seemed
very young and Maisky became very eloquent about him, maintaining that he was in the thirties and a typical peasant. However,
I debunked that by discovering that he was in the last war, though
as a boy and was forty-two, so there was not so much in years
between him and Nye. It seems that he is a Major-General on
the staff of the army. He appeared very keen and a tough fighter
and I liked him.

A long cold drive back. On the way we stopped at a village not
far from Klin where we saw half a dozen wretched German pris-

oners. They appeared to be little more than boys although three of them were N.C.O.s. We were allowed to speak to them and they complained much of the cold. They were miserably clad in thin overcoats with only a poor cardigan and no gloves. They said that they were kept in an unheated hut and appeared half-starved with cold. They were captured yesterday. One came from Sudetenland, another from Dresden and a third from Mann-heim. They talked freely but were scarcely the representatives of a victorious army. They looked pleasant enough boys and I felt very sorry for them. God knows what their fate will be, but I can guess. Hitler's victims.

The last stage of the drive home was difficult in the dark and our driver showed uncanny skill in keeping to the road. We only lost it once, but that was almost enough for me, for I was dozing in the back and caught my head an awful crack against the roof.

I talked to Maisky pretty frankly about the Russian attitude to the agreements during our trip and told him that no one would be pleased with the failure he was imposing upon us, except those who did not want to see our two countries friends. Nye thought that I had shaken him, but Cripps reported on our return an unsatisfactory two and a half hours' talk with Molotov.

The Foreign Minister had been quite unyielding and concluded the conversation by saying: "In the absence of a settlement of the frontier question, no sound basis would be created for relations between Great Britain and the Soviet Union."

★   ★   ★   ★   ★

On my return to Moscow, I found a reply to a telegram I had sent asking for the War Cabinet's views about Stalin's insistence on our immediate recognition of the 1941 Russian frontiers. My colleagues agreed that I could not go further than I had already done in say-ing that I must discuss the question of frontiers with them and with the United States and Dominion Governments on my return to Lon-don.

During the next day I tried to work out an acceptable text, but I had soon to admit that the gap was not to be bridged by any mere formula. Stalin having rejected my proposal of tripartite conversations with the Americans, I could see no prospect of signing any agreement. I therefore went to our last meeting, on the evening of December 20th, with nothing more than the draft of a short communiqué.

But when I got to the Kremlin I found that my talk with Maisky had evidently had some effect. Stalin, while still insisting on our recognition of the Soviet frontiers, which I could not grant, seemed to have dropped the general suspicions which had been so evident two days earlier. He said that he had previously overlooked the necessity for my consulting the United States and had thought we had more freedom of action than we actually possessed. Whether the treaties were signed now or later, he was sure that Anglo–Soviet relations would improve. Stalin produced a draft communiqué which was longer and more forthcoming than mine. I accepted it with relief that, for the time at least, the Soviet Government had ceased to ask for what I could not give.

Much of our last discussion was concerned with the military situation. I said that the position in Malaya was bad. We were doing our utmost to send reinforcements, but it might be difficult or impossible to get them to their destinations in time. In these circumstances, it would have been a help if the Soviet Union could have relieved the pressure upon us. All Japanese air-power was concentrated against us and the Americans. I understood that Stalin could not help us in the Far East for the reasons he had given me and, for the same reasons, we could not help him by creating a second front. One of the divisions which we had hoped might form the basis of a British force to be sent to south Russia had now had to be diverted to Malaya. Later I said I expected that, in view of the very serious situation in the Far East, the Prime Minister would want to know Stalin's exact position:

EDEN: I understand you to say that you cannot do anything now, but that in the spring the position will be, or may be, different. Have I got this right, or how exactly did you put it?

STALIN: If the Soviet Union were to declare war on Japan, we should have to wage a real war by land, on sea and in the air.

It would not be like the declarations of war on Japan by Belgium and Poland. Consequently we have to make a careful estimate of the forces involved. At present we are not ready. A considerable number of our troops were removed from the Far East to the Western front. New troops are being got ready but we shall require about four months before they are fully prepared.

I think it would be far better for the Soviet Union if Japan were left to attack us. This would create a better political and psychological atmosphere amongst the Soviet people. War would be unpopular with our people if the Soviet Government were to take the first step. If, on the other hand, we were attacked, the feelings of the Soviet people would be very strong. We have seen this in the present war in the West. Hitler attacked us, and because we were attacked, the Soviet people have shown a wonderful unity and great heroism and readiness to sacrifice themselves. We would prefer that Japan should attack us, and I think it very probable that she will do so—not just yet, but later. If the Germans are hard pressed it is likely that they will urge the Japanese to attack us, in which case the attack may be expected about the middle of next year.

EDEN: I fear that the Japanese may meanwhile adopt a policy of dealing with their opponents one by one, and may try to finish with us before attacking the Soviet Union.

STALIN: Great Britain is not fighting Japan alone. She has allies in China, the Dutch East Indies and the United States of America.

EDEN: The main attack at the moment is on Malaya, where our allies cannot help us much.

In conclusion I said:

The next six months are going to be difficult. We have got to stick it out, and we shall do so. But it is a very uncomfortable situation. You may like to know that I have received a telegram from the Chiefs of Staff saying that we shall go through with the Libyan campaign and shall not call it off in order to send reinforcements to the Far East. The Far East must hold out until we can afford to send reinforcements.

STALIN: I think that is quite sound. The weakest link of the Axis is Italy, and if this link is broken the whole Axis will collapse. If the British had attacked Italy in 1939, or before then, they would now be masters of the situation in the Mediterranean.

When the last meeting had been going for about an hour and a half, Stalin suddenly said: "Would you like to dine with me, and your party? What time would suit you? Nine, or ten?" I accepted for ten o'clock and sent a message to our delegation, some of whom had already embarked on their evening meal. I was rather taken aback at the invitation because I knew how difficult the conditions were in Moscow. Food was very scarce, even milk being hard to come by. We were told that not long before our arrival Stalin had moved the N.K.V.D., and perhaps some of the police also, up to the front. As a consequence there had been some looting in which our Embassy amongst others had suffered, the whole of the diplomatic corps being at Kuibyshev.

However, whatever the shortages in the city, these had not invaded the Kremlin and the banquet, which took place in the Empress Catherine's rooms, was almost embarrassingly sumptuous. After the usual vodka and caviar came bortsch, sturgeon and the unhappy little white sucking pig which looked up at one from the dish with its black caper eye, and meats of various kinds. After the vodka we drank a variety of Russian wines, including champagne. Of these I preferred a pleasing and quite light white wine from Georgia. Stalin, I noticed, stuck to a red wine which appeared to be sparkling and which he drank from a bottle at his side. I eschewed the Russian champagne which I have always found too heavy for my taste and my stomach.

I was on Stalin's right with Molotov opposite him, Marshals Timoshenko and Voroshilov were also among our hosts. Early in the evening I learnt that the next day was to be Stalin's sixty-second birthday so, when the hour struck, I proposed his health, wishing success to him and to Soviet arms. Timoshenko, then much a hero for his recent victories, appeared to have been imbibing before we had met. Stalin seemed rather embarrassed at the signs of this and said quietly to me: "Do your generals ever get drunk?", to which I replied, I hope diplomatically, "They don't often get the chance." Stalin asked about our experience of fighting in North Africa and about our commanders on land and sea. I spoke of Wavell and Cunningham and asked about the winter fighting in Russia. We both rehearsed our recollections of our earlier meeting in Moscow six years before and discussed its aftermath, the rise of Nazi power and the failure of France, Soviet Russia and Britain to pursue common policies. Each gave and argued his version.

After dinner we sat in a circle and returned to this theme, when Stalin made a defence of the Ribbentrop–Molotov Pact, for which he brazenly gave Molotov the discredit. He spoke of his lack of confidence in the French armies, his uncertainty about western policies and our failure to send missions of sufficient authority to Moscow soon enough. I countered with complaints of the secrecy and uncertainty of Soviet policies and the activities of the Communist Party in a country like France.

Stalin spoke of Molotov's visit to Berlin in 1940 and of the British air raid which had compelled him to take refuge with Ribbentrop in a dugout, telling the story of Ribbentrop's confidence that the British Empire was finished and of Molotov's reply: "If the war is over, why are we in this dugout and whose bombs have put us here?" Molotov smiled smoothly and nodded.

The evening was long but relaxed. For many of the Russians present this could have been the first occasion for months, perhaps since the Nazi invasion of their land, that they had been able to enjoy such a feast, and enjoy it they did. Even so, it had for me a feeling of unreality, which was not due to the hunger, even misery, in our midst, or to the German armies, so near that their gunfire was almost within sound. Within these gilded rooms the atmosphere was unhealthy, because where one man rules all others fear.

Later that morning I telegraphed to the Prime Minister:

> . . . Our work has ended on a friendly note. Final discussions with Stalin were the best and I am sure that the visit has been worth while. We have allayed some at least of the past

suspicions. Stalin, I believe, sincerely wants military agreements but he will not sign until we recognize his frontiers, and we must expect continued badgering on this issue. Meanwhile our position and that of America is completely safeguarded. Banquet lasted until five this morning, Stalin's birthday. We drank your health and some others. Stalin spoke very warmly of you.

On December 21st and 22nd I had talks with Knatchbull-Hugessen and Sir Reader Bullard, the British Ambassador in Tehran. Both had come up to Moscow to see me, despite the formidable difficulties of travel, as I wanted to get their first-hand accounts of recent events in Turkey and Persia. Our party finally left Moscow by train on the evening of December 22nd. We spent Christmas at sea and, after an uneventful voyage, reached London on December 30th, grateful to H.M.S. *Kent* and her brave crew.

3

THE IMPERIAL WAY
February–December 1941

The Greater East Asia Co-Prosperity Sphere — A stiff interview with the Japanese Ambassador — Uncertainty over the United States' attitude — Japan in Indo-China — General Tojo becomes Prime Minister — H.M.S. *Prince of Wales* and H.M.S. *Repulse* go to the Far East — War on December 8th Japanese time — The United States fleet is decimated

JAPAN'S LEADERS were lured on by imperial ambition, however much they might pretext economic needs to excuse their policy. The attempt to subdue China, which by 1940 had lasted four years, tested the country's military strength and drained its material resources. Three non-Asian powers were in the way of the further spread of Japanese conquests, France, the Netherlands and Great Britain, each with substantial colonial territories. Behind these, but detached, stood the United States, whose threatened interests were mainly strategic and commercial.

The fall of France had the same consequences on the Far East as on the Middle East, leaving the British Commonwealth much exposed, although the hostile force which it now faced alone was not, as yet, actively aggressive. On August 1st, 1940, Prince Fumimaro Konoye formed a Government to exploit the opportunity created by France's weakness. Mr. Yosuke Matsuoka became the Foreign Minister and defined Japan's mission as the "imperial way" to a Greater East Asia Co-Prosperity Sphere.

Its area was not modest. The trials of the Japanese war criminals later revealed that it was to include, after two more wars, not only southeast Asia, but Ceylon, parts of Canada and of the United States, Central America, the West Indies, Australia and New Zealand.

More immediately, Japan would need to replace the seventy to eighty per cent of her trade which was being conducted with the United States and the British Empire. To do this a smaller, self-supporting "sphere" had to be created. The pressure was turned upon Vichy France, which yielded, first acknowledging the pre-dominance of Japanese political and economic interests in the Far East, next accepting the right of Japanese armed forces to pass through Indo-China and finally surrendering on September 22nd the right to occupy Hanoi and six aerodromes in the north. Five days later Japan signed the Tripartite Pact with Germany and Italy.

The Japanese Government had prepared plans against Thailand and the British and Dutch colonial territories, but these entailed the risk of war. Tokyo had, therefore, first to seek security against attack from the Soviet Union and the United States. Nazi diplomacy was slow to understand this and Ribbentrop tried to persuade Japan on February 23rd, 1941, to attack Hong Kong and Singapore as a complement to Hitler's secret plans against Russia. The Japanese, however, were not yet ready.

Early in the same month of February, our Intelligence reports made me think that the Japanese might be contemplating an attack upon Malaya. The answer which their Ambassador, Mr. Mamoru Shigemitsu, had given to my Parliamentary Under-Secretary, Mr. R. A. Butler, at an interview on February 1st, did not carry conviction. The Ambassador had said that Japan's purpose was not solely dictated by Germany. The Japanese Government had undertaken the Tripartite Pact, he argued, in order to extricate themselves from the difficulties of their policy in China. Against this laboured pretext I minuted: "How can it possibly achieve this?" I thought that I should see the Ambassador and speak my mind, though this course had its dangers, for if he were to judge that I was bluffing, I might make the position worse.

Meanwhile reports came through from Tokyo, Bangkok and Hanoi of a possible Japanese advance into Thailand and southern Indo-China. I was also told of evidence that the Japanese Embassy in London might be packing up. Added together, these straws seemed to show that an attack upon British territory was at least possible.

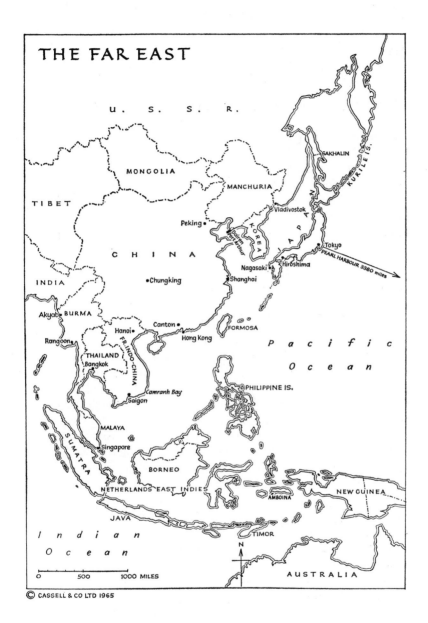

THE FAR EAST

U. S. S. R.

MONGOLIA

MANCHURIA

TIBET

Vladivostok

Peking •

KOREA

Port Arthur

SAKHALIN

KURILE IS.

J A P A N

Tokyo

PEARL HARBOUR 3380 miles

Nagasaki • • Hiroshima

C H I N A

INDIA

•Chungking

•Shanghai

Akyab• BURMA

Canton •

FORMOSA

Rangoon•

Hanoi •

Hong Kong

FR. INDO-CHINA

THAILAND

Bangkok•

Camranh Bay

Saigon

P a c i f i c

O c e a n

PHILIPPINE IS.

MALAYA

•Singapore

BORNEO

SUMATRA

NETHERLANDS EAST INDIES

AMBOINA

NEW GUINEA

JAVA

TIMOR

I n d i a n

O c e a n

N

AUSTRALIA

0   500   1000 MILES

February 5th: Saw Quo Tai-chi [the Chinese Ambassador] in afternoon. He seemed to me less buoyant than usual though his words were confident. I fear that internal position in China is bad, for all that poor Quo says. Later we got news which seemed to show Jap preparations for some *coup,* perhaps against us.

At noon the next day I spoke to the War Cabinet of possible Japanese intentions. The Prime Minister then referred to the dropping of mines by the Germans in the Suez Canal, which might result in closing it for about fifteen days. This, he said, could have been done by Germany to show Japan what she could do to prevent Britain sending reinforcements from the Middle East to the Far East.

February 7th: I spent an hour and forty minutes with Shigemitsu. I spoke slowly from a brief so that he might take it all down. He appeared taken aback at what I had said and doubted whether Tokyo would like the message.

I told the Ambassador that it seemed to me that the state of relations between our countries required a full and outspoken discussion between us. Japan's actions showed that it was her intention to extend the sphere of her operations and to dominate the whole of East Asia. Our Ambassador in Tokyo had reported that there was a general feeling among the Japanese that a crisis in the Far East would develop in the next few weeks. I did not know why the Japanese should think that, or who was going to provoke such a crisis or against whom such action was contemplated. Were we to believe that some forward move was planned by Japan, to synchronize with the German offensive against Britain? If so, were we to assume that British territories in the Far East were in danger of attack by Japan? It was difficult to understand why the increasing atmosphere of crisis was being created in this country, where the purpose of statesmen appeared to be to show that some gigantic convulsion was impending.

It was impossible, I went on, for His Majesty's Government to ignore these signs and portents. Great Britain had possessions in the Far East, and while she had no aggressive intentions towards any power, she had also no intention of sacrificing those possessions at the dictation of any power. Nor were we prepared to subscribe to a theory that Japan alone was entitled to control the destinies and to dominate all the countries of the Far East. There were peoples in that part of the world for whose safety and well-being Great Britain was responsible, and she intended to discharge her obligations to them. If British territories were attacked, there should be no room for doubt that the British people would defend them with the utmost vigour.

I said that reports had reached me that all news favourable to British arms was suppressed in the Japanese newspapers and that the idea was encouraged in Japan that the British Empire was weak and ready to collapse. His Excellency, who had seen Great Britain at war, both in the last conflict and now, would understand the quality of the spirit and determination of our people. I felt sure that he would not have left his Government in doubt as to the unity and strength of purpose of the Empire. We were absolutely convinced that, backed by our vast resources and with the increasing help in munitions which the United States was providing, we could not fail to secure final victory.

The Ambassador was perturbed and asked several times if I wanted him to transmit to Tokyo all that I had said. He seemed to fear the reaction. I had, however, considered my words carefully with Sir Alexander Cadogan, who had himself been an Ambassador in the Far East, and I told Shigemitsu that I wanted everything I said reported to his Government. He could only reply that what I had told him was serious, though he would not have estimated the situation to be as grave as our Ambassador had reported.

After he had left me, the Ambassador went down the passage to see Cadogan and told him of his concern at the reception of my message in Tokyo. Cadogan went into the next room to telephone to me a report of the Ambassador's words, but we agreed to stand by what I had said. I was in a muck sweat when I put the telephone down.

★   ★   ★   ★   ★

We were uncertain about the firmness of the American attitude
on the Far East. At times the outlook appeared hopeful, as when
Mr. Hopkins and Mr. Herschel Johnson, the United States Chargé
d'Affaires, had luncheon with me and some members of the Foreign
Office.

February 8th: We had important and valuable talk. Far East
and Balkans. I think the Americans are really willing to help in
the former, though Hopkins naturally cannot commit them. Hopkins for instance said as he left: "You have said nothing in all this
about Hong Kong, but I know that you are worrying about it.
Well, I am pretty certain what the President would do if Hong
Kong were attacked, but I guess I cannot tell you about it."

At the time I thought this a broad hint. Even so, as I wrote to
the Prime Minister the same day, I saw no hope for a joint declaration by the United States and the British Empire, such as the Chiefs
of Staff looked for, that any attack on the Netherlands East Indies,
or on British possessions in the Far East would involve Japan in
immediate war with all the powers concerned. My minute continued:

> . . . it is clearly of the first importance that the United States
> should, independently, go as far as they can in making plain
> their attitude to the Japanese Government. I have spoken in
> this sense to Mr. Hopkins at luncheon today, and I am sure
> that he fully appreciates the gravity of the situation. I particu-
> larly emphasized the menace to the Cape route which must re-
> sult from Japan's entry into the war. I think that Mr. Hopkins
> will telegraph to the President urging at least some step beyond
> the ordinary execution of manœuvres at Hawaii. He then told
> me that he thought the most effective results would be pro-
> duced by the President sending for the Japanese Ambassador
> and making plain the United States' interests in Far Eastern
> affairs in words of one syllable.

On February 11th I telegraphed to Lord Halifax, asking him to
try to encourage the Americans to do just this. In the event, on

February 14th the President used much the same language as I had to Shigemitsu, to the new Japanese Ambassador, Admiral Kichisaburo Nomura, who had come to open conversations in Washington.

Meanwhile Mr. Matsuoka, anxious to secure his country's northern flank, was off on a tour to Moscow, Berlin and Rome. Hitler and Ribbentrop were in a difficulty. They dared not divulge their secret plans against Russia, and so they could not effectively discourage Matsuoka from negotiating a neutrality pact with the Soviet Union, which was signed on his return to Moscow on April 13th. Nor can Hitler much have liked Stalin's words when seeing Matsuoka off the same day at the railway station: "Now that the U.S.S.R. and Japan have arranged the matter, the Japanese will straighten out the East, the U.S.S.R. and Germany will take care of Europe and later, between them, they will take care of the Americans." By this date we had warned Stalin so that he should have known better. If he did, this pretence of faith in Hitler could have been tactical.

★ ★ ★ ★ ★

The difficulty of determining world strategy at a time when our resources were so stretched, even including those of a benevolently neutral United States, was illustrated by an incident which could have had wide repercussions. Somewhat unexpectedly, Colonel Frank Knox, United States Secretary for the Navy and Mr. Henry Stimson, Secretary for War, approached Rear-Admiral V. H. Danckwerts, of the British naval mission in Washington, with a proposal that a large part of the United States Pacific fleet should be moved into the Atlantic. Admiral Danckwerts had discouraged this suggestion, conscious no doubt of the deterrent effect upon Japan of the American fleet at Hawaii, provided that it was well balanced.

At a Defence Committee on April 30th Mr. Churchill was indignant that a move which he regarded as of great psychological importance should have been given a cold reception. The First Sea Lord, Sir Dudley Pound, however, who always kept a cool hold on strategic realities, was firm that from the point of view of winning the Battle of the Atlantic, there was no advantage in moving such a large fleet. Our Naval Staff wanted six battleships, two aircraft

carriers and four eight-inch cruisers to be kept at Hawaii, releasing
a rather smaller formation to reinforce the Atlantic. This proportion was probably the correct one at the time, though in the event
three-quarters of the fleet remained in the Pacific. Not one of us
even guessed what was to be the fate which awaited those ships at
Hawaii.

★   ★   ★   ★   ★

Equally urgent was the problem of the Netherlands East Indies
where our Dutch allies were showing themselves characteristically
resolute. I wished to make a declaration with them on the defence
of our territories in the Far East. To the Defence Committee I
wrote in a memorandum on May 15th:

> We are already allied to the Netherlands Government against
> Germany. Thus, if the Netherlands East Indies were attacked
> by Germany's ally, our moral obligations, as well as our vital
> need to secure our communications with Australia and New
> Zealand and our obligations in this respect to the two Do-
> minions, would make it impossible to stand by and see the
> Netherlands East Indies overrun. . . .

It seemed to me that if the United States Government were to remove part of their Pacific Fleet into the Atlantic, it would be more
than ever necessary that we and the Netherlands should, by a firm
declaration, try to convince Japan that we would protect our joint
interests in the South Seas. The Defence Committee agreed,
though I eventually preferred to give this warning privately through
our Ambassador in Tokyo to the Japanese Foreign Minister, which
was done.

> *June 13th:* Said *au revoir* to Shigemitsu who is returning to
> Japan on a visit. I fear that it may be "good-bye," not because I
> think war with Japan any more probable than it has been for
> many months, but because Japanese Ambassadors who have
> friendly feelings towards this country, as Shigemitsu certainly has,
> have a knack of not returning.

This estimate proved to be true.

A few days later the German invasion of Soviet Russia created Japan's opportunity. Resisting the Nazi temptation to join in the attack, the Japanese prepared to concentrate on expanding their Greater East Asia Co-Prosperity Sphere, regardless of the risk of war with Britain and the United States. I soon had reports of their intention to occupy bases in southern Indo-China and these led me to hold urgent consultation with the Dominions, the Netherlands and the United States. The Americans, it seemed, intended to freeze Japanese assets and to impose a complete embargo, at least on the export of certain key commodities. I wrote in a memorandum for the War Cabinet:

> A complete embargo, in the literal sense of the stoppage of all current trade between the United States and Japan . . . would be likely to force the Japanese to choose between two grave alternatives, namely, completely to reverse their pro-Axis policy, or to proceed with their southward move to the point of war with the Netherlands East Indies and ourselves in an endeavour to obtain control of sources of raw materials. Even a complete embargo on oil *might* have this effect.
>
> Faced with these alternatives, and particularly if we, and perhaps the Dutch, acted in complete conformity with the United States, Japan might well choose the first alternative; nevertheless, the risk remains that she would choose war with us, hoping that the United States would not intervene in time. The question therefore arises whether we are prepared to go the whole way with the United States if they desire to take such drastic action; and, if not, whether we should attempt to restrain the United States.

On balance, I advised against attempting to put any brake upon the American purpose, whatever that might prove to be. I wrote: "The risk of creating another Simon–Stimson incident* and of seriously weakening the ties between us and America is real." My own view, as I said boldly, but not perhaps unwisely, was that "the

* *Facing the Dictators,* pages 523–4.

risk of the United States not intervening in a war between ourselves and Japan is small."

I did, however, advise that if called upon to go to lengths which involved a risk of war, we ought to ask for an assurance of armed support from the United States, should the Japanese attack either ourselves or the Netherlands East Indies, as a result of action jointly agreed upon. The War Cabinet accepted this counsel. On the same day, July 21st, the Vichy Government yielded to the Japanese demand for bases in southern Indo-China; by the end of the month Japanese troops had occupied Saigon and Camranh Bay. The United States, the Netherlands and ourselves then carried out the freezing measures.

There remained the question of whether I could tell the Netherlands Government that Britain would give them military support if their territories in south-east Asia were attacked. Both the New Zealand and Australian Governments wanted me to do this, irrespective of the attitude of the United States, which was inhibited by its constitution. On July 30th I wrote to the Prime Minister:

> All that is suggested is that we should let the Dutch know that we will help them, in the event of a Japanese attack, to the best of our ability. . . . The Dutch are at present forced to rely on the hope that this will be so, but our hesitation is increasing their anxiety which, if not allayed, will soon grow into dangerous suspicion. . . .

Mr. Churchill agreed to my proposal. The next day I had a conversation with the American Ambassador when I suggested to him, among other things, that, apart from any private assurance his Government might feel able to give either to the Dutch or to ourselves, the United States Government might be willing to give a public warning.

However, at his meeting with Mr. Churchill in August at Placentia Bay, Newfoundland, the President was very prudent. The Prime Minister understood that Roosevelt had agreed to make a statement in Washington to the Japanese Ambassador, though in the event this fell short of what we had hoped for. The President limited his warning to the Ambassador to action affecting the interests of the United States. At best the Japanese would now only be uncertain whether an attack against us or the Netherlands East Indies would lead to war with the United States.

Meanwhile a fresh turn was given to events when the Japanese asked for the renewal of negotiations in Washington. The informal and somewhat dilatory discussion which followed between the American Secretary of State and the Japanese Ambassador, grated upon the Japanese military. At their demand the Imperial Conference on September 6th in Tokyo secretly agreed that, if in a month's time Japan's minimum demands had not been accepted in Washington, the decision for war would be taken.

Our Ambassador in Tokyo warned us that there was little hope of the Japanese Cabinet surviving, if the discussions with the United States broke down or were unduly prolonged. I thought this a Japanese manœuvre to put pressure on Britain to exert an influence in Washington favourable to Tokyo, and on October 1st I minuted that we should not do so. A fortnight later Prince Konoye resigned, rather than fulfil the decision of the Imperial Conference for war if the discussions broke down. The menacing General Hideki Tojo succeeded him.

★　　★　　★　　★　　★

The situation seemed to me daily more strained for another reason. As I wrote on September 30th, in a memorandum for my colleagues, Japan was faced with the prospect of economic isolation unless she transformed her policy. There was no sign of a change of heart in Japan, though there might be some division of opinion as to how the hand was to be played. Against that general background we had to decide our course, and I suggested that "a display of firmness is more likely to deter Japan from war than to provoke her to it."

Despite our exposed position, I was convinced that to show weakness would be to invite Japanese pressure and, worse still, leave the Americans with the impression that our tactics were to appease the enemy, possibly even at their expense. We should thus at once divert upon ourselves the full threat of Japanese ambitions and weaken any sense of American responsibility for our consequent troubles.

My standpoint had its critics. Anxiety was expressed by Lord

Hankey, the Paymaster-General, at the effect upon supplies to Russia if Japan interrupted the Vladivostok route. Never, he said, had there been a time in our history when a cautious Far Eastern policy was more necessary. On this I commented:

> The old appeasement again. Of course we do not want to fight Japan, but I fear that Lord Hankey will never learn that to be gentle with aggressors does not avoid hostilities. . . .

To him I wrote a letter:

> The situation as I see it is described in my paper on Far Eastern policy . . . of September 30th. Japan is approaching a serious decision. What her choice will be we cannot foresee, but in my opinion the most likely way to keep her quiet is to convince her that any further adventure on her part will meet with formidable and combined opposition.

As tension tightened I raised the question of naval reinforcements to the Far East and this was discussed at the Defence Committee on October 17th. The Admiralty favoured the despatch of half a dozen of our older and slower capital ships. The Prime Minister did not like this. The new German battleship *Tirpitz*, he pointed out, compelled us to keep on guard a force three times her weight, apart from the power of the United States in the Atlantic. The presence of one modern capital ship in Far Eastern waters could have a like effect on the Japanese naval authorities and thereby on Japanese foreign policy.

I agreed with this argument, as did my colleagues. *Repulse* was already in Indian waters and the intention was that *Prince of Wales* should join her at Singapore, being accompanied by the aircraft carrier, *Indomitable*. No decision, however, was taken until three days later, when the discussion revolved around the question whether *Rodney* or *Prince of Wales* should be sent. The balance of the argument appeared to favour *Prince of Wales*, the more modern ship, but the only conclusion that day was to send the ship to Cape Town, where the news of her arrival would, all were agreed, be salutary. A decision about her onward journey would be taken after she had got there. However, on November 11th, before the ship had reached Cape Town, the Admiralty ordered *Prince of Wales* and *Repulse* to meet in Ceylon and proceed together to Singapore. Unhappily, *Indomitable*, which was to have sailed in their company, ran aground on November 3rd in Jamaica and had to be docked, thus further exposing the other ships to hostile air power.

At last, on December 5th, Lord Halifax telegraphed that he had seen the President who agreed to warn Japan against any attack on Thailand, Malaya or the Netherlands East Indies. Roosevelt considered that the warning should be given independently by the United States, Great Britain and the Netherlands, his own Government issuing it first, so that it should not appear that he was following our lead.

> *December 4th:* A good message from Roosevelt about the Far East. To my intense relief was able to induce Winston to agree to full assurance to Dutch on the strength of it.

But the President's decision was too late, for the hour was long past when deterrent words could influence Japanese plans. On December 7th, all Japanese naval and military commanders were told that war would begin on December 8th, Japanese time. The decision had been ratified by the Emperor in council a week before.

In the early morning of what was, by American time, Sunday, December 7th, Japanese planes, based on aircraft carriers three hundred miles away, destroyed the greater part of the United States Pacific fleet, then lying at anchor in Pearl Harbour. This action, grievous as it was at the time for American naval power, doomed the signatories of the Tripartite Pact. They could not, in the end, withstand the combined resources of the United States, the Soviet Union and the British Empire.

The hawk's dive upon the American fleet was followed by a political decision which was to determine how the Allied victory was to be won. Hitler and Mussolini declared war on the United States on December 11th. This was a gratuitous act, for neither the German nor the Italian Governments had advance knowledge of the Japanese intention. Had the Nazi and Fascist powers held their hand, the total American effort must have been directed to the Pacific, leaving Russia in Europe and the British forces in North Africa to bear alone, for some years at least, the military might which Hitler and his satellites could have hurled against them.

The consequences of such a shaping of events can be conjectured; they would have been costly; they could have been fatal. Loyalty is not a word commonly associated with Hitler and Mussolini. This unique occasion, on which they displayed it together towards a third nation, sealed their fate.

4

A LOW EBB

January–August 1942

Far Eastern disasters — My memorandum on Russia in Europe — The fall of Singapore — The Leadership of the House of Commons — Disturbing Roosevelt diplomacy and tactics — The Anglo–Russian treaty and the second front — Mr. Molotov arrives in London — The United States jumps the gun — General Rommel's successes in the Western Desert — A vote of censure — Peace feelers from some Germans

SINCE HITLER'S ATTACK on Russia, we had an immeasurable ally. The Soviets, though nearly crushed at the outset, survived and were now inflicting defeats on the invader. In the last month of 1941, the United States in her turn had been the victim, but was now arrayed with us in the full and closest partnership of arms. With the growing weight of American power beside us, we knew that Hitler could not triumph. Our lonely year was over.

In spite of which many blows fell, during the early months of 1942, on the three countries which had now to fight together. In the Far East a succession of disasters overwhelmed Malaya, the Philippines, Singapore, the Dutch East Indies and Burma, exposing the whole Pacific and Indian Oceans to the enemy. In the Middle East we once again lost the ground gained by Auchinleck's winter offensive and at midsummer Rommel stood near the gates of Alexandria and the Nile Delta. In Russia the German summer offensive penetrated farther than in the previous year, deep into the Caucasus and to the Volga at Stalingrad. Not until the autumn did the tide of battle begin to flow in our favour.

Politically, Britain's relations with her great allies were now my chief concern until the end of the war. I accepted the fact that the United States must in time become the dominant partner in Anglo–

American councils. In 1942 this was not so. Her wealth and pro-
ductive capacity were not yet at full stretch and her armed forces
were only beginning their training and deployment. Our effort, on
the other hand, after more than two years of war, was nearing its
peak.

The balance of power between us brought its problems. How to
handle our relations with Soviet Russia, the policy to be followed
towards de Gaulle, and the future of the British Commonwealth
presented varying facets almost daily. I had to judge how far in
meeting them I could, at the Foreign Office, insist on my point of
view, how far be unreservedly with Mr. Churchill in his sentiment
for his transatlantic allies. These were conundrums which rose up
scores of times, in different shapes and sizes. If we did not always
get the right answers, our country still spent itself without stint and
beyond the recovery of the wealth and authority we had known.

There were also the strategic tugs-of-war among the United States
Chiefs of Staff, and between them and our own, about the demands
of the Pacific theatre and those of Europe. Though these appeared
from time to time to be resolved in conference, they were apt to
break out again and they had a significant influence on the course
of the war. Admiral Ernest J. King, United States Chief of Naval
Operations, in whose mind the Pacific enjoyed a sacred priority,
had more of his way in executing allied policy than in formulating
it. While the British were less divided in their opinions, they knew
that they would have to rely increasingly on American material aid,
without which they would be hard driven to do more than survive.

With our other major ally the path was rougher. Though Soviet
Russia's immediate interests in the war were the same as ours, in
the peace they might conflict with what we and much of the world
thought right. It was this contingency that I wished to guard
against, if I could. I was given to saying at this time that the failure
of the British Empire and Russia to agree their policies in advance
had made possible three great conflicts, the Napoleonic war and the
two world wars.

We had to fight in unison, which was the only way to shorten the
war. Consequently, our relations with Soviet Russia seemed to be
a swaying contest between what common sense declared we ought
to do and what experience proved practicable. Perhaps it must

always be so when dealing with a power which is confident that its faith must dominate the world, to the exclusion of all others.

★   ★   ★   ★   ★

The disasters in the Far East were arousing criticism in Parliament and in the country. Eighteen months after the nadir of the fall of France, this evidence that we were still unable to withstand attack seemed to many to show that the direction of our affairs was at fault. In particular, the critics thought the burden of being Prime Minister, Minister of Defence and Leader of the House of Commons was too much for Mr. Churchill to carry. The tone became sharp.

January 21st: Defence Committee after dinner, when we discussed situation in Malaya on basis of Wavell's last telegrams. It looks increasingly critical, and it is very strange that so little should have been done all these years to protect the fortress against land attack.

After meeting, Max [Beaverbrook] and I and [A. V.] Alexander [First Lord of the Admiralty] had drinks with Winston. We spoke of Australia and domestic situation. Max and I urged patience with former and understanding of seriousness of latter if news from Malaya continued to deteriorate, as it probably would. Winston was tired and depressed, for him. His cold is heavy on him. He was inclined to be fatalistic about the House, maintained that bulk of Tories hated him, that he had done all he could and would be only too happy to yield to another, that Malaya, Australian Government's intransigence and "nagging" in House was more than any man could be expected to endure. I urged reforms in Whips' Office and organization of pro-Government speakers. Max backed me in latter, citing example of last war. But Winston would not be interested, arguing that Ll.G. was young and therefore right to insure against future, but that he was sixty-seven.

In this atmosphere it was not easy to concentrate upon our political arrangements with the Soviet Union, yet it seemed all the more necessary in view of what I felt was the growing evidence of Soviet power which we would have to face after the war. On January 28th I wrote in a memorandum for my colleagues:

> On the assumption that Germany is defeated and German military strength is destroyed and that France remains, for a long time at least, a weak power, there will be no counterweight to Russia in Europe. . . . Russia's position on the European continent will be unassailable. Russian prestige will be so great that the establishment of Communist Governments in the majority of European countries will be greatly facilitated, and the Soviet Government will naturally be tempted to work for this.

Stalin would soon, I explained, expect a detailed answer about his 1941 frontiers and it would be better to give it in agreement with the United States.

In our own minds there was never any question that the frontier with Poland must be excepted from any recognition of Russian western boundaries. More difficult was the position of the Baltic States. President Roosevelt understood the argument of Soviet security. He was less convinced of what seemed to us self-evident, however little to our taste, that Russia would not be prepared to accept in victory frontiers there which were shallower than those across which she had been attacked. We did not want to recognize any Soviet position in the Baltic States, but it seemed inescapable that, if Hitler were overthrown, Russian forces would end the war much deeper into Europe than they began it in 1941. It therefore seemed prudent to tie the Soviet Government to agreements as early as possible. The United States Government were not, at this stage of the war, so convinced. On the contrary, they became more tolerant of Soviet demands as Russian military victories developed and the likelihood of sharper Soviet appetites grew.

I forecast something of this later in my memorandum:

> There is bound to be difficulty in practice in harmonizing day-to-day Anglo–Russian co-operation with Anglo–American co-operation. Soviet policy is amoral: United States policy is exaggeratedly moral, at least where non-American interests are concerned.

In America there is still a widely-spread feeling of distrust and dislike of Russia, which the Pact with Hitler and Russia's attack on Finland greatly augmented. As United States opinion, however, becomes more realistically minded under the stress of war, this feeling may be gradually modified, especially as Russian assistance would be valuable to the United States of America in preventing a revival of Japanese militarism in the Far East. The question of the Baltic States is the first example of this conflict of principle between the United States and the Soviet Government. . . . If it came to a direct conflict of policies and we had to choose between the United States of America and the Soviet Union, we should no doubt decide that Anglo–American co-operation is more indispensable and the more natural because it rests on broader and older foundations than Anglo–Russian co-operation.

On the other hand, we shall wish to abstain from any action which would intensify the Soviet Government's already existing suspicion that we look forward to an Anglo–American peace in which Russian interests would be thwarted or ignored.

In practice this means that, in order successfully to reconcile American and Russian susceptibilities and to co-ordinate our policy with both of theirs, we shall have to consult the United States Government in all our discussions with the Soviet Government, and try to obtain their approval or at least their acquiescence in all Anglo–Soviet arrangements. Wherever possible we should work for tripartite consultations and tripartite solutions. . . .

I mentioned two alternative proposals which might be made to the Soviet Government if we and the Americans agreed that we could not meet the full Russian frontier demands. The first was that we should support, when the time came, Soviet demands for bases in countries neighbouring Russia on the Baltic and Black Seas. The second, suggested by Lord Halifax, was that we should endorse at the peace settlement a Soviet demand to control the defence and foreign policy of the Baltic States. On all likely forecasts we could hardly hope to get better results than these, unpalatable though they might be.

Some of the War Cabinet were doubtful of the wisdom of agreeing to Stalin's demands, even with Poland left on one side, while
others supported them more enthusiastically than I could. The
hesitants among my colleagues felt that there was as yet no certainty
of a Russian victory over Germany. While we would do all we
could to avoid a compromise peace between the two countries,
should this happen it would be better not to have frontier obligations towards the Soviet Union. Finally we resolved our differences
and, on February 10th, I was able to instruct Lord Halifax to approach President Roosevelt and the State Department and to put
the problem to them.

I had already given Mr. Winant a full account of my conversations with Stalin. On February 6th the Ambassador told me that he
had instructions to send all the information he could get about any
post-war commitments which we had made or were discussing with
other Governments. In reply I sent him the full texts of our engagements. Maisky was also busy and complained that it was already
six weeks since I had left Moscow. He feared the effect of the delay
without any indication of our view.

★   ★   ★   ★   ★

Despite the overwhelming vote of confidence given to the Government by the House of Commons on January 29th, uneasiness persisted. The surrender of Singapore on February 15th shocked and
grieved the country. The conduct of the war came under criticism
and there was a sense of troubled discontent.

February 16th: On arrival in London found message from Winston asking me to lunch. He greeted me with: "I am in a trucu-
lent mood." I told him I had gathered this from his broadcast
[on Singapore]. Nonetheless he gradually softened to the extent
at least of admitting that changes would have to be made, though
he is still reluctant to make them soon. We agreed that [Mr.
Arthur] Greenwood [Minister without Portfolio] must go, though
Attlee would struggle to prevent this, that K. W. [Kingsley Wood]
was a weakness. . . . Winston is also much troubled about
M.A.P. [Ministry of Aircraft Production]. Possible new colleagues

were also discussed, Cripps in particular. I said I was convinced
that C. was no self-seeker and would try to play his part fairly in
the team. Winston agreed. We also thought that Oliver L.
[Lyttelton] would do well at War Office.

February 18th: Winston summoned me urgently after questions. I found Max [Beaverbrook] with him. Latter vehement
against Cripps as Leader of the House. James Stuart [Chief
Whip] also there but left when I arrived. I had only twenty
minutes before I left to take chair for Cripps [at a private meeting
at the House of Commons organized by the Empire Parliamentary Association]. Winston asked me whether I could take Leadership of House and keep Foreign Office. I said I would like to
think about it an hour or two. When could I see him again?
W: "Can you lunch?" A: "Unhappily not, I have South American lunch." W: "I must have my sleep after lunch." We finally
fixed 5.30.

In point of fact Winston did not have his sleep, for at 4.30
Stafford C. arrived in a high state of excitement to say that he
had been with Winston for two hours and that he had decided
to come in and help. I said, "Good, in what capacity?" S: "Leader
of the House. Unless you want it, that is what I should like
most."

Further talk with Winston at 5.30, Attlee was also there. . . .
We agreed to meet again after dinner, at 10.15. A very long sit-
ting followed. First of all James [Stuart], Winston and I talked.
I told them that Max and others thought I should lead the House.
Winston was doubtful: "You are a doer, not a talker." Stuart
against. He maintained Cripps would be welcome to our people
because unwelcome to Labour. We also discussed Cabinet of five
against seven. I favoured five or rather four, but Winston wanted
[Sir] John Anderson [Lord President of the Council] included. As
Max said to him later: "He is agreeable and always agrees with
you." Anderson is, I believe, a good committee man, but zero in
Cabinet. We discussed other posts, War Office, etc., all this with
Attlee who had meantime arrived.

February 19th: Winston sent for me in the morning and told
me that he had decided to choose the seven formula and to take
Max at his word [on leaving the War Cabinet]. I agreed to con-

tinue at Foreign Office but did not want to accept Cripps' suggestion of Ministry for External Affairs, if this meant to leave Foreign Office, as it did. Winston agreed.

Cripps' proposal was for a single Ministry combining the Foreign Office, Dominions Office and Colonial Office under one Minister in the War Cabinet.

Dick [Law, Parliamentary Under-Secretary of State for Foreign Affairs] and Jim [Thomas, Lord Commissioner of the Treasury] very perturbed at new layout. They do not think that it will satisfy country and they are angry that Cripps is Leader of the House and not me. I told them that Alec [Hardinge] and Winant do not share their views on last, but they were not to be comforted.

The new War Cabinet was announced the same night, February 19th. Its numbers were reduced from nine to seven. Churchill retained the Ministry of Defence but gave up the leadership of the House of Commons to Cripps, who became Lord Privy Seal. Attlee became Deputy Prime Minister and Dominions Secretary. Oliver Lyttelton was brought back from Cairo to become Minister of State with general supervision over production. Ernest Bevin, John Anderson and I retained our old positions. Kingsley Wood ceased to be a member of the War Cabinet but remained Chancellor of the Exchequer. Beaverbrook and Greenwood resigned.

February 20th: The new Cabinet has had a good press, better than I had expected. Saw Winston in morning, when we discussed other posts. He still favours P.J. [Grigg] for War Office and despite the undesirable precedent of promoting civil servant to be political chief of his own Department, there is much to be said for it. I believe that P.J. would do it well. [He was appointed on February 22nd.]

Despite this smooth start, more changes were needed within nine months. For me the enduring advantage was the accession of Lyttelton. No man understood better the true loyalty of a colleague.

He could be firm without provocation and cool without bravado, so that his opinions were respected and often fruitful.

Meanwhile our discussions with the Americans about the Russian treaty became tangled. The President, whom Halifax saw on February 17th, seemed at first prepared to contemplate Soviet control over the defence and foreign policies of the Baltic States. Sumner Welles, however, with whom Halifax had a conversation next day, spoke at length of the need to build the new world on principle. Although he too acknowledged Russia's need for security, he thought this could be provided by the dismemberment of Germany.

Two days later Welles told Halifax that the President had decided to make a direct approach to Stalin and was confident he could reach agreement with him. Halifax demurred at this, pointing out that it was with us that Stalin wished to sign a treaty and that this procedure might put me in a difficult position. Here was the first of several occasions when the President, mistakenly as I believe, moved out of step with us, influenced by his conviction that he could get better results with Stalin direct than could the three countries negotiating together. This was an illusion.

The War Cabinet discussed the American attitude on February 25th and, with their agreement and Winant's endorsement, I gave him a memorandum expressing our objection to direct exchanges between the President and Mr. Maxim Litvinov, now Soviet Ambassador in Washington, on the subject of the British treaty with the Russians. I suggested instead that there should be tripartite conversations in London after Winant came back.

While these arguments were being bandied, Maisky was active. He tried to put pressure on the Government by talking indiscreetly to journalists, telling them of Stalin's demands, chiding us for slowness in answering, complaining of what he called our excessive dependence on American approval, and stressing that Stalin would not be willing to discuss military matters until the frontier question was settled to his liking. These tactics were not new, Maisky had used them before and would use them again, but they were provoking.

When Halifax saw the President and Harry Hopkins on March 9th, he found it impossible to dissuade Mr. Roosevelt from direct negotiation. The President proposed to tell Stalin that, while everyone recognized Russia's need for security, it was too dangerous to put anything on paper now. But there was no need to worry about the Baltic States, since their future clearly depended on Russian military progress and, if Russia reoccupied them, neither the United States, nor Britain, could or would turn her out. I did not like the method of this statement, because I was sure that it would fail to satisfy Stalin and because it seemed to me to give us the worst of all worlds. We would be ungraciously conniving at the inevitable, without getting any return for it.

In the event the President's interview with Litvinov did not quite take the shape that he had forecast with Halifax, probably as a result of the Ambassador's arguments. While he told Litvinov that he could not subscribe to any treaty, secret or public, which dealt with frontiers, until the war had been won, he added that he was entirely in favour of facilitating the complete future security of the Soviet Union. He promised that after the war the United States would support Russian efforts to achieve "legitimate" security.

As a reply to this conversation, Litvinov was instructed by the Soviet Government merely to tell the President that they had taken note of his communication. Maisky explained to me that his Government, not having approached the United States themselves, nor asked for the American point of view, did not think that anything else was called for. He now hoped that we would conclude our treaty with Soviet Russia.

This the British Government decided to attempt. I told Maisky on April 8th that we were ready to negotiate and asked that the discussions should take place in London. I added that if, as we hoped, our efforts were rewarded, we should welcome a visit by Molotov to sign the treaty.

*   *   *   *   *

At the beginning of April proposals for future operations in western Europe were taking shape in Washington. The United States Chiefs of Staff, with the approval of President Roosevelt, put forward a plan for a second front in Europe in 1943. They also proposed that a smaller operation should be prepared for the autumn of 1942, either to take advantage of a sudden German disintegration, or to forestall an imminent Russian collapse.

General George Marshall, the United States Chief of Staff, and Mr. Harry Hopkins arrived in London on April 8th to discuss these plans. Once Anglo–American agreement had been reached, President Roosevelt intended to invite Russian representatives to Washington. I was disturbed at these American projects. I did not believe in early German disintegration and I was sure that we could not help the Russians by a landing on the European continent in 1942. It could only be a costly disaster.

April 10th: Saw Winston after luncheon. We spoke of American plan. He feared General Staff would say "Yes" and make this a pretext for doing less elsewhere.

At this time we accepted the United States' plan for a landing in France in 1943 and a possible emergency landing in 1942 but, three months later, the Americans acknowledged that an autumn landing was impracticable that year and agreed to an operation in North Africa instead.

Meanwhile the enemy air attack on Malta was at its height and convoys were almost unable to reach the island:

April 11th: We ought never to have allowed our margin of fighters [in Malta] to fall so low. Everyone knew of the threat. Nine Spitfires at a time flicked off an old freighter is not good enough. We always seem to need brilliant improvisation, especially the Air Ministry and that is not the way.

April 18th: Some talk with Winston in morning about American report of Laval and Darlan having taken over from Pétain and an optimistic telegram from Roosevelt that he and Welles thought an independent [French] move in North Africa possible. Would we consider what we could do, etc. Americans have always been too optimistic about Vichy, and enquiry showed that this story was only based on newspaper report and not on [Admiral William D.] Leahy [United States Ambassador at

Vichy]. Winston much disappointed for he had been very hopeful and even wanted to bring back Harry Hopkins and Marshall.
But they would not be stopped.

★　　★　　★　　★　　★

Negotiations with the Russians over the text of the treaty crept
forward. The draft which I gave to Maisky on April 13th contained a clause specifically excluding the Russo–Polish frontier
from any promise of a return to 1941. The Soviet counter-proposal
omitted this article, and also a reference which we had included to
our two Governments acting with others in post-war Europe.

April 24th: Saw Maisky in afternoon. Then about 5 p.m. to
Winston who had just woken up. He was in tearing spirits. Said
he could not remember where he was on waking, he had had
such deep sleep and he was striding about his room in vest and
drawers with cigar in his mouth, whisky and soda at his side and
calling for Nellie to produce his socks! We spoke of Government
and I urged him to bring as many of Cabinet into his plans as
he could. He agreed though arguing this must slow up machine.
However Cripps, Oliver and I he thought pretty powerful with
himself.

April 27th: Luncheon with Winston alone. He was in better
form than I have known him for ages. We spoke of painting and
pictures, the light on the Horse Guards, the right tactics in politics and so forth. He strongly impressed upon me the importance
of not being afraid to drop out for a bit. He ought to have gone
for a tour of the Empire when he was out of office. It was a
mistake to believe that if one had once played a great part one
would be forgotten. I said that I thought Ll.G. had made a mistake in not retiring after the last war. He recalled a conversation
he had with Ll.G. about it early in 1919 when motoring in
France. Lothian [then Lloyd George's private secretary] had
advised him to retire and he had asked Winston's opinion.
Winston had recalled his obligations to those who had worked
with him. On another occasion Ll.G. had told him that he had
been asked on the same day to lead Liberal and Tory parties.

On May 5th I told Maisky that while we hoped for collaboration with the Soviet Government, both during and after the war, he must know that we had also to act with the Dominions, the United States and our other Allies about the post-war settlement. I had not liked the Russian omission of the reference to this obligation, which had been in our draft.

I then spoke of Poland, and said that the Russian draft seemed to assume that the British Government would have nothing to do with Soviet–Polish negotiations about their common frontier. Our undertaking to Poland, I reminded him, must be clearly safeguarded and, unless we were met on this, we could not sign the treaty. As for pacts with Finland and Roumania, which Maisky now maintained must be approved at the same time as the treaty, this demand had never been made when I was in Moscow. It was despairing to try to negotiate with the Soviet Government when they invariably raised their price at every meeting.

Maisky promised to telegraph all this to his Government. When I rang him up two days later he said he would let me know as soon as he received a reply, but that he had been hoping for further word from me. I retorted that there was no likelihood of this, to which the Ambassador replied that if this was our last word, he feared agreement would not be possible. I made no move and no reply came from Moscow. Negotiations were at a standstill until Molotov arrived in England.

I had been casting around in my mind for alternatives and, at Sir Alexander Cadogan's suggestion, I submitted to my colleagues the draft of an entirely different treaty. The main purpose of this was to offer the Russians a post-war alliance against German aggression, instead of the recognition of their frontier claims. I wrote:

> With the disappearance from the Treaty of any mention of frontiers it would no longer be necessary for us to safeguard the Polish position and to reassure our other Allies in Eastern Europe by the insertion of special stipulations about the confederation of these States and about collaborating in the post-war settlement with the other United Nations.
>
> If Mr. Molotov, on arrival, proves unwilling to meet us on

the above two points, it will, I believe, be of little use to embark upon prolonged discussion of alternative formulae for getting over the difficulty. On the other hand, it would be highly undesirable from both the Russian standpoint and our own that his visit should end without the signature of a Treaty, which is widely expected both here and abroad.

My alternative draft treaty, I concluded, might offer a solution in the event of such a deadlock. Even if rejected by the Russians, it would strengthen our position.

★   ★   ★   ★   ★

Molotov arrived in London on May 20th in an uncompromising mood and discussions began the next day. At the first meeting, which was attended by the Prime Minister, Attlee, Cadogan and myself, with Molotov and Maisky on the Russian side, Molotov revealed that, of the two questions he had come to discuss, the second front was more important than the Anglo–Soviet treaty. This, he said, would be better postponed if it was not possible for us to agree to the minimum Soviet conditions as set out in their draft.

When the Foreign Minister spoke of minimum conditions, he explained that his Government insisted on recovering the territory violated by Hitler, and they could make no concessions about this. Furthermore, it was not sufficient simply to restore what existed before the war; the Soviet Government must secure their territory on their north-western and south-western frontiers. Without some guarantee, as in the proposed pacts with Finland and Roumania, no one in the Soviet Union would approve the treaty. Poland was the most delicate question, but the Soviet Government would do their best to come to terms with Poland over frontiers. In reply, Mr. Churchill tried to make the Soviet Foreign Minister understand the British purpose in undertaking treaty negotiations, no easy task with a man of Molotov's temperament.

When Cadogan and I sat down to detailed discussion of the treaty with Molotov and Maisky that afternoon, the question of Poland soon came to the fore. Molotov said that he was ready to sign a treaty with Poland on the basis of the Curzon line, with minor modifications in favour of the Soviet Union, or on the basis of the line occupied in 1941, which the Russians preferred. To agree to leave the Polish frontier unsettled was a Russian concession which should be matched by us: the British Government should therefore not maintain their support of the Polish cause.

I replied that it was not a question of taking sides, but of our treaty with Poland signed before the outbreak of war. I must also safeguard the British position, stated in July 1941 with Russian acquiescence. When I was in Moscow the Soviet Government had accepted to leave open the question of the Polish frontier; I was therefore surprised to find that they now seemed to think they were entitled to ask some further concession from us.

The next day's meeting brought us no nearer agreement about Poland. I therefore informed the War Cabinet that I proposed to put the alternative treaty before Molotov. This I did on the afternoon of May 23rd. Molotov showed no enthusiasm and said he thought it would be impossible to discuss it with his Government by telegram. However, he agreed to stay longer in London, if need be, to complete the treaty discussions before he went on to Washington. The final stages are recorded in my diary:

May 24th: Some talk with Office and then meeting with Russians at 4 p.m. They produced several concessions, notably on Polish issue. I pressed my second draft strongly and Molotov was less unreceptive on the subject. Maisky drew me on one side at one moment and said: "I cannot understand your attitude. We have made many concessions, yet you seem as though you did not want agreement." . . . After further discussion I agreed to submit conclusion to Cabinet, though holding out no hope they would agree.

Rang up Winant on return to Binderton, and urged him to see Russians soon. He said he was doing so tonight and we discussed what he would say. He rang me up later and said that he thought all had gone well. He had spoken plainly and Russians had been "frightfully nice." Between my two talks with Winant, Maisky had rung up to say that, on further examination, Molotov was ready to discuss our new draft and thought that something could be done on basis of it. Could we discuss it tomorrow? I agreed and fixed 3 p.m. Telephoned to Winston who was greatly cheered. Bed after midnight, much relieved, though many a slip is possible yet.

May 25th: Winston and I had long talk with Molotov and Maisky who arrived at 10 p.m. W. spoke of progress of war and told them of Libya and our production and other matters. Molotov drew plans of the most anxious sectors of the front for Russia, Leningrad, Moscow and Kharkov. We also spoke of Treaty, when he said that he had received authority to sign. We discussed drafts together. Winston talked America to them, rather too much I thought. Anyway I put in that our war production was still greater than theirs [the United States'], for Winston spoke almost as though we were doing scarcely anything.

After they left Winston congratulated me most warmly on Treaty developments. He said that if it came off it would be much the biggest thing I had done. He was particularly delighted that we should have thought of second draft.

May 26th: A morning spent on Treaty texts. Saw High Commissioners who were delighted, and also Turkish Ambassador who was pleased and Polish Ambassador who was non-committal but must have been relieved. Cabinet at 1 p.m. when final position was explained and Prime Minister voiced congratulations. Luncheon at Soviet Embassy. Found Molotov somewhat harassed because Harriman had denounced Treaty to him. It soon emerged that he knew nothing of later draft. . . . Russians seemed genuinely pleased at the outcome, and for us it is a great relief.

The Russian motive in accepting the new text, which contained no mention of frontiers, after battling so long and so obdurately for our recognition of their "minimum conditions," is obscure. The chief purpose in the Soviet Government's negotiation was to secure a second front in Europe as soon as possible. At some stage in our talks Molotov probably became convinced he could not get his way over frontiers and decided that more was to be gained in the military field by accepting our new terms, and going to Washington with the Treaty signed, than by failure to agree.

Molotov returned to London on June 9th, bringing an explosive message with him. In Washington he had induced the Americans to agree to a communiqué which spoke of "full understanding" having been reached "with regard to the urgent tasks of creating a second front in Europe in 1942." We were not consulted about this wording and could not have agreed to it, with its implication of a definite pledge. If it meant anything, it was a promise of a second front that year, which we did not believe possible. Yet we could not give the enemy the comfort of conflicting communiqués, so we repeated it, while being explicit to Molotov about the difficulties of a cross-Channel operation in 1942, the main burden of which would fall on British forces.

> *June 9th:* Molotov and Maisky dined with Winston, Clem [Attlee] and I also there. Long talk after dinner, mainly explanation by W. of second front problems. I think that this did much good. At least it helped to increase confidence. Party broke up after 1 a.m.
>
> *June 10th:* Adjournment to Soviet Embassy for luncheon, to which Russians have invited Poles at my suggestion. Party probably did some good, though nobody could call it a great success. Left Molotov and Sikorski still talking at 4 p.m. [Mr. A. E.] Bogomolov [Soviet Ambassador to the Allied Governments in London] is an unhelpful creature, to all appearances a poor substitute for Maisky.

That evening the Prime Minister gave Molotov, before he left on the final stage of his journey home, an *aide-mémoire* explaining that it was not yet possible to say whether the plan for a landing on the Continent was feasible that year. We could therefore give no promise. Despite this document, the Soviet Government affected to believe, and gave their people to understand, that a second front had been promised. Later in the summer, when the Americans admitted that the operation could not take place, Russian reproaches, particularly against Britain, became violent.

★   ★   ★   ★   ★

> *May 30th:* Wellington Koo [now Chinese Ambassador] came to luncheon. Long talk afterwards on Anglo–Chinese relations.

He admitted misunderstandings and seemed sincerely anxious to improve matters. We agreed on a programme including loan, military plans and a trip by him to Chungking. . . .

Rommel began his new offensive in the Desert on the night of May 26th–27th, and established a bridgehead among the British minefields.

June 7th: Winston rang up twice in morning. First about Libya battle, as to which we agreed that reports were disappointing. We were both depressed by extent to which Rommel appears able to retain offensive. "I fear that we have not very good generals," said W. He was also depressed by Chiefs of Staff sudden decision to cancel their own previous plans to take certain place in north [Petsamo]. I had not heard of this change. W. feared it had to do with Tovey's extreme reluctance to continuing Russian convoys. "The politicians are much abused, but they get little help or inspiration from their service advisers," was W's comment and it can hardly be denied.

Later he spoke about China. There also he wants us to plan ahead for offensive action to relieve Chiang [Kai-shek] who is obviously hard pressed. Military appear to take a leisurely view and I undertook to raise political issue with him to emphasize urgency. Then at least we can get examination.

A week later Rommel broke out of his bridgehead and in severe fighting gained possession of the ridges between El Adem and "Knightsbridge."

June 14th: Libyan battle is raging fiercely. Rommel still seems to have the initiative and either his resources are much greater than our people judged, or his losses have been considerably less than they estimated. On their calculation he should have few tanks left, yet he always comes up strong.

The highlight of this tragic period was the surrender of Tobruk on June 21st. News of this reached the Prime Minister while he was in conference with President Roosevelt in Washington. He felt the humiliation bitterly. A few hours later he telephoned to me, at what was five in the morning, our time. He asked for news of the position at home. The New York newspapers, he said, were full of the impending fall of the Government. I told him that I had heard not one word of this. Of course there was much grief. No doubt there would be blame for the Government, but so far nothing had happened to shake us.

General Auchinleck, who took over direct operational command of the Eighth Army on June 25th, decided that it was not possible to make a final defence at Mersa Matruh and chose instead the Alamein position.

June 28th: War Office rang up at dinner time with an account of the battle. It is clear that we are back behind Matruh, but this may not be as bad as it sounds if our armour has not been heavily engaged and if we are adding to its strength meanwhile. But as to all this we are in the dark. Poor Jumbo [General Wilson] always longed to fight the Matruh battle. It was in his view the perfect set-piece battle. Strafer [Gott] can only have abandoned the project because he was too weak in armour.

These new disasters caused a fresh outbreak of discontent with the Government's conduct of the war. On his return from Washington Mr. Churchill faced a censure motion in the House of Commons tabled by Sir John Wardlaw-Milne. Sir Stafford Cripps marshalled our forces, and he did it badly, choosing Oliver Lyttelton, a new hand in the House of Commons, to reply first for the Government. Lyttelton was soon in trouble, despite his courage and his knowledge, simply through not being familiar with the personalities and practices of the House. When he sat down beside me at the finish he was dripping with sweat and muttered: "I don't know if this is your idea of fun, but it's not mine." But it did not matter. The Government's critics ranged from Sir Roger Keyes on the right to Mr. Aneurin Bevan on the left and they got into each other's way, the Government finding safety in the strange assortment of their suggestions. In the division lobby they mustered only twenty-five votes.

July 2nd: Winston wound up with one of his most effective speeches, beautifully adjusted to temper of the House.

Work at the Office. Then dined with him alone except for his brother. Much discussion of war situation. Winston said repeatedly that we had not done as well as we should. "I am ashamed," etc., and we discussed too the problems of the Army, its Trade Union outlook, paucity of talent, etc. I urged Winston to see Ralph [Assheton, Parliamentary Under-Secretary, Ministry of Supply] about his "Churchill" tanks.

Then Winston broached possibility of another journey [to the Middle East]. I didn't like it and told him I thought he wouldn't be able to help and would be in the way. "You mean like a great blue-bottle buzzing over a huge cowpat!" said Winston. I said this was just what I did mean! At this moment Brendan [Bracken] appeared and took up the running strongly against the project, especially on grounds of risk. But this W. would not have. Anyway he had made his testament in my favour before he went to United States and he was not indispensable. Argument was inconclusive.

As the outcome of a request from His Majesty, Mr. Churchill had advised the King to ask me to form a new Government in the event of his death on the journey.

★　★　★　★　★

At this moment when our fortunes were at a low ebb I received reports of peace-feelers from groups of Germans said to be opposed to Hitler. The chief strength of this opposition was apparently in the army, that same army which had again and again given way to Hitler against its own better judgment. Successes were acceptable to it so long as they continued. A peace-feeler might therefore only be an attempt to save the German army from destruction and to salvage as much as possible of Hitler's territorial gains.

Even more important was the possible reaction upon our allies, notably the Soviet Union, through whose territories the German armies were then thrusting towards Stalingrad and into the Caucasus. There was an evident risk that suspicion might be sown in the Russian mind. I therefore repeated the instructions already given to our missions abroad that these rumours, which were now current in two or three capitals, should be ignored. On May 11th I told the War Cabinet what I had done and they approved. I asked Lord Halifax on June 8th to tell the United States Government what we thought and our reasons, and telegraphed:

> We have been careful to make no response whatsoever to such approaches since we suspect that they may be inspired by the German secret service who have made a special study of the strategy and tactics of the peace offensive. If our suspicions are correct, no doubt the German Government would be quick to take advantage of any response we might make, with the object of trying to sow discord between us and our allies and of checking the tempo of our war effort.
>
> You might add that we do not doubt that elements of opposition to the Nazi regime exist in Germany, that these elements may well become more vocal and their organization more crystallized in the next few months; but that unless and until they come into the open with deeds they are not worth consideration.

On the other hand, I asked Halifax to draw the attention of the American Government to recent statements by some of my colleagues and myself, devised to make our policy towards a future Germany as positive as it was safe to do.*

Dr. George Bell, Bishop of Chichester, had lectured in Sweden during May and June, 1942, under the auspices of the Ministry of Information. On his return the Bishop asked to see me, which he did on June 30th. He told me that two anti-Nazi German Protestant clergymen had come to Sweden to meet him. The Bishop left a memorandum with me reporting in detail what the German clerics proposed. This showed that the group they represented intended to overthrow the existing rulers, who were to be replaced by anti-Nazi members of the army and administration, former trade union leaders and churchmen. The Allies were invited to announce that, once Hitler was overthrown, they were prepared to negotiate with another Government. The names of General Ludwig Beck, Chief of Staff until 1938, Herr Karl Goerdeler, Mayor of Leipzig,

---

* *Freedom and Order,* page 159.

and other notable figures were given as deeply involved in the movement.

I asked the Foreign Office to examine this and to probe all the parallel information we had from secret and other sources and, after some preliminary correspondence, I wrote to the Bishop on August 4th:

> I am very conscious of the importance of what you say about not discouraging any elements of opposition in Germany to the Nazi regime. You will remember that in my speech at Edinburgh on May 8th I devoted quite a long passage to Germany and concluded by saying that, if any section of the German people really wished to see a return to a German state based on respect for law and the rights of the individual, they must understand that no one would believe them until they had taken active steps to rid themselves of their present regime.*

> For the present I do not think that it would be advisable to go any further in a public statement. I realize the dangers and difficulties to which the opposition in Germany is exposed, but they have so far given little evidence of their existence and until they show that they are willing to follow the example of the oppressed peoples of Europe in running risks and taking active steps to oppose and overthrow the Nazi rule of terror, I do not see how we can usefully expand the statements which have already been made by members of the Government about Germany. I think those statements have made it quite clear that we do not intend to deny Germany a place in the future Europe, but that the longer the German people tolerate the Nazi regime, the greater becomes their responsibility for the crimes which that regime is committing in their name.

* *Freedom and Order,* page 159.

5

"TORCH"
July–November 1942

Heavy losses in the convoys to Russia — The Prime Minister prepares for Moscow — The death of General Gott — Appointment of General Montgomery to Eighth Army — I feel the strain — Mr. Dulles gives his views — Difficulties with Sir Stafford Cripps — Trouble with our Allies over Operation "Torch" — El Alamein — Allied landings in North Africa — The United States and Admiral Darlan — General de Gaulle refuses to become involved — Field-Marshal Smuts and Mr. Churchill — I take on Leadership of the House of Commons

THE CONVOYS to Russia's northern ports were the most brutal duty of the war. The ordeal was almost beyond human endurance, the losses appalling and the gratitude negligible. During the summer months of 1942, the Nazi navy and air force concentrated upon the destruction of these fated ships which linked America, Great Britain and Russia by sea.

On July 14th, 1942, Mr. Maisky told me that reports from the Russian front were very grave and he wanted to know if there was any news of the latest convoy carrying military supplies to Archangel. I said that I regretted to have to tell him that the news was bad. Only five ships had got through out of the forty which had sailed; it was possible that two more might yet do so. The losses in shipping and material must have been very heavy; so far as we knew, about a hundred tanks out of six hundred had arrived and forty aircraft.

The Ambassador expressed concern and asked what our plans were for the next convoy. I said that it was obvious that we must take some account of the experience of the last one. To send convoys out and have nearly all the ships sunk was of no help to the Russians, or to anyone but the enemy.

As a result of these losses, the War Cabinet decided that the next convoy must be postponed. The remorseless duty was taken up again a month later with no happier fate.

July 24th: Went to see Winston, who reported on a somewhat stormy interview with Maisky last night, when the latter brought a rough answer from Stalin [to the news of a convoy's postponement]. I told Winston that this was to be expected, but he was not to be easily soothed. Asked me to see Maisky, which I did, also Winant.

Last named was very critical of us for not starting up second front. I reminded him that his people did not suggest anything before October which would be useless for Russia and even then scale could not be enough, on American plan, to affect Eastern front. He had no arguments, but was obstinate and said we should ask Americans for what we wanted by given date and put it up to them. I told him I saw no use in this since we both knew American contribution must be of the smallest this year. I have never seen Winant so put out. He dislikes "Gymnast."

This was the plan for an operation in French North Africa and was renamed "Torch." The weakness of our Middle Eastern position was still the elongated communications. Our front was maintained by sending supplies round the Cape at heavy cost in ships and time. If we and the Americans could establish ourselves in North Africa and work eastwards, communications would be eased and we could attack the Axis in Africa from the east and west. The invasion of Italy would be in sight.

★   ★   ★   ★   ★

July 29th: Nothing very difficult about Parliamentary Questions but many Members came and lobbied me at question time and before a division in the evening. They seem in poor spirits which is perhaps not surprising as the war is now going.

On the same day I wrote of an interlude when Cranborne and I had luncheon at the Palace, "just the four of us." It is a measure of that period of strict rationing that I singled out for mention a slice of cold ham. Luncheon a few days later at the Brazilian Embassy was "made eventful by the appearance of oranges. All guests to be seen with eyes starting out of their heads, and luscious nectarines cheerfully spurned."

On July 29th I dined with the rest of the War Cabinet at No. 10 Downing Street to meet the King. I sat on the other side of the Prime Minister. He suggested that he should make a visit to Egypt. I did not pay much heed, for he had proposed this before. When the King had gone, however, Mr. Churchill suddenly said at 1 a.m., "Now, we'll have a Cabinet," and proposed that he should leave for Egypt two days later. Mr. Attlee nodded his head. Nobody else said much, except Mr. Bevin, who approved. I thought that they were all as surprised as I and only learnt afterwards that some of them were not. I asked whether the doctor approved, but I was also troubled by the risks of the journey, though it was clearly useless to speak to the Prime Minister about these; they would only whet his appetite.

The next morning Cadogan showed me a personal telegram from Sir Archibald Clark Kerr, our Ambassador in Moscow, suggesting an early visit by the Prime Minister to Stalin. I wrote in my diary that "A meeting in Astrakhan, or even Moscow, with Joe [Stalin] at a time like this might indeed pay a dividend."

July 30th: Took the telegram round to Winston and he jumped at it. W. agreed to a Cabinet before luncheon.

At meeting he asked me what I thought. I said that on reflection I had liked less and less idea of his visit to Egypt. That I should have advised against journey for that alone. But that this new development seemed to me to put a different complexion on whole business, and if Joe were prepared to invite him I thought he should go. All this of course subject to doctor's all clear. The others agreed.

On August 1st I had luncheon with the Prime Minister and Mrs. Churchill, when Lord Beaverbrook and Mr. Brendan Bracken, as well as the Prime Minister's brother, Major John Churchill, were the other guests. Both Beaverbrook and Bracken wanted to go with him. The Prime Minister and I walked up and down in Downing Street garden while we discussed whether either of them should do so. He felt the need for company, especially in Moscow, but finally decided to travel with Brooke and Cadogan, but with no other Minister.

Mr. Churchill reached Cairo on August 3rd and three days later sent his verdict on the Middle East Command. He had decided to appoint General Alexander Commander-in-Chief and General Gott to command the Eighth Army. My colleagues were delighted, but none more than I.

Late on the night of August 7th the War Cabinet was in Downing Street considering a telegram from the Prime Minister, who had made proposals for the division of authority between Alexander and Gott, when a private secretary came in white-faced. He brought a message to the table with the comment: "I fear that this is bad news." It was from Churchill and announced that Gott's aircraft had been shot down and he had been killed. I felt not only grieved but shaken. The war had been going badly for us and it seemed that we could never get the right commanders in the right places. Now that we thought all was set fair, this unexpected blow had fallen.

However, in war there can be no pause and we agreed to the choice of General Bernard Montgomery, whose name General Brooke had proposed to the Prime Minister and General Smuts in Cairo.

★ ★ ★ ★ ★

Mr. Churchill's Soviet assignment was as unpalatable as any man could face, but by the end of it Stalin had ceased to insist that a second front should be opened in 1942. Though he saw the advantages of the plan for an Anglo-American landing in North Africa, it did not halt the spate of Soviet propaganda for a second front by all means, scrupulous and otherwise:

August 16th: Troubled by plan, at present unknown to Russians, for switch of twelve squadrons of R.A.F. [from Egypt] to south Russia. They cannot arrive before October, by which date battle of Caucasus will in all probability have been decided. On the other hand it is most dangerous to weaken Alexander now, for the defeat of Rommel will greatly facilitate "Torch."

Another example of dangerous dispersal. U.S. replacements, for which Winston calls, will not arrive to time. Felt so strongly about this that I rang up Portal and found his reaction the same. He was delighted to get my backing and, at my suggestion, he enlisted Attlee too, to whom I spoke on telephone.

The plan was scotched.

I had asked Sir Alexander Cadogan to try to arrange for Mr. Churchill to see M. Panayotis Kanellopoulos, the Greek Minister of Defence, during his stay in Cairo. Cadogan sent a message reminding the Prime Minister of this, and was summoned forthwith to the bathroom, where he heard Mr. Churchill splashing as he threw his sponge up and down: "Kanellopoulos, Can'tellopoulos, Kanellopoulos." "All right, I'll see him," was the final verdict.

At the end of the month I saw Field-Marshal Dill, who was in London on a visit from Washington.

August 30th: Had a talk with Jack [Dill] yesterday about Greece; Oliver [Lyttelton, Minister of Production] was also there. He [Dill] was quite unrepentant that we were right to go there. Politically, no doubt: militarily, on balance, "yes." He said that we had worked the whole thing out very carefully at the time and had never had any illusions about the difficulty of the choice. He knew O'Connor had believed that we could press on towards Tripoli with a small column. He did not believe that it could in fact have achieved much. He was very steady and firm about the whole business.

The consistent overwork which I had to shoulder was occasionally relieved by reminiscent conversations of this kind. At other times it was responsible for more gloomy entries, which give the reckoning of responsibility in these war years even upon a strong constitution in the prime of life.

September 6th: I am bothered about money. There is no security in politics, and I feel that, for boys' sake and my own old age

I ought to take something that will last a few years and at least allow me to put by my private income, which at present I am overspending at £1000 a year or more. Moreover I do not really feel confidence in myself as No. 1 at home and it looks as if, *faute de mieux,* I might drift that way. . . .

Truth is I feel too tired to tackle these post-war problems. I am desperately in need of a change and do not know enough of economics.

Meanwhile work went on:

September 16th: A difficult meeting with American correspondents. They had been having tea with Maisky, who had evidently filled them up with criticisms of us for not opening second front, with hints that we had not kept Russians fully informed, that Americans had wished to attack and we had not, etc. Maisky is overstepping bounds of an Ambassador's privilege and a row before long would not surprise me.

★   ★   ★   ★   ★

"Torch" continued to be an issue, not least on the diplomatic front. On September 4th Mr. Richard Law, my Parliamentary Under-Secretary, reported from Washington a conversation with Mr. Sumner Welles, who expressed great disquiet about General de Gaulle. He thought the time would soon come when we would have to sever our association with him. He accepted Law's reply that it would be a great shock to French opinion, but still seemed to think that we might have to face it. If de Gaulle came in with the occupying armies and established a provisional government, he could never be removed.

I did not share these opinions. In a memorandum for our Washington Embassy, I wrote that if de Gaulle were to accompany the forces entering France, he would have to take his chance with the French people. If he did set up a provisional government, I saw no serious prospect of his being able permanently to maintain himself in power, even if he wished to do so.

At this time I was told of the views of Mr. John Foster Dulles, who was in London on an unofficial exploratory mission. The United States, he said, was in favour of larger national *blocs* in Europe, resulting from the confederation of equals, but would not welcome the creation of *blocs* of lesser states, concentrated round one or another great power. He interpreted a plan of M. Lie, the Norwegian Foreign Minister, for North Atlantic defence as one whereby the smaller states of western Europe would become satellites of Great Britain, and said the United States Government would not smile upon it, nor would they enter into such a combination.

On this I minuted on July 25th:

> American views are of interest, but ours are even more important where Europe is concerned. I am sure that the Scandinavian *bloc* plan [a neutralist *bloc* advocated by Sweden] won't work, but I am not sure about this new project either. . . .
>
> As regards America, we should always consult U.S. Government, but our object should be to bring them along with us. They know very little of Europe and it would be unfortunate for the future of the world if U.S. uninstructed views were to decide the future of the European continent. Our diplomacy should be equal to this task. . . .

★ ★ ★ ★ ★

At the end of August the Prime Minister learnt that Sir Stafford Cripps, Lord Privy Seal and Leader of the House of Commons, had developed serious doubts about "the effectiveness of our machinery for the central direction of the war."* On September 21st Cripps told Mr. Churchill that he felt it was his duty to resign from the Government.

October 1st: Stafford asked to see me urgently and came in at 6 p.m. He said that he and W. had reached the parting of the ways. In response to further questions it seems that he saw W. at 11 p.m. last night and that they went at it until 2.30 a.m. The first hour W. attacked him, so S.C. says, told him that he raked

* Churchill: *The Second World War*; Vol. IV.

up criticism from all quarters, that if he went out he would have no future, neither Tories nor Socialists supporting him. S.C. retorted; then matters were calmer but without agreement.

I told S.C. that all this scarcely affected major issues of war or major decisions of policy on which we were all agreed. He, however, cited instances of how badly war was run and eventually said he might accept a job outside this country, e.g. Co-ordination of Supply in U.S.

The Prime Minister then asked me to dinner, but since my son Simon was in London for the evening on leave from his Royal Air Force training, I could not manage it.

Round to W. at 11 p.m. Found Attlee there and persuaded him, with some difficulty, that crisis should be postponed. W. convinced that S.C. has Machiavellian political plot. I don't believe it.

At this point Mr. Lyttleton came in:

S.C. had spoken to him as though resignation already decided upon. W. up in arms and unwilling to treat. Attlee and I stuck to it that S.C. had not so spoken to us. Eventually agreed that A. and I should see S.C. and discuss American project and Ministry of Aircraft Production, which is another alternative, *without* seat in War Cabinet. S.C. seemed to like idea of both, especially the latter. A. and I also did our best, on general grounds, to convince S.C. of folly of causing rift in ranks at this critical moment. I think that we made some impression. Back to W. who in turn was easier to convince against the deep laid plot theory.

October 2nd: Winston rang me up early to say that he was impressed with Stafford's readiness to take another job, did I see any objection to his asking him to postpone whole question until after "Torch." I said none and reminded him that I had suggested this before. He said that he would see S.C. and put this. Just before luncheon W. sent for me and told me he had done so. S.C. had seemed impressed, but expressed desire to talk it all over with me. I undertook to do my best.

He came along at 3.15 and we went at it for an hour. I told

him that national interest was only thing he could consider, that this was not moment to rock the boat. Later, if "Torch" failed, we were all sunk, if it succeeded, he was free to act as he wished. If it were fifty-fifty, we could think again. I asked him to think of effect on troops of an attack on central direction of war at this particular moment. He agreed that there was force in all this, but argued that my course left all difficulties unresolved and that truth was that he was convinced we should all get on much better without W. anyway. But he would think it over and write to W. tomorrow. This last only I repeated to W. and urged strongly on him that this was no time for crisis, with most critical month ahead. He agrees now.

All idea of Supply co-ordination in U.S. or Ministry of Aircraft Production had to be dropped because S.C. insisted upon a letter from him to P.M. explaining why he had done this. He showed me draft of such a letter at our meeting this afternoon. I told him that no P.M. could accept it.

October 3rd: Stafford rang me up and read over his proposed reply to Winston. Thank Heaven it postpones the resignation until "Torch" is launched. The more I think of it the more I am convinced how crazy it would be to have a political upheaval here, even a minor one, just now. Rang up Winston and told him that I thought that the Cripps letter was good enough. I think that he was relieved, though he is certainly exasperated by Cripps. The hostility between them is bound to deepen, but the essential is that it should not burst at a time most damaging to the nation.

In the midst of all this argument, I had to attend an official luncheon at the Soviet Embassy in my honour and, not surprisingly, my diary concludes on Saturday night: "Tired after a very strenuous week."

October 6th: An after dinner Cabinet in Cabinet War Room, which I always dislike; mostly about a telegram to Stalin on the lines of which we agreed. Oliver [Lyttelton] and I had a drink with Winston after: "Like being asked into the pavilion," Oliver said.

October 8th: Simon [my son] had breakfast with us and left during the day for Oxford and his air training. It is sad to see him go, and he is so very young. Not yet eighteen. . . .

Max [Beaverbrook] expressed concern at Winston's health and described him as "bowed" and not the man he was. Brendan [Bracken] also said that W. was very "low" yesterday when Max saw him. I told him that his powers of recuperation were very great and I was not worried.

I was, however, concerned about the fact that the declarations which were being prepared for the President of the United States to issue at the opening of "Torch" contained not a single word about the British share in the operation. This was on the pretext that the British were most unpopular in North Africa, which proved to be a legend. I telegraphed about this omission to Halifax on September 28th, but I was not able to secure more than a reference to the participation of the United Nations.

The trouble with Mr. Maisky which I had foreseen a month earlier had now blown up and, on October 15th, I asked him to come to see me. He would, I said, recall that some little time ago the Prime Minister had given him full information about "Torch," under the pledge of absolute secrecy and that he himself had replied that, as an old conspirator, he could be trusted with a secret. We had received information, from sources which we must regard as absolutely trustworthy, that on at least two occasions the Ambassador had spoken to journalists about "Torch."

Mr. Maisky interrupted me at this point to say vehemently, "No! No!," but I continued that unfortunately our evidence was such as we could not ignore. The Ambassador repeated that he had never at any time spoken to anybody about "Torch," though he must tell me that there were a great many rumours flying about Fleet Street. Too many people appeared to know about "Torch." I replied that that was an entirely different question. I was not concerned with indiscretions by our own people. Those were for us to deal with. I was asking him about reports of what he had said. The Ambassador reiterated that there was no truth in them. I went on that our accounts of his conversations went further than I had told him, and also attributed to him the sentiment that "Torch" would not be regarded by the Russians as the opening of a second front. The interview was an uncomfortable one for us both and the Ambassador seemed put out and somewhat resentful. However, it was a duty I had to face.

★　　★　　★　　★　　★

October 17th, Chequers: Looked in on Winston about 10.30 and told him I wanted to go on to Binderton for luncheon. He agreed, when Pug [Ismay] rang up and said mysterious French message had arrived, so all plans changed again. We awaited this, which only arrived about 1 p.m.

The message concerned offers to the United States Government from Admiral François Darlan, Commander-in-Chief of the French Forces and Vice-President of the Council, and from General Henri Giraud, living in retirement in unoccupied France. Both asked for the supreme command of any American expedition to French North Africa and claimed that they would be able to rally the troops there to the Allies.

At the preliminary reading of the account which Ismay had sent, at which Smuts, Pound and Mountbatten, now Chief of Combined Operations, were present:

> I felt suspicious, which may be just my nature, but it seemed too much like the way Germans would play their hand if they wanted to know our plans and delay them. After luncheon Smuts proposed adjournment to London to discuss with Americans. Off we went, Winston in high tide of enthusiasm.

We reached London and met, at No. 10 Downing Street, Lieutenant-General Dwight D. Eisenhower, Allied Commander-in-Chief, Major-General Mark Clark, his deputy, and Brigadier-General Bedell Smith, his Chief of Staff. Our own Chiefs of Staff also attended and we agreed that contact should be made with Giraud only, but that there would be no change in the chain of command for "Torch." Giraud's representatives in Algiers having suggested that a secret American mission should be sent to meet them, General Clark was asked to handle this.

On October 27th, President Roosevelt sent the Prime Minister the draft of a press release for issue immediately following the landings. It included the statement that the operation "provides an effective Second Front assistance to our heroic Allies in Russia." The Foreign Office wanted this paragraph omitted, as it might have stirred up controversy, but Cadogan and I liked the reference. The Russians alleged that the Americans were ready for a second front in Europe and that we deterred them. I saw no need to point out this snag, preferring to let the text stand, since the matter was, after all, the President's business. Mr. Churchill fully agreed with my conclusion.

There now followed in a matter of months a series of engagements ending in victory for the Allies: El Alamein, the landings in North Africa, Stalingrad and Guadalcanal. They marked the turning point of the war. On the day of the North African landings, I saw the Spanish and Portuguese Ambassadors to tell them.

> *November 8th:* Terrific day and strenuous one, marred for me by heaviest of colds. Many talks with Winston on telephone during morning and interview with [the Duke of] Alba and [Dr. Armindo] Monteiro. A good reply from [Dr. Antonio] Salazar [Portuguese Prime Minister] early, but nothing from Madrid, except a muddled American interview, until late. Then very satisfactory accounts, first from American and then from Sam [Hoare, Ambassador in Madrid]. It is evident that latter greatly exaggerated difficulties, for whatever reason.
>
> Lunched with Winston and de Gaulle. Latter was reasonable and less *blessé* than usual.

De Gaulle's position was strengthened by reports from Gibraltar that Giraud was showing a grasping appetite. The Prime Minister had rung me up to complain about this.

We had wished to warn the General beforehand of what was afoot, but since over two hundred and fifty thousand American soldiers were on the high seas, the President had strongly urged the Prime Minister to refrain. Nevertheless, I knew that de Gaulle had gleaned hints about the operation. He now commented favourably upon the choice of General Giraud as a leader in North Africa. Giraud had signed no armistice. He had escaped from Germany and was without reproach. The Americans, de Gaulle added, were right to go to North Africa, but wrong should they subsequently foster any division between the various elements ready to fight the Axis.

It may be that my broadcast to the French people of July 14th had reassured de Gaulle as to our intentions, for he referred to it in later years.* I said:

> I am addressing you, the whole people of France, on your National Day, on behalf of the whole British people. I address you not only as friends, but as allies, for in the two years which have passed since the events at Bordeaux you have proved yourselves faithful allies by continuing the struggle against the common enemy. . . .
>
> Thanks to General de Gaulle's decision to fight on, a decision which deprived the Bordeaux capitulation of all moral value, France has never been absent from the battlefield. The French troops who fought so gallantly against overwhelming odds in the Battle of France have found worthy successors in the heroes of Bir Hakeim.
>
> No less heroic has been the conduct of those Frenchmen who have continued the struggle inside France. . . .
>
> For us the full restoration of France as a Great Power is not only a declared war aim and the fulfilment of a pledge made to a sister nation, but also a practical necessity, if post-war reconstruction is to be undertaken within the framework of that traditional civilization which is our common heritage. . . .

Meanwhile, though the landings had met with little resistance at Algiers, the Americans were opposed more strongly than they had expected at Oran and Casablanca, despite the many warnings we had given them. The next day General Clark and General Giraud saw Admiral Darlan. Although demanding the supreme command for himself, Giraud had, it seemed, not ruled out the possibility that Darlan would come over to the Allies, and his last words on leaving Gibraltar for Algiers had been: "I have taken my decision. I am going to look for Darlan."

* *Mémoires de Guerre;* Vol. II.

Soon after the landing, Giraud had to accept that he himself could effect nothing. Whereupon Clark decided that it would save time and lives if an agreement were made with the Admiral.

November 10th: Winston asked me to go through telegrams with him after party [for all Ministers]. It seems that Laval, Ribbentrop and Ciano are to meet at Munich. I am worried for the French fleet.

I had good reason for this fear, which would have been stronger had I known that Hitler was also at the meeting. The next day he occupied all France, as predetermined. Gestures of respect were made towards the fleet at Toulon, but on November 26th, when no doubt could linger that the Germans meant to take the ships into their power, their Admiral scuttled them, a melancholy conclusion to an armada about which there had been so many hopes, fears and premonitions.

★   ★   ★   ★   ★

November 11th: Talk with Winston on telephone. His speech [in the House of Commons on the Western Desert victories and the North African landings] has gone very well. Main discussion about progress of fighting and unsatisfactory character of almost all Frenchmen!

For these two days I was laid up and hoarse with a cold and sore throat:

November 12th: Several talks with Winston on telephone. He begged me not to go to House today, but wants me available at Chequers on Saturday night for staff talks with himself, Smuts and Chiefs of Staff. Meanwhile he sent over to me Chiefs of Staff paper written before success of "Torch." It is certainly thin gruel so far as next year's operations are concerned.

The fragmentary reports from North Africa about relations with the French were disturbing, and on November 11th the Prime Minister had to send a telegram to remind the President that we were under quite definite obligations to General de Gaulle and his movement. I learnt on November 13th of an agreement between Giraud and Darlan by which the former would be the military and the latter the political head of the French organization in North Africa. Although I had instructed Mr. Mack, our representative with Eisenhower, to speak of our concern at this development, I thought it was time that Lord Halifax should be asked to warn the United States Government directly. Winant agreed with me and I telegraphed:

> I think you should make it plain to the President or Mr. Hull that the inclusion of Darlan in French administration in North Africa would be most unpopular here, unless he had delivered the goods in the shape of the French navy. Nor would de Gaulle or any of the French Movement be willing to collaborate with Darlan, and all hopes of unifying the French Empire in the war against the Axis would be frustrated.

When Halifax saw Mr. Hull in the President's absence, on November 14th, the Secretary of State's feeling appeared to be much the same as ours, nor did Admiral Leahy, now the President's Chief of Staff, dissent when Halifax spoke to him. The touchstone for him was whether Darlan could produce the French fleet. Halifax emphasized to Leahy the need for the United States to avoid political commitments to Darlan at this stage, or until we could judge more safely what, if anything, was his value.

The same day I motored to Chequers for luncheon alone with Mr. Churchill.

> [Afterwards] he began to talk of [Cabinet] reconstruction. Paper and pens were produced and we sat until 4 p.m. W. anxious to put the changes through next week. In particular he doesn't want to go on in uncertainty as to Cripps' attitude.
>
> *November 15th, Chequers:* Just before conference at 11 a.m. telegram came through from Eisenhower announcing an agreement with Darlan. Didn't like it a bit, and said so. Conference next discussed future strategy and Italy in particular.

The telegram told us that Darlan, together with Giraud, General August Noguès, Resident-General in Morocco, and other French notables, were to form a provisional government and co-operate with the Allied forces. The danger of acute divisions between the French was so evident to me that I spoke to the Prime Minister about it later that evening.

As a result, we saw General de Gaulle together the following morning. De Gaulle was firm that he could not be a party to any arrangement, however temporary, which gave authority to Darlan. Not even the immediate military advantage, he said, could justify having dealings with a traitor. The General added that he must make public his own position and dissociate himself from the negotiations in North Africa. The Prime Minister asked that he should delay doing so for a day or two, but de Gaulle, who had already postponed his *communiqué,* replied he must put it out that day. The General was unemotional and did not blame us, but he was decided and we did not feel that we could insist further.

Worse was to follow. Gaullist sympathizers and other friends of ours in the French zone of Morocco were ill-treated by the local French authorities. I asked Lord Halifax on November 17th to let Mr. Hull know how strongly we felt about this. It would be difficult enough to make French opinion, and British opinion too, accept the necessity for collaboration with Darlan even as a temporary measure. We could not justify such a policy if it became known that the Allies were either unwilling or unable to prevent the continued victimization of those who had remained faithful to the Allied cause in the dark days. I asked Halifax to press for instructions to the United States authorities in Morocco to secure the immediate release of all British and Allied internees. Even this modest request was slow to be realized.

On November 17th, President Roosevelt announced at a press conference in Washington:

I have accepted General Eisenhower's political arrangements for the time being in Northern and Western Africa. . . . The present temporary arrangement in North and West Africa is only a temporary expedient, justified solely by the stress of battle.

In an off-the-record comment he stigmatized Darlan as "a devil and no good." Supping with him was still to give us much trouble. Another gloss was given to the policy of the White House when Roosevelt told M. André Philip and M. Adrien Tixier, two honourable and representative Frenchmen: "Certainly I'll treat with Darlan since Darlan gives me Algiers, and tomorrow I'll deal with Laval, if Laval gives me Paris." *

★   ★   ★   ★   ★

Field-Marshal Smuts called on me to say good-bye on his return to South Africa.

November 19th: He said that my position was very difficult because W.'s mind had a stop in it at the end of the war and he, Smuts, quite understood that I must have a foreign policy on which to work with Allies here, with Americans and Russians. I begged him to take the chance of his journey with Winston [who went to see Smuts off] to do this. He promised.

We then spoke of Cripps and impending [Cabinet] changes. Smuts approved these. I said that I didn't want to lead the House. He said that he feared I must. W. had spoken to him of his utter confidence in me and it was necessary to spare W. every possible burden. No one else could take this on.

Late this evening when I was in bed W. rang up, I suppose from Portsmouth or Bristol, and said that Smuts wanted to say good-bye. The grand old man told me he had done his best and had helped, he thought. I thanked him and we said good-bye, on my side with real emotion.

The friendship of Churchill and Smuts always fascinated me. They were such contrasting personalities; the one with his neat philosophic mind, the other a man "so rammed with life." I remember one evening, in particular, alone with them at Chequers. The horizon was beginning to clear and the talk was of future military plans. Mr. Churchill paced up and down the room, cigar in hand, his thoughts ranging widely. Smuts sat quietly in his chair,

* De Gaulle: op. cit.

commenting occasionally and, almost literally, pouring water into the Churchillian wine. Yet the partnership was incomparable.

★　　★　　★　　★　　★

November 20th: Winston very active on telephone after tea. I don't like the text of Darlan–Eisenhower agreement and I tried to explain that though Eisenhower might argue that Part I was only a preamble and bound no one, he was unhappily wrong in such a conclusion. We wrangled away at intervals throughout the evening. He wanted to telegraph to Roosevelt to agree to Protocol. I wouldn't agree and wanted to send considered reply and criticism. He wouldn't agree to this, so eventually we decided to send nought and wait for the Americans. One of our telephone talks lasted over half an hour. I cannot get W. to see the damage Darlan may do to the Allied cause if we don't watch it. He can make rings, diplomatically, round Eisenhower. At a moment of the shouting match W. said: "Well, D. is not as bad as de Gaulle, anyway."

On the morning of November 21st the Prime Minister and I continued the discussion. I still wished for some amendments and told Mr. Churchill that they might have been a help to Roosevelt, who was clearly trying to avoid an agreement with Darlan which conflicted too sharply with his own published declaration of four days earlier.

November 21st: W. became impatient: "Do you agree or don't you?" "I should like a chance to read R's reply and consider it." "Then you don't agree. Very well, Cabinet at 12." An hour later he rang up to ask me to luncheon and to ask after my cough. Cabinet was an argument between us. Bobbety helped me, but nobody else took much part. I am certain that Darlan has outwitted our people and that process will continue.

Lunched with Winston at Buck's. W. in splendid form, certainly seemed to bear no malice for our set-to. Much talk of Smuts. W. said he was as he imagined Socrates might have been. When we got back to No. 10 Winston made me come in to con-

sider the [Cabinet] moves afresh. He sent for the Prof [Lord
Cherwell, personal assistant to the Prime Minister] to cross-
examine him about [Colonel J.] Jay Llewellin's [Minister of Aircraft Production until November 22nd, then Minister Resident
for Supply in Washington] performance. He had told me before
that he suspected Prof didn't want Cripps in that job [Aircraft
Production]. Then he showed me his letter to Jay. I urged him
to see him, as fairer to Jay. He said that he preferred to write
and to see people afterwards. He had done so with the Auk
[Auchinleck] even. I said I preferred to see people. A letter
seemed somehow to shirk an unpleasant duty. Much discussion
on this. Eventually it was found that it was already so late that
he would have to see Jay anyway!

The Government changes were announced the next day. I took
over the Leadership of the House of Commons from Sir Stafford
Cripps, who became Minister of Aircraft Production, giving up his
membership of the War Cabinet. Some such solution was the only
outcome possible after Cripps' express criticism of the Prime Minister's conduct of the war. There was also another side to the decision. Cripps had been a little too ascetic and inhuman to be an
entirely happy choice as Leader of the House. He was inclined to
treat his fellow Members as a pedagogue and to reprove them if
they did not match up to his standards, which they seldom did.

I remember that one day arrangements had been made for a
debate on the progress of the war and, as often happened, the Prime
Minister was to open this with one of his splendid statements and
I was to wind up. The House of Commons was then meeting in the
morning but, as I had much work to do in the Foreign Office, I
only went across about luncheon time. As I came in Cripps was
talking to one or two Members in the lobby and I asked him how
the debate was going. He told me with a frown that the House
was already up. He was not influenced by my expression of delight,
adding sternly that Members should take their duties more seriously and that rising so soon would produce a bad effect on spectators: "Walter Lippmann was in the Gallery." My sense of relief
was not modified by Cripps' woebegone tale.

If I had had time, I should have enjoyed my new job, but meetings of the Defence Committee, the War Cabinet and the work of the Foreign Office were sufficiently onerous. I had to be almost continuously at hand in the House of Commons during the day, while the Defence Committee often sat late into the night. This meant a ruthless burning of the candle at both ends for the best part of three years, for which excess there is always a price to be paid.

Leading the House of Commons is not something which can be rushed, even in wartime. Most Members of Parliament are prima donnas. They like attention, which is a time-consuming form of flattery. Make them feel that they are all that matters and they will purr. Let them suspect that they are not the centre of events, but only a short and unwelcome interlude in an overcrowded day, and they will exact a merciless tribute from your time. War conditions also obtruded another paradox. Though the Government was a coalition of all the parties and had therefore the support of virtually the whole House, where responsibility was spread so wide many felt that they could leave its actual discharge to others. There was always the danger that what all were supposed to do, too few could be found to do.

6

DARLAN AND DE GAULLE
November 1942–January 1943

I have misgivings about the Franco–American Agreement — The Vichy French in North Africa — The House of Commons and my Jewish declaration — Admiral Darlan assassinated — Coldness between General de Gaulle and General Giraud — The United States and the future of France — The Casablanca Conference — The French Generals meet at last

ON NOVEMBER 22ND the Agreement was signed by General Clark and Admiral Darlan. Four days later, I wrote to the Prime Minister:

> In his statement of the 17th November, with which we have publicly said that we are in the fullest agreement, President Roosevelt stated emphatically, first that General Eisenhower's political arrangement was temporary and that no permanent arrangement would be made with Admiral Darlan; and secondly, that public opinion in the United Nations would never understand the recognition of, and reconstitution of, the Vichy Government in any French territory.
>
> On both these points the situation seems to be deteriorating and the tone of the French authorities in North Africa to be hardening.
>
> Admiral Darlan makes it clear that he interprets the word "temporary" to mean "until the liberation of France is complete" and we can be sure that he will use all his skill and resource and power of decision to fortify himself in his present position.
>
> Darlan has also made it clear that he regards himself as holding his authority from the Marshal [Pétain].
>
> All this seems to me to run counter to the President's statement, and I do not think we can safely allow this state of

affairs to continue, once the military situation allows us to take steps to change it.

I am as conscious as anyone of the operational advantages of the present arrangement during the present critical period; and I realize the potential value to us of agreement between Darlan and [M. Pierre] Boisson [Governor-General of French West Africa]. But Boisson's own statements have been equivocal, and it is not yet clear whether he means actively to come into the war and to give us the facilities we may require in his territory.

From the purely military point of view we should run grave risks if we continued to deal with these men. Already the United States military authorities have grave doubts about Noguès and are unhappy about the situation in Morocco. My strong opinion is that no one who maintains his allegiance to the Marshal can be trusted wholeheartedly on the side of the United Nations. We are dealing with turncoats and black-mailers and until the French administration and armed forces are in better hands, it would not be safe to arm them with modern weapons.

But there is above all the moral aspect. Our appeal to the French people, whose resistance has been steadily stiffening, is now stultified. In Europe as a whole the "filthy race of quis-lings," as you once so aptly called them, will take heart since they now have reason to think that if only they happen to be in authority when the forces of the United Nations arrive, they will be treated as being the government of the country.

I think the time has come for us to exchange views with the United States Government on the ways and means of giving effect to the President's statement.

The Prime Minister decided that he would prefer to wait for the time being. His inclination was to let the Americans sort out the situation themselves, but the form of government which we had helped to set up was well illustrated by a decree from Darlan. Dated November 30th, this opened:

We, Admiral of the Fleet, High Commissioner of French Africa acting in virtue of powers conferred upon us by the Marshal of France, head of state, order. . . .

and was "made in the name of the Marshal of France." I asked Mr. Mack to come back on December 3rd from General Eisenhower's headquarters for consultation, when we briefed him with our opinions.

December 5th: I am much troubled by Darlan developments. Americans seem completely to ignore political issue at stake, and we risk running into grave trouble.

Sent Winston yesterday strong draft telegram to the United States. . . .

In the minute to the Prime Minister which accompanied the draft I said that if General Eisenhower

is going to make political statements it is surely necessary that he should have some guidance. At present he has none.

I had a talk to Winant about this this morning. He tells me that the difficulty is to find an American who can do the job. No doubt this is true, but all the same I think that we should press for responsible political guidance for the Commander-in-Chief, whose thoughts are rightly concentrated on the immediate battle.

The draft telegram to our Ambassador in Washington went off with the Prime Minister's approval:

In spite of President's statement that political arrangement with Darlan was temporary, Darlan appears to be digging himself in more and more firmly. His administration is in effect a Vichy regime, and it appears that some of our best friends, like Generals Béthouard and Mast, are still without active employment.

It therefore seems to us now a matter of urgency that the United States Government and His Majesty's Government should send political representatives of high authority to Algiers. Political developments in North Africa cannot fail to have far-reaching effects in Europe and in the world at large, of which General Eisenhower can hardly be expected to be conscious.

It would also be the function of these representatives [of the two Governments] to try to secure such changes in the regime in North Africa as would facilitate an agreement between the North African administration and de Gaulle and thus unite the French Empire once again.

★ ★ ★ ★ ★

Soon after the Anglo–American landings, negotiations between General Eisenhower and M. Boisson had been opened. On December 3rd a deadlock was reached. Boisson would not consent to release Allied or Free French prisoners unless de Gaulle released Vichy prisoners. The President appealed to the Prime Minister, who told me on December 4th that General de Gaulle should be requested to agree.

I replied the same day that I saw small prospect of this. Half an hour after midnight the Prime Minister wrote that it was absolutely necessary for him to know whether de Gaulle refused to release the internees or not. He hoped that the utmost pressure would be put upon him. This message was telephoned to me on Saturday morning, December 5th.

December 5th: Today, on my instructions, Strang produced a firm draft about Dakar, refusing to be squeezed by Boisson or to undertake to squeeze de Gaulle. Had expected vehement reaction from Winston, but to my surprise after a first outburst that I had not tackled de Gaulle and insisted, he rang up a second time to say that he had read the draft and that it was "a very good piece of work." He is incalculable.

The telegram said that we could see no possibility of obtaining de Gaulle's agreement, because Boisson had handed over his Gaullist prisoners to Vichy and the Germans. There was, therefore, no advantage to de Gaulle in the exchange. On the strength of this the

President rejected Boisson's conditions and secured a satisfactory agreement.

★   ★   ★   ★   ★

December 7th: A troublesome day, even for Monday. Oliver [Lyttelton] lunched with me. Maisky turned up at No. 10 with message from Joe [Stalin, saying that he could not leave the front]. This was disappointing as to meeting [of Churchill, Roosevelt and Stalin]. Winston asked me to stay when he had gone and began to argue that Thursday's [December 10th, secret session] debate [on the developments in North Africa] must be postponed. I contested this, and argument got us nowhere. I told him House would resent postponement and country's suspicions of Darlan business be increased. He said that my leadership of the House was "febrile," and that not one person in a hundred was worried about Darlan anyway. I urged Cabinet should be asked. He wouldn't have that. Meanwhile my appointments waited.

Eventually agreed that Attlee and I and James [Stuart, Chief Whip] should wait after Cabinet. Great wrangle, but we stood firm and Winston gave in. James said that there was a silence after I had gone while W. sat looking in front of him and James felt he should offer a bar of chocolate.

On December 8th Lord Halifax lunched with the President and spoke to him in the sense of my telegram of three days before about the danger of Darlan digging himself in. Roosevelt evidently did not contemplate any early action to dispense with the Admiral's services and mentioned some kind of commission for French North Africa. Anti-Darlan feeling might be placated by the reduction of Darlan's status to that of membership of such a body, he thought.

Lord Halifax said that public opinion in the United States and Great Britain, in France and in the occupied countries would not be greatly soothed by the arrangement the President had sketched. Roosevelt's reply was that no doubt the Czechs would come and ask him whether it was our intention, as we liberated their country, to make terms and work with a quisling Czech. He would answer:

"Not necessarily. Everything will depend on circumstances, and whatever we have to do for military reasons during the war will not prejudice your freedom of choice later."

On December 8th General de Gaulle and General Catroux dined with me. I asked de Gaulle whether, if Darlan were to disappear from the scene, it would be possible for him to reach an agreement with the French authorities there. The General said that Darlan was the one obstacle, no one else mattered. His regime would fade away as soon as he himself had disappeared and sounder elements would be left. The solution would be to establish an enlarged National Committee at Algiers, with General Catroux as High Commissioner or Delegate-General and with General Giraud in charge of military affairs, which were, in fact, his only interest. I said that one of the troubles was that the Lafayette tradition was standing in our way. The Americans were convinced that they knew better how to handle French affairs than we did.

The same day, December 8th, a message from Mr. Alvary Gascoigne, Consul-General in Tangier, added evidence to my argument. This the Prime Minister asked me to condense into a telegram for him to send to the President, and as such it was despatched on December 9th. Our reports, Mr. Churchill declared, showed that Fascist organizations continued their activities and victimized our former French sympathizers, some of whom had not yet been released from prison. Well-known German sympathizers, on the other hand, who had been ousted at the Allied landing, had now been reinstated. There had been cases of French soldiers being punished for desertion because they tried to support the Allied forces during the landings. There was an almost complete absence of control on the frontier of the French and Spanish zones in Morocco. Axis agents were crossing in both directions. Military operations would be endangered. There was no Allied control of postal and telegraph censorship.

This telegram was repeated by the United States Chiefs of Staff to General Eisenhower on December 11th. Eisenhower replied two days later by denying that any of the unsatisfactory conditions we mentioned existed, except for defective frontier control. Eventually, out of this and later complaints, arose the arrangement by which Mr. Robert Murphy was appointed the President's Personal Representative at General Eisenhower's headquarters, while Mr. Harold Macmillan became Minister of State at Algiers. In this way Mr. Macmillan, who had been Under-Secretary for the Colonies, retained his position as a member of His Majesty's Government, which helped his authority, with good results for us all.

★   ★   ★   ★   ★

December 17th: The last day of the House for a few weeks. Read my Jewish statement at end of Questions.

I reported that, after receiving reliable information of the barbarous and inhuman treatment to which Jews were being subjected in German-occupied Europe, His Majesty's Government had been in consultation with the United States, the Soviet and other Allied Governments. As a consequence, a declaration was being made public in London, Moscow and Washington, at the same day and hour as I spoke, condemning

> in the strongest possible terms this bestial policy of cold-blooded extermination. The Governments declare that such events can only strengthen the resolve of all freedom-loving peoples to overthrow the barbarous Hitlerite tyranny. They reaffirm their solemn resolution to ensure that those responsible for these crimes shall not escape retribution. . . .

December 17th: It had a far greater dramatic effect than I had expected. After Jimmy de Rothschild had made a feeling little speech the whole House rose [and stood to mark in silence its support of the declaration] on the motion of a Labour Member [Mr. W. S. Cluse]. Lloyd George said to me later: "I cannot recall a scene like that in all my years in Parliament."

★   ★   ★   ★   ★

The arrangements for the conference between the Prime Minister and President were now under way. Its value was reduced by Stalin's refusal to attend, but so were the difficulties of choosing the meeting place.

December 19th: Winston rang up once or twice to conjecture the contents of the note this weather-bound courier is to bring [from Roosevelt]. He expects a rendezvous, since only the answer "yes" or "no" is required, according to Hopkins. The delay is maddening for no plans for the future can be made meanwhile. "I don't know whether I should stand on my head or sit on my tail," Winston complained this morning.

In the evening he rang up to give me good news of German difficulties on Tripoli front.

A few days later the decision was taken in favour of a conference at Casablanca during the middle of January.

The assassination of Admiral Darlan on Christmas Eve dramatically transformed the position in French North Africa. Only six days previously General de Gaulle had spoken to Mr. Charles Peake, our representative with the French National Committee, of disbanding his organization. From the opening of the North African operations, Darlan had appeared to be the only stumbling block to French unity. But things had turned out differently, de Gaulle continued wryly, and it seemed that it was not Darlan and the things for which he stood, but de Gaulle and the things for which he stood, which were in danger of impeding the unity of the Allies.

On the day of the assassination itself, General de Gaulle told Mr. Peake that it was a detestable crime. His view of the situation was the same as he had expressed when he had dined with me and General Catroux on December 8th. Now that Darlan had disappeared, he saw no obstacle to co-operation between himself and Giraud, provided they were left to do the job.

The next day, December 25th, General de Gaulle sent to the United States Embassy a message for transmission to General Giraud, which suggested a meeting between them as soon as possible on French territory. The staff at Grosvenor Square apparently did not regard the message as urgent and it was not sent off until late in the afternoon of the next day. I considered that the telegram ought to be repeated to the President and this was then done.

December 26th: Tired. There is always a reaction after these long periods of work and strain, and the spring seems to uncoil more and more. A cold day. Some walking and work at the timber, and too much activity on the telephone.

I was not alone in feeling the physical and mental burden. As the months passed we were all to show it, even the Prime Minister, and sometimes we would express it in impatience or intolerance of each other.

December 27th: Some talk with Jim [Thomas] on telephone in evening. He is worried as to whether I can carry on two jobs for long. He is probably right, but he and Dick [Law] appear to contemplate my becoming a King Lear at the Foreign Office.

This was a further reference to the plan to appoint a Minister of External Affairs, who would supervise the three Ministers in charge of the Foreign, Dominions and Colonial Offices and represent them in the War Cabinet. I did not favour it.

On December 29th General Giraud replied without enthusiasm to General de Gaulle's offer, pretexting an unfavourable atmosphere for the meeting following Darlan's assassination and suggesting an emissary from de Gaulle in his place. De Gaulle replied with an impassioned appeal for a meeting between himself and Giraud. This, like other messages in this exchange, was delayed, sharpening de Gaulle's suspicions that the Americans feared his influence. He also began to suspect that the British and United States Governments were going to make an agreement with Giraud over his head, which led him to publish a blunt statement that internal confusion was steadily growing in French North and West Africa.

I watched these unhappy exchanges and minuted for the Foreign Office that it was a pity every phase of them was discussed in the press. No doubt it was the fault of the Free French, but it was an unwise method of negotiating.

★   ★   ★   ★   ★

Early in the New Year I telegraphed to Washington that our two Governments ought now to consider their future relations with the French Empire. The solution I advocated still seems to me sensible, but it took months to realize. It was to establish in Algeria, on the soil of a department of France, a single authority, in place of the French National Committee and Giraud's administration in Algiers. Our two Governments, and no doubt others, should recognize this authority as a *de facto* administration, provisionally exercising sovereignty over certain departments of France and over the whole French Empire, pending the establishment of a government chosen by the French people themselves. It should not be recognized as even a provisional government, but would maintain informal relations with other foreign governments and be admitted to the United Nations.

The same day as I telegraphed, Mr. Harry Hopkins lunched with Lord Halifax who asked him what was at the back of the American mind about North Africa. Hopkins said that some people, including the State Department, felt that we wanted to set up something like a provisional government. Whatever we might say, this would have the effect of hampering the future liberty of the French people. On this telegram I minuted on January 5th:

Prime Minister to see.
    I am not much impressed by Harry's argument. The Frenchman is a politically-minded animal and we shall have no peace until one authority speaks for all, and not much then.

The Prime Minister replied the same day:

    The French cannot be wholly denied some form of national expression in their present phase.

I telegraphed to Sir Ronald Campbell in this sense, but when he spoke to Mr. Cordell Hull, the Secretary of State answered that to suggest as our first aim some form of union between the Fighting French and the French in North Africa would be a new departure on our part. He thought that we were backing de Gaulle's idea that he alone should have civil authority while Giraud should have military command. I replied to our Ambassador on January 15th:

> [The British Government] are not backing de Gaulle for first place in North Africa. It is for him and Giraud to come to terms if they can. . . .
>
> De Gaulle may well have political ambitions in North Africa. Whether or not he achieves them will be for Frenchmen to settle. It is certainly not our policy to seek to impose him. We had indeed been inclined to think that after "Torch" his role might decline in the face of new rivals in North Africa. But things have turned out otherwise and the Darlan episode has increased his prestige. He can in any event bring a valuable contribution to the common fund, namely a substantial part of the French Empire and a great and resounding name in France. I should hope that the United States Government will come to look upon him with a more sympathetic eye.

★ ★ ★ ★ ★

On January 13th, Mr. Churchill and, on January 14th, Mr. Roosevelt, arrived at Anfa, near Casablanca, for their conference. General Giraud joined them the next day, when the Prime Minister telegraphed to me asking me to invite General de Gaulle to Casablanca. I asked de Gaulle to come to the Foreign Office on the morning of January 17th.

The General expressed no pleasure at the message from Mr. Churchill. He said that he had wished to meet General Giraud immediately after the assassination of Admiral Darlan, but General Giraud had not been willing. The time was not now so opportune. Nor did he feel happy at the idea of meeting General Giraud under the auspices of the other two great Allies. He would be too much in the position of a man under pressure to compromise, when he knew that he should not compromise.

I asked General de Gaulle whether he now wished to come to terms with General Giraud. He replied that he was prepared to meet him, alone, at Fort Lamy, in the Chad territory. The right course now was for General Giraud to rally to the Fighting French.

He would become a member of the National Committee and would be appointed to command the forces in North Africa.

I told de Gaulle that I thought it inconceivable that, after the Prime Minister and the President of the United States had agreed to promote this meeting, he should be unwilling to play his part. I had no doubt myself that the Prime Minister had explained to the President the position of General de Gaulle, and here was an opportunity for him to do so in person, which was precisely what he had been intending to do by a visit to the United States.

The General said that that was a different proposition. If the President wished to see him, he, de Gaulle, could always call upon him in America; but no one could invite de Gaulle to meet anybody on French soil.

I replied that I should deplore a refusal by him to meet allies and to co-operate with them to try to bring the war to a victorious end. Finally General de Gaulle agreed to think the matter over and either to come to see me or to send me a written reply.

At five o'clock the General came back, handing me his refusal of the invitation. His note said that he did not consider that an exalted Allied forum, *un très haut aréopage allié,* around the Giraud–de Gaulle conversations, together with the suddenness of the proposal, created an atmosphere designed to bring about a really useful arrangement. He was telegraphing again to General Giraud to repeat his proposal for an immediate meeting.

I once more pointed out that the Prime Minister's proposal provided for just such a meeting. The General reverted to his fear of "pressure." He still hankered after an independent encounter with Giraud, but I held out no hope of this. I told him that he was throwing away an opportunity for an arrangement with Giraud, supported by the two principal Allied leaders. This would have greatly helped the war effort. Nothing I said, however, could influence the perspective in which he saw events.

These exchanges I reported to the Prime Minister by telegram, and to the War Cabinet the next morning, January 18th. As we now know, at least part of the cause for General de Gaulle's refusal had been that he had been invited by the Prime Minister alone.* During these difficult days I enlisted the help of General Catroux,

* Charles de Gaulle: *Mémoires de Guerre;* Vol. II.

who had always shown himself a patient and tactful counsellor to
de Gaulle. Probably his arguments had more effect than mine, for
when a sterner reply came back from the Prime Minister, though a
little modified by the War Cabinet, the General accepted, admittedly without enthusiasm.

While the discussions with de Gaulle were still at their peak, I
received a message from Roosevelt: "I have got the bridegroom,
where is the bride?" In Casablanca the marriage between de Gaulle
and Giraud eventually took place, with as good a result as could
be expected from a shotgun wedding.

★   ★   ★   ★   ★

On January 20th Mr. Attlee and I received a telegram from the
Prime Minister announcing that, when the President returned to
the United States, he proposed to visit Marrakesh and Cairo and
fly on to Turkey or at least to Cyprus. He wished to meet the
Turkish authorities, in complete secrecy, and to discuss the whole
future with them. I did not much care for this plan, nor did Attlee
and the War Cabinet, whom we felt that we had to consult. Parliament and the nation would, my colleagues considered, want to hear
the Prime Minister's account of the meeting as soon as they could
and not be dependent upon the President, but it was the Turkish
part of the business which troubled me. I did not think that we
should get any results in that stubborn quarter. So Attlee and I
telegraphed to the Prime Minister:

> Our experience in 1941 was that a promise extracted from
> them in Cyprus was promptly gone back on in Ankara. We
> do not want you to court either a rebuff or a failure.

However, the Prime Minister was not to be stayed and we yielded
with, as I wrote, "the poor comfort that we have had the best of
the argument and shall suffer the worst of the consequences."

The Prime Minister returned to England on February 7th. He
immediately set to and said that he had been angry with me for my
obstruction of his Turkish plans and had resented my enlisting the
War Cabinet against what he wanted to do. He had drafted and

cyphered, but not sent, a violent personal telegram. The President, he said, had been much surprised at the difficulty he had had with the Cabinet.

I replied that his position was not the same as Roosevelt's. He had referred to me and it was my duty to express a view. Mr. Churchill went on that he must be allowed to go where he liked when he was abroad and that he had studied Europe for forty years. The Foreign Office were always on small points like chrome and ships in Sweden. Anyway, if he had been killed, Mr. Churchill told me, it would have been a good way to die and I should only have come into my inheritance sooner. "There is old Anthony thinking all I want is a joy ride. He has got it all wrong," he had said to himself at the time, and the Prime Minister paused and regarded me, but, "I bear no rancour."

7

ENTER ROOSEVELT
January–March 1943

My idea of the United Nations Organization — The Prime Minister and M. Flandin — We suspend convoys to Russia — The death of the Speaker — My paper on the future of Germany — I visit President Roosevelt — The United States comes to the forefront — Divergence of views on France — "Wallonia" — The President conjures with Europe — General Marshall and I visit the forces — My ancestors in America — A speech in Annapolis — President Roosevelt and the Far East — Mr. Welles versus Mr. Hull — An off-the-record dinner with Mr. Hopkins

By the last weeks of 1942, the time had come to examine with the United States and Soviet Governments some of the problems we would have to face after the war. The Allies had the strategic initiative, victory could be foreseen and I considered we now had to prepare for it politically.

On December 2nd, speaking in the House of Commons, I laid down two conditions for any international organization, if it were to have a chance to achieve its purpose. First, it should represent the powers which meant to keep the peace and which must have the unity and will to agree upon positive decisions. Secondly, the organization must have the force behind it to give effect to them. I accepted that success would depend, in the first instance, on understanding between ourselves, the United States and Russia, and reasoned that this opportunity was open to us. It was symptomatic of the hopeful temper of the times that two Members of Parliament, Major Maurice Petherick from the right, and Mr. William Gallacher, our sole communist Member, should have joined in expressing their approval to me afterwards. This was the policy which the nation wanted, but which the Soviets were to destroy.

A few weeks later I sent to the Cabinet my first paper about a United Nations organization. It was a plan for political and economic world councils, which depended on the victorious great powers agreeing on a common world policy and being prepared to act together to enforce it.

> Failing this, we shall be confronted by the prospect of a world in precarious balance, with the great powers, each with its circle of client States, facing each other in a rivalry which will merge imperceptibly into hostility.

Unhappily, this proved only too accurate a forecast.

While regional groupings should be encouraged, my paper continued, there must not be a kind of "limited liability" system, whereby one power was solely responsible for keeping the peace in a given area. On the contrary, it was essential to assume that the great powers were in principle equally interested in maintaining the peace everywhere in the world, and that they would act together whenever and wherever it might be threatened.

I thought it likely that the United States would insist on China being regarded as a great power, but there was not much that I could do about relations with that country. A formal step was the signature of a treaty renouncing our extra-territorial rights. The ceremony took place in Chungking on January 11th. While it could have no immediate effect, the Chinese Government attached importance to this token that the epoch of inferiority to the western world was at an end.

But the key lay in Moscow and I was determined to try to do business with the Kremlin despite its communist carapace. Our Ambassador had been home for consultations and his return to his post could be just the opportunity I wanted. On February 4th I instructed Sir Archibald Clark Kerr to tell Molotov of the progress we were making in shaping our policy and to ask the Soviet Government for any ideas they had. In particular I proposed that three-power consultations should now be held on post-war arrangements for Western, Central and Eastern Europe. These were essential if we were to avoid chaos when Germany collapsed. It must be excluded, I said, that any one of the great powers should run a policy of its own behind the backs of the others. The problems of Eastern Europe would be particularly important and I thought it desirable to begin to concert the necessary plans in good time.

I also asked the Ambassador to make further inquiries from Molotov about the Soviet attitude to confederations in Eastern Europe. The Russians had more than once told us that they would have no objection to this in principle, but we had recently learned that they were pouring cold water on the Polish–Czech negotiations.

January 29th: Lunched with Beneš and after it we surveyed the complicated Polish–Russian–Czech triangle. Not much that is good to discuss and Russian policies all dark and uncertain.

It already seemed likely that the Soviets intended to divide and rule their western neighbours, so that the sooner these matters were aired, the better.

★   ★   ★   ★   ★

President Roosevelt had sent me a message by Mr. Mack on January 4th saying he looked forward to seeing me again soon, but mentioning no place. I had not met Roosevelt since 1938 and spoke of this message to the Prime Minister, who telegraphed to the President suggesting an early visit. Mr. Roosevelt responded: "the sooner the better."

I originally intended to leave for the United States on February 22nd, but the Prime Minister fell ill and could not take charge of the Foreign Office in my absence. My journey was therefore postponed until March. On the evening of February 24th the Prime Minister's chief private secretary, Mr. John Martin, rang me up to say that he thought I ought to see a telegram which Mr. Churchill was despatching to our Minister Resident in Algiers. I sent for the telegram and saw that the Prime Minister was urging that every opportunity should be taken to press for the admission of M. Pierre-Etienne Flandin into the French North African administration.

I did not think this a wise move or likely to be welcome to the French, but I did not attach much importance to it. I told the

Foreign Office that I would talk to the Prime Minister about the telegram in the morning and to hold it up meanwhile.

On my way to the House of Commons I called on Mr. Churchill. He looked flushed and clearly had a fever. After referring to one or two matters of business I then added, expecting no trouble: "By the way, about that telegram you thought of sending last night to Algiers. . . ." "Thought of sending? What do you mean? I sent it." I replied: "No, it hasn't gone yet. I wanted to talk to you about it first." Churchill gripped the counterpane with both hands and growled: "By what right do you interfere with my private correspondence?" I said that the message I had been shown was not private correspondence. "How did you know about it?" "You know," I answered, "that the Foreign Secretary sees all important messages." He retorted that he was not dead yet and would send any telegrams he chose.

As his temperature was clearly mounting by leaps and bounds I said, "All right, we'll talk about it later," and left, adjuring the private secretary on my way to send for his doctor, Sir Charles Wilson, and Mr. Brendan Bracken and to ask them to persuade the Prime Minister not to send any more telegrams until his temperature was normal again.

I had no sooner reached the House of Commons than I was told that the Prime Minister wanted to speak to me on the telephone. I said I could not do so as I had to be in the Chamber and persisted in this refusal all day. At length, after the House rose I called in to see Mr. Churchill, who was reclining benignly in bed with the telegram on the counterpane.

He asked after my day in the House and my son's progress in the Royal Air Force and other casual topics before at last he glanced at the telegram and added: "Oh, by the way, you remember that message I intended to send? Perhaps we had better not send it." He took it up and tore it through. We then agreed a variant that if any suggestions were made about appointing Flandin to some modest post, all the circumstances should be reported to the Prime Minister before any opinion adverse or otherwise was expressed.

This was characteristic of Mr. Churchill and of something very lovable in him. First the indignation sparked by fever, then reflection and a generous acceptance expressed without half-tones or hesitation; these were the successive stages which endeared him to those whom he berated. There was nothing I could say that evening, but he knew how I felt and the deep affection that was unspoken.

Meanwhile our Ambassador's approach to Molotov did not gain us much information, though the Russians seemed pleased, even surprised, that we had consulted them about Eastern Europe before the Americans. Molotov was also receptive about tripartite talks, if vague about dates.

On an immediate problem the Russians were obstructive. Our Arctic convoys had to have air cover, and, to provide it, the Air Ministry wished to send squadrons of Royal Air Force Hampdens to operate in north Russia. The Russians at first agreed to provide accommodation for the air crews and ground staff, but they made difficulties when they learned that they numbered seven hundred all ranks. On February 24th Maisky wrote to tell me that the Russian authorities could not accommodate even the five hundred originally proposed by the Air Ministry. They suggested that, instead, we should hand over the aircraft to be flown by Soviet pilots. This proposal ignored the technical difficulties of co-operation between aircraft and naval escorts, and had to be rejected.

February 26th: Difficult Allied Supplies Executive meeting. The Turkish position is particularly troublesome. Winston's visit has let us in for shipping commitments we simply cannot hope to meet, as we feared. Interview with Maisky in afternoon which was grim.

I gave Maisky a memorandum explaining that additional air protection was indispensable for the safety of the convoys and that it must be provided by British squadrons under British control, if it was to be of any use. We could not allow the safety of the convoys to be imperilled by trying to operate the squadrons with fewer men than were essential. It was impossible to believe that accommodation could not be found for the numbers involved, and we asked the Russians to withdraw their proposal and agree that we should operate the aircraft. I also complained of recent Russian action in ordering some of the British naval wireless transmitters at Polyarnoe and Archangel to close down. These communications were needed for the movement of the convoys. Finally I told Maisky that the matter had been considered by the Chiefs of Staff and the War Cabinet and that, if the Soviet Government felt unable to meet us, we should have to review the whole question of continuing the convoys.

In reply the Russians withdrew the order closing down the wireless transmitters, but maintained their refusal to receive the Royal Air Force squadrons. Convoys to north Russia were then suspended from March until the late autumn of 1943. The bulk of the escort vessels were used for operations in the Mediterranean in the summer, while strong Nazi naval forces were concentrated in north Norway. In these conditions the Home Fleet could not manœuvre east of Bear Island and therefore could not protect the convoys on the final stage of one of the sternest ordeals of the whole war.

★   ★   ★   ★   ★

At the beginning of March a sad duty confronted me as Leader of the House of Commons. The Speaker, Captain Edward Fitzroy, whose family had been friends with mine from my earliest years, had fallen seriously ill in the middle of February.

March 3rd: Lunched with Winston after an interesting Cabinet at which we discussed precedents for Speaker dying in office. Clerk was sent for and 1789 precedent discovered. Winston so delighted that he read the whole thing from the Journal, amidst swelling protests that the luncheon hour was past. I didn't mind so much since I was lunching with him anyway! . . .

Before the coffee stage message reached me to go to House at once. On arrival found that Mr. Speaker had died. Said what I could and adjourned the House. W. discussed Speakership with Gwilym Lloyd-George [Minister of Fuel and Power] and asked him if he would accept. G. said frankly, yes. I talked to him after and warned him that House was likely to want Clifton-Brown [the Deputy Speaker].

Colonel Douglas Clifton-Brown was in fact elected on March 9th, though Lloyd-George would, I believed, have made the better

Speaker. The decision is, of course, one for the House of Commons and not for the Government, and rightly so.

★　　★　　★　　★　　★

Since my visit to the United States was postponed, I was able, on March 8th, to send my colleagues a paper on the future of Germany. This foreshadowed later policy.

There was no dispute that Germany must be disarmed and prevented from rearming. The question was whether anything more should be done to weaken or destroy the political unity of the country and thus guard against renewed attempts to dominate Europe. My Foreign Office advisers believed that separatist tendencies might arise and could be encouraged under Allied occupation, but they were hardly likely to disintegrate Germany. While, my paper explained, the victorious powers could impose dismemberment, with the passage of time they would probably lack the will to insist upon it. Nor could a policy of handing large areas of German territory, complete with their populations, to neighbouring states, be made to last. Frontier rectification might be possible and even necessary in some areas. Poland could probably absorb East Prussia and part of Silesia, but neither France nor the Low Countries seemed likely to be able to assimilate the Rhineland or the Ruhr. The best long-term solution seemed to be a voluntary federation in Germany.

Though I had not at this time come to a fixed decision about Germany's future, any hesitation about the dismemberment of the country was due more to doubts as to whether it could be made to last than to scruples about its harshness. I was interested, therefore, when Maisky said that the Soviet Government, while wishing to see Germany broken up, would countenance some kind of federal union between the parts. The Ambassador told me this on March 10th, when he came to give me his views on Europe before I left for Washington. He said he hoped that I would not make any binding commitments about the post-war settlement. I replied that my conversations would be exploratory; we would inform his Government fully about them.

Maisky repeated that Soviet Russia was determined to keep the

Baltic States after the war and to have bases in Finland and
Roumania. The Russo–Polish frontier should be the Curzon line,
with minor adjustments. I asked the Ambassador about confederations in Europe and he replied that his Government were not, in
general, attracted by them. They might not oppose a Balkan confederation which excluded Roumania, or a Scandinavian one
which excluded Finland, but their attitude to a Polish–Czech confederation would depend on the complexion of the future Polish
Government. If, after the war, Poland were democratic and friendly
towards Russia, relations between the two countries would be good.
Most of this was stubbornly negative.

I arrived in Washington on the evening of March 12th, when
Lord Halifax was my host for the greater part of an official visit
which lasted nearly three weeks. Mr. John Winant returned to
Washington for my stay.

My first meeting with President Roosevelt was at dinner on March
13th, Harry Hopkins and Winant being the only other guests. While
the talk was general, I gained the impression, as I think I was meant
to do, that the President intended to do all he could to keep the
United States in the forefront after the war. Unquestionably Roosevelt had the power, for he was head of a mighty country which was
coming out into the arena. He would be able to alter the whole
pattern of its policy, guiding it from isolation to an active part in
world affairs.

My next conversation, with Mr. Cordell Hull two days later, was
less encouraging about where we might be led. We talked for two
hours, with the emphasis on French problems. The Secretary of
State persisted in his dislike of General de Gaulle and showed scant
sympathy for the Free French. I reported to the Prime Minister:

> . . . Mr. Hull unburdened himself of his grievances, which
> were in the main that, while he had been pursuing a policy of
> maintaining relations with Vichy in which His Majesty's Gov-
> ernment agreed, he had been subject to much criticism in the
> British press and by the Fighting French; the mud batteries

had been turned on against him. I explained along the usual lines that while there had been agreement as to the desirability of American representation at Vichy, the British people felt neither sympathy nor admiration for Pétain and Vichy dominion. Nothing either you, or I, or anybody else, could say would alter this. . . .

Most of my numerous talks with American officials on French affairs were, however, concerned with the future, and here I already found our policies at odds with those of the United States. The Americans did not want to see a sole French authority established, even it it were not recognized as a government. They preferred to deal with individuals and were content to see General Giraud and General de Gaulle fall apart. They also wanted to act separately with the local French in the Pacific Islands and in Martinique. I wondered whether this was connected with the desire which the President had expressed to me to place some of the Pacific Islands under international control.

This dispersion of authority was contrary to my doctrine and I explained in all our conversations that the British Government would much prefer to deal with a single French authority, even if we did not regard it as a government in quite the same sense as the other European governments in exile. Nor could I agree to another American project, that Allied forces landing in France should administer liberated French territory. It seemed to me that Roosevelt wanted to hold the strings of France's future in his own hands so that he could decide that country's fate. I did not like this and preferred a French civil authority to work with the Allied forces from an early stage.

On the night of my talk with Hull I dined alone with the President and Harry Hopkins. Mr. Roosevelt expatiated happily to me about his views on European problems. He thought that after the war armaments in Europe should be concentrated in the hands of Britain, the United States and Russia. The smaller powers should have nothing more dangerous than rifles. He seemed to be ignoring the obvious difficulty of disarming neutral countries, but I did not take the idea as a serious proposal and it passed with little comment.

We then discussed in some detail the Russian demands, as explained to me by Maisky before I left London. Somewhat to my surprise, Roosevelt did not seem to foresee any great difficulty over the Polish question. He thought that if Poland had East Prussia and perhaps some concessions in Silesia, she would gain rather than lose by agreeing to the Curzon line. In any event Britain, the United States and Russia should decide at the appropriate time what was a just solution, and Poland would have to accept. The President was also prepared to agree to the Russian demands about Finland, nor did he take exception to the Russian claim to the Baltic States, although he hoped it might be possible to arrange plebiscites there.

The big question which rightly dominated Roosevelt's mind was whether it was possible to work with Russia now and after the war. He wanted to know what I thought of the view that Stalin's aim was to overrun and communize the Continent. I replied that it was impossible to give a definite opinion. Even if these fears were to prove correct, we should make the position no worse by trying to work with Russia and by assuming that Stalin meant what he said in the Anglo–Soviet Treaty. I might well have added that Soviet policy is both Russian and communist, in varying degree.

On the future of Germany the President appeared to favour dismemberment as the only wholly satisfactory solution. He agreed that, when the time came, we should work to encourage separatist tendencies within Germany and foresaw a long "policing" of that country. More surprisingly, he thought that the three Powers should police Europe in general. I pointed out that the occupied countries, as they then were, would want to put their own house in order and I thought we should encourage them to do so. We should have our hands quite full enough with Germany.

Roosevelt next showed anxiety about the future of Belgium and described a project which he had mentioned to Mr. Oliver Lyttelton a few months before, for a new state called "Wallonia." This would include the Walloon parts of Belgium with Luxembourg, Alsace-Lorraine and part of northern France. I recorded on this point that "I poured water, I hope politely, and the President did not revert to the subject."

In the Balkans, Mr. Roosevelt favoured separating Serbia from Croatia and Slovenia. I told him that in principle I disliked the idea of multiplying smaller states, I hoped the tendency would now be reversed and that we should aim at grouping. I could not see any better solution for the future of either the Croats or the Slovenes than forming some union with the Serbs.

Though I enjoyed these conversations, the exercise of the President's charm and the play of his lively mind, they were also perplexing. Roosevelt was familiar with the history and geography of Europe. Perhaps his hobby of stamp-collecting had helped him to this knowledge, but the academic yet sweeping opinions which he built upon it were alarming in their cheerful fecklessness. He seemed to see himself disposing of the fate of many lands, allied no less than enemy. He did all this with so much grace that it was not easy to dissent. Yet it was too like a conjuror, skilfully juggling with balls of dynamite, whose nature he failed to understand.

Hopkins recorded that the President had urged the British to give up Hong Kong as a gesture of "good will." Hopkins' account goes on:

> In fact, the President had suggested a number of similar gestures on the part of the British, and Eden dryly remarked that he had not heard the President suggest any similar gestures on our own part.*

★ ★ ★ ★ ★

At one of my early meetings with the President he suggested that I should visit some of the factories working for Britain. I suppose that I showed only limited enthusiasm for this, being unintelligent about machinery, for General George Marshall, who was present, spoke up: "Lend me Mr. Eden for a few days, and I will show him our army training." I acclaimed this with delight.

Dill and I spent three days with General Marshall, working northward by aeroplane from Biloxi, on the Gulf coast east of New Orleans. Our first stop was Montgomery, Alabama, where the Air Force cadets had asked to mount and command their own parade for me. This they did superbly, despite the inevitable little white

* Robert E. Sherwood (Ed.): *The White House Papers of Harry L. Hopkins*; Vol. II.

dog frisking its way between them and the saluting base. Afterwards Dill and I spoke to the cadets and to a number of our own seasoned Royal Air Force pilots who were helping them in their training.

General Marshall had been at much pains to emphasize the Anglo–American occasion at every parade. Giant flags of our two countries flew on the cars and fluttered over the saluting bases. Excusably, our national anthem was not always familiar even to the officers present and when it was being played I once heard a hoarse whisper behind me "Why the heck do we salute at *My Country, 'Tis of Thee?*"

At the camps we were shown over the barrack and mess rooms, which were very splendid compared with anything we had at home, and at Fort Bragg we talked to officers and men of an airborne division and watched them do a parachute drop. I was much impressed. The years passed and, early in 1945, I was with Mr. Churchill and General Marshall when they spoke of the renown won by the 82nd Airborne Division in the Ardennes. Marshall turned to me: "You will remember them, because they remember your visit to Fort Bragg."

We returned to Washington on March 24th and next day I went to see the naval yards at Norfolk, Virginia, where some of our battered warships were being swiftly and proudly mended.

One evening the President said to me: "Anthony, you'll have to make a speech to us before you go home. Where shall it be?" After some talk, I suggested San Francisco, where I could remind the West Coast that we were with them in the Japanese war until the end. Roosevelt liked the idea, until he discovered that Madame Chiang Kai-shek, then the prima donna in American favour, was on the Pacific Coast. "It will have to be nearer home," the President commented, adding after a pause: "I know where you must speak, in Annapolis, and the State Legislature of Maryland will meet to hear you and we will link you up with all the other State Legislatures across the country." I was rather taken aback. "Surely," I said, "they don't want to be reminded of the colonial past." "Don't they just," Roosevelt said. "You'll see."

This was the connection. Early in the seventeenth century when the first Charles was king in Britain, George Calvert, first Lord

Baltimore, was granted a charter to colonize a part of North America, later to be named Maryland after Queen Henrietta Maria. For a hundred and forty years this family ruled Maryland, only paying in tribute to their sovereign two Indian arrows once a year. They were Roman Catholics, but their religious policy was toleration, rare enough to be remarkable in its time. The seventh and last of his line was clever, but a rake, and left no legitimate heirs. His sister Caroline Calvert was my great-great-grandmother, having married Sir Robert Eden, the last colonial governor of Maryland.

Eden had, so his brother complained from the Foreign Office, "a predilection for the Americans," and was a personal friend of George Washington. The War of Independence over, he returned to the United States, where General Washington, now President, entertained him to dinner in a house which I was shown at Annapolis. Unhappily Eden was smitten by a fever and died suddenly before he could make arrangements about his wife's property in Maryland or for the return of his family to America. His widow and children stayed in England, but Maryland is still the only State of the Union to use the coat of arms of a family as its State flag. In Annapolis the State House had been built during my ancestor's term of office. When I spoke in its beautiful hall on March 26th, his portrait on the wall behind me, all this and more resulted in a welcome which made me feel that I was an Annapolis boy who had made good.

I judged this an opportunity to express some of my ideas about the post-war world. It also seemed advisable, in the climate of American opinion, to lay special stress on China:

> In the period between the two wars the intentions of the peace-loving nations were excellent, but their practice was weak. If there is one lesson we should have learnt from the distresses of those years, it is surely this: that we cannot shut our windows and draw our curtains, and be careless of what is happening next door or on the other side of the street. . . . We cannot have prosperity in one country and misery in its neighbour, peace in one hemisphere and war in the other. And if we try to have these things, we shall be back on the old road to world war. We shall never find security or progress within heavily defended national fortresses. The United Na-

tions, and in particular the United States, the British Commonwealth, China and the Soviet Union, must act together in war and peace. . . .

And one thing, I am sure, is above all essential. Never again must the civilized world be ready to tolerate unilateral infraction of treaties. For that would be to sap the whole foundation of the secure international life, which it is our principal purpose to restore.*

Unfortunately these hopes have once again been disappointed, more sharply this time than in the first years of the League of Nations. The United Nations applies two standards, with consequent loss of respect, being indulgent with newly emerged dictatorships and stern with European democracies which were once colonial powers. So are new tyrannies fostered while the peoples of formerly rich territories, as in Indonesia, suffer impoverishment that their ruler may buy arms and the Papuans are bereft by the United Nations of an old tolerance and subjected to a new despotism. Of course, this and comparable events will have consequences.

★   ★   ★   ★   ★

On my return from Annapolis I spent the weekend at the White House as the guest of the President and Mrs. Roosevelt. Here on March 27th I had my most formal meeting with Roosevelt and his advisers. It was the only occasion when I saw Cordell Hull and Sumner Welles together. Their relations were vinegar, although the Secretary of State when speaking of his Under-Secretary in his absence was acidly correct, to foreigners at least.

Lord Halifax and Mr. Strang were with me and we worked through an agenda which had been prepared beforehand. Afterwards I sent a long telegram to the Prime Minister:

. . . The first point raised by the President was the structure of the United Nations organization after the war. The general idea is that there should be three organizations. The first would be a general assembly at which all the United Nations would

* *Freedom and Order*, pages 186–95.

be represented. This assembly would only meet about once a year and its purpose would be to enable representatives of all the smaller powers to blow off steam. At the other end of the scale would be an executive committee composed of representatives of the Four Powers. This body would take all the more important decisions and wield police powers of the United Nations. In between these two bodies would be an advisory council composed of representatives of the Four Powers and of, say, six or eight other representatives elected on a regional basis, roughly on the basis of population. There might thus be one representative from Scandinavia and Finland and one or two from groups of Latin American states. This council would meet from time to time as might be required to settle any international questions that might be brought before it. . . .

The President said it was essential to include China among the Four Powers and to organize all these United Nations organs on a world-wide and not on a regional basis. He made it clear that the only appeal which would be likely to carry weight with the United States public, if they were to undertake international responsibilities, would be one based upon a world-wide conception. They would be very suspicious of any organization that was only regional. We have strong impression that it is through their feeling for China that the President is seeking to lead his people to accept international responsibilities.

The President had already, in his earlier conversation with me, purred his satisfaction at Madame Chiang Kai-shek's description of Mr. Willkie as adolescent and himself as sophisticated. He now claimed that China would neither be aggressive nor imperialist but would be a useful counterpoise to the Soviet Union. He said that in future dealings with China, the element of commercial exploitation should be excluded. I agreed with this last comment but, on the political aspect, said that much would depend on the kind of situation which would later exist in China. About this I was pessimistic, fearing that the country might go through a revolution after the war.* There followed a discussion of the fate of some Far Eastern and Pacific territories. My telegram continued:

* *The White House Papers of Harry L. Hopkins*; Vol. II.

In the Far East the policy is to be "Japan for the Japanese." Manchuria and Formosa would be returned to China and southern Sakhalin to Russia. The Japanese mandated islands in the Pacific would pass under the trusteeship of the United Nations. All other Pacific islands, with the exception of the two groups mentioned below, would remain under their present sovereignty British, French or whatnot, but would have a common economic policy, such as is to be set up in the West Indies. The French Marquesas and Tuamotu Islands would pass to the United Nations, for use respectively as stages on the northern and southern air routes across the Pacific from Caribbean area to Australia and New Zealand. Korea and French Indo-China would pass under international trusteeship; for the former the trustees might be the United States, the Soviet Union and China. Timor was most important for Australia and would also have to be dealt with. . . . [The President] suggested in passing that places like Dakar and Bizerta were of the greatest importance for the defence respectively of the United States and Mediterranean. His idea was that the United States should act as policeman for the United Nations at Dakar and Great Britain at Bizerta.

I remarked that the President was being very hard on the French, from whom the strongest opposition was to be expected. He admitted this, but said that France would no doubt require assistance for which consideration might be the placing of certain parts of her territory at the disposal of the United Nations. Welles reminded the President that the United States Government had gone on record for the restoration of French possessions. The President said he thought that this referred only to North Africa but Welles observed that there was no such modification. The President said that he thought in the ironing out of things after the war this kind of position could be rectified. . . .

At the close of the discussion Hopkins said that it was important to bear in mind three points: first, that there should be no attempt to set up a European council, for this would give free ammunition to the isolationists, who would jump at the chance of sitting back in a similar regional council for the American continent; secondly, that the discussions should not have the appearance of an Anglo–American attempt to settle the future of the world; and thirdly, that in our future policy towards China, exploitation should be excluded.

Finally we discussed once again the dismemberment of Germany, which the President thought would make for the security of Europe. Hull admitted that, despite study, he had not yet made up his mind, while I was inclined to favour it. All of which will now be seen as a mixed bag of ideas. A number of them, not always the best, lived on to win more formal shape. The future of the French territories, however, was to cause something of a running fight between the United States and ourselves.

*   *   *   *   *

There were other topics more insistent than the post-war world and much time was taken up with our immediate problems of shipping. On March 29th I telegraphed to the Prime Minister:

> I spoke to the President and Hopkins separately and together after dinner last night on the subject of our import programme. I impressed upon them that this question was one which concerned them as intimately as it did us. Our protection and maintenance of the life of our people was as intimately their concern as the output of their factories on the Pacific coast. If, as a result of non-fulfilment of our import programme, our production was to suffer, the result would be of the utmost seriousness for the Allied war effort.
>
> All this was accepted, though Harry Hopkins maintained that even our own people did not think it possible to reach the figure of twenty-seven million tons for this year; twenty-five and a half millions was the utmost. I said that the essential thing was to regard our import programme as a first charge that had to be fulfilled, and not to treat it as something that could be cut into at intervals for the sake of some military emergency.
>
> The President said that great efforts were being made to meet the shipping situation and it is certainly true that Hopkins' activities in the last few days have been strenuous in this regard. . . .

When all possible cuts had, however, been made, the President was clearly apprehensive as to whether we could find in the next few months the shipping which was imperatively necessary to carry out our many commitments, especially if losses continued at the present level. If any downward revision were necessary it was clear that he would prefer a modification of "Anakim" [a plan for the recapture of Burma] rather than interference with, or insufficient support of, any of the other operations agreed on at Casablanca.

He said that if it were found indispensable to cut out "Anakim" then we should concentrate on "keeping China going by air." He scribbled down headings of his views on this and kindred matters and asked me to talk them over on my return. There is of course no question of any decision being arrived at here. In fact the whole conversation was in the nature of thinking out loud by the President, and of searching for methods to meet our shipping needs. . . .

During these weeks I had also some discussion, principally with Harry Hopkins, about progress with the atom bomb. I was conscious of the effect these developments might have on the course of foreign policy and the power of nations and they formed, of course, a frequent topic of conversation between the Prime Minister and myself. My exchanges with Hopkins on this subject are printed as Appendix E.

There was at this time a strange dichotomy in the conduct of American foreign affairs, the President preferring to work through Sumner Welles, yet having regard for his Secretary of State's authority, especially with the Senate. I liked Mr. Cordell Hull, and right up to the time of his death I would never visit Washington without calling upon him in his retirement. But these were the days of his authority. Looking like an old eagle, and gently weaving his pince-nez, he had almost old-fashioned good manners. For all the years I knew him I was never more than Mr. Eden to him. Yet it was impossible to forget the beak and the claws. I could never watch him without recalling the song of his native Tennessee about the Martins and the Coys. I felt that he too could pursue a vendetta to the end.

On the evening before I left, Mr. Hull gave a farewell dinner party. A few hours earlier I had been in the State Department saying good-bye to some of those who had helped us in our work. As I took leave of Mr. Sumner Welles, I checked myself, adding in all innocence: "But, of course, I shall see you at the dinner tonight." Mr. Welles flushed up, but replied firmly: "I have not been asked."

Late that night Harry Hopkins took me off to the Carlton restaurant for some oysters and "to let our hair down." I told him frankly what I had thought of the conversations, to which he replied that the President had enjoyed trying his ideas out on me. I was not to worry, what I had said would sink in; he, Hopkins, would make sure of that. I was only partly comforted, in spite of which we spent a pleasant hour, as it was almost impossible not to do in Harry Hopkins' company.

We spoke of anything and everything without, on my part at least, even a shade of official afterthought. I made no notes of the talk at the time and did not report it home. Yet it had for me a certain consequence. After the war, during the life of the Labour Government, Mr. Churchill rang me up to ask me whether I had seen the proofs of Mr. Robert Sherwood's book *The White House Papers*. I said I had not. "Well, you had better ask to see them," came the reply, "because there are some things in them put down to me which I shall question. You may have to do the same."

When I wrote to Mr. Sherwood, he sent me the texts which concerned me, while firmly pointing out that these papers were now the property of the United States Government and were therefore sacrosanct. I could have no objection to that, but I was astonished to find among them an account of this same supper and relieved to read its relative discretion. The moral of this is that a true friend can be trusted to report even one's indiscretions discreetly, but it is quite a risk to take. Diplomacy is never off the record. The only advantage of pretending that it can be is to pursue diplomatic ends by undiplomatic means.

★ ★ ★ ★ ★

I finally left Washington on March 30th and flew to spend three days in Canada. There followed full discussions with the Canadian

Government and I addressed a session of Parliament. Highly as I valued this compliment, there was for me no less interest in visiting one of the centres of the Empire Air Training Scheme with which I had been so much concerned in its early days, for my elder son was soon to join it as an embryo pilot.

8

OUR OLDEST ALLY
April–June 1943

A proposition that I should become Viceroy of India — General Wavell appointed — Mr. Attlee and I send a telegram about the French — The Prime Minister influenced by Washington — We meet in Algiers — The problem of the Azores — I advocate diplomacy towards Portugal — President Roosevelt favours fragmentation of the French — A cause for dissension

THE MARQUESS OF LINLITHGOW had been appointed Viceroy of India in 1936. The normal term of office was five years but, because of the war, the Viceroy had been asked to stay at his post. By the end of 1942, however, it was thought that the time had come for a change. Though the political situation had been to some extent frozen by Sir Stafford Cripps' mission in the spring of that year, the problems were still alive. New energies and initiatives were also needed in the military field, as we began to prepare offensives in the war against Japan.

When I arrived back from the United States in April 1943, it was evident that a new appointment could not be delayed much longer. I am not sure who first suggested that I should be the next Viceroy. It may have been the Secretary of State for India, Mr. Amery; he certainly urged this course strongly in the next few weeks. Mr. Churchill, though at first opposed to the idea, became more receptive and we had many talks on the subject. He at once realized that I would not wish to limit my political career by accepting a peerage, the precedent for Viceroys. There was, he said, no need for that, and I must still be available to return to England to take charge if anything happened to him.

Of this, however, I was sceptical and so was the King. In a letter

to the Prime Minister of April 28th, His Majesty set forth his views
about me:

> From the point of view of the general conduct of the war he
> is, I know, very much in your confidence. He is, so to speak,
> your Second-in-Command in many respects, and, while I appre-
> ciate your readiness to let him go, I cannot help feeling that
> you might well find the loss of his assistance and support too
> great an addition to the heavy burden which you already have
> to bear.*

The King also spoke to me without reserve on May 8th, suggesting that my appointment might be reconsidered later but that for
the present I was indispensable at home. I had also my doubts
whether, once absorbed in Indian affairs, I could remain sufficiently
in touch with events at home to take over if need be. But the
Prime Minister would not accept this. I would remain a member of
the War Cabinet, he said, and be kept continuously informed of
their proceedings.

He also promised me wide powers and full backing from home for
any recommendations I made. I was sure that Mr. Churchill meant
this, but I knew that he had strong views about India and that
Delhi might think differently from Downing Street. This prospect
in itself would not, of course, have swayed me, but I had no illusions
about it.

The Prime Minister never urged the post upon me and his mood
about it changed as mine did, though not at the same moments.
My own inclinations were in favour of going and the fascination as
well as the complexities of India and her future tempted me. Yet I
was not sure that it was fair to leave the Foreign Office and the
Leadership of the House of Commons at this critical phase of the
war.

April 21st: Went round to see Winston after dinner about
some telegrams. He then opened up on the subject of India and,
to my surprise he was positively enthusiastic. Said what a calam-

* John W. Wheeler-Bennett: *King George* VI.

ity it would be to win the war and lose India, that I was his chief lieutenant and only really intimate friend among his colleagues and that, though he would hate to lose me, etc., etc. In short Winston's imagination has clearly caught fire, encouraged no doubt by the difficulty of finding anybody else and by the fun of reconstructing his government which he proceeded to do straight away! . . .

April 25th: Alec H. [Hardinge] telephoned to me after dinner about the Indian plan. He does not like it and thinks I must stay here to have some influence on Winston. In peace-time the move would be right, but he had doubts whether there was much to accomplish there now. Anyway he thought that the King would be against a hurried decision. He shared my view that once out there I could not be regarded as W's successor.

Hardinge said he was sure that the balance of advantage was against my going.

No decision had been reached by the time Mr. Churchill left on May 5th for a conference with President Roosevelt at Washington. If, as many of his colleagues advised him and as I myself was reluctantly beginning to accept, I could not go, the question was, who might. One possibility was Mr. Oliver Lyttelton, another Sir John Anderson. During his voyage across the Atlantic, the Prime Minister's mind was revolving these choices and the allied problem of the military commands in India. On May 9th he sent me a wireless message saying that he was inclined towards Mr. Lyttelton. I had also been talking over the problem with Mr. Amery and Lord Cranborne; the former was still very anxious that it should be me and he followed up his championship with friendly persistence. I therefore replied to Mr. Churchill:

I agree as to increasing seriousness of Indian military situation. Have talked to Amery and latter has spoken to Lyttelton. Amery has impression that Lyttelton is ready but not keen to go. In view of growing responsibility of charge he urges strongly that possibility of my going should not be ruled out. We are continuing discussions but am sure no final decision can be taken before you return.

There the matter rested for some weeks, while I pondered the decision and grew increasingly to feel that I ought not to leave London, despite the appeal of a job of this magnitude and of work so much on one's own. I had to admit that inter-allied relations now mattered no less than Indian politics and that in leading the House of Commons, I was taking a burden off the Prime Minister. He must not be allowed to resume those duties and there was no obvious alternative, in view of the Conservative majority. Moreover, the War Cabinet was now working well as a team; it seemed rash to disturb this by what would have to be a major reconstruction.

June 8th: Long talk alone with Winston late into the night about India. He keeps on repeating that I am the only appointment that could redeem the situation and adds that if he were my age he would go. But he as readily admits the disadvantages.

June 9th: Called in to see Winston on my way to answer Parliamentary Questions. He showed me alternative plans for Viceroy on the assumption that I or Oliver [Lyttelton] should go. Most of them on the assumption of Oliver. We discussed them for a while and both agreed that it was a great misfortune to have to take any important piece out of the War Cabinet machine now that it works well. I then went to my P.Qs. [Parliamentary Questions] and Oliver came in. O. told me on the bench after that W. had asked him if he would go and he had replied: "I will do whatever I am told." W: "That is exactly what Anthony says, making it quite plain at the same time that he has no intention of going."

Told Attlee on the bench that I had been suggested. He was hot against it. "Who is going to lead your party?"

Finally the dilemma was resolved. Rather than disrupt the War Cabinet, the Prime Minister decided to recommend the King to appoint General Wavell as Viceroy. At the same time he decided to separate the command of operations in South-East Asia from the office of Commander-in-Chief, India. General Auchinleck succeeded Wavell in the latter post and shortly afterwards the Supreme Allied Command, South-East Asia, was set up with Admiral Lord Louis Mountbatten as its chief.

Before his appointment was announced Wavell wrote to me a letter of characteristic modesty:

June 17th, 1943.

What a surprise, and what a shock! I wish you had been able to take it. I went to a theatre the other night where an announcement was made that the leading lady was unable to play and that an understudy had to take up the post at very short notice. I recall the groans of disappointment of the audience. . . .

Well, well,
Yours apprehensively,
Archie Wavell.

★   ★   ★   ★   ★

Meanwhile French affairs made only uncertain progress. Despite everything that I could do in London or Mr. Macmillan in Algiers, the meeting between General de Gaulle and General Giraud did not come easily, American policy adding its share to the difficulties. The United States Government were still against setting up a single French authority in France in advance of an Allied landing, in order to secure the support of the French people and gradually take over the administration behind the fighting line. They were also, as ever, suspicious of, and hostile to, General de Gaulle. They feared his dynamic personality and were inclined to discount the support which Gaullism was receiving from the resistance movement in France.

The new meeting was not arranged until May 21st when General Catroux, who had been working hard as intermediary, brought a message to London from General Giraud accepting the most recent proposals of the French National Committee. All seemed set fair when, on the same day, a sudden squall blew up from another quarter.

The Prime Minister had been for nearly a fortnight in Washington and subject, of course, to repeated American denunciation of the Free French leader. He now telegraphed suggesting that his colleagues should urgently consider whether de Gaulle should not now be eliminated as a political force.

May 23rd: Cabinet at 9 p.m. *re* de Gaulle and Winston's proposal to break with him now. Everyone against and very brave about it in his absence.

Attlee and I replied to the Prime Minister immediately after the meeting:

> . . . We had no idea that de Gaulle situation was rankling so much just now. We are fully conscious of the difficulties which de Gaulle has created for us, and of your position under heavy pressure from the Americans. We do not, however, consider that the policy which you so strongly recommend is practicable for the following reasons.
>
> The latest phase of the Giraud–de Gaulle negotiations indicates that union is nearer than it has been at any time. De Gaulle has been invited by Giraud to Algiers subject to the acceptance of two conditions and it seems probable that he will accept.
>
> . . . It has been the policy of His Majesty's Government and the U.S. Government for the past four months to bring the two generals together and this policy was blessed by the President and yourself at Anfa [Casablanca]. If, as we believe, it was the right policy then, it is in our view even more the right policy now when both generals appear to be on the point of achieving the union which they were then pressed to bring about.
>
> Our information is that the failure of the two generals to reach agreement has caused disappointment in France. There is much evidence that de Gaulle's personal position in France is strong. . . . Mr. Macmillan reported on May 4th that local opinion in Algiers was becoming more and more insistent on the need for immediate union and we understand that the postponement of de Gaulle's proposed visit to Algiers at the beginning of April caused considerable excitement in North Africa and did not enhance Giraud's reputation. He has also reported that the Frenchmen in Tunisia were predominantly Gaullist in the broadest sense.
>
> Moreover the wider interests of France render union between the two bodies a necessity. What prospects would there be of

union in France itself after the liberation if the Frenchmen outside France are now incapable of reaching agreement between themselves?

We are advised that there is no likelihood of any of the present members of the French National Committee continuing to function if General de Gaulle were removed by us. The same is probably true of the Free French Fighting forces. . . .

Is there not also a real danger that if we now drove de Gaulle out of public life at this moment when a union between the two French movements seems on the point of being achieved, we would not only make him a national martyr but would find ourselves accused by both Gaullists and Giraudists of interfering improperly in French internal affairs with a view to treating France as an Anglo–American protectorate? If so, our relations with France would be more dangerously affected than by a continuance of the present unsatisfactory situation.

. . . We suspect that Murphy is becoming impressed by the evidence of rising Gaullism in North Africa which must be reaching him and that he prefers to ascribe this to Gaullist propaganda rather than admit that he was as wrong about Gaullist strength in North Africa as he was about anti-British feeling there. The fact is that Giraud's retention of unpopular men and Murphy's continued reluctance to insist on their removal have helped de Gaulle very considerably in North Africa.

Mr. Churchill replied next day, accepting to await the results of the meeting between the two generals. He would tell the President that the matter would be considered again on his return to London.

General de Gaulle came to see me on May 26th before leaving for Algiers. I told him that we were pleased that he and General Giraud seemed about to reach agreement. Throughout all these years our policy had been unchanged: we wished to see a strong and united France, playing her part in world politics. Amity between the French elements prepared to fight the common enemy was clearly a necessary step on this road. General de Gaulle said that he fully shared our view as to the need for co-operation between our two countries. He hoped that France would again be able to play her part. In the post-war world, he thought, there would be two

great powers, Russia and the United States, and it was desirable
that Britain and France should work together, situated as we were
between the two.

★   ★   ★   ★   ★

The Prime Minister flew from Washington to Algiers, with General Marshall, to continue discussions on the operations which were
to follow the forthcoming invasion of Sicily.

May 29th, Binderton: Guy [Millard, one of my Assistant Private Secretaries] rang through in early afternoon to say that telegram had just come through from P.M. asking me to come out
to join him. Alec H. [Hardinge] was fortunately staying with me
so that I was able to discuss with him. Also spoke to Attlee.
Decided to leave tomorrow evening from here.

I took off from West Hampnett in Sussex, landed in Cornwall
and left for Gibraltar at two o'clock in the morning.

Rather cold in early stages and dreary, for we had to sit in dark,
no blackout. The dawn was beautiful and warming.
May 31st: Governor met us. Some talk about plans, then to
his house for bath and breakfast. . . .
Left for Algiers noon. Uneventful flight. Macmillan met me
and we motored direct to Admiral's [Cunningham] villa. Long
talk with Winston there. He is worried about French negotiations and strongly anti-de Gaulle, in part at least as a result of
stories told him by [Gen. Alphonse] Georges [who had just been
brought out of France] whom I met later at dinner and who
struck me as a reactionary old defeatist. Winston said I might
have to intervene if matters took a turn for the worse. I explained my reluctance and we agreed that matter was not immediate anyway, since we were off for forty-eight hours to the
front. Winston then asked what I thought of going on to Russia to see Joe [Stalin], the two of us or one of us. Asked me to
think it over and let him know tomorrow.
Staff Conference at 5 p.m. All went well. Americans very

friendly in their greeting to me. I like Eisenhower and Marshall.

Mr. Churchill's idea was that he or I should explain the results of the Washington conference to Stalin in person. While I had not been in Washington, I felt that from the point of view of his health, the Prime Minister ought not to go on another long journey by air. I therefore said that I was ready, if it was really necessary for anyone to make the journey. I discussed the matter with Brooke, who nobly undertook to travel with me.

Happily, on further consideration the idea of a personal visit was dropped. I thought it undesirable anyway, unless the Americans were represented at the same level. There was no need for us to bell the bear. Instead the Prime Minister and the President sent a message to Stalin setting out the conclusions of their conference, including the decision to launch an all-out invasion of the Continent in the spring of 1944. Inevitably, Stalin took the news of the further postponement of the second front badly. His messages during June reached such a pitch of acrimony that for several weeks Mr. Churchill dropped all personal correspondence with him.

The Staff Conference fascinated me, for it showed the instinctive distrust of the Americans for any military operations which committed them further into Europe, except by a cross-Channel invasion. Their reluctance was perfectly natural, but it was also costly. Fear of entanglement in the Balkans and of British schemes to lure them there diverted the Americans from thoughts of Vienna and Prague and gave the Soviets too wide a field. This was all for the future, the present compromise was Sicily, with the least said of the Italian campaign to which it must lead.

The next two days with the Prime Minister among our soldiers and airmen were for me about the happiest of the war. I had no work to do, only to ride with Mr. Churchill, or with Air Marshal Sir Arthur Coningham, in an open car, either at informal parades or between lanes of cheering troops and airmen. They were relaxed and happy in their victory, as they had every right to be.

The final negotiations between de Gaulle and Giraud were concluded on June 2nd, fortunately without the need for any intervention by me, and the event was duly toasted and wined at an Allied luncheon two days later. In the interval the Prime Minister and I enjoyed some bathing expeditions which were so agreeable that we more than once lamented our failure to take two days' holiday, but war did not permit and we left for London in the aftermath of our feasting.

★   ★   ★   ★   ★

In the year 1373 England and Portugal signed a Treaty by which the two countries would be "friends to friends and enemies to enemies." This was the oldest Alliance in our history and had been bravely upheld down to and including the first world war. The second world war presented graver complexities. When the British Commonwealth stood alone, Portugal would only have been another liability which we could not meet, but with the Nazi invasion of Russia and the Japanese assault upon Pearl Harbour, the picture began to change. Enemy forces being deeply engaged in distant theatres, the use of the Azores became more attractive, as the commitment towards our ally became less dangerous for either party to the Treaty. Hitler had other ventures upon his hands than to attack Portugal through a stubbornly reluctant Spain, and the air bombardment of Lisbon became a risk which, even in anger, he had now less resources to take.

We now know that on May 14th, Hitler rejected for the last time any idea of marching through Spain upon the Straits of Gibraltar, adding gloomily that the Axis must face the fact that it was saddled with Italy. Mussolini had been pressing for this action as a final thrust against the Allies in North Africa. As Tunis fell Field-Marshal Kesselring, the German commander in southern Italy, and Admiral Dönitz added their voices to Mussolini's. Hitler refused. He knew that Spain would not now enter the war on the Axis side and insisted that German occupation of Spain without the consent of the Spaniards was out of the question. Although Dönitz had also recommended the occupation of Portugal, Hitler did not even mention that country.*

As the campaign in North Africa reached its final stage, Admiral

---

* *Führer Conferences on Naval Affairs, 1943*; Chapter Three.

Sir Dudley Pound revived a proposal which he had made a while before, that the Government should ask the Portuguese to grant us facilities in the Azores. Experience in the Battle of the Atlantic had shown that the presence of even a single aircraft over a convoy greatly hampered German U-boat operations.

Without the use of the Azores and in order to gain the greatest possible air protection, our Atlantic convoys had to follow a northerly route. This was often affected by bad weather and ice and inevitably became known to the enemy. A southerly route which had air protection would be particularly valuable in winter. It would enable us to vary convoy routes when U-boats were concentrated in the north and to economize shipping by using more direct sailings across the Atlantic. We should also benefit from being able to fuel naval escorts in the Azores, and from the use of the islands as a staging post on the air supply route from the United States to the Mediterranean.

Mr. Churchill and the Chiefs of Staff discussed the Azores on their way across the Atlantic to meet the President, and on May 10th the Prime Minister sent the War Cabinet a message saying that he would be prepared to approach the Portuguese Government for facilities and to let them know, if they made difficulties, that we intended to take over the islands. He thought that Dr. Salazar, the Portuguese Prime Minister, might find it easier to bow to *force majeure* than to assent to such a violation of Portuguese neutrality.

I did not think this a correct reading of the chances. I thought that we should try to get the facilities we needed, but that the best method was to invoke the Alliance. The Portuguese took pride in this, as we did. If they responded, we should get Portuguese goodwill as well as the facilities. Sir Ronald Campbell,* our experienced Ambassador in Lisbon, had recently been home and had told me that he shared this opinion. We should also be spared the invidious role of attacking our oldest and smallest ally. All this, quite apart from the strain on our shipping and other resources involved in fitting out an expedition to capture the islands. The

* This Sir Ronald had been Ambassador in Paris in 1940 and is not to be confused with the other Sir Ronald Campbell who was H.M. Minister in Belgrade in 1941 (Book Two, Chapter VII), and then Minister in the Embassy in Washington (Book Three, Chapter V).

Defence Committee agreed with this judgment when they met to
discuss the Prime Minister's telegram that evening.

After the meeting Attlee and I replied to Mr. Churchill. We
told him that we thought the Portuguese would respond if the
Alliance were invoked and the idea came from our country alone.
We were opposed to the forcible seizure of the Azores. We agreed
that there was no question of guaranteeing to defend the Portuguese mainland, but we could offer to help in organizing defence
against air attack and to protect Portuguese shipping. The Defence
Committee favoured making an early contact with the Portuguese
Government and we proposed to recall Campbell for briefing the
moment we knew that the Americans agreed.

Mr. Churchill answered us on May 21st, saying that the Combined Chiefs of Staff strongly recommended that the Allies should
have the use of the Azores as soon as possible, as a military necessity.
He did not think the Portuguese Government were likely to agree
and he could not see any moral substance in the objection to overriding Portuguese neutrality. It was a painful responsibility, he
said, to condemn ships to destruction and seamen to drowning
because our inhibitions prevented us from taking the steps that
would save them. He asked the War Cabinet to empower him to
tell the Americans on May 24th that if they would agree to share the
responsibility, the Combined Chiefs of Staff should make a plan
to take the Azores at the earliest possible moment.

The War Cabinet were not influenced by the charge of indiffer-
ence to our drowning seamen and held firmly to their opinion that
we should first make a diplomatic approach to Dr. Salazar. The
Portuguese were strongly pro-British, but they did not feel the
same sympathy for the United States. They suspected that whereas
we would withdraw at the end of the war, the Americans might
prefer to stay.

We put these and other arguments to the Prime Minister at once
and pointed out that action could, in any event, not be taken in
the next few weeks without impairing other operations and weakening the escorts for our convoys at a critical time of the year.
We asked that decision should be postponed until Mr. Churchill
came home and we could discuss it with him. The Prime Minister
was not yet persuaded. On May 24th, after a further meeting of
the War Cabinet, Attlee and I telegraphed to him:

We understand operation could not take place for two months at earliest, which gives us time to consider how it could be staged. We are convinced that it would be better to try first a diplomatic approach. His Majesty's Ambassador, when here, told us he thought there was a chance of Salazar giving us what we want. Salazar's temperament being what it is, he is less likely to give way to an ultimatum. We feel it would be better to invoke the Alliance and state our case. If he rejects that he will have shown that the Alliance is of little value. We should then be in a better moral position than if we, without any approach, suddenly threatened to seize the territory of an Ally.

We would however agree that preparations should go ahead now and that we should approach Salazar before the operation, at a time to be agreed upon. . . .

Mr. Churchill now consented to reserve the British decision on the operation until his return.

★　　★　　★　　★　　★

Back in London, the Prime Minister still held to his opinion about the Azores. He argued, at a Chiefs of Staff meeting which I attended on June 7th, that he could see no reason to believe that we should get what we wanted by a diplomatic approach without the display or threat of force. I was not against a display of force, but insisted that I must have a few days in which to persuade the Portuguese to yield to our arguments. The Chiefs of Staff, keen as they were to enjoy the facilities of the Azores, were unhappy at the calls to be made on our escorts and shipping. So diplomacy had its chance.

The next day Dr. Salazar asked our Ambassador for new Anglo–Portuguese staff conversations because of the changed military situation. This, Campbell thought, might mean that we could make an appeal to the Alliance now that the threat of a German invasion of the Peninsula seemed to be past. I was encouraged to persevere with our method.

June 18th: Monteiro [Portuguese Ambassador] came to see me in afternoon and I opened "Lifebelt" [the Azores]. He took it quite well. If it lay with him I think it a little better than even money he would accept, Salazar a little worse. But there is a chance.

I explained to Dr. Monteiro how important facilities in the Azores were to us for shortening the war. We were not, I said, asking Portugal to take a step which would place her in danger. I supposed that the great majority of the Portuguese people wished the Allies to win; we were now offering Portugal a chance to play a part in accelerating our victory. If Portugal felt able to do this, she would not find us ungrateful and the ancient Alliance would take on a new lease of life. I gave the Ambassador two papers setting out the facilities for which we were asking and the reasons why we needed them for the defeat of the U-boat menace in the Atlantic. In return Britain offered to discuss measures of assistance against possible German air attack on the mainland, and protection for Portuguese shipping and trade. We also gave assurances about the maintenance of Portugal's sovereignty over all her colonies.

On the same day Sir Ronald Campbell made his approach to the Portuguese Government. Dr. Salazar, who had apparently not been expecting an appeal to the Alliance, promised to consider sympathetically the request for facilities. On June 23rd he gave our Ambassador a note agreeing in principle to provide the desired facilities, but asking for conversations on the conditions for granting them and on the action to be taken to deal with the possible consequences for Portugal. I had suggested, on June 20th, that I might go out to Lisbon soon to conclude discussions and sign any agreement which might be necessary. Dr. Salazar turned the idea down, on the ground that a visit from me could not be kept secret and that it would be impossible to reach any conclusions in the short time I could spare.

After this rebuff I had to find some other way to clinch matters, for dawdling was dangerous and costly.

The formation of the French Committee of National Liberation at Algiers on June 3rd did not make all smooth in French affairs.

There was friction about the military command. General de Gaulle was convinced that the French forces needed complete reorganization and that General Giraud was not the man to do it. The United States authorities were equally determined that Giraud should retain control of the army. They also insisted that M. Boisson remain Governor-General of West Africa, because they feared an extension of General de Gaulle's influence there. The President sent General Eisenhower a strongly worded telegram in this sense and asked the Prime Minister to support him.

June 11th: Winston rang up early to tell me of telegram from F.D.R. about de Gaulle crisis. American hatred is keen and maybe they want Dakar too. But de Gaulle has done much to shake all confidence in him. Discussion in office and then talk to Winston about his draft reply, fitted into a morning full of engagements.

Across to No. 10 to say God speed to Alex [Gen. Alexander]. Telegrams about fall of Pantelleria [captured on June 11th] were discussed. We thought it a good omen.

Beatrice and I motored home. It looked and smelt lovely as usual. We are glad not to be giving it up for a splendid palace at Delhi.

President Roosevelt's anger against General de Gaulle continued to mount. He seems to have thought that an enlargement of the Committee of National Liberation, announced on June 8th, but not apparently noticed in Washington until about June 16th, was due to political machinations by the General. On June 17th he again proposed to Mr. Churchill that "we must break with him."

June 18th: W. rang up and read over to me a long telegram from Roosevelt about de Gaulle. It seemed pretty hysterical to me and Winston didn't really try to defend it. We shall be hard put to it to keep in step with Americans, or rather pull them into step with us, over the French business, and not commit some folly which will give de Gaulle a martyr's crown or control of the French army or both. F.D.R.'s mood is now that of a man who persists in error. It has all that special brand of obstinacy, like Hitler at Stalingrad. Attlee also rang me up during day. He didn't like W's reply to F.D.R. Nor did I much, but I had secured one amendment and failed to secure more. I therefore suggested he should try. He did, and secured another.

In the end a compromise was reached about the command of the French forces; it was a partition like that between Octavius Cæsar and Mark Antony. This did not matter so much as that the Americans now extended their distrust to the Committee of National Liberation, thus making its recognition a cause of prolonged controversy between the allies.

9

THE FREE FRENCH
July–September 1943

The French Committee of National Liberation — Mr. Churchill
and I both write papers — Reconciliation — Slow progress over
the Azores bases — The Agreement signed — Resignation of
Signor Mussolini — The Quebec Conference — Deadlock over the
French — A fishing expedition — Mr. Maisky leaves London —
The Moscow Conference is fixed

THE FRENCH COMMITTEE of National Liberation, as soon as it was
formed, had presented a note asking for recognition as "the body
qualified to ensure the conduct of the French effort in the war as
well as the administration and defence of all French interests."
However, the crisis over the command of the French forces and the
agitation of President Roosevelt, which communicated itself to Mr.
Churchill, over the enlargement of the Committee, made me postpone for a few weeks any attempt to push recognition.

I then reminded my colleagues in a Cabinet paper on July 2nd
that they had agreed we ought to build up the authority of the
civilian members of the Committee. The most effective way of
doing so was to give the Committee some recognition and not to
back one General or the other. I wrote that a number of our allies
had already recognized the Committee, while the Soviet Government had only delayed doing so at our request. I suggested a
formula for recognition which we would discuss with the United
States Government.

The Prime Minister still said that it was too soon. The Committee's desire to be recognized was our best means of ensuring
good behaviour. On July 6th we heard from Algiers that General
Eisenhower and Mr. Murphy were now advocating immediate recognition, so Mr. Churchill agreed to send my formula to the Presi-

dent for his comments. Mr. Roosevelt's reaction was to tell Eisenhower and Murphy not to recognize the Committee under any condition without his approval.

July 8th: Defence Committee began with a fierce argument about the French. A reply from F.D.R. had encouraged W. to say that nothing would induce him to recognize Committee, coupled with a tirade against de Gaulle. I retaliated that Americans had mishandled French problem from beginning, their treatment of de Gaulle would soon make him national hero. Alec C. [Cadogan] backed me and was told he had been "frequently wrong." A turbulent and rather ludicrous interlude.

★   ★   ★   ★   ★

Two days later Mr. Roosevelt told the Prime Minister that he was prepared to "accept," not "recognize," the French Committee as the temporary *de facto* authority for civil administration in France, on two conditions. The first was that complete authority must be reserved to General Eisenhower to do whatever he felt necessary to secure effective military operations. The second was that the French people must be given the opportunity to choose their own government freely. The President said that he was instructing his officials to modify the British draft in order to make these points clear.

July 12th: Dined with him [Prime Minister]. Stimson and the Winants also there. Stimson left soon after dinner and we had a fierce but friendly argument about French in Cabinet room until 2 a.m. I told W. again all I felt. He maintained that de Gaulle could not be allowed to dominate Committee and he must see how things worked out before recognition was accorded. Admitted that if we broke on this I should have much popular support, but warned that he would fight vigorously to the death. I told him I wasn't contemplating resignation. We agreed each to put our ideas down on paper.

My paper began by describing what we had learnt about United States policy towards France:

So far as I have been able to piece together the various indications I have received, I would say that they [United States Government] did not wish to see a strong central administration for the French Empire built up in Algiers. They would have preferred if possible to deal separately with each part of the French Empire. They dislike the growth of an independent spirit in any French administration anywhere and consider that any French authority with whom they deal should comply without question with their demands.

Later I added that there were grounds

for believing that some at any rate of the governing authorities in Washington have little belief in France's future and indeed do not wish to see France again restored as a great imperial power.

Our views and policy, I wrote, must be different:

Our main problem after the war will be to contain Germany. Our treaty with the Soviet Union, which is designed to secure the collaboration of the Soviet Union for this purpose on Germany's eastern flank, needs to be balanced by an understanding with a powerful France in the west. These arrangements will be indispensable for our security whether or not the United States collaborate in the maintenance of peace on this side of the Atlantic.

Our whole policy towards France and Frenchmen should therefore be governed by this consideration. . . . In dealing with European problems of the future we are likely to have to work more closely with France even than with the United States, and while we should naturally concert our French policy so far as we can with Washington, there are limits beyond which we ought not to allow our policy to be governed by theirs. . . .

Europe expects us to have a European policy of our own, and to state it. That policy must aim at the restoration of the independence of the smaller European Allies and of the greatness of France. . . .

We have intimate dealings with the French in Syria and Madagascar, and we have French forces stationed in this country. We have to live and work with France in the future. From both the political and the legal point of view it is inconvenient not to have formal relations with the authority whom we in fact recognize as responsible for all the French territories and armed forces which are collaborating with us in the war.

July 13th: Sent Winston my memorandum at lunchtime as agreed. Surprised to get further letter from him, rather formal. Went over to see him at 7 p.m. and asked him why. He said he didn't like my paper and thought we might be coming to a break.

This was far from my purpose and was perhaps a sign that the war years could bear even upon him.

Sir Winston has printed part of his paper in his war memoirs.* To my mind the danger was that American policies towards France might jeopardize their relations and ours with that country for years to come.

The Prime Minister and the President were also prone to argue that as we had encouraged the growth of Gaullism in France, so we could equally well weaken it. Even were it true that we could influence public opinion in France to this extent, which seemed to me highly doubtful, the argument overlooked the damage which such action would do. The resistance of the French people themselves, even more than the re-entry of French territories into the war, was vital for the future of France as well as important to our military operations. It ought not to be weakened by us.

Fortunately this controversy between the Prime Minister and me did not last long.

July 19th: Staff meeting at 10.30 after which I stayed and talked to Winston until after 1 a.m. He admitted, to my surprise, that I had been right about Portugal and finished up by offering to telegraph to Roosevelt about recognition of French Committee. Altogether many changes since last week. All this

* *The Second World War*; Vol. V.

was wedged in, of course, between much talk on progress of the war and future plans. Winston was in very good form and could not have been more friendly.

July 20th: After dinner went across to No. 10 at Winston's request. He showed me his message to President about recognition, which is admirable. He remarked that he seemed now to have swallowed my thesis whole, to which I said that it would be truer to say that he was asking Americans to face up to realities of our situation.

"Munich Mouser" [a black cat which Mr. Churchill found at No. 10] is dead. He died in the F.O. this afternoon. Winston says that he died of remorse and chose his death-bed accordingly. He feared he had been thrown on the ash can. He would have been ready to give him burial in the garden of No. 10. Yes, I said, R.I.P. Munich Mouser would look well there. We laughed a good deal about the poor cat.

Mr. Churchill sent his telegram to President Roosevelt next day. He suggested that the British Government might find it necessary to proceed independently of the United States.* The President in reply did not refer to any of Mr. Churchill's arguments. He maintained his suspicions of General de Gaulle and the Committee, and held out no hope of recognition.

I thought at first that this message must have crossed the Prime Minister's, but it turned out to be a reply. It left us on either side of the fence.

★ ★ ★ ★ ★

Meanwhile negotiations with the Portuguese Government over the grant of airfields and fuelling facilities for naval escorts in the Azores were proceeding jerkily. To get matters moving I told our Ambassador in Lisbon that I might be paying him a visit. He replied that the Portuguese were showing good will in meeting our desire for speed and that Dr. Salazar would regard a new proposal for a visit by me as trying to rush him.

* Churchill, op. cit.

July 24th: "Lifebelt" [the Azores] becomes troublesome again with Salazar dilatory and Winston impatient. We shall have to force the pace, at least to extent of determining a day [for our entry].

August 2nd: Motored to London. Lunched with Winston, alone with family. Discussed various matters after, including French National Committee. W. is round at last to recognition, but F.D.R. it seems is further away than ever. We also spoke of "Lifebelt" without reaching agreement.

We had a row about this last at Defence Committee after dinner. Something of a shouting match going on for an hour or more. W. maintaining that we could have taken the islands in June, July or August but for my insistence on approaching Salazar, that he had himself been pleased with progress at first, but that now it was clear that S. was merely fooling me. I retorted that we had been absolutely right, that we had stopped him making unprovoked attack on an ally and that anyway he had not been in a position to do the last until end of August. Brooke said that we had gained some ships for "Husky" [landings in Sicily] by my plan.

No result at meeting but we reached agreement after W. and I had talk about other things after meeting alone. As I said good night he said he was sorry if he had been obstreperous at meeting, but he felt that S. was intolerable. I replied that I feared that I had been obstreperous too. "Oh you, you were bloody!" On which note we said good night.

A fortnight later the agreement was signed and October 8th was accepted as the date of our entry into the Azores. It was many months before facilities were granted for American aircraft to operate from the islands under British insignia. I was on my way to Moscow when the time came to tell Parliament the outcome of our negotiations, but Mr. Churchill made splendid use of the opportunity and no listener could have guessed that any other thought had ever crossed his mind but to embrace our oldest ally in enduring affection.

★   ★   ★   ★   ★

July 25th: Winston rang up about 11.30 p.m. to announce the great news that Musso had resigned. After some jubilation and reminiscence of the humiliation of Neville and Edward's visit to Rome, we discussed next moves. W. made it plain that he wanted to treat with King and Badoglio [the new Prime Minister]. I said I thought it likely this Government would not last. Certainly it would not be able to make Italians fight. Badoglio might be the Max of Baden. W. agreed and that we were in the presence of an event of utmost consequence.

The new Italian Government lost little time in deciding to make contact with the Allies, while still trying to avoid an open breach with the Germans. This involved intricate and sometimes burlesque exchanges, with much toing and froing of envoys, crossing and double-crossing in Lisbon, Tangier and Sicily, but all ending up on September 3rd on terms which were sensible rather than drastic. This was the date of the Anglo–Canadian landing on the Italian mainland.

July 25th: A lovely day at last and despite plenty of work enjoyed the sunshine. Winston rang up before luncheon when we had a long talk about "Quadrant," French situation and other problems.

"Quadrant" was a proposal for an Anglo–American meeting at Quebec. On the night before the Prime Minister left we spoke again of the need to keep the Russians informed as far as we could. The clamour for a second front was unabated. Mr. Churchill admitted the problem but held that we could only do our best by our conduct of the war. He was sure that he had to go to Quebec to see Mr. Roosevelt and I agreed. Moreover, if he could persuade the Americans to put more effort into the invasion of Italy, this should have some effect on our relations with the Russians. Our talk had, however, a consequence. Before leaving for Quebec, Mr. Churchill drafted a message to Stalin which was sent as from the War Cabinet, in which he brought up once more our proposal for a tripartite meeting.

This time Stalin agreed that a meeting should be held as soon as possible and suggested that responsible representatives of the three countries should meet first, to make arrangements and draw up an agenda. I advised the Prime Minister to reply at once, agreeing in principle, and he did so. On August 18th he and the President sent a joint message to Stalin again urging a meeting of the three leaders. If this could not be arranged, they agreed to a meeting at the Foreign Office level. This exchange was the origin both of my second wartime visit to Moscow and of the Tehran Conference.

★   ★   ★   ★   ★

On August 16th Sir Alexander Cadogan and I left London by air for Quebec, arriving two days later after weather delays in Ireland. I was soon absorbed in Anglo–American relations both towards the Russians and towards the French. First came a talk with Mr. Harry Hopkins about the proposed meeting of Foreign Secretaries. The Russians, I argued, were chiefly interested in two subjects, the second front and their western frontiers. Hopkins said there was a third, the treatment of Germany after the war. I replied that I thought two and three were related. If I went to meet Molotov or Stalin, accompanied by some American opposite number and made plain, first that there would be no second front this year, then that we had not advanced at all in our consideration of the Russian frontier claims or the future of Germany, I thought the meeting was almost certain to do more harm than good. Hopkins agreed and added that if Mr. Welles went, Mr. Hull would certainly do his best to torpedo the meeting. I remarked that this sounded altogether an agreeable enterprise for me to set out upon.

Next afternoon I called on the American Secretary of State, Mr. Cordell Hull:

August 20th: More work after luncheon and then talk for more than two hours with old Hull. Most of it was about recognition of French Committee. I failed to make any impression and we both got quite heated at one time when I told him we had to live twenty miles from France and I wanted to rebuild her so far as I could. This was a first, though small, step. He retorted by accusing us of financing de Gaulle, with implication that our money had been used to attack him, Hull, for a long time past. I like the old man but he has an obsession against Free French which nothing can cure. I eventually suggested we each take our own course.

W. and F.D.R. did not get back from fishing expedition until 8.30, so that our dinner was unpleasantly late. Talked to W. while he was dressing on my day with Hull, etc. He was ready enough to agree with my line as to French. Dinner was not very agreeable meal. I sat between President and Hull. Hull appeared anxious to go to bed. When he eventually rose to go, about midnight, W. was scandalized and exclaimed in reply to Hull's protest that it was late, "Why, man, we are at war!"

The party at dinner had consisted of the President, the Prime Minister, Cordell Hull, Harry Hopkins and myself. I explained my anxieties about the conference. Mr. Roosevelt said that we would not be plenipotentiaries and that, if the Russians raised the question of Finland or the Baltic States, the American representative would say that he had no instructions and would refer home. The Prime Minister asked what would be the good of that, since the United States Government would not be able to give an answer. The President replied that he could then keep silence. Mr. Churchill observed that this could hardly improve relations. I said that a meeting in such conditions could only make matters worse.

Finally the President mentioned a proposal of his that the Four Powers should set up an international security organization. This was to cover the interim period before the final peace treaties could be signed. The outline as presented to us was still sketchy, but Mr. Churchill and I said that we liked it and would put it to the War Cabinet when we both got home.

On August 21st I again discussed the French Committee with Mr. Hull and found that we were no nearer agreement. During one of our talks he said: "My, Mr. Eden, I had no idea you were such a politician." I asked him if he knew Lloyd George's definition of a statesman: "A statesman is a politician with whom one happens to agree." I was sorry that by that standard I could not apply the name to him that day. Hull laughed and matters became a little easier, but the Committee still stuck in the American throat. We finally concluded that however undesirable it might

be, our two Governments would probably have to recognize the
Committee in different terms. This was what happened.

Mr. Hull and I had a brief but useful discussion about Soviet
frontiers on August 23rd. We agreed that if our two countries had
to make concessions, we must be ready to table our needs in return. I gave Mr. Hull a note about probable Russian demands,
pointing out that neither the British nor, as far as I knew, the
United States Government had ever given the Russians any hint of
their views. My chief concern was that if these questions were left
until the Soviet armies re-entered Poland, Polish-Soviet differences
would be all the harder to solve.

The Conference over, the Prime Minister and I parted company
for some relaxation. Mr. Churchill set off for the Lake of the
Snows. I and my party motored to Lake Jacques Cartier, sixty-seven
miles from Quebec and separated from the Prime Minister by a
mountain range. The next morning our fishing expedition was
delayed in starting because Nicholas Lawford, my Private Secretary, had to motor thirty miles and back to receive an important
message. This turned out to be from Mr. Churchill, would we
lunch or dine. Evidently the beauties of the scenery and the teem-
ing trout were not absorbing him sufficiently. We spent the day
happily fishing. Next morning at seven o'clock Lawford was again
sent for to receive yet another message from Mr. Churchill, would
I join him and the Chiefs of Staff for dinner on his side of the
mountain. This involved returning to Quebec and then driving
by another road to the Prime Minister's camp. I gave in and made
the journey to the Lake of the Snows.

August 26th: Charles Wilson [the Prime Minister's doctor]
came in. He spoke to me apart about W. He is worried, says
that he appears to be unduly depressed by troubles that are not
immediate and to be unable to shake them off.

When W. arrived I admit that he confirmed C.W.'s diagnosis.
He did not look at all well and was a bad colour. He said to me
that he felt the need for a longer change. I urged him to take it.
[This he did.]

He said it had been absolutely right to bring me out, fussed
about the party in our Clipper. "I don't know what I should do

if I lost you all. I'd have to cut my throat. It isn't just love,
though there is much of that in it, but that you are my war
machine. Brookie [Sir Alan Brooke], Portal, you and Dickie
[Mountbatten]. I simply couldn't replace you."

Then we had talk on politics. All this while W. was splashing
about in his bath, most of the time by the light of one candle,
the lights having fused.

★   ★   ★   ★   ★

The Russian Ambassador, Mr. Maisky, came back to London at
the end of August to pack up before returning to Moscow to become Deputy Commissar for Foreign Affairs. I had several talks
with him before he left, when he described to me the situation he
had found in Moscow. Russian casualties had been enormous and
the destruction appalling. We were thought not to share the Soviet
desire to finish the war as soon as possible, while American material aid was more in evidence than ours. I replied that the Russians spoke as though the air factor were of no account. They had
told us that there were only three hundred German fighters on
the Russian front; moreover to knock Italy out of the war was not
an unimportant contribution.

Maisky was interested in possible operations in the Balkans. I
told him that we should co-ordinate our policies in those countries
and that we might talk at the Conference about what could be
planned. Maisky appeared to like this idea. He said his Government attached importance to the Conference reaching conclusions
on military and on political questions, immediate and post-war. I
replied that military matters were hardly for Foreign Secretaries
who at the most would be accompanied by military representatives,
but accepted that we ought to reach conclusions about the political
pattern.

Maisky then said that after the war we could each have a sphere
of influence in Europe, the Soviet Union in the east and Britain
and America in the west. He did not think this a good plan, but
by means of it we could exclude the Russians from French affairs
and the Mediterranean and they would claim the same freedom in
the east. If, however, as the Soviet Government would prefer, we

could all accept that Europe was one, then we must admit each other's rights to an interest in all parts of the Continent. There was no dispute, I said, that we preferred the second choice and our Conference might find a form of words to express our will.

★　★　★　★　★

Much of September was spent in arguing where the Conference was to be held. Mr. Churchill and I strongly pressed the claims of London. The Russians, as usual, were reluctant to leave their own soil, even though Stalin was not going to take part. The arrangements were further complicated by doubts as to who would be the American representative. Telegrams flowed between London and Washington, where the Prime Minister stayed on till the middle of the month, and between Washington and Moscow.

September 10th: Felt depressed and not very well all day, partly, I think, because of exasperating difficulty of trying to do business with Winston over the Atlantic. Two telephone calls during the day. Roosevelt has had his way again and agreed to Moscow for the Foreign Secretaries' conference with alacrity. His determination not to agree to a London meeting for any purpose, which he says is for electoral reasons, is almost insulting considering the number of times we have been to Washington. I am most anxious for good relations with U.S. but I don't like subservience to them and I am sure that this only lays up trouble for us in the future. We are giving the impression, which they are only too ready by nature to endorse, that militarily all the achievements are theirs and W., by prolonging his stay in Washington, strengthens that impression.

A fortnight later Mr. Hull had decided to attend the Conference himself, despite his age and his dislike of travelling.

September 26th: Heard that F.D.R. had suggested to Joe [Stalin] that Hull should attend meeting and that it should be held in England. Good; but it is what I proposed six weeks ago and F.D.R. and Hull turned down. I suppose that they have been unable to find suitable man to represent them in Moscow.

But Stalin still insisted on Moscow, and eventually Hull agreed to go so far. The Conference was fixed to begin there in the middle of October.

10

A RUSSIAN FORTNIGHT
October–November 1943

Service discussions in Cairo — General Montgomery to breakfast — *Nul et non avenu* — The Foreign Secretaries' Conference in Moscow — I ask to see Marshal Stalin — He criticizes British sailors — The Conference bogs down — I see the Marshal again — Mr. Molotov gives a hint about Japan — A meeting with the Turks in Cairo — The Middle East Defence Committee

ON THE EVENING of October 11th, 1943, I arrived in Cairo on my way to Moscow. General Ismay and Mr. William Strang, Assistant Under-Secretary in the Foreign Office, were with me. I had hoped that Mr. Cordell Hull would join me in Cairo so that we could fly on together, but he was delayed. While waiting for him I had four days of consultations on political and military problems.

October 12th: Hot by our standards. A swim and sunbathe by myself in early morning after a stuffy night of rather indifferent sleep. Found that Winston had been trying to reach me on the telephone. He did actually reach me during the conference but line was difficult and little more than "It's good to hear your voice."

Had meeting at 10.30 a.m. with First Sea Lord [Sir Andrew Cunningham] who had been sent on from Tunis by Winston, Jumbo [Gen. Wilson], Airchief [Air Chief Marshal Sir Sholto Douglas, Air Officer Commanding-in-Chief, Middle East] and other Cunningham's [Admiral Sir John Cunningham, Commander-in-Chief, Levant] representative. A thorough examination of our problems followed and an agreed telegram to Winston [about operations in the Aegean] was despatched in the evening. I did not much enjoy presiding over this gathering, because

I don't like butting in on other people's jobs in their own theatre. However, they were all very friendly about it. This was followed by dissertation by S.O.E. [Special Operations Executive] on their problems, all of which gave me scant comfort about our future. In fact I became increasingly depressed. Large crowd of G.H.Q. personnel in street when I came out who were cheerfully enthusiastic and clapped vigorously, which somehow seemed strange for soldiers.

Another meeting at Embassy with First Sea Lord and Pug [Ismay] about military mission with Badoglio. Then home to [Mr. R. G.] Casey's [Minister of State, Middle East] for a swim, after which series of meetings with Rex Leeper [Ambassador to Greece in Cairo] and Ralph Stevenson [Ambassador to Yugoslavia in Cairo] about their problems. Those of the former are particularly hideous.

The King of the Hellenes had been our loyal friend, but his return to Greece was not unchallenged. The Government established in Cairo were torn by disagreements and had little authority, while comparable rivalries split the two main resistance movements. We had been supporting both with arms and money and trying to make them form a common front, but on October 8th E.L.A.S., the People's National Liberation Army, expecting an Allied invasion of the Balkans, launched a strong attack on E.D.E.S., the National Democratic Greek Army, with the evident intention of being in sole control of the country when the Allies arrived. Such was the situation when I reached Cairo.

October 13th: Spent a day with Jumbo with the troops, enjoyed morning very much. Yorkshire Hussars, 4th Hussars, Staffordshire Yeomanry, 7th Rifle Brigade, Nottinghamshire Yeomanry. All in good heart and it was good to see them. Found several old friends. Some talk with Jumbo between units. We spoke of old campaigns. He was still rocklike that we were right militarily to go to Greece [in 1941]. He maintained that the few tanks that went there would have made no difference to Libyan campaign. Apart from other considerations, their tracks were so bad that their radius was limited for enclosed country, negligible for desert. Jumbo asked 4th Hussars officers about this and they backed him. But he maintained that Military Mission over-estimated value of Greek Army and that the only change he would make if he had to take decision again would be to travel lighter. . . .

October 14th: Day of heavy engagements beginning with King of Greece. Meeting of Defence Committee.

October 15th: [M. Emmanuel] Tsouderos [Greek Prime Minister] arrived at 11 a.m. and we went thoroughly through all Greek questions again.

I told M. Tsouderos of a suggestion I had made to the Middle East Defence Committee in Cairo that we should build up in Athens an authority under the Archbishop, Damaskinos, which could represent the Greek Government when the Germans withdrew.

October 16th: Monty [Gen. Montgomery] joined me at breakfast and we had a talk. He wanted to know about future commands, but I told him I wasn't free to tell him. He was clearly very keen for No. 2 in "Overlord" to Marshall and expressed confidence in its feasibility. He said that there had been deterioration in German command, not in troops. Kesselring was poor compared with Rommel. ["Overlord" was the Anglo–American landing in France fixed for 1944.]

Left Cairo West soon after 8 a.m. Easy flight to Habbaniya where the heat seemed intense after flying at 10,000 feet. Lunch with R.A.F. A few words to men on aerodrome and then into the plane which had been standing in the midday sun and was hotter than any Turkish bath. We dripped inside and then rose to 15,000 or higher when we needed overcoats. These changes of temperature are an unpleasant strain. Sat beside the pilot as we flew over the Persian mountains. Reached Tehran about 4.30 p.m., rather exhausted.

October 17th: Some news of Hull at last. He reaches Tehran today. Called on Shah in fantastic modern palace built by his father. The marble is itself beautiful in colour and superb in quality, but the whole thing has an over-glittering effect despite cypress and sunshine. Shah himself was an intelligent and agreeable young man who chats away fluently in excellent French. He seemed to have a clear enough understanding of his country's troubles which are indeed grievous and chiefly due to corruption and selfishness, especially in the Majlis.

Then to Gulhek where lunched with the Holmans [Mr. Adrian Holman was Counsellor at the British Legation in Tehran and came on to Moscow with me]. A lovely summer Legation. Lunch was in a very fine modern Persian tent which has belonged to our Consul at Shiraz, with flowers and fountain playing and goldfish swimming while we drank vodka and pomegranate juice. Altogether very Persian and enjoyable. . . .

On to call on Hull, etc. at United States Legation. The old boy was in quite good spirits considering his ordeal. Useful talk.

★   ★   ★   ★   ★

On arrival in Tehran I received a telegram from the Prime Minister about the Arctic convoys to Russia. On October 1st, in response to a Russian request for their resumption, Mr. Churchill had informed Stalin that we planned to send four convoys to North Russia between November and February. He had, however, given a warning that this was not a contract to be fulfilled whatever the circumstances, and had also set out a list of complaints about the difficulties made by the Russians over the treatment of our sailors and arrangements for their relief. After nearly a fortnight Stalin sent an offensive reply. On October 18th the Prime Minister saw the new Soviet Ambassador in London, Mr. Feodor Gusev, and handed Stalin's message back to him, using the correct diplomatic phrase for that action.

Once or twice in conversation over the years, Mr. Churchill had asked me whether I had ever used the expression *nul et non avenu* in handing back a document from a foreign embassy. I said, never. On this occasion the message should not have been sent, so the words were apt, though their significance was no doubt lost on Mr. Gusev, who had little English and no French. However, the Ambassador understood quite enough to know that he was outside the door with the peccant document back in his pocket, as I was soon to learn in Moscow.

October 18th: Took the air at 8 a.m. for Moscow. Good and uneventful flight. Fine view of tops of Caucasus above the clouds and of Volga, a few miles east of Stalingrad. But the country generally appears flat, treeless and monotonous from the air until near Moscow, when the forests and country roads are just such as to recall a country squire driving home in the pages of a Russian novel.

Usual greetings on arrival. Molotov very affable. First meeting at my suggestion this evening. I want to get on as fast as I can. We discussed publicity and other minor matters quite pleasantly.

The three Governments had agreed an agenda and each protagonist had one subject to which he attached particular importance. The Russians were concerned for a second front in Europe in the spring of 1944. The subject nearest to Hull's heart was a Four-Power Declaration on war aims and an international organization to keep the peace. My purpose was to get agreement to set up machinery for consultation between the Allies on European questions connected with the war, for they were crowding in upon us. All these major objectives were realized.

I wanted also to discuss a number of European problems with Molotov and to establish, if we could, a common policy in the Balkans. Hull, with his long interest in trade policy, wanted to consider economic questions. Molotov wanted to secure a Russian voice in the affairs of Italy. On these topics we made uneven progress. The Conference also agreed to re-establish a free and independent Austria.

"Measures to shorten the war" had been put at the top of the agenda and Molotov unmasked his batteries at once. He asked for immediate action to ensure the Anglo–American invasion of northern France and inquired whether the spring of 1944 was still the date. He also proposed optimistically that the three powers should invite Turkey to enter the war immediately and that Sweden should be approached to provide air bases.

We were soon in physical trouble. At our first formal meeting, on October 19th, the room was reasonably warm, but Mr. Hull liked to work in a temperature of about ninety degrees and he sent for his overcoat. The Russians, being ever polite hosts, responded, and at the next meeting the heat was such that I thought I would faint. Happily the three Powers were able to agree on a compromise temperature.

Marshal Voroshilov and Major-General Gryzlov attended with Molotov and the Soviets did not conceal their suspicions as they pushed and probed our intentions. General Ismay and his American colleague, Major-General John Deane, were, however, a match for them. With exemplary patience they answered every question and explained every detail of complicated cross-Channel operations, with which the Russians, being land animals, were unfamiliar. After exhaustive sessions they were, I thought, convinced that we meant to launch "Overlord" as soon as we could in 1944, which was a diplomatic triumph for Ismay and his colleague.

The Conference then discussed Turkey. I agreed that Turkey's entry into the war was desirable, the only question was timing. Britain had, I said, made it clear to the Turkish Government that the war material we were supplying to them was intended for use against Germany. If, however, we asked them to enter the war now, they would call for the forces which we were pledged to send if Germany were to attack, and these no longer existed in the eastern Mediterranean. Moreover, now that we had airfields in Italy, we did not need Turkish bases from which to bomb the Roumanian oilfields. On balance it seemed, therefore, that Turkey as an active ally might be more of a liability than an asset.

Of Sweden, I said opinion in that country would be much affected by the Russian attitude to Finland. If the Soviet Government would indicate their intentions about Finnish independence, Sweden might be reassured. Sweden would ask for air protection and this technical aspect would have to be studied. Molotov refused to be drawn about Finland and Hull declined to comment on any military matters.

October 20th and 21st: Weather still fine and sunny. A walk round ill-kept garden is only exercise possible. My appearances in Moscow streets are made in a bullet-proof motor car, the inside of which is heavily scented. The window can only be opened with difficulty but I have at last found a way.

The food here is good, though there is rather too much of it by our standards. There never was a country where two standards of living were more plainly marked, the official and the rest. Perhaps I should add a third, the army. Our Russian hosts certainly look better in health than they did two years ago; that is to say people like Stalin and Molotov. The people in the streets show little change, the impression of drab dreariness persists.

On October 19th I had told Mr. Molotov that I thought I should see Marshal Stalin, so that I could put to him the War Cabinet's position on the convoys. Molotov said that he would try to arrange a meeting. He added that his Government greatly valued the convoys and had sadly missed them when they were suspended.

Even so, the opening of the meeting with Stalin on the evening of October 21st was, as my diary records, "sticky." After some preliminaries the Marshal said:

> The Prime Minister is offended and will not accept my reply. I understand that Mr. Churchill does not want to correspond further with me. Well, let it be so.

He spoke glumly, as if we did not want to fight the war as Allies. I replied that this was not our position and never had been. The Prime Minister had, however, resented the tone and content of Stalin's message of October 13th about the convoys, justifiably, as I thought. That was why he had returned it to the Ambassador. He had, however, instructed me to discuss the position with Marshal Stalin and that, if he wished, I was ready to do.

This relaxed the atmosphere and we began to do business, Stalin showing a readiness to get to grips with my account of the major naval operation which every convoy entailed and of the continuing struggle of the anti-U-boat warfare. I had most difficulty over my proposal to increase the number of men we should need on shore.

Then came a comment which I found inexplicable, but which Stalin appeared sincerely to believe. He said that if only our sailors in North Russia had treated the Russians as equals the difficulties would not have arisen. If we would do so now we could have as many men as we liked.

I showed my astonishment. Our sailors, I said, were the last people in the world to look down on others. The real difficulty, which I did not mention, probably was that the Russians had shut off our sailors from contact with their own people. After more talk, I promised to give Molotov a list of our needs next day and see what we could agree.

Stalin then gave me details of the situation at the Russian front and spoke of Turkey, Sweden and Bulgaria. On his own front, the Marshal said, German resources were now limited and, while the weather permitted, the Russians would have to continue operations so as not to allow the enemy to recover. He admitted that the Anglo–American campaign in Italy had helped the Soviet Union; the Germans no longer moved fresh reserves to the Soviet front.

Hitler had made a great mistake at Stalingrad. All conquerors perished when they could not apportion their aims to their capacity. Hitler was an able man but not profound, only superficial. He could not estimate the military situation. He was greedy and thought too much of prestige.

That night I wrote in my diary of Stalin:

October 21st: He, of course, understands to the full our contribution to the war; it is a danger to the future that his people don't and now the Americans are making claims to a share in the bomber offensive which is by no means justified, but further dims our glory. Joe was friendly enough to me personally, even jovial. But he still has that disconcerting habit of not looking at one as he speaks or shakes hands. A meeting with him would be in all respects a creepy, even a sinister experience if it weren't for his readiness to laugh, when his whole face creases and his little eyes open. He looks more and more like bruin.

Archie [Clark Kerr] was very pleased with the talk.

After a discussion with Molotov the next morning I telegraphed to the Prime Minister:

My talk with Molotov went well. He agreed to granting of visas for fresh men we need and for reliefs, and to meet us on other minor matters connected with convoys. Visas will be given on their arrival in North Russia.

Destroyers may therefore sail at once.

★   ★   ★   ★   ★

At the Conference meeting of October 23rd, I spoke of Yugoslavia. I said that for some time we had had representatives with both the royalist and the partisan guerrilla movements. I hoped that as a result of the Conference the two movements could be advised to avoid conflict with each other. Mr. Molotov had no immediate comment to make and Mr. Hull did not support me. I decided to raise the question again with Molotov later.

Next morning I sent the Prime Minister a progress report:

> You may like general indication of how we are getting on and of our plans.
>
> We are making fair progress though we have yet to tackle the most contentious issues, e.g. Poland and Yugoslavia. I hope that at least there will emerge from this Conference machinery for the better ordering of our work henceforth. In particular there is a good prospect that we shall obtain agreement to set up commission in London. If we can get this then the Conference will have justified itself. We may also get agreement on American Four-Power Declaration and make progress on a number of minor issues. . . .
>
> But the work is heavy and not very rapid, language difficulty causing inevitable delay. There is also much drafting to be done. . . .

The Conference had now been going about a week and was churning along ever more slowly, until I began to wonder whether anything would be finally settled. During one of our adjournments, at which the Russians provided refreshments and opportunities for talk, Hull asked me to join him at a table in the corner. He was unhappy and began to gesticulate with his pince-nez. We were getting nowhere, he said, and were being strung along. What were we to do about it and had I any suggestions.

I said I shared his sentiments and I might have an opportunity to talk with Stalin within the next day or two about the Italian campaign, on the Prime Minister's instructions. If Mr. Hull would give me authority, I would use this occasion for a talk with Stalin, with or without Molotov, and tell him what our feelings were. Hull agreed at once and so after our meeting I told Molotov that I would need to see Marshal Stalin again. He did not seem pleased, but said that he would let me know what could be done.

The next evening, October 27th, I was summoned and went with Clark Kerr and General Ismay on our mission to discuss the battle in Italy and its possible effects on "Overlord." Stalin showed reasonableness even when I could give him no undertaking that a postponement of "Overlord" could be avoided. During an interval in the proceedings I told Stalin of my conversation with Hull. He said: "What do you want?" I replied: "Decisions on the subjects we have been discussing for more than a week." Stalin nodded and said he would talk to Molotov.

I became hopeful, but the next two days were as abortive as their predecessors and when we had finished I had to tell Hull that evidently I had failed. However, on the afternoon of October 30th the atmosphere appeared suddenly to change. Molotov became brisk and business-like, he was always a superb workman, as skilful at disentangling as at stalling. In an hour or two we had reached conclusions on all the ten days' discussions.

During this visit to Moscow, Hull and I had been charged with arranging a meeting of the three heads of Governments. Stalin did not want to leave Russia and Molotov told me that his presence was indispensable to the conduct of the fighting on the Russian front. I was rather sceptical about this, but it was probably true. For instance, on the evening when we were discussing convoys, Stalin was called to the telephone in the room where we were talking, a very rare occurrence. Our excellent interpreter, Major Birse, told me afterwards that from Stalin's end of the conversation he was giving a decision about targets to bombard in the Crimea.

That same evening, Stalin took me to one side and spoke about

Molotov. If he himself could not go to a conference outside Russia, that, he said, would not be so grave a matter, because Molotov had his full confidence; it would be as if he were there himself. I said that I was sorry, but this would not do, the other two heads of Governments could not make long journeys except to meet him. Reluctantly he assented, but I was impressed by Stalin's opinion of Molotov. They were a formidable pair.

But there was one ominous void in our discussions. In recent months the Soviet armies had advanced some two hundred miles on the central and southern sectors of the front. Once they were into Poland, our negotiating power, slender as it was anyway, would amount to very little. With this in mind I had two talks with Mr. Hull, but I found him most unwilling to make any move. He argued that he had no instructions about Poland and that he could not go beyond his authority. This seemed to me unnecessarily reserved, because I was not suggesting detailed discussion about frontiers. The Polish Government had told me they were not ready for this, only that we should show keen concern for Poland's future. But I was unable to shake Mr. Hull.

Nevertheless, I decided to raise the subject on October 29th and began with a reference to the absence of diplomatic relations between Poland and the Soviet Union. I said that we were concerned because we had played no small part in bringing about the Soviet–Polish Agreement of 1941. The present position created embarrassment for us all. There was a particular problem on which the Combined Chiefs of Staff had asked for guidance. So far we and the Americans had flown in explosives in small quantities to help the resistance movement in Poland. I wanted to know if we should go further and send arms.

Molotov's reply was discouraging. He thought that arms could only be given into safe hands and he doubted if there were any safe hands in Poland. He also hinted pretty broadly that the question of Polish–Soviet relations was the concern almost exclusively of those two countries. Hull said that when two neighbours got off speaking terms, the other neighbours did not inquire what the trouble was about, but merely hoped that the two neighbours would get back to terms; which seemed a detached view of neighbourliness. I said that before I left London both the Polish Prime

Minister and Foreign Minister had seen me and assured me of their desire for good relations with the Soviet Government.

Mr. Molotov did not respond to this, though he admitted that the Polish Division was fighting heroically against the Germans on the Soviet front. I pressed on and said I hoped that other Polish divisions would soon be doing the same in Italy. Molotov attempted to contest this and pretended that General Kasimierz Sosnkowski, the Polish Commander-in-Chief, did not want them to. I replied that this was not so and that the troops would be used. It was partly our fault that they had not been in action earlier. This scrapping left a sour taste in my mouth and it was not much comfort to reflect that Molotov could always make the most of a negative.

On October 28th Mr. Cordell Hull had received his Government's views about Turkey and Sweden. On Sweden they coincided with ours. We could not afford equipment and supplies for that country, which would certainly be demanded if we tried to get bases. The Americans shared our doubts about asking Turkey to enter the war, when we had not the resources to meet the extra calls which would be made upon us. On the other hand the Prime Minister and I did not want to give a flat negative to the Soviet proposal. With Hull's agreement I went with Ismay and our Ambassador to see Molotov again on October 31st.

I proposed to the Foreign Minister that we should ask for the use of airfields in south-west Anatolia which we needed, as Ismay explained, for operations in the Aegean, and for permission for two or three merchant ships escorted by submarines to pass into the Black Sea carrying important stores for Russia. Molotov did not like this gradual approach. As I telegraphed to the Prime Minister:

> He repeated again and again that if the three Great Powers were really of the belief that Turkey should come into the war, she would have no option and he harped on the fact that although the conference had in the main gone extremely well, it had been a great disappointment to his military colleagues that not a single suggestion put forward by the Soviet Delegation for shortening war had been accepted, and further that

no alternative proposals to that end had been put forward by
either United States or ourselves.

The Conference eventually agreed that we should do our best to
get Turkey into the war in 1943, but that the first step must be to
secure the air bases which were necessary for us. Molotov showed
no enthusiasm for the idea that British submarines should enter
the Black Sea. I asked him if he would like to send a representative
to Cairo with me to meet the Turkish Foreign Minister, but he
replied that he was content to leave the matter in my hands.

Molotov had shown himself unwilling to discuss the Balkans, so
that once again with Hull's agreement, I spoke to him privately of
Yugoslavia on October 30th. We discussed General Mihailović, his
Četniks and the Partisans. I told him that we were pressing the
Četniks to take action against the Germans and asked him to advise the Partisans not to take action against the Četniks. Molotov
said that his Government had little contact with the Partisans and
would like to send a mission to them. It would be in contact with
the British Mission and might operate from British-controlled territory. I welcomed this idea, thinking it better that a Russian mission should work in contact with our own people rather than
operate on its own.

The Conference was now finished. Our labours had been ar-
duous, spread over a fortnight of almost continuous sessions. Yet
on balance this meeting, and maybe that in Tehran later, showed
the Russians more forthcoming than they were afterwards to become. It was the high tide, if not of good, at least of tolerable,
relations between us. As I telegraphed to the Prime Minister on
November 2nd:

> When I came here I had no conception of how much they
> wanted this Conference to succeed. There were of course checks
> and setbacks, but general progress was cumulative and we
> ended at the top. Our exchanges since the Conference have
> been on a still more intimate footing.

Experience was soon to show that the Soviet attitude would
harden with the growing certainty of victory. Once Russian soil

was clear of the German invader and we and the United States were committed by action to the second front in France, confidence swelled until the Soviets felt little need to listen to their allies, and none to cherish them.

Before I left, however, Mr. Molotov appeared to give me some encouragement for the immediate future. He was speaking of the far eastern war and I made a remark indicating that there might be a considerable gap in time between the collapse of the Germans and the collapse of Japan.

Molotov disagreed and said that the interval would be short. Once Germany had surrendered, even the Japanese would understand the truth of their position. I purposely expressed scepticism and maintained that the Japanese were very good fighters and capable of maintaining a tough battle on their own. Molotov repeated his conviction and was, I thought, clearly giving me a broad hint of Russia's intention to take part in the Japanese war.

★   ★   ★   ★   ★

I reached Cairo again on the evening of November 4th and immediately conferred with Mr. Casey and with our Ambassador arrived from Ankara, as well as with General Wilson and Air Chief Marshal Douglas. In a further talk next morning we agreed to ask the Turks for the use of bases to be made available for ten squadrons of the Royal Air Force, together with anti-aircraft and other army units. The whole force should arrive in Turkey in just over a month.

The Turkish delegation, whom I had invited from Moscow, arrived at midday and we began our talks at once. M. Numan Menemençoğlu, the Foreign Minister, was accompanied by his Secretary-General, M. Acikalin, and a younger Foreign Ministry official. As I telegraphed to the Prime Minister afterwards, we had a long, tough day. My persuasions were the less effective as both the Foreign Minister and Acikalin seemed to be particularly deaf, and, at one point, when I appealed to the younger official, he too seemed to have difficulty in hearing what I said. No one can be so deaf as a Turk who does not wish to be persuaded.

The strength of the Turkish position lay in their doubts about

Soviet intentions after the war. They feared the growth of Soviet power and that we and the United States would then be far away and unwilling to help them. The weakness of their position was an unfounded suspicion that there had been some deal between us and the Russians, as a result of which the Russians had abandoned their demand for a second front and we had agreed to put pressure on Turkey, which would end in her being involved in war with Germany.

It took me the best part of three days of ding-dong argument, including a final private talk with Menemençoğlu, to persuade him that there was no truth in this tale and I was not sure even then that I had succeeded. He fell back on the claim that Allied bases in Turkey could not be separated from the question of Turkey's entry into the war. He must have more reassurance that it would be in Turkey's ultimate interest to enter the war before he could consider such a step.

I argued that Turkey would obviously be in a better position with the Russians if she were to align herself with the Allies at this stage. Menemençoğlu protested the dangers; Germany, he said, was in a position to react strongly. If the Allies had a large force near at hand in the Balkans, it would be another matter. Finally the Foreign Minister volunteered that he thoroughly endorsed our policy towards Russia and said that the Moscow decisions had exceeded his expectations, but he could not promise that his Government would be prepared to discuss Turkey's entry into the war. The many hours' debate ended in a draw, which was success for the Turks.

On November 7th I attended a meeting of the Middle East Defence Committee to discuss Greece. Matters there were even worse than they had been three weeks earlier. The fighting between E.L.A.S. and E.D.E.S. continued, and E.L.A.S. had murdered a New Zealand officer, Lieutenant Hubbard. They were now openly flouting General Wilson's authority. The propaganda of E.A.M., the National Liberation Front, a political group controlling E.L.A.S., was attacking Britain as well as the Greek King and Government and General Zervas. It was agreed that we must break with E.A.M. and E.L.A.S. and try to form non-political bands in the E.L.A.S. areas. At the same time we should ask King George to declare that he would not return to Greece until the people invited him to do so. He should agree to establish a Regency Council at the time of the German withdrawal.

My conversations in Cairo convinced me that this was the right course both from our point of view and from the King's. Now that there was no question of his return as Commander-in-Chief of the Greek Army with an Allied landing, his position in the future would be stronger if he followed it. So long as E.A.M. could say that Britain intended to impose the King on the country by force, they would retain their non-Communist following, and this could not be allowed to happen.

11

CONCERN FOR POLAND
November 1943–January 1944

Polish–Russian relations — Anglo–American Conference in Cairo — Thanksgiving dinner with President Roosevelt — General Chiang Kai-shek — The Americans wish to hold the stage — The Tehran Conference — The Russian–Polish frontier problem hardens — The Turkish President in Cairo — Difficulties with the King of the Hellenes — The Partisans are headed by Marshal Tito — The Soviets closing in on Poland

I SPENT LESS than a fortnight in England between my return from the Moscow Conference on November 10th and setting off again for the Conferences in Cairo and Tehran. During these days I concentrated on the three countries which had occupied so much of my time and thoughts during my visits to Russia and the Middle East: Greece, Turkey and Poland.

The Polish Government in London were in a position of acute embarrassment through no fault of their own. The fact of being in exile weakened their authority and increased their natural reluctance to propose any concessions which would affect Poland's future.

This was soon evident when, in my first conversation with the Polish Ministers after my return, they seemed distressed that we had made no more progress with the Russians about their country's future. The Polish Ambassador repeated this criticism on November 17th, but I had to remind him that his Government had themselves asked me not to mention the frontier question in Moscow.

Count Raczynski then explained that if Poland's friends told the Government that they must accept such and such a settlement in order to safeguard the future of the country, this would be different.

He implied that any settlement must be underwritten by Britain and the United States.

After this talk I decided that the best hope was for us to work out the possible lines of a Polish–Russian settlement and take it up with the Russians. I asked the Foreign Office to draw up such a plan for me. They advised that the only possible solution to the frontier question was the Curzon line, though we should try to persuade the Russians to let Poland keep Lwow. In return, the Soviet and British Governments and, if possible, the United States Government, should give Poland a definite assurance that she would receive East Prussia, Danzig and Upper Silesia.

The paper continued that, if we were to impose a frontier settlement on the Poles, we should have to get assurances from the Russians to allay Polish fears. Diplomatic relations ought to be restored at once and the Polish Government encouraged to accede to the Soviet–Czechoslovak Treaty. There would also have to be assurances that the Government would be enabled to go back and take part in administering Poland as soon as military necessities allowed, and that elections would be held freely without outside pressure. The first draft of the paper suggested that Britain ought to join the Soviet–Czechoslovak–Polish Treaty too. I commented on this:

> This is a very able paper and I should like to take it out [to Tehran] with me. I have only one doubt as to policy. Should we join any tripartite arrangement there may be? I am reluctant to do this. It is an engagement in an area where our influence cannot be great and where militarily we should be ineffective. Our good offices I would certainly offer, but our engagement? I should not like this. . . .
>
> If this is our plan, we who go out will have to consider how to put it to the Russians.

M. Stanislaw Mikolajczyk, the Polish Prime Minister, came to see me on November 22nd. He said he understood that Poland was on the agenda for the Tehran Conference. I replied that the conference was to be a military one, but I hoped that there might be an opportunity to discuss Polish problems. All I asked was that the Polish Government should not prevent me from raising the question

if I got the chance. I would do my best, though the Polish Government should not expect too much from the Conference. There
might be some difficulty with the Americans, who seemed disposed
to put off discussing territorial questions till the end of the war;
I thought this was unwise. M. Mikolajczyk said he certainly did not
wish to dissuade me from discussing Poland. I was therefore prepared to make a new move, if I saw an opening at the Conference.

★   ★   ★   ★   ★

On November 15th we received the reply to the requests I had
put to the Turkish Foreign Minister in Cairo. It was much as I
had expected. In principle, the Turks accepted their country's entry into the war, but in practice they refused to move until the
military implications had been cleared up. They would not be
content to grant us air bases, arguing that this would inevitably
lead to war with Germany. M. Menemençoğlu told our Ambassador
that his Government wanted conversations with us alone first; if
they received a triple invitation to come into the war they would
refuse.

The Chiefs of Staff were now on their way to Cairo. I therefore
telegraphed to ask them to consider the military aspects of the
Turkish reply with their American colleagues when they arrived.
I also wrote a message for the Prime Minister, who had left for
Cairo, but then decided to take it with me rather than telegraph it.

I have been turning over in my mind what should be our
next step with the Turks, since we are committed to getting
Turkey into the war by the end of the year, and time is running short.

By the time I reach Cairo, the Chiefs of Staff should be in a
position to tell us something about the military implications
of the Turkish reply. What the Turks are after is some statement from us about our future Balkan strategy and the part
they can play in this, but even though the Chiefs of Staff may
be able to offer Turkey sufficient air squadrons and ground
defences to enable her to play a defensive role, I doubt whether
we can give the Turks much comfort on this score.

If my assumption proves correct, then our chances of leading the Turks from a vague acceptance of the principle of co-belligerency to a definite commitment of when they will come into the war are not rosy, and the prospects of conversations between the Turks and ourselves alone are pretty poor.

Nevertheless, I think we are entitled to proceed to such conversations without the fear of any criticism from the Russians. . . . If we alone cannot get what we want out of the Turks, will a tripartite approach really do the trick? . . .

★　★　★　★　★

I left London on November 23rd and arrived in Cairo next day, accompanied by Sir Alexander Cadogan. The Prime Minister and the Chiefs of Staff had already been in Cairo for three days and had begun meetings with President Roosevelt and the United States Chiefs of Staff and with General Chiang Kai-shek.

November 25th: A day with but little achieved. Motored to Mena to pick up Winston and after some preliminary talks about a number of matters we went on together to see Chiang [Kaishek]. Talk mainly military for which Dickie [Mountbatten, Supreme Allied Commander, South-East Asia] joined us. It appeared satisfactory. On to President's house where much time was spent with photography. We stood about and sat about for hours, a desperate waste of time.

Then after some gossip with Harry [Hopkins] went back to luncheon with Winston alone. Long wait before any food came. W. very kind and friendly though he accused me of looking sulky and being in bad temper. Wasn't conscious of it and think it was only lack of sleep, which I told him. Also said that we didn't seem to be getting anywhere with our work. He agreed. F.D.R. [Roosevelt] was "a charming country gentleman," but business methods were almost non-existent, so W. had to play the role of courtier and seize opportunities as and when they arose. I am amazed at patience with which he does this. W. admits that our war progress in the last two months has been below level of events. He showed me memoranda he had prepared for our Chiefs of Staff and repeated many times that during the last two months he had felt to be fighting with hands tied behind his back.

My afternoon was spent in conversations about French and Greek problems.

Dined with President. Thanksgiving. He was a charming host and party was easy and pleasant with a good regimental band to enliven and deafen us. Some desultory political talk at intervals about Greeks and Yugoslavs and Poles. I told President I thought we should take up last with Uncle Joe [Stalin]. He appeared to agree, but he is an uncertain quantity.

I was much impressed by Chiang. He is smaller and slighter than I had expected, very well made, with small and beautifully shaped hands and feet. He would be difficult to place in any category and does not look a warrior. He has a constant smile, but his eyes don't smile so readily and they fix you with a penetrating unswerving look, in marked contrast to Uncle Joe's habit of looking at one's navel. His strength is that of the steel blade.

Madame [Chiang Kai-shek] surprised me. She was friendly, a trifle queenly perhaps. Obviously used to getting her own way, but an industrious and earnest interpreter and neither sprightly nor touchy as I had been led to expect. I liked them both, Chiang particularly, and I should like to know them better.

The most troublesome question which concerned me was how to get the three Allied leaders working together upon the problems which would beset us the moment hostilities ceased. These included how to occupy and administer defeated Germany. If nothing was settled, Soviet Russia would gain, because the chances were that her troops would be the first to reach German territory. The Russians having agreed during our Moscow conference on joint examination and advice to our Governments by the European Advisory Commission in London, I was eager to get it going. After a meeting with Winant and Mr. John McCloy, United States Assistant Secretary for War, I wrote:

November 26th: Americans seem inclined to run out and I

had to use some pretty plain language about it. Winant seemed to think afterwards that this had been useful.

Later, when I returned to London I received a commentary from Lord Halifax about this apparent American lack of enthusiasm for the work which the Commission had to do. He attributed it to a wish to keep Washington as the centre of gravity for war planning, the Combined Chiefs of Staff were already established there. This was true, but we were now to deal with planning for peace and London had been accepted by their own Secretary of State, at the Moscow Conference, as the site for that work and we had to get on with it.

November 26th: French and Greek problems followed. Wang [Chung-hui, Secretary-General of the Chinese Supreme National Defence Council] came to luncheon and he and I and Alec [Cadogan] had a talk afterwards. We had to be firm about Tibet.

The Chinese wanted us to recognize their old claims upon Tibet.

In afternoon discussion with Harry [Hopkins], Wang and Alec about communiqué which was put into pretty good shape and agreed. Then tea at Chiang's, back to Embassy for a talk with Dickie [Mountbatten] about his problems. He has a "tough assignment" as the Americans say.

W. came to dinner. Small party and he was in tremendous form. Net result was 2 a.m. before bed. Much discussion about the past and my poor old resignation came up again together with 1940 and War Office experiences.

This Conference was among the most difficult I ever attended. Our fortunes in the Far East were militarily at their lowest ebb. Singapore and our whole position in South-East Asia had been lost. Australia had been endangered. The contribution which we could make towards retrieving this situation was slight, and our American allies were impressed, almost to the point of obsession, with the merits of General and Mme. Chiang Kai-shek and their Government. I sensed that even the future of Hong Kong was in question with them.

There was nothing for it but to wait and hold our end up as best we could, leaving most of the talk and the proposing to others. Though the role of attendant listener was uncongenial to him, the Prime Minister played it faultlessly all these days, so that we came through without the loss of any feathers, if not with our tails up. The Conference agreed that the territories which Japan had seized by force must be returned, and that Korea must be independent.

November 27th: Called at 5.45 a.m. Miles [Lord Killearn, Ambassador in Cairo] motored with me to aerodrome where we met Winston. Flew in York to Tehran. Pleasant and easy journey. W. had lost his voice, I think from too much talk last night, and was sorry for himself until he had a stiff whisky and soda, at 8.45 a.m. He appeared on aerodrome as Air Commodore in khaki drill and amazed me by translation into blue before we touched Tehran. His travelling wardrobe must be prodigious.

When we arrived at the airport at Tehran I was somewhat surprised to be instructed to get into a car and drive off on my own to the British Embassy where we were to stay. I asked about the Prime Minister and was formally but mysteriously told that other arrangements had been made for him.

Off I went in much state, surrounded by a cavalcade of cavalry at the trot. All went well until we reached the gates of the Embassy compound where a characteristic Persian donkey and its owner had firmly established themselves and took much shouting, gesticulation and police activity to dislodge. I had time enough to reflect that if anyone wanted to toss a bomb into the car, I was a sitting target. We swept up to the Embassy where I found an indignant Mr. Churchill, of whom I asked: "Where have you been?" He replied: "They brought me the back way." Among other things, he thought it wrong that I should be the decoy duck. These diversions were apparently the result of a security precaution of which we were soon to hear more.

November 28th: Little was achieved today. Late last night Molotov sent for Archie [Clark Kerr, Ambassador in Moscow] and

Harriman [United States Ambassador in Moscow] and said there would be a "scandal" which would mar the conference if we weren't careful. This turned out to be possible attempt on life of somebody by German agents. Consequently President must move into compound of Russians or ourselves. Most of the morning was spent over this. [He moved into the Russian Embassy.] Lunched at Embassy and Winston remained in bed so that Americans and ourselves had had no previous meeting on military affairs when conference opened. President talked of Far East and U.J. of eastern front, but future Anglo–American plans inevitably didn't go so well.

Winston and I dined with President. U.J. and Molotov and two Ambassadors made up the party. This was quite a pleasant evening, but dinner broke up early because President was not feeling well. He certainly seemed to be below par in the talk we were having at our end of the table and Harry told me he was afraid he was going to faint.

When we adjourned W. and I and U.J. and Molotov went into the next room and in a corner began some general talk. U.J. mellowed and W. eventually raised Poland. The opening moves did not go too badly. If we could get on to the business soon we might be able to hammer something out. A difficulty is that Americans are terrified of the subject which Harry called "political dynamite" for their elections. But, as I told him, if we cannot get a solution, Polish–Russian relations six months from now, with Russian armies in Poland, will be infinitely worse and the elections much nearer.

Before the party broke up there had been a spell of conversation among the six of us sitting in a circle with our coffee and cigars. The exchanges were general and for the most part about the progress of the war. After a while Churchill remarked: "I believe that God is on our side. At least I have done my best to make Him a faithful ally." Stalin looked up at the translation, grinned and added: "And the devil is on my side. Because, of course, everyone knows that the devil is a Communist and God, no doubt, is a good Conservative."

★　★　★　★　★

From my point of view as Foreign Secretary, the most important discussions of the Conference were those on Poland and on Turkey. President Roosevelt was reserved about Poland to the point of being unhelpful. He mentioned his political difficulties to us, but it was not until long afterwards that I learned he had also explained them to Stalin. He told the Marshal that for electoral reasons he could not take part in any discussion of Poland for another year, nor be publicly associated with any arrangement. This was hardly calculated to restrain the Russians.

On December 1st the Prime Minister extracted from Marshal Stalin, with Molotov present, a definition of the Russian frontier demand. It brought us no comfort. They asked for the Curzon line, with Lwow to go to the Soviet Union. Stalin also claimed Königsberg and the northern part of East Prussia, while two days earlier he had advocated moving the Polish–German frontier as far west as the Oder. Explicit in what he wanted, he was less precise about re-establishing diplomatic relations with the Polish Government and made the outrageous accusation that they were closely connected with the Germans. He said that he drew a distinction between the exiled Government and Poland. Though the Prime Minister contested his accusation of collaboration, it seemed to us that Stalin actually believed it.

One incident in the discussion on Poland was revealing of the Russian state of mind. Stalin had claimed that Soviet Russia adhered to the frontiers of 1939, because they appeared to be ethnographically the right ones. I asked if this meant the Ribbentrop–Molotov line. "Call it what you like," Marshal Stalin replied. Molotov protested that it was generally called the Curzon line, but I said no, there were differences which were important, whereupon the Prime Minister produced the map we had prepared showing both the Curzon line and the 1939 line.

At this point our meeting broke up into groups and the discussion went on for some time, Molotov countering with the Russian version of the Curzon line and a text of a wireless telegram from Lord Curzon giving all the place names. The argument made no progress and I began to have little hope that we could reach a settlement which the Poles could accept.

Stalin had changed his mind about Turkey since the Moscow Conference. He was now sure that she would not enter the war and did not seem to care. The Combined Chiefs of Staff emerged as lukewarm, because they believed that Turkey would not come in unless we committed ourselves to operations in the Aegean. As this would mean delay for "Overlord," which none of us wanted, Stalin now opposed putting pressure on Turkey, though he thought we should go on asking for the air bases.

My feelings at the close of the Conference were less easy than they had been in Moscow. I found the sudden shifts in Stalin's policies disturbing and could not fathom the apparent American unwillingness to make ready with us for the Conference in advance. Above all, I began to fear greatly for the Poles.

★   ★   ★   ★   ★

We arrived back in Cairo on December 2nd. President Ismet Inönü and his advisers came to meet us two days later. The result of our talks with them should have surprised no one. Fear of Russia was not mentioned again; instead the Turks based their reluctance on their country's military unpreparedness, which was genuine. The total result of three days of argument was that the Turks agreed to preparations being made for air bases to be ready for us by February 15th, 1944. In the interval, supplies to Turkey would continue, British specialists in civilian clothes would be infiltrated and military talks would be held. On February 15th the Allies were to ask permission to send aircraft into the bases. Thus the final Turkish decision was postponed for another two months.

The Turkish party left Cairo at midday on December 7th. The Prime Minister and I went to see them off. On the airfield President Inönü embraced Mr. Churchill in farewell. This attention delighted the Prime Minister, who said as we drove back into Cairo: "Did you see, Ismet kissed me." My reply, perhaps rather ungracious, was that as this seemed to be the only gain from fifteen hours of hard argument, it was not much to be pleased with. Mr. Churchill said no more to me, but that night, when he went to bed he remarked to his daughter Sarah: "Do you know what happened to me today, the Turkish President kissed me. The truth is I'm irresistible. But don't tell Anthony, he's jealous."

One day the Prime Minister came into the Embassy to meet Nahas Pasha at luncheon. Despite some failings, the Egyptian

Prime Minister had stood loyally by the Treaty which he had taken a lead in negotiating with me in 1936. He had proved himself a stalwart friend when troubles and dangers had thickened around us. One of his foibles, not unknown in politicians of other lands, was a conviction that he had never acted in error, nor, he explained to us solemnly, even once in contradiction to the dictates of his conscience. Mr. Churchill looked at him for a moment with an expression in which incredulity and humour were mingled and replied: *"Moi, j'ai toujours traité ma conscience en bon camarade."*

★ ★ ★ ★ ★

On November 22nd the War Cabinet had approved the new policy for Greece which I had worked out in Cairo on my previous visit. They had agreed that the Prime Minister and I should set it going. However, our plan now received an unexpected setback at the hands of President Roosevelt, of all people.

I saw the King of the Hellenes in Cairo on December 3rd and put to him the arguments in favour of a declaration that he would not return to Greece until asked to do so by the Greek people. I recommended that King George should consider asking Archbishop Damaskinos to head a Regency Committee in Athens when the Germans withdrew. I hated having to give this message, but I was sure it was in the King's own interest that he should act in this way. He listened to me quietly but made little comment and I thought it probable that, after reflection and taking counsel, he would follow the course I had suggested.

The next day his Prime Minister, M. Tsouderos, and the American Ambassador, Mr. Lincoln MacVeagh, both urged him to accept my advice. On December 6th the King called on President Roosevelt. The President told him that the war was not nearly over yet and that it would be a great mistake for him to make the proposed declaration. This intervention was the more irresponsible because I had spoken some days before with Winant and Harry Hopkins, who had agreed with me, and I knew that the State Department also approved our policy.

I feared the worst when I went round to the final meeting with the President. We had quite a wait and Harry Hopkins came up to me saying: "You know what's going on in there? The King of Greece is with the President." He added that my policy was not going well. When the President emerged, he was cold towards me and complained of the way I had been treating the King. I replied that the action I had taken was, I felt sure, in the King's own interest and that if my advice was not followed he would soon be without Ministers. I pointed out that I had kept the United States Government informed at every stage.

The President said no more for the moment but he did not appear mollified. The next morning, on his drive to the airport with the Prime Minister, he complained bitterly to Mr. Churchill of my conduct. He said that I was trying to deprive the King of his crown and that I had no right to do this. The Prime Minister argued back, but admitted to me afterwards that the President had been much wrought up on the subject.

On December 7th, King George came to luncheon with Mr. Churchill and myself at the British Embassy, when we reproached him for what he had said to the President. The King, however, was not to be persuaded that he had done wrong. Eventually he did agree to add to a letter which he had written to M. Tsouderos a phrase to the effect that he would reconsider the date of his return to Greece with the Government at the time of liberation.

Winant was as much upset at this turn of events as I was. I suspect that he shared in the Presidential reproof. Certainly he continued to uphold our policy. I disliked the whole affair very much, for I had the greatest regard, indeed affection, for the King and I knew that he had complained to Field-Marshal Smuts that the British now wanted to be rid of him. It seemed to me doubtful whether anything Mr. Churchill and I had said would convince him that this was not true. In the final resort the King did take our advice, but I am not sure that our friendship and confidence were ever entirely restored.

★   ★   ★   ★   ★

Yugoslav affairs were reaching a new complexity. In discussions in Cairo with Stevenson, General Wilson and Brigadier Fitzroy Maclean, head of our Military Mission to Tito, I heard of reports that Mihailović was unco-operative and was told of evidence that some, at least, of his subordinates were working with the Germans and their puppets. I was unhappy about this and it was decided by the Prime Minister, Wilson and myself that Mihailović should be asked to carry out an operation so that we might further test his intentions. General Wilson therefore sent a message to Mihailović on December 8th asking him to attack two specified bridges on the Belgrade to Salonika railway, which, in the event, he was never able to do.

King Peter and his Government had been warned several times of our difficulty in continuing to support Mihailović while he was being inactive. On December 10th, after I had left Cairo, Mr. Churchill saw the King and his Prime Minister, M. Purić. He told them that in the near future the British Government might suggest that General Mihailović should be dismissed, and that they might decide to withdraw support from the Četniks.

While these exchanges were going on, we learned that on November 29th the Partisans had set up a Council of National Liberation with an Executive Committee headed by Tito, who was now a self-styled Marshal. Then, on December 17th, came a Partisan radio broadcast demanding recognition for the Council and attacking both the Yugoslav Government and King Peter. This made me increasingly reluctant to advise the King to dismiss General Mihailović and risk alienating his only supporters in the country. As I telegraphed to the Prime Minister on December 20th: "The moment seems to have come when we ought ourselves to make a direct proposal to Tito in order to bring matters to a head."

The difficulty of deciding upon the terms of this proposal was not eased by the fact that Mr. Churchill was now ill in Tunisia, Mr. Stevenson and Brigadier Maclean were in Cairo, and I was in London. A lengthy triangular exchange of telegrams followed. At one stage I suggested that King Peter might go to Partisan headquarters, but Stevenson and Maclean replied that this would be impracticable. On December 23rd I suggested that the Prime Minister might have a meeting with Tito to try to bring him to a better frame of mind. There might even be a meeting between him and the King in the presence of the Prime Minister.

Stevenson replied that he and Maclean thought it unwise to

bring up the issue of the monarchy at all with the Partisans, who were unalterably opposed to the King. The Ambassador cited, amongst other reasons, the military need which must prevail over political considerations. I was reluctant to give up any attempt to bring the King and the Partisans together, even though the chances of success were small. Accordingly, Maclean was instructed to ask Tito to refrain from further polemics and tell him that for the sake both of Yugoslavia and of the common war effort, relations ought to be established between the Partisans and the King.

Meanwhile a note brought to me by Mr. Gusev on December 20th gave hope that the Russians would exert their influence on Tito. The note said the Soviet Government agreed with us that the Partisans and the King and Government ought to work together. They were ready to do everything possible to find a compromise between the two sides. I told Mr. Gusev that his Government could help by telling Tito to stop polemical pronouncements. The Ambassador said he thought they might well favour this, but he did not know how much influence they had with Tito nor how good their means of communication were. I replied that I understood the Soviet Government were in wireless communication with Tito.

This, of course, was true. Since early in 1942, Tito had been in wireless contact with Moscow and had been asking for material help. All he received were exhortations such as: "Achieve a true united national front of all enemies of Hitler and Mussolini in Yugoslavia, in order to attain the common aim, the expulsion of the invaders and would-be conquerors." * The Soviet Government were informed in advance of the Partisans' intention to set up a National Committee on November 29th, but not of the declaration attacking the King and Government. This independent action, without waiting for approval, infuriated Stalin who saw it as a "stab in the back for the Soviet Union and for the Tehran decisions." † Not knowing all this at the time, we supposed that Moscow had great influence over Tito.

When the Prime Minister was ill, Tito sent him a message of good wishes. The terms of Mr. Churchill's reply became the subject

* Moša Pijade: *About the Legend that the Yugoslav Uprising owed its Existence to Soviet Assistance.*
† Vladimir Dedijer quoted in Fitzroy Maclean: *Disputed Barricade.*

of some correspondence between us. I telegraphed to him on
January 1st:

> I am doubtful whether we should tell Tito now that we are
> prepared to have no further dealings with Mihailović. First,
> because we here, at any rate, have not yet got conclusive evi-
> dence of his misbehaviour, and secondly because tactically it
> would seem better to keep this up our sleeve as a concession
> to Tito if he is prepared to discuss working with the King at
> all. . . .

And again on January 1st, after repeating a suggestion that King
Peter should go to Yugoslavia:

> As regards Mihailović, I do not recollect any decision in
> Cairo to demand his dismissal before the end of the year.
> Maybe this was after I left. I still feel that it would be a
> mistake to promise Tito at this moment that we will break
> the man, not merely by depriving him of supplies, but by
> forcing the King to dismiss him.
>
> First, I think Tito would look upon it as a sign of weakness
> on our part to volunteer this promise to him.
>
> Secondly, we are by no means sure that we could force the
> King to dismiss Mihailović unless we had something concrete
> to offer him in the way of collaboration with Tito; otherwise
> the King would say that we were asking him to deprive himself
> of the last and only link which he had with his country.
> Thirdly, if we have a public and spectacular breach with
> Mihailović, our case against him for treachery must be un-
> answerable. I am still without evidence of this. . . . I hope
> therefore that we may keep the Mihailović issue open a little
> longer until we have got our proofs. . . .

Mr. Churchill agreed to modify the references to Mihailović in
his letter to Tito, but decided not to include my proposal about
King Peter going to Yugoslavia. He gave Maclean discretion when
to raise the subject in discussion with Tito.

★　　★　　★　　★　　★

Count Raczynski called on me on December 17th, a week after my return from Cairo and as the Soviet armies were approaching the Russo–Polish frontier. I told him that from our discussions with Stalin, it was clear that there were two aspects of the Polish–Russian problem. The resumption of relations was one and the future status of Poland, with her frontiers, was another. I mentioned Stalin's complaints that the Government had instructed Poles in Poland not to co-operate with the Russian partisans and his accusation of collaboration with the Germans.

The Ambassador explained that owing to severe German reprisals, the Poles had recently restricted themselves to action against the most prominent and criminal Germans. On the other hand, the Russians had been dropping agents all over Poland, who by their activities brought down reprisals on the population. It was inevitable that there should be some feeling against them. There was also the danger that Russian agents might penetrate the Polish underground organization and break it up when the Soviet armies arrived. Count Raczynski said he was sure his Government would be able to draw up a declaration refuting Stalin's allegations and proposing co-operation. I said that I thought this the right course. Count Raczynski then asked about frontiers and I gave him a general indication of what Stalin had said.

When M. Mikolajczyk, with M. Tadeusz Romer, the Polish Foreign Minister, and Count Raczynski, came to see me on December 20th I asked whether he could give me a statement that there was no contact between Poles and Germans and vouch for the Poles' readiness to discuss with the Russians their plan of campaign against the Germans. This I thought necessary in order to escape the dangers of a false position. On the frontier question I told M. Mikolajczyk that I knew Mr. Churchill thought there was a basis for agreement and was most anxious to bring it about.

On December 22nd I again repeated all this to M. Mikolajczyk and then telegraphed to the Prime Minister:

> Mikolajczyk explained that all his communications from inside Poland showed his people were expecting Poland, as a reward for Polish suffering and fighting, to emerge from this war with [the] victors, her eastern provinces intact and her western provinces increased.

Mikolajczyk was not comforted

by the offer of large areas of German territory which he fears a weakened Poland would have difficulty in digesting. But nonetheless we are pegging away and I do not despair.

I was surprised a few days later to learn that Mr. Zinchenko, a member of the Soviet Embassy staff, had said that he thought his Government would welcome a suggestion from the Poles for direct negotiations. I minuted on this on December 28th.

Our chief desire is to do our best for the Poles. If they were likely to fare better with the Russians in direct negotiations I should not wish to stand in the way. If Polish–Russian relations were to become like Czech–Russian relations, why should we worry? But assuredly I do not want to throw the poor Poles to the Russian wolves. That was never in my thought, even though my power to help them may be limited. I am nonetheless intrigued by Mr. Zinchenko's remarks. Russians don't speak like that as a rule without instructions, and it is conceivable that Russians would offer Poles better terms direct than through us.

We received one or two other hints that the Soviet Government would like to deal directly with the Poles. Dr. Eduard Beneš, the Czechoslovak President, went to Moscow in December to sign his treaty with the Russians. When he came back he conveyed the same impression.

On January 5th the Polish Government published a statement on the lines I had suggested. It proclaimed the unequalled Polish record of resistance to the Germans, reaffirmed the instructions already given to the underground forces and offered co-operation with the Soviet military authorities. I told Mr. Churchill:

The result was, I think, fair and we did our best to get it a favourable press but we were not wholly successful. The truth is that in the present atmosphere of overwhelming Russian victories there is public impatience with the Poles. This may not be just but it is the truth.

I also saw Gusev last night and asked him to do what he could to ensure that the Russian reaction to the Polish statement was as favourable as possible, but I am not optimistic about this. . . .

My optimism was not increased by a passage in a message from Stalin to Churchill on January 7th:

I feel bound to say, inasmuch as you have touched on this subject, that if one is to judge by the last declaration of the Polish emigrant Government and by other expressions of Polish representatives, then, as is apparent, there is no foundation for reckoning on the possibility of bringing these circles to reason. These people are incorrigible.

The Soviet reply to the Polish statement, when it was published on January 11th, was not unreasonable, however, except for the repetition of an attack on the Polish Government. After a day or two of discussion with M. Mikolajczyk and his colleagues, and some persuasion, the Poles put out a further announcement, which repeated their desire for an agreement with the Soviet Union "on terms which would be just and acceptable to both sides." The Polish Government, they declared, was therefore ready to discuss with the Soviet Government, with British and American participation, "all outstanding questions, the settlement of which should lead to friendly and permanent co-operation between Poland and the Soviet Union."

Naturally I pressed this offer on Mr. Gusev, to whom I showed it on January 14th, before publication. I told him that the Polish Ministers authorized me to say that "all outstanding questions" included frontiers. The Polish Government, I went on, had had a very difficult time in making this decision. They could not be expected to accept the Curzon line before negotiations started, but the answer represented a real effort to reach a settlement. I asked Gusev to tell his Government that they should not reject this offer, which I knew was sincerely meant and which at last offered a chance of negotiations leading to a settlement of differences which were acutely embarrassing to us all.

January 15th: Papers have given Polish declaration a warm welcome. This may have some effect on Russians, though I am not optimistic.

The final word in this exchange of public statements came with the Russian reply published on January 17th. It rejected negotiations, on the ground that the Polish Government had not accepted the Curzon line and did not wish for neighbourly relations with the Soviet Union. This reply, as I told Gusev, was like a blow in the face.

There was worse to come. In the Balkan countries the story of the next eighteen months shows how the British Government attempted to shape their policies to counter Soviet designs. Poland was much more difficult for us. This was the ally for whose sake we had gone to war with Germany, yet whose territory was most remote from us. The Polish Government and people looked to Britain for help. We knew we had to go on trying, but the result was beyond our reach to decide.

12

BEFORE D-DAY
January–June 1944

A meeting with the Poles at Chequers — Marshal Stalin's discourteous reply — Marshal Tito and King Peter — I ponder the
future of Germany — The Commonwealth Prime Ministers' Conference — A paper on a "United Nations" — My minute on
foreign policy in post-war Europe — Arguments over the liberation of France — The burdens of my dual role — The bombing
of occupied France — General de Gaulle is invited to England
— His discussions with Mr. Churchill misfire — My conversation
with Mr. Bevin on a National Government — D-Day — She
Stoops To Conquer

IN THE SPRING of 1944 the Soviet armies crossed the Polish frontier,
making the need for an agreement between the Polish Government
in London and the Kremlin more urgent but no easier. The Prime
Minister and I had several meetings with M. Mikolajczyk and M.
Romer in an attempt to narrow the chasm, but it was, and it now
appeared had always been, unbridgeable.

The Resistance movement in Poland would not countenance any
discussion of territorial changes, while the Polish forces fighting at
our side had been recruited chiefly from the eastern provinces
which the Soviets were claiming. All the same, after months of
discussion, the Polish Government showed themselves ready to
consider a compromise.

January 19th: Some talk [with the Prime Minister] on Russian
business, which seems to get worse and worse. We are to see Poles
together tomorrow.

This was a task which neither Mr. Churchill nor I relished, but we
had to try to get a statement from them on the Curzon line. While

Mikolajczyk and some of his immediate colleagues could admit the inevitability of this, at least it must take time to convince a majority among the exiles in authority. We had to persevere.

> *February 6th:* Winston rang up early about Polish business and begged me to come over to luncheon at Chequers. I agreed, I admit reluctantly, for I feel pretty tired and need the Sunday break. All the Poles to luncheon. Two hour session afterwards. They were told the worst. There is just the outside chance of a settlement, not more, but I have seen such chances come off before.

The Polish Prime Minister and Foreign Minister were at this meeting. They announced that the underground in Poland were prepared to come into the open and meet the conditions of the Soviet commanders without any prior agreement between the two Governments. As against this, M. Mikolajczyk told us that the underground were determined to maintain Poland's territorial integrity. This was natural enough for men who were risking their lives in a Poland remote from our discussions, but Mikolajczyk added that the fact that he was willing to discuss frontier questions had troubled the Poles in his own land.

Three days later I spoke to the Soviet Ambassador, telling him that the Prime Minister and I were anxious to reach a solution, not only because of the Polish question itself, but because failure would have repercussions on all Anglo–American–Soviet co-operation. The British people could never forget that they had gone to war on account of the invasion of Poland. I told him that, as leader of the House of Commons, I knew there was a growing feeling among many members that Poland must be given a fair deal. When I added that the Poles were suspicious that the Soviet Government did not wish their Government to return to Warsaw, but would prefer to set up a communist administration, Mr. Gusev emphatically denied this.

I referred to the difficulties which were caused by Russian demands for changes in the Polish Government. It was essential that the Government should be given a chance to make its own arrangements, if it so desired. The Ambassador remarked that three men only had been cited. I said I hoped this did not mean that there would be any more; any increase in the numbers would make our task impossible.

Two months of our efforts at negotiation were greeted by Marshal Stalin with a message to the Prime Minister on March 3rd which was discourteous in tone and abrupt in its misrepresentation of Polish claims. On this I minuted the next day for the Foreign Office that the answer was "cavalier as well as dusty." Commenting on a draft proposal for the reply I added in the same minute:

> I don't like even to refer to the possibility that we should break with Polish Government in London. I should prefer to ignore the issue but, if it has to be mentioned, should it not be on basis "of course we shall continue to recognise Polish Government in London.". . .
>
> But over and above all this, Soviet attitude on this business raises most disquieting thoughts. Is Soviet regime one which will ever co-operate with the West? . . .

Later in the month:

> *March 25th:* Telephone fairly quiet until W. rang up in evening. He seems to have enjoyed his trip with American troops, but much perturbed by very bad message from Uncle Joe during the day about Poles. That aspect of our problems grows daily worse. I share his anxiety and truly don't know what course to advise with least damage to our affairs.

A few days later when the Foreign Office tried, quite properly, to present the Soviet Government in not too bad a light, I regretfully could not agree, writing of a senior official's comments:

> . . . I should dearly like to accept his summing up, for I share entirely his valuation of Anglo–Soviet understanding. But I confess to growing apprehension that Russia has vast aims and that these may include the domination of Eastern Europe and even the Mediterranean and the "communising" of much that remains.

On May 19th the Polish Foreign Minister gave me news, for my own information and that of the Prime Minister alone, which seemed to show an improvement in Soviet–Polish relations. The Polish Government had heard that the Soviet Government would like to establish contact with some Pole representing the Polish Government in London. The contacts would be entirely unofficial and secret. Moscow wished to make them very soon and the Polish Government wanted to know if His Majesty's Government had any objection. The Minister added that not a word was being said to the Americans. The risk of leakage was very great.

I said that I was glad to hear this news, but it did not very greatly surprise me. There had been one or two indications that the Soviets would prefer to talk to the Poles direct. So far as we were concerned, we had no objection whatever. On the contrary, we saw the advantages and could only hope that the conversations would be successful. They took place principally between M. Miko-lajczyk and Mr. Lebedev, now Russian Ambassador to the Allied Governments in London.

★   ★   ★   ★   ★

At this time, communists in Yugoslavia were playing their hand after the pattern of their comrades in Moscow. At the end of January, Brigadier Fitzroy Maclean suggested that we should ask Tito to enter into contact with King Peter for the joint prosecution of the war. The Prime Minister and I thought this worth a try. Marshal Tito, however, would not play. He claimed that his own National Committee should be recognized as the only Government. This reply was stiffened a few weeks later by a decision of the Yugoslav Anti-Fascist Council that the King could not return before the end of the war.

On March 31st I wrote to the Prime Minister:

> The best thing that we can do for King Peter now is to try to ensure that he puts himself on as good a wicket as possible internationally. . . .
>
> He should try to raise himself above the internal dissensions of his country (1) by making a suitable public declaration to

the effect (a) that his only desire is to unite his people in the face of the invader, (b) and that all internal political issues should be postponed until after the enemy has been driven from the country and (c) that then his people must have an opportunity of expressing their will freely in regard to the future regime of Yugoslavia and that he will abide by their choice, and, (2) by forming an administration which would accept the above declaration and would be expressly dedicated to collaboration with all those elements in Yugoslavia, who are actively resisting the enemy, regardless of their political colour. . . .

We should therefore advise him to form a new Government on the above basis, not as part of a bargain with Tito, but in order to improve his own position during the next phase. . . .

I had much sympathy with King Peter. After a luncheon alone with King George vi and Queen Elizabeth, when we had a discussion about Balkan sovereigns, I wrote:

March 10th: Of them all I like little King Peter the best. He is at least lively and not to blame for his troubles.

The King had several conversations with Mr. Churchill or myself and subsequently he summoned Dr. Ivan Šubašić from retirement in the United States. Šubašić was generally respected and had been appointed Ban, or Viceroy, of Croatia by Prince Paul in 1939; he was also known to be acceptable to Tito. At the end of May, the King charged him with the formation of a new Government. He was to make contact with all resistance elements in Yugoslavia before deciding on its final composition.

Meanwhile German activity in Yugoslavia had made the island of Viš, which was under Allied control, a more acceptable headquarters for Marshal Tito than the mainland. Dr. Šubašić visited him there and, on June 18th, we learnt that he had reached what he considered a satisfactory agreement. The Royal Government and the National Liberation Committee would co-ordinate their efforts against the enemy. The National Liberation Committee would not consider the monarchy an obstacle to collaboration, both sides accepting that the peoples of Yugoslavia would decide the organization of the State after the war.

Šubašić seemed to think that if the system of collaboration between the King and Tito could be started, he might later be able to tackle the question of the King's position in more favourable conditions. I was rather sceptical about this, but I thought the attempt worth making. Mihailović was no longer even an apparent obstacle. He had ceased to be Minister of War when the Purić Government was dismissed and at the end of August his High Command was dissolved by royal decree.

★ ★ ★ ★ ★

While arguments were bandied with the Communist powers, at least as much thought had to be given, in the opening weeks of 1944, to the future of Germany and how to present whatever we intended to do about it. There could be no question of denying the unconditional surrender formula. All the same, I thought that a statement by the three heads of Governments to the German people could be helpful if, as I wrote in a minute for the Prime Minister on February 8th,

> made at the right psychological moment and provided its terms were not such as to expose us later to a charge of bad faith.

Mr. Churchill and I were both conscious that, while Anglo–American demands were going to be stern, those of Soviet Russia would be without restraint or pity. Nor would it be easy to reach agreement with our two allies on any statement at all. In spite of these difficulties, I thought that I should prepare a draft and give it to the Cabinet. The Prime Minister acquiesced, although he was not convinced that the moment had come. Mr. Churchill did not like to give his time to anything not exclusively concerned with the conduct of the war. This seemed to be a deep instinct in him and, even though it was part of his strength as a war leader, it could also be an embarrassment.

★ ★ ★ ★ ★

May 1st: Opening of [Commonwealth] Prime Ministers' Conference at noon with much photography etc. All went well. Lunched with W. Smuts and Ike only other guests. Ike produced some last-minute problems about the date [of D-Day], which Navy had landed him with this morning. I think that he was sorry he had, because afterwards he received so much advice. Smuts tried to break party up from 2.30 p.m. and got up from table. He and I talked at window, Smuts making occasional sorties to the table to replace the stopper on the brandy bottle. W. ignoring all and continuing the address to Ike on way to handle British Admiralty, pretty good stuff based on years of experience.

Smuts lectured me on W., said: "He may be mentally the man he was, he may be, but he certainly is not physically. I fear he over-estimates his strength, yes, he over-estimates his strength and he will wear himself out if he is not careful." Some of which W. may have heard and was probably meant to hear.

May 4th: Foreign Affairs [at Commonwealth Prime Ministers' Conference]. I gave my account as best I could, despite frequent interpellations by W., so that even at the end of the session neither of us had finished. All the same there was time for Dominions to express themselves a little, if only in reply to some of W.'s interruptions, and they did so. It soon became apparent that they were whole-hearted in approval of our foreign policy, and this was not in a passive sense but with vigorous active approval. Fraser [now Prime Minister of New Zealand] and [Mr. John] Curtin [Prime Minister of Australia] both made this very clear and, just as we were about to leave, Mackenzie King held us back a few moments to add his quota. All this in marked contrast to 1937 and I admit that I find it very gratifying.

This was my first meeting with Curtin. His outlook and intentions proved to be close to mine. We became friends and when I went on a private visit to Australia and New Zealand a few years after the war, it was at the invitation of Labour Governments in both countries. I was the more sad that Mr. Curtin's sudden and early death prevented me from renewing our friendship in his own home.

Spurred on by this support, I sent the Prime Minister the same day a summary of Foreign Office papers entitled "Future World Organization." I hoped that he would allow me to circulate these documents to the Dominion Prime Ministers, not as committing him or any of his colleagues, but simply as an official study. They described the United Nations Organization with a council, an assembly and a secretariat, much as it was afterwards composed. I also advocated a military staff committee to be attached to the council which would have enabled us to use the established machinery for military co-operation. Members would place military forces at the disposal of the council. This system could have been reinforced by the joint garrisoning or occupation of certain areas.

My paper concluded: "Its name might well be 'United Nations,' which is now a phrase to which we are all accustomed."

On May 8th the Prime Minister replied with a memorandum of his own, which showed a preference for regional councils and later these documents were discussed with the Dominion Prime Ministers:

> *May 11th:* In morning a very good meeting of Dominion Prime Ministers. They all took my line and not W.'s about future world set-up. This was very helpful, in particular they were nervous of regional councils and for the same reasons.

Their principal motive was a reluctance to be included in regional councils limited geographically to their own part of the world, when their future could be as much affected by events in areas where they would not be represented. In other words, regional councils would make the effective working of the British Commonwealth more difficult.

I then submitted another paper to the Prime Minister which incorporated his ideas and mine as possible alternatives. As I explained to Mr. Churchill on June 2nd, some of the alternatives to my original proposals were criticized by all the Dominions representatives to whom they were submitted. One important exception was, however, preserved: the project for a regional council for Europe which, in the Prime Minister's paper, included the United States and Soviet Union as well as ourselves. The Dominions approved of this concept and it was incorporated in the directive taken by Sir Alexander Cadogan to the Dumbarton Oaks Conference on a future world organization.

★   ★   ★   ★   ★

In May 1944 it became the War Cabinet's duty to consider a paper on post-war employment presented by Lord Woolton, as Minister of Reconstruction, and based upon the report of an able committee of officials. This was a formidable document of about thirty printed pages, founded in the main upon Keynesian theories. At this time the nation had been holding a number of "weeks" entitled Salute the Soldier, Salute the Sailor, and so forth, to spur the war effort. Though Mr. Churchill did not enjoy excursions into economic affairs, least of all if they dealt with the period after the war, he invited Lord Woolton to expound the document briefly; a difficult assignment which Lord Woolton nevertheless contrived to despatch with skill. When, however, an attempt was made to arrange for early publicity for these intentions, the Prime Minister looked up with a light in his eye and exclaimed: "I see what you mean, a Salute the Slump Week!"

Stimulated by a despatch from Mr. Duff Cooper, our Representative with the French National Committee at Algiers, I wrote on July 2nd a minute on Britain's relations with her neighbours in Europe after the war:

> . . . What are we doing to discuss these matters with our Western associates? So far as I know, nothing at all. Indeed I have never spoken on these matters to Van Kleffens [Netherlands Foreign Minister], Lie, Spaak or Massigli [French Commissioner for Foreign Affairs]. They have not been encouraged in their various timid advances and they may soon return to their lands. I trust that they will, but then shall we not have missed an exceptional opportunity? Should I not speak to them of these things, and openly, and soon? Should I not later invite Massigli and associate him with our discussions? Should I not tell U.S.A. and U.S.S.R. what I propose? It is no doubt good that many papers should be prepared, but this seems an occasion for action, and I should like a meeting to discuss it.

On July 11th I wrote to thank Duff Cooper:

> I am going to circulate your despatch to the Cabinet, to-
> gether with my comments. Generally speaking, I agree with
> many of your conclusions, but not with all your arguments.
> However, you will see what my views are when you get a copy
> of the paper, and this should reach you fairly soon. In any case,
> I propose in the near future to make a few general remarks to
> the representatives of the four Western Allies, so as to prevent
> them from getting down-hearted and pave the way for subse-
> quent and perhaps more concrete action. . . .

I wanted first to discuss mutual defence arrangements, which
seemed to me indispensable, whatever form the proposed world
organization took, and I wanted to act soon. It was no excuse for
us to be without a foreign policy in Europe simply because we
were waiting for the United States.

In a further reply to Duff Cooper's despatch, on July 25th, I
wrote:

> It is clear to my mind that any World Organization which
> may be constituted must be reinforced by various systems of
> alliances. In parenthesis, I would here point out that efforts
> on the part of some people in this country to foster and
> strengthen an alliance against Germany and Japan, were in the
> thirties always impeded by those who declared that such action
> on our part would only succeed in creating an Axis, which
> might not otherwise have been formed. We must not fall into
> this type of error again. . . .

Though there was a danger of the Soviet Union pursuing a policy
of expansion in Europe,

> It is above all important that any proposals for closer asso-
> ciation between ourselves and the Western European allies, or
> even with the States of Western Europe, should be for the sole
> purpose of preventing a renewal of German aggression. It

would be fatal, as I see it, to let it be understood that there is any other purpose in such an association.

Any durable system in Western Europe should, I considered, be based:

(a) on the Anglo–Soviet alliance,
(b) on an expressed intention never again to permit the revival of a powerful Germany, and
(c) if possible within the ambit of a World Organization, itself resting on an alliance, or close understanding, between the United Kingdom, the United States and the U.S.S.R.

In practice the extent to which we could work towards "the formation of a group of the western democracies bound together by the most explicit terms of alliance" was limited by various factors.

There is no doubt that, rightly or wrongly, the American Administration is suspicious of proposals which tend, in their opinion, to divide up the world into a series of *blocs*. Not only do they fear that such *blocs* would become mutually hostile, but they also believe that their formation would tend to reinforce those isolationist elements in the United States who are above all anxious that their country should undertake no commitments in Europe, but rather concentrate on preserving its power and influence in South America, and possibly in the Far East as well. . . .

Only by encouraging the formation of some World Organization are we likely to induce the Americans, and this means the American Senate, to agree to accept any European commitments designed to range America, in case of need, against a hostile Germany or against any European breaker of the peace. It is quite on the cards, indeed, many would say it is likely, that the American Senate will never enter into such general obligations, but the chance remains, and so long as it does it would be folly to throw it away by undue emphasis on policies which cut across the lines on which the present American Government is working. For there is surely no doubt that in the event of our obtaining such an obligation, there would be small reason to fear German, or indeed any other, aggression in Europe for a long period to come. . . .

I then advocated a common European defense policy, adding that if we could secure the standardization of armaments, that would be a further advantage. My reply to Duff Cooper continued:

> But as I see it, you aim higher than this, and contemplate what would be a sort of union, at any rate in the economic sphere. Though this is perhaps outside my province, I rather question whether we could arrive at anything like an economic union unless we had a political union as well; and whether we shall all of us be ready for a political union, even after the present war, seems to me to be open to the gravest doubt. You will already have noticed that M. Van Kleffens has publicly repudiated Field-Marshal Smuts' suggestion that Holland, among others, might join the British Commonwealth of Nations. As for France, I cannot imagine that if, for instance, the Prime Minister's offer of 1940 was extended to a Provisional Government under General de Gaulle, it would have the slightest chance of acceptance. In all these circumstances it rather looks as if plans for some closely integrated Western Union would be doomed to failure. . . .

During the week of July 19th I made a start by speaking to the Belgian, Netherlands and Norwegian Foreign Ministers about joint defence. I told them that we had to wait for the result of a conference which Mr. Hull was soon to hold at Dumbarton Oaks before embarking upon full-scale discussions. At that conference Britain would make it clear that she proposed to go ahead with defence talks with the Western European allies and that she considered herself free to do so.

The varied problems of our nearest neighbour were now pressing in upon us. On February 9th I wrote to the Prime Minister that my policy for the liberation of France had four stages:

(1) The planning stage, when the Supreme Commander will deal with representatives of the French Committee of National Liberation;

(2) the early operational stage, before a provisional government is formed in the liberated part of France;

(3) the provisional government stage, during which arrangements will be made for holding elections, which can hardly be held until a year or eighteen months after liberation; and

(4) the establishment of a constitutional French Government as a result of the elections.

During the following weeks the discussion went back and forth in Whitehall and across the Atlantic, in the main over the draft instructions to the Allied Commander-in-Chief on how he was to handle these matters. The influences at work in the White House were mostly adverse. Mr. McCloy told our Ambassador of Admiral Leahy's advice to the President, that Marshal Pétain was the most reliable person to whom the Allies could look for help in rallying the French, when the Allied troops entered France.

Roosevelt's position was more obdurate and negative than that of Mr. Churchill. A typical example of this was his teasing message to the Prime Minister of February 29th. The President ironically denounced the paternity of Belgium, France and Italy, and told the Prime Minister that he should bring up and discipline his own children. As they might be his bulwark in future days, Mr. Churchill should at least pay for their schooling.

Mr. Duff Cooper wrote that everybody was quite sound about France "except the Prime Minister and the President." * Apart from any sentiments he might harbour towards General de Gaulle himself, Mr. Churchill was naturally reluctant to be at odds with the President if he could avoid it. Nevertheless he was usually patient with the arguments which I pushed remorselessly in dozens of messages and conversations.

My own conviction was that the Resistance movement in France and indeed the majority of French opinion, was overwhelmingly behind de Gaulle and that, if we were to treat the National Committee of Liberation shabbily or with apparent mistrust, we should

* Duff Cooper: *Old Men Forget.*

damage Anglo–French relations at the very moment when they might soon play an influential part in the world again. General Eisenhower's view, that it was important to be in agreement with General de Gaulle on how to handle civil affairs in France, was mine also. Mr. Winant was sympathetic and so was Mr. McCloy.

On February 29th I thought that a fresh approach might move the Prime Minister to take action:

> I like your idea, which you mentioned at luncheon yesterday, of inviting General de Gaulle to pay a visit to this country. . . .
> But it seems to me that such a visit would most conveniently take place nearer the time of "Overlord" [landing in France] and that it would be a mistake to invite de Gaulle until the directive to the Supreme Commander about the civil administration of France has been settled and the French Committee informed of the role which the Allies intend it to play. . . .
> When it has been settled I see every advantage in inviting General de Gaulle to London.

March 4th, Binderton: A disturbed day from Chequers. Much telephoning and too many messages. In particular W. wanted to send messages to Halifax agreeing with President's attitude to French, which I don't do at all. President's absurd and petty dislike of de Gaulle blinds him. It would be folly for us to follow him in this. . . .

In these last weeks before D-Day we were to confront a harsh dilemma, which is inescapable in a war fought across the territory of an ally. Perhaps I felt it the more because I knew its people and respected them for all they had contributed to a civilization now being burnt out and to be replaced by something more mechanical and less sympathetic.

I was disturbed by a minute which General Ismay had sent to the Prime Minister on behalf of the Chiefs of Staff on March 30th. General Eisenhower had put to them a request by his Air Commander-in-Chief that permission be given for certain railway targets in occupied territory to be attacked. This was to be carried out by day or night as part of the bombing preliminary to "Overlord."

The whole question of our bombing policy was therefore raised by me in the War Cabinet that same day. Up to that moment, I explained, attacks in France and Belgium had been limited to targets where the loss of life to civilians could be reduced to the minimum. The Chief of the Air Staff replied that if these restrictions were continued, it would only be possible to bomb one-sixth of the railway centres which the Commander-in-Chief considered should be attacked. I said that the reputation of the Royal Air Force for accurate bombing stood very high, but it would be lost if these attacks were carried out. Moreover, the attacks would affect our position in France and Belgium *vis-à-vis* Russia and would handicap us in re-establishing our relations with these countries after the war. The Cabinet concluded that the bombing should be continued on the restricted basis only, but the argument did not end there.

On April 5th I minuted for the Foreign Office: ". . . Does Department realize that casualties will be greater than total suffered by all in Britain since war began? . . ." That evening I repeated my point of view before a Defence Committee, where it found much support, adding that targets such as dumps and camps should be more attractive than railway centres. It was again agreed that the restrictions on bombing should be upheld.

★　　★　　★　　★　　★

By this time the physical effort of combining the Foreign Office with the leadership of the House of Commons, to say nothing of the Defence Committee and the War Cabinet, was beginning to tell. Here are some sample extracts from my diary.

March 16th: W. dined. After dinner Brendan [Bracken] raised division of my labours.

We discussed this but were soon in difficulty about finding a substitute for me at the Foreign Office.

General result that we made no progress at all, rather the reverse and W. muttered to me as we joined the others: "You will have to go on as you are for a few months longer."

March 24th: A troublesome day in Secret [Session] in House about tank situation. Had to be there nearly all the time which played havoc with my work. Hate these endless crises first in Foreign Office, then in House. One or other would be bad enough.

Some talk to Brendan Bracken when House rose. He is convinced that I should give up Foreign Office. I am so weary I hardly care so that I am released from one.

March 26th: Sunday. Politically a most harassing day. Winston rang me up at least three times, during one of which he read me out the greater part of his speech though it was coming to me by despatch rider. Winant telephoned twice and Alec [Cadogan] and the office several times. I had heavy boxes and two speeches of my own to prepare. Very exhausting.

The next evening the Prime Minister asked me to go round after dinner when we had a talk on many matters including my future place in the Government. He agreed that a divorce must be made between my two jobs, but was apprehensive about the Foreign Office, where he did not want to work with any of my possible successors.

March 27th: Later on unhappily the morning papers came in with many strictures on W.'s speech and an attack on me in *Daily Mail.* W. was furious and it took me long to persuade him that it didn't really matter.

To add to the complexities at this time I had no real confidence in the new Soviet Ambassador, Mr. Gusev, as a channel of communication with Moscow. His knowledge of our language was limited and I thought his perceptions slow.

March 28th: Some talk to Gusev after [dinner]. Tried to impress upon him the difficulties Russian methods make for us. He appeared to understand, but God knows whether he did. One misses Maisky very much, for it was always possible to have a heart to heart with him.

Which is perhaps the reason why Mr. Maisky did not stay with us.

April 5th: Saw Winston at question time in House when he again urged me to hold on and at 7 p.m. and again after a Defence Committee about 12.30 a.m.

We didn't talk of my future all the time! But he said in the late night final that I was clearly overpressed. Urged me to get a doctor's report and above all to get three weeks' rest and review matters after that. He could not have been kinder. "You are my right arm; we must take care of you," and much more to the same effect.

I accepted the Prime Minister's decision.

★　★　★　★　★

The Defence Committee after my return, on April 26th, resumed discussion of the restricted scale of bombing upon which we had insisted. Mr. Attlee asked what the reactions of the population in France had been.

I replied that it took some time to get information out. The little that had so far been received showed that French opinion, while deploring the necessity for the attacks, accepted the results. If the attacks were continued for a long period, however, the French would become resentful. I said that I would like the policy to be given up, but, as a compromise, I wanted bombing to continue only where the casualties were likely to be small.

The whole question was again referred to the War Cabinet the next day. Here we were told that the first estimate of casualties had been reduced. I argued that it was the length of time during which the attacks were to be kept up which made them so serious. I did not believe that they were essential and advocated that our effort should be diverted to other targets. The Cabinet's conclusion was to restrict targets to those where the estimated casualties did not exceed one hundred to one hundred and fifty. As a result, General Eisenhower suspended attacks on twenty-seven of the seventy-four centres until May 5th.

On the evening of May 2nd the Prime Minister told the War Cabinet of a message from the Supreme Commander. General Eisenhower had written that he had weighed the political considerations. The targets which would entail heavy casualties would be left until the end of the programme, but the restrictions the War Cabinet had suggested would, we were told, emasculate the whole plan.

After Sir Archibald Sinclair and the Chief of Air Staff had supported these arguments I replied that I was perturbed at the possible reaction of European opinion. After the war Eastern Europe and the Balkans could be largely dominated by the Russians, whereas the people of Western Europe would look to us. If the attacks were continued we might well find that they regarded us with hatred. It had in the past been necessary to take decisions in favour of courses of action which entailed horrible results. I would be quite prepared, I said, to take such a decision now if I were convinced that it was a case of victory or defeat, but it was not.

Faced with this dilemma, Mr. Churchill telegraphed to the President, which only revealed that Roosevelt would not impose any restrictions on military action by the commanders which might in their opinion militate against the success of "Overlord," or cause additional loss of life to the Allied forces. As Mr. Churchill wrote later, "This was decisive." *

The Prime Minister and I, however, continued to be depressed by reports of the effect which Allied bombing was having in France. On May 28th he wrote to me: "We will talk about this tomorrow. Terrible things are being done." We did talk, but events were by then beyond our control, for the Royal Air Force programme was more than nine-tenths completed and, although that of the United States was only half-way through, the President had already refused to intervene.

There can be no dispute that, despite the reduction which our representations had imposed upon it in its earlier phase, the bombardment was enough. On May 15th the German Transport Ministry had reported:

> . . . in Belgium and Northern France, the raids carried out in recent weeks have caused systematic breakdown of all main

* *The Second World War,* Vol. V.

lines; the coastal defences have been cut off from the supply
bases of the interior. . . .*

Even more remarkable was the endurance of the French Resistance. The members of the railwaymen's union itself never
weakened in their efforts to sabotage the railways, which the enemy
were still desperately trying to work. Their courage was unwaver-
ing despite ruthless German vengeance for acts of sabotage and
the casualties their own allies had to inflict as they prepared their
advance.

★   ★   ★   ★   ★

At this juncture Mr. Duff Cooper proposed that de Gaulle should
be invited back to Britain. During a Cabinet meeting on the
evening of May 30th the Prime Minister told us that he was preparing to issue this invitation on D-Day. I said I was unhappy about
this, because I expected that once we and the Americans landed
in France, General de Gaulle would feel it essential to make some
statement. If he did so in Algiers without having consulted us, it
might well be unhappily phrased, and we had to consider the consequences of this possibility upon our future relation with France.
De Gaulle should therefore arrive before D-Day.

The Prime Minister decided that the Chiefs of Staff should consider the military implications of my proposal, but they feared that
the departure of the General from Algiers would give the enemy
a very good clue to the imminence of "Overlord." The next morning, May 31st, I discussed this point with the Prime Minister and
he accepted that General de Gaulle must be told about "Overlord" before it was launched. This being so, it was evidently safer
to tell him in England than in Algiers. The invitation was finally
sent off and de Gaulle arrived in time for luncheon with the Prime
Minister on June 4th.

That morning I had motored over from Binderton to the Prime
Minister's special train at Droxford, near Portsmouth. This was
an imaginative but uncomfortable exercise on Mr. Churchill's part.
The accommodation was limited and there was only one bath,
adjoining his own compartment, and one telephone. Mr. Churchill

* Major L. F. Ellis: *Victory in the West*, Vol. I.

seemed to be always in the bath and General Ismay always on the telephone. So that, though we were physically nearer the battle, it was almost impossible to conduct any business.

I arrived in time to walk down the railway line with de Gaulle. The Prime Minister, moved by his sense of history, was on the track to greet the General with arms outstretched. Unfortunately de Gaulle did not respond easily to such a mood. He was offended at the failure to make any agreement with the French Committee for the civil administration of France, and may also have been genuinely uncertain about the purpose of this somewhat strange railway meeting. Mr. Bevin and Field-Marshal Smuts were other guests on the train. Smuts, usually so invaluable as a soothing influence, was handicapped by a previous statement of his which the French remembered with bitterness, to the effect that France would never be a great power again.

In the course of the tense conversation which followed, de Gaulle remained firm that agreement should have been reached with him about the civil administration of his country which must follow our landing, while the Prime Minister became increasingly exasperated at what he regarded as the General's obduracy. Finally Mr. Churchill declared that, if it came to the point he would always side with the United States against France. I did not like this pronouncement nor did Mr. Bevin, who said so in a booming aside. The meeting was a failure.

When the opportunity came for a few words alone together, I did all that I could to thaw de Gaulle's resistance and reminded him that General Eisenhower had always been receptive to working with the French Committee of National Liberation. We then drove to General Eisenhower's headquarters. The meeting which followed with the Commander-in-Chief seemed to go well. Unhappily there was apparently some misunderstanding about Eisenhower's declaration to the French people, which he had shown to de Gaulle and upon which de Gaulle thought that he was being asked to comment. When he did so the next day his observations were too late, the declaration having already been printed. This created further offence, more through mischance than from anybody's fault.

In view of the train's cramped facilities for work, I decided to retreat on Binderton that evening, where my private secretaries were anyway installed. Before leaving, however, Bevin and I had a talk during which we spoke of the impending battle and then of the political future.

Bevin appeared to think that it might be necessary to continue the National Government into the immediate post-war period and asked me if I knew what Churchill's intentions were. I replied that I did not. He said that if the old man were to retire then he and I, he was sure, could work together, if that were the right thing to do. This course would present no difficulties to him. He would not care which office either of us held. I replied, "Neither would I." There was, however, one thing that he must have. "What?" I asked. "The nationalization of the coalmines." The trade unions would have to have that.

General Smuts had seen us at our talk and when it was over and I was alone he asked me, "What were you and Bevin talking about for so long?" I told him and he commented with characteristic crispness, "cheap at the price."

June 5th: Wrote paper for Cabinet on French situation and its reactions on Anglo–French–United States relations.* Rather liked it! It is so rare in these hard-pressed days that I have a moment to write a paper myself and I am never happy at having to re-shape other people's expression of my own ideas.

W. rang up later to say that, despite appearances, forecast was good and operation would proceed tomorrow as planned, an immense relief. Motored to London where I soon found myself in midst of French drama.

June 6th, D-Day: News good in morning except for one American beach. A meeting about French when I asked Duff to see de Gaulle and try to induce him to let his [liaison] officers go. Heavy work until luncheon during which de Gaulle's broadcast was brought to me. Decided not to attempt to alter only peccant paragraph which referred to government of France. . . .

That day I wrote to the Prime Minister:

* Printed as Appendix F.

What I suggest is that you should authorise me to repeat to [M. Pierre] Viénot [Diplomatic Representative of the Free French] that we are prepared to discuss these civil affairs matters with the French Committee. . . . At the same time I hope that you will also feel able to send a message to the President urging him to authorise Winant to sit in with us. The result of our work would of course be *ad referendum* to you and to the President. . . .

In this connection please see the President's message [of February 29th]. If the President renounces the paternity of France, surely he must allow us to do the schooling in our own way. The present position is unfair to H.M. Government and dangerous to Anglo–American relations.

June 6th: . . . Brief rest in afternoon. W. rang up about 7 and long argument ensued about de Gaulle and French.

Again soon after midnight W. rang up in a rage because Bevin and Attlee had taken my view. Argument continued for forty-five minutes, perhaps longer. I was accused of trying to break up the Government, of stirring up the press on the issue. He said that nothing would induce him to give way, that de Gaulle must go. Said I had no right to "bully" him at a time like this and much more. There would be a Cabinet tomorrow. House of Commons would back him against de Gaulle and me and any of Cabinet who sided with me, etc., etc. F.D.R. and he would fight the world. I told him that I heard that [Admiral Raymond] Fénard [French naval representative in United States] had arrived with a personal message from F.D.R. to de Gaulle. He did not like that. I didn't lose my temper and I think that I gave as good as I got. Anyway I didn't budge an inch.

Two hours later Brendan [Bracken] rang me up to say that he had been called lackey of Foreign Office, etc., but that, in the middle, message from F.D.R. came inviting de Gaulle to United States.

June 7th: Dined with de Gaulle. He was personally trying, I think, to make himself pleasant, but politically stiff. He is convinced that this is only way to get anything out of Americans and ourselves, whereas so far as W. is concerned the tactics could not be worse. It is my failure that I have never been able to persuade de Gaulle of this.

I told the General that we wished to discuss with the French Committee the problem of civil affairs in France. We would keep the United States Government informed and would do what we could to encourage them to participate. I also told him that I supposed he would need the help of some of his colleagues for these conversations.

General de Gaulle then made a long lament. He said that he had never been so unhappy about our relations as now. He had been grateful for the Prime Minister's action in receiving him on his arrival and telling him of the battle. But still nothing had been arranged about civil administration in France.

I told the General that our intention was to discuss just this problem. It would be days, perhaps weeks, before we commanded any territory except beaches. In the meantime let us work together to agree a plan. The General asked what would be the value of such a plan unless the Americans would also agree and made further complaints. I said that these things were no doubt important, but they must be weighed against the immense Anglo–American effort to liberate France. De Gaulle interjected: "I understand that and we feel with you for the losses which your army will suffer." I continued that what we were asking him to do was to work with us so that the civil administration of France could be set up:

> If you would accept and if you invite your Ministers to come here to help you, I think that there is a fair chance of a solution satisfactory to you, to us and to the United States. If you refuse our invitation, there is nothing more that I can do. The choice lies with you.

The General said that he understood, but continued to complain about our dependence on American policy. I retorted that it was a fatal mistake in national policy to have too much pride. "She stoops to conquer" was an action which we could each of us find useful to observe at times. Having pondered over this de Gaulle repeated the difficulty he felt in entering into conversations which might lead nowhere. They would give a false impression of an agreement which did not exist, while the Supreme Commander issued a series of edicts which affected the future of France.

M. Viénot, who was present, at this stage put in a plea that the conversations on civil affairs should go forward. General de Gaulle replied that M. Viénot could certainly conduct them himself. This was done, with satisfactory results.

Meanwhile the question of a visit to France by de Gaulle was also discussed and finally accepted by the Americans and ourselves. I gave a dinner for him at the Foreign Office on June 13th, the eve of his journey. Mr. Attlee and others of my colleagues were present. During the meal a letter came from the Prime Minister, questioning whether the General should go to France the next day, in view of his attitude over the liaison officers; de Gaulle had forbidden these officers to do their job in the absence of a civil affairs agreement. There was, Mr. Churchill wrote, still time to cancel his visit. But the others present, and especially Attlee, supported me in maintaining the original decision about the General's journey across the Channel.

June 16th: Saw W. at his request at 10.30 a.m. Some further talk about de Gaulle.

The Prime Minister continued to protest against him and his methods, with foreboding for the future. I replied that he might be right, but if so we could do nothing about it at this late hour; the "French must deal with him."

After luncheon in the House of Commons I went to see the General in Carlton Gardens. This was the first time I had done so. I was received with some ceremony, a guard of honour being drawn up outside, with officers posted at intervals up the stairs. De Gaulle talked easily for twenty minutes. As I commented at the time, "he is at his best as host."

The General said that he was very grateful for the hospitality and courtesy extended to him during his visit. Although he admitted that there had been tensions in our discussions, he was glad that he had come and he thought we had made progress. He was in a more reasonable mood than I had ever known him and added that, despite the obstacles, he wanted above all to work closely with ourselves and the Americans.

As France was liberated, its administration fell without question into the hands of the Resistance which acknowledged General de Gaulle as its chief and this chapter of our difficulties, the cause of so many hard feelings, naturally resolved itself. Whatever de Gaulle's gifts or failings, he was a godsend to his country at this hour, when France must otherwise have been distracted by controversy or bathed in blood.

13

FAR EASTERN STRATEGY
June–September 1944

Assessing General Montgomery — Flying bombs — Soviet influence in the Balkans — The Prime Minister and his Generals — Hammering out a Far East strategy — An attempt to assassinate Herr Hitler — Optimism of the Poles — Mr. Churchill in Italy and I in Normandy — Marshal Tito levants to Moscow — The agony of the Warsaw rising — The Quebec Conference — The Morgenthau Plan — The Prime Minister and I decide to go to Russia

IN THE MONTH of June, France and the great enterprise now launched there preoccupied us all.

June 17th, Binderton: [Lieut.-Gen. Henry] Crerar [commanding First Canadian Army] and his Chief of Staff [Brig. C. C. Mann] came to dinner and [Group Captain William] Crisham [R.A.F. Sector Commander, Tangmere] and his second in command, called, I think, Ward. Crerar was very optimistic about the campaign. He maintained that Germans had already committed their strategic reserve and that whole thing might be over as a campaign in sixty days. He said Monty was a good field commander but not a great man.

I ranked Montgomery higher, as supreme in his own job. One should not ask for more.

June 22nd, London: Staff talk after dinner, W. and I and Chiefs of Staff, about next stage. Macmillan also there. A pretty useful survey. . . .
Also some talk about flying bomb. Portal stressed high proportion of wounded, but figures I saw later don't bear this out. The

people are good and patient, but this thing gets on their nerves and must be taken seriously. I have a suspicion that Air Staff take it a bit too lightly.

I had suggested to the Soviet Ambassador on May 5th that our two countries should agree that during the war Britain would take the lead in Greece and the Soviet Union in Roumania. President Roosevelt immediately manifested unhappiness at the idea of "spheres of influence" in Europe,* though my suggestion was a limited one, intended to confine as far as possible the conflicts which were already developing between Russian policies in the Balkans and our own.

> *June 22nd:* Went into W.'s for a drink afterwards when we found two messages, one from F.D.R. and one from [Lord] Moyne, [Minister of State, Middle East] showing that U.S. Ambassador to Greece had himself given this message [about spheres of influence] and much else away to the press. A slight sense of exasperation on W.'s part, and on mine, and so to bed about 1 a.m. Woken by flying bomb.

The Russians had shown little interest in Greece until the spring of 1944, when they began to criticize our policy and come out openly in support of E.A.M. This was a signal to me of the difficulties which the Russians would cause us and pointed the danger of a link-up between pro-Soviet movements in Yugoslavia, Albania and Greece.

Some weeks earlier I had asked the Foreign Office to produce a paper on this subject. "There are unhappily increasing signs," I minuted, "of Russia's intention to play her own hand in the Balkans regardless of our desires and interests, e.g. in Greece." The resulting document was circulated to the Cabinet on June 7th, and reported that the Russians were using the Communist-led movements to gain a predominant position in South-East Europe.

Britain was in fact partly responsible for this development in Yugoslavia and Greece. When these insurgent activities first appeared, the Foreign Office had often warned of the clash between

* Churchill: *The Second World War,* Vol. VI.

our short and long-term interests and had forecast the situation which now faced us as a result of our deliberate choice. Military needs had overpowered political forebodings.

It is obviously difficult in war to take account of political presages for the future world at peace, or to decide how far the attempt should be made and at what cost. We can declare that any policy which would result in a better peace should be carried through if the price in prolonging the war be not too high. But the nicety is in the calculation, for it is not true, as is sometimes said, that wars do not by their duration decide anything. The second world war decided that the United States and Soviet Russia should rule the world; the longer it lasted, the more established the rule. If there had been no dictatorships using war as an instrument of policy in the nineteen-thirties, Europe would have continued to play the leading part for many years.

I referred in my paper to the apparently better behaviour of the Soviet Government over Greece, but added:

> We should not be lulled into a state of false optimism by these satisfactory developments. The national army may not materialize, E.A.M. may break loose again and the Soviet Government may yet fish in troubled waters. We should therefore make the most of the present favourable atmosphere to organize some counterweight to the force of attraction which, no matter what happens to E.A.M., Russia is still likely to exercise in post-war Greece.

I advised that the only practicable policy to check the spread of Russian influence throughout the Balkans was to consolidate our position in Greece and Turkey. Even this involved intricate politics:

> As regards Greece, we should have to set about now building up a regime which after the war would definitely look to Great Britain for support against Russian influence.
>
> As regards Turkey, we should have to abandon our policy of trying to force Turkey into the war under the implied threat that, if she does not come in, we shall leave her to "stew in her own juice" after the war. . . . Although the Soviet Govern-

ment now take the line that they are not interested in whether Turkey comes into the war or not, they have probably never liked the Anglo–Turkish alliance, and the present deadlock in our relations with Turkey suits them very well. They cannot be expected to relish the prospect of a renewed Anglo–Turkish "get together," more especially when they appreciated, as they soon would, the policy behind it.

Meanwhile we had to determine our strategy at the armies advanced up Italy and the decision was not solely ours. By midsummer our differences with the Americans on this account had begun to loom.

June 24, Binderton: A glorious day of unbroken sunshine. Some telephoning to W. about war situation. What Alex [Gen. Alexander, Allied Commander-in-Chief in Italy] shall do, whether he shall part with a portion of his army, if so where it shall be employed. After half an hour or so of discussion about this, W. said that he would send me advance copy of paper he was proposing to do. Then more talk of French. President has sent another querulous telegram [about responsibility for civil affairs in France]. W. wants to reassure him but I don't want to do so too much. We must get on, in fact we are. Winant arrived in evening and we had more talk about this. He understands what a jam we shall be in if President turns down our joint work.

June 25: Another talk in morning on telephone with W., mainly about strategy again and telling me of his paper.* "I have laid an egg" was the opening sentence. . . . Another flying bomb brought down, this time three hundred yards short of the house, glass broken again and telephone gone as well. Rather disturbed night in consequence.

★ ★ ★ ★ ★

During this time problems of future strategy in the Far East and the British contribution to the war against Japan were being debated and determined, not without occasional hard feelings.

* Churchill: op. cit.

July 6th: After dinner a really ghastly Defence Committee nominally on Far Eastern strategy. We opened with a reference from W. to American criticism of Monty for over-caution, which W. appeared to endorse. This brought explosion from C.I.G.S.

Sir Alan Brooke reproached the Prime Minister with lack of confidence in his generals. Mr. Churchill was hurt and indignant, since he took pride in his knowledge of strategy and his close relations with the commanders. I tried to pour oil by suggesting that the size of our Monday meetings was part of the trouble; it would be good if we could confine criticism to the Defence Committee's intimate circle. The C.I.G.S. cordially agreed. My diary continued:

Result was that our discussion of Far Eastern strategy was meaningless when it was not explosive. I agreed with Chiefs of Staff on their paper [proposing to form a British naval force in Australia to operate on the left flank of Gen. Douglas MacArthur's advance in the south-west Pacific] which seems to me to offer the best way of bringing our weight to bear, which is not a heavy weight in the Far East. I should have preferred "Culverin" [a proposed operation in northern Sumatra] but Chiefs of Staff are emphatic that resources are not available to do this until some time after German war is over. Result may be to do nothing if we wait so long. W. kept muttering that resources were available, but produced no evidence and ended up by accusing us all of trying to corner the Prime Minister or take it out of him or some such phrase. Finish 1.45 a.m.

I called this "a deplorable evening" which it certainly was. Nor could it have happened a year earlier; we were all marked by the iron of five years of war.

July 14th: A few questions in House about secret session, the majority don't want it, and then to Defence Committee, when another two hours on Far Eastern strategy. "Two hours of wishful thinking," Attlee called it on a slip to me and he was not far wrong. The Far Eastern war is going to be a problem for our people and what I like about Chiefs of Staff plan is that it gives us the nucleus of an Imperial force at an early date and upon this we can build. "Culverin" is attractive, but I fear probably beyond our strength, if not at first stage then at second. Moreover, since it is remote from the centre of conflict with Japan, if we cannot see it through we shall be regarded by Americans as having played virtually no part in defeat of Japan.

Work in Office, then to see W. on a number of points which we settled happily.

August 8th: Had to leave by car for London early to be in time for Staff meeting on Far East. Three meetings during day on Far Eastern strategy and at the end we were further off than at the beginning. W. harks back to "Culverin" always and generally seemed very tired and unwilling to address himself to the arguments. As a consequence Brookie [Sir Alan Brooke] became snappy at times which didn't help much. Portal was the most constructive of Chiefs of Staff and, after the first meeting, I piped away.

My anxieties are two:

First that our offer of fleet to co-operate in main attack on Japan should be clearly stated as our preference; [operation towards] Amboina [Island and Borneo], etc., after which Chiefs of Staff hanker so much, being my second best. Secondly that we should decide to make attack on Rangoon as soon as possible and with the intention of exterminating Japs in Burma, thereby not only freeing Burma but liquidating this heavy Burma commitment which locks up so large a British–Indian force.

Dickie [Mountbatten] came to have a talk in afternoon. He didn't care for Amboina plan and begged me to make myself heard. He insisted this was only chance of a decision. If Rangoon couldn't be done any other way, why not Australian division from MacArthur's area to play their part. Dickie was very unhappy. This was before afternoon meeting. At the finish he was very content. But it remains to convince Chiefs of Staff.

August 9th: Talks continued all this day, the discussion eventually taking reasonable shape.

August 10th: Another Far Eastern meeting just before luncheon. We are, I think, "home" as far as our plans are concerned and I don't think we could devise better. But we are very late.

The conclusion was to prepare for an amphibious landing at Rangoon and to build up a naval task force for the Pacific.

★   ★   ★   ★   ★

The agreement reached on June 16th between Marshal Tito and the Yugoslav Prime Minister, Dr. Šubašić, had seemed a step towards forming a united Government in Yugoslavia. Tito, however, had not helped by refusing to meet the King. He was confident that his movement would gain control over Serbia later on and was not prepared to help Šubašić any further in the quest for unity. I minuted to the Prime Minister:

> Tito seems to be trying to run out on his agreement with Šubašić, and his suggestion that purely military conversations [with Gen. Wilson] should be held at some later stage somewhere on the Italian Adriatic coast, merely means that he wants to extract further concessions without giving anything in return. He has put his signature to an agreement with Dr. Šubašić and has nominated two members to the latter's Government. He has, therefore, no real excuse for declining to meet Šubašić or to discuss political matters with him further.

July 16th, Sunday: Box in morning and then talk to W. about some tiresome developments in Yugoslav situation. We were both irritated with local people because they have not carried out our instructions, with result that Tito gets away with it, whereas he wants pulling up.

July 17th: Lunched alone with W. He was in pretty good spirits. My face fell when W. said that when coalition broke up we should have two or three years of opposition and then come back together to clear up the mess!

Mr. Churchill used to enjoy this tease and practise it in diverse forms, whether I fell for it or not.

July 19th: Interview with [the Duke of] Alba [Spanish Ambassador in London] in p.m. who was very insistent that I should help Spain with penicillin now, in return for light which Richard Eden had brought from Spain in his translations in 16th century. Alba sees every problem in setting of ancestry.

Richard Eden, who is not even definitely known to be a member of my family, had translated Spanish works on discovery and science.

July 20th: Difficult meeting of Armistice and Post-War Committee in afternoon. This was followed by Cabinet, during which I got news of attempt on Hitler's life. Ernie B. [Bevin] at once said that it was Nazi stunt to popularise H. Brendan [Bracken] said it was Goebbels' work. I said it was hard to tell so far, but I didn't think so.

July 21st: Hetta [my cook] rang up in morning with most exciting news that Simon was home. Late in evening he rang up himself. His voice sounded assured and lively, with a Canadian accent.

House in morning when I dealt with a number of questions on business and declined to speak of Germany. Quite sure that my diagnosis of H. [Hitler] business was right and that there has been some real trouble in Germany.

★ ★ ★ ★ ★

By the beginning of the summer of 1944 the prospects of a Polish–Russian settlement again seemed to the Poles more hopeful. M. Mikolajczyk went to the United States early in June and came back encouraged by his talk with President Roosevelt. The President had told him that he was opposed to territorial changes being settled before the end of the war and promised that, at the appropriate time, he would help Poland to retain not only Lwow, but also Tarnopol and the oil areas in eastern Galicia, and see that Poland received Königsberg as well as the rest of East Prussia and Silesia. I commented on this in a minute to the Foreign Office:

> The President will do nothing for the Poles, any more than Mr. Hull did at Moscow or the President himself did at Tehran. The poor Poles are sadly deluding themselves if they place any faith in these vague and generous promises. The President will

not be embarrassed by them hereafter, any more than by the specific undertaking he has given to restore the French Empire.

Mikolajczyk had also been cheered by a version of Stalin's attitude which he had heard from the Polish–American professor, Oscar Lange, who had recently been in Moscow. On June 22nd Mr. Churchill and I warned the Polish Ministers not to be too optimistic about such reports and not to show themselves more rigid towards Russia because, at the moment, the Soviet attitude seemed more conciliatory.

Stalin had some reason to wish for agreement with Mikolajczyk for, as his armies had advanced into Poland, they had found strong popular support for the exiled Government and a numerous and well-organized Home Army. Yet, on June 23rd, Mr. Lebedev abruptly broke off the talks he had been holding with the Poles.

June 29th: Poles dined with me. I like Mikolajczyk and every time I see him I like him better. But I feel that he has many internal troubles, in particular I suspect with the President [M. Wladyslaw Raczkiewicz]. Though he was careful not to let it appear he was, I am sure, depressed by the setback in Russian talks and not easy in his mind when I hinted that Poles might have made use of the better atmosphere to make some salutary changes in their own set-up.

June 30th: House quiet and soon over. Lunched there. Cuthbert Headlam tackled me about political future. He thought young were very Left. I asked him how he visualized next General Election. Did he think those who had been working together should now set about attacking each other? He said this was crazy to him, but admitted difficulty of renewing this Parliament by any means such as coupon election.

The Poles had recently revived the idea that M. Mikolajczyk should visit Moscow. They wanted us to propose this to Stalin, but I was not enthusiastic. President Roosevelt had just tried and had not succeeded. I thought that if we were also rebuffed, it would then be difficult if not impossible for the Poles to renew their proposal. The Prime Minister agreed with me, but we told Mikolajczyk that if he liked to make a direct approach to Stalin, Mr. Churchill would support him in a message. This succeeded, to the extent that Stalin replied that he would not refuse to receive the Polish Prime Minister.

On July 23rd Russian forces occupied Lublin, west of the Curzon line, and Stalin told Churchill that the Polish Committee of National Liberation intended to set up an administration "on Polish territory." He said he could not consider this Committee as the government of Poland, though it was possible that, in due course, it would serve as a nucleus for the formation of a provisional Polish government "out of democratic forces."

When I warned Mr. Gusev against any Russian recognition of the Committee, he gave me the impression that the Russians hoped a new government might be formed if M. Mikolajczyk and members of the Committee were to meet in Moscow. Mikolajczyk himself, while deeply suspicious of the Committee, decided to leave at once for Moscow, taking M. Romer and M. Grabski with him.

July 27th: During [Cabinet] proceedings message came in that Molotov had told A.C.K. [Archibald Clark Kerr] that Russians would send plane to fetch Mikolajczyk at Tehran. An immense relief. I would have been inclined to bet that Stalin would find a pretext — there are some — to postpone indefinitely M.'s journey to Moscow. Alec [Cadogan] had thought the same and we could only repeat for the many hundredth time that Russians were to us incalculable.

In answer to another message from Mr. Churchill about a Polish settlement, Stalin said that he regarded the formation of the new Polish Committee as a good start in the unification of Poles friendly to Britain, the U.S.S.R. and the United States. It could be, I thought, but I feared make-believe.

July 30th: W. rang me up before dinner and we had half an hour's talk on many matters. He took a more cheerful view of U.J.'s reply on Poles than I did. He may be right. Truth is that, like many communist messages, it is capable of several interpretations.

August 4th: A day of meetings, interview with W., etc. Eventually, under pressure from him, decided to give up attempt to reach Ditchley before dinner. So that Nicholas and I dined only with Winston. I have never seen W. in greater form. He, of course, completely fascinated Nicholas who listened and looked all eyes and ears. Stories of his young days at Harrow, how he was for two terms, or two years, I forgot, bottom of the whole school, how his father was famous then and when the school filed by, as it frequently did, spectators used to point at him and say: "Look, there he is, the very last of all." How he hated Harrow and implored his mother not to send him back, even for his last half. Long quotations from *Henry VI* and advice to "read only Shakespeare," etc., etc. All this to the accompaniment of a good dinner and the best possible bottle of champagne. Finally, when I got into the car I found Nicholas bubbling with excitement and he confessed that £2 had been thrust into his hand with injunctions not to tell "him."

★   ★   ★   ★   ★

Both Mr. Churchill and I were unhappy about the reluctance of our American ally to exploit victory in Italy and so enable us to play a more influential part in Central Europe. Though the United States argued that this was for strategic reasons, we were not convinced that political inhibitions about becoming "involved in the Balkans" did not play a part.

July 1st: Long telephone talk with W. about strategy: we have to give way to U.S. Argentine: we have to give way to U.S. [by withdrawing our Ambassador]. I wish that I could persuade W. to be more vigorous in support of my French thesis. We are in the right there and have a right to have our say and our way.

I now wanted to recognize the French Committee's assumption of the title of Provisional Government, but Churchill was unwilling to move faster than Roosevelt. Suddenly the President himself moved a step forward.

July 11th: Reuter message came in before dinner showing that President has put out his intention at press conference to recognize French as *de facto* authority. Took this round to W. whom I had to see anyway before dinner. He didn't like it, the more so since it was so close to what I forecast would happen.

Back [after dinner] to W. with whom I discussed and agreed many things. He was in a mellow mood, in part I think because he felt I had been right about French.

Finally escaped at 2 a.m., W. remarking: "You and I have some heavy burdens to bear together."

On August 4th the Eighth Army reached Florence, when the withdrawal of Alexander's troops for a landing in the South of France compelled a halt of three weeks before the offensive against the Gothic Line. Mr. Churchill decided to go to Italy. He wished to see how Alexander was preparing for the offensive and also to meet Tito, who could be flown from Viš for the occasion. I lent the Prime Minister Mr. Pierson Dixon, my Private Secretary, for his tour.

When I saw Churchill on the evening of August 10th, he dictated a minute putting Attlee in charge of home affairs, with the chairmanship of the War Cabinet, while I was to take the chair at the Defence Committee and the Chiefs of Staff meetings, and the Chiefs of Staff were to keep in touch with me. I told the Prime Minister that I did not care about the chairmanship, but only wanted Ismay to keep me posted with events. What happened to this minute I have no idea, for I never heard of it again. Perhaps Sir Edward Bridges, as Secretary to the Cabinet, persuaded Mr. Churchill to withdraw it.

While the Prime Minister was away I flew to Normandy for a short visit, landing at La Molay on the morning of August 19th. On my way to Arromanches I saw first a rest camp and then a hospital. Ever since the first world war and the memories of casualty clearing stations, I have not been good at military hospitals, but this one was a revelation. Its swift, aseptic handling of the wounded and injection of pain-killing drugs were far removed from the mud and stretcher bearers of Flanders, though the initial wounds were as savage and searing.

Mulberry Harbour was in full operation, but as I watched it suffered its first casualty, a ship was mined and sunk just outside. The next hour or two were spent with the French, and in particular with the Préfet, in battered Caen, and in the evening at Bayeux

with the French Regional Commissioner, M. Coulet. All around
me was evidence of the price which Normandy was paying, with
stoic acceptance, for an Allied advance after so many years of
waiting.

While I was lunching with Supreme Commander, General Eisenhower, he said that I had just missed General de Gaulle whom he
had received that morning. He had told him that the Leclerc division would be the first to enter Paris and that de Gaulle would be
with them, together with Koenig as Military Governor. I congratulated Eisenhower on this happy move to end much argument within
the Anglo–French–American triangle. Certainly throughout this
business the Supreme Commander had never failed to practise
patient diplomacy. In his guest camp that night, an air raid and a
bomb in the next field gave me the only reminder of war as I had
known it twenty-five years before.

General Montgomery having asked me to come to see him, I
motored to his tactical headquarters near Falaise that evening.
There he expounded to me his own plan for future operations,
then under discussion between him and the Supreme Commander.
Montgomery was already looking keenly and far into the future,
beyond any present argument. He asked me about our relations
with the Belgian Government and what help we could expect in
the use of Belgian harbours and from the civilian population. As
Falaise had only just been captured, I was astonished that his mind
was already ranging so wide. Montgomery explained that the
Channel ports had not the capacity he needed and that if the
battle unrolled as he planned, he must have the use of Antwerp.
This was imaginative generalship at its lucid best.

★   ★   ★   ★   ★

Mr. Churchill in Italy was seeing Marshal Tito and Dr. Šubašić,
both together and separately. On hearing the Prime Minister's account, I telegraphed to him on August 15th that his conversations
with Tito seemed to have been most successful. I was, however, as
I told the Prime Minister, perturbed that the Yugoslav Prime Minister, himself a Croat, had endorsed Tito's view that there was no
gulf between the latter's movement and the Serb people. Mr.

Churchill and I were agreed that we must prevent the Partisans' major effort being directed against the Serbs, even if they be Mihailović Serbs.

I was in charge of the Government for a few days before the Prime Minister returned to England on August 29th, while Mr. Attlee was also away in Algiers. During this period M. Massigli arrived, on August 21st, to sign the long-delayed French civil affairs agreements. After the President's statement of July 11th there was, to all appearance, little difficulty in reaching a settlement. The documents had been initialled in Washington on August 16th, but the final signature in London between General Eisenhower and General Koenig, and between M. Massigli and myself, had already been postponed. I now learned that General Eisenhower was still without final instructions to sign, and that Mr. Roosevelt would not be in Washington until August 23rd.

After discussing this situation with Massigli, I told Halifax that since I could not allow our guest to leave London without having signed, this being the primary purpose of his visit, or ask him to stay on indefinitely, we would sign on August 25th, the last possible day. Perhaps this had its effect. In any event the President approved the documents and the four signatures were duly affixed, to the accompaniment of simultaneous communiqués in London and Washington.

August 25th: After luncheon, in succession Nye and Ismay, former mainly about our impending attack in Italy and both about Ike's proposal to take over direction of operations himself. His plan and Monty's are not the same, latter implying greater concentration of force towards Pas de Calais and Flanders. This to me appears more attractive, but much depends upon estimate of Germany's remaining strength in the west.

We agreed to refer whole business to Joint Planners and J.I.C. [Joint Intelligence Committee] and to have papers ready against P.M.'s return. We also agreed that Ike was well within his rights in taking over command and might well have done so sooner had he wished. We could only intervene on the basis of the plan, which it was open to us to argue about with Combined Chiefs of Staff. Ike's plan involved splitting his force into two and with anyone but him there would be some suspicion that he preferred this to Monty's, because it gave fair pretext for his assumption of command.

Ike is of course under strong pressure from U.S. to do this, but he is too straight a man to give way to this. Another complication is that his staff is hardly organized, nor indeed competent, to conduct a battle. But if he leaves this to Monty and [Gen. Omar] Bradley [commanding United States Twelfth Army Group] no great harm should result.

August 29th: Decided to fix Cabinet for 6.30 so that W. should have time to get there. Looked in at Annexe on chance that he might be arriving and walked into him in passage as I was leaving for Cabinet. He seized my hand. "Ah, there you are, dear Anthony, come into my room, I want to talk to you." This was followed by a hurried whisper from Clemmie: "He has a temperature of 103°." In his bedroom while undressing and tumbling into bed he told me what had happened: a sudden chill a few hours from home. Fortunately, as he said, for a few hours earlier he would have been stuck at Rabat.

Extracted myself as soon as I could for he showed every desire to discuss all our problems and I felt the whirl of approaching doctors, etc. Slipped out and sent [Lord] Moran in and went down to Cabinet. Told them briefly the position without details of the temperature.

Later reports in the evening were better.

On August 31st Mr. Churchill, somewhat disenchanted by his meeting with Tito, sent me a minute remarking upon our responsibility for supplying Tito with arms with which he could subjugate Yugoslavia. In view of the minutes I had been sending him for many months, I commented to the Foreign Office that we hardly needed this reminder. The Prime Minister had indeed persistently championed Tito despite our warnings.

My reply to Mr. Churchill said:

> I have certainly never lost sight of this danger, which has arisen largely because our policy towards Yugoslavia has had to be dictated on grounds of short-term military expediency rather than those of long-term political interest.

It was for this reason that we for so long deprecated the policy of forcing the King to break with Mihailović before we had secured the position of the anti-Communist Serbs in post-war Yugoslavia, and that we have for some time past been trying to bridge the gulf between the King and the Yugoslav Government in exile on the one hand and the Partisans on the other, in the hope that by securing a united front we could prevent the arms we are giving to Tito from being used against his opponents when the day of liberation comes. . . .

Marshal Tito had agreed with Dr. Šubašić at their meeting in August that the National Committee would produce a draft plan for the creation of a new Government. But when reminded of this by Šubašić, who wanted an early answer, Tito dismissed the question as unimportant. The Prime Minister was then in Quebec, so I telegraphed to Tito myself on September 11th:

> I am surprised to see from the reply which you have sent to Dr. Šubašić's message suggesting that immediate steps should be taken to form such a united Government, that you do not consider the matter as of immediate importance.
> I cannot agree with you. The occupying armies may be forced to evacuate the greater part, if not the whole, of Yugoslavia in the near future. It is therefore, in our view, of the utmost importance that immediate steps should be taken to form a united Government which would be in a position to assume control of the country at the moment of liberation, and which His Majesty's Government would be able to recognize as the Government of Yugoslavia during the Peace Settlement. I beg you therefore to give this matter your urgent consideration.

I followed this up with instructions to Clark Kerr to discuss the situation with Molotov and to ask the Soviet Government to use their influence with Tito in the same sense. Tito, however, had no liking for this growing pressure. On September 21st he levanted from British protection at Viš and flew to Moscow. The Communist had homed to his lair, which nearly became his cage.

★　　★　　★　　★　　★

Mikolajczyk's talks in Moscow marked some progress, super-ficially at least. Stalin was reported as forthcoming and as not wish-ing to force Communism on Poland. He did not now insist on Polish acceptance of the Curzon line before a regular Government had been set up in Warsaw.

M. Mikolajczyk, when I saw him on his return on August 14th, appeared to attribute the improvement in Stalin's attitude to the power of the underground army, which had done much serious fighting. The Polish Premier thought that Stalin would use the Committee to see how far he could get Mikolajczyk to fall in with his own views, but that he would throw it over if it proved incapa-ble of keeping liberated Poland quiet. He was therefore hopeful of reaching agreement with Stalin about the principles on which his administration should be set up in Poland.

I was not too confident that this improvement would last, particu-larly as Mikolajczyk attached importance to Soviet help to the un-derground army fighting in Warsaw. If no Russian help were forthcoming, he said, Russo–Polish relations would be irremediably damaged.

The Warsaw rising had begun on August 1st. It was set off by the local Polish commander without consultation with us and without co-ordination with the Soviet forces advancing on the city, though the Poles had tried, and continued to try, to establish contact with the Russians. However, the Soviets had themselves a direct respon-sibility, for it was their organization, the so-called Union of Polish Patriots, which had called on the population to rise on July 29th. When Mikolajczyk arrived in Moscow two days later, Stalin prom-ised that he would send help to the insurgents.

It is true that a German counter-attack held up the Soviet advance and that it was not the Russian habit to assault a city frontally. Yet, when all is said, the conclusion seems inescapable that Stalin, sur-prised by the vigour and success of the rising, was content to see the underground and the remaining political and intellectual leaders of Poland destroyed. It did not suit him that the Poles should liberate their capital themselves; nor could he allow Mikolajczyk and his followers to return to Poland with their underground organ-ization intact. He now refused to let American aircraft land on Soviet airfields after dropping supplies on Warsaw. British aircraft, many with Polish pilots, flew to their extreme range from the Mediterranean, but could hardly affect the issue.

During September 3rd the Prime Minister and I had further conversations about the Polish agony. At one point we considered a message to Roosevelt, asking him to join Churchill in telling Stalin that the next convoy to Russia would not sail because of his attitude to Warsaw. The weakness of this idea was that Stalin's armies alone could save Warsaw, which we then believed from our reports, wrongly as it proved, could only hold out for a few days. I thought it might be better to help the Poles more directly by an attempt to gatecrash the Soviet airfields. Only the United States air force had negotiated the right to land on these after bombing in Germany. Mr. Churchill agreed that we should discuss this and other suggestions in the War Cabinet next morning.

When the War Cabinet met they endorsed the idea that the Prime Minister should try to toughen the President by asking him again to consider an air operation to drop supplies on Warsaw. It was also agreed that the Prime Minister should send another message to Stalin in the name of the War Cabinet, warning him of the effect of his action on future Anglo–Soviet relations. This did eventually result in one operation by the Americans, which could not, unhappily, be enough. The heroic Polish resistance ended on October 2nd after heavy loss of life.

September 4th: Lunched alone with W. Spoke of our various problems and plans during his absence [at the Quebec Conference]; also of political situation. He is firm that this Parliament must be renewed pretty soon and insists that we shall only lose by delay while the glamour wears off. He had February in mind. I think that he is right but confess I cannot look at general election as cheerfully as he does. I loathe the things. . . .

Went back to my office for number of duties. Then Cabinet at 6.30. Didn't last long, despite the battle progress in France and Italy we had to review. W. was I think tired and did not look at all well. He liked our draft messages to U.J. and F.D.R. about Polish affairs* though they had been pretty hurriedly scratched up.

* Churchill: op. cit.

September 5th: W. rang up twice before he got off. Both times on War Office matters and Polish affairs. He insists I take on W.O. matters until P.J. [Grigg] returns. Relieved to find when I summoned Nye and [Sir Frederick] Bovenschen [Permanent Under-Secretary, War Office] and Home Guard General [Maj.-Gen. Sir James Drew] that P.J. is due back tomorrow. We had some talk about Home Guard and I was firm that drills must stop and that they must be thanked when they did stop. Nye agreed about first, subject to consultation with Commander-in-Chief, which he will hold tomorrow. Failed to convince them of second, but returned to charge and Cabinet endorsed my views in evening.

I should rather have liked to broadcast "Farewell" to Home Guard as I broadcast "Hail" more than four years ago, but P.J. will be back and will no doubt want to perform.

★ ★ ★ ★ ★

Many of M. Mikolajczyk's compatriots blamed him for failing to secure effective help for Warsaw, though he had done everything that he could. The Prime Minister and I encouraged him, but on the morning of September 5th he came to tell me he must resign. After three hours of strenuous argument I was able to persuade Mikolajczyk that such action could only weaken the Polish cause, perhaps destroy it.

September 5th: In evening further meeting with Air Staff about help to Warsaw, which is an impossible proposition.

On September 12th a telegram arrived from Mr. Churchill in Quebec, suggesting that I should join him there. The War Cabinet had already prepared a plan for partial demobilization at the armistice and for the use of the manpower which would then be at our disposal. They also wanted to increase the pay of those left in the services after the defeat of Germany. Bevin wished to announce the plan very soon, but Churchill wanted to discuss the details further when he came home. So my colleagues thought it useful that I should try to win the Prime Minister's favour for the scheme.

September 13th: A good night's sleep, having refused to accept a midnight call from Quebec. Delighted to hear when I got down to the office that we had received Russian clearance for [American] operation to Warsaw. Meeting about Poland, and discussion of plans for departure. Luncheon with Winant and some Congressmen. Winston rang up in afternoon to ask if I was "on the wing." I gave him Polish news with which he was pleased. In morning also discussed pay and Stage II demobilisation plans which I have to try to agree with W. It will be a tough task.

Saw Šubašić and lectured him about getting a Serb into his Government. This briefly, after long talk with Poles, who are much more cheerful.

Eventually left for Hendon about 5 p.m. Good flight to Prestwick, working on the way. Dined there, rather gloomily in vast mess, but infuriated to learn soon afterwards that weather was too bad to fly. After some discussion agreed to leave for Iceland at 4 a.m. and retired for a few hours' rest.

September 14th: Up at 3.45. Cup of coffee and then to aeroplane. It has one bed made up, but otherwise no amenities. Four-hour flight to Iceland went easily. Reykjavik is not quite so grim as I had expected. A certain beauty here and there of mountain and loch. I don't care for the prevailing colours, like the mauves and greens of a bad water-colour or an oleograph. We motored into the town. Saw some very fair young Nordic types of both sexes. But it is a land of gales and volcanoes and I would hate to live there.

Left at 10 a.m. local time, Royal Air Force having been most kind, and began our interminable flight to Canada, nearly thirteen hours which seemed as many days, only relief being when we landed unexpectedly at Quebec instead of Montreal. Passed Greenland on the way, rather fine distant line of snow mountains, and flew over a sharp little iceberg. Otherwise no incident. Finished my book and felt very bored. Not expected at Quebec which was a relief as I was desperately unshaven, so fled hurriedly to Frontenac. Bath, shave and drink. Refreshing.

Alec [Cadogan] turned up and we went round together to see Winston. He was with F.D.R. and [Mr. Henry] Morgenthau [United States Secretary of the Treasury] and Prof. [Lord Cher-

well, Paymaster-General] in conference about Lend Lease. They
seemed glad of interruption and we talked of many things,
Russians, Poles, Dumbarton Oaks, etc. until time to dress for
dinner.

Dined approximately same party plus Mackenzie King. Sat
next to President. Thought he looked very drawn. W. said afterwards that he had deliberately taken off weight. Even so he didn't
look good to me. W. looks much better and Mackenzie a very
fit old man. Slipped off to bed at reasonable hour. Felt deaf and
tired.

On September 1st Lord Halifax had telegraphed to me that Mr.
Morgenthau was urging upon the United States Government that
the occupying powers in Germany should not go out of their way to
maintain or re-establish the German economy. Morgenthau apparently thought that a severe inflation, as happened after the first
war, would burn into German minds that war spelt economic ruin.
Halifax warned me that this question might come up at Quebec.

I decided that we ought to let Mr. Churchill know of this and
suggested to my colleagues that we should send him a message. In
the event, I left for Quebec and had intervened on the subject at
the Conference, before it arrived or I knew its contents. On the
morning of September 15th I joined the Prime Minister and the
President, who were by now in agreement in their approval of
the plan. Cherwell had supported Morgenthau and their joint
advocacy had prevailed. Large areas of the Ruhr and the Saar
were to be stripped of their manufacturing industries and turned
into agricultural lands. It was as if one were to take the Black
Country and turn it into Devonshire. I did not like the plan, nor
was I convinced that it was to our national advantage.

I said so, and also suggested that Mr. Cordell Hull's opinion
should be sought for. This was the only occasion I can remember
when the Prime Minister showed impatience with my views before
foreign representatives. He resented my criticism of something
which he and the President had approved, not I am sure on his
account, but on the President's.

When the message from London arrived the next day, this fortified my opinion. There were good arguments, the Foreign Office

and the Treasury admitted, for weakening Germany economically as a security measure, but if Germany were unable to manufacture she would also be unable to pay for imports. World trade would suffer and our exports with it. This made nonsense of Mr. Morgenthau's claim that his plan would bring economic benefit to Britain.

When Hull learned of the scheme he was as much against it as I was, with an added spice of indignation towards Morgenthau for prowling on his preserves.* The plan was quietly put away.

September 15th: Had some talk in morning with W. about the pay and demobilisation business. Found him very troublesome on the line "I won't be rushed or bullied. I'm not one of Bevin's boys," etc. He said he would discuss with officials I had brought out, on way back in ship. I explained why this wouldn't do and eventually persuaded him to see [Sir Eric] Speed [Permanent Under-Secretary, War Office] and [Sir Godfrey] Ince [Permanent Under-Secretary, Ministry of Labour] after dinner. To my horror, an Admiralty man had also turned up, from I don't know where, to announce he didn't agree. However we made some progress.

Incidentally I also tried today to get President and P.M. to recognise French as Provisional Government. A pretty hopeless discussion, each going off in turn on a tirade against de Gaulle. W. did however go so far as to say that he would rather have a de Gaulle France than a Communist France, a distinct advance!

September 16th: Another rather poor night, followed by a pretty wretched day in which there was much hanging about. A difficult meeting with W. and our own Chiefs of Staff. W. wanted to alter some of their report which they had already agreed with difficulty with Americans. Naturally our people were most reluctant to go back to Americans. W. however was in a tiresome mood, fastening on many minor points of wording. I urged that he should make a statement of his own, which could be taken note of at meeting, and make minimum changes in Staff paper. Brooke pleased with this suggestion and I undertook to press it on W., and did so afterwards.

Full plenary meeting went off well and I thought Americans

* Cordell Hull: *Memoirs,* Vol. II.

patient and reasonable. Marshall is a grand chap; I have always liked him very much. Dill looks ill and tells me his blood is weak. I had him in for a drink and a chat in evening.

Pug [Ismay] and Brooke tell me that they had a pretty terrible time on board with W. [when it had been very hot and sticky in the Gulf Stream for two days], and Moran told Bob Dixon: "He glared at me as if I had invented the Gulf Stream." . . .

Lunch, at which Athlones [the Earl of Athlone was Governor-General of Canada] presided, then degrees, press conference, which went well.

President had kindly asked me to Hyde Park, but really I thought I must get home. Couldn't go there without seeing Hull, who isn't invited. I don't want to go to Washington in election year. W. explained to President at luncheon. He said: "He's got to come, I'll kidnap him. I want him to talk to Harry," etc. This last I should have much liked, but I held to my decision.

In retrospect, my refusal seems to me like a missed opportunity, but at the time I was much charged with the House of Commons leadership, as well as with the Foreign Office, and was probably too conscientious about the discharge of the double duty.

Said goodbye to President alone after press conference. He said that, win or lose, he would come to us after the election, end of November. He was very friendly, sitting at his desk in an almost completely packed up room, apparently writing in a notebook. He has no secretaries with him like Martin [Mr. Churchill's Private Secretary] and Co., and it was his chief policeman who arranged my interview. Altogether a strange set-up.

Dined at Citadel. Athlones again. Malcolm [Macdonald, United Kingdom High Commissioner in Canada] and [Lord] Leathers [Minister of War Transport] and Prof. and Clemmie and W. A fairly good party but W. lingered long afterwards. Eventually disappeared and he followed me a few minutes later. Quite good tactics. We got through draft on this wretched pay business which is really about all I have achieved by this journey.

Poor night, slept badly. Composed most of reply to debate [due a few days hence] in still watches of the night.

September 17th: Glorious day of brilliant sunshine and warm, so that we regretted not to be spending it bathing. Work in my room, then with Malcolm to Lieutenant-Governor's house which has much charm. Then on to the Citadel. Various jobs with W.; a final clearing up. I gave him suggested draft of what he and F.D.R. might say jointly from Hyde Park to U.J. He said he liked it. Also discussed meeting place for Bulgarian [armistice] negotiations. He favoured letting Russians have their way in this.

Lovely drive to plane, flight to Montreal and then on board "Commando." Comfortable but cold for a spell during night and bumpy.

★   ★   ★   ★   ★

As soon as the Prime Minister reached London, I told him that M. Mikolajczyk had no answer from the Russians about the proposals put to them three weeks before. It did not seem to me that we were making any progress at all. We agreed that Mr. Churchill should suggest to Stalin that either he or I should visit Moscow to discuss both Poland and the Balkans, as well as war plans. I was reluctant to face another journey immediately, the more so because it was unlikely to settle anything. Yet I could see no choice but to make the attempt, though routine work would have piled up mercilessly in the interval. This entry for Saturday September 30th, is typical of many weekends:

Heavy boxes to clear off in morning. Much work after luncheon. More work after and between tea and dinner.

October 1st: Guy [Millard, one of my Private Secretaries] read good telegram from U.J. welcoming W. or self to Moscow. This is encouraging, but we shall have tough battle over Polish business. Talk to W. about it twice on telephone. He was highly excited and we plan for Saturday night.

14

WITH THE POLES IN MOSCOW
October–December 1944

An evening with Queen Mary — Moscow — The Russians haggle
over the Balkans — Marshal Stalin and I discuss prisoners — The
Poles arrive — Arguments over the Curzon line — An evening at
the Bolshoi Theatre — The future of Germany — I fly to Athens
— Freedom of the City is conferred on me — Field Marshal Alexander's H.Q. at Siena — Paris is liberated — A military parade
on the *Champs-Elysées* — My minute on Western Europe — Mr.
Harriman and the Poles — Russia recognizes the Lublin Government — Question of a Regency in Greece — Mr. Churchill and
I in Athens — We hold a meeting — Archbishop Damaskinos

To PROVIDE a cover plan for our journey to Moscow, it was arranged
that I should speak in Bristol * on the afternoon of October 7th,
before flying off that night. In the interval I dined at Badminton
where Queen Mary was staying and, with an apology for having
no evening clothes, I explained what I was about. I found the audience which followed fascinating. Queen Mary knew Europe inti-
mately as one who had been brought up with its problems and
personalities. Her experiences were still pertinent even when the
power of those of whom she spoke had passed to others.

The King had expressed a wish that the Prime Minister and I
should not fly in the same aircraft in wartime. The C.I.G.S. and I,
therefore, took off from Lyneham on the night of October 7th while
Mr. Churchill chose an aerodrome nearer London. We met the
next morning for breakfast in Naples. The Prime Minister then
remarked on the amount of work we had still to do before we met
the Russians and proposed that, in order not to waste time, we
should travel together on the next stage of the flight which would

* *Freedom and Order*, pages 266–71.

be in daylight and over territories far removed from any possible enemy action. Accordingly I transferred to his aircraft, but we had both forgotten the fact that it would be nightfall before we reached Cairo. As ill luck would have it, we made a very indifferent landing, so that I was hardly surprised to learn that the aircraft had damaged its undercarriage and was unable to fly on. We were badly caught out and in the end had to complete the whole journey to Moscow in one aircraft after all.

I was not hopeful for the outcome of our mission. The Russians had already grabbed the territory they wanted, so that the Curzon line was no longer the real issue. It was what happened in Poland that mattered. While we would argue that an early union between the Government in London and the National Committee in Lublin was desirable, I was unhappily conscious that the Soviet Government had every motive to play for time. The longer their puppets had to extend their rule and destroy the official underground movement, the worse for free Poland. Unfortunately the Russians did not lack arguments with which to stall M. Mikolajczyk and they had only to bring up again their objections to President Raczkiewicz, or the Constitution, or the Government's refusal to accept the Curzon line publicly.

Our best chance was to protest the damage to Anglo–Soviet relations which must result from failure to agree a fair settlement for the Poles, but this was an uncertain weapon.

October 9th: Slept little, late and was eventually woken about 9 a.m. by the steward. W. only person still asleep. He soon woke up and we had an excellent breakfast of cold pheasant and white wine which he provided. Country looked pleasant in the sunshine and autumn colouring. Less gloomy than any previous impression of Russia that I can recall.

Landed triumphantly at wrong aerodrome some miles from Moscow. Not very good. Pug [Ismay] considers this journey provides many strong arguments why Air Ministry should not control civil aviation. Half an hour later landed happily where we should. Usual ceremonies at airport.

Maisky and Vyshinsky whisked me off to Embassy while P.M. went to his *dacha* which neither of us had realised was forty-five minutes away. Some talk with M. and V. who were certainly friendly enough. Then joined W. at his *dacha* in time for late luncheon.

Some talk of plans, then I went back and had first meeting with Molotov. This was friendly and easy, so was our first meeting with U.J. after dinner. He agreed that Mikolajczyk should be sent for and to have "another try" to settle Polish affairs.

W. came back to Embassy for a drink and we both went to our sleep much cheered.

October 10th: A pretty trying day. After work at Embassy went to lunch at our conference building. Terrible and interminable ceremony with many speeches lasting until 4 p.m. or later. No chance to eat anything and had to drink in desperation. These things are only bearable at night.

After the luncheon I had a brush with Molotov. As I told the Foreign Office in a telegram:

> I had a pretty vigorous exchange with Molotov on the Bulgarian situation, Maisky acting as interpreter. I said that a number of reports had reached us this morning showing that the Bulgarians were behaving with increasing insolence towards ourselves. They had even dared to place our officers under house arrest in Grecian Thrace. Such a state of affairs was intolerable. I must ask that Soviet authorities issue immediate instructions to their Marshal [F. I. Tolbukhin] in Sofia to compel Bulgarians to put an end to this state of affairs.
>
> Molotov seemed embarrassed by these charges and begged me to believe we should together discuss whole Balkan situation when he felt sure that agreement could be reached on all points. The Soviet Government had no desire to pursue a separate policy. He continued that he had a secret to tell me. Marshal Tito had recently been in Moscow. At the Marshal's express request visit had been kept secret. Its object had been to agree upon joint military action in Yugoslavia. The Soviet forces in that country were relatively weak and collaboration of Partisans was indispensable to them for effective action against German armies. This was reason of visit.

I replied that we took the strongest exception to Marshal Tito's behaviour and to the fact that we had not been told of the visit. Marshal Tito had been living on the island of Viš under the protection of the Royal Navy and the Royal Air Force. If he had had the courtesy to tell us that he was going to Moscow we should have wished him *bon voyage*. But neither he nor Soviet Government had thought fit to tell us anything about it although it was we who had armed and equipped Marsal Tito and made his military operations possible. As a result, I must repeat that we felt strongest resentment at what had happened.

Molotov hurriedly put all the blame on Marshal Tito. He said he was a peasant and did not understand anything about politics: that he had the secretiveness of his type and had not dared to impart his plans to anyone. He repeated once again that he would be only too glad to discuss all these matters with me later this evening.

I told Molotov that he must understand the effect that events of this character must have on our relations. There were many people in England who said that Soviet Government was pursuing its own policy in the Balkans without the slightest regard to us. Marshal Tito's visit and behaviour of Bulgarians fully justified this criticism and the position of His Majesty's Government in consequence became impossible. More explanations about ignorance of Yugoslav peasants followed. . . .

At the previous evening's meeting with Marshal Stalin, Mr. Churchill had made his "percentage" proposal for the Balkans.* As I had to follow it up with Molotov, we met again at seven o'clock. Stalin had admitted that Greece was primarily a British concern, but Molotov showed a disposition to haggle over the percentages for the other countries. Finally I told him that I was not interested in figures. All I wanted was to be sure that we had more voice in Bulgaria and Hungary than we had accepted in Roumania, and that there should be a joint policy in Yugoslavia.

This went on until 9 p.m. when I found to my horror that I was dining with W. at his *dacha* and not at his town house as I had supposed. Therefore long drive and late dinner.

* Churchill, *The Second World War*, Vol. VI.

W. rather upset by my report. I think he thought I had dis-
pelled good atmosphere he had created night before. But I explained this was the real battle and I could not and would not
give way.

October 11th: A day of lovely sunshine in contrast to yesterday's grey skies. Up late. Luncheon in Embassy, small and
pleasant party, then sat for brief spell in sunshine. Molotov at 3
p.m., when all was as smooth as it had been rough yesterday and
we obtained what we wanted on almost all points. I should say
90 per cent overall. In particular they will summon Bulgars out
of Greece and Yugoslavia tonight.

I had learned with relief that Tito had now invited the Yugoslav
Prime Minister to meet him in Serbia. I suggested to Molotov that
we should send them both messages of encouragement.

That evening we entertained Stalin and Molotov to dinner at the
Embassy. Our guests arrived at 9 p.m.

Dinner went well. Fortunately we were able to get through a
part of it before the toasting began. Quite a bit of talk with U.J.
through Pavlov [the Soviet interpreter] who sat between us. He
was pretty outspoken in criticism of Labour Party as at present
led. He also maintained, as he has done before, that if W. and I
had been in Government at Munich time, or in 1938, events
would have been different. We had some talk of Poles, too, on
usual lines. Then he spoke of wine and stores captured from
Germans in Crimea, I suppose he meant stores of Russian wine,
and offered me two hundred bottles. When I pleaded space in
aircraft he said it would be managed somehow.

At one moment our conversation took an unexpected turn.
Stalin began to talk about the Soviet "volunteers" whom we had
captured with the German army in France and now held in England. He said that he would be extremely grateful for any arrangements which could be made to get them back to Russia. I used this
opportunity to speak of our own prisoners. Many of them were in
camps in East Germany and in Poland and I was becoming anxious
about their fate. Our Military Mission in Moscow had been trying
to make arrangements ahead of time with the Russians to rescue

and collect these men, but they had only met with obstruction and delay.

I remembered how, during one of my earlier meetings with Stalin at the Foreign Ministers' Conference in 1943, he had told me that if ever I was in serious difficulty on any point I could come to him. This seemed the moment to recall his offer. I told him that we would do all we could about his men, though shipping difficulties were considerable. We would try to find troop-ships to carry them and the necessary naval escort. Stalin repeated that he would be deeply in our debt if we could arrange this matter for him.

I then asked that his Government should give in return all the help in their power to our prisoners in Poland and Germany, as and when the Red Army reached the camps in which they were held. Stalin said at once that certainly this would be done. He would make it his personal charge and he gave me his word that every care and attention would be given to our men.

All the same it took time and effort to get this pledge fulfilled, in part probably because the Russians lacked the means as much as the will. It was only at Yalta that an agreement was signed providing that officers should be sent to the Soviet Union to collect and look after our liberated prisoners. Even this was not carried out. Our officers were never allowed to go beyond Odessa, and we received many reports of bad organization and unsatisfactory treatment of our men on their long journey.

After dinner we sat round and talked until four o'clock in the morning. In the first phase, Molotov, Harriman and I discussed Poland. Then we all joined up and Stalin talked about Europe, often impressively as I thought, even when I disagreed with his conclusion. Mr. Churchill, on the other hand, was more responsive, even in his approach to foreign affairs. For instance, he admitted that evening, not for the first time, that his attitude to Italy had been changed by the welcome the cheering crowd had given him. He was not pleased when Stalin said that the crowd had supported Mussolini all right.

We also spoke of Yugoslavia, when Stalin said that Tito thought the Croats and Slovenes would refuse to join in any government under King Peter. He himself had the impression that the King was ineffective. I replied that I was sure the King had courage and I thought that he had intelligence. Mr. Churchill interjected that the King was very young. "How old is he?" asked Stalin. "Twenty-one," I answered. "Twenty-one!" exclaimed Stalin with a burst of pride, "Peter the Great was ruler of Russia at seventeen." For that moment, at least, Stalin was more nationalist than communist, the same mood as had seen the disappearance for the time being of the portraits of Marx and Engels from the Kremlin rooms and their replacement by Kutuzov and Suvorov.

October 12th: Slept until nearly noon. Some work, then luncheon with W. alone at his town house. An interminable meal of tepid meats and the inevitable cold sucking pig, with soup arriving somewhere near the end. W. held forth about Kings, inveighed against [M. Georgios] Papandreou [Prime Minister of Greece], said he would take no more interest in Greece, complained that we were dropping [King] Zog in Albania, etc. I argued that it was impossible to regard kings in most of these Balkan lands as other than coming and going like a Labour Government at home. More argument about France which didn't advance matters much; the drip drip of water on a stone.

My pessimism was exaggerated for no one was wiser than Mr. Churchill in giving weight to arguments which he had resisted at the time if, on later reflection, he judged them sound. Two days afterwards he telegraphed to President Roosevelt that we could now safely recognize General de Gaulle's administration as a provisional government of France. The President was still inclined to dally, but with one of those sudden changes of mind which were characteristic of him and placed his actions in the lead, he was the first to notify the French a few days later that recognition would be granted on October 23rd.

★   ★   ★   ★   ★

M. Mikolajczyk, with his colleagues M. Romer and M. Grabski, had now reached Moscow.

October 12th: Long talks with Poles in evening. Was puzzled by their apparent reluctance to take over Government in Poland until whole country was freed.

This was probably because Mikolajczyk was conscious that his greater strength would lie in Poland west of the Vistula, which the Russians had not yet reached.

Next day we had our first full meeting with the Russians and the Polish Ministers, Harriman attending as observer for the President. We made no progress, Stalin calling for public acceptance of the Curzon line and Mikolajczyk being unable at that moment to give it. I sympathized with his dilemma, for he knew how urgent it was to reach agreement with the Russians and the Committee, yet he could not move far ahead of his colleagues in London and their followers in Poland. Without them he would have small chance to help his country, for Stalin had no interest in men without power.

Later that evening we met the representatives of the Lublin Committee. They seemed creepy to me. "The rat and the weasel," I murmured to the Prime Minister in reference to two of them, Bierut and Osóbka-Morawski, who were fulsome, not to say servile, to the Russians. Ready of course to concede the Curzon line, Osóbka-Morawski was soon criticizing Mikolajczyk and the parties supporting him. This was too much for us and we were glad to break up.

In spite of this experience, the Prime Minister felt that we must make a further effort with the Polish Ministers, using every method of argument and menace on the frontier question, but all to no avail. Five days more of hard discussion followed, the Poles trying by all means to persuade Stalin to give up Lwow. Mikolajczyk said that if he could only get this concession, he and his colleagues would accept the rest of the Curzon line. At their request and Mr. Churchill's, I went to see Stalin to make a final remonstrance and appeal. Stalin showed no resentment, neither did he yield, listening attentively but merely saying that he was committed to the Ukrainians. On October 16th I telegraphed to the Foreign Office:

> And so at this time, after endless hours of the stiffest negotiations I have ever known, it looks as though Lwow will wreck all our efforts.

M. Mikolajczyk, who had shown a calm courage throughout this ordeal, decided that he must return to London, to try to persuade his colleagues that the Curzon line must be accepted as part of a general settlement. His final talks with Stalin and with Bierut even raised his hopes of reaching agreement on a new government.

★ ★ ★ ★ ★

On the night of October 14th Stalin entertained us to a lavish performance at the Bolshoi Theatre. There was much polite clapping and enthusiasm. Towards the end of an interval for refreshment the Prime Minister and I were shown where we could wash our hands. Here Mr. Churchill suddenly became excited by a thought which came to him to help in the Polish dilemma and he began to expound it eagerly to me. After repeated efforts I had at last to stop him with a reminder that the audience must have been waiting quite a while. When we returned to the box the Russians, scrupulous hosts as ever, made no comment.

However, three nights later Stalin asked us both up to his flat for supper. As we came into the little entrance hall, he nodded to a door in the corner saying: "That's where you can wash your hands if you want to, the place as I understand it where you English like to conduct your political discussions."

Stalin's room was quietly and conventionally furnished, with nothing to distinguish or mar it. The conversation round the supper table was of methods rather than of large political issues. Our host discoursed on diplomacy and how the leading nations practised it, until somehow the conversation went back to the years of his captivity in Siberia. He told us of the fish he was obliged to catch for food and of the stark conditions of life in those northern latitudes, but without complaint.

During the night after the Bolshoi entertainment, the Prime Minister gave us quite a fright by running a high temperature. Lord Moran feared pneumonia and we prepared to send for nursing help from wherever we could get it. I had disagreeable visions of how we should be placed if Mr. Churchill were to develop pneumonia in his Moscow *dacha*, but he rallied splendidly. In the interval I took his place at the second of the military discussions at which both Russians and Americans were present. This dealt with Soviet intervention in the Japanese war.

The Soviet Chief of Staff, General Antonov, was the official Russian spokesman. He was lucid and fluent, but he always looked to Stalin for confirmation and it was Stalin who answered the questions. He explained how much time it must take him by the Trans-Siberian Railway to make up for his present weakness in the Far East. I expressed scepticism about the assumption that the Japanese would stand by and watch while the Russians reinforced. Stalin did not disagree. He added, with a near approach to a smile: "If they do attack, they will at least solve what will be my most difficult problem with my own people. It will be obvious who is the aggressor." Stalin undertook to take offensive action against Japan about three months after the end of the war with Germany, but he posed two conditions. The necessary stocks of weapons and supplies must be built up and the political terms clarified.

On October 17th Mr. Churchill and I had an inconclusive discussion with Stalin and Molotov on Germany's future. The Marshal said that Germany must be deprived of her metallurgical industry and of all shipping and aviation. As he went on to oppose any grouping of states in central Europe, I became more wary of the advantages the Soviets might seek in a weakened and divided continent. While the pretext of nationalism which must tangle attempts to unite Poles and Czechs and Hungarians was plausible enough, it was put forward with an unction which made me uneasy.

We left Moscow on October 19th. Mr. Churchill went on to London after one night in Cairo. With his approval I decided to stay a little longer and then to visit the army in Italy, at the invitation of Field-Marshal Alexander. However, before these agreeable plans could develop, I received a message from Mr. Rex Leeper suggesting that I should go to Athens. British forces having landed on October 5th, he had returned with the Greek Government a fortnight later on the German withdrawal, and had some teasing problems to face. I accepted and took Lord Moyne with me from Cairo.

October 25th: Called at 6.30. Motored to Heliopolis. Spoke to about two thousand airmen, then took off for El Adem, where I lunched with Royal Air Force. . . .

Beautiful afternoon flight, the Greek islands and Athens looking lovelier than ever. It was a strange feeling to return on the
heels of a fleeing enemy.

Rex met us and we drove to Embassy. Papandreou called. He
was surprisingly confident, and probably rather over-optimistic.
I am not too sanguine myself about the political situation, but it
is the financial problem that dominates all. Unless we can get
that right all our efforts will have been wasted.

Jumbo [Wilson] came in to dinner with Commander-in-Chief,
Mediterranean [Admiral Sir John Cunningham] and others.
Leeper produced wonderful meal in circumstances.

Worked hard after dinner. First discussed military plans with
Jumbo and Cunningham. Approaches to Salonika and shortages
of landing craft and minesweepers set some pretty problems.

I am not satisfied about rate of unloading supplies. C. was
gloomy and not too helpful.

Then we turned to financial business and after some hours of
plunging about in the dark produced a few decisions and I telegraphed to P.M.; but I am not satisfied that we are at the bottom
of the business yet.

My telegram to Mr. Churchill set out the difficulties as we saw
them:

> Moyne and I have arrived and had a first look round. The
> political situation on the surface at least is fairly satisfactory,
> but it yet remains to be seen how far the authority of the Gov-
> ernment can be established beyond Athens. Papandreou, whom
> General Wilson and I saw separately tonight, showed con-
> fidence in his ability to handle the situation and he clearly has
> considerable popular backing. On the other hand, E.A.M. is
> active and we should be unwise in my judgment to under-
> estimate its strength. I had some talk with Papandreou about
> this and the situation of the King. I will telegraph later about
> this.
>
> Most immediately urgent question, however, is runaway in-
> flation which is so serious as to resemble the situation of Ger-
> many after the last war. As you know I do not pretend to

understand these things but we have tried tonight, with the help of expert advisers on the spot, to see what we can do to deal with the problem. Unless we can deal with it, Papandreou or any other representative of the Government will be swept away and anarchy will take its place. . . .

I put forward various requests for transport and goods, and asked the Prime Minister to send out a first-class Treasury expert. He replied that Sir David Waley, Under-Secretary at the Treasury, would come as soon as possible, and I decided to stay in Athens until he arrived.

October 26th: Work in morning and then to Grande Bretagne [Hotel] for luncheon with Greek Government. Drove to Piraeus afterwards through cheering crowds. Port position far from satisfactory. Daily clearance at present only one thousand four hundred tons which includes military supplies. They hope to get it up to two thousand five hundred by Monday [October 30th]. But we must do better than that. Cunningham and Jumbo were with me and we stirred things up a bit. I fear that one of the troubles of this campaign, which is really a political and not a military campaign, is that most of the staffs are the leavings of other commands. We went aboard the cruiser *Orion.* As ever I was immensely impressed by smartness and quickness of Royal Navy. All the men looked so fit and bright and keen.

Drove back with Papandreou and then to theatre with him. Much enthusiasm but pretty dreary performance for me who do not understand one word of Greek. Poet Laureate was the worst. He apparently read letters that had been addressed to him in his praise. However they eventually brought the curtain down upon him after one or two ineffectual efforts to make him stop by clutching at him through the drop scene. The best was the Greek dancing.

After the play we had meant to drive back in our respective cars and I said goodbye to Papandreou at the box. But as his open car was drawn up when we got to the door he invited me into it and we drove off. To our amazement we found the streets packed with people who had assembled during the theatre. They clapped frenziedly and were so dense as eventually to bring the car to a standstill. Battley [my detective] was very worried because the town has still plenty of German agents and any of them could have lobbed a grenade or emptied a pistol into the car and probably got away. All this he explained later.

I confess that at the time my one anxiety was lest the car would crush or run over someone. It was an amazing experience. "C'est du délire," P. said, while Walter Moyne's comment was: "It is good that there is one country where we are so popular."

Dined with Jumbo. Some talk about the Greek campaign [of 1941] and old times generally, and then a further meeting in an attempt to straighten this unhappy tangle out. I am still much troubled.

October 27th: While I was shaving Bob [Dixon] informed that Athens wished to confer freedom of city upon me at Acropolis this morning. It is a queer world. Papandreou came to fetch me and we drove up through streets fairly well filled. Here and there groups of E.A.M. chanting their slogans which was slightly irritating. At the Acropolis the crowd found a new variant: "Edèn. Edèn." But the crowds were generally less impressive than the spontaneous gatherings of yesterday. The ceremony itself was short and impressive. We stood on the site of the temple of Roma to emphasize humiliation of Italy. Weather was unfortunately misty which limited the view.

Harold Macmillan arrived at lunch-time and we had brief talk. Then C.O. of 11th Battalion 60th [Rifles] came to fetch me and I went to see his battalion. It is always pleasant to be among riflemen. He had paraded one company and I inspected them and spoke to them. Then I had tea in the officers' mess.

Back to Embassy and further meeting at 6.30 p.m. which lasted more than two hours. We still struggle manfully. Dinner at Embassy, more work afterwards and bed about 2 a.m.

I now sent Mr. Churchill a further report:

> We have had a further day of discussion and action on supply and monetary problems. As a result I feel happier about the former. . . . The monetary business is devilish, Waley

arrives tomorrow for which I am most grateful. . . . I find the political situation extremely difficult to assess. There are so many uncertain factors, not least being the mercurial character of these people. Moreover we have only seen Athens. One thing is certain, that at present the only factor that really unites all the Greeks is their devotion to Britain, to whom they look perhaps rather too much for guidance and salvation.

As regards the strength of E.A.M., their present importance lies in the fact that they are the only really organized party, but I still doubt whether in Athens at any rate they have any deep hold on loyal people. This does not mean that they could not and would not stage a *coup d'état* if the Government's hold on the country were weakened. . . .

Communist members of the Government asked to see me and in agreement with Papandreou I received them this morning. Their professions of loyalty to the Government of National Unity and their assurances of their intentions to work with us could not have been more profuse. All the same I have no doubt that if we had not made our position pretty clear to Bear we would have had a good deal of trouble with them.

The King's position is difficult to pronounce upon because he is just never mentioned. This should not necessarily be taken as a comment wholly unfavourable to his prospects. On the contrary there are many who think that by the line he is following he is beginning to gain ground. . . . I am sure that advice given to him up to date has been sound in his own interests, for if he were to come in at this moment when E.A.M. is the only armed force in the country except for our own troops and three thousand Athens police, we should soon have civil war.

Papandreou has issued a decree calling on four classes from twenty-six to twenty-nine. . . . We hope to deliver to him within six weeks enough uniforms and equipment to allow him to have about thirty thousand men under arms. Agreement has been reached with E.A.M. Ministers that E.L.A.S. are to be demobilized. When that has happened and there is a National Army instead of an E.A.M. Army, the political position may undergo something of a transformation. At the moment E.A.M.

are bullies in the background, who but for our presence would certainly come to the fore. If we can tide over the next six weeks, we should have considerably reduced the menace to the state.

October 28th: Still no news of Waley. Talk with Harold [Macmillan] and Jumbo in morning and we discussed number of projects for handling this situation. After luncheon Rex [Leeper] and I drove towards the mountains on the Marathon road and got out for a walk. Very pleasant, lovely country, autumn crocus out. Only excitement created by a number of rifle shots fired uncomfortably close as we reached the road again. Battley definitely doesn't approve.

Finally Sir David Waley arrived and I was able to leave for my visit to Italy. I sent Mr. Churchill a prognosis on October 30th:

> Dr. Waley has arrived and has prescribed for the patient, though no final decision as to the date of the operation [currency stabilization] will be taken until after the examination of the patient, Papandreou, tomorrow. Dr. Waley inspires confidence though he repeats the usual warning that all depends on the patient's will to live.
>
> At any rate there is nothing more that family friends can do for the moment, . . . but I am by no means confident that this little country will be able to regain its stability without other and maybe terrible upheavals. It is so desperately poor in all natural resources and the Germans have so well planned their work of dislocation and destruction.

A rough and stormy flight over southern Italy and the Apennines was not the best preparation for the official dinner which Macmillan and I found awaiting us in Rome. However, Sir Noel Charles was a considerate host and I spent a pleasant evening in discussion with the Italian Prime Minister, Signor Ivanoe Bonomi, whose intentions were excellent, but whose Government was unfortunately none too stable. After a visit the next morning to Mussolini's room in the Palazzo Venezia, where lovely pictures had replaced the politics,*

* *Facing the Dictators,* page 229.

I set off for Field-Marshal Alexander's headquarters near Siena.

A torrential downpour of rain which lasted several days almost immobilized us and destroyed my hopes of seeing the battle front, but at least I understood the conditions in which the army and air force had to fight. My host's company, impervious alike to the weather or enemy action, redeemed the chagrin I must otherwise have felt.

★   ★   ★   ★   ★

Paris had been liberated by a French rising on August 23rd. When I returned to England, I found preparations in progress for a visit to that city, to which General de Gaulle and M. Georges Bidault, the Foreign Secretary of the newly recognized French Government, had invited Mr. Churchill and myself. Our colleagues were not very happy about the trip, being anxious for the Prime Minister's safety. I felt doubly responsible, for the Prime Minister, of course, was raring to go and I was equally enthusiastic. At a last-minute tussle I admitted that there were risks, but it was accepted that they should be taken.

The days chosen were November 10th, 11th and 12th and the scene at the military parade in the Champs-Elysées on Armistice Day was unforgettable. Among a people whose spirit was free again the troops marched proudly by, while the crowds acclaimed with cheers and tears of relief and happiness.

Years before in an acrimonious discussion at a time when there were difficulties between us and de Gaulle, the Prime Minister had corrected the General when he had referred to relations between "France and England," and spoke of "General de Gaulle and England," suggesting that he was not France and might not be so accepted by his countrymen. The General had been much offended. As we now stood, Mr. Churchill on the General's right and I on his left, de Gaulle turned to me and said quietly: *"Regardez-moi ce peuple en révolution."*

We were lodged at the Quai d'Orsay in the same rooms as the King and Queen had occupied on their state visit to France a few months before the outbreak of war. The next morning I wanted to consult the Prime Minister about some telegram which had arrived from the Foreign Office. I went to seek him in his bedroom. It was empty, but through the open bathroom door I heard splashing and then a voice called out: "Come in, come in; that is, if you can bear to see me in a gold bath when you only have a silver one."

★   ★   ★   ★   ★

During this visit, France, as I was soon to report to the House of Commons, was like a man emerging from a darkened room into a blaze of light, dazed for a moment and grateful still to his friends for understanding and encouragement.* Our journey had a political consequence. The Foreign Office on my instructions had been examining the so-called western *bloc* with the Chiefs of Staff. Mr. Churchill, though still sceptical about this, was now prepared to discuss it. He wrote to me that all the Western European countries were hopelessly weak and asked how Britain could afford to defend them before a strong French army had been re-created. I replied:

> I entirely agree with you that it would be both absurd and highly dangerous for us to enter into any commitments for the defence of Norway, Denmark, Belgium or Holland, except in conjunction with the French and as part of some general plan for containing Germany evolved under the ægis of a World Organization. On these two points the Foreign Office has never had any doubts and I have repeatedly made them clear myself.
>
> I further agree with you that the Western European countries behaved very foolishly between the two wars and were grossly unprepared to meet the blow when it fell. But our own record in this period was not entirely praiseworthy and we only escaped their fate by the skin of our teeth and thanks to the Channel. It has always seemed to me that the lesson of the disasters of 1940 is precisely the need to build up a common defence association in Western Europe, which would prevent another Hitler, whencesoever he may come, pursuing what you have so aptly called the policy of "one by one." The best way of creating such an association would obviously be to build up France and we can only hope that during the period of the occupation of Germany such a build up will be possible. . . .

---

* *Freedom and Order,* pages 277–9.

There seems every reason to start thinking about it now, since if our Western European Allies and more especially the French have the impression that we are not going in future to accept *any* commitments on the Continent it may well be, as you suggest, that they will come to the conclusion that their only hope lies in making defence arrangements, not with us, but with the Russians. And surely the development of long-range missiles proves that somehow or other, if we are to retain our independence, we must obtain some kind of "defence in depth."

As I see it, then, a properly organized Western Europe can provide us with depth for defence and large resources of manpower which would greatly ease our burden and enable us to avoid a huge standing army which would cripple our economy. Hitler's strategy of "one by one" not only gave him ideal bases from which to bombard us and assault our sea communications, but also deprived us of a manpower pool of over sixty millions. Consequently, we have once again had to strain ourselves to the utmost to raise a large army as well as a powerful air force and navy, and even then we could not have hoped for victory without the manpower of Russia and America.

Meanwhile, Hitler has himself had the labour of millions of these Western Europeans, which has greatly helped him to keep up the numbers of the Germany Army. This situation might be avoided in the future if we have some system whereby France in the first instance and the smaller Western European Allies in the second agree to organize their defences together with us according to some common plan.

I see no reason to suppose that such an arrangement would result in the maintenance by us of a huge standing army, though I think we should have to reconcile ourselves to making a rather larger land contribution than the famous two divisions which was all we had to offer last time. . . .

★   ★   ★   ★   ★

Soon after the Paris visit I had to retire to bed with a throat infection.

November 17th: Felt a little better in morning but still not too good. [Dr.] Rossdale came in and didn't want me to go to House or to Walter's service [the memorial service for Lord Moyne, who had been assassinated in Cairo on November 5th by Jewish terrorists]. Worked in bed until luncheon time. Winston came in for half an hour. Sweet of him. We talked of many things, foreign and domestic. Changes in Government in particular, and remedies for sore throats. He wanted to spray me with his penicillin.

Off home after luncheon and a rather tiresome interview with King of Greece. I like him and am really trying to help, but he is curiously obtuse.

King George admitted that his position had improved as a result of staying outside Greece. He seemed optimistic about the results of a plebiscite. I said that I could not judge of this, for I had not heard the question canvassed while I was in Athens. At the moment the immediate Greek concern was with the means of existence.

November 18th–19th: Three bad messages from F.D.R. These last are unhelpful. Snarky to the French and generally arrogant and aloof, ignoring our invitation to him to come here altogether. I am told that Leahy now has the ear. Whatever the reason the result is a bad augury for the new regime [the President had been re-elected for a fourth term on November 7th].

The President had refused to agree that the French should attend at the next three-power meeting to discuss Germany. He was not forthcoming about equipment for the new French army, although he warned Mr. Churchill that after the defeat of Germany, American troops would be brought home from Europe as quickly as transport would allow. The Prime Minister was hoping for an early meeting, but the President sent him a copy of a message he had sent to Stalin, explaining that he did not wish to leave Washington before his inauguration in January.

One of the subjects which Mr. Churchill wanted to discuss was, as usual, Poland. When I returned to London at the beginning of November, I found that M. Mikolajczyk had made little progress in converting his colleagues to the acceptance of the Curzon line, even as part of a package deal with the Russians and the Lublin Committee. In order to strengthen his hand, the War Cabinet had assured the Polish Government that they would support the extension of Polish territory in the west as far as the Oder, even if the Americans did not agree.* The Poles now thought it essential to get a clear expression of the President's attitude.

Mr. Averell Harriman arrived in London with Roosevelt's reply on November 21st:

> Dined with W., Averell and family. Talk after dinner about Polish affairs and Averell showed us answer Americans were returning to Polish questions. It is not worth much to the Poles, but I don't expect that they counted on more, though they may have hoped for it. We discussed how situation must be handled and A. asked whether he should offer to raise Lwow again with Russians, as F.D.R. had given him discretion to do. I favoured him offering to do this to Poles. W. didn't much like it, on grounds that Russians would only refuse. I maintained that it was important to Mikolajczyk to be able to show his people that he had done everything in his power. Moreover, though I didn't say so, I thought it would do Americans no harm to have a crack at this for themselves and Russians no harm either. We have made the running so far.
>
> *November 22nd:* Cabinet lasted until 1.45. Further long Cabinet in afternoon which I left about 6.30 p.m. though I believe it went on much longer. Someone has only to start any new hare and W. cannot resist chasing it himself across many fields by which time it is pretty difficult to pull up others.

A Cabinet as conducted by Mr. Churchill could be a splendid and unique experience. It might be a monologue, it was never a dictatorship. The disadvantage, to those with specific duties to perform or departments to run, was the time consumed. All the same, none of us should have grudged these Cabinets, enlivened by the sweep and dive of the Prime Minister's discourse.

Mr. Harriman delivered President Roosevelt's letter to M. Mikolajczyk on November 22nd. Two days later the Polish Prime Minister told him that he would not ask the Americans to press once

* Count Edward Raczynski: *In Allied London.*

more for Lwow. All the parties in the Polish Government, except his own Peasant Party, misdoubted the Russians' good faith to such an extent that they were opposed to any concession about the frontier before the peace settlement. M. Mikolajczyk and his associates felt that if there were only a ten per cent chance of an arrangement with the Russians working, it should be taken. But since they did not have general support, Mikolajczyk felt bound to resign.

Stalin now had no further motive to stay his hand. At the end of December the Russians recognized the Lublin Committee as the provisional Government of Poland.

★　★　★　★　★

Soon after my conversation with the King of Greece on November 17th, I had received a message from Field-Marshal Smuts suggesting that it was time for the King to return to Greece and restore the constitutional position while E.A.M. was being eliminated. I replied on December 1st:

> The large measure of success which has attended our operations in Greece and the absence of any serious disturbances may give a misleading impression of the situation in the country. This is in fact extremely precarious, and would be far worse if it were not for M. Papandreou's skill and determination and the powerful support which we are able to give him. The Greek Government's authority extends at present only to Athens and Piraeus and the immediate neighbourhood. Of the rest of Greece the greater part is under E.A.M. control. . . .
>
> I am convinced that for the King to return to Greece at this moment would be playing straight into E.A.M.'s hands, for it is the one issue on which they might be able to whip up opposition both against the Greek Government and against the British forces. It would gravely weaken M. Papandreou's own position and our ability to help him, for there would be very strong criticism both in this country and in Greece if it could be suggested that British troops were being used to reimpose the King against the wishes of the Greek people.
>
> The question of the monarchy is not the burning issue of the

day and it is essential that it should remain dormant until the Greek Government have been able to establish their authority over E.A.M. and E.L.A.S. The outcome should not be long delayed, for the crucial date is likely to be December 10th when the E.L.A.S. guerrillas are to be disarmed and demobilized.

Even as this message was being despatched to Field-Marshal Smuts, E.A.M. Ministers had left the Government and the trial of strength had begun. Instructions were at once sent to General Scobie and Mr. Leeper to restore order in Athens and Piraeus. But this could not resolve the political problem of a weakened Government. Leeper pointed out on December 10th that neither Papandreou nor any other politician had sufficient standing to meet this situation. The King could not be present. The only way in which a settlement might be reached was for the Archbishop of Athens to be appointed Regent.

With the War Cabinet's approval, Mr. Churchill and I put this suggestion to the King of the Hellenes on December 12th. The King refused, because his people, he told us, would take the appointment of a Regent to mean that he was abandoning his cause and his duties. From Athens Mr. Macmillan endorsed Leeper's recommendation, saying that each side feared reprisals if the other won.

Mr. Churchill and I saw the King again on December 14th and 16th. On each occasion he told us that while he would feel bound to follow his Government's advice, the recommendations he was receiving from M. Papandreou and the other politicians were by no means all in favour of a regency. We already knew from Leeper's reports that the Greek Ministers were not unanimous, and the War Cabinet decided on December 18th to wait for a few days before pressing the King again. The Prime Minister was influenced by the fact that Archbishop Damaskinos had been appointed to his see under the Germans, and by the King's belief that he was tender towards E.A.M.

Opinion in Parliament and the country was confused and disturbed by events in Athens. Owing to our earlier support and our efforts to bring about unity between the guerrilla bands, the true character of E.A.M. had never been publicly explained. Many regarded the rebels as good left-wing democrats and gallant resistance fighters, and feared that British troops were being used to suppress Greek political freedom.

However, on December 8th, a debate in the House of Commons which Mr. Churchill opened and I wound up, ended in an encouraging victory for the Government. Though our purpose, as I explained, was to enable the Greek people to express their own will, we must insist that the expression should be through the ballot box and not by the bomb. On December 11th Mr. Bevin carried the Trades Union Congress with him in support of our action. But criticism continued and on December 20th the House again debated the situation.

December 20th: Feeling pretty weary. Went to House where I saw W. during Questions. He still maintained, as he did when I spoke to him on telephone this morning, that he would speak and argued that we both should. I went to our room after Questions and discussion continued. He seemed tired and eventually began to say what points he would make if he were to speak. I knew then that he wouldn't. All parties were anxious that he shouldn't for fear of further altercation with Bevan and Gallacher and Co.

In my speech I confined myself to giving facts to counter the wilder accusations about British action. In speaking of the Regency I revealed that it had been proposed by Leeper; but I could not as yet say that the Government had strongly urged it upon the King.

December 21st: Very difficult Cabinet on Greece. W. has his knife into the Archbishop and is convinced that he is both a quisling and a Communist. In fact, as Alec [Cadogan] puts it neatly, he has taken the place of de Gaulle. Brendan [Bracken] was maddening and supported W. knowing absolutely nothing of the matter, and also attacked Leeper. This brought me out and I said if Cabinet had no confidence in Leeper they had better say so and say the same of Foreign Secretary at same time. W. rejoined, rather mournfully for him, that there was no doubt of Cabinet's support of Foreign Secretary. What was in doubt was Cabinet's confidence in him. Embarrassing pause. But W. clung to his opposition to Regency of Archbishop, or "dictatorship," as he insists on calling it.

December 22nd: More evidence in morning that King of Greece is not telling us the truth about evidence he is getting from Greece on Regency. [M. Athanasios] Aghnides [Greek Ambassador], whom I trust, gives a different version to that of the King. Went to see W. who was still in bed. After some argument during which he upbraided Leeper and Macmillan, whom he describes as our two "fuzzy wuzzies," he agreed that we should send for the King.

This we did at 3 p.m. and in course of talk it was quite clear that he had held back at least one message from Papandreou. Even W. admitted this. But I doubt whether interview did much more than confirm King in W.'s support of him, last sentence being to remind King that Charles I had lost his head by fighting but had perpetuated crown and Church.

Historical as these exchanges were, they provided no means of reconciling the two sides in Greece. On December 23rd I sent the Prime Minister this minute:

It may be of some help if I try to put down the reasons why I still think, after our conversation with the King of the Hellenes yesterday evening, that a Regency in Athens will prove necessary.

It is hardly conceivable that Papandreou can continue in office after E.A.M. have accepted Scobie's terms and preside over a broad-based Cabinet including E.A.M. We desire such a Cabinet for the post-armistice period and a new Prime Minister will presumably have to be found to head it. The King's idea appears to be that he could form such a new Government from London by telegraph. This hardly seems possible. Much negotiation is likely to be required on the spot and for this a trusted Regent could be of great service. If there is no Regent it looks as though our representative will have to do the job. I cannot see Papandreou organising the Government that is to succeed him.

The principal E.A.M. weapon throughout this business has

been to pretend that it was our intention to impose the King upon his people. There is no doubt that despite all our protestations this has been pretty widely believed. The appointment of a Regent together with a statement by the King as he put it to us last night to the effect that he will not return until after a plebiscite would, I belive, go far to remove this fear and to ease the tension when the armistice comes. If, on the other hand, the King continues to attempt to carry out Cabinet-making from here I fear that suspicion of him and his motives would be intensified and our difficulties correspondingly increased.

Characteristically Mr. Churchill decided that the way out of the impasse was to reconnoitre for himself.

December 24th: W. rang up in morning to say that he was considering going to Athens, probably tomorrow night. Suggested I should go instead. Then W. said we ought both to go. But weather unlikely to be favourable. We were in touch on telephone all day and then to my horror at about 5.30 p.m. he rang up to say weather was good and we must be off tonight. Hell. I was looking forward to quiet family Christmas.

I felt it all the more hardly because this was my son Simon's final leave before he flew off to the Far East for the Burma campaign.

When we arrived at Athens the next day, we conferred with Field-Marshal Alexander and Macmillan and Leeper, even before leaving our aircraft. Macmillan told us that they had been considering whether it would help to summon a conference of all the Greek political leaders and invite E.L.A.S. We thought that this might be useful. Later in the evening Mr. Churchill and I saw M. Papandreou and Archbishop Damaskinos on board H.M.S. *Ajax* and told them about the plan. The Archbishop agreed to preside over the conference. His bitterness over the atrocities committed by E.L.A.S. soon converted Mr. Churchill from his former distrust.

Criss-crossing the empty streets, I spent the next morning getting into touch with the American Ambassador, the French Minister and the head of the Soviet Military Mission to invite them to come to the conference as observers. Colonel Popov seemed uncertain, but after some argument he bravely undertook to consult his superiors. In the event all three accepted, which had its significance for our meeting.

The Prime Minister and I drove in armoured cars to the Greek Foreign Office through the gloom of a winter evening. When we entered the room all was in murky shadow except for a long table down the middle. There a few hurricane lamps broke the darkness and played upon the glittering epaulets of the chief of the Soviet Mission, as he sat with his French and American colleagues at the end of the table.

The Archbishop presided with Mr. Churchill on his right and I next to him. Papandreou sat opposite with General Nikolaos Plastiras beside him, resplendent in uniform and waxed moustaches. The E.L.A.S. delegates had not arrived and the conference began. In the half light the tall figure of the Archbishop was majestic in black robes. When Damaskinos had welcomed us, Mr. Churchill began his reply. He had not got very far before there was the sound of scratching at the door. The shadows dissolved to reveal the E.L.A.S. delegates being disarmed before they approached to take their places at the end of the table, facing the representatives of our allies, where Colonel Popov's uniform no doubt had its effect. At the conclusion of Mr. Churchill's speech, all the foreign representatives withdrew to the sound of the gunfire of the civil war without, leaving, we devoutly hoped, the Greek parties to come to terms.

Field-Marshal Alexander and I were following the Prime Minister when we noticed a figure rapidly skirting the wall, for all the world like an old cock pheasant running down a hedge. He proved to be an elder statesman, M. Sophoulis, and he was firmly headed back to join the rest of the company.

The next day the Archbishop came to the Embassy to tell us the outcome of the meeting. All, he said, were in favour of a Regency; M. Papandreou had promised to advise the King accordingly. The Archbishop was ready to become Regent and it was finally agreed that he should do so with British support. Meanwhile operations had to continue until Attica was free or until E.L.A.S. had accepted General Scobie's terms.

Mr. Churchill and I left Athens in the afternoon of December 28th and flew first to Caserta.

December 29th: Up early after a most uncomfortable night on the hardest of pillows. W. unexpectedly punctual and pleased with his prowess. Left at 7 a.m., I with Commander-in-Chief, Mediterranean. Uneventful flight.

At six o'clock the same evening Mr. Churchill and I reported to the War Cabinet in London on our conversations and on the advice we proposed to give the King of Greece. From the Cabinet we went back to the Annexe at a quarter past ten for a meeting with the King, which unfortunately lasted with intervals until half past four in the morning.

[The King] tried hard to avoid the word "Regent," secondly to modify sentence that he would not return until his people had expressed their will. I had eventually to recall that it was ambiguity on this issue that I had tried to clear up in Cairo more than a year ago, and it was failure to do so that was at least in part responsible for our present troubles. W. was very firm and steady.

Eventually King George agreed to a declaration appointing the Archbishop as Regent and promising that he would not return to Greece unless summoned by a free and fair expression of the nation's will.

Archbishop Damaskinos at once took office and appointed as Prime Minister General Plastiras, a republican who had been many years in exile. A truce was soon signed with E.L.A.S.

Greece's troubles were by no means over, but at the least the Greek people would now have a chance to choose their destiny without fear.

15

STALIN THE NEGOTIATOR
January–April 1945

Preparations for the Yalta Conference — Mr. Bevin — Preliminary discussions in Malta — Arrival of President Roosevelt — We proceed to the Crimea — The President and the Conference — Mr. Churchill and the Conference — The hooded Georgian — Controversy over Poland — Sevastopol — We fly to Greece — The Russian-directed *coup d'état* in Roumania — The Soviets renege on Yalta — I doubt the validity of a United Nations' Conference — Death of President Roosevelt — Marshal Stalin details Mr. Molotov for San Francisco

MEETINGS of the three war leaders had their merits, though orderly despatch of business was not one of them. Before Mr. Churchill and I went to Athens there was no sign that the next encounter was yet in the offing. I wanted another meeting of Foreign Secretaries to pave the way, as our conference in Moscow had prepared the ground for Tehran. When it became probable that the main meeting would take place at the end of January, I still thought that some preliminary discussion was essential to its success.

January 4th: A heavy morning's work, the most important item being a talk with Alec C. [Cadogan] about a meeting of the three great men. I am much worried that the whole business will be chaotic and nothing worth while settled, Stalin being the only one of the three who has a clear view of what he wants and is a tough negotiator. P.M. is all emotion in these matters, F.D.R. vague and jealous of others.

I therefore wrote to Mr. Churchill, saying I hoped that the Foreign Secretaries could meet at least a week in advance, perhaps in

Cairo. We should, I thought, be in great difficulties if this were not done and there were "neither agenda nor orderly preparation of any kind." I had my forebodings that accommodation in Yalta might be haphazard and scattered, making informal meetings difficult to arrange.

I gave Mr. Churchill a list of some of the questions which might come up for discussion. This included Germany, a subject on which he was still unwilling to take decisions. On the same day as my minute to him, January 4th, the Prime Minister sent me a report from Lord Keynes which said that President Roosevelt had not made up his mind on several fundamental issues and apparently did not intend to do so for some time. I noted on this:

> Of course it is always attractive to postpone decisions, but the President's waiting on the side-lines has its dangers also. Europe will take shape or break up while he stands by and it will be too late afterwards to complain of frontiers or of the nature of conflicts, e.g. Poland and Greece.

January 5th: Talk to W. on telephone, who is just back from France. There the battle still sways and its outcome is yet uncertain. He thinks Americans have lost one hundred thousand men. Russian attitude towards Poles bad and I am still anxious, as I told W., about meeting of Big Three. There is still no preparation, no agenda, and no agreement as to how long meeting will last. There is much work to be done and I doubt if they will get down to it. Therefore I urged preliminary meeting of three Foreign Secretaries. W. was doubtful and said we should do better all together.

However, Mr. Churchill was anxious that the British and American Staffs should have talks before going to Yalta and, in telegraphing about this to President Roosevelt on January 8th, he also put forward my suggestion of a Foreign Ministers' meeting.* The President replied that the United States Secretary of State, Mr. Edward Stettinius, could not be away from the United States for as long as himself. He said that Stettinius would join him at

---

* Churchill: *The Second World War*; Vol. VI.

Malta and that the conference at Yalta should not last more than five or six days.

This was all too short and I was the less disposed to accept the dismissal of consultation. On January 10th I asked Mr. Churchill to return to the charge and propose that Stettinius should come to Malta in advance, even if Molotov could not be invited. The President replied that the Secretary of State would, after all, reach Malta on January 31st, and with this I had to be content. He also promised to send Harry Hopkins to London first.

> *January 12th:* Terrible Cabinet, first on Greece. . . . Whole thing lasted four and a half hours. Really quite intolerable. I was in pretty bloody temper in first half for everyone started taking a hand at drafting messages for me, including Bevin. Everything takes many times longer to decide than is necessary.

This action of Bevin's was entirely out of character. I have many reasons to remember how constantly he supported me in the War Cabinet and remained friendly to me after the Conservative Party defeat. I was at a small luncheon one day given by the Austrian Ambassador, Herr Lothar Wimmer, to Mr. Bevin as Foreign Secretary. Lord Cranborne and Lord Addison were the other guests. During the meal the Ambassador pressed Bevin to pay a visit to Vienna. "Yes," he replied, "and I'll bring Anthony along with me. It'll show that we have one foreign policy." Bevin's opinions were rough-hewn and big and, though he had his personal prejudices, the in-fighting of party politics did not appeal to him. Our friendship was never marred by any serious difference and lasted until his death.

★　★　★　★　★

Even the weekend brought no relief:

> *January 13th:* Two boxes to get through, worked like a slave. Another box at luncheon but not so bad. Work after tea.

Yugoslav affairs were again in uneasy balance. When Dr. Šubašić came back in December from his prolonged visit to Moscow, he gave an account of his agreement with Marshal Tito which I considered "as good as we dared hope." There followed negotiations about the King's position in these new conditions.

On January 2nd I minuted in the Foreign Office:

> I have some sympathy with the King if his argument is that he doesn't want to give the Communist dictatorship a cloak of respectability, if royal approval is respectability these days.

Even so it appeared that King Peter's only hope of reigning again, a slender one, was to accept the agreement. The British and American Ambassadors should then, as I told Mr. Churchill, "do all they can to see that it is carried out as fairly as they can contrive." The Prime Minister and War Cabinet approved this course.

King Peter finally endorsed the formation of a Regency Council. Both it and the new Government took office at the beginning of March.

★   ★   ★   ★   ★

Harry Hopkins flew to London on January 21st. I spent several evenings with him and the Prime Minister, talking over all our problems. On one of these occasions Mr. Churchill, in the best of spirits, held forth to Hopkins about British affairs in a form which our guest could not resist and which had much wisdom in it:

> W. gave me a lecture on the use of the box in the House, with illustrations, which was very entertaining. Naturally I was also touched by his kindness to me. He told Harry that we were H.M.G., that if for any reason we came into real conflict, the Government must break up; all this with a gay recital of our methods of work together. Incidentally it was the only evening when I got to bed as early as 1.15 a.m. The other evenings I had found much of a trial with talk of Greece, Poland, France and a hundred subjects Parliamentary and foreign, with the result that I was so tired most of the week that I made very little sense in the House.

The discussion on the use of the despatch box turned upon the question of the speaker's height. For a man of short or medium stature there was no problem, but if the speaker were six foot or more, his eye was farther from the box and there was a temptation to lean or drape himself across it. Mr. Churchill was strongly against this. "Whatever your height, stand back from the box," was his advice, "no attempt should ever be made to conceal the use of notes, better to flaunt them than to pretend not to be using them and take sidelong glances. If it is difficult to read the notes, then it is better to have special spectacles made." I believe Mr. Churchill used to do this himself; a master of his craft as an orator, he was never ashamed to learn the tricks.

On January 26th I sent the Prime Minister a note of the Russian political demands which I expected to be raised at Yalta. These would be linked to a Soviet entry into the war against Japan. Stalin might also revert to the idea of revising the Montreux Convention governing the Turkish Straits, which he had raised first at Tehran and again on our last visit to Moscow. I thought it well to warn the Prime Minister not to be too forthcoming on either of these issues:

> it would be better for us merely to note what they [the Russians] have to say without entering into discussion and without giving them too much encouragement of our support. It may well be that we shall want to ask for *quid pro quos* even though we may not get them. In any case I do not think we should indicate straight away that we regard any proposals put forward by the Russians as well founded.

On the Far East I had been disturbed by a Chiefs of Staff minute reporting that, on present evidence, Russia was unlikely "to display any major interest in the Far East except in an area consisting of her present Far Eastern possessions, together with Manchuria, Korea, Sakhalin and the Kuriles." But, I continued in my note to the Prime Minister, this was a very important exception:

> There may perhaps be little argument about a Russian claim to recover possession of South Sakhalin which was ceded to Japan by the Treaty of Portsmouth in 1905. The Americans may look more closely at any claim to take the Kuriles. But a most difficult issue is likely to arise over Manchuria and Korea.

We do not yet know what Russia's requirements are likely to be, but their conformity with the Cairo Declaration, for which we ourselves share responsibility, will be closely scrutinized by the Chinese, the Americans and others; and it is possible that these requirements can only be satisfied at the expense of incessant friction with the Chinese who may receive American support and expect ours also.

At all events there is here a potential cauldron of international dispute. It seems advisable therefore, at this stage, to go warily and to avoid anything like commitments or encouragement to Russia.

A forecast to be fulfilled at a terrible cost years later, but I was wrong in my estimate of American support for their Chinese ally at the Conference.

Mr. Churchill replied that he would not be prepared to resist a Russian demand for the freedom of the Straits. With regard to the Far East, too, he would not be able to oppose the kind of Russian wishes I had mentioned, if granting them led to a quick end to the Japanese war. I answered on January 28th, agreeing that there was no difference of principle between us but explaining:

What I have in mind is this: the Russians will presumably want from the Conference (1) Recognition of the Lublin Government; (2) A readiness on our part and that of the Americans to consider proposals for a new Montreux Convention; (3) Some requirements, we do not yet know what, in the Far East.

We want (1) a free and independent Poland. Stalin has promised this to us before, but he is not at present fulfilling his promise. Unless we can get a free and independent Poland our future co-operation with him, whether we will or not, is bound to be affected. (2) On another plane we have a similar situation to deal with in Persia where the Russians are not observing the terms of the Tehran Pact agreed between us and them and the Americans. We want nothing for ourselves, but we shall be hard put to it to get what we want for others, particularly Poland. It was for this reason that I suggested that we should not make concessions about what Stalin wants except in return for concessions in respect of what we want.

It may be said that any concession to Stalin in the Far East will be in return for his part in the Far Eastern war. But I would submit that Stalin has his own reasons for wishing to come into the Far Eastern war and it is this that influences him, although no doubt he will try to get further advantages if he can.

That same night I joined the Prime Minister and Mrs. Churchill for a film at the Air Ministry, "a Californian colour fantasy with Deanna Durbin." The scenery and the sunshine did me good in our dark wartime London evening. I went back with the Prime Minister to his room afterwards, when he showed me a letter he had written to the King, at his request, with advice on the political succession, should he and I both be killed on our journey. The King had told me the week before that he had asked for this. Mr. Churchill and I employed ourselves speculating on what would happen and came to the conclusion that on the whole our colleagues would lead much quieter lives.

The next day we left by separate aeroplanes for the meeting with President Roosevelt.

January 29th: Up early after much too short a night, barely five hours. Motored with Bob to Northolt. Still very cold. Fast flight to Malta, but we flew high and were not given oxygen with the result that I arrived with a headache, not feeling too good. Read a Maugham novel and dozed. Flew straight over Binderton which looked fragile in the snow.

Met by captain of *Sirius* [Capt. Patrick Brooking] at aerodrome and after a brief talk with Harriman motored to the ship. Alec [Cadogan] and I went for a walk late in evening which did me good. Talked to one or two soldiers on the way who seemed very cheerful. Nothing gives me more comfort than when a soldier's face lights up with pleasure when he recognizes one. I suppose this is vanity, but I hope not entirely. The truth is that I like our people and to be with them.

January 30th: We crossed the harbour and berthed at opposite side to *Orion.* As soon as we had tied up we went ashore, took our cars and motored round the island. . . .

Back about 4.30. We walked the last two miles in, and, as we approached the docks, were given a great welcome by Maltese who followed us to the ship, cheering. All rather like the Pied Piper.

Went across to see Winston at 6.30 on his summons. Brookie and I went into his cabin and were staggered when he told us that he had had temperature of over 102° last night. Perfectly normal now. Alec told me that he was sure it was all due to excitement. W. and I and Brookie had talk over work of Combined Chiefs of Staff so far, prospects on Western Front, Alex's [Field-Marshal Alexander] future, etc. It is hard to believe that Germans can hold out long if Russians enter Berlin. Much depends on whether Russians can carry through their forward sweep now, or whether they must rest and refit and start afresh, perhaps after six weeks' interval. My own betting is that they will make Berlin.

Alec and I dined with Winston, Harriman also there. We had some quite good preliminary talk on our conference problems and then left them to their bezique.

The following day Stettinius and Hopkins arrived.

We dined at Government House. Sat between Lady Schreiber [wife of the Governor, Gen. Sir Edmond Schreiber] and an American Admiral; quite pleasant. Managed to break the party up about midnight, encouraged thereto by Alex and other fellow guests. W. had talk with Ed [Stettinius] and when I came up was deprecating standing pat on American voting formula [for United Nations] against Russians. He also held forth against Western pact. Some argument between us on both issues.

February 1st: After a preliminary turn on deck [of H.M.S. *Sirius*] Ed and I and our helpers sat down to a review of the conference work. We found ourselves in complete agreement on all major points. They seemed to me to give rather too much weight to World Council and too little to Poland, in the sense that unless the Russians can be persuaded or compelled to treat Poland with some decency there will not be a world council that is worth much. But this is more a matter of emphasis than anything else since they seem fully alive to seriousness of Polish issue. I certainly did my best to underline this and to urge upon Ed that it was their turn to take up the burden on this issue. We would back them to the full but a change of bowling was needed, and we would both have to do all we could.

I suggested to the Secretary of State that we should propose withdrawing all foreign troops from Iran as soon as the supply route to the Soviet Union could be dispensed with. I wanted to break the Russian stranglehold on Iran and this seemed one way to do it.

When Stettinius asked me about the Russian interest in warm-water ports I told him, as I had told Mr. Churchill, that I felt we ought to put all the things we wanted from the Russians against the things we had to give. This would apply both to the Straits and to the Far East. If the Soviets decided to enter the Far Eastern war it would be because they thought it was in their interest to do so. There was no need for us to offer them a high price, and if we were prepared to accede to their territorial demands in the Far East we should see to it that we got a good return in other directions.

On Germany we agreed that, with the Russians nearing Berlin, it was urgent that the three powers should work out a common political and economic policy.

We had large luncheon party in *Sirius*. Marshall and Brookie, Cunningham [First Sea Lord] and Pug [Ismay] and Harriman besides Americans staying in the ship. Party went quite well I think though rather crowded.

Went for walk rather late in afternoon for a brief spell in Governor's garden where Lady Schreiber met us and insisted upon picking oranges for us. Just before luncheon I took Ed for a short walk in the docks when Malta gave a splendid display of loyalty which, I think, greatly impressed him. Caps off and clapping all the time.

Ed and Harry and I dined with Winston. Some talk of Poland

and conference and of our past record in Italy and Greece. Evening passed off satisfactorily and we got home early.

On the morning of February 2nd I was woken by the ship's band busy practising *The Star-Spangled Banner*. At half past nine President Roosevelt's cruiser hove in sight. As the great warship sailed into the battered harbour every vessel was manned, every roof and vantage point crammed with spectators. While the bands played and amid so much that reeked of war, on the bridge, just discernible to the naked eye, sat one civilian figure. In his sensitive hands lay much of the world's fate. All heads were turned his way and a sudden quietness fell. It was one of those moments when all seems to stand still and one is conscious of a mark in history.

February 2nd: Winston and I lunched on board with him [the President]. I thought he looked considerably older since Quebec; he gives the impression of failing powers. Sarah [Oliver] and Anna B. [Boettiger], F.D.R.'s daughter, Leahy and [Mr. James F.] Byrnes [Director, Office of War Mobilization] made up the party. Pleasant but no business whatsoever done. So a dinner was arranged specifically for this purpose which was no more successful than the luncheon. Impossible even to get near business. I spoke pretty sharply to Harry about it, when he came in later, pointing out that we were going into a decisive conference and had so far neither agreed what we would discuss nor how to handle matters with a Bear who would certainly know his mind.

As a result of these two failures, there had been no Anglo–American consultation except my meetings with Stettinius. The President was so unpredictable that the Prime Minister and I became uneasy at this void. The day had been a sad one for me, for I had learned of the death of three able young members of the Foreign Service and of my personal detective, Inspector Battley. Flying out from London to join us, their pilot had failed to find Malta in the mist, the aircraft came down in the sea off Lampedusa, and they, with eleven others, had drowned.

★ ★ ★ ★ ★

February 3rd: Took off about 1 a.m. Good flight to Crimea; only last part bumpy. Landed about 10 a.m. their time. Molotov, etc. met us. Some refreshments in a marquee on snow-covered aerodrome, part of a grim and treeless plain. Alec and Harry [Hopkins] and I went off together by car. Long drive. Last part through fine mountain scenery, reminiscent of the shores of the Bosphorus.

February 4th: Conference opened in afternoon after various calls which passed off pleasantly enough. Military session was a success, Russians being obviously pleased to learn of our plans. Dinner with Americans; a terrible party I thought. President vague and loose and ineffective. W. understanding that business was flagging made desperate efforts and too long speeches to get things going again. Stalin's attitude to small countries struck me as grim, not to say sinister. We were too many and there was no steady flow and brisk exchanges as at Tehran. I was greatly relieved when whole business was over.

Roosevelt was, above all else, a consummate politician. Few men could see more clearly their immediate objective, or show greater artistry in obtaining it. As a price of these gifts, his long-range vision was not quite so sure. The President shared a widespread American suspicion of the British Empire as it had once been and, despite his knowledge of world affairs, he was always anxious to make it plain to Stalin that the United States was not "ganging up" with Britain against Russia. The outcome of this was some confusion in Anglo–American relations which profited the Soviets.

Roosevelt did not confine his dislike of colonialism to the British Empire alone, for it was a principle with him, not the less cherished for its possible advantages. He hoped that former colonial territories, once free of their masters, would become politically and economically dependent upon the United States, and had no fear that other powers might fill that role.

I do not believe that the President's declining health altered his judgment, though his handling of the Conference was less sure than it might have been. On one occasion when this was causing me special concern, Harry Hopkins came up behind me and said: "The President's not looking very well this afternoon." "Then,"

I replied, "we'd better adjourn now before we get into serious trouble." Adjourn we did.

For those who attributed Roosevelt's decisions to illness, it must be remembered that though the work of the Conference was strenuous enough to keep a man even of Churchill's energy occupied, Roosevelt found time to negotiate in secret, and without informing his British colleague or his Chinese ally, an agreement with Stalin to cover the Far East. This document was, in my judgment, a discreditable by-product of the Conference.

When the Prime Minister and I were told of it on the last day, I did not want him to sign. We were not pressed to do so and, in front of Stalin and Roosevelt, an argument arose between Mr. Churchill and myself. We agreed to call in the assistance of Sir Alexander Cadogan, who had been our Ambassador to China and who shared my view that we ought not to be parties to the agreement. The Prime Minister, however, felt that whether we liked it or not, our authority in the Far East would suffer if we were not signatories, and therefore not parties to any later discussions.

There was force in this, of course, but I still regret that we signed. It was unjust to take decisions affecting the future of China without consulting her and in the absence of her representatives. The negotiations were not conducted for Roosevelt by his Secretary of State, Mr. Stettinius, who knew none of the details. He was kept out of them almost as completely as were the Prime Minister and myself.*

★   ★   ★   ★   ★

Winston Churchill's strength lay in his vigorous sense of purpose and his courage, which carried him undismayed over obstacles daunting to lesser men. He was also generous and impulsive, but this could be a handicap at the conference table. Churchill liked to talk, he did not like to listen, and he found it difficult to wait for, and seldom let pass, his turn to speak. The spoils in the diplomatic game do not necessarily go to the man most eager to debate.

Stalin sometimes led him on. At Yalta on one occasion Stettinius

* Edward R. Stettinius: *Roosevelt and the Russians.*

introduced in a report from the Foreign Secretaries a mention of territorial trusteeship. As Stettinius later explained, this was intended principally to deal with the territories which might be taken from Japan. I had, however, been suspicious of possible wider applications and had not liked the topic when Roosevelt brought it up in Washington in 1943.* Churchill considered that the intention of the report might be aimed at the British Empire and he was not the man to let this go by. He launched out eloquently in defence. Though the Prime Minister's vehemence was a warning signal to the Americans it appeared to give most pleasure to Stalin. He got up from his chair, walked up and down, beamed, and at intervals broke into applause. This embarrassed Roosevelt and did not really profit anybody, except perhaps Stalin, who was able to please himself and point the division of his allies at the same time.

Marshal Stalin as a negotiator was the toughest proposition of all. Indeed, after something like thirty years' experience of international conferences of one kind and another, if I had to pick a team for going into a conference room, Stalin would be my first choice. Of course the man was ruthless and of course he knew his purpose. He never wasted a word. He never stormed, he was seldom even irritated. Hooded, calm, never raising his voice, he avoided the repeated negatives of Molotov which were so exasperating to listen to. By more subtle methods he got what he wanted without having seemed so obdurate.

There was a confidence, even an intimacy, between Stalin and Molotov such as I have never seen between any other two Soviet leaders, as if Stalin knew that he had a valuable henchman and Molotov was confident because he was so regarded. Stalin might tease Molotov occasionally, but he was careful to uphold his authority. Only once did I hear Stalin speak disparagingly of his judgment and that was not before witnesses.

At Yalta the Foreign Secretaries met in the morning and the Heads of Government in the afternoon. At several meetings I had pressed Molotov for agreement to withdraw troops from Iran and he had turned me down pretty sharply. Stettinius gave me support, but after a day or two he pointed out that I was getting nowhere

* Sherwood: *The White House Papers,* Vol. II.

with this attempt and only exacerbating things, and asked if it
would not be better to drop it. I said I could not do that, there
was too much at stake.

I therefore decided, if the Prime Minister approved, to avail myself for the second time of Stalin's promise that I could come to
him if I was in difficulty. Mr. Churchill did not want to raise the
matter formally and encouraged me to go ahead. So after the
meeting that afternoon I went up to Stalin and reminded him of
what he had told me. As soon as I mentioned the name Iran he
laughed. "You should never talk to Molotov about Iran. Didn't
you realize that he had a resounding diplomatic defeat there? He
is very sore with Iran. If you want to talk about it, talk to me.
What is it?" I told him that I thought the time had come to make
a joint plan for the withdrawal of our troops when hostilities ceased.
He nodded and said: "Yes, I understand. I'll think about it."

I was not sanguine of the outcome, but the first step was taken
that summer with the withdrawal of British, Russian and American
troops from Tehran. Maybe Stalin thought this the best way to
handle matters in view of Molotov's failure the previous autumn.
When the Soviets had demanded an oil concession, the Iranians
countered with a law that none could be discussed without parliamentary approval. Russian withdrawal from Azerbaijan proved
much more difficult and, when it came, owed most to the ingenuity
of the Iranians themselves.

★   ★   ★   ★   ★

February 6th: Meeting at noon at Americans' about dismemberment [of Germany]. I had wrangle with Russians, Stettinius not
appearing to seize the points very quickly. Molotov wished to
tie us hand and foot to dismemberment before enquiry was made.
I refused to do this and stuck to my point. Maisky on the way to
luncheon began: "I don't understand your attitude," and I bit
him, reminding him that we were still an independent power.
My obstinacy did good, I think. Anyway, after luncheon Stalin
greeted me most warmly at conference and said: "You have won
again." I didn't know what he meant at first, but when Stettinius
put issue to conference Molotov withdrew his amendment.

I was ready to consider the dismemberment of Germany in the context of future European security, but not to commit myself in advance to decisions for which Molotov was showing increasing eagerness in order to aggrandize Soviet power.

The subject that took up most time at Yalta was once again Poland. After my talk with Stettinius at Malta, I had written to Mr. Churchill saying that we had very much the same ideas about a possible solution. The present state of affairs ought not to continue, with the Russians recognizing one Polish Government in Lublin and ourselves another in London. The only remedy Stettinius and I could see was the creation of a new provisional Government, pledged to hold free elections as soon as possible. This would include representatives of all the political parties and elements from the Lublin Government, from Poles abroad and Poles in Poland. "If," I continued, "the Russians persist in their present policy, that would only neutralize the efforts of all those in our two countries most anxious to work with Russia."

The territorial problem was less difficult, except for the question of Poland's western frontier. We had been willing the previous autumn to agree to a frontier up to the Oder in order to help Mikolajczyk's Government, but this had been conditional on agreement being reached between him and the Russians. We had no such commitment to the Lublin Poles, and there had never been any question of our agreeing to the Western Neisse. Even the line of the Oder would severely tax the Polish capacity for absorption. I ended my minute:

> If the Russians refuse to accept any solution such as that outlined above, the present deadlock must continue. That would be bad, but a simple recognition of the Lublin Government would be worse.

On this basis we argued at Yalta.

February 6th: First talk on Poland. President and P.M. were both good, but Stalin gave us a very dusty answer. I am sure that we must come back hard on this. Dined with Winston and we discussed this and line to take tomorrow. Averell came round later with suggested draft letter from President to Stalin. It was on the right lines but not quite stiff enough. I suggested some amendments which Winston and A.H. approved and he took draft back. We heard later that President had accepted them in their entirety.

February 7th: Foreign Secretaries' meeting at Molotov's villa. Made some progress on various topics. A luncheon followed with usual inevitable toasts. After more talk with Molotov on various matters had a short walk in American garden before 4 p.m. meeting. Dumbarton Oaks first. . . .

The Russians, I wrote, caved in. They accepted a conference to succeed the one at Dumbarton Oaks, which had made a first sketch for an international organization after the war. At this point Mr. Churchill unexpectedly spoke up against such a meeting in wartime. This was another example of the Prime Minister's reluctance to see any energies diverted to peacetime tasks, but the abrupt reversal was

not unnaturally resented by Americans since we had long ago agreed to such a meeting. Then came Poland and Russians again made some concessions, which give hope though we are still far from where we want to be.

A more cheerful dinner with W. and Sarah and Alex. Work after dinner on Russian text *re* Poland, our people produced a good draft.

Once agreement was reached that the United Nations Conference should soon take place, the Foreign Secretaries next discussed where it should be held. All favoured the United States, we as strongly as the Americans. For our purpose was to try to commit our allies as far as we could in support of the United Nations and to reduce the risks of a later withdrawal, as with the League of Nations after the first world war.

Perhaps for the same reason, some of the Americans were against the choice of a populous centre in the eastern States and canvassed a site in the middle west. For this I felt little enthusiasm and later suggested California to Stettinius. San Francisco was in my mind, because I thought it geographically well placed. I had also been disappointed not to be able to see the city on my last visit to the United States. Stettinius worked the oracle.

February 8th: Not such a good day. Stuck again over Poland. Americans produced a text something like ours of last night though not so good. Sent ours round to Russians in morning.

February 9th: After a heavy day of little progress on Poland it was agreed to refer this, like all else, to Foreign Secretaries. Worked at texts again and I made out my minimum which was American text discussed in morning with some improvements of ours, especially at beginning and end. Former were intended to put whole business in better perspective, latter to show our continuing responsibility and intention to supervise.

Met at 1 p.m. Found the Russians unprepared even to consider our draft, so I fairly let them have it, told them something of British opinion, said I would far rather go back without a text than be a party to the sort of thing they wanted, etc.

That afternoon at the plenary session, President Roosevelt observed that the differences between ourselves and the Russians were largely a matter of the use of words. He was deluding himself. After much more dogged argument, we finally reached agreement on words, but it was not long before we learned that the difference of intention remained untouched. Only if a genuinely representative new government had been formed in Poland quickly, would the pledge of free and unfettered elections have had any meaning. This was true of all we did at Yalta, it was the execution which mattered. For the moment the outward appearances had been preserved, as they had to be if we were to win an early victory.

Meanwhile the Americans had brought forward a draft declaration on liberated Europe. This too, though admirable in intention, was soon to be denied by Soviet action.

★   ★   ★   ★   ★

February 12: Up about 9 a.m. and left about 10.30 for Sevastopol. Many farewells. Early part of drive went well, but drivers

didn't know the way, with the result that we took a wrong turning which Alec and I both thought was wrong and said so, and
then found ourselves in a town name of which they didn't know.
I insisted that they should ask, through Archie's [Clark Kerr] very
moderate Russian, and it turned out to be Balaclava, so that I was
delighted at their mistake. Port was attractively placed and must
have been pretty before heavy damage of the war. We turned
round and tried to reconstruct battle and charges on our onward
way. I don't think that we were very successful.

Reached Sevastopol earlier than we expected, after two hours'
drive, all the first part through lovely scenery. But when we
reached the town we got hopelessly lost and spent an hour wan-
dering about the shattered streets in search of our ship. The Russians had not the faintest idea where it was or how to find it.
Indeed this was the first thing they had really muddled, and one
of the most inconvenient.

However eventually reached *Franconia* in time for late luncheon with Winston. Alec and Sarah and Archie Kerr joined us.
W. was going off to visit Balaclava with Alex and said he had
put it off until afternoon so that I could go with him, and also
no doubt because he didn't want to get up. I wouldn't go, for I
really felt too tired and the need for much sleep. We had an admirable Liebfraumilch for luncheon, delicious after pretending
to savour these Russian wines which are drinkable, no more.

Molotov came on board at 3 p.m. and after W. had left I
showed him over the ship and said a last goodbye, the men cheering him, not without encouragement, as he went over the side.

Then to bed for two hours. Dined with Winston and Alex and
Sarah. Some good talk at dinner but also much order, counter-
order, disorder of plans. Eventually decided on at least another
day of rest here which is good.

February 13th: Lay in bed until noon, after a good night, reading and doing some work. Then walk up and down the deck
with Archie, giving him a line for his Polish negotiations. Talked
to some gunners.

Then to see W. at Tommy's [Commander C. R. Thompson]
request when we discussed plans for the hundredth time and
agreed both to leave for Athens tomorrow. Luncheon with him.

More sleep in afternoon which was perhaps a mistake for I woke up irritable and slept badly in the night, indeed hardly at all. I have a great weakness to be so fretted by little things.

February 14th: Up about 7 a.m. Ready half an hour before time to go ashore, so took opportunity to thank *Franconia* on the ship's loudspeaker or whatever it is called. Went ashore ahead of W. Very friendly send-off from the crew. Long and for the most part tedious drive to Saki. Much snow had fallen and the latter part was grimly monotonous.

A last gulp of vodka in a marquee at the aerodrome, the usual ceremonies, with yet a little more imperialism, this time the guards had standards, and we were off. We soon flew into sunshine and reached Athens after a beautiful flight over islands and abreast of mountains. We saw Olympus in its glory and the rough bear-brown and barren coastline of so much of Greece. All indescribably beautiful and miserably poor.

Our plane is faster than W.'s so that we had to circle round for a bit to wait. We met on the aerodrome, exchanging the Stanley–Livingstone handshake. Then motored to the Regency and thence to Constitution Square in car with Harold [Macmillan]. W. and I had a brief talk to Regent in his room; nothing remarkable. W. spoke to a vast throng in the square. Estimates varied wildly, according to political beliefs, from four thousand to one hundred thousand.

One American journalist described it later as like a pre-war Hitler demonstration, which it certainly was not. Very few banners or slogans. One felt the majority were just devoutly thankful. The feeling was different from that on the evening when Papandreou and I drove from the theatre to the Embassy. I confess that I thought this less moving, perhaps because you cannot call upon the populace to assemble in a square without taking some of the spontaneity out of it.

W. and I had some talk with Greek Ministers afterwards. Then drove to Embassy and to a bath. Soon after dinner, which Primrose [Mrs. Leeper] had miraculously prepared for more than thirty people, Archbishop came round and W. and I had another talk with him. I can see that His Beatitude is much troubled by economic and financial position and I think that he is quite right to

be so. We are back where we were before E.A.M. revolt in this
respect, and with a rather worse situation except that spring is at
hand in this heavenly country.

February 15th: Awoke early to another day of glorious sunshine
and this clear crisp invigorating air. Worked in the sun until
10.30 when our meeting commenced with a review of what is being done to create a new Greek army. Much impressed by local
Chief of Staff, [Brig. Hugh] Mainwaring. Discussion was useful
as well as another on economic issues in which I soon found myself floundering. I then spoke with Alex and Harold and Alec
alone about staff problems, command and finally Yugoslavia and
Italy. Altogether a heavy morning.

Enjoyable afternoon seeing troops, Brigade Headquarters 139
Brigade, Leicesters, 5th [Sherwood] Foresters and 16th Durhams
[Light Infantry]. W. and I saw this Brigade in Tunis with others
of this 46th Division which has had hard fighting since.

Then on to Piraeus where we saw ships unloading and dockers
gave a fervent welcome. No congestion now in the port or on the
quays, rather a shortage of incoming supplies. Good work has
been done here. Tea with the Consul [Maj. Warden-Baker], a
kindly and agreeable old boy, where we dawdled because Scobie
assured me that I was not to see 23rd Armoured Brigade as I had
hoped. When we drove back to Embassy found to my horror that
I was expected [by 23rd Armoured Brigade], and that we were
late, which I hate to be on such an occasion. Spoke to a number
of them, they are very fine men, and then had a drink in officers'
mess. Liked the Brigadier [Brig. Robert Arkwright] and indeed
all of them.

Back to Embassy. Met another T.U.C. delegation, just come
out from home. Talked to [Mr. Thomas] Rapp [Consul-General
at Salonika], then to Regent's for dinner. He was a perfect host
except that I found that informal speech I made in response to
toast of my health appeared in next day's newspapers. I had
thought we were at private dinner.

Afterwards Rex [Leeper] and I and Harold M. and Waley with-
drew to talk to Greek P.M. [Gen. Plastiras], Minister for Foreign
Affairs [M. Ioannis Sophianopoulos] and Finance Minister [M.
Georgios Sideris] who is also Minister of Supplies. An absurd ar-

rangement. I am afraid that I was blunt to the verge of rudeness on the need for Greeks to bestir themselves. But they are now in the mood to rely entirely upon us and that way lies disaster for them and for us. I had concerted general line with Rex beforehand and he didn't seem unduly perturbed.

February 16th: Up at 6.30 and off to Corinth. Drove there, or rather to some small town nearby, with Rex and Primrose. Lovely road. Met [Maj.-Gen. Cyril] Weir [commanding 46th Infantry Division] at his headquarters and drove with him to Corinth. Saw a few men there and luckily some more of 23rd Armoured Brigade. They are a grand lot. We had a gossip. They were very outspoken about E.L.A.S. and sore about press and M.Ps. Nor were they disposed to take it lightly. I rather felt that they thought Winston and I might have been rougher with the opposition, and said: "Send those M.Ps. out here and we will teach 'em." Also they complained that they had only seen parachute boys. "We would have taught 'em some more." Refreshing.

Townspeople turned out and cheered wildly, but I prefer the quiet welcome of our English boys. They are splendid. It would be the highest honour to serve and lead such men. But how is one to do it through party politics? Most of these men have none, as I believe that I have none. And how is this General Election to express any of this, for they could not be farther from the men of Munich in their most extreme form, for whom I have to ask the electors to vote. It is hell.

Curiously enough W. doesn't seem to feel any of this and is full of the lust for electoral battle, and apparently content to work with men afterwards, with many, probably most, of whom he doesn't agree. No doubt he is confident that he can dominate them, but I feel it a responsibility to ask the electorate to vote for them.

Priggish no doubt, but when the battle was almost over, the fervent and comparatively young in years and politics were protesting at a return to old forms and faces.

★   ★   ★   ★   ★

The atmosphere of the next weeks, after my return to England, was strange. On the one hand all felt the exhilaration of approaching final victory. Eisenhower's armies crossed the Rhine in March. By the middle of April, the American Ninth Army was over the Elbe, while Montgomery's forces had reached Bremen. On the eastern front the Russians, after their rapid advance in January, had reached the Baltic, though they were not across the Oder below Breslau. Marshal Malinowsky entered Vienna on April 7th. After the long winter pause in Italy, Alexander's final offensive opened on April 9th.

Yet, following in the wake of these military triumphs, more trouble was piling up for Europe. At Yalta the Russians had seemed relaxed and, so far as we could judge, friendly. If they were going to modify their attitude, there seemed no reason to think that they would do so abruptly. Within a few weeks all this had changed.

The Soviet motives will probably never be known for certain. At the time Mr. Churchill and I were inclined to think that some pressure must have been exerted in Soviet councils. The Russians had recoiled after previous meetings with the Western Allies, as if Stalin needed to demonstrate that he was still pursuing Soviet interests. Perhaps now that the war was nearly over, the withdrawal was all the more abrupt.

There can be little doubt that the changing chessboard of war influenced Stalin's political moves. At Yalta the military situation was still conspicuously in his favour. The sweeping Russian offensive in January had reached to within a hundred miles of Berlin, whereas the Western armies were only just ready to resume the attack after the German breakthrough in the Ardennes. The speed of the Anglo–American advance in Germany soon altered this balance. The preposterous Russian accusations over the first Nazi surrender offer in Italy were to show the depth of Soviet suspicion of a Western victory. Stalin may have felt he had better consolidate his position in eastern Europe while he still had a free hand.

The Russian-directed *coup d'état* in Bucharest at the end of February must have been planned before the Yalta Conference ended, and it instantly showed up the hollowness of the Declaration on Liberated Europe. Although at my instance the Roumanian Prime Minister, General Nicolae Radescu, was given asylum in the British

Legation, there was nothing we could do for Roumania. Mr. Churchill felt himself prevented from vigorous protest by the "percentage" agreement which Stalin had observed during the crisis in Greece, but even if the agreement had never been made, we had not the power to deny Soviet action in the greater part of the Balkans, where the Russians could claim to be setting up their own security system against Germany. It was better to reserve our arguments for areas where we had special interests and the means to back them.

Mr. Churchill was now inclined to withdraw from further interest in Yugoslav affairs. In two minutes to me, on March 10th and 11th, he wrote that he was reaching the conclusion that Britain's role should become one of increasing detachment and that our inclination should be to back Italy against Yugoslavia at the head of the Adriatic. We could still hope to save Italy from Communism. I replied on March 18th that a policy of withdrawal would not be wise:

> Our present policy towards Yugoslavia is, I think, realistic and not overambitious. It recognises that Yugoslavia has not the same long-term strategic and political importance for us as Greece or for that matter as Italy, and that Yugoslavia lies outside or rather on the edge of the area of our major interests. It is based on the "fifty-fifty" agreement, the principle of which is in effect that Yugoslavia should be a sort of neutral area between British and Russian zones of influence.
>
> Since a half share of influence in Yugoslav affairs does not fall to us naturally, the agreement has meant in practice that we have to exert ourselves to produce some influence on Yugoslav affairs to counterbalance the otherwise overwhelming Russian influence. . . . My idea has been that by aiming in this way to make Yugoslavia as far as possible a "neutral" area, we shall be providing an important protection to our position in Greece and to a lesser extent in Italy as well. . . . From the political point of view it seems to me that we should not draw out and leave the whole business to Tito and Moscow.

On March 19th the Russians served notice on the Turkish Government to bring the Turco–Soviet Treaty to an end. This move presaged a campaign of pressure upon Turkey in which our interests would be concerned. But worst of all was the Russian behaviour over Poland. As soon as the Moscow Commission of the two Ambassadors and Molotov met, it became apparent that the Russians did not intend to give true effect to the Yalta decisions. By the fourth meeting on March 5th, deadlock was complete.

Parliamentary uneasiness about Poland had persisted since the debate in the House of Commons on the Yalta Conference. The War Cabinet wanted to warn Stalin that we might have to explain to Parliament that the Yalta agreement had failed. President Roosevelt, however, was not prepared to go so far and many days of argument were needed before new instructions could be sent to Clark Kerr and Harriman. In the circumstances there was a certain irony in the preparations for the conference at San Francisco, to set up what was now becoming known as the United Nations Organization.

> *March 18th, Sunday, Binderton:* Sunshine and pretty sharp east wind. Some work and talk with Gil [Winant] in morning. Told him of risks I saw in San Francisco trying to attempt too much. It should stick to security business. We should only get into trouble if we dived off into trusteeship, etc. These could be tackled later. Gil appeared to agree and on Monday showed me excellent message he had sent.

★   ★   ★   ★   ★

On March 21st I addressed the Scottish Unionist Conference at Glasgow. I wanted to warn those idealists who felt that the new Organization would in itself solve the world's conflicts and spoke of our nascent difficulties with Russia. On domestic politics I said that I should profoundly regret the ending of the Coalition Government.*

The next day there was a meeting of the War Cabinet:

> *March 22nd:* W. spoke of danger of our breaking up before German war was over. Labour men didn't respond much, then

---

* *Freedom and Order,* pages 326–35.

E.B. [Bevin] complained that W. had accused them [in a speech to the Conservative Party conference on March 15th] of going back on nationalization. This he showed he resented. W. said he hadn't meant to infer that and instanced incident as showing our growing difficulties. I said my conviction was unchanged, that if country could express itself we should go on as we were until end of Japanese war. W. agreed. H.M. [Morrison] said real difficulty was in domestic legislation where our differing views on state and private enterprise were causing delay and difficulty. But even that isn't quite true, because if we once made up our minds to go on together we could work out a programme, compromising no doubt on that, but it would be a programme.

March 23rd: Talk with Moley [Sargent], [Christopher] Warner [Head of the Northern Department, Foreign Office] and [William] Allen [Assistant Head of the Northern Department] about Russo–Polish affairs. I hope it is only this vile throat, but I take the gloomiest view of Russian behaviour everywhere. We don't yet know how Russians will react to our last Anglo–American message, but if it is still negative a breakdown seems inevitable. Then there is Molotov's refusal to go to San Francisco and Russian behaviour to Turkey. Altogether our foreign policy seems a sad wreck and we may have to cast about afresh.

That evening I retired home with laryngitis and on the following day came the news that Molotov had rejected the two Ambassadors' definition of the work of the Moscow Commission.

March 24th, Sunday: Bob [Dixon] arrived for luncheon. Much work and trouble during day over Russian behaviour everywhere. Monty is over the Rhine on a four-division front.

I wrote a pessimistic minute to the Prime Minister:

I think it well to let you have my first reflections on Clark Kerr's telegrams. . . . May be they will prove too gloomy when we have Clark Kerr's full report of his interview. . . .

Of course Molotov doesn't want a breakdown, he wants to drag the business out while his stooges consolidate their power. We cannot be parties to this and must force the issue. How to do this presents a number of problems which we must face up to.

At least there should now be a message from you and President Roosevelt to Stalin. It is for consideration whether it should cover other topics besides this. Should there also be a public statement before Easter?

Is there any other way by which the Russians can be forced to choose between mending their ways and the loss of Anglo–American friendship? This is the only method by which we can hope to attain anything approaching a fair deal for the Poles.

Finally: is it of any value to go to San Francisco in these conditions? How can we lay the foundations of any new World Order when Anglo–American relations with Russia are so completely lacking in confidence?

Mr. Churchill was in Germany watching Montgomery's forces crossing the Rhine, but he telegraphed his agreement that we must now ask the United States where they stood. The War Cabinet approved a message to President Roosevelt, which was sent on March 27th.*

April 1st: Some telephoning during day with W. Americans and ourselves are mercifully agreed as to how to handle Polish business. I doubt whether Russians will give way enough.

We now began to hear reports that sixteen Polish underground leaders, invited to Moscow for talks, had disappeared. These stories increased my concern. I had so little hope of a Russian change of attitude that I asked the Foreign Office to draft a communication to Molotov, announcing the British withdrawal from the Commission. I sent the draft to the Prime Minister, commenting:

We should not accept to continue in a Commission that has become a farce. It is better in the interests of future relations between the Russians, the Americans and ourselves that we should speak plainly. I hope the Americans will also take this view.

* Churchill, op. cit.

I was racking my brains to know what to do about the San Francisco Conference. It was impossible to ask the United States to postpone it, but I felt keenly the difficulty of supporting the Yalta formula on voting in the Security Council, when collaboration between the great powers was already displayed in failure.

On April 5th I had a conversation with Lord Cranborne, who was also very unhappy about the position. I told him that if Stalin's reply to Churchill and Roosevelt was as rigid as Molotov's answer to Clark Kerr and Harriman, I would have to make an unvarnished statement about Poland in the House. Then, at San Francisco, when the voting proposal was discussed, I would not withdraw British support, but would declare that its success depended on the determination of the great powers to respect scrupulously the rights of their smaller neighbours. Since I could not honestly say that this attitude was at present being adopted by all the great powers, British approval of the voting formula would be conditional and subject to revision.

When it came, Stalin's reply gave slight promise of yielding and while we were considering what answer to make the situation was transformed by President Roosevelt's death on April 12th. Stalin agreed, as a gesture of respect, to send Molotov to San Francisco after all. It was now for Stettinius and myself to take him on.

16

THE SAN FRANCISCO CONFERENCE
April–June 1945

I attend the funeral of President Roosevelt — My impression of President Truman — General Marshall on the Far Eastern war — The San Francisco Conference — M. Masaryk's address — International differences begin to show — V.E. Day — I am despondent about the future of U.N.O. — Domestic politics — Resignation of Mr. Churchill — The caretaker Government — Field-Marshal Wavell's problems in India — I fall ill before the General Election campaign

I WANTED to be sure that the delegation which I was taking to the San Francisco Conference was a strong one and so, on March 8th, I had suggested to the Prime Minister that it should include Mr. Attlee and Lord Cranborne as well as Lord Halifax. My own departure for the United States was finally made in some haste. The Prime Minister at first proposed to attend President Roosevelt's funeral himself, but at the Cabinet on April 13th he asked me to go in his place.

The next day I was at the White House, taking part in a simple but moving ceremony. Afterwards Mrs. Roosevelt asked me to go to see her. She said how touched she was that our country had sent a special representative and added that as the immediate responsibilities we had all to share were so heavy, she thought that I should meet her husband's successor at once. A moment or two later I was introduced to the new President and to Mrs. Truman. I could not help feeling sympathy for this courageous but unassuming man, who had now to take decisions of the first importance without having had any opportunity to follow their development over the years. Such were, in those days, the limitations of the Vice-President's office.

There was much to discuss and agree before the San Francisco Conference opened on April 25th:

April 15th: Went with Edward [Halifax] to see Harry [Hopkins] in bed. He looks frail, but maintains he is better. He gave us a pretty frank talk on the situation which I asked Edward to put on paper to Winston and which he did well.* The only point he softened was that Harry was emphatic that it would have been an error for W. to have come over now and that Truman, who knows absolutely nothing of world affairs, would have been terrified. . . .

After luncheon [Mr. James] Dunn [Assistant Secretary of State] and [Mr. Charles] Bohlen [from the State Department] came round and we agreed draft of message which they said President would want to get off to Stalin tonight. I then telephoned W. and explained what we had done. He was greatly pleased, said that he had been talking to Smuts in interval and that he was about to telegraph and tell me to go ahead and do as I liked about the Polish message. Mikolajczyk has put out a good statement about Poland which should help if Russians really want a compromise.

The next day Lord Halifax and I went to the White House to call upon the President. I telegraphed to Mr. Churchill:

My impression from the interview is that the new President is honest and friendly. He is conscious of but not overwhelmed by his new responsibilities. His references to you could not have been warmer. I believe we shall have in him a loyal collaborator, and I am much heartened by this first conversation.

April 16th: Edward and I went later in morning to hear President [speak to Congress]. We were shown into room with all Cabinet. Very kindly welcome.

Ed [Stettinius] told us afterwards that President had asked him to stay on for 'Frisco, but I doubt whether he will last longer

* Churchill: *The Second World War,* Vol. VI.

than that. I shall be sorry if he goes. He is not brilliant, but he is a good friend to our country and easy to work with.

Leahy and Byrnes and Stimson came to dinner. Byrnes was full of suggestions for amending Dumbarton Oaks. Leahy made himself very agreeable as did old Stimson. He was against any world organization for the present and would run the world by means of a grand alliance of the big three which, after all, is not too successful just now.

Mr. Harold Stassen had luncheon with me the next day. Formerly Governor of Minnesota, he was at this time a United States delegate to the Conference. We found a meeting of minds easy, I thought because we shared left-wing Tory opinions.

★　★　★　★　★

April 18th: Up early and motored with Edward [Halifax] to War Department where Marshall showed his maps and graphs. This is a function that takes place every morning and it is very well done by specially trained young staff officers. Better than any map room.

Marshall's stern report forecast a prolonged struggle in the Far East, if conventional weapons only were used. The sober reserve with which he recited his appraisal made it all the more disturbing. He was, I knew, no alarmist.

I referred to these and other events in a telegram to the Prime Minister:

> Thank you for your telegram No. –. I strongly share the view that Montgomery should take Lübeck. A Russian occupation of Denmark would cause us much embarrassment. The fears of Scandinavian countries would be greatly increased and I seem to remember that one of the causes of dissension between the Russians and the Germans in their honeymoon period in 1940 arose out of certain Russian demands for control of the Kattegat. Foreign Office would no doubt be able to check this.
>
> I also agree about [advancing on] Linz. I had never contem-

plated that we could agree that French zone should march
with the Russian. Therefore, apart from graver considerations
you mention, it seems all to the good that Americans should
enter Stuttgart. Further I am sure that you still have Prague
in mind. It might do the Russians much good if the Americans
were to occupy the Czech capital, when no doubt, they would
be willing to invite Soviet Ambassador to join United States
and ourselves, in contrast to the behaviour the Russians have
shown us. . . .

I have had two long conversations with General Marshall
since I have been here and at his suggestion I attended the
account of current operations on every front, which is given
him at the opening of his day's work. This lasted for more
than an hour. He seemed to take a more optimistic view of
the position in Germany than Eisenhower gave you. On the
other hand, Marshall is of course at a distance from this theatre.

What interested me most, however, in our discussion was his
view of the Far East campaign. The Japanese are doing all
they can to build up their strength on their mainland. They
have, it seems, brought one or two divisions back from Korea
and also one from Manchuria and have now about twenty-five
divisions in Japan, though of varying quality.

Marshall was inclined to think that the Russians underestimate the extent of the challenge they would have to meet if
they engaged the Japanese on a large scale by land. He thought
that they would have very heavy losses. He emphasized the
difference between a landing on islands where the Japanese
garrison was limited and a major engagement with a large
Japanese field army.

When I instanced Burma as an example of how the Japanese could be beaten in the field he accepted this, but reminded
me how overwhelming was our strength in this theatre, by
land and in the air, something like four or five to one. Russians would have no comparable superiority in the Far East.
He also said that he did not wish to attack the mainland of
Japan until after the Russian armies had engaged the Japanese
in Manchuria.

I need hardly say that this is for you alone. It may be that

I shall have an opportunity for some further talk with Marshall before I go to San Francisco.

April 18th: From there [War Department] to Jack Dill's grave in a beautifully chosen site at Arlington. Decided to write to Marshall about this, for it is all his work.

On to the big Naval Hospital to see Hull. He was up and dressed and talked away for nearly an hour. Much better than I had expected to see him. He told me that F.D.R. had told him on his return from Yalta that Winston was overworked and definitely failing. I couldn't help smiling, and assured him I saw no sign of it.

Picked up Edward and we went on to Senate for luncheon. They were very friendly; indeed a remarkable contrast to two years ago. I had not prepared any speech, nor indeed any thoughts, and just rambled a bit for a quarter of an hour. Edward however seemed very pleased and so did they. Even [Senator Robert] La Folette had nothing to say of which I could complain. I am indeed rather worried by the enthusiasm they all now show for San Francisco, lest we should fail to achieve anything.

Before the Conference, Halifax advised me to spend a brief weekend at Mirador, the lovely house in Virginia an hour's drive from Washington, which had been lent to him. He also interposed himself, although I did not know it, between me and telephone calls from the Prime Minister, in the thought that a few hours' rest were overdue to me. As a result, I received something of a rebuke from Mr. Churchill on April 19th, saying that a whole series of most urgent matters were now coming through and would require very quick handling. During my absence in Virginia it would be necessary for him to deal direct with the Ambassador, who must remain at his post. My delinquency, however, was not serious and our affairs did not suffer.

★   ★   ★   ★   ★

Before leaving London on April 13th, I had instructed Sir Alexander Cadogan to write to Mr. Winant, pointing out how important and valuable it would be if the American forces could press forward into Czechoslovakia and liberate Prague, supposing that military considerations allowed. No reply having been received, Sir Orme Sargent, who was deputizing for Cadogan, told the Prime Minister what I had done, repeating our conviction that such action by the Americans, were it possible, might make the whole difference to the post-war situation in Czechoslovakia and might well influence that in nearby countries.

On April 26th the Prime Minister, who felt as strongly as I did, telegraphed to me in San Francisco asking me to speak to the Secretary of State. I said that I would do so and that a message from Mr. Churchill to the President would be most helpful, adding of my friend, the Czechoslovak Foreign Minister: "Poor Masaryk is here a depressed prisoner of the Russians." Two days later, Stettinius told me that he entirely shared our views and had sent word accordingly to the President and Admiral Leahy.

Even before this, during the interval between President Roosevelt's funeral and the Conference, I had had discussions with Stettinius and Molotov on the subjects at issue between us, and one of these was Czechoslovakia. On April 22nd, during a talk on Poland, I took the opportunity, which Mr. Molotov offered by a reference to the Soviet–Czechoslovak Treaty of December, 1943, to remind him that His Majesty's Government had no information about Czechoslovakia, since we had not been allowed to send an Ambassador. Molotov said that the Ambassadors could proceed when the military situation cleared up. At present there were Soviet troops in Czechoslovakia. I pointed out that the presence of British and American troops in Western Europe had not led us to deny the Soviet Government the right to appoint diplomatic representatives to France or Belgium. Molotov did not answer.

On April 28th M. Jan Masaryk addressed the delegates at the Conference, concluding a brief but deeply moving speech with a sentence which I thought he intended as an appeal. Having spoken of the suffering inhabitants of the terrible concentration camps and ghettos, he added: "My country, Fellow Delegates, has been one concentration camp since 1939. . . ."

Truman's reply to Churchill was disappointing. He accepted the attitude of General Eisenhower, who had reported that he would not attempt any move which he deemed militarily unwise.

There would, however, have been no danger from the Germans in occupying Prague, but Eisenhower halted his advance short, after seeking the opinion of the Soviet commander.

The failure to take Prague meant that the Red Army was able to put its creatures firmly in command. When Masaryk returned from San Francisco he was faced with a gradually deteriorating situation. Out of loyalty to the memory of his father and to President Beneš, he stayed on at his post while Communist participation in the Government grew into control. The only escape for him then was the final release from this world, which came in violence two years later.

★ ★ ★ ★ ★

The uncertain political outlook at home began to make itself felt in California. On April 28th the Prime Minister telegraphed to me:

> You seem to be forging ahead through many difficulties at San Francisco. You made a brilliant speech and are *facile princeps*. I note that you speak of results in four weeks. This is longer than I bargained for. I hoped you and Attlee would be back by May 15th. The bye-election at Chelmsford [when a Common Wealth Party candidate had defeated his Conservative opponent], making all allowances for special conditions, airborne v. chairborne, etc., shows clearly how impossible it will be for us to hold office for a moment longer than is necessary after our Labour colleagues have been called out. It seems to me most likely that electioneering will begin the moment after the end of the German war, and you will probably find it in full swing before you return. . . .

Mr. Churchill made no pretensions to classical scholarship, but would say of his Latin tags: "They are few but faithful."

I replied to the Prime Minister's telegram two days later, with an account of our difficulties:

> It is really impossible to forecast how things are going to work out here. We start at 9 a.m. tomorrow with a free for

all, the South Americans and Molotov being the chief pro-
tagonists. The South Americans want Argentine admitted and
won't allow two Soviet Republics [Byelorussia and the Ukraine]
to function at San Francisco until she is. We could watch this
with detachment except that the moment the South Americans
raise their demand, Molotov returns to the charge over [the
admission of] his Warsaw Poles.

As regards dates, I asked for four weeks, which demand was
greeted with very tepid applause because most of the delegates
were reconciled to six weeks. I did not say I would remain
here myself for the whole of the four weeks. . . .

On the whole we are a pretty good Empire party here. Smuts
has been most helpful at every point and we [the delegates] are
giving him the chairmanship of the most important commission [on the General Assembly]. Mackenzie King has intermittent colds in head and feet, brought on by the imminence
of his general election, but on the whole he is in good heart
and very helpful. [Dr. Herbert] Evatt [Australian External
Affairs Minister] and [Mr. Peter] Fraser [New Zealand Prime
Minister] are making clear to the Americans and all concerned
that we do not control their votes. . . .

In a further telegram to the Prime Minister I reported that I
had told Field-Marshal Smuts

that if things continued to go fairly smoothly I planned to
leave for home in about a week [May 12th]. He cried out
against this and said that he feared that Stettinius had not the
strength to carry the thing along alone and pleaded for at
least a day or two beyond that. In fact I think that much will
depend on how we get on in the next two or three days. At
the moment progress is painfully slow. . . .

I was sad to be out of Europe on V.E. Day and in no way exaggerated my feelings when I ended a telegram to the Prime Minister,
"I hate not to be with you." San Francisco faced the Pacific and
its thoughts were quite naturally directed that way, too. All the
same I learnt that the town was to go dry that night. Being fore-
warned in time, I was able to collect a few bottles to share at the

dinner to which I invited the Dominion Prime Ministers to pass an evening of thankfulness and reminiscence. We had shared so much together, but even in the hour of victory there could not be much confidence about the pattern of things to come.

★   ★   ★   ★   ★

The Prime Minister replied to my congratulations the next day:

> Thank you so much for your charming telegram. Throughout you have been my mainstay. There are grand rejoicings here and today they are to have a Russian emphasis.
>
> You and Attlee really must come back. I have to take a very difficult decision in the next week in which you are both needed. . . .

That same day I had telegraphed to Mr. Churchill:

> I want to get back very badly, but I am sure you will understand how much we shall open ourselves to attack if it could be said that my departure from here had brought the Conference tumbling down. You must forgive my seeming conceit but there is a real danger of this. . . . I have tried to strike a balance between the needs of home and here and I think I can just make Sunday [May 13th]. . . .

The Prime Minister now asked my opinion as to the date of the General Election, the alternatives being June and October. I would have been in favour of continuing the coalition until the end of the Japanese war if that had been practicable, but as between June and October there seemed no advantage in so brief a postponement. I telegraphed:

> . . . Dangers of present situation need no emphasis. I sometimes feel that we are entering period like that of second Balkan war transferred on to world stage. We are clearly in a stronger position to handle foreign affairs as a National Government, and we shall have need of all our strength in the next few months.

Against this, will international situation be any easier in October or need for National Government any less then? As far as I can judge, all signs point to greater difficulties in October than today. An election in that month is likely to be even more harmful in relation to the international situation than an election in June. Yet in October no further postponement will be possible.

What therefore we have to balance is the limited advantage of prolonging Coalition on an uneasy basis until October against risk of election at an even more dangerous period in international affairs than now and increased chances of a Socialist victory in October. After carefully weighing all these conflicting considerations I hold to the opinion I had previously expressed that from the national point of view the balance of the arguments is in favour of an election in June.

In later years Mr. Churchill and I often discussed this exchange of telegrams and he, naturally enough, would probe the question of whether our party would have fared better in an election later in the year. I do not think that it would. Political trends were boxed off by the war, not deflected.

The work of the Conference, during the three weeks that I was there, was heavy and the methods used by the great powers in handling it were criticized, I think undeservedly. We had asked in advance for comments on the proposals published after Dumbarton Oaks and Yalta, for I wanted to show that the new organization would be something other than a field for the disputes of the great powers. The response was voluminous, about which there could be no complaint, but if we were to examine the suggestions put forward, and there were over a thousand pages of them, we had to meet frequently, if not secretly, in what had become a city of a thousand and one correspondents.

The British role was not prominent, but this was deliberate; we thought it to the common advantage that the United States should play the lead in their own country, and we had memories of the past. Perhaps if the constitution of the League of Nations had been debated and decided in New York or California, that body would have had a better chance of survival.

At intervals our Charter discussions were rudely broken into by the multiplying reports of brutal Russian behaviour in Poland. It was not until May 3rd that Mr. Molotov admitted to the arrest of the sixteen leaders of the Polish underground. I recorded for the Prime Minister the conversation which Mr. Stettinius and I had with him the next day:

> . . . I said that, if the sixteen now arrested included a number of those who were on the list given to the Soviet Government in Moscow [for inclusion in the Warsaw Government] I was amazed to hear that they should be accused of terrorism because we knew them to have been good patriots all through period of German occupation and democrats who favoured good relations with Russia. . . .
>
> Mr. Molotov said he had only received this news aout 6 p.m. yesterday in a telegram from Moscow which had given no names or details. . . .
>
> I again asked for the fullest particulars. I said that I would report what Mr. Molotov had told me but that in the circumstances I would not continue discussion of Polish affairs here. . . .
>
> Mr. Stettinius said that in the name of the United States Government he could endorse all that I had said. . . .
>
> I have never seen Mr. Molotov look so uncomfortable.

Although the Poles were not sentenced before June, some to long terms in prison, from this moment I became increasingly despondent about the future of a United Nations, which depended upon the unity of the war-time allies.

It was characteristic of Stettinius to take account of my absence when the drafting of the Charter of the United Nations was complete. He sent me a message that a space had been left for me to sign at the head of the British delegation, but I was soon out of office and I never did.

★　　★　　★　　★　　★

On May 14th I reached Washington from the west, at two in the morning after a flight of some two thousand miles prolonged by bad weather. I telegraphed to the Prime Minister:

If I am to do any good here I simply must have two days in this place. Stimson has asked to see me this morning for a talk on special subject in which you know his interest [the atom bomb].

I explained that a meeting with General Marshall and Field-Marshal Wilson was to follow and then a visit to the President.

[Mr. Joseph] Grew, who is in charge of State Department, sent me a message at the airport that he wants to see me and has many things to discuss. . . .

The subject of the atom bomb I talked over with Stimson that morning and with Field-Marshal Wilson later in the day. At this stage there was still no certainty as to what this fearful, but untried, weapon could do, and some scepticism even among the initiated.

When I saw the President, we first decided on the need for a joint meeting with Stalin. Both Truman and Grew referred bitterly to the failure of the Russians to keep their word on the agreements reached at Yalta. Leahy was also present and suggested that if a meeting took place with Stalin, the United States Government would be well advised to make it clear to the Russians that credits and loans would be dependent upon their showing a more co-operative spirit.

The mood of our discussion was expressed in my final comment to the Prime Minister:

In general, I was struck by the President's air of quiet confidence in himself. He said at one point in our talk, "I am here to make decisions, and whether they prove right or wrong I am going to take them."

★ ★ ★ ★ ★

When I returned to London on May 17th, I found the members of the Government increasingly absorbed with the domestic political scene.

May 21st: Whit Monday. W. rang up in morning and we spoke of Yugoslav affairs which are better, and of general election. The press don't look hopeful for acceptance of our offer [to Labour to continue Coalition until the defeat of Japan]. I never thought that there was much chance of it, though I much want it. W. had strong impression from Attlee twice that he would recommend acceptance, but I think that this was only Attlee's timidity in an interview.

After dinner Jock Colville [Prime Minister's private secretary] rang me up with Attlee's reply and W. asked for comment. I could only say it was what I had expected though sharper in tone. It invited the retort, "If it is impossible to hold together for a purpose, to beat the Japs, how is it possible to hold together without one?"

The Prime Minister was of the same mind and two days later he submitted his resignation to the King. Mr. Churchill had now to make ready a caretaker government pending his appeal to the nation.

May 22nd: To W. [after dinner] where I stayed until 2.30 a.m. busy with first lay-out for new Government. Not too bad.

There were some who were not sanguine about the results of the election.

May 23rd: Luncheon to Norwegians, the last of the National Government's parties. Lie said he was impressed by what our young officers told him of left-wing views in the army, which it seems officers share. He thought we should have had a better chance at election if W. had retired, a view which I know is incidentally shared by Oliver Stanley. Whatever the problems of the future I find this impossible to accept.

May 24th: Dined with Winston and Clemmie alone. A pleasant party. W. was tired and Clemmie not impressed by his list of Ministers. . . . Later, and most unfortunately, Brendan came in and began to talk of Bretton Woods [Conference] and impossibility of his accepting Board of Trade unless he knows our attitude to that.

Earlier he had criticized list. This brought explosion from W. in which Brendan soon joined. In fact they were soon shouting at each other. In vain I called, "Oh, do be quiet, you two," they had a grand old row. James [Stuart] and I went out after a while and when we came back half an hour later, row seemed at exactly the same stage.

There was on that rumbustious evening no indulgence in those "smoothings or smirchings" which Mr. Churchill used to deplore between those who worked around him in the war.

★   ★   ★   ★   ★

The sense of purpose which had held so many diverse personalities together now began to weaken. Churchill and Cripps had always been as disparate as a lion and an okapi.

One day during the negotiations for the formation of the care-taker Government, Cranborne and I were standing by the fireplace outside the Cabinet room, waiting to see the Prime Minister, when the door opened and Stafford Cripps came out. "What have you been doing in there?" Cranborne asked, and Cripps replied that Churchill had asked him to stay on in the Government, "but of course I can't do that, much as I admire the old man. We do not think alike." Cranborne and I said we were sorry, though we were not in fact surprised. As he turned to go, Cripps murmured: "It might have been different if it had been Anthony who'd asked me." I like to think that this was not just a Wykehamist's good manners.

May 27th: Winston rang me up during luncheon, much troubled by his two talks with [Mr. Joseph] Davies [former United States Ambassador in Moscow]. He [W.] had understood that President contemplated a first meeting alone with Stalin, W. coming in later. Naturally W. had reacted violently against this. Altogether D. had made an unfavourable impression. I replied that D. was a vain amateur and might well have delivered his message badly. W. agreed and begged me to see him and have a good talk alone and check up on his impression. This I undertook to do.

The next day Mr. Davies lunched with me. My impression was not more favourable than the Prime Minister's. I told him why we could not possibly agree to the President's plan, as he had reported it to Mr. Churchill. Mr. Davies appeared to accept this, but asked that he should not have to take back a despatch in this sense. Having had a talk with the Prime Minister earlier, I was able to agree that Davies should do the explaining to the President, while the Prime Minister would merely send a telegram thanking for the visit and reaffirming our position. Mr. Davies seemed relieved at this.

May 29th: Further long talk with Davies. It didn't amount to more than an appeal for Russia. He is the born appeaser and would gladly give Russia all Europe, except perhaps us, so that America might not be embroiled. All the errors and illusions of Neville C., substituting Russia for Germany.

As victory drew near, so did trouble. Wavell, now Viceroy of India, had his share. To help meet it, he wished to set up a new Executive Council without British members, except for the Viceroy and Commander-in-Chief. He proposed to summon a conference of representative Indian leaders to advise him on the Council's membership. The Secretary of State for India, Mr. Amery, was in sympathy with Wavell, but about how to do the job there were almost as many opinions as counsellors.

May 30th: Dined with Archie Wavell at Athenæum, very late. He was much troubled about his Indian Policy. We had a good talk afterwards and I found his arguments convincing. I urged him to put them to Cabinet as he had just put them to me. Unhappily Leo [Amery] is an unlucky advocate though a deeply sincere one, while Simon, I am sure, is hostile in true snake style. For Simon some months ago had informed me at No. 10 that Wavell was a foolish, woolly-headed old man.

May 31st: Archie did well at Cabinet. I had been able in a brief talk with W. earlier to prepare the ground a little, though I thought it wiser not to tell him that I had had a long talk with Archie. When Archie had finished, I said, if I remember right

I spoke next, that I felt much comforted by what he had said, which was a different plan from what we had been given before.

P.M. was inclined to agree and Simon somewhat peevishly said that India Committee had never heard plan in this form before, whereat Wavell retorted that he had never been asked to state his plan to the Committee. All went much better, though poor Leo with the best of intentions nearly muddied the waters again once or twice. It was agreed that India Committee should redraft, or examine, Wavell's statement, and I don't think there will be any further trouble. Great relief.

★　　★　　★　　★　　★

The price of indulgence in over-work, like any other, has always to be paid in the end. I had no serious illness through all the harassments of the war years, but in the last days of May I began to suffer a gnawing internal pain. My doctor diagnosed a duodenal ulcer and commanded some weeks' complete rest. I was exasperated and unhappy at this development on the eve of the General Election campaign, which the Prime Minister had just announced. Having a speaking engagement in Warwickshire that day, I decided to divert my return journey through Chequers and tell Mr. Churchill myself.

He was in bed at the time, mulling over some party literature in preparation for his first broadcast of the campaign. He accepted the verdict glumly, but without question. We agreed that I should go at once to my Sussex home, lie up and continue with as much of my Foreign Office work as the doctor would allow and, if possible, give a political broadcast from there towards the end of the campaign. This I did, Mr. Churchill's doctor, Lord Moran, having travelled down to Binderton and confirmed the diagnosis.

I was able to read and reflect, and there had been little time for either since the war began.

June 6th: Bob [Dixon] brought down quite a fan mail of letters of sympathy from friend and foe (political!) alike. Oliver Lyttelton and Stafford Cripps wrote particularly pleasant letters to receive.

June 14th: Moran wants to insist on four weeks without work except for the one broadcast. He has persuaded Winston to agree, and I did so, reluctantly.

Earlier in the year I had been asked to be Honorary Air Commodore of No. 500 (County of Kent) Squadron, Royal Auxiliary Air Force, in place of the Duke of Kent who had been killed flying on duty.

June 21st: Airman arrived who commands 500 Squadron, [Wing Commander H. N.] Garbett by name. I liked him. Much talk about the squadron which interests me. Anything to do with men is always intriguing and I always seem to have to do with papers.

I remember much sunshine that month, but in every other respect it was a wretched period. A message reached me that my elder son, recently promoted a Pilot Officer in the Royal Air Force, was missing from a flight with supplies in mountainous country in Burma. He and his crew had failed to return to their base at Akyab. I knew that the casualty rate had been high and his letters had been graphically descriptive of the weather conditions, so that I could have little hope. Though intermittent reports reached me in the next few weeks, adding to the tension, it was not until the time of the Potsdam Conference that the aircraft was found, crashed into the mountain side on its return from the second sortie that day.

★　★　★　★　★

I asked Arthur Mann, now in retirement but, as always, a discerning judge, to come to help me with the broadcast which I was to give on June 27th. He arrived, speaking with gloomy foreboding of the election outcome. He did not think that our aims had been intelligently worked out, nor happily presented. "Your party is losing," was his summing up.

I decided to cut party polemics to a minimum and present the future in which I believed, but some reply had first to be made to our critics:

It has been suggested by Sir Stafford Cripps and others that in order to have good relations with the Soviet Union we should have a Socialist Government in this country, because, so the argument runs, British Socialists are more sympathetic to the Russian objectives than are Conservatives and Liberals. My friends, such an argument is not merely false, it is dangerous. It would be just as reasonable to argue in reply that in order that this country should have good relations with the United States, the home of free enterprise, it is essential to return to power in this country a government which believes in free enterprise, that is to say, a government drawn from the Conservative and Liberal Parties. But, personally, I would never use such an argument. International relations are not governed by such considerations as these. . . .

Later I spoke of domestic issues:

Frankly, I cannot follow Sir Stafford Cripps when he speaks as he did the other night as though State control was all that was virtuous and private enterprise all that was evil. There is no moral issue in this. The issue is, which system will give our people more prosperity at home, whether in agriculture or in urban industry, which will give us the better chance of selling our goods in the markets of the world, as we must sell them if we are to maintain and improve our standard of life in this country, as we all want to do. It is no good just to hiss out the word "profit" as if it were the equivalent of "sin" and to think you have proved anything thereby. . . .

The National Government stands for free enterprise and for the encouragement of individual initiative here at home, but these tendencies must not be allowed to develop in a way that conflicts with the public interest. Do not imagine that the choice before you at this election lies between complete State socialism, as expounded by the Socialist Party, and an anarchy of unrestricted private enterprise. Private enterprise and government control can and should exist side by side. . . .

There are certain enterprises which are by their nature public services though they may have been originally created by the enterprise of individuals. . . . But there is a third and by far the biggest category. These are the industries which, by their variety and diversity of character, call in a special degree for the qualities of initiative, individuality and imagination. It is just these qualities which we shall most need in the post-war years.*

* *Freedom and Order*, pages 346–55.

17

VICTORY AND DEFEAT
July–August 1945

The Soviets get tough over Turkey — The Potsdam Conference
— My minute on Russian policy — Marshal Stalin is told about
the atom bomb — An interlude with the 11th Hussars — The
General Election — Devastating results for the Conservatives —
The Prime Minister resigns — He holds his last War Cabinet —
Reflections on Mr. Churchill's Cabinet — A conversation with
Mr. Bevin at Buckingham Palace — I decline the Garter — A
sad evening — I am canvassed for Secretary-General of U.N.O. —
Power as a habit — The Japanese surrender — Mr. Churchill
invites his colleagues to a final dinner — Journey's end

TOWARDS the end of June I was able to deal with some of my more
important Foreign Office work at home, but my physical recovery
was far from complete and I was haggard in fact as in looks. This
made my work burdensome and also explains, if it does not excuse,
some impatience on my part.

The Turks had asked the Soviet Government for a new Turco–
Soviet Treaty. The reply showed a rough appetite. The Soviets
demanded in return the cession of the provinces of Kars and Arda-
han, the grant of bases on the Turkish Straits and a revision of the
Montreux Convention by Turco–Soviet agreement.

July 3rd: Told Bob [Dixon] how much I disliked Russian attitude, especially in Turkish affair, from press accounts. I was
sure we should make our position clear at all points to them,
otherwise they would go on prodding for a weak spot as usual.
Moley [Sir Orme Sargent] arrived in time for luncheon and found
him in full agreement. He said he found the Americans de-
plorably weak; I said that we couldn't allow them to dictate our

foreign policy and if they were wrong we would have to show independence.

Our recognition of the new Polish Government in Warsaw was
also a cause of argument.

July 4th: Too much telephone trouble all day over Turkish
and Polish affairs. Very tiresome conversation over both, and all
things, with Winston at about 9 p.m. I had to remind him over
and over again of promises I had given Parliament about a free
election in Poland and all parties being represented in Government. If we just had list voting [from a list of candidates prepared by the Government itself] it would be a farce. He kept
repeating Truman wouldn't wait. I replied that our position was
different. Americans knew little of Europe, we were of it and
would be watched on this.

I refused to yield. Over Turkey he was as difficult, saw no need
to say anything to Russians about their demands on Turkey. I
explained danger of this with Russians who were always ready
to take silence for consent and would push on. If we didn't mean
to agree we should enter a *caveat* now.

The United States Government would not join us in a statement
supporting the Turkish refusal of these demands, and the Prime
Minister accepted that we should have to act alone and ask the
Soviet Government to bring the matter up during the Conference
at Potsdam, which was to be held later in the month. The British
Government, he instructed our Ambassador at Ankara to tell the
Turks, would do so even if the Russians did not. No agreement
was reached at Potsdam but the Turks proved able, with British
and United States support, to withstand the Soviet demands.

These struggles led to gloomy thoughts:

July 5th: Am beginning seriously to doubt whether I can take
on F.O. work again. It is not work itself, which I could handle,
but racket with Winston at all hours. Alec [Cadogan] told me on
telephone today that he [Churchill] had promised Truman to
recognize new Polish Government tomorrow. Yet Polish reply

shows many points still unsatisfactory which should be cleared up
first.

I returned to London on July 10th to take charge of the Government for a few days while Mr. Churchill, the election over, was re-
cuperating at Biarritz. We left together for Potsdam on July 15th,
Mr. Attlee accompanying us to ensure continuity whatever the outcome of the election.

The Russians clearly considered this a peculiar arrangement. At
first I thought they suspected us of contriving to secure extra representation at the Conference, but Mr. Attlee was so subdued and
terse a figure that this hardly seemed possible. So they remained
perplexed, though convinced that Mr. Churchill and I had really
come to stay.

The meetings about Poland's frontiers were the most tough and
disagreeable. They were also unsuccessful, we being able to do no
more than hold our own, the Americans keeping to their same position, but now with less conviction. I was sure that the Polish western frontier should not be further west than the Eastern Neisse. I
would have preferred it to be farther east than that and had said
so many times both to the Prime Minister and in discussion with
Poles, Russians and Americans.

I thought that this, only moderate, restraint was much in the
Polish interest. If that country were to attempt to absorb large
areas of territory which had been German in tradition, industry and
life, they would lay up troubles for themselves in the future. But
these Polish spokesmen became increasingly Communist creatures,
and it suited the Kremlin both to deprive Germany of as much eastern territory as possible and to create as much bitterness as could
be contrived between Poles and Germans, a useful secondary influence in support of Soviet authority in Warsaw.

July 17th: Devastation of Potsdam terrible and all this I am
told in one raid of fifty minutes. What an hour of hell it must
have been.

Back [from visit to Sans Souci] just in time for meeting. Americans very direct and tabled series of papers which must have surprised Russians considerably.

The new President appeared to favour a business-like approach which was in contrast to his predecessor's practice of playing it by ear.

> We had an anti-Chinese tirade from Winston. . . . Dined alone with him and again urged him not to give up our few cards without return. But he is again under Stalin's spell. He kept repeating "I like that man." I am full of admiration of Stalin's handling of him. I told him I was, hoping that it would move him. It did a little.
>
> Depressed and cannot help an unworthy hope that we may lose, or rather have lost, this election. If it were not for the immediate European situation I am sure that it would be better thus, but that is a big "if," I admit.

The same day I wrote a minute for the Prime Minister:

> You mentioned in conversation yesterday that the Russian policy was now one of aggrandizement. This is undoubtedly true. And, considering in this light the additions which Molotov told me yesterday he wished to make to our Agenda, I find them disquieting. Russia has no direct interest in such matters as Tangier and the Levant, nor in countries to be placed under trusteeship. This last is, in any event, a matter for the new World Organisation and not for us here. We had much difficulty with the Russians about trusteeship at San Francisco. The truth is that on any and every point, Russia tries to seize all that she can and she uses these meetings to grab as much as she can get.
>
> At previous meetings such as Tehran and Yalta we have met in the knowledge that Russia was bearing a heavy burden in this war, and that her casualties and the devastation of her country were worse than anything that we or the Americans were suffering. But now all this is over. Russia is not losing a man at the present time. She is not at war with Japan and yet she is doing her utmost to demand more of China than was agreed.
>
> To meet this situation we have not many cards in our hand.

One of them, however, is the possession of the German Fleet. I agree with the Admiralty view that it would be best if this Fleet were sunk. But, in any event, we must not, I am sure, yield a single German ship in our possession until we have obtained satisfaction for our interests, which the Russians are treating with contempt in all the countries where their authority holds sway. Our oil interest in Roumania is one example of this. On the political side there are many subjects with which I have troubled you in earlier minutes, but most urgent is to get agreement over the withdrawal of troops from Persia. The independence of that country is important to us. Unless we can begin the withdrawal soon, it is clear from Bullard's telegrams that North Persia will be completely sovietized.

All this brings me to the question of Russian access to the great seas. I know that you feel that her demands in this respect are just, and personally I agree with you that there is no reason why Russia should not be allowed free access to the Mediterranean. At the same time, I feel that it would be unwise to speak about this to the Russians at this meeting. We told them before that we were in favour of revising the Montreux Convention. What has been their response? To make other demands of Turkey which would result in placing Constantinople under Russian guns and would probably be the first stage in the subjection of Turkey to Russia. One must also remember that while we agree that the Russians should be free to enter the Mediterranean, they have not yet freedom to get out of it. Having achieved what they desire about Turkey, Russia's next request may be for a position at Tangier where they may give us much trouble.

And is their interest in the Lebanon a first stage to an interest in Egypt, which is quite the last place where we want them, particularly since that country with its rich Pashas and impoverished fellaheen would be a ready prey to Communism? If we were to talk generously to the Russians this time about access to the wider oceans, I fear that they would only regard it as an indication that we had not been shocked by their demands on Turkey, and would proceed to make more and more demands on Persia and on other countries in the Middle East.

Forgive this sermon, with all of which I feel sure you will agree. But reading through our briefs and documents again last night I am deeply concerned at the pattern of Russian policy, which becomes clearer as they become more brazen every day.

July 19th: Molotov came to luncheon. Bob [Dixon] indignant because he brought his own soldiers and stationed them with tommy guns in the garden. Even then it seems that he claimed there was inadequate protection when the photographers turned up, though his people had asked for them. It must be grim to spend a life guarded like that. No wonder the man is a most able but ruthless automaton.

★   ★   ★   ★   ★

On July 17th the President told the Prime Minister that the first atom bomb had been exploded at Alamogordo. Despite this reported success, there was still some uncertainty about the bomb's effectiveness and Admiral Leahy continued frank in his doubts. Later, when Mr. Churchill and I saw Mr. Truman and Mr. James Byrnes, now Secretary of State, on July 22nd, it was decided that we must drop an atom bomb on Japan if she did not accept unconditional surrender. The Russians had previously rejected Japanese approaches to mediate on their behalf, which they later reported to us. These moves were not significant, because they were not from any quarter in Japan where power then lay. The second bombing at Nagasaki was carried out without consultation with us.

Mr. Churchill and I had previously discussed together the problem of telling Stalin and, if so, whether before the explosion of the bomb or after. If we did tell him would he ask for the know-how at once? A refusal would be awkward, but inescapable.

There were embarrassments every way, but on balance I was in favour of telling Stalin. My chief argument was that the United States and Britain would have to refuse the secret information. They would be better placed to do this if Stalin had already been told that we possessed this weapon and meant to use it. There was not much to this, but the Prime Minister thought it the better way.

On the question of when Stalin was to be told, it was agreed that President Truman should do this after the conclusion of one of our meetings. He did so on July 24th, so briefly that Mr. Churchill and I, who were covertly watching, had some doubts whether Stalin had taken it in. His response was a nod of the head and a brief "Thank you." No comment.

July 25th: We had a [Foreign Secretaries'] meeting in morning, uneventful. After it was over Molotov, surrounded by Vyshinsky, [Mr. Arkady] Sobolev [political adviser to Soviet administration of Germany], etc., expressed his good wishes in the warmest terms, saying that they all hoped for my success, and much more besides. I must be a very bad Foreign Secretary and give way too often that they should want me back. Americans also very warm in their good wishes, to an extent which was almost embarrassing in Attlee's presence. A talk with Byrnes after. W. came in and said he was off to aerodrome, would I drive with him? I explained I was going later and separately.

Much has been written of the influence of personalities on the course of their countries' foreign policy, but this can be exaggerated. My experience of likes and dislikes is that they may make the work of diplomacy congenial or tedious, but they do not influence policy. After some years of practice, it is almost instinctive to treat the work to be done as an exercise. Admittedly the confidence or lack of it felt in an allied representative, or the degree of suspicion towards an opponent, can modify tactics but they do not change purposes.

Even this Conference had not been without its agreeable interlude. I was much complimented when the 11th Hussars invited me to be their guest at a commemorative dinner. This Regiment served with 7th Armoured Division, the Desert Rats, from the earliest days of the African campaign until their entry into Berlin. The honour was the more welcome when I realized that I was the only civilian present and, on going in to dinner, was greeted by the strains of my Regimental March. Since the 60th had served alongside the 11th

Hussars throughout the African campaign, this thoughtful attention was paid to me not as a politician, but as one who had served with my Regiment in an earlier war.

As a souvenir of the evening they had kept for me a fragment of Hitler's desk, but I felt I would rather be reminded of the Regiment than of the Führer, so they mounted for me their Regimental badge instead.

★   ★   ★   ★   ★

After luncheon on July 25th I flew home to learn the election results. I was not too happy about them. In one of my son Simon's last letters from Burma he had hinted that many of the fighting forces were not likely to vote for us and, from the contacts I had in the army, I shared his opinion. However, Mr. Churchill was receiving confident predictions and I saw that my doubts were not welcome.

From Down Ampney aerodrome I motored in the afternoon to Ditchley, Mr. Ronald Tree's house, taking my son Nicholas with me. That evening my agent, who was an experienced campaigner, telephoned to me with an optimistic forecast of the position in my constituency. In particular he believed that the service vote was strongly favourable. I was surprised and pleased, and my first instinct was to telephone to the Prime Minister to cheer him. My second, prompted by Mr. Tree, was more prudent. The good news might only be local.

July 26th: Nicholas and I left Ditchley soon after 9 a.m. and were at Warwick about 10. We had a pretty long wait when we got there, count taking more time than we expected. Tables were remarkably even, all but two showing two to one in my favour over Labour.

As I learnt afterwards, mine was one of the six or seven largest Conservative majorities in the country.

Declaration [of poll] to small crowd in rain about noon. Motored on to Leamington, where there was much larger crowd, apparently all supporters. Socialist mayor read out figures. Much enthusiasm. Rumour had it that we were doing badly elsewhere so stopped at Conservative Club where gloomiest reports were confirmed.

Drove on to Snitterfield which we reached in time for one o'clock news. Worse than ever. It is evident that we are out. Rang up Winston and said what I could.

Mr. Churchill's mood at that moment was not to resign, but to meet Parliament as a Government and let Labour turn us out. I counselled no decision about that until more returns were in. If defeat were then beyond dispute, it would be better to go at once. The Prime Minister grunted and asked me to get back to London as soon as I could.

Through the pouring rain we drove to Stratford and a fervent demonstration, where I could only tell my damp but cheering supporters, many of the services among them, that the heart of England had been wiser than the limbs. From there I completed my tour of the constituency and had a depressing drive back to London.

During the journey I felt troubled about the effect abroad of the Prime Minister's defeat and who would succeed me at the Foreign Office. Just before Parliament reassembled at the end of May, Mr. Churchill had given a reception at No. 10 Downing Street for his War Cabinet colleagues. I had had a talk there with Mr. Ernest Bevin, asking him what office he would take if his party won. He said he hoped the Treasury. I expressed my astonishment: "Whatever for? There will be nothing to do there except to account for the money we have not got." Bevin shook his head and persisted that he had always been interested in financial questions. I knew this was true, but I thought his work there could not compare in significance with the Foreign Office, at this time of attempted peace-making. I told Bevin so and begged him to think it over. He said he would, but I do not believe that I did more than give him food for thought. Anyway he was not the man to anticipate his winnings.

Now, I wondered, would he or another be Foreign Secretary. If the issue were in doubt I resolved to do anything I could to slant events, for I was sure that Bevin was the man for the job.

When I went to see the Prime Minister at the Annexe on my arrival in London, he told me that he had already resigned. He said that he had offered the new Government my help at Potsdam for a while, if it were needed, but he had been told that it was not. We had agreed to make the offer if defeated. I then dined with Mr. Churchill and his family.

We did not speak much of the future, it hardly seemed possible. My own feeling was one of overwhelming sympathy for this man, to whom his country owed so much and for whom this was a devastating, and especially a personal, defeat. He had been deeply moved by the large enthusiastic crowds he addressed in every city in the land during the campaign, though in truth they were only saying: "Thank you. You have led us superbly. We shall always be grateful to you." He could not be expected to sense that there was also something valedictory in their message. He would not have been Winston Churchill if he had.

★　★　★　★　★

July 26th: Saw Attlee at his request soon after 10 p.m. Bridges took me up and asked me to press for return to Potsdam not later than Saturday [28th], for Attlee was speaking of further delay. Gladly did so when A. asked my opinion. Also advised him to take his Foreign Secretary with him. In answer to question said I was available if required, but position was different to when A. came with W. and me. Election was now over and I should certainly not be hurt or criticise if they went without me. He seemed relieved.

Returned to W. and reported this. Then Bob came with me across to F.O. He tells me my successor may be Dalton. This would be very bad; it should be Bevin.

Thus ends this staggering day. Before campaign opened I thought Labour would quite likely win, and Bobbety and I both expressed that view at San Francisco. But I never expected such a landslide as this. Nor do I think it need have been. We fought the campaign badly. It was foolish to try to win on W.'s personality alone instead of on a programme. Modern electorate is too intelligent for that, and they didn't like being talked down to.

Finally while there is much gratitude to W. as war leader, there is not the same enthusiasm for him as P.M. of the peace. We should, I think, have probably been beaten anyway, but Labour majority should have been smaller.

July 27th: At noon W. held farewell Cabinet. It was pretty grim affair. After it was over I was on my way to front door when W. called me back and we had half an hour alone. He was pretty wretched, poor old boy. Said he didn't feel any more reconciled this morning, on the contrary it hurt more, like a wound which becomes more painful after first shock. He couldn't help feeling his treatment had been scurvy. "Thirty years of my life have been passed in this room. I shall never sit in it again. You will, but I shall not," with more to the same effect.

I replied as best I could that his place in history could have gained nothing by anything he might have achieved in this room in the post-war years. That place was secure anyway. This he accepted and at length we parted. I couldn't help reflecting as I walked down the passage on all that the experience of these war years in that Cabinet Room has meant to me. I cannot believe I can ever know anything like it again.

Nor have I, for thus ended nearly six years at a stretch as a senior Minister in the Government, almost all of it as a member of the War Cabinet. As I look back, the dominating impression is one of work and yet more work, much of it against time, but made bearable or even welcome, by a heightened sense of purpose. Arguments there were, even sharp debate and occasional outbursts of anger or indignation, as was inevitable between men of character and opinions so constantly together, but no continuing tension or intrigue, on the contrary respect, friendship and even affection among those who bore the chief burden. I doubt if it would have been tolerable otherwise.

The War Cabinet which Churchill assembled came to function with the sense of authority and power which this crucial period demanded. It was the combined creation of the Prime Minister's leadership and the men he chose. The Labour members, Attlee, Bevin and in the later years Morrison, though so diverse in character, added up to a total of efficiency and were unshakeably reliable in crisis. The earlier phase provided a different kind of stimulant.

The dynamism of Lord Beaverbrook whether in agreement or contradiction was never dreary, and it meant much to the Prime Minister. Outside the War Cabinet, but also within Mr. Churchill's
closest councils, Brendan Bracken was always at hand, perceptive
as well as utterly loyal, courageous in the championship of an unpopular cause or of a man under a cloud.

It must seem fantastic to modern eyes that throughout this time
the whole Government of the country and direction of the war in
its every aspect should have been the responsibility of the War
Cabinet and the Defence Committee. The former was composed
of six or seven members, three of whom, Mr. Churchill, Mr. Attlee
and myself, doubled on the Defence Committee, with Mr. Lyttelton
added to us on his return from Cairo.

The machinery for the military and political conduct of the war
had been discerningly built and it worked, withstanding all strains,
including the exhausting eccentricity of hours dear to the Prime
Minister. Churchill knew how to get the best out of it and though
he never spared himself he never wasted himself either. Don't be
put upon, he once said to me, and he lived up to his advice. The
Chiefs of Staff as professionals of proven ability, had to endure and
to know when to accept any of the variety of theories and suggestions constantly put to them. Equally they were free to propound
their own ideas and did so, even if the timing could be a matter of
nice judgment.

All in all, as I walked out of Downing Street that summer afternoon, I could not expect to be enlisted in such company again.

★   ★   ★   ★   ★

July 28th: Left for Palace soon after 10 a.m. to give up seals.
I was regretful at parting. The King told me that Bevin was to
be my successor at the Foreign Office. I said that I was delighted
for I was sure that he was the right choice.

Found Simon [who had just taken leave as Lord Chancellor]
waiting for me when I came out. He asked me to drive him away;
he haunts me these days. At this moment Bevin arrived and

asked for talk so that I sent J.S. off in my car. Told E.B., at his request, something of the problems. After this we spoke of the election. He was critical of W.'s tour. Said he went to most of the places afterwards. It had done us harm, especially in London.

"The people nowadays like dignity. They don't even like you to mention your opponent. . . ."

He said that he had asked for Treasury and that only at 5 p.m. previous evening had he been told he was to take F.O.

Mr. Churchill had been insistent that I should allow him to recommend me for the Garter. When I saw the King he mentioned this and asked if I knew that he had offered it to the Prime Minister, who had refused. I said that I did not and that, in those circumstances, I could not accept it. The King replied that he had thought I would feel like this.

The next day I explained to Mr. Churchill what I had done about the Garter, which he acknowledged, though he disagreed, saying that my position was not the same as his. Having just been rejected by the nation, he could not take it, whereas for me it was a fit reward for my work as Foreign Secretary.

August 1: W. and I dined at 8.30 alone at penthouse at Claridge's. He deplored my having been ill and said that as a result he had no one to consult, that if I had been at his side he would not have made mistakes in broadcasts, which is not true though very generous, because each must say what he thinks. But we agreed that there was anyway a strong leftward undertow. We spoke of Hendaye where he will go, and he urged me to join him. Finally I left him alone at midnight. It is a staggering change of fortune from a week ago when at his nod came running secretaries to Chiefs of Staff and behind this was real power. Of course he feels the blow heavily and his pride is hurt. But maybe it is for the best for his reputation in history. . . .

Fate plays strange tricks. If Churchill had retired in the hour of victory, being then over seventy years of age, and I had succeeded him, the Conservative Party would have lost the General Election and the verdict have been: if only Churchill had led them, the Tories would have won.

My own future was now all uncertain, but I was too saddened by my son's death to care. For a time I was canvassed to be the first Secretary-General at the United Nations. Field-Marshal Smuts and Mr. Peter Fraser were active in this, while M. Paul-Boncour was a champion within the circle of the four great powers. The Russians, too, were said to be not unwilling. Mr. Trygve Lie was an enthusiastic protagonist on my behalf. Though he was ultimately to become Secretary-General himself, he wrote:

> . . . I regarded him [Mr. Eden] as an ideal choice for Secretary-General. I am not sure that he would have accepted, but he did not object when I told him I should like to sound out the Labour Government and Moscow. However, the matter was never pressed, but I was quickly given to understand that the Labour Government in Britain was not favourably disposed.*

I took no step to promote my candidature, but if this offer had been made to me, it could hardly have been refused.

The Labour Government having quashed the idea, Mr. Churchill and I went through the years of opposition still together. This was a period of few rewards, though the rebuilding of the Party's confidence and fortunes was fascinating. In the event, our redressed Conservative philosophy was not so much the brain child of backroom boys as is sometimes proclaimed today. The two Olivers, as we would call them, Stanley and Lyttelton, to say nothing of Lord Woolton and his brilliant Central Office team, and the work of Mr. Henry Hopkinson and our new Parliamentary Secretariat, all played their influential part with varying renown. As chairman of the Committees which brought so many plans and manifestoes into form, I have reason to know that a balance was kept between these elements. It was their amalgam which gave results.

More than twelve years had passed since Mr. Churchill and I had first worked together, before the General Election of 1951 placed the Conservative Party precariously back in power, with a majority of

* Trygve Lie: *In the Cause of Peace.*

seats but a minority of votes, to confront the events described in *Full Circle.*

It is a common happening that those in power, as their tenure of office continues, find themselves less and less able to contemplate relinquishing it. The vows they made earlier that they would give way to a younger man when the years begin to blunt their faculties, when illness begins to twist their judgment, these they choose to ignore. Power has become a habit they cannot bear to cast off. Mr. Churchill, by his indubitable stature and his weighty talents, belied this process. What neither he nor I could have foreseen was that when at last I stepped into his place, I should have so short a run. Thirty years of political work at high tension and a feckless disregard for my health were to claim their forfeit.

EPILOGUE

On August 14th, 1945, Japan surrendered. The six years of ordeal were over, from the edge of defeat through a balance of strength to victory. Everywhere the nation was rejoicing. That evening Mr. Churchill invited a number of his former colleagues in the Conservative Party to dine with him in a private room at Claridge's. Dinner was something of an unreality to me because it seemed so strange that Churchill was not at the centre of the national celebration instead of dining apart, in an hotel.

When dinner was finished, we adjourned to another large room where the wireless was turned on in a corner and we sat and listened in a circle. After a while Mr. Attlee barked out a few short sentences, then gave the terms. The Japanese had surrendered. The war was over.

There was a silence. Mr. Churchill had not been asked to say any word to the nation. We went home. Journey's end.

APPENDICES

APPENDICES

APPENDIX A

EXTRACTS from Mr. Eden's speech, foreign affairs debate, House of Commons, May 19th, 1939:

This problem falls approximately into two parts. Each of those parts is important in itself, but they are absolutely distinct, and it is important, if we are to come to wise decisions, that we should not confuse them. . . . The political issue is whether we want the closest possible relations, political and military, with the French and Soviet Governments. . . . The second problem . . . is to embody this expression of our desire . . . in a diplomatic instrument which shall have the maximum deterrent effect, while taking account of the difficulties which we know to exist in regard to third parties, or, more strictly speaking, fourth parties. . . .

It is my conviction that it would be a gain to peace if an understanding could be arrived at between this country, France and Russia, and the sooner, the more complete, the more far-reaching that arrangement, the better. . . .

Let me turn to the purely strategic aspect of this question. . . . We have undertaken commitments to go to the help of Poland and Roumania. There can be no question of turning back from that. The whole House and the nation supported the Government in giving these commitments. If we were ready to undertake them it is inconceivable that we should not be anxious now to build up the peace structure as a whole in Eastern Europe. To use a military metaphor, what we seem to have done is to occupy an outpost line in Eastern Europe. It is essential that we should consolidate the main front behind that line. I assume that the Government share this view. I can hardly believe, unless they did share it, that they would have undertaken these tremendous obligations. *If you are go-*

*ing to build a deterrent it is folly not to build the most powerful deterrent in your power.** The Prime Minister, speaking at the Albert Hall the other day, spoke of a conversation with M. Blum, in which M. Blum said that in his judgment the greatest danger of an outbreak of war was that there should still be doubts in the minds of certain governments — we may as well name them, Germany and Italy — as to our seriousness of purpose. I entirely agree with M. Blum. This country can certainly not carry conviction more effectively in the minds of these two governments than by two steps — compulsory National Service on the one hand, and an arrangement with Russia on the other. . . .

The basis of arrangement should be a tripartite alliance between this country, France and Russia based on complete reciprocity; that is to say, that if Russia were attacked we and France would go to her help, and if we or France were attacked Russia would come to our aid. Then, if any other nations of Europe were victims of aggression and called for help, we should make it clear that we would be prepared, all three of us, to give that help at once and to the fullest extent of our resources. . . .

If we make a tripartite arrangement between three great powers, it could certainly be so drafted as to make it plain that it would not come into operation in respect of Russia's neighbours or in respect of anybody else except with their consent or at their invitation. . . . As far as I can follow from what has been told us in the Press, the Russian proposals make exactly as much allowance for the position of third parties as ours. In fact the arrangement we are proposing to Russia is concerned exclusively with Russia's immediate neighbours. We could have a form of arrangement which would cover Europe as a whole and which, therefore, would be much less invidious to Russia's neighbours. . . .

After the events of March, or, as some of us would prefer to put it, after the events of last autumn, there were in principle two courses open to the Government and to the people of this country. We could have disinterested ourselves entirely in Central and Eastern Europe and we could have sought to live what lives we could on the western fringe of Europe while nations in Central and Eastern Europe were called upon to stand and deliver one by one. . . . There was only one other course, and that was to join with other

* Author's italics.

peace-loving nations to put a stop to acts of aggression which must ultimately lead to disaster. . . . The Government have embarked upon trying to construct what has been called the peace front. I would beg them to pursue that course with the utmost vigour and conviction, for only thus can peace be saved.

APPENDIX B

MEMORANDUM from Mr. Eden for the Prime Minister dated September 3rd, 1940:

With the close of the Ribbentrop–Ciano–Mussolini conversations, the moment is ripe to attempt to visualise the enemy's intentions in the military sphere in the next few months.

While we have no information of what passed in Rome, we can be fairly sure that Ribbentrop urged more vigorous Italian action in Africa, and that in reply the Italians pleaded geographical difficulties, shortage of aircraft, and perhaps of A.F.Vs. [Armoured Fighting Vehicles] also. Ribbentrop is likely to have gone some way to meet Italian requirements, and it is therefore probable that German pilots, as well as aeroplanes, will shortly make their appearance against Malta and in Africa. Germany has ample resources in Armoured Divisions to spare one for Africa if she wished. We must therefore anticipate an intensification of fighting in Africa in the next few months.

It is an advantage of victory in the field that the victorious Commander thus opens up for himself a number of promising alternatives, from which he can choose as many favourable ones as his resources can command. This is what Hitler is now doing. He has three courses open to him which, as viewed from Berlin, might lead to final victory, and he is pursuing all three.

(1) The invasion of Britain. This needs no comment. Were Hitler able to gain air superiority, to establish his land forces in strength, and finally to defeat our Army in this country, he would have achieved his main purpose. But the conquest of Britain is

proving an increasingly formidable task, and Hitler is therefore simultaneously pursuing alternative (2).

(2) He seeks by air and submarine warfare to blockade us into submission. The attacks on London Docks, on the Mersey and the north-western approaches are all parts of this plan.

Finally, should Britain still hold out, there is alternative (3).

(3) The conquest of Egypt and the capture of the Suez Canal, with the object of depriving our Fleet of the use of Alexandria as a base and cutting our communications with the East, dealing at the same time a very heavy blow at our prestige.

A victory in Egypt would have this further advantage for Hitler, that it would deprive us of the only front in the strictly military sense that still remains to us, and would remove the danger to him of offensive action by us against his weaker ally, Italy.

All the evidence that we get goes to show that there is no enthusiasm for the War in Italy, even at present, though the Italian people have suffered little so far and have even enjoyed some spectacular success.

If these considerations have any weight they point to the need for maintaining a consistent policy of strengthening our forces in the Middle East. The balance between African and European needs will never be easy to strike, but we must always bear in mind that it is in Africa and the Mediterranean only that opportunities for early offensive action can be found, and that it is against Italy that such action is likely to have the greatest psychological effect. If, for instance, the Italian advance into Egypt were repulsed, and we in our turn captured Rhodes, the consequences in Italy must be far-reaching, perhaps even decisive. Turkey and Greece would take heart — the former might perhaps even take action. Spain, now dangerously uncertain, would be steadied, while all African France would surely rally to us.

It is therefore my earnest hope that we shall be prepared in the sphere of the Army soon to take the admittedly serious risks involved and despatch further fully-equipped forces to the Middle East. By fastest convoy they now can complete the journey, even round the Cape, in five to six weeks. If some of the equipment can go through the Mediterranean so much the better.

If the Italians can be held in Africa now, we should make every endeavour to enable our forces to take the offensive against them in a few months' time.

If the Germans go to Italy's aid, as well they may, the centre of war will shift southwards to Africa. If so, the stakes in that Continent will only become the greater.

APPENDIX C

Minute from Mr. Eden to the Prime Minister dated September 24th, 1940:

Many thanks for your comments and criticisms on my paper. I will deal with them in full, for I do not want you to think that the projects we put forward here have not first been carefully examined in all their aspects.

I take the Far East first. It seems to me difficult to maintain now that the Japanese threat to Malaya is not serious. They have enforced an agreement on the French which has given them air bases in Indo-China. United States opinion is clearly apprehensive that Siam is the next victim, and that country is, of course, incapable of any resistance. There is every indication that Germany has made some deal with Japan within these last few days, and it seems, therefore, wise to make some provision for the land defence of Singapore, even though in present conditions that must be more modest than we should like. Of course, if Singapore is to be retained as a naval base, it is not sufficient just to hold the Island, we have to command at least enough of the mainland to ensure that the enemy cannot land and bring the Fort under the range not only of his aircraft but even of his guns. However, it is now decided that two Indian Brigades are to go to Malaya to try to fill this role.

I had read the Chiefs of Staff paper on the use to be made of Indian reinforcements and had understood that the division for Basra and the two other divisions for Iraq were to be made available for the Middle East generally. You will remember that it has always been our policy to hold one Indian division for Iraq for the protection of the oilfields. This was the Niblick Division which is now in Egypt and the Sudan. I sincerely hope that these three divisions from India will never be used in Iraq, but it is necessary that they should have ancillary troops available for that role. My hope is that all these divisions will in due course play their part in fighting in the Middle East.

As regards the waste of troops in Kenya, General Wavell has within the last few days issued instructions for the transfer of one K.A.R. battalion from Kenya to the Sudan. This leaves in Kenya:—

Rifle Strength
    7 East African Bns.
    6 West African Bns.
    *6 South African Bns.   (includes 3 Bns. due to arrive late October, 1940)

M.G. Strength
    1 East African M.G. Bn.

Artillery Strength
    20 3.7 Hows.   (includes 4 guns for E.A. Lt. Bty. due from India end of Sept. 1940)

    *8 4.5 Hows.
    *12 18-pdrs.   (due to arrive from South Africa late October, 1940)
    12 2-pdr. A.T.   (due to arrive from U.K. mid-October, 1940)

A.F.V. Strength
    *12 Light Tanks   (South African)
    *44 Armoured Cars   (due to arrive from South Africa late October, 1940)

You will see from these figures that Kenya is weak in artillery. The following forces will be available to General Wavell in the Sudan when the reorganisation he is effecting there is complete:—

* [Original footnote] Not fully trained and, so far, not employed.

Rifle Strength
  2 British Bns.
  7 Indian Bns.
  1 East African Bn.
  S.D.F. Units   (equivalent of 3 Bns.)

M.G. Strength
  1 British M.G. Bn.
  6 M.M.G. Coys. S.D.F.   (equivalent of a battalion and a half)

Artillery Strength
  20 3.7 Hows.   (includes 4 due to arrive from India
                                         October, 1940)
  16 18-pdrs.
  16 4.5 Hows.
  4 37 mm. Bofors A.T.

A.F.V. Strength
  1 Squadron R.A.C.   (probably 15 light tanks)

A company of Royal Armoured Corps and a battery of artillery have moved from Egypt to the Sudan within the last few days.

I think that it is clear from these dispositions that General Wavell shares your view and mine that the defence of the Sudan is of greater importance than the defence of Kenya, for his fighting power in the former territory is definitely stronger. Incidentally, the Royal Air Force in the Sudan is also stronger than the S.A.A.F. in Kenya.

As regards the Mountain Battery, I was myself a little surprised that General Wavell should have decided to send this to Kenya, but it is, of course, a very small affair — only a four-gun battery — and he already has a number of these guns in the Sudan with the Sudan Defence Force.

As regards the alleged waste in Palestine, the number of British troops there has been greatly reduced. The only fully equipped units that remain are two Infantry Battalions and two Cavalry Regiments; there are also nine Cavalry Regiments that form the Yeomanry Division, but these have only a training scale of equip-ment and some of them may be moving shortly to Egypt for internal security duties. The regular British Infantry Brigade has already moved to Egypt. There were originally two Australian Brigades each of four battalions in Palestine. These General Blamey has made into three brigades of three battalions each, scraping from odds and ends to complete the ninth battalion. One of these brigades is fully equipped and now in the Western Desert; the second brigade is partially equipped and has, we believe, already arrived in Egypt; the third brigade has only the lightest scale of training equipment and remains in its training quarters in Palestine. All the artillery in Palestine, including the guns of the Cavalry Division, have already been moved to Egypt.

As regards regular troops in the Canal Zone, in Cairo and Alexandria, these total:—

2 Bns. at Alexandria.
1 Bn. at Cairo.
3 Bns. on the Canal.

I do not include in these figures General Wavell's general reserve of one Regular Infantry Brigade recently moved to the neighbourhood of Cairo from Palestine. It has to be remembered that some of them constitute a reserve for fighting in the Desert or for the close protection of The Delta. It also has to be remembered General Wilson would not wish to concentrate in the neighbourhood of Mersa Matruh more troops than he judges necessary for the impending battle, because maintenance and transport is the determining factor in Desert fighting; also the greater the concentration of M.T. the greater the target he would present to an Italian Air Force much stronger than our own. When we send six Blenheims to bomb Sidi Barrani, the Italians send more than thirty to bomb Mersa Matruh.

I hope that you will, therefore, agree that the Egyptian command is making the best use possible of the troops at its disposal.

Finally, as regards Malta, after telegraphic exchanges with General Dobbie it has been agreed to reinforce him with one battalion and a battery of 25-pdrs. This he thinks will serve him better than two battalions. I did read Dobbie's Appreciation of the front he is to hold, and confess that I was not greatly impressed by it. You will recall that a great part of the island of Malta has no front properly so called at all but is sheer cliff down to the sea. We estimate the useful front he really has to defend is little more than about 3,300 yards per battalion. At the same time I am horrified at the suggestion that we have no command of the sea at Malta. Surely if there were an attempted invasion of the Island on the scale you suggest, an Expeditionary Force of 20,000 to 30,000 men from Italy supported by the Italian Fleet, the Royal Navy would have the opportunity of which it has dreamed.

APPENDIX D

DRAFT PREFACE by Field-Marshal Earl Wavell to a proposed account of the Greek campaign, 1941:

1. The British Expedition to Greece in the Spring of 1941 has been one of the most discussed operations of the war. It is also certainly one of the most interesting, both from the view of policy and of strategy. On the political side the preliminary negotiations with Greece, with Turkey and with Yugoslavia were most complex and dovetailed into each other in a manner which has not been generally understood.

The Campaign also involved consideration of our relations with the Dominions, whose troops formed a large proportion of the Expeditionary Force.

On the strategical side, the problems and lessons of the Campaign are also of very great interest.

2. Owing to lack of information on the above, a number of legends and misunderstandings have grown up around the Greek adventure: e.g. that our disasters were due to undue optimism on the part of the Foreign Secretary about Turkey and Yugoslavia; that we forced troops on Greece against her will; that the expedition was doomed to fail from the first; and that had we not undertaken it we should have been able to seize and hold Tripoli at once and thus have

secured ourselves in the Mediterranean at an early date and have avoided the subsequent campaigns and losses in North Africa.

Two accounts recently published — General Papagos' first story of the advents leading up to the German invasion of Greece, and General De Guingand's book "Operation Victory" — have given a somewhat one-sided history of events and do not contain the full story from the British point of view.

3. We are also now in a position to judge from captured German documents of the effect of the Greek adventure on the enemy's plans and conduct of the war, so that the ultimate effect of our intervention in Greece can now be estimated.

4. For the above reasons we have considered that an account of the genesis of the British campaign in Greece, from the British point of view, should now be made public by a relation drawn up by two of the principal actors, one on the political side and one on the strategical side: the Right Hon. Anthony Eden was Foreign Secretary at the time, and Field Marshal Earl Wavell, who as General Sir Archibald Wavell was Commander in Chief in the Middle East at the time and was mainly responsible for the execution of the campaign in Greece. These two, together with the late Field Marshal Sir John Dill, were the principal figures in the negotiations which preceded the undertaking of the campaign. The account has also been checked by others who took a part: Field Marshal Lord Wilson (then General Sir H. Maitland Wilson), who commanded the British forces; Admiral of the Fleet Viscount Cunningham of Hyndhope, Naval Commander in Chief in the Mediterranean at the time; Air Marshal Sir Arthur Longmore, A.O.C. in C.; and others.

The narrative is not intended in any sense as an apology for the action taken. That mistakes were made, both in the political and military sphere, will be admitted; but it is hoped to make clear to the public the extremely interesting story of these events and of their effect on the war.

In a joint narrative of this kind, written by two principal actors there is always the difficulty of pronouns. It was therefore decided to compile the account in as impersonal a way as possible, and to avoid personal pronouns altogether. We hold ourselves, however, jointly responsible for the accuracy of the story and for any opinions expressed.

APPENDIX E

(*i*) TELEGRAM from Mr. Eden to Mr. Hopkins dated April 13th, 1943:

Have you any news for me about the very secret matter we discussed. You will realize that we have various decisions to take if there has to be a separate development.

(*ii*) Letter from Lord Halifax to Mr. Eden dated April 14th, 1943:

Harry came up last night and opened up on the secret scientific matters that you had spoken to him about. Without trying to repeat all he said the gist of it came down to this:

He had very little doubt that both on the American side and on the British side there was a tendency to hold back information from one another, since this scientific research was necessarily largely in the hands of persons who had been and would be again in the employ of big business, and who therefore had their eye on post-war interests on either side. He was inclined to think that the only way of meeting this situation was for the President and the Prime Minister to agree that the pooling of knowledge system should not be confined to the war, but to carry over into post-war times.

The issues involved were too big to be decided by any lower authority, and unless the thing could be handled on the broadest lines, he foresaw considerable possibility of trouble.

He asked me not to telegraph to you about it and his thought was not sufficiently precise at this stage to justify saying anything to you, but I know that Winston has it very much in mind and may possibly like to know how Harry's mind was working. Don't however, let anything be said or done that would get back from Harry to me at

658APPENDICES

this stage. He is very much concerned about it all and had been having much talk with Vannevar Bush. He said that Winston was pressing him on the matter but that he had nothing definite to say at the present time.

P.S. I have just seen your Tel. with message for Harry, which I am passing on at once. But I doubt if he will have much to say at the moment for the reasons I have given in my letter.

(*iii*) Telegram, sent by Lord Halifax, from Mr. Hopkins to Mr. Eden, dated April 15th, 1943:

Your message regarding secret matter received. I am going to send you on Monday a full telegram about the matter. On further enquiry I find it has many ramifications and I therefore am anxious to send you my views fully. Delighted that you returned safely.

The later telegram giving Hopkins' views never arrived, and Mr. Churchill's journey to Washington in the following month provided the opportunity for another approach. The course of relations, however, continued chequered until the Quebec Agreement, signed by the Prime Minister and the President on August 19th, 1943.

A year later at Quebec, Churchill and Roosevelt pledged each other at Hyde Park that:

Full collaboration between the United States and the British Government in developing Tube Alloys for military and commercial purposes should continue after the defeat of Japan unless and until terminated by joint agreement.*

Unfortunately the fulfilment of these just hopes was to confront many difficulties. With victory, governments became more concerned with national peacetime needs. It was perhaps inevitable that in these conditions British interests should suffer; it is certain that they did so.

* Richard G. Hewlett and Oscar E. Anderson, Jr.: *The New World, 1939–1946.*

APPENDIX F

DRAFT MEMORANDUM by Mr. Eden dated June 5th, 1944:

1. I am deeply concerned at the situation which is developing in respect of Anglo–French–American relations. Owing to the attitude of the United States Government we have been unable to make any agreement with the French Committee of National Liberation as to civil administration in liberated French territory. We have therefore placed the Committee in a category below the exiled Governments of Norway, Holland and Belgium. Such a differentiation is not justified. The French Committee controls areas and forces much greater than those of all the other three put together. Though on a strictly legal basis the French Committee has less right to recognition, I am convinced that it has more authority in France than, for example, the Belgian Government enjoys in Belgium. The French Committee of National Liberation controls the Resistance Groups in France and de Gaulle has agreed that these Groups shall receive General Eisenhower's orders through General Koenig.

2. Failure to reach agreement with the French Committee in the sphere of civil affairs will not be understood in this country. Such failure will also have serious repercussions on Anglo–American relations. It will increase the personal authority of General de Gaulle, who is more intractable and xenophobic than his colleagues, and confusion and dismay will result to our friends in France and Western Europe generally.

3. General de Gaulle has arrived here on the invitation of the Prime Minister and with the President's approval. He will broadcast on D-Day and his collaboration in the military field is assured. It was never seriously in doubt, for it is in General de Gaulle's interest to collaborate in this sphere. He too wants to bring about Germany's defeat at the earliest possible moment. The more whole-heartedly

he helps to do this, the more will his own authority be enhanced, the wider spread will be the public sympathy extended to him and the louder the criticism of H.M. Government and the United States Government that no arrangement has been made with the French Committee.

4. General de Gaulle's own attitude deepens my concern. He has brought no political advisers with him and shows no eagerness to conclude any political arrangement with us. He argues that he approached the Americans and ourselves last September, that he has received no reply, and that now in the heat of battle it is too late to discuss these matters. He considers that when France is freed, the unchallengeable nature of the Committee's support will be made plain. His position will thus be further strengthened and further criticism will fall only on H.M. Government and the United States Government. General de Gaulle can bear this with comparative equanimity.

5. All these developments, if they are allowed to proceed unchecked, will be harmful to Anglo–American relations. Parliament and public wish to see an arrangement reached with the French Committee of National Liberation. If General de Gaulle returns to Algiers without any progress being made, protest will be loud unless it can be shown that General de Gaulle is alone to blame for this failure. This cannot now be shown because it is the United States Government's refusal to be represented at the discussions with General de Gaulle in London which gives the General his pretext for not bringing political colleagues with him. It must be admitted that General de Gaulle has played his hand skilfully, but the President of the United States has done as much for him as he has done for himself.

6. I now suggest that we should
    (i) once more approach the United States Government using as many of these arguments as may seem appropriate, and urge them to authorise Mr. Winant, or to propose some other United States representative, to discuss with us and with the representatives of the French Committee of National Liberation all outstanding issues affecting the civil administration of France. This would include

the vexed issue of currency which is likely to be the first of which the public will become aware.

(ii) repeat to General de Gaulle that we wish to discuss the civil administration of France with representatives of the French Committee of National Liberation, and that, for this purpose we hope that he will at once summon M. Massigli and any other Ministers he considers necessary to London.

(iii) warn the United States Government that we shall have to make public our own position in respect of (i) and (ii).

This document was prepared as a Cabinet Paper. It was never so issued, events having overtaken it, but I reproduce it as a summary of my reflections at the time.

References
and Sources
Index

REFERENCES AND SOURCES

Lord Avon, and Houghton Mifflin Company, wish to express their thanks to those authors and publishers who have kindly allowed them to reprint extracts from copyright material in *The Reckoning*. (Throughout the text page references for quoted passages apply to British editions where these exist.)

BOOKS BY LORD AVON

The Earl of Avon, *The Memoirs of Anthony Eden: Facing the Dictators.* Boston: Houghton Mifflin, 1962; London: Cassell, 1962.

Sir Anthony Eden, *The Memoirs of Anthony Eden: Full Circle.* Boston: Houghton Mifflin, 1960; London: Cassell, 1960.

Anthony Eden, *Places in the Sun.* London: John Murray, 1926.

Foreign Affairs. New York: Harcourt Brace, 1939; London: Faber & Faber, 1939.

Freedom and Order: Selected Speeches, 1939–1946. Boston: Houghton Mifflin, 1948; London: Faber & Faber, 1947.

Days for Decision: Selected Speeches, 1946–1949. Boston: Houghton Mifflin, 1950; London: Faber & Faber, 1949.

OFFICIAL AND ANONYMOUS PUBLICATIONS

Documents On British Foreign Policy, 1919–1939; Edited by E. L. Woodward and R. Butler. Third Series, Vol. I. His Majesty's Stationery Office, 1949.

Documents on German Foreign Policy, 1918–1945; From the archives of the German Foreign Ministry. Series D, 1937–1945. His Majesty's Stationery Office: Vol. I, 1949; Vol. XI, 1961; Vol. XII, 1962.

Foreign Relations of the United States, 1941. Vol. II. United States Government Printing Office, 1959.

Führer Conferences on Naval Affairs, 1943. Admiralty, 1947.

The History of the Times (Stanley Morison). Vol. IV, part ii. London: The Times, 1952.

PERIODICALS AND ARTICLES IN PERIODICALS

National-Zeitung, March 14, 1938. Essen, Germany.

De Witt C. Poole: "Light on Nazi Foreign Policy" in *Foreign Affairs,* No. 25, October, 1946. New York.

V. T. Fomin in *Voprosui istorii,* No. 6, June, 1957. U.S.S.R.

BOOKS

Winston S. Churchill, *The Second World War,* 6 vols. Boston: Houghton Mifflin, 1948–1953; London: Cassell, 1948–1954.

Count Galeazzo Ciano, *Ciano's Diary, 1937–1938.* London: Methuen, 1952. Published in the United States under the title *Hidden Diary, 1937–1938* (New York: E. P. Dutton, 1953).

Alfred Duff Cooper, *Old Men Forget.* London: Rupert Hart-Davis, 1953; New York: E. P. Dutton, 1954.

Charles de Gaulle, *The Edge of the Sword.* Translated by Gerard Hopkins. London: Faber & Faber, 1960; New York: Criterion Books, 1960. *Mémoires de Guerre,* Vol. II. Paris: Plon, 1956; translated by Richard Howard, *War Memoirs:* Vol. II, *Unity.* London: Weidenfeld & Nicolson, 1959; New York: Simon & Schuster, 1960.

Major L. F. Ellis, *Victory in the West,* Vol. I. London: Her Majesty's Stationery Office, 1962.

Keith G. Feiling, *Life of Neville Chamberlain.* London: Macmillan, 1946; New York: St. Martins Press, 1946.

André François-Poncet, *Au Palais Farnèse.* Paris, Arthème Fayard, 1961.

Richard G. Hewlett and Oscar E. Anderson, Jr., *The New World, 1939–1946:* Vol. I, *A History of the United States Atomic Energy Commission.* University Park: Pennsylvania State University Press, 1962.

Cordell Hull, *The Memoirs of Cordell Hull,* Vol. II. London: Hodder & Stoughton, 1948; New York: Macmillan, 1948.

Trygve Lie, *In the Cause of Peace: Seven Years with the United Nations.* New York: Macmillan, 1954.

Sir Fitzroy Maclean, *Disputed Barricade: The Life and Times of Josip Broz-Tito.* London: Jonathan Cape, 1957. Published in the United States under the title *Heretic: The Life and Times of Josip Broz-Tito* (New York: Harper & Brothers, 1957).

Lord Morrison of Lambeth, *Herbert Morrison: An Autobiography.* London: Odhams, 1960.

General Alexandros Papagos, *The Battle of Greece, 1940–1941* (English edition). Athens: J. M. Scazikis, 1949.

Moša Pijade, *About the Legend that the Yugoslav Uprising owed its Existence to Soviet Assistance.* London: Yugoslav Embassy, 1950.

Count Edward Raczynski, *In Allied London.* London: Weidenfeld & Nicolson, 1962.

Deneys Reitz, *No Outspan.* London: Faber & Faber, 1943.

Robert W. Seton-Watson, *A History of the Czechs and the Slovaks.* London: Hutchinson, 1943; New York: Transatlantic Arts, 1944.

Robert E. Sherwood, *The White House Papers of Harry L. Hopkins: An Intimate History*, Vol. II. London: Eyre & Spottiswoode, 1949. Published as a revised edition in the United States under the title *Roosevelt and Hopkins: An Intimate History* (New York: Harper & Brothers, 1950).

Edward R. Stettinius, *Roosevelt and the Russians: The Yalta Conference.* Edited by Walter Johnson. London: Jonathan Cape, 1950; New York: Doubleday, 1949.

Viscount Templewood, *Nine Troubled Years.* London: Collins, 1954.

Sumner Welles, *The Time for Decision.* London: Hamish Hamilton, 1944; New York: Harper & Brothers, 1944.

John N. Wheeler-Bennett, *King George VI: His Life and Reign.* London: Macmillan, 1958.

INDEX